MYTH
AND
TRAUMA

Myth and Trauma:

Higher Self Ancient Wisdom, and their Enemies

David Warner Mathisen

BEOWULF BOOKS   PASO ROBLES, CALIFORNIA

Copyright 2020

David Warner Mathisen

All rights reserved.

No part of this book may be reproduced or transmitted in any form or by any means, electronic or mechanical, including photocopying, recording, or by any information storage-and-retrieval system, without permission in writing from the publisher.

Published by Beowulf Books, Paso Robles, California

Mathisen, David Warner.

Myth and Trauma: Higher Self, Ancient Wisdom, and their Enemies /
David Warner Mathisen.

1. Mythology.   2. Astronomy.   3. Spirituality.

ISBN 978-0-9960590-8-4

Dedicated to

the spirit of George Orwell
and his opposition to fascism

the spirit of Margret and H. A. Rey
and their celebration of curiosity

the spirit of Martin Luther King, Jr.
and his courageous work to heal the wounds of
centuries of injustice

and to
Social uplift

and

an end to
oppression, colonialism, imperialism,
racism and the privatization of
the gifts given by nature
and the gods to
all
Men and Women

and ultimately
to **You**
and your own recognition of
and reconciliation with

your Self

Contents

Introduction	i
1. A vision of the Infinite	1
2. Figures in the stars	25
3. The importance of Hercules	47
4. Mighty battles with Serpents and Dragons	79
5. Gods of thunder and of wind	103
6. Positive or Negative?	145
7. The Divine Twin	163
8. "Reach hither thy finger . . ."	201
9. The Master of the Chariot	221
10. Ophiuchus	251
11. A still small voice	287
12. Collaborators against the gods	313
13. The cult of Mithras	347
14. The path of Perseus and the path of Midas	413
Concluding Thoughts	489
Notes	515
Image Credits	532
Bibliography	535
Index	543

Introduction

If you want to oppress people, and take away the natural resources given by nature to those living in a land, it is easier to do so if they are traumatized.

The concept of *psychological trauma* is not new: we can see that this concept was deeply understood well before the very first ancient texts which we can examine were written down. What is newer is the application of the word "trauma" (which typically refers to a physical wound) to psychological and emotional issues and not just to physical injury.

Dr. Gabor Maté, a respected healer and author and speaker on the subject of trauma and its detrimental effect on our lives, says plainly that: "What trauma actually is, fundamentally, is a disconnect from the self." [1]

When men and women are disconnected from the self, it is easier to exploit them, and more difficult for them to counteract that exploitation.

The good news, however, is that the world's ancient myths speak very clearly about this subject, and about the way to overcome trauma (and to repair the accompanying disconnection from the self).

Unfortunately, although the world's ancient myths (and ancient scriptures, and sacred traditions) convey this very positive and beneficial message, they have been twisted and even inverted in order *to* traumatize, rather than to heal trauma.

Literalism, and especially literalist interpretations of the scriptures we call the Old and New Testaments of the Bible, have caused and continue to cause enormous trauma and suffering in the lives of men, women, and children around the world.

Introduction

I do not deny that these scriptures can and do have a positive impact on the lives of many individuals, despite the ways that literalist interpretation twists and inverts their message at many points, but this positive impact only testifies to the positive power inherent in the ancient wisdom *in spite of* the misinterpretation to which these ancient stories have been subjected, and not *because of* that misinterpretation.

The world's ancient myths -- to include the stories of the Bible -- actually teach us how to recover from trauma, and especially how to repair the most significant byproduct of psychological trauma, which is the *alienation from our essential self,* from our authentic self, our higher self.

This alienation from the self creates a tremendous void, and an ache for reconnection -- and leading medical doctors, psychologists, and healers are now realizing and teaching that this alienation lies at the root of virtually all forms of addiction, depression, severe anxiety, and even chronic physical illness.

The incredible ancient wisdom bequeathed to every culture on earth in the form of their original myths, scriptures and sacred stories reveals a clear understanding of the source of the problem, teaching that the authentic self is never lost and is actually always available, even if buried and suppressed by "the ego" or "the mind" (which itself is a defense mechanism that we create as a way of coping with pain and trauma).

When we are taught that the ancient myths (including the stories of the Bible) are historical, literal, and terrestrial, it implies that they are actually about someone else, someone external to us, and this in turn implies that we must seek somewhere outside of ourselves for the remedy to the alienation we feel, when in fact the solution cannot be found outside but only within.

This book will explore the ways in which the world's ancient myths point us towards the reconciliation with our essence, and the repair of the trauma which caused us to become alienated from who we really are. But in order to see how they do that, we

Introduction

must examine the little-known *system of celestial metaphor* upon which the ancient myths, from virtually every culture on our planet, are constructed.

The ancient myths can be shown to be metaphorical, rather than literal -- and they can be proven to be metaphorical rather than literal because the figures and events described in the myths relate directly to specific constellations and heavenly features, and to celestial cycles including the cycles of the earth, moon, sun, visible planets, and even the ages-long cycle of precession.

The evidence which establishes the fact that the world's myths have their foundation in an extremely ancient world-wide system of celestial metaphor is simply overwhelming in its volume. This book will provide irrefutable evidence of their metaphorical nature, which must be established in order to help us to realize that the myths are not pointing us towards external solutions to the alienation we feel within (as literal interpretations always tend to do, because literalizing and historicizing the texts naturally externalizes the characters and events).

Even beyond this important understanding, the fact that the ancient myths are built upon a system of *celestial* metaphor teaches another important truth -- because the use of the *stars and heavenly cycles* as the foundation for the metaphor was by no means accidental. The ancient myths employ the celestial realms as a means of picturing the *infinite realm* -- and indeed, when we gaze out into the universe on a clear, dark night, we are gazing out into an infinite realm.

As it turns out, the ancient myths tell us that our essential self, our higher self, connects us to the infinite realm, the realm of pure potential: the realm of the gods.

In this book, we will first see abundant and undeniable evidence that the myths of the world are indeed built upon a common foundation of celestial metaphor -- and then we will explore how understanding their esoteric language can help us to grasp their profound message of reconciliation with who we are, at our essence.

The myths point us towards the recovery of that self, from whom we have become alienated. That reconnection is in fact always available to us -- because our true self is never lost, and is always there, waiting for our return, ready at a moment's notice.

There are forces in this world who would very much prefer to keep the vast majority of men and women traumatized, alienated, and disconnected from themselves. This book will touch upon some of the ways in which they seek to do that -- and once you understand the pattern, you will begin to recognize it in places that are not discussed at length here.

It is my hope that the format of this book will help each reader to see through the lies we have been taught about the world's ancient wisdom, by learning the language that the ancient myths themselves are actually speaking -- which is a metaphorical language, an esoteric language, and a celestial language.

As we begin to hear what the ancient treasure of the myths, entrusted to every culture on every continent and island on our planet, are trying to tell us, we will start to see the path they illuminate for our journey to recover our connection to our own essential self. It is a journey that no one else can take for us -- but the myths can show us the way, if we dare.

We will begin in a lonely desert, under an open sky, filled with stars . . .

Chapter 1

A vision of the Infinite

Join me as we travel to a desolate and rocky wilderness, far from human habitation, part of my multi-year research project pursuing the ancient wisdom given to humanity in remote antiquity.

Night is falling and the sun is setting. A traveler, journeying alone and on foot, has been making his way through a rocky and deserted landscape, from the ancient settlement of Beersheba, a site with evidence of human occupation going back at least as far as the Copper Age, and whose name may be translated "Well of the Oath" or "Well of Seven" (and hence, "Place of Seven Wells").

The lonely traveler is on his way to the distant region of Haran, which according to present scholarship is thought to have been located in the northern region of Mesopotamia and in fact to have been situated in the proximity of the ancient city of Urfa (recently given the more honorific designation of "Sanliurfa"), not far from the incredible stone circles of Göbekli Tepe which only began to come to light in the late 1990s and early 2000s after being deliberately buried under tons of earth not later than the year 8000 BC or BCE.

As the sun begins to set, the weary traveler finds a space to rest for the night, under the open sky. He positions a stone or stones to use for his pillow, and stretches out on the ground and prepares to go to sleep.

As the final glow of the sun fades in the west, a cool desert breeze crosses over the barren landscape moving from the west to the east, and countless stars begin to appear in the velvet-black sky. The young traveler has much to contemplate as he lays his head upon the stone pillow and tries to make himself comfortable on the desert floor. He has set out with his father's blessing to seek out his uncle, the brother of his mother, in distant Haran. His

Chapter One

father has specifically charged him with taking a wife from among his uncle's daughters, and sent him away with a benediction wishing him many children and the inheritance of the land through which he will sojourn.

As the young man's conscious thoughts begin to give way to the onrush of sleep, the images he sees within his closed eyelids become more and more animated, until he crosses over the boundary into the realm of sleep, and enters the world of dreams.

His dreams have a vividness and power that is impossible to describe to the waking mind. In this realm of dreams, color and motion take on an unworldly reality, one with which we are all familiar because we ourselves go there too, when we sleep. He sees a glorious ladder, set up with its base upon the earth, stretching upwards into the sky, the top reaching all the way to heaven. Holy angels of indescribable beauty can be seen ascending and descending upon this celestial ladder.

And, as the text of Genesis chapter 28 tells us (for that is where we encounter this story of the traveler making his way from Beersheba to Haran), above the ladder, the actual figure of the LORD is standing ("behold, the LORD stood above it," the text declares in verse 13), and says to the dreamer these words:

> I *am* the LORD God of Abraham thy father, and the God of Isaac: the land whereon thou liest, to thee will I give it, and to thy seed; and thy seed shall be as the dust of the earth, and thou shalt spread abroad to the west, and to the east, and to the north, and to the south: and in thee and in thy seed shall all the families of the earth be blessed. And behold, I *am* with thee, and will keep thee in all *places* whither thou goest, and will bring thee again into this land; for I will not leave thee, until I have done *that* which I have spoken to thee of.[2]

When the traveler awakens from his sleep, he exclaims: "Surely the LORD is in this place; and I knew *it* not" (verse 16).

What has just happened?

Is this ancient record telling us the story of a unique encounter with the divine, given to one privileged individual, specially selected for reasons we cannot begin to fathom, but certainly far from our own experience, living as we do in our uninspiring quotidian routine of traffic lights, workday frustrations, grocery lines and bills to pay via computer or mobile app?

Or is there more to this story, some hidden clue which will unlock an ancient truth -- long forgotten -- capable of speaking to us even in this modern day, indeed even in this very present moment?

To answer this question, we must travel to a vantage point where we can behold one of the most distinctive and breathtaking features of our night sky: the glorious column of the Milky Way galaxy itself, which rises up out of the southern horizon[3] and arches over our heads like a great pillar of fire -- if we can find a place to observe the night sky far enough away from the light pollution created by the streetlamps and city glow that washes out the view of the heavens within and around so many of our modern population centers.

I myself live in an area where the stars are clearly visible from my house and within my neighborhood on most cloudless nights -- but in order to really observe the heavens in all their glory, I drive to a secluded pass high among the hills which overlook the Pacific Ocean, where on a moonless night the countless stars are absolutely breathtaking in their splendor.

We venture out into the hills, passing farms and vineyards, leaving behind the lights of the towns and cities, for a singular reason.

For the past ten years, I have been exploring the overwhelming evidence which demonstrates that the world's ancient myths, scriptures and sacred stories are based on the stars -- including the stories collected into the scriptures of the so-called Old and New Testaments of the Bible, as well as the myths and sacred traditions of virtually every other culture on our planet, from ancient Egypt to ancient Mesopotamia and ancient India to ancient Greece, ancient China, and ancient Japan, to the cultures of Africa, Australia, North America, Central America, South America, the islands of the vast Pacific, and many more.

Chapter One

Once we begin to understand this system, and to become familiar with the correspondence between the various characters and events which recur in world myth and the characteristics of specific constellations and their position within the great heavenly cycles (involving the motions of our planet in relation to the other planets, as well as the sun and the moon), we realize that an episode in ancient myth such as the vision of Jacob described in Genesis 28 can best be analyzed by examining the figures in the night sky, as opposed to trying to match the events described with any terrestrial coordinates.

Thus, to analyze the famous story of "Jacob's ladder," we do not need to travel to the arid desert of the northern Negev (or the Naqab, to use its Arabic name) in the Levant: we can instead turn to the sky. As we drive along the two-lane California highway through the deepening gloom, we are in fact situated within the same latitudinal band that encompasses the supposed journey of Jacob from Beersheba (positioned at about 31° north latitude) to Haran (positioned at roughly 37° north latitude), although half a world away if measured by longitude.

By the time we reach our destination, just over the crest of the ranges which separate the inland valleys from the coastal regions and the glimmering Pacific itself, the sky is a deep black. A cold breeze blows off the ocean from the west and sweeps up over the hills, as the denser air hanging above the water rushes in over the land that has been warming in the sun all day, although this situation will reverse by morning, as the land cools down at night.

We turn off onto a wide gravel turnout, facing south and west, with a dazzling view of California's Central Coast stretched out below us. The gravel crunches under the tires of the car as we coast to a stop and turn off the engine and the lights.

I climb out and sit down on the hood of the car. It's warm from the engine. Leaning back against the glass of the windshield, as if on a lounge chair, and facing towards the south, it is perhaps not as comfortable as Jacob's campsite on the desert floor, which

A vision of the Infinite

featured a rock for a pillow (not recommended for the windshield-lounge chair). The coastline stretches out below, curving away beneath the night sky.

Above, the stars rise in the east from behind the ranges we have just crested, and wheel overhead before sinking down into the west to disappear into the ocean. Facing to the south, the path of the planets is indicated by the band of zodiac constellations, arcing above the southern horizon. During the months of the year when Sagittarius and Scorpio dominate the night sky between the hour of sunset and the hour of midnight, the shining band of the Milky Way rises almost straight up between the Archer and the Scorpion, its widest and brightest region flanked by these two zodiac constellations, which themselves are enormous when seen in the sky in person, far more impressive than can be conveyed by the diagrams in this book or in any planetarium app on a screen, such as the excellent free and open-source program Stellarium which is used to create the star-charts presented here:

Far from any light pollution, the sheer volume of stars overhead is almost unbelievable. No image on the flat page can do it justice. The column of the Milky Way rises in the south like a splendid pathway.

Chapter One

Here, for ease of identification, I have outlined the Milky Way band. Notice that it is brightest and widest near the bottom of the star-chart, where it is rising up out of the southern horizon:

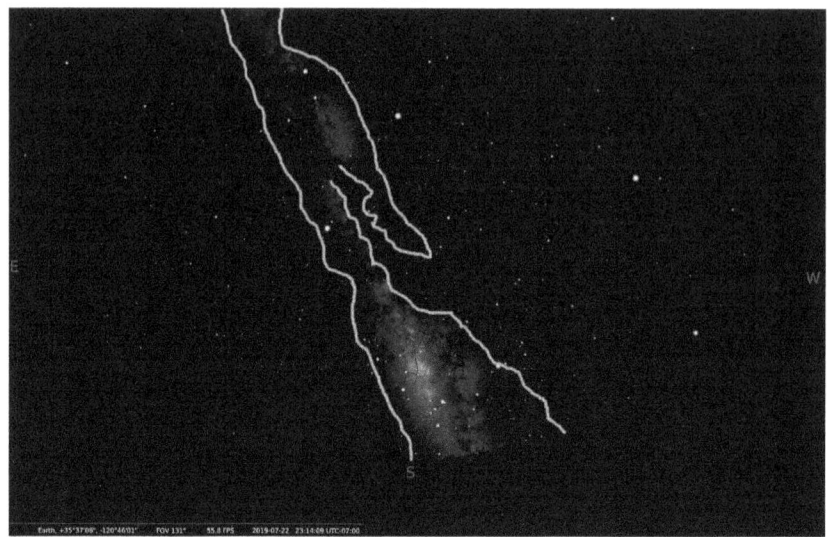

Below is the same star-chart shown above, but this time with the colors inverted such that the dark night sky becomes light, and the shining stars become black dots. This inverted color scheme will be used for the majority of star-charts in this book, because it is much easier to see the constellations against a light background:

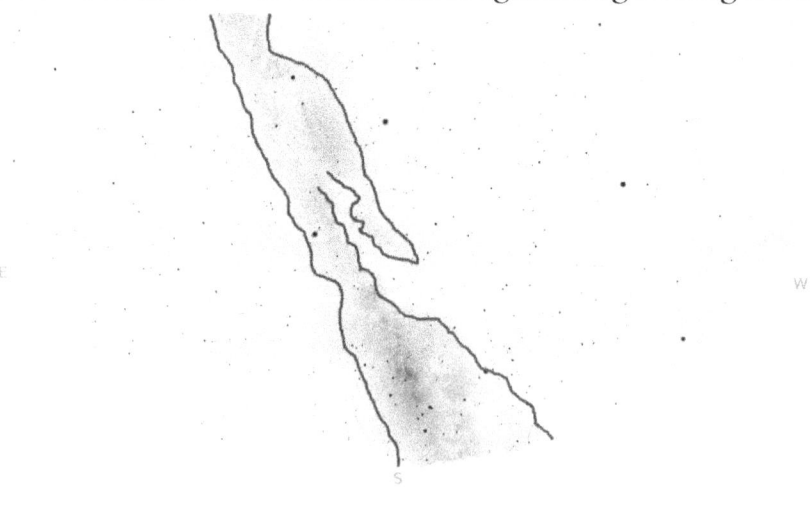

A vision of the Infinite

The Milky Way itself forms a great "ring" in the heavens, because it is actually a massive spinning whirlpool of stars which forms an enormous disc of stars, within which we ourselves are situated. It is believed to have a massive bulge at the Galactic Center, so that we can think of our galaxy as being shaped like an enormous fried egg, some 200,000 light-years in diameter (that is to say, so wide that it takes a beam of light 200,000 *years* despite traveling at a speed which traverses 186,000 miles every *second*).

If you can imagine our earth and our solar system situated within the flat disc of this enormous "fried-egg shaped" whirlpool, containing perhaps as many as 400 billion stars, you can understand why from our vantage point looking out into the night sky, the great disc of our galaxy appears as a great ring of light or cloudy band in the night sky. This ring or band is the disc of the galaxy itself, which we are situated within, such that we see it "edge-on" because we are inside of it.

Think of a great fried egg composed of billions of stars floating freely in space (no frying pan), and imagine yourself within the fried white (or albumen) of that egg, about halfway between the yolk in the center of the fried egg and the edge that marks the boundary of the fried egg's edge. If you imagine yourself on a planet that is spinning on its axis within the egg-white, you can envision the fact that the flat disc of the fried egg will appear as a ring, and that as our earth turns on its axis, we will see the "ring" appear to make a full revolution around us (although what appears to be a ring is actually the disc of the galaxy, within the flat disc of which we ourselves are situated).

As we turn, making a complete revolution within each of our earth days (almost, but not quite, twenty-four hours in length), we *would* be able to see the galactic disc (which looks to us like a ring) make a full revolution around us (although it is actually our planet which is making a revolution on its axis, and causing the galactic ring to make what appears to be a full revolution in the sky), except for the fact that the sun is up for around half of that

Chapter One

time, which means that we won't be able to see the "ring" of the galaxy during the time that the sun is in the sky.

Half of that time, we would be looking towards the great bulge at the center of the galaxy (the Galactic Center, which is like the "yolk" on our fried egg) and the other half of that time we would be looking towards the "outer edge" of the fried egg (in the direction that is away from the Galactic Center or the "yolk").

In the diagram above, the sun's location in the "Orion Spur" of the whirlpool-like arms of the Milky Way's swirling spiral is indicated, and beyond it we see the glowing center of the galaxy where the density of stars is the greatest. If you imagine our earth rotating *into* the page as it rotates on its axis (see arrow that I have added to the same diagram, on the following page), you can then understand why this rotation causes the entire disc of the Milky Way to seem to "flip" around us once per day (and to look like a "ring," because we are inside the disc itself), and how this "flipping" of the Milky Way in the sky exposes us first to the half of the "ring" containing the Galactic Center, and then to the half which we will see when we are looking *away* from the Galactic Center, towards the outer edge of the galactic disc.

In the diagram above, I've added an arrow intended to convey the idea of the direction of our earth's daily rotation on our axis (from the bottom of the "C"-shape towards the top), which causes the galactic disc (appearing to us as a great ring in the sky) to "flip" around us once per day.

The brightest part of the galactic band, of course, will be the part when we are looking towards that Galactic Center, containing the densest region of stars in the galaxy -- and we see that part of the Milky Way when we are looking towards the constellations Scorpio and Sagittarius. When we are turned in that direction (and when the sun is not in the sky -- in other words, when it is night) we see the brightest and most distinctive part of the great Milky Way band, rising up between the constellations Scorpio and Sagittarius, and stretching up from the horizon to arch over our heads like a glorious shining ladder or "stairway to heaven."

Chapter One

When we understand that the brightest portion of the Milky Way band, the portion we see when we are facing the Galactic Center, is the portion we see when we are facing the constellations Sagittarius and Scorpio, then we will begin to understand the vision described in Genesis 28 involving the dream of Jacob and the ladder which reaches from the earth all the way to heaven. This brightest portion of the Milky Way column, seen from earth, forms the "stairway to heaven" described in the dream!

Below is a star-chart depicting the brightest portion of the Milky Way, rising between Sagittarius and Scorpio. It is the most glorious part of the Milky Way band, a shining column rising up like a heavenly stair or ladder:

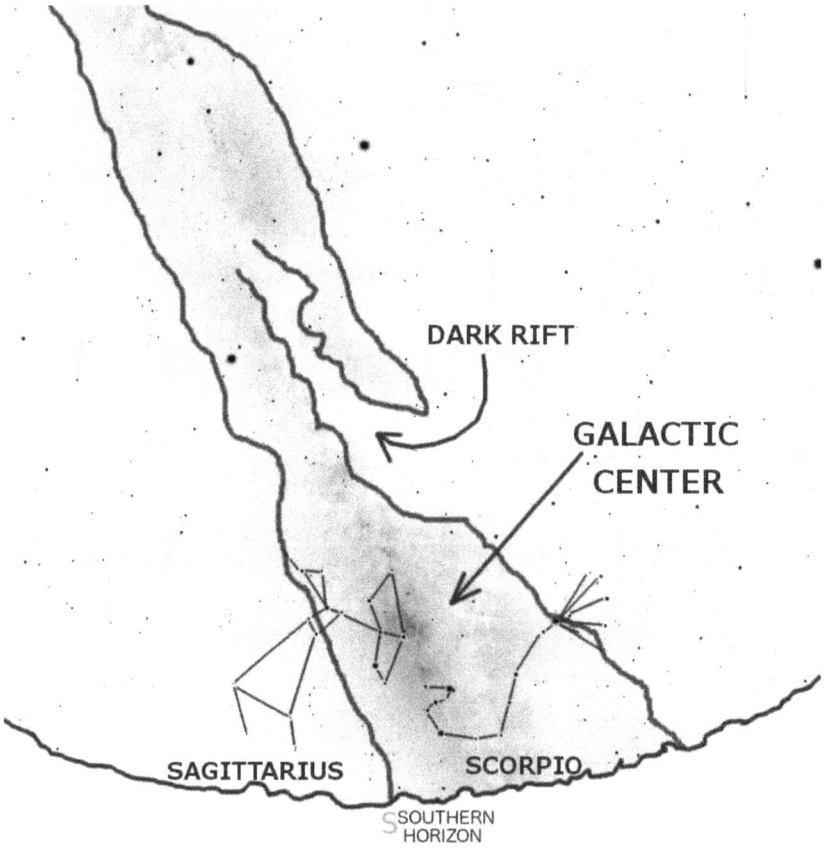

Remember that the colors are inverted in the image, which means that everything light-colored in the star-chart above is dark in the night sky (and the ground, bounded by the horizon, is dark as well, because it is night-time). The Milky Way, which appears as a darker band in the chart, is brighter and lighter in the sky, but when inverted it appears dark. The brightest part of the Milky Way, corresponding to the Galactic Center, is indicated in the chart with an arrow. Just above this brightest region is a dark pathway (lighter in color in this inverted chart) known as the Dark Rift, which plays an important role in many Star Myths around the world.

Let's explore the evidence that this shining column of the Milky Way, beginning at its brightest and widest region in the vicinity of the zodiac constellations of Sagittarius and Scorpio and stretching upwards like a ladder whose base is set upon the earth but whose top reaches into the infinite heavens, forms the stairway to heaven described in the ancient text of Jacob's dream.

Above the figures of Sagittarius and Scorpio, we see the two great winged figures of the constellations Aquila the Eagle and Cygnus the Swan, one appearing to be flying upwards from the horizon (Aquila, for viewers in the northern hemisphere) and one appearing to be flying downwards (Cygnus).

These are the two "great birds" of the Milky Way -- very distinctive and recognizable constellations which are easily visible in the night sky during long portions of the year. Both constellations contain a good number of fairly bright stars, making their outlines easy to identify, and each constellation contains one very bright star which is so bright that it is almost impossible to miss.

The brightest star in the constellation Aquila the Eagle is Altair, the center star in a small line of three stars (not as large or distinctive as the three stars in the belt of Orion, because the other two stars on either side of Altair are not nearly as bright as is Altair, but still fairly easy to identify).

Chapter One

The rest of the constellation Aquila looks something like a great bat or manta ray in the heavens when seen in person in the heavens -- it is outlined in the chart below.

The brightest star in the constellation Cygnus the Swan is Deneb. This bright star forms the point at the base of two triangles which are the easiest part of Cygnus to see in the heavens. I have outlined that part of the Swan with heavier lines in the chart below.

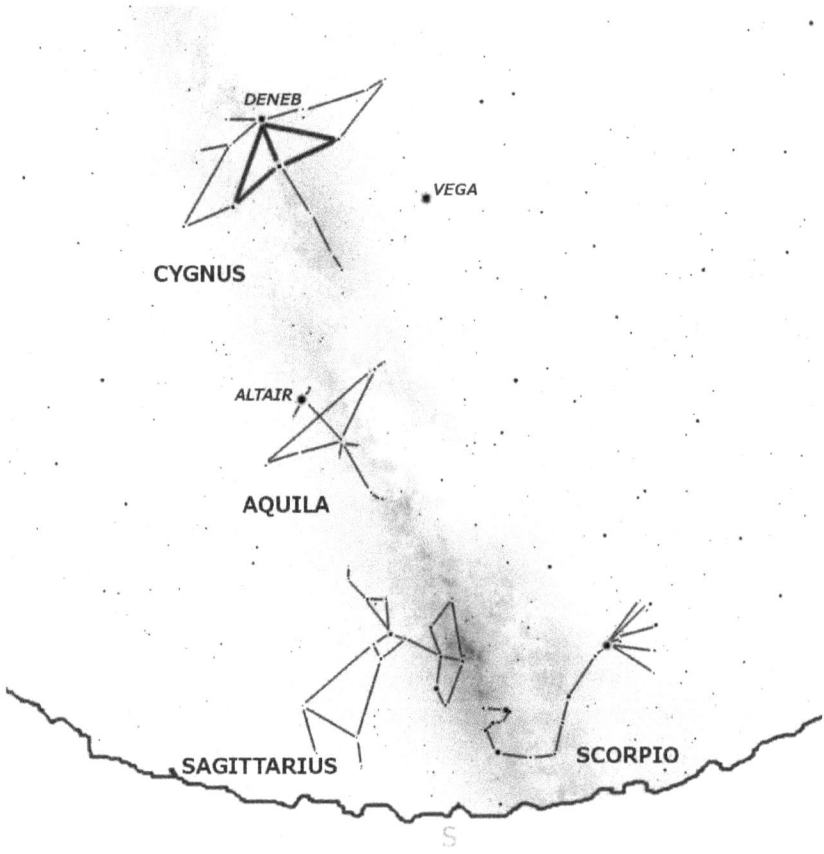

In this chart I have left out the outlining of the Milky Way band itself, but by now you should be able to recognize it as it rises up between Sagittarius and Scorpio. Note that the two great birds, the Swan and the Eagle, are actually "within" the galaxy's shining

A vision of the Infinite

column, although higher up from the southern horizon relative to Sagittarius and Scorpio (these charts are drawn from the perspective of an observer in the northern hemisphere).

The three bright stars of Altair, Deneb, and the extremely bright star Vega (in the constellation of Lyra, not directly involved in this particular story of Jacob's ladder) are often referred to as the "Summer Triangle" of stars, and they are quite easy to identify in the heavens (for observers in the northern hemisphere). These three bright stars are labeled in the chart using italicized letters, to keep the star-labels separate from the constellation labels (which are not italicized).

Note that one of the two great birds of the Milky Way appears to be flying upwards, while the other bird appears to be flying downwards. Aquila the Eagle is closer to the southern horizon from our vantage point, and appears to be flying *upwards* along the Milky Way. Farther up in the heavens we see the beautiful Swan of Cygnus, and this great bird appears to be flying *downwards* along the same Milky Way.

In other words, we have a beautiful winged figure ascending along the Milky Way (Aquila the Eagle) and another beautiful winged figure (Cygnus the Swan) descending along the same Milky Way.

Returning to the ancient text of Genesis 28, we read in the description of the vision of Jacob: "And he dreamed, and behold a ladder set up on the earth, and the top of it reached to heaven: and behold the angels of God ascending and descending on it" (verse 12).

Thus, from our vantage point atop the windy ridgeline overlooking the Pacific coast, watching the glorious panoply of stars slowly wheeling by over our heads as the hours of the night pass by, we ourselves can gaze upon the very "ladder" described in the story of Jacob's dream: the blazing column of the Milky Way galaxy itself, rising like a pillar of luminescent smoke from the

13

Chapter One

southern horizon (where its base is "set up on the earth"), with its top reaching upwards to heaven!

And upon this shining ladder, which connects heaven and earth, we can see the angels ascending and descending: the beautiful winged figures of Aquila and Cygnus, one of which appears to be flying upwards and the other of which is flying downwards.

But just in case some skeptical reader is not yet fully convinced that we are indeed gazing at the very region of the night sky which forms the celestial foundation for this vision of Jacob's ladder described in Genesis chapter 28, the text itself supplies us with still further clues and evidence to positively confirm our identification.

The very next verse declares: "And behold, the LORD stood above it" (verse 13).

This passage thus opens up for our contemplation a subject of truly profound importance: the heavenly constellation which will consistently be seen to play the role of the God of the Bible in the texts themselves.

There is a constellation positioned in the heavens above the constellations we have been discussing and above the brightest part of the Milky Way, a constellation of tremendous significance in all of the ancient Star Myths found in cultures literally around the globe, a constellation which very often plays the role of the most powerful god or deity or hero in any pantheon of ancient myth, and a constellation which can be shown to very consistently play the role of the God of the Bible in the scriptures themselves.

That constellation is the constellation Hercules.

On the facing page, I have included the same star-chart showing the now-familiar region of the night sky containing the brightest part of the Milky Way ("Jacob's ladder" in this story), and below it an engraving from 1860 showing an artist's depiction of the Jacob's ladder scene. And in the star-chart, I have added the outline of Hercules.

A vision of the Infinite

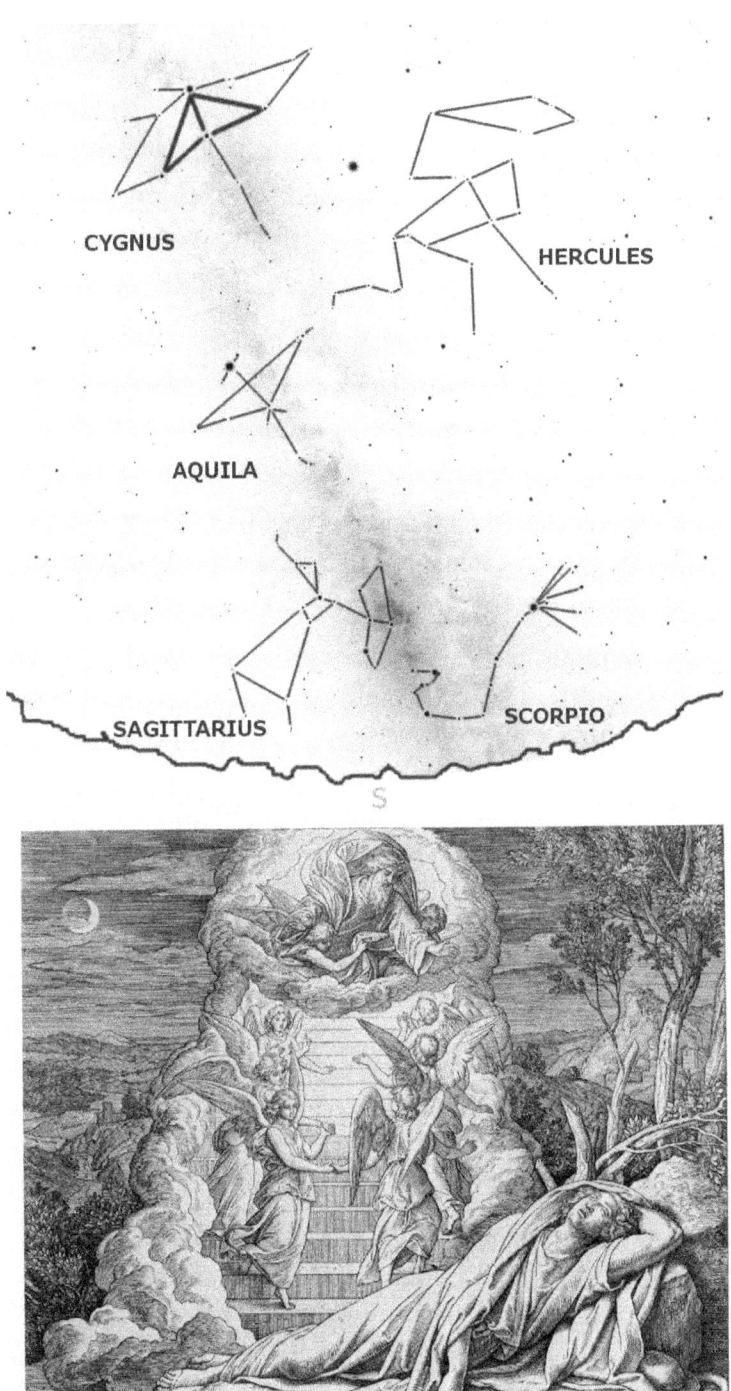

Chapter One

The details in the engraving correspond quite closely to the celestial figures in the region of the heavens we have been discussing -- so closely in fact that it can hardly be denied that the celestial foundation of this particular episode in Genesis was known to some in previous centuries. And this 1860 engraving is by no means the first artistic rendition of the story of Jacob's dream to include very specific details corresponding to the heavens above: artistic depictions from centuries earlier consistently include details which evoke the Milky Way (particularly its brightest and widest region, including the feature of the Dark Rift) and the surrounding constellations.

In the artwork shown on the preceding page, we see that Jacob's ladder itself is depicted as a shining column with billowing clouds on either side, evocative of this particular region of the Milky Way band.

The angels ascending and descending the stair can be seen to correspond to Aquila and Cygnus (although it could certainly be argued that the angel lowest on the stair in that engraving, on the left of the sleeping form of Jacob as we face the image, has been envisioned by this artist as corresponding to the graceful form of the constellation Sagittarius).

At the top of the scene, above the shining stairway just as described in the text, we see that the artist has depicted the God of the Bible. Note that he is depicted leaning forward and reaching downward with his outstretched arm, and that his head is slightly inclined -- all features which can be seen to correspond directly to the outline of the constellation Hercules in the night sky.

The constellation Hercules itself has its other arm raised, brandishing what looks like an enormous weapon, but in the artist's rendition this arm becomes a billowing cloak or mantle, arching up over the head of the Almighty (but still corresponding to the "upper arm" of the constellation, which arches overhead in the outline of Hercules).

A vision of the Infinite

Additionally, the constellation Hercules has a distinctive square-shaped head. In ancient myth and sacred tradition around the world, figures associated with this constellation will often have some feature which evokes and points back towards this square-shaped head of the constellation Hercules. In this case, we see that the artist has depicted the God of the Bible with a very full beard -- and this characteristic is certainly part of a long tradition of other such artistic renditions. Other figures associated with this same constellation will also very often have a full beard (including the hero Heracles or Hercules himself, from the myths of ancient Greece and Rome).

Note as well that the artist has depicted Jacob as lying at the same angle and in the same general location which the constellation Scorpio occupies in the heavenly scene.

The text also explicitly states that Jacob uses a *stone* or *stones* for his pillow (Genesis 28: 11). If Scorpio plays the role of the recumbent figure of Jacob in this episode (which seems to be a likely interpretation, given the matches we have already seen involving the *Milky Way in the role of the shining ladder stretching from earth to heaven*, and the great winged figures of *Aquila and Cygnus flying upwards and downwards along this Milky Way band to play the role of the angels* ascending and descending along the heavenly stair, and the positioning of the *constellation Hercules above to correspond to the textual statement* that "the LORD stood above it"), is there a constellation close to Scorpio which could play the role of the "pillow made of stone" upon which Jacob rests his head according to the text?

Indeed there is.

In my earlier interpretations of this passage of scripture, such as the discussion published in *Star Myths of the World, Volume Three: Star Myths of the Bible* (2016), I argued that the identity of the stone was most likely associated with the constellation Ara

Chapter One

the Altar, which is a block-shaped constellation and could certainly play the role of the stone used by Jacob as a pillow.[4] It is located not far beneath the "tail" end of the constellation Scorpio, and thus could be envisioned as the pillow, if Jacob is associated with Scorpio and his head is envisioned as lining-up with the tail-end of the Scorpion.

However, if the head of Jacob aligns with the head of the constellation Scorpio (as I believe is a likely interpretation, and as the artist in the 1860 engraving has depicted in his artistic envisioning of the scene), then we should consider other candidates to play the role of the stone or stones upon which Jacob rests his head prior to his dream.

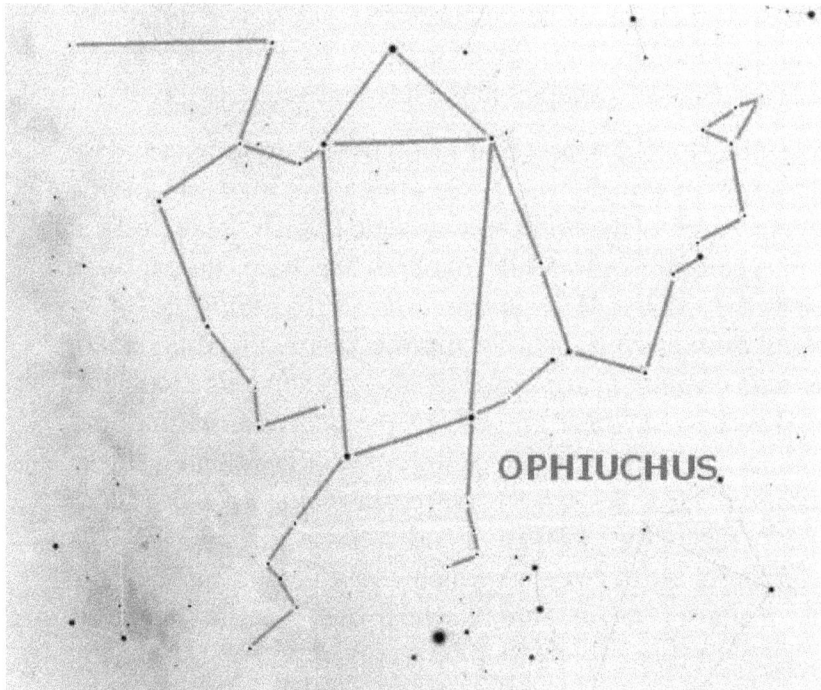

The constellation just above the head-end of the constellation Scorpio is a tall, oblong-shaped constellation of tremendous importance in the ancient Star Myths given to cultures around the world: the constellation Ophiuchus. The constellation is shown in the star-chart above (the stars of Scorpio can be seen just below, although not marked on this chart).

A vision of the Infinite

Due to its distinctive shape, Ophiuchus can be shown to play a wide variety of roles in the world's ancient myths. Often, Ophiuchus will play a human or human-like (anthropomorphic) figure, either male or female, including many important gods or goddesses in various myth-systems from around the globe. However, in addition, Ophiuchus can also be envisioned as a door, a gate, or even a cave, due to the door-like outline of the central body of the constellation. And, Ophiuchus can be shown to play the role of a mountain or great rock in other myths (as well as appearing at times as an ant-hill!). Thus, I believe it quite likely that the stone upon which Jacob rests his head is in fact associated with the constellation Ophiuchus, above Scorpio:

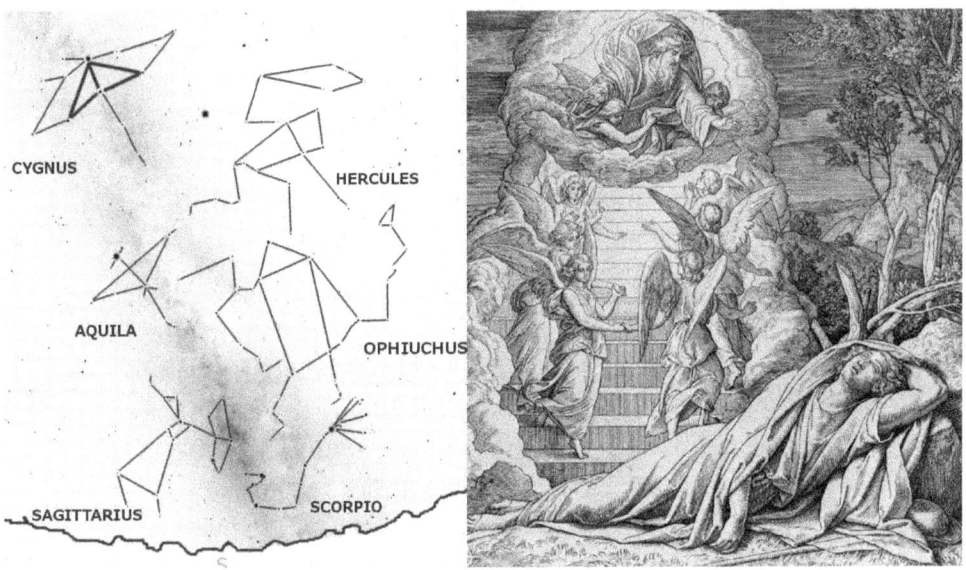

If you look above the upturned face of the figure of the sleeping Jacob in the engraving on the right, you will see that the artist has depicted not only the "stone pillow" upon which Jacob rests his head but also a mountain with a triangular peak (in the distance). This mountain clearly corresponds to the position of Ophiuchus (look again at its location in relation to the cloud-lined "stairway to heaven" which corresponds to the Milky Way).

Should still further evidence be required to support the identification of Jacob with Scorpio (and thus to support the

Chapter One

probability that Ophiuchus plays the "stone" upon which Jacob rests his head, when he sees his vision of the stairway to heaven), we can turn back to the description of the birth of the two twins Jacob and Esau, described in Genesis 25. In that chapter, Esau is described as being born first, but immediately thereafter Jacob emerged into the world, born with his hand grasping the heel of his twin brother Esau.

Sure enough, as I also discuss in *Star Myths of the Bible*, Ophiuchus and Scorpio can be envisioned as being fraternal twins, born to the recumbent figure of Virgo the Virgin, with Ophiuchus above and Scorpio below -- thus Ophiuchus (corresponding to Esau) is the "first-born."[5] However, Scorpio appears to be "grasping the heel" of Ophiuchus just above (and as examined elsewhere in *Star Myths of the Bible* and in some of my other publications and videos, this relationship between Scorpio and Ophiuchus also explains the verse about "bruising the heel" found in Genesis 3: 15 during the episode of the expulsion from Eden).

Thus, the description of Jacob's birth, taking hold of his brother Esau's heel, found in Genesis 25: 26 provides powerful confirmation of the identification of Jacob with Scorpio in at least some of the episodes of Genesis, and strengthens the argument presented above which suggests that the sleeping Jacob in this scene corresponds to Scorpio, with his head resting on the "stone" of Ophiuchus, seeing in his vision the "stairway to heaven" formed by the Milky Way, with the angelic figures of Aquila and Cygnus appearing to "ascend and descend" on the same shining column.

The LORD stands above, and pronounces a benediction upon Jacob in his dream. The God of the Bible in this scene clearly corresponds to the powerful figure of the constellation Hercules. This correspondence can be confirmed again and again using evidence found in other episodes in Biblical scripture, as we will see.

A vision of the Infinite

Some readers at this point may be wondering what could possibly be the significance of the foregoing discussion, while others may already be feeling a bit lost.

For those who feel this discussion has been going a bit too fast -- don't worry! We will fill in some of the "stepping stones" in the upcoming pages as we explore the world's ancient myths and their foundation in celestial metaphor, how the system works and evidence that this ancient system is in fact operating on a world-wide basis.

But, granting that the above analysis correctly interprets the story of Jacob's dream and its origins in the celestial patterns of the constellations and heavenly features (including the Milky Way galaxy itself), what could be the intended message of such a passage?

We will explore that question further in the upcoming pages as well, but for starters it will rapidly become clear that the stories and characters described in the scriptures of the Bible are based upon the *very same system of celestial metaphor* which forms the foundation for virtually all the other ancient myths, scriptures, and sacred stories preserved among cultures around the world, on every inhabited continent and island, from Europe to Africa to the Americas to Australia and India and Asia and the islands of the vast Pacific.

This conclusion, which can be backed up by overwhelming evidence (some of it contained in my previous books, which thus far total over 5,000 pages of content, including diagrams and star-charts, and which are supplemented by over 1,200 published blog posts and dozens of videos I've made for my website and posted on YouTube and Vimeo, and yet all of this only barely begins to scratch the surface of the evidence which is available in the world's myths), points to the inescapable conclusion that the religions which have been built upon the stories and figures of the Biblical scriptures do not have an exclusive claim to truth,

21

Chapter One

contrary to their claims and behavior of the past seventeen centuries or more.

The demonstration that the stories and personages in the pages of the Old and New Testaments are based on the stars, heavenly figures, and celestial cycles should not, however, lead to the mistaken conclusion that this means they are not themselves "true." As I have emphasized before many times, the world's ancient myths can clearly be seen to be designed to impart profound truth, intended for our benefit and blessing. Their demonstrable basis in celestial metaphor indicates that they are not *literal* – but the words "literal" and "true" do not signify the same idea, despite the fact that their meaning is often conflated by those who have been taught that the scriptures of the Bible must be literal in order to be true.

The figures in the stories of the Bible, just as in other sacred stories from other cultures around the globe, can be shown to be based on celestial metaphor, corresponding in most cases to specific constellations. The consistency with which this correspondence can be demonstrated rules out the possibility that we are merely dealing with a coincidence or with an isolated instance in any one passage or episode.

And if the figures and events are based upon celestial metaphor, then (as will become increasingly clear as we proceed) the texts are not recording literal history involving terrestrial persons who lived long ago.

And we can now begin to answer the question posed earlier, after observing Jacob's famous dream and hearing his reaction upon waking from his vision, when we asked whether this ancient record was telling us the story of a unique encounter with the divine, given to one privileged individual in ancient times, specially selected for reasons we cannot begin to fathom, and certainly far from our own experience.

The answer to that question is: "No."

A vision of the Infinite

This majestic passage of ancient scripture, describing the unforgettable and evocative vision of the lonely traveler lying asleep upon the desert floor with a stone for his pillow and towering above him a shining ladder connecting heaven and to earth, with the glorious vision of the angels themselves ascending and descending upon the stair, and the LORD above, looking down and pronouncing a blessing, is not restricted in its scope to a single historical personage on a single historical date and a single terrestrial location.

As I will argue and attempt to demonstrate in this volume, the ancient myths employ celestial metaphor in order to depict for our understanding something which is infinite, and indeed something which is invisible. The world's ancient myths employ figures from the most awe-inspiring canvas available in nature -- the heavens above, which are indeed infinite in their depth -- in order to convey truths about a realm which is beyond the natural, a realm which is beyond the finite, and yet which (as this story of Jacob's ladder dramatizes) is intimately connected with our seemingly-ordinary reality.

When Jacob awakens from his vision, he immediately declares that surely the presence of the divine *is* (present tense) in the very place where he himself is, "and I knew not!"

The truth of this declaration is not limited to some ancient moment, in a place far away, for one particular individual only: indeed, it can be shown that the individual described in this story, and the events of the episode itself, are not based upon events in the life of a literal individual in a remote time of terrestrial history.

The story is certainly *true*, but it is also certainly not *literal*.

It is a metaphor, intended to convey to our understanding a profound truth.

What is the truth which this ancient myth is intended to convey?

Certainly the answer to that question is multi-layered, and its exploration could fill volumes and volumes, without ever exhausting the subject. But for certain one central truth which this incredible ancient story is intended to show to us, and to impress upon us on the deepest possible level (far more deeply than if it were simply stated as a logical argument), is proclaimed in the text itself by Jacob, immediately upon emerging from his vision.

The Infinite is already present, right where we are – even though we do not perceive it.

This often overlooked and unappreciated reality applies to every individual man and woman, at every geographic location and in every situation, even though society and circumstance seem to conspire to prevent our realization of this truth, articulated by the figure of Jacob and dramatized so powerfully in the story of his vision on the journey to Haran.

Chapter 2

Figures in the stars

Go out on a clear night, preferably at a time when the moon is not dominating the sky with its reflected glow, and despite a sky full of stars, you may still have some difficulty identifying the outlines of the specific constellations described in the previous examination of the story of Jacob's vision.

This difficulty results from the fact that we are never formally introduced to the constellations in our modern curriculum of "education," making it quite possible and indeed quite common for most individuals to be able to go through thirteen consecutive years of required schooling (not counting any pre-kindergarten years), followed by four years of undergraduate study at a college or university, and even further years of graduate study after earning a bachelors degree (in order to receive a masters or even a doctorate), without ever once receiving a single minute of instruction regarding the constellations and their outlines and locations in the night sky, their significant stars and their names, and their relationship to the celestial mechanics which create the various cycles which order our lives (days, weeks, months and years) and cause the changing seasons.

Certainly someone with a bachelor's degree (let alone a masters or a doctorate) would be considered "educated" in our modern society. And yet if you were to ask a randomly-selected individual from virtually any walk of life, even one selected from among those who have successfully passed through the very highest levels of education in virtually any of the myriad subjects for which advanced degrees are awarded, to sketch for you the general outlines of the constellations Sagittarius or Ophiuchus, that successful graduate would likely find such a request difficult or (more likely) completely impossible to complete.

Chapter Two

The constellations and their significance have been removed from our modern awareness. Those who want to learn to identify them must do so on their own, generally without assistance from others, and with little guidance regarding which resources will be helpful and which will actually be misleading and counter-productive.

Much of the material purporting to help us to mentally envision and then to enable us to find the constellations seems deliberately engineered to do the very opposite: to obfuscate and confuse and to make the constellations even more difficult to picture in our minds than they already were, more difficult to locate in the night sky, and certainly more difficult to juxtapose with the figures and events described in the stories of the Bible, in order to perceive the undeniable evidence that the world's ancient myths and scriptures (to include those of the so-called Old and New Testaments) are all based on these constellations.

This statement holds true whether we are talking about printed materials in books and magazines, or digital aids including apps and web resources. The depiction of the constellations seems designed to degrade rather than enhance the ability to envision the constellations in our minds or in the night sky.

As a result, even those who have made some effort to become familiar with the stars of our night sky may still feel somewhat insecure if asked to describe or draw the outline of even the most important constellations.

This situation even holds true for those who study and practice aspects of astrology, and who are intimately familiar with the names of the zodiac constellations, their order of progression throughout the year, and who generally ascribe great importance to the heavenly cycles, in brave defiance of the pervasive apathy or even outright hostility towards the idea that the motions of the stars and the knowledge of the constellations might be a subject of utmost importance.

Thus, even who have taken the time to become quite knowledgeable about astrology and who could easily describe numerous traits and influences relating to Capricorn or Aquarius or Virgo or Aries might have difficulty sketching out the stars of these constellations on the back of a napkin, or pointing them out to you in the night sky itself.

This lamentable state of affairs is not new, and it is not the fault of the men and women of the general public, as a famous author (whose work is familiar to almost every reader of this book) wrote over sixty years ago, in 1952.

According to the biography on the website of his publisher (Houghton Mifflin Books), Hans Augusto Reyersbach was born in Hamburg, Germany on September 16, 1898.[6] It was and remains the second-largest city in Germany, after Berlin, and is situated in northern Germany just a hundred miles south of the southern border of Denmark, along the Elbe River which flows east and southeast from the North Sea. The online biography page from Houghton Mifflin says that as a child, growing up "near the world-famous Hagenbeck Zoo" in Hamburg, young Hans "developed a lifelong love for animals and drawing."[7]

An article published in the *New York Times* in 2010 explains that after graduating from the University of Hamburg, Hans "moved from Hamburg to Rio de Janeiro as early as 1924, and sold bathtubs and sinks along the Brazilian Amazon."[8] There, after about eleven years in Brazil, the young man, now 36 or 37 years old, was pleased to learn that a family friend, Margarete Elisabeth Waldstein, was moving to Brazil as well.

Margarete, born in 1906, was an artist and a photographer. She had studied art at the Bauhaus in Dessau, as well as at Kunstakademie Düsseldorf and the University of Munich. In 1935, when she moved to Brazil, she would have been 28 or 29 years old. The Reichstag fire had taken place two years earlier, in 1933, cementing Nazi control of the government of Germany, and Margarete felt she had to leave the country of her birth.

Chapter Two

That same year, the two announced their engagement to be married. The *New York Times* article from 2010, describing a museum exhibit containing their work as well as memorabilia from their lives, describes "a wedding invitation sent out in 1935, soon after Hans Augusto Reyersbach shortened his last name to Rey, and Margarete Waldstein shortened her first name to Margret."[9]

And it would be under these names that the pair of artists and later authors would become famous, as Margret and H. A. Rey. Margret convinced Hans to leave his previous employment selling tubs and sinks, and the two founded the first advertising agency in Rio de Janeiro.[10]

The *Times* article goes on to explain that during a belated honeymoon to Europe in 1936, the couple fell in love with Paris, and moved there for the next four years."[11] "It was here that Hans published his first children's book, after a French publisher saw his newspaper cartoons of a giraffe and asked him to expand upon them," Houghton Mifflin informs us -- and the rest is history.[12]

Together, Margret and H. A. Rey created a book about a giraffe named "Raffy" and his nine monkey friends -- and its reception caused the Reys to realize that one of the monkeys "deserved a book of his own, so they began work on a manuscript that featured the lovable and exceedingly curious little monkey."[13]

However, in June of 1940, the Nazis were approaching Paris, and Hans and Margret -- who as German-born Jews, and with Margret's father a former member of the Reichstag, had reason to fear the Nazis -- decided to flee before the Germans arrived in the city. The biographies of the Reys recount that Hans acquired bicycle parts to assemble two bicycles, and as the Nazis rolled into Paris, the couple rolled out just ahead of them:

> Early in the morning of June 14, 1940, the Reys set off on their bicycles. They brought very little with them on their predawn flight -- only warm coats, a bit of food, and five manuscripts, one of which was *Curious George*. The Nazis entered Paris

just hours later, but the Reys were already on their way out. They rode their makeshift bicycles for four long days until reaching the French-Spanish border, where they sold them for train fare to Lisbon. From there they made their way to Brazil and on to New York City, beginning a whole new life as children's book authors.[14]

In New York, Margret and Hans established residence in Greenwich Village, and *Curious George* was published soon after, in 1941, becoming an instant success. They would write six more Curious George books together, which sold many tens of million of copies. In 1963, the couple moved to Cambridge, Massachusetts, where they would live the rest of their lives.

And yet, while the adventures of the memorable character Curious George made the Reys world-famous, and while I myself certainly remember reading the original series of books as a child (and having them read to me, before I was old enough to read them myself), it is another book written by H. A. Rey which has had a much greater impact on my life, an impact which continues to this day.

In 1952, the Houghton Mifflin Company of Boston published a book by H. A. Rey entitled *The Stars: A New Way to See Them*, the importance of which simply cannot be overstated. In it, Rey laments the very phenomena we have been discussing in this chapter: the widespread lack of familiarity with the outlines of the constellations themselves, induced by suggested outlines for the constellations which are in fact deleterious to the ability to envision the constellations and find them in the night sky.

Delineating the scope of the problem, Rey writes:

> Of course one can enjoy the stars without knowing them. But if you know them at least a little the pleasure is infinitely greater. It is fun to watch them announce the seasons, to see them rise at the expected times and places and follow their paths year in, year out, more reliable than anything else.[15]

Chapter Two

And yet, Rey notes, although becoming familiar with the stars is "both enjoyable and useful," the deck seems to be stacked against those who want to look at the stars. The problem, he says, going directly to the heart of the matter, lies in the way our instructional materials represent the constellations:

> The constellations have such intriguing names -- somehow we expect the books to show us groups of stars in the shape of a Lion, a Whale, a Virgin, and so forth. But they show nothing of that sort.[16]

Instead, Rey observes, the depictions consistently fall into one of two equally unhelpful categories: either they show elaborate artistic depictions overlaid upon the stars, which cannot be seen when we go out into the night sky to search for the constellations, and which have no direct connection to the actual stars, or they take a more modernistic approach and connect the stars in a seemingly-random manner, creating in his words "involved geometrical shapes which don't look like anything and have no relation to the names."[17]

Neither way is of much use to us if we are trying to gain familiarity with the actual layout of the stars of any particular constellation (let alone trying to learn and become familiar with *all* of them!) and neither way is much use to us if we are trying to find any particular constellation in the sky, as Rey explains.

Not mentioned by Rey in his book, but equally if not more important: neither of the unhelpful methods he criticizes enable us to see the connections between the constellations and the characters and episodes in myth or in ancient artwork; indeed, these two methods of badly representing the constellations seem almost designed to obscure these connections and prevent the discovery of the truth that the world's ancient scriptures and sacred stories are based on celestial metaphor.

One would think that, nearly seventy years after the publication of Rey's brilliant 1952 book calling attention to the utter uselessness of these two unhelpful schools of depicting the constellations, and

Figures in the stars

providing his suggested remedy, which solves all of the problems detailed above, the benighted systems of depicting the constellations criticized by H. A. Rey would be a thing of the past.

But one would be wrong to think so.

Below are contemporary examples of each type of unhelpful outline, presented for the constellation Sagittarius, which we encountered in the preceding examination of the vision of Jacob. First, an example of the kind of flowery and "allegorical" (as Rey called them) outlines in which an artist freely sketches an artistic depiction around the stars, with little or no connection to the stars themselves:

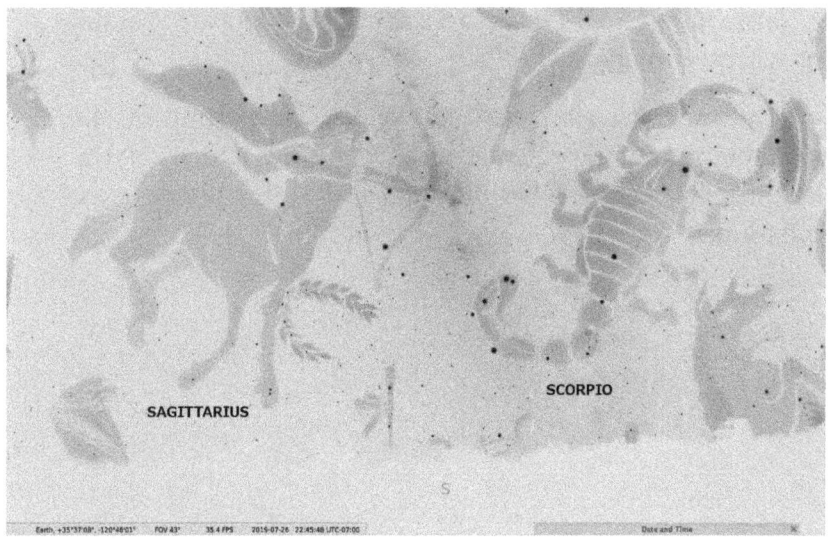

In the star-chart above, we see the very same region containing the constellations Sagittarius and Scorpio that we examined during the preceding discussion of the dream of Jacob's ladder: you can see the thickest and brightest part of the Milky Way band rising up between these two zodiac constellations (because the chart is inverted, the bright column of the Milky Way appears as darker clouds against a light background, instead of as a bright and shining feature against the dark background sky).

I call the outlines added in the chart above "flowery" artwork (Rey refers to them as "allegorical drawings"). Look at the

31

Chapter Two

depiction of the constellation Sagittarius: it takes the form of a centaur, pointing its bow in the direction of Scorpio. But, as Rey's book says of such depictions:

> This may look decorative but the drawing has little to do with the stars. You cannot *see* it in the sky. It is confusing rather than helpful.[18]

Indeed, if you look closely at the artistic depiction of the centaur over the stars of Sagittarius on the preceding page, you will have to admit that you could probably place that same flowery artwork over any other bunch of stars just about anywhere else in the night sky. Going out into the night with that image in your mind for the constellation Sagittarius and then trying to locate it in the heavens will be virtually impossible.

Below is a star-chart showing the exact same portion of sky shown on the preceding page, and connecting the stars using the default constellational outlines included in the free open-source app Stellarium:

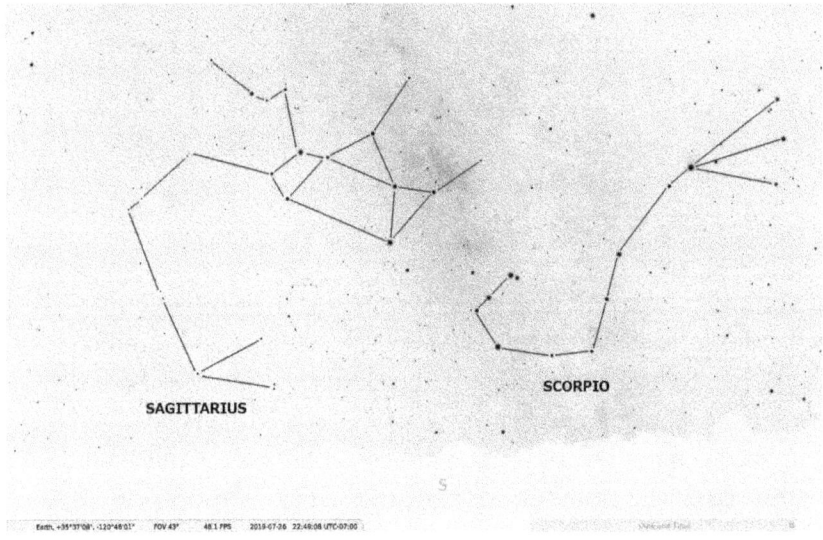

This type of outlining is typical of the "geometrical figures" that Rey described in his 1952 book, and which continue to appear in books, websites, star-gazing publications and even in apps which purport to help people find the constellations.

The outline for Scorpio in this particular case is not terribly bad, but Scorpio is a very simple constellation which, when you see it in person, fairly jumps out at you from the sky in the sinuous shape seen in this chart (and Rey's suggested outline is not much different). The graceful outline rather resembles a serpent, and as it turns out, Scorpio appears in the world's myths more often as a serpent or a dragon (and often as a serpent with multiple heads, as seen here) than it appears as a scorpion (although it does appear as a scorpion in some significant myths and scriptures).

Turning to the outline of Sagittarius, we can immediately perceive the truth of H. A. Rey's criticisms of these random-looking modern geometric outlines. The jumble of lines bears no resemblance to a centaur holding a bow, or indeed to anything else. Trying to remember that outline and then finding it in the heavens would be difficult. Even if you stared at it for some time, it would be difficult to reproduce on a paper from memory, and it would even be difficult to connect the stars on a printout of the same chart containing the stars of the above region of the sky (unconnected) in a pattern resembling the pattern shown.

More significantly for our purposes in this book (that is, exploring the ancient Star Myths and their meaning for our lives, and exploring the evidence which demonstrates that the world's ancient myths are built upon a common system of tremendous antiquity), neither of the systems of depicting the constellations presented in the two previous examples (neither the "flowery" nor the "geometric") are of much use at all in perceiving the connections between the myths and the stars.

As it turns out, Sagittarius is one of the most important constellations in the celestial system underlying the world's ancient myths. The constellation plays the role of numerous extremely important figures, including many different gods and goddesses, and heroes and heroines, in myths from cultures around the globe. And yet, if all we had to go on were the random-looking jumble of lines shown on the preceding page as

Chapter Two

our way of envisioning Sagittarius, these connections would be extremely difficult to perceive.

There are in fact a great many pieces of ancient artwork which have survived to the present day and which can be convincingly proven to incorporate artistic details which point directly to connections between specific mythical figures and specific constellations -- but we will be all but oblivious to those ancient clues if our way of envisioning the constellations is limited to the egregious methods against which H. A. Rey raises his complaint in his 1952 book.

Below I present perhaps my favorite example of proof, one I have presented in previous books but which illustrates the principle so powerfully that I include it again here, not only for those readers for whom this book may be the first of my books that they encounter, but equally for those who have seen it before, because it drives home the incredible importance of what Rey gives us in *The Stars: A New Way to See Them* (a book far less well-known than the stories of Curious George, but so important to history).

First, here are the constellations Sagittarius and Scorpio, with outlines added *as suggested by H. A. Rey* in his book:

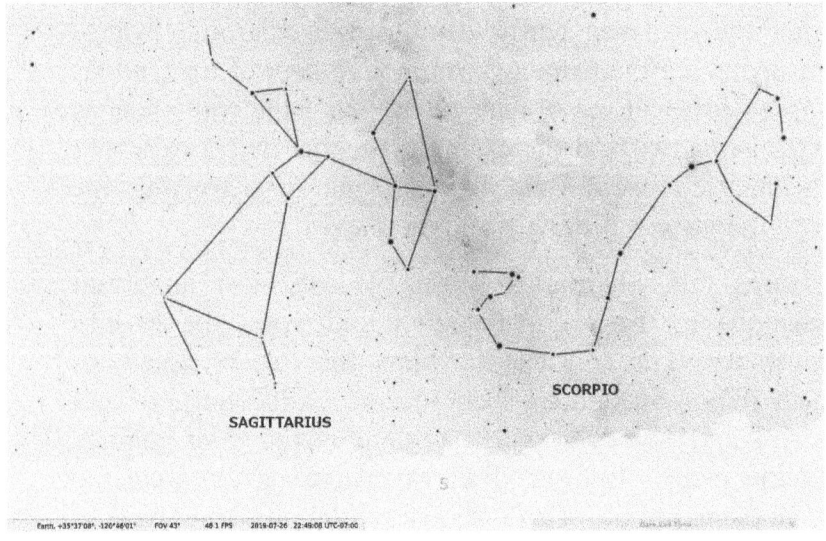

Figures in the stars

These outlines are elegant, and they are memorable. If you study them, you *will* be able to sketch them out from memory, if necessary -- and you will be able to find them in the night sky. Most importantly of all, however (at least for the discussion in this book): Rey's outlines consistently match up with specific details mentioned in ancient myths from around the world, and even with ancient artwork.

Consider the illustration below, of an ancient red-figure bell-krater from the Attic region of Greece, thought to have been crafted in the period between about 500 BC and 475 BC. The vase depicts Artemis, slaying the unfortunate young prince Actaeon (or Acteon):

When I first encountered this artwork (first as an illustration in Beazley's 1918 *Attic Red-Figured Vases in American Museums*, although I later visited the ancient Greek vase itself, in person), I was astonished. Clearly, the ancient artist has chosen to depict the goddess Artemis in such a way as to evoke the constellation Sagittarius, and Actaeon in such a way as to evoke Scorpio.

35

Chapter Two

On the opposite page I have placed a photograph of the artwork on the bell-krater itself above the constellations Sagittarius and Scorpio -- with the constellations outlined based on the system presented by H. A. Rey in his 1952 book on the stars.

That the ancient artist, thought to have composed this masterful artistic scene in the first part of the fifth century BC, has depicted the goddess Artemis in a position which is based directly upon the outline of the constellation Sagittarius is undeniable.

In order to illustrate some of the many points of correspondence between the artist's depiction and the stars of the constellation itself, I have added the letters "A," "B," and "C" to each of the illustrations.

Letter "A" in the star-chart and in the ancient artwork calls our attention to the fact that the body position of the goddess as depicted on the vase is nearly identical to that of the constellation as outlined by H. A. Rey in 1952. The bend in the knee, near the location of the letter "A," makes the connection very easy to recognize.

Note also the length of the dress or skirt worn by the goddess, and the correspondence to the outline of the constellation in the night sky, as well as the position of the feet in the artwork and in the outline of the stars. It should be self-evident that the artist of this ancient depiction of the goddess was aware of the distinctive features of the constellation Sagittarius (and, what is more, was envisioning that constellation in the same way as that suggested by H. A. Rey in his system of outlining, published in his 1952 book, millennia later).

Moving now to the letter "B" in both the artwork and the outline of the constellation, we focus on the bow held by the goddess, and the level at which she is holding the bow as she points it towards the doomed prince. The correspondences between the constellation as outlined by Rey and the artwork from the early fifth century BC are undeniable: the manner in which the artist

Figures in the stars

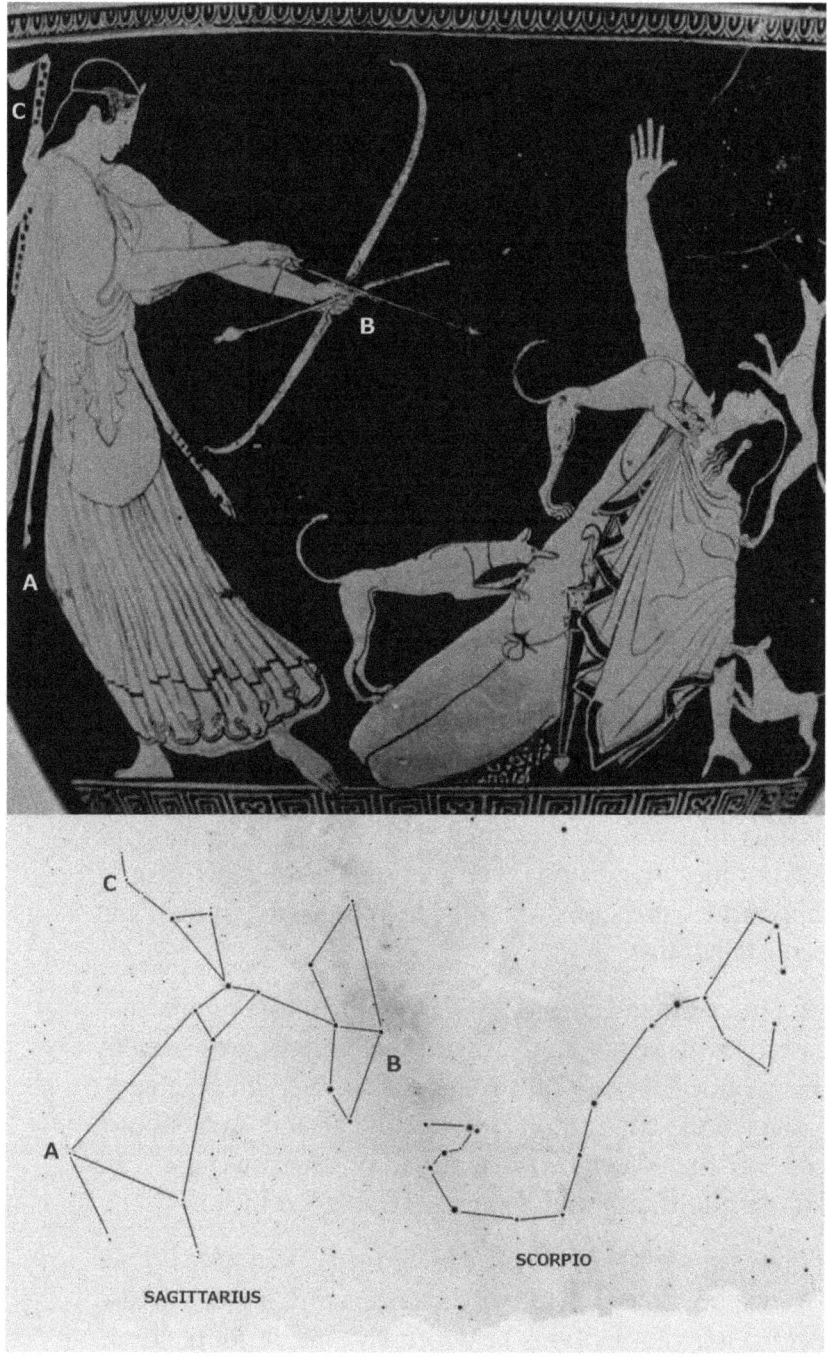

SAGITTARIUS

SCORPIO

37

Chapter Two

has depicted the goddess holding the bow argues very strongly that the constellation Sagittarius is being deliberately evoked.

Finally, note that the ancient artist has included something strapped or slung over the shoulder of the goddess Artemis, decorated with what appears to be a tassel. This tassel (attached perhaps to a quiver or perhaps a sword slung over the shoulder) is indicated by the letter "C" which I have added to the artwork in order to call attention to this specific artistic detail.

As we can see by the corresponding letter "C" in the star-chart diagram below the artwork, the constellation Sagittarius itself has a distinctive feature above the "head" of the constellation, consisting of a line of stars rising up above the triangular head of Sagittarius.

The inclusion of this detail by the ancient artist should confirm beyond all reasonable doubt that the ancient masterpiece depicting Artemis slaying Actaeon on this red-figure vase from a period close to 500 BC is deliberately based upon the outline of the constellation Sagittarius -- and indeed upon the very outline of the constellation as suggested by H. A. Rey in his 1952 book (an outline very different from any other way of connecting the stars of Sagittarius that we are presented with in any of the horrific suggested outlines found upon websites such as Wikipedia or in mobile apps which are supposed to be helping us to envision and find the constellations)!

Pause for a moment and consider the enormity of the significance of this assertion. If we are familiar with the outlines presented by Rey in his wonderful book on the stars, then we will be able to readily perceive the connection between the ancient depiction of the scene of the slaying of Actaeon by Artemis and the constellations Sagittarius and Scorpio. If not: good luck.

I myself grew up with Rey's book *The Stars: A New Way to See Them*, from the time I was very young (and in fact I also remember having another book he wrote, specifically for children, presenting the same system of constellational outlines and entitled *Find the Constellations*, first published in 1954). Thus, when I first saw the incredible artwork on the bell-krater depicting Artemis and Actaeon, I immediately recognized the correspondence (I had at that point been exploring the connections between the myths and the stars for some years).

However, if all we had to go by were the two types of unhelpful systems for depicting the constellations that were illustrated previously, we might stare at the bell-krater containing the beautiful artwork from the fifth century BC for many hours, and never perceive what should be obvious to the most casual observer!

Think about it: if all you had ever seen to depict the constellation Sagittarius had been the geometric outline shown earlier, would you have noticed any of the correspondences between the constellation and the artwork, such as those marked "A," "B," and "C" in the preceding comparison?

And, similarly, if all you had to go on in order to locate Sagittarius in the sky had been the flowery illustration of a centaur laid over the stars, the connections would have been equally difficult to detect. The flowery illustration preserves even fewer of the distinctive features of the constellation itself as formed by the position of the stars in the sky.

The more modern-looking "geometric" method of connecting the stars does at least stick to the stars themselves, unlike the "flowery" artistic rendition, which only conforms to the stars very loosely. However, the modern geometric patterns seem to have been almost deliberately designed to *obscure* as many of the distinctive features of the constellations as possible.

Looking at the diagram below, we see how the modern, non-Rey method of outlining the stars of Sagittarius seems to go out of its way to obfuscate the details that the ancient artist saw as indicative of the constellation Sagittarius and which that artist included in the artwork of the Artemis and Actaeon scene.

Chapter Two

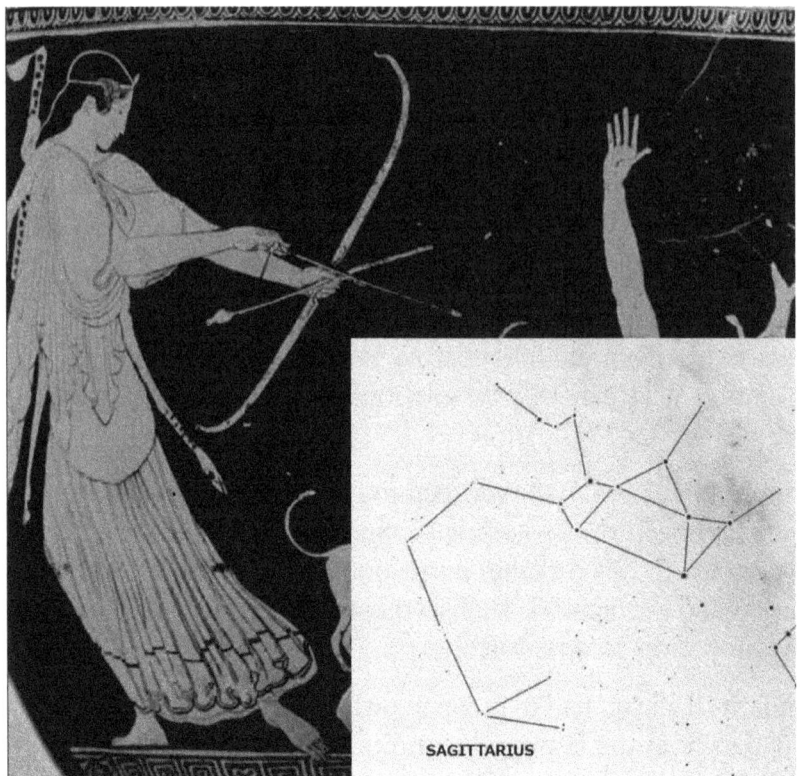

The bend in the knee or the position of the legs is completely obscured in the atrocious outline offered by these "modern" methods. There is no way to tell where the "head" of Sagittarius is located in the jumble of lines presented in the outline above, let alone the "tassel" feature. It would even be difficult to figure out where the distinctive "bow" of Sagittarius is located, using the hideous modern outline shown here.

Indeed, when we look at what is being offered in the atrocious modern outlines (against which H. A. Rey was rightly indignant, saying that they were actually "confusing rather than helpful"[19]), we realize that if someone wanted to prevent modern men and women from perceiving the celestial foundations of the world's ancient myths and scriptures, they would simply have to ensure that the only outlines presented to them as means of envisioning the constellations fall into the two categories illustrated previously, which Rey railed against in his book (the two systems which I we could describe as the "flowery" system and the "geometric random-jumble" system).

If we never saw Rey's outlines -- outlines which can be shown, over and over, to match up with specific details in ancient myth and even with specific details in ancient artwork -- then we would be blissfully unable to see the connections, even if they were staring us right in the face (the way these connections absolutely stare us in the face in the artwork depicting Artemis and Actaeon presented in this chapter).

In fact, we would be in precisely the condition which George Orwell warns us about in the appendix he included at the end of his famous book *Nineteen Eighty-Four*, an appendix entitled "The Principles of Newspeak." There, Orwell explains that manipulating vocabulary and language enables manipulation of the very ability to think altogether. If men and women do not have access to words regarding concepts that the oppressors do not want them to think about, then those men and women will not even have the ability to frame those concepts in their minds. Orwell writes:

> The purpose of Newspeak was not only to provide a medium of expression for the world-view and mental habits proper to the devotees of Ingsoc, but to make all other modes of thought impossible. It was intended that when Newspeak had been adopted once and for all and Oldspeak forgotten, a heretical thought -- that is, a thought diverging from the principles of Ingsoc -- should be literally unthinkable, at least so far as thought is dependent on words.[20]

In just the same way, if men and women have no access to the "vocabulary" of the constellations, then they will be rendered just as incapable of framing "heretical" thoughts regarding the connection between the scriptures of the Bible, for instance, and the stars of the night sky -- regardless of the overwhelming and very clear evidence that the figures and stories described in those ancient texts are based on a system of celestial metaphor.

Chapter Two

This is what makes the publication in 1952 of H. A. Rey's book *The Stars: A New Way to See Them* such an incredibly important event in human history. For H. A. Rey's suggested system of envisioning the constellations, correcting the problems of both of the other systems prevalent at the time (and still prevelant to this day, nearly seventy years later), provides us with a kind of "Rosetta Stone" by which we can begin to decipher the ancient code within which the figures in the myths correspond to specific constellations in the heavens.

Rey's book does not actually go so far as to explain that ancient code, and the connections between his outlines and the figures and events in the myths. To my knowledge, he himself never directly revealed any "smoking gun" that would indicate to the reader that what he was publishing in *The Stars: A New Way to See Them* was in fact the very same ancient method of envisioning the constellations which underlies the stories in the Bible and the myths and sacred stories preserved by virtually every other culture around the world.

However, he does drop what I would consider to be a very strong hint at one point, early in the book. On page 16, after presenting example after example of "the old way" of depicting various constellations, and contrasting the atrocious outlines of "the old way" with the wonderful outlines of "the new way" which he proposes in his book, Rey makes the following statement (or perhaps we should say, "understatement"):

It may even be that this new way is not so new after all.[21]

He then goes on to speculate that perhaps in some extremely remote time in humanity's past, "long before recorded history began," people looking up at the stars and began to arrange them into groups, and perhaps (Rey goes on), just perhaps "we are doing here precisely what" those ancients were doing, in a time before the earliest history known today.[22]

Figures in the stars

Is it possible that when Rey suggests that he is doing "precisely" the same thing that was done in a time before *known* history even began to be recorded, he means exactly what he says: that the outlines he is sharing with the reader are *precisely* the outlines which were known even *prior to* the conventionally admitted "earliest civilizations" -- that he is sharing the outlines which are employed in this incredible ancient system which underlies the myths of the world, even those found in the earliest surviving texts of ancient Mesopotamia and ancient Egypt?

I find this possibility, that Rey knew much more than he lets on in his text, both extremely compelling and extremely intriguing. We cannot dismiss the idea out of hand, because the outlines presented by Rey in his text turn out to be *the key* to unlocking the ancient mysteries. We have already seen one very powerful example in this chapter, with the amazing artwork on the bell-krater depicting Artemis and Actaeon. The correspondence between the outline and the artist's depiction make it quite clear that the ancients must have been using the very same system of envisioning the constellation Sagittarius that H. A. Rey proposes in *The Stars: A New Way to See Them*.

And we will have occasion to see many more equally astonishing examples as we proceed through our examination in this volume, including passages in ancient scripture and examples of ancient artwork which line up precisely with the outlines proposed by Rey for other important constellations (not just Sagittarius).

This raises the question of how H. A. Rey came by the system which he shares with the world in his 1952 book. It is a question I have often contemplated, ever since I began to see the connections between the stars and the myths, and to realize that the system presented by H. A. Rey provides us with the vocabulary to begin the work of translating the language of celestial metaphor which the ancient myths are speaking.

The possibilities are numerous, and at this point we should be careful not to rule any of them out without good reason.

Chapter Two

First, it is of course possible that Rey came up with this system on his own, independently of anyone else, and that with his own artistic talent and artistic eye, he perceived the most elegant way to connect the constellations in a way that matches up with their traditional names and the figures they purport to represent (a powerful hero in the case of Hercules, for example, or a beautiful maiden in the case of Andromeda).

It is also possible that Rey was somehow privy to an ancient tradition, which had been passed down in secret for centuries prior to his decision to reveal it to the world. He and his wife Margret seem to have come from very interesting families, and to have had quite an extraordinary array of experiences during their twenties and thirties, including travel to Brazil and the Amazon, but also including education (in Margret's case) among some of the most respected but also innovative and even iconoclastic and avante-garde artistic academies and institutions in the world.

It is even possible to speculate that Rey may have come across or been given exposure to some aspect of the world's ancient wisdom during his eleven years traveling into the depths of the Amazon on a regular basis as part of his job. As Graham Hancock describes in his most-recent book, *America Before: The Key to Earth's Lost Civilization* (2019), the remains of hundreds of enormous, geometrically-sophisticated earthworks have recently been detected (using new technologies such as Lidar) in the Amazon jungle of South America, a vast region the size of the Indian subcontinent and one which has been only minimally explored by archaeologists to date, and yet a region which appears to hold vital secrets regarding humanity's ancient past.

It is even possible to speculate, and we should again not rule it out, that Rey may have received inspiration regarding the outlines of the constellations from some type of contact with the spiritual realm. At this time we do not actually know the origin of the amazing ancient system of celestial metaphor which underlies the world's myths. It may be that this system itself was imparted to humanity from the divine realm in some manner. It may also be

Figures in the stars

that this system was received through the process of communicating with the other realm through practices such as the ingesting of plant medicines, including those which are known to have been preserved among the cultures of the Amazon (such as the plant medicine ayahuasca).

If the system itself originally came to humanity through inspiration of this nature, then it is certainly possible that individuals at later points in time might somehow tap into the same source. We should not completely rule out the possibility that either Hans or Margret Rey somehow gained insight into the outlining system underlying the myths through inspiration of this nature, although at this point all of the above suggestions are purely speculative, and not based on any direct evidence other than the fact that the system Rey published in 1952 can be shown to match up with ancient artwork literally from around the world, and to help to unlock celestial connections in myths from cultures on every inhabited continent and island of our planet.

Another intriguing question to consider is the question of why would Rey (or perhaps others with whom he might have been in contact) choose to publish aspects of this ancient system at the time that he did? This question is particularly pressing if indeed Rey was privy to some ancient knowledge which had been preserved and passed down in secret for many centuries, prior to the publication of his 1952 book on the stars.

Recall the history of the tumultuous early years of the marriage of Margret and Hans: seeing the permanent suspension of human rights in Germany following the Reichstag fire in 1933 and the seizure of power by the fascists in Europe, involving the imprisonment in concentration camps of those deemed to be enemies of the state. Recall that the couple had to flee in the pre-dawn hours on bicycles to escape Paris before the Nazis occupied the city in 1940, and that by making their way to the Americas the couple may very well have escaped with their lives.

Rey's book *The Stars: A New Way to See Them* was published in 1952, a mere seven years after the cessation of open combat in the Second World War. Perhaps this proximity to that horrific conflagration helps explain the publication of this system, if indeed Rey was privy to some ancient and previously secret tradition.

It is even possible to speculate that the Reys, or others with whom they were in contact, perceived in the forces of darkness which had seized power in the country of their birth a manifestation of a more ancient evil which had been working for centuries to oppress and tyrannize humanity, including through the suppression of the very same system of knowledge in which the constellations portrayed in the 1952 book have always played a vital role.

Whatever the answer (and it is a question to which we may never have an answer), it is simply impossible to overstate the importance of the publication of *The Stars: A New Way to See Them*, and the importance of the system of outlining the constellations contained within.

As we've seen, we cannot even begin to grasp the connections between the stars and the myths until we can envision the constellations -- and there appear to be forces at work which even today seek to prevent men and women from being able to envision the constellations.

Armed with the outlining system provided to us by H. A. Rey in his watershed book, we now turn our attention to another one of the most important constellations in the ancient system of celestial metaphor underyling the world's ancient myths: the constellation Hercules.

Chapter 3

The importance of Hercules

These are the stars of the constellation Hercules.

This constellation is one of the most mythologically important constellations in the ancient myths and scriptures of the world.

In a pattern we have already seen, perhaps in order to prevent men and women from discovering the truths discussed in this book, the outlines we are usually given for connecting the stars of this constellation are almost universally atrocious and unhelpful.

Chapter Three

For example, if you look for the constellation outline suggested by the International Astronomy Union (the IAU), you will find an image which connects the stars in the manner shown below:

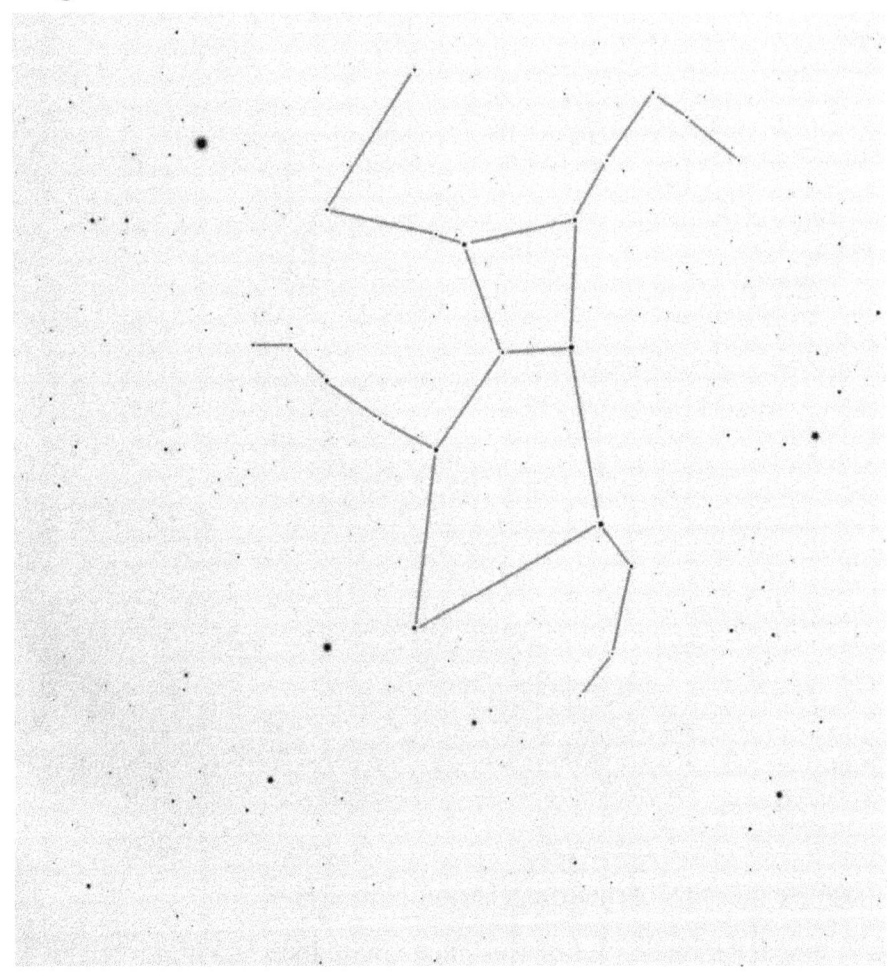

This outline is singularly unhelpful for envisioning or remembering the constellation, or for finding it in the night sky.

What exactly does the outline above, endorsed by the IAU, represent? It appears to depict some type of nightmare insect with a bloated and misshapen abdomen. It can hardly be said to represent the constellation's namesake, the semi-divine hero

The importance of Hercules

Hercules (or Heracles, to give him his ancient Greek name), son of Zeus.

And yet, if connected in a different way, the stars of this constellation do in fact resemble the ancient hero Heracles or Hercules. Here are the very same stars, connected with a different outline -- the outline suggested in 1952 by H. A. Rey:

Note that in this outline, which we have already encountered in the vision of Jacob, the figure of Hercules has a distinctive square-shaped head, a body position resembling a deep lunging or kneeling posture, and two arms, one reaching forward or downward and the other raised overhead and brandishing a

Chapter Three

formidable weapon, perhaps an enormous club, sword, mace, or other instrument of war:

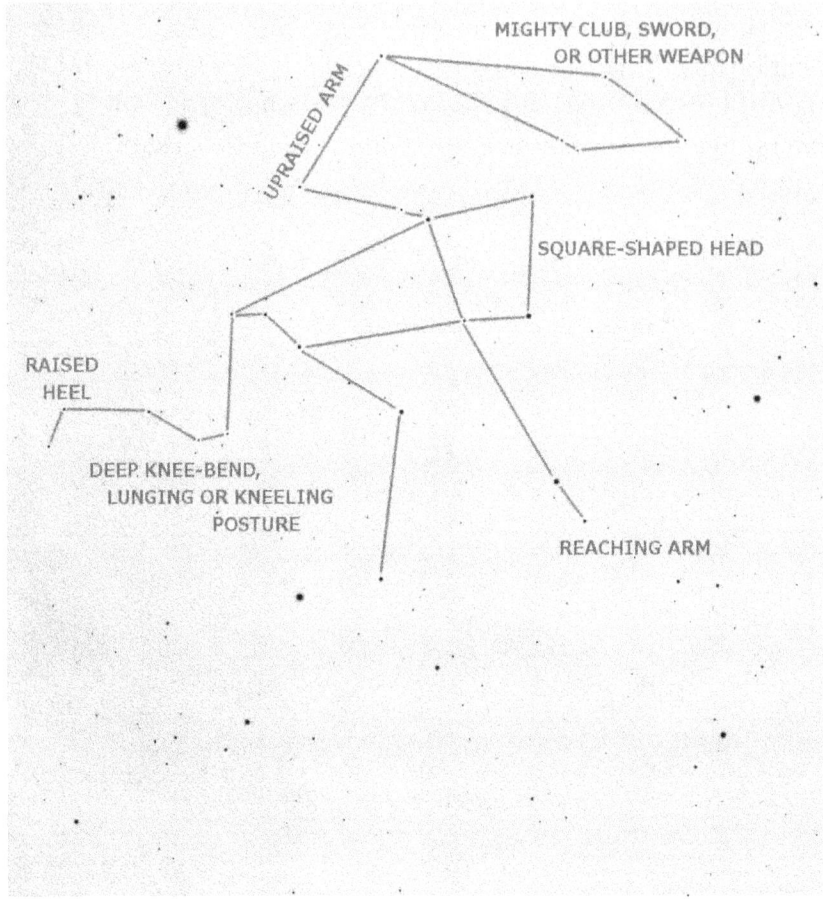

As we have already seen, and as H. A. Rey himself appears to have hinted, even though Rey titled his book *The Stars: A New Way to See Them*, there is abundant evidence that the above method of outlining or envisioning the constellation Hercules is actually extremely ancient.

Indeed, all of the distinctive features of the constellation Hercules noted on the previous page can be shown to parallel ancient artistic conventions employed by ancient artists when depicting the hero Heracles himself, such as the artwork on the ancient Greek vase shown below, thought to date to about 530 BC:

The importance of Hercules

It should be immediately obvious to even the most casual observer that the ancient artist of this scene has chosen to depict Heracles in an outline nearly identical to the outline given for the constellation Hercules under the system suggested by H. A. Rey in 1952!

Most obvious of course is the upraised arm brandishing a weapon corresponding in shape and position to the weapon held aloft by the constellation. However, note also the square-shaped head of the hero, depicted here (as so often in ancient artwork of Heracles) with a full beard and wearing the head of a skinned lion as headgear, giving the head of Heracles a very square shape. Note also the hero's forward-reaching arm, matching the outline of the constellation.

Below we see the same ancient artwork, this time with the image of Heracles isolated and all the other figures removed, in order to highlight the similarities to the outline of the constellation itself in the night sky:

51

Chapter Three

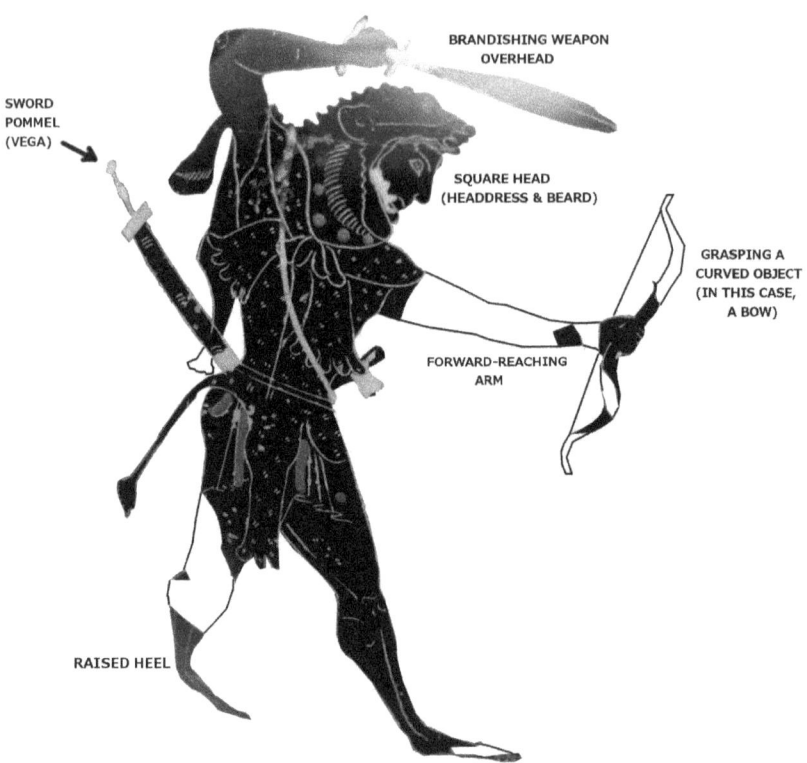

We can now see even more clearly the similarities to the *constellation* Hercules in this ancient depiction of the hero Heracles from a vase dating back to around 530 BC. In addition to the weapon held aloft and brandished over the square-shaped head, we also note the raised rear heel of the figure as depicted, as well as the fact that the outstretched arm is grasping a *curved* object: in this case, a short bow (if you turn back to the original image of the artwork and look carefully, you can see this small bow held in the hero's forward-reaching arm).

The fact that the artist has depicted the hero holding a curved bow in his forward-reaching hand is significant: this detail is a distinctive feature often included in artwork of figures associated with the constellation Hercules. Why? Directly in front of the constellation Hercules in the night sky is the arc-shaped

52

The importance of Hercules

constellation of Corona Borealis, also known as the Northern Crown -- and we can imagine the forward arm of Hercules grasping this arc in the sky:

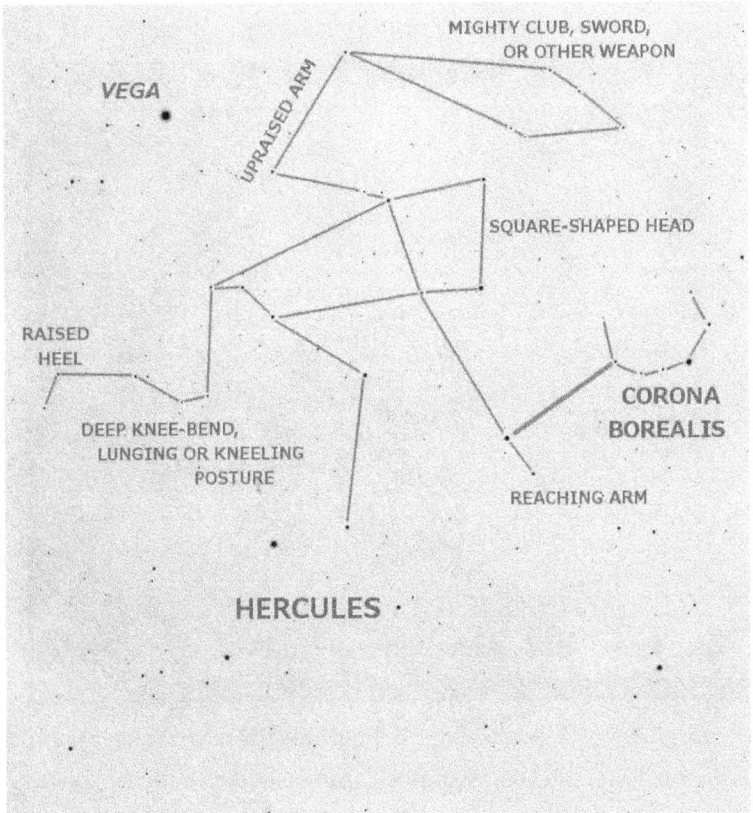

In addition, note the pommel of the sword of the hero, indicated with an arrow in the labeled artwork on the preceding page: this sword pommel corresponds to the location of the bright star Vega in the heavens, in the constellation Lyra, not far from Hercules in the sky (Vega is labeled in the star-chart above, and we mentioned this star earlier when introducing Cygnus and Aquila and the "Summer Triangle" of stars).

These correspondences constitute extremely compelling evidence that the outline suggested by H. A. Rey for the constellation Hercules was known and understood in ancient times – and that

Chapter Three

the hero Heracles in myth (the hero known as *Hercules* to the Romans) corresponds to this constellation in the sky.

Below we see another example of ancient artwork depicting the hero Heracles, from an ancient amphora dated to about 540 BC:

Note once again the square-shaped head of the hero, the raised heel on the rear foot, and the weapon brandished overhead. Note also the forward-reaching arm of Heracles: the hand not brandishing the weapon overhead is depicted as reaching forward, which is a detail that again matches the actual stars of the constellation as we see them in the night sky.

Indeed, if we look closely enough, we can see that this forward-reaching hand is again grasping a curved object -- in this case, the curved helmet-crest of the hero's opponent. The fact that the forward-reaching arm is grasping a curved object in a completely different piece of ancient artwork adds credibility to the argument that the ancient artists were following conventions based on the actual constellation Hercules (and nearby Corona Borealis) when they depicted the hero Heracles in their art.

The importance of Hercules

Below is a close-up of the same artwork, showing that the artist has indeed depicted the forward-reaching hand of the hero grasping the curved helmet-crest of his opponent:

Again, this detail helps to establish the fact that the ancient mythological figure of Heracles, who is being depicted in these pieces of art, was himself associated with the constellation in the night sky we know today by the name of Hercules. The forward-reaching arm of the hero in the artwork corresponds to the forward-reaching arm in the constellation in the sky, which is close to, and which can be envisioned as grasping, the curved arc of the constellation Corona Borealis (the Northern Crown).

In order to demonstrate that these two pieces of artwork are by no means anomalous, but are in fact representative of many ancient depictions of the hero Heracles, we will consider a few more. In the artwork below, from a red-figure vase thought to date to around 450 BC and located today in the Louvre in Paris, we see the hero depicted in the same characteristic posture corresponding to the outline of the constellation:

55

Chapter Three

Note once again the weapon held aloft over the head and pointing forward (in this case, the great *club* most-commonly associated with Heracles or Hercules, and the hero's favored weapon). This matches the configuration of the constellation in the heavens as seen in the stars on the opposite page.

Note too the square-shaped head effect, created by the combination of the hero's full beard and the lion-skin headdress he wears over his head. And notice once again the distinctive lunging-forward posture of the hero's body, corresponding to the outline as envisioned by H. A. Rey in *The Stars: A New Way to See Them* (including the characteristic upraised heel on the foot of the rear leg).

Perhaps most intriguingly, note the fact that the ancient artist has also depicted the hero's forward-reaching arm as being in the act of *grasping a curved object*: in this case, grasping the great curving horn of a supernatural being with a bull-like body and anthropomorphic head, often identified as Achelous (a river god).

The importance of Hercules

When comparing the details of the artwork on this Achelous vase from 450 BC with the stars of the constellation Hercules in the night sky, there can be very little doubt that the ancients envisioned the constellation in the same manner suggested by Rey in his 1952 book -- and that they also often envisioned the forward-reaching arm of the constellation as grasping the curved arc of Corona Borealis:

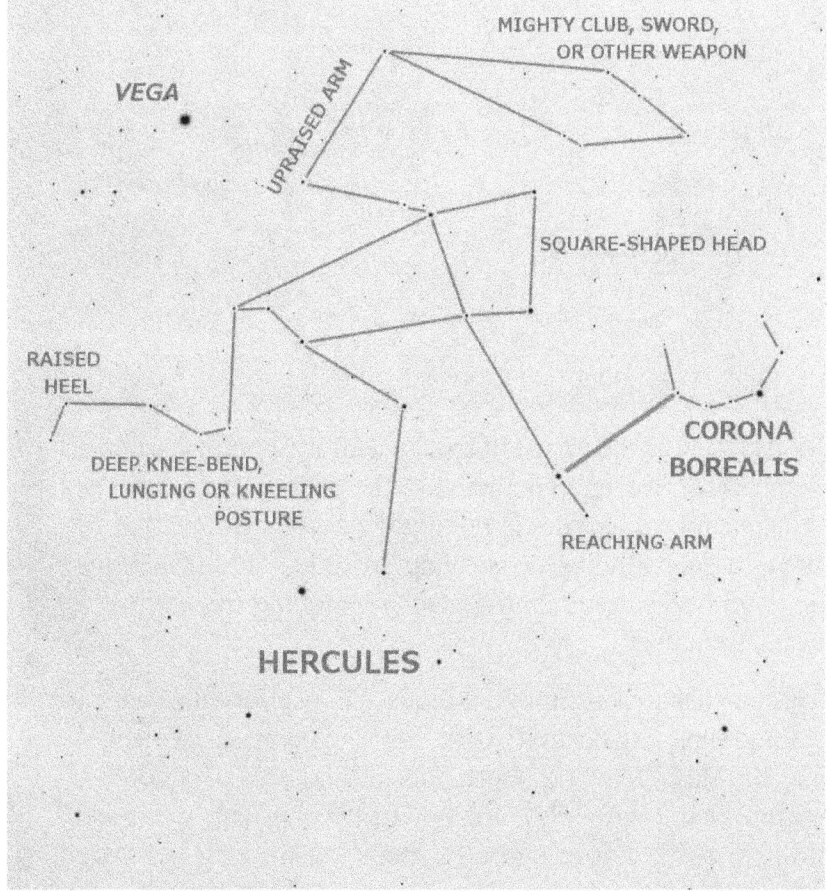

Below is one more image of the hero Heracles as depicted by an ancient artist, this time on a *hydria* (or water jar) thought to date to the period between 530 BC and 520 BC, presently located in the Museum of Fine Art in Boston:

Chapter Three

If we look closely at the image in this ancient artwork, we can see that Heracles is once again depicted in the posture characteristic of the constellation Hercules in the night sky. We can see that he is shown in a deep lunging or kneeling attitude, with his rear leg extended and heel raised, almost exactly matching the outline of the constellation itself.

Note that in this ancient image, Heracles is not reaching out to grasp something associated with the arc-shaped Northern Crown. In this artwork, both his arms are around the supernatural being with whom he is wrestling, usually identified as Triton. Instead, Triton himself is depicted wearing a crown: this crown probably corresponds to Corona Borealis in this case as well (I have argued elsewhere that Triton in this scene probably corresponds to the important constellation Ophiuchus, located directly below Hercules and Corona Borealis).

Note that all of these correspondences would have been extremely difficult or even impossible to perceive if we used the

The importance of Hercules

benighted outline of the constellation Hercules suggested by the International Astronomy Union or one of its similarly unhelpful variations which are repeated in various other sources in print or online purporting to depict the constellations.

Intriguingly, figures associated with the constellation Hercules often battle serpentine monsters. The hero Heracles is depicted in the foregoing artwork in a battle with a being who has a serpentine body (in this case, Triton, whose long fish-like tail is depicted as humping upwards in the middle and resembles some kind of sea serpent or sea monster). However, Heracles is by no means the only figure in ancient myth described as battling such a creature -- and as we will see, a great many of those mythological figures who battle serpentine beings of some sort can be shown to correspond to the very same constellation Hercules in the night sky!

Below we see an image of the god Zeus battling with Typhon, from an ancient *hydria* thought to date to the period between 540 BC and 530 BC, presently located in the Staatliche Antikensammlungen (the "State Antiquities-Collection") museum in Munich, Germany. Note that Zeus has been depicted in the very same posture which we have seen to be characteristic of the constellation Hercules in the night sky:

The numerous correspondences between Zeus as depicted in this ancient artwork and the constellation Hercules should be beyond

Chapter Three

question. For ease of comparison, the outline of the constellation, with distinctive features labeled, is reproduced below:

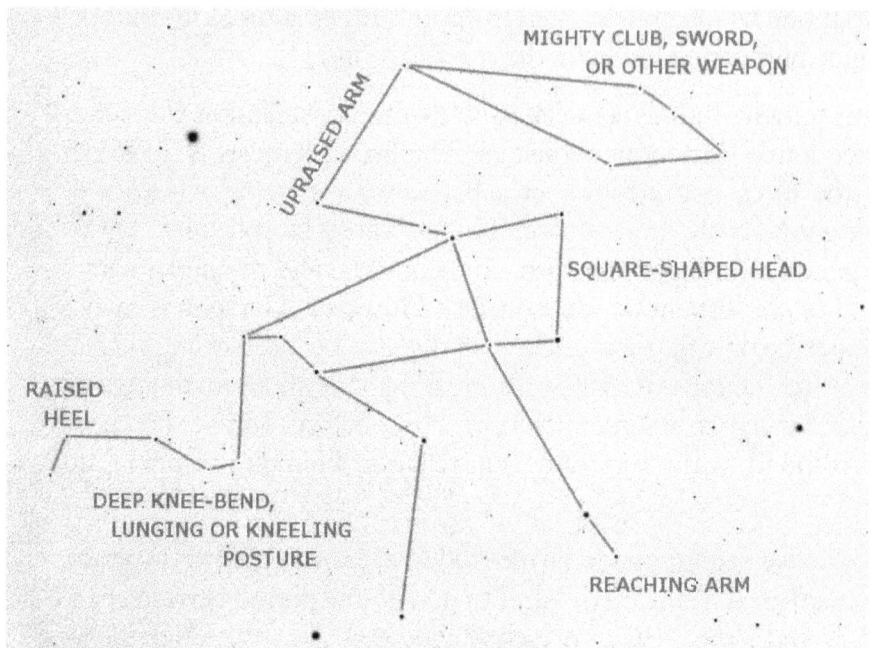

This and other depictions of the god Zeus in ancient artwork, as well as descriptions of the god in numerous surviving ancient sources, confirm a correspondence between Zeus and the constellation Hercules. This establishes some very important points, the first of which is the fact that the constellation which we call Hercules in the night sky is associated with *many other* mythological figures *in addition to* the hero Heracles or Hercules himself. Just because the constellation is known as "Hercules" does not mean that this constellation is exclusively associated with that hero (the same can be said for the constellations Perseus, Andromeda, Casseiopeia, and Cepheus).

As we will see, it is very evident that the *constellation* Hercules is associated with other important figures in myths around the world, far beyond the myths of ancient Greece. Even in ancient Greece, however, the constellation is associated with mythological figures other than Heracles, as evidenced by the association of Zeus with the very same stars in the heavens.

The importance of Hercules

This point, in fact, is critical to the understanding that characters and episodes in ancient myths and scriptures from all around the world appear to be based upon the very same constellations, envisioned the same way, within a common system of celestial metaphor of extraordinary antiquity, already in use within the mythology of the most ancient civilizations known to conventional historians (such as the civilizations of ancient Mesopotamia, ancient Egypt, ancient India, and ancient China).

There are, of course, only a limited number of constellations -- and thus, these same constellations will appear in many different roles, in much the same way that actors will take on different roles in different Hollywood movies, often wearing different costumes and different hairstyles and even speaking in different accents, but ultimately recognizable once we become familiar with the various actors who play these different roles.

Similarly, the different constellations (like famous well-known actors in the movies) will often appear as different characters playing different roles across different mythologies -- and will even play different roles *within* the same myth-system (or even within the same story or episode!), such as Hercules playing the role of both Zeus and of Heracles within the myths of ancient Greece. However, as with actors in the movies, these roles that a specific constellation plays will often have very similar characteristics, even across cultures separated from one another by vast distances.

One other interesting fact to note is that nearly every constellation will appear in some myths as a male figure, and in other myths as a female figure. We have just seen evidence, for example, that the constellation Hercules plays the role of both the god Zeus and the hero Heracles (who is the son of Zeus) -- and yet in my book *Star Myths of the World, Volume Two: Mythology of Ancient Greece*, I discuss evidence which suggests that the same constellation also plays the role of the dreaded Gorgon sisters in the myth of Perseus, the Gorgons of course being female.

61

Chapter Three

Below on the left we see an ancient depiction of a Gorgon. Note the "fringe" of serpents around the entire head, forming a squarish outline similar to the square-shaped heads that characterize other Hercules-related figures such as the god Zeus and the hero Heracles (who are usually envisioned with a full beard, giving their heads a squarish appearance). Note also the posture in which the Gorgons are almost invariably portrayed in ancient artwork: the body position itself indicates a correspondence to the outline of the constellation Hercules in the sky.

The deep lunge and raised rear heel are very characteristic of the constellation Hercules. In the case of the Gorgons, we do not see the characteristic brandishing of a mighty club or other weapon, however. Instead, we see wings. We can establish from other artwork that the "weapon" overhead in the constellation Hercules was sometimes envisioned as wings instead of as a weapon of war (just as the "weapon" feature became a billowing *cloak* in the depiction God above Jacob's ladder shown previously).

To the right of the Gorgon art above we see artwork depicting Achilles dragging the corpse of Hector, and behind Achilles the ancient artist has added a winged figure, usually interpreted as the spirit of the departed Patroclus. This figure is most certainly

The importance of Hercules

depicted in the position and posture of the constellation Hercules, and note once again the wings instead of a weapon brandished overhead. We can be very certain of this identification, because the other figures in the scene correspond to constellations which surround the constellation Hercules in the sky: the charioteer (Achilles) corresponds to the constellation Boötes, located in front of Hercules in the heavens. The chariot itself corresponds to Ophiuchus, which plays the role of a war-cart in other myths (notably in the Sanskrit epic of the Mahabharata, which contains the Bhagavad Gita). And the body of Hector, being dragged by Achilles, corresponds to the constellation Scorpio, beneath Ophiuchus. The text of the Iliad tells us that Hector's hair raises a great cloud of dust as his corpse is dragged: this column of dust corresponds to the bright band of the Milky Way, which rises up through the constellation Scorpio in the heavens.

Returning to the illustration of the ancient artwork depicting Zeus battling Typhon, shown again above, another important point to notice is the fact that the enormous weapon outlined in the stars of the constellation Hercules was envisioned as the thunderbolt weapon of the god Zeus, and not just as an earthly weapon such as a club, sword or mace. This is a very important point, because figures associated with Hercules are often found in myths around the world to be wielding the *most powerful weapon* in any pantheon of deities – often a thunderbolt weapon, as in the case of Zeus.

63

Chapter Three

The weapon held aloft by the constellation Hercules is indeed the largest and most formidable-looking weapon held by any of the constellations. Therefore, figures associated with this constellation will often play the role of the most powerful god or hero in any particular set of myths around the world.

Figures who wield a thunderbolt-weapon in myths from around the world include but are certainly not limited to: the god Thor in Norse myth (undoubtedly associated with the constellation Hercules, as explored in depth in *Star Myths of the World, Volume Four: Norse Mythology*), the god Xango or Shango in the myths of Africa (and particularly the Yoruba tradition, as discussed in *The Ancient World-Wide System*), the god Indra in the Vedic scriptures of ancient India (also discussed in *The Ancient World-Wide System*), and the triple sky-deity introduced in the Popol Vuh of the Maya civilization, whose three related aspects (we are told in the Maya text) are introduced as follows: "First is Thunderbolt Huracan, second is Youngest Thunderbolt, and third is Sudden Thunderbolt. These three together are Heart of Sky."[23]

Below is artwork from one of the few surviving Maya codices not destroyed by the European invaders during the sixteenth and seventeenth centuries, the so-called "Dresden Codex" (so called because it was shipped from Central America to Spain and ended up in the State library in Dresden, Germany). It is the oldest surviving text from the Americas, dated to the 1200s or early 1300s, well prior to Columbus.

The importance of Hercules

Clearly, the figure found in this Maya text, which was created *prior to* the European invasion, has been depicted by the original artist in the same distinctive posture characteristic of the constellation Hercules. The Hercules constellation outline published by H. A. Rey in 1952 is provided beside the image from the Dresden Codex, showing the unmistakable similarity.

The posture alone of the figure in the illustration should confirm that the Maya, well prior to any known European contact, were envisioning the constellation Hercules in the *very same manner* which informs the artwork from ancient Greece that we have been examining (and which can also be shown to inform artwork from ancient Egypt, ancient Mesopotamia, ancient India, and many other cultures, as I have demonstrated in previous books).

Beyond the distinctive deep-knee posture which characterizes Hercules figures, we also see the distinctive square-shaped head of Hercules incorporated in the artwork from the Maya codex -- not through the inclusion of a full beard (as with depictions of the god Zeus or the hero Heracles), but rather through the incorporation of boxy, square-shaped headgear. We see similar square headgear in the depictions of the figure of Tiki in the artwork of the cultures of the Pacific.

In addition to the square shape of the head of the constellation in the sky, we can also see that the outline of stars causes the head of the constellation Hercules to appear slightly bowed forward, as if nodding gravely. This aspect of the constellation is incorporated into surviving repositories of ancient Greek myth, including the texts of both the Iliad and the Odyssey, in which we are frequently told that Zeus nods his head in assent to certain requests, signaling his granting of specific permission. The depiction on the Maya codex of the figure in the Hercules posture can be argued to have his head slightly forward as well, enhancing the correspondence with the outline of the constellation itself.

In fact, if we look closely at the illustration from the Dresden Codex, we will perceive that the artist has included what looks like an eagle or other bird of prey on the shoulder of the lunging-forward god in the illustration. Below is the same image, this time with the outlines of what I believe to be the attendent eagle enhanced for greater visibility:

The inclusion of this eagle adds yet another parallel to Hercules-figures in other myth-systems around the world. Certainly it is well-known that the god Zeus is associated with the great eagle in the myths of ancient Greece, as is the god Jove or Jupiter in the myths of ancient Rome.

This association is almost certainly due to the close proximity of the constellation Aquila the Eagle to the constellation Hercules, as we saw in the star-chart illustrating the celestial foundation of the dream of Jacob in the first chapter (see page 19).

Aquila is located adjacent to the extended rear foot of the constellation Hercules, and just above the shoulder of Ophiuchus. Thus deities associated with Hercules, as well as those associated with Ophiuchus, will often have an affiliation with a great eagle. In the myths of ancient India, as discussed in *The Ancient World-*

The importance of Hercules

Wide System, the god Vishnu has as his close companion the great eagle, Garuda. Vishnu can be shown to be identified with the constellation Ophiuchus, rather than with the constellation Hercules. But the presence of the eagle or eagle-like bird in the illustration shown above from the Dresden Codex adds further confirmation to the argument that this figure's Hercules-like posture is intentional, and that he is associated with that constellation in the heavens.

As if all these details are not enough to seal the identification, the final confirming detail in the Maya illustration, of course, is the presence of a thunderbolt – the clear hallmark of a figure who corresponds to the powerful constellation Hercules in the heavens:

When juxtaposed, the similarities between the ancient image of Zeus battling Typhon and the image of the thunderbolt-bearing deity from the Dresden Codex of the Maya are unmistakable. Look at the thunderbolts in the two pieces of artwork above -- their shared characteristics are quite remarkable.

Indeed, both depictions of the thunderbolt-weapon share clear similarities to the depictions of the Vajra, the thunderbolt-weapon of the Vedic storm-god Indra which serves as a transcendental symbol in many later forms of Hinduism and Buddhism, and which is known as the Dorje in Tibetan sacred tradition.

Chapter Three

Below is a Vajra thunderbolt, which is a sacred symbol often depicted in art and used in ceremony in certain Buddhist traditions to this day:

The similarities to the thunderbolt depictions in the ancient artwork of Zeus in his battle with Typhon and in the Maya artwork from the Dresden Codex should be obvious: in each case, the weapon features a kind of "central shaft" which forks outward at the ends. Below are close-ups of the thunderbolt-weapons depicted in the ancient Greek and Maya artwork:

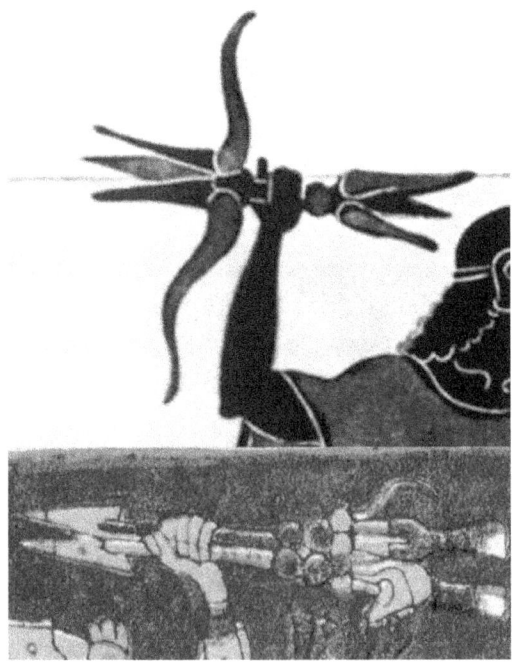

The importance of Hercules

Clearly, there appears to have been a world-wide tradition of associating the thunderbolt-weapon with figures connected to the constellation Hercules. I would suggest that the distinctive shape of the Vajra weapon, with its four prongs (or lotus-petals) surrounding a central pyramid-like shaft or pillar may be derived from the massive weapon brandished overhead by the constellation Hercules, which can be envisioned in myth as a great club, as a massive sword, as a tremendous mace, as a mighty hammer (as in the case of the god Thor), as a powerful axe (as in the case of the god Xango or Shango), and as a thunderbolt.

Below, the now-familiar outline of the constellation Hercules is presented, and I have added arrows pointing to important stars on the mighty weapon being brandished overhead. The stars indicated by these arrows may well be the inspiration for the thunderbolt-weapon pattern, including the Vajra with its four petals surrounding a central shaft:

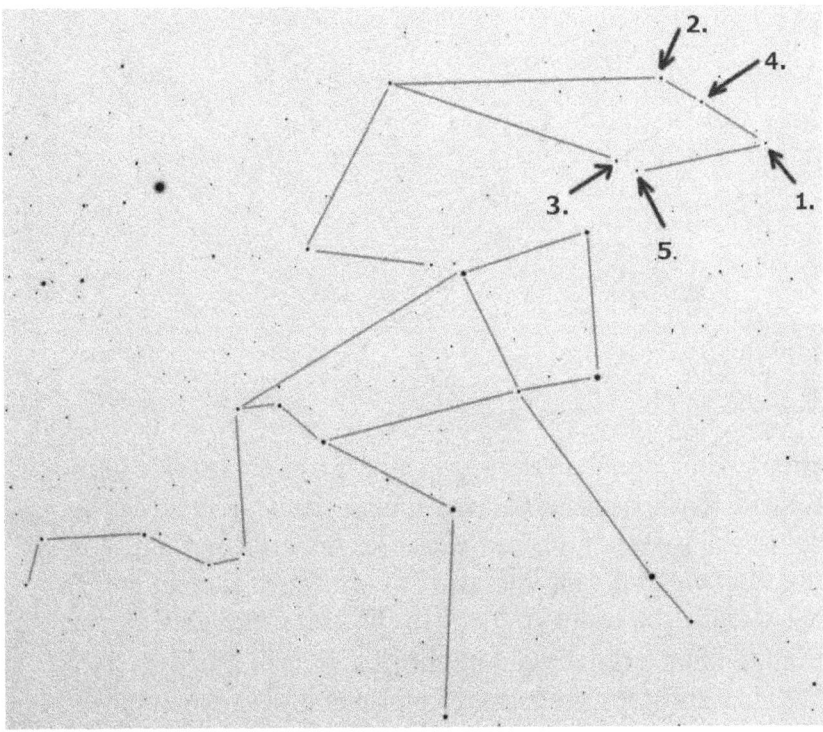

69

Chapter Three

Can you see how the stars indicated could give rise to the Vajra or thunderbolt shape, in which there is a central shaft (created by the star furthest to the right in the diagram, numbered as "one" in the star-chart) with four petals branching out (the other four stars indicated by arrows, numbered "two" through "five" in the star-chart)? Can you also see how the actual stars in the outline of the constellation suggest the "gathering together" of the branches back at the "handle" of the weapon, where it is held by whatever deity is envisioned as holding the thunderbolt?

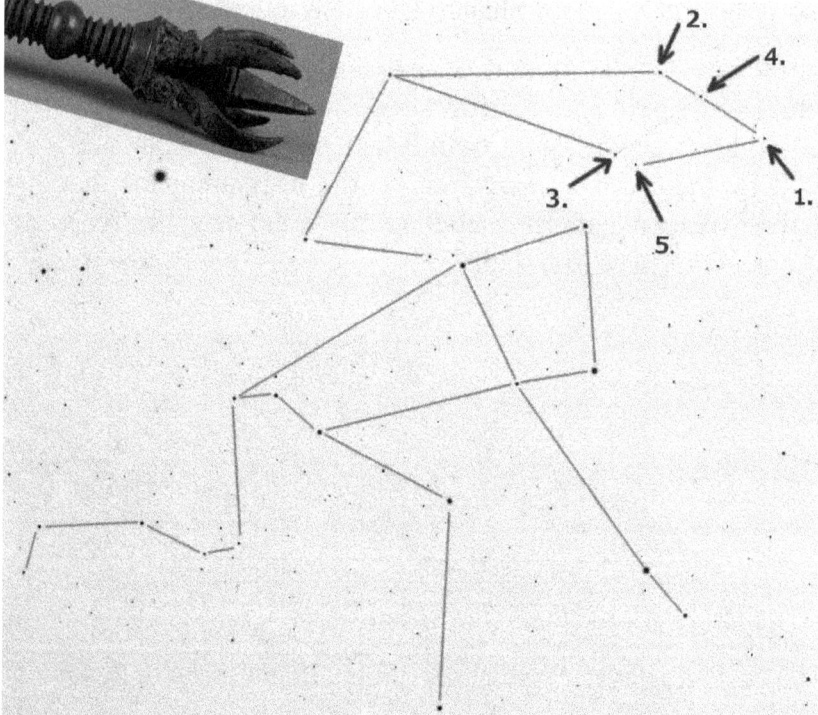

These four stars (numbered 2, 3, 4 and 5) on either side of a central shaft (envisioned as a line running from the star at the "handle" of the weapon, where the arm of the Hercules-figure is grasping the weapon, all the way to the star at the point, designated with the number "one" in the star-chart above) can also be envisioned as creating a mighty hammer or a mighty axe. If stars 2, 3, 4 and 5 are connected to form a kind of rectangle or quadrilateral (instead of being envisioned as the branching petals

The importance of Hercules

of a lotus, as in the traditional Vajra, or as the branching bolts of a lightning-bolt), then the Hercules-figure will appear to be grasping an enormous hammer (as in the case of Thor), or an enormous axe (as in the case of Xango), or even an enormous mace (as in the case of the god Hanuman in the myths of ancient India, or in the case of Hanuman's human relative Bhima, who is also a Hercules-figure and whose favored weapon is a tremendous mace).

Note that the Vajra or Dorje thunderbolt-weapon is often depicted with its petals gathering back together at the extreme tip of the weapon, as shown in the representation below:

This gathering back together is not surprising either, given the shape of the weapon brandished overhead by the outline of Hercules, and the fact that it does appear to come together in a point at the tip.

The fact that these Vajra weapons, and the thunderbolts held by artistic depictions of Zeus and others such as the ones shown here, have a kind of "doubled" shape does not initially appear to match the weapon brandished overhead by the outline of Hercules, as envisioned by the system published by H. A. Rey in 1952. Nevertheless, it is quite undeniable that figures carrying the thunderbolt-weapon have characteristics which clearly indicate association with the constellation Hercules (such as the depiction of Zeus holding the thunderbolt while executing a deep lunge, in the battle with Typhon shown in the ancient artwork presented in this chapter). Thus, it is possible that the "mirror image" of the

Chapter Three

great weapon held overhead was a form of mythical "artistic license" in the ancient artwork.

Another possible explanation, however, is that the stars of the constellation Lyra (located adjacent to the constellation Hercules in the sky) could sometimes be envisioned as forming the "other half" of the mighty thunderbolt-weapon wielded by these Hercules-figures in myth:

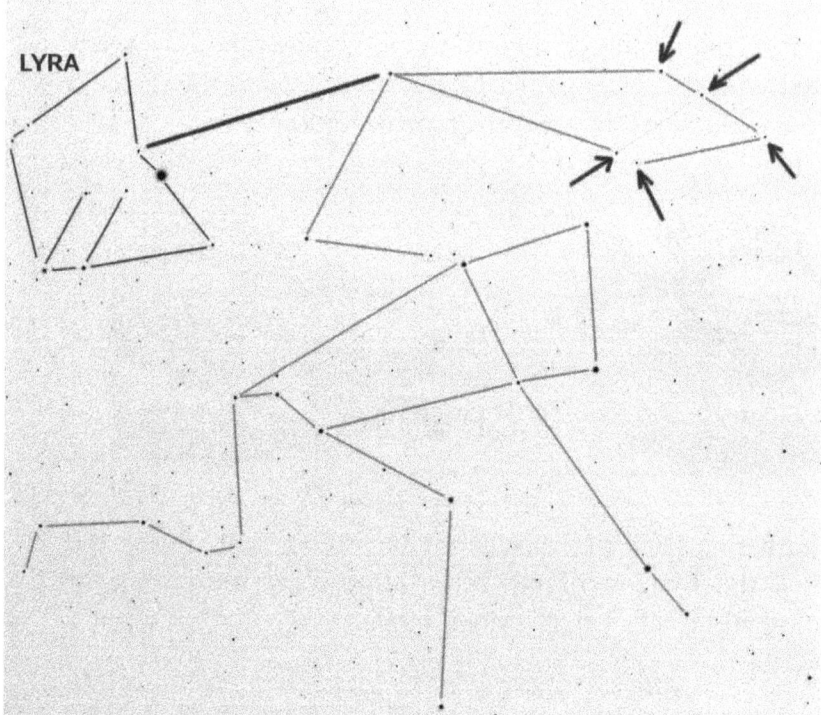

This interpretation is not certain, but I believe it is a possibility for some of the thunderbolt-weapons envisioned within the ancient system and depicted in the ancient art, including the double-sided Vajra or Dorje. Note especially in the thunderbolt-weapon held by the god Zeus in his battle with Typhon that the thunderbolt is not depicted as being perfectly symmetrical: the "back-half" of the thunderbolt is actually depicted as being significantly wider and larger than the "front-half" of the thunderbolt that Zeus is holding in this ancient artwork:

The importance of Hercules

This depiction of the thunderbolt brandished by Zeus as being larger on that half than on the half that is closer to the god's head would be consistent with the theory that in some cases the stars of Lyra were envisioned as forming part of the branching two-sided thunderbolt-weapon. As we can clearly see in the star-chart on the page opposite, the constellation Lyra is much wider (or perhaps we should say "taller") than the outline formed by the stars that make up the "weapon-outline" over the head of Hercules. Also, the stars of Lyra (and especially the bright star Vega) are brighter and easier to see than the stars of the sword or club of Hercules. These details could explain the asymmetrical appearance of the double-sided thunderbolt brandished by Zeus in the ancient artwork shown above.

In any case, it should be established beyond reasonable doubt at this point in the discussion that thunderbolt-wielding gods the world over, including the god Zeus as shown in the ancient artwork presented in this chapter, as well as the thunderbolt-wielding divinity with an eagle on his shoulder shown in a nearly-identical posture by the oldest-known surviving Maya codex, were anciently envisioned as corresponding to the constellation Hercules -- and that the ancients were using the very same method of envisioning the constellation Hercules that H. A. Rey

Chapter Three

presents to the world in his 1952 book entitled *The Stars: A New Way to See Them.*

These are remarkable conclusions, but they are backed up by undeniable evidence. It should be pointed out that the constellation Hercules does not simply "leap out of the sky" at the viewer, and it is by no means "obvious" that different cultures would all choose to envision Hercules in very much the same way -- let alone automatically associate the stars of this constellation with the wielding of a thunderbolt-weapon, and choose to associate their thunderbolt-wielding god with this particular set of stars.

Indeed, it is by no means intuitively obvious that cultures around the world, having no apparent contact with one another, would all choose to pattern their myths and sacred stories on the stars in the first place! The fact that virtually all of them do, and that they appear to ascribe similar characteristics to the very same constellations in the sky, points to the strong probability of some kind of connection -- most likely, some kind of descent from a common and even more ancient source, perhaps some culture or cultures predating the world's oldest known civilizations by many thousands of years.

As we've already seen, H. A. Rey published a book in 1952 which appears to supply (by and large) the system of envisioning the constellations used within this ancient world-wide system. In this chapter we've seen incontrovertible evidence that the way Rey suggests we envision the constellation Hercules matches up with the way the ancients did envision this constellation, as shown in countless pieces of ancient artwork from around the world (and many more examples, from many other cultures, could be added to those shown thus far).

Indeed, the reader is invited once again to consider how difficult it would be to make the connection between *the artwork* presented in this chapter showing gods and heroes and monsters who are associated with the constellation Hercules, and *the outline of the constellation itself*, if all we had to work with were the confusing and counterproductive outlines supplied by sources such as the International Astronomy Union and if we did not have the ancient key, supplied to us by H. A. Rey in the pages of his transformative text.

The artwork we've seen, along with other ancient artwork found around the world, declares in no uncertain terms the constellation it is referring to when depicting a Hercules-figure. It is as if the ancient artists, through their work, are coming right out and telling us, through the artistic conventions that they include in their art, that we are looking at a figure associated with that constellation. And yet, if all we ever learned were Hercules outlines such as the meaningless scribble promoted by the IAU, those ancient artists could scream to us at the top of their lungs (through their art, figuratively speaking) that they are showing us Hercules, and we would be unable to understand what they were trying to say to us. Like the populace whose language has been replaced by Newspeak, envisioned by George Orwell in his dystopian writings, we would be unable to so much as frame the conceptual ideas in our minds, because we would be lacking the mental pegs upon which to hang those ideas.

In Orwell's description of Newspeak, he explains that the removal of vocabulary was seen by the oppressors of humanity as a desirable goal to be pursued as its own end, in order to *strip away* the ability of men and women to even think about concepts.

He writes:

> The word *free* still existed in Newspeak, but it could only be used in such statements as "This dog is free from lice" or "This field is free from weeds." It could not be used in its old sense of "politically free" or "intellectually free," since political and intellectual freedom no longer existed even as concepts, and were therefore of necessity nameless. Quite apart from the suppression of definitely heretical words, reduction of vocabulary was regarded as an end in itself, and no word that

Chapter Three

could be dispensed with was allowed to survive. Newspeak was designed not to extend but to *diminish* the range of thought, and this purpose was indirectly assisted by cutting the choice of words down to a minimum.[24]

The analogy to what has been lost, via the removal of our vocabulary for hearing and understanding the message of the ancient myths, makes a rather direct parallel.

The message of the world's ancient wisdom concerns our freedom, including our political and our intellectual freedom, as well as our reconnection with who we really are, at the very deepest level.

And yet, there is evidence of a campaign as insidious as the deliberate reduction of vocabulary described by Orwell in his warnings about Newspeak, a campaign which has been waged for at least seventeen centuries (and probably for much longer than that) to not only suppress the ancient wisdom but to render men and women less and less capable of grasping the concepts of freedom and abundance that the myths want to tell us about, to deliberately diminish our "vocabulary" to the point that we have no way to grasp what they are saying, and can only gape at them without comprehension of their message, no matter how brilliantly and ingeniously that message is delivered to us by the ancient sources.

As with Orwell's example in which the word "free" would still be allowed to be used, but only in situations disconnected from any association with actual personal freedom having to do with the ability of individual men and women to exercise power ("political freedom") and achieve greater levels of enlightenment and self realization ("intellectual freedom"), the campaign to eliminate the uplifting message of the myths allows the people to continue to consider the ancient myths and their gods and goddesses, devoid of understanding of their higher meaning and ability to empower and enlighten.

The importance of Hercules

We are allowed to have our gods, but only in the diminished way that Newspeak allows us to have the word "free" -- in the sense of "free from lice" or "free from weeds."

However, the ancient meaning contained in the myths never actually disappeared, just because the enemies of that meaning (the enemies of the gods . . . and the people) campaigned tirelessly to eradicate the understanding of that ancient meaning, any more than the original meaning of the word "freedom" ever really disappears, even if the proponents of Newspeak work tirelessly to eradicate awareness of the concept.

It is as if the Declaration of Independence had been kept around, even as men and women were systematically stripped of their ability to comprehend the meanings of the potent words it uses -- as if the speeches of Martin Luther King, Jr. had been preserved for our listening, even as the capacity of men and women to grasp the concepts of justice and equality of which Dr. King spoke so eloquently was deliberately taken from them.

Such documents and such speeches would still retain their potency, their danger to oppressors and their ability to empower the oppressed, should those original meanings ever be revived and remembered.

If an ancient dictionary which included the original meanings of words such as "freedom" and "justice" were discovered, and men and women could begin to recover their awareness of those meanings, then the words in the ancient documents and speeches regarding those subjects would immediately come back to life, as those same men and women would begin to read and to hear them in an entirely new way, with entirely new understanding.

The same is true of the world's ancient myths. We find ourselves today in largely the situation described by George Orwell in *Nineteen Eighty-Four*, when Oldspeak has been almost entirely replaced by Newspeak when it comes to the language of the ancient myths. Certainly there remain some few individuals who can still understand their original meanings, can still speak and understand their original language (particularly among peoples and cultures whose connection to their original myths and sacred traditions was not attacked until more recent centuries, as opposed to cultures in which the ancient ways were obliterated by literalism a thousand years or more before the present day).

But because of treasures such as the 1952 book published by H. A. Rey, which like the Rosetta Stone provides us with a way of deciphering the hieroglyphics with which the ancient myths are written, we can slowly and cautiously rebuild the dictionary which enables us to hear again those ancient messages in their more complete power and glory, and experience (like someone many thousands of years in the future listening to a speech by Martin Luther King and understanding for the first time the meaning of the words he is using) the thrill of comprehending what their message holds: a message with tremendous potential to transform, to uplift, and to emancipate.

Chapter 4
Mighty battles with Serpents and Dragons

When the great hero Heracles opened his eyes and rubbed his forehead, the madness had passed. He had been driven temporarily insane by the goddess Hera, the queen of Olympus and wife of Zeus.

Hera had born a grudge against Heracles since even before his birth: his mother was the beautiful mortal woman Alcmene, whom Zeus had seduced one night by taking on the likeness of Alcmene's husband Amphitryon, causing the night to last three times its normal duration while Zeus and Alcmene made love.

Upon recovering his senses, Heracles was horrified to discover that during his madness, he had slain his own beloved wife Megara and their three sons (casting them into a fire).

Overwhelmed with grief and remorse, the powerful hero exiled himself, eventually making his way to Delphi, where he sought out the Delphic Oracle and the Pythia -- the priestess of Apollo at Delphi -- in order to inquire of the god where he should go and what he should do to atone for the heavy guilt which he bore.

The Oracle at Delphi and its sacred spring was said to have once belonged to a tremendous female serpent or dragon, known as the Python -- but the god Apollo with his irresistible arrows had confronted her in single combat, grievously wounding the Python and driving her into a deep fissure beneath the earth, where the great serpent eventually perished.

It was said that fumes from the body of the Python still issued from the chasm where the serpent had disappeared, and the priestess would sit above this fissure upon a golden tripod and enter a trance state, a state of reverie induced by the venomous fumes. Thus, she was known as the Pythia. While in the trance-

Chapter Four

state, she would receive the words of the god Apollo, and relate them to mortals.

The god told Heracles through the Pythia that he must go to the sacred city of Tiryns, an extremely ancient settlement situated at the north end of the Argolic Gulf, one of the deep inlets that cause the Peloponnese to resemble a hand with downward-pointing fingers (the gulfs being the deep bays between those "fingers" – and the Argolic Gulf being the gulf that defines the easternmost "thumb" of the Peloponnese, with Argos and Tiryns being located along the top of that gulf, where the web of skin between your thumb and the rest of your hand would be). To this day, visitors to Tiryns can see the great "cyclopean walls" and passageways, constructed of mighty stones so large that the ancients, according to Pausanias (c. AD 110 - c. AD 180), attributed their construction to the Cyclopes themselves.

At Tiryns, as the Oracle informed the penitent hero, Heracles would have to perform ten labors for his cousin, Eurystheus, the mean-spirited and jealous king of that land. Thus began the famous Labors of Heracles (or Hercules), the first of which involved the slaying of the famous Nemean Lion, whose skin was invulnerable to any edged weapon (Heracles therefore had to strangle the beast with his bare hands).

The second task which Eurystheus assigned to the hero was the requirement to slay the Lernaean Hydra. The Lernaean Hydra was one of the fearsome offspring of the terrifying half-nymph, half-serpent Echidna, by the powerful monster Typhon (encountered in the previous chapter), Typhon constituting the final and most powerful challenger to the god Zeus in the battle for the right to rule from Olympus. In some accounts Typhon is described as having fifty heads, and in others as having a hundred. In most accounts, Typhon has two great serpents instead of legs, issuing from where his thighs would have been.

There are many variations to the cataclysmic battle between Zeus and Typhon, but in one of the most well-known of these, Typhon hurls mountains towards Zeus in an attempt to crush the upstart god, but Zeus turns each projectile back with a thunderbolt of his own, and eventually these same mountainous missiles batter and beat down Typhon himself.

Wounded but not completely slain, Typhon retreats, and Zeus delivers the decisive blow by slamming a great mountain down on top of the monster -- by most accounts, Mount Aetna. Buried beneath this mountain, Typhon is imprisoned for the rest of time, occasionally erupting forth in fury (spewing out smoke and lava upon the surface) but unable to escape. By this victory, Zeus ascends to rule the cosmos from his throne on Mount Olympus.

Echidna herself retreats to a remote cave, but the monstrous offspring of Typhon and Echidna remain on earth, including the dreaded Hydra as well as the three-headed hound Cerberus, the Sphinx of Greek myth, and (according to Hesiod) the Nemean Lion slain by Heracles in his first assignment from Eurystheus. Other ancient accounts attribute a variety of other famous monsters to the offspring of Typhon and Echidna as well.

Thus it was that the massive hero set off down the coast of the Argolic Gulf towards the region of Lerna, where (according to the ancient records) the Hydra dwelt among the dank and putrid swamps surrounding the deep natural spring or well of Amymone, which fed the river Lerna.

Approaching the edges of the swamp, the road gave out, and Heracles dismounted from his chariot. His charioteer was his young nephew Iolaus, son of Iphicles, the twin of Heracles by the same mother Alcmene but by the human father Amphitryon rather than by Zeus (Amphitryon had returned home from the battlefield the day following Alcmene's tryst with the Olympian god, and thus Iphicles was born one day after Heracles: this pattern of two twinned figures, one with divine characteristics and one with "ordinary mortal" characteristics, is very common in world myth, and very significant, and we will examine it more fully in a later chapter).

Chapter Four

Leaving the chariot and allowing the horses to graze, the pair set off into the gathering gloom of the swamp. Iolaus lit a torch and carried it aloft. Unsettling noises could be heard in the distance, their source unseen beyond the mist and the looming trees with their gnarled branches hanging with "old-man's beards" of moss and lichen.

Deeper and deeper into the swamps they went, sloshing through muddy fens and stagnant water, sometimes barking their shins on fallen trunks and branches rotting beneath the dark surface out of sight.

At last the ground begins to gain slightly in elevation as they approach the hill beside the well of Amymone. Through the thick mist that hangs over the swamp, they perceive the den of the great Hydra, a yawning cave mouth opening in the side of the hill.

Heracles takes his powerful bow from across his chest and places multiple arrows between the fingers of his bow-hand. Holding their tips briefly within the fire of the torch offered by Iolaus, the hero shoots them in rapid succession into the mouth of the monster's den.

A deep rumble issues from the depths and increases into a terrifying din, and the ground beneath their feet begins to tremble as the Hydra emerges from her lair, all nine heads writhing in unison, joined to a serpentine body of massive girth and length, far larger than even the biggest constrictor known today. The offspring of Typhon and Echidna, now fully grown and indeed very ancient herself, she immediately spies the hero and rushes forward to devour him, gathering speed as she attacks, her nine serpent heads dripping with venom.

Heracles grips his club tightly and lunges forward to meet the monster, delivering a massive blow which crushes the first Hydra head to jelly:

Mighty battles with Serpents and Dragons

In the ancient artwork above, from an Etruscan vase thought to date to about 525 BC, the hero is not depicted in his customary Herculean garb of lion-skin, but his posture is unmistakable and clearly patterned upon the constellation Hercules in the heavens, with deep lunge and extended rear leg, brandishing his club overhead and reaching forward with his other arm.

Some ancient accounts tell us that instead of crushing the heads with his club, Heracles instead uses a curved blade to sever the Hydra heads at the neck -- the curved blade being characteristic of the hero Perseus, from whom Alcmene the mother of Heracles was descended (Perseus being her grandfather, and Andromeda her grandmother).

Whether he cuts them off at the neck or crushes them with his club, for every head that is slain two new heads grow from the stump, such that Heracles seems to be going backwards in his efforts to slay the Hydra.

At this point in the battle, some ancient accounts also tell us that a great crab emerges from the swamps and seizes Heracles by the

Chapter Four

foot (we can see that the ancient artist has included the crab in the scene upon the Etruscan pottery pictured on the previous page).

Heracles dispatches the crab with one swing of his club (or his sword). Then, suddenly inspired by the goddess Athena with the way to defeat the seemingly-invincible Hydra, the hero calls to Iolaus to take his torch and sear the end of each neck as soon as Heracles cuts off the head.

In this way, the monster is soon left with but a single serpent head -- the central head of them all, which unlike the others is immortal and can not be slain. Heracles cuts off this final immortal head and buries it underneath a great rock. The massive serpent coils for a few minutes in agony, its burned neck-stumps thrashing blindly, and finally lies still.

Thus ends the second of the Labors of Heracles, the slaying of the horrible Lernaean Hydra. Eurystheus complained that this success would not count towards the ten required labors, because Heracles had received help from Iolaus in the form of the burning of the necks of the monster with his torch. Thus the original ten labors eventually became twelve, due to the disqualification by Eurystheus of this one and of the later cleansing of the Augean Stables.

Turning again to the night sky, we can readily discern that this entire episode from the myths of ancient Greece is based upon the same system of celestial metaphor which forms the foundation for the characters and episodes in other myths from around the globe. Examining a star-chart containing the same region of the sky we have been examining thus far, we find constellations with clear connections to the mighty hero Heracles, as well as his chariot-driving companion and nephew Iolaus, the torch carried by Iolaus which helps Heracles to finally prevail, and of course the many-headed and serpentine monster who plays the terrifying Hydra herself:

Mighty battles with Serpents and Dragons

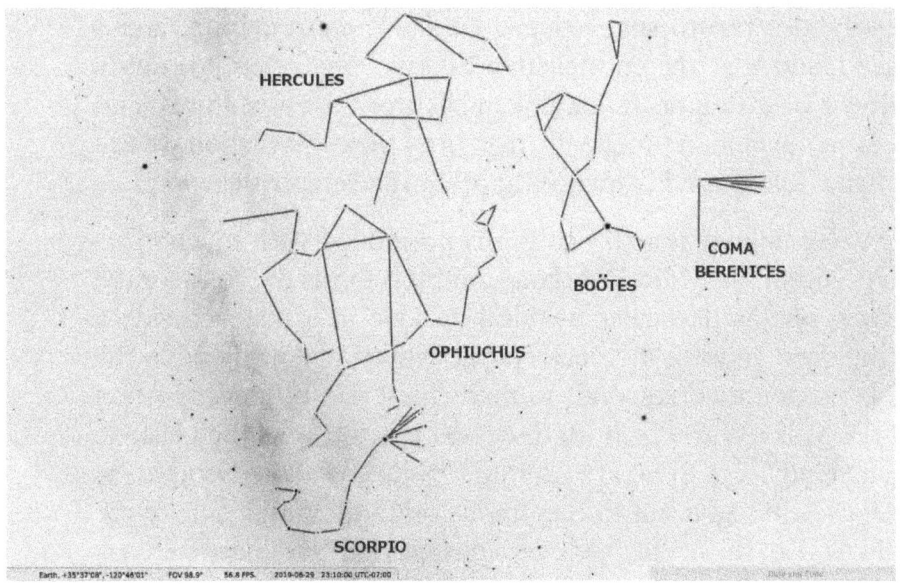

Above we see a star-chart showing the same region of the heavens which we examined previously in our discussion of the vision of Jacob from Genesis 28. At the bottom of the chart we see the constellation Scorpio, situated near the brightest and widest portion of the Milky Way, which rises up like a shining column (remember that colors are inverted in these charts) from the bottom of the picture near the word "Scorpio" to the top, inclined towards the left as we face the image. Scorpio can clearly be envisioned as a great serpent with multiple heads -- and is often envisioned this way in the world's ancient Star Myths. Scorpio plays the terrible Hydra in this famous episode of the encounter between the hero Heracles and the Lernaean Hydra.

Some readers may wonder how the constellation Scorpio could play the Hydra, when we have another constellation not far away which actually bears the name of "Hydra" to this day. It is prudent to avoid jumping to conclusions based simply on the names by which we know the constellations: this system can be shown to be incredibly ancient (it can be shown to be fully mature prior to the inscription of the Gilgamesh tablets and the tablets containing the Enuma Elish of ancient Mesopotamia, for instance). It is best to examine all the evidence and explore all the

85

Chapter Four

possibilities before suggesting a celestial interpretation, and I have found that the constellation Scorpio very often portrays a serpent or a dragon in ancient myths from many cultures, and does so much more frequently than does the constellation we call "Hydra" (although Hydra does appear in ancient myth as well).

As we've already noted, Scorpio is positioned with much of its body within the Milky Way band, and this forms the basis for the setting of this particular mythical episode in a marsh beside a great river. Indeed, the deep spring or well of Amymone in the story no doubt corresponds to that widest and brightest portion of the Milky Way which we discussed previously as the Galactic Center, adjacent to Scorpio and to Ophiuchus above Scorpio (as well as being adjacent to Sagittarius on the opposite side of the Milky Way from Scorpio, a constellation we have already discussed and one which will enter into this discussion presently).

Note also that Scorpio when seen in person is actually tremendously large and awe-inspiring, composed of relatively bright and visible stars, and can easily suggest the towering form of the monstrous Hydra, with her great serpentine body branching into multiple heads, the central head of which is immortal -- most likely corresponding to the Scorpion's brightest star, Antares, as we saw in a previous examination of another mythical episode involving Scorpio: the "Oracle at Aulis" involving a serpent devouring eight chicks and their mother in a tree before being turned to stone, described in the Iliad and discussed in *Star Myths of the World, Volume Two: Myths of Ancient Greece.*[25]

The "hill" where the mythical Hydra makes her lair, described explicitly in some of the ancient accounts of this episode, undoubtedly corresponds to the constellation Ophiuchus, situated directly above Scorpio and adjacent to that wide and bright region of the Milky Way (the "well of Amymone" in this story). Ophiuchus can be shown to play the role of a hill or mound or mountain in numerous Star Myths from around the world.

Mighty battles with Serpents and Dragons

The hero Heracles in this story, of course, corresponds to the constellation Hercules, and his companion Iolaus almost certainly corresponds to the nearby constellation Boötes, who can be definitively shown to play a charioteer in many Star Myths, both in ancient Greece and in myths from many other cultures (in the myths of ancient India, for instance, and also in the Norse myths, as discussed in *The Ancient World-Wide System* and in *Star Myths of the World, Volume Four: Norse Mythology*).

Indeed, we've already seen positive confirmation that Boötes can play the role of a charioteer, in the ancient artwork depicted on page 62 of this volume, where we saw Achilles dragging the corpse of Hector. Behind Achilles (who in this ancient artwork is driving a chariot) we see a winged figure corresponding to the location of the constellation Hercules, thus confirming that Achilles in the chariot corresponds to Boötes in that artwork, since that constellation is located immediately in front of Hercules in the night sky, as seen in the star-chart below:

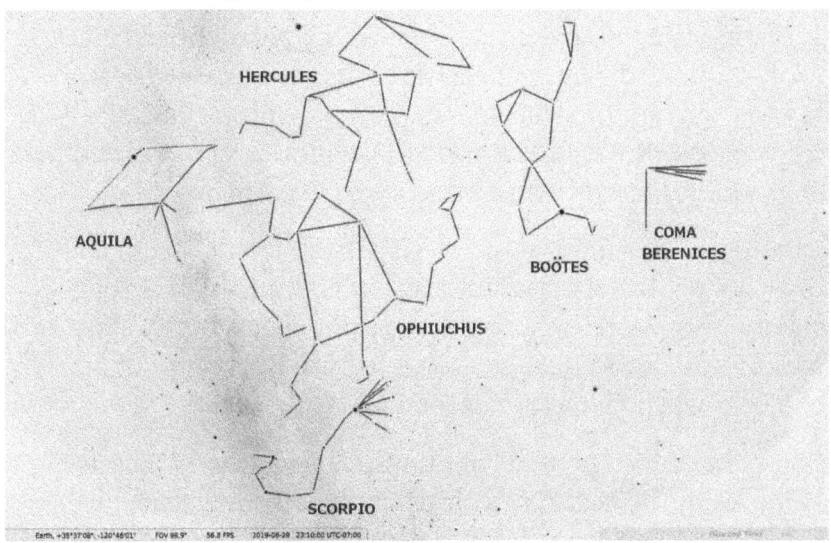

Thus, we can be quite confident that Iolaus, the nephew of Heracles who acts as his charioteer in this story, corresponds to the constellation Boötes. Notice how Boötes can actually be envisioned as driving a chariot with the constellation Hercules in

Chapter Four

the back of it! This configuration actually appears elsewhere in world myth as well, such as in the Norse myths, when Loki acts as the charioteer for Thor in several adventures -- Loki corresponding to the constellation Boötes and Thor to the constellation Hercules, as I discuss in *Star Myths of the World, Volume Four*.

Note the location of the constellation Coma Berenices in close proximity to Boötes. Coma Berenices is a beautiful constellation, rather faint but well worth finding in the heavens if you have a clear sky and a dark location for viewing the constellations (and if it is the right time of year for finding Coma Berenices). The constellation's name means "Berenice's Hair," and it figures in many myths and legends around the world involving the theft of hair (the reader may be aware that Loki in fact steals the beautiful hair of Thor's wife, Sif, in one episode in the Norse myths).

Coma Berenices plays other roles in world myth besides hair. I have demonstrated that Coma Berenices sometimes appears as a "whisk" (sometimes described as a whisk of peacock feathers, such as in some of the ancient Sanskrit epics of ancient India), and also as a flaming torch (such as in the story of Iphigenia, who in some versions of the Greek myths becomes or is associated with the goddess Hecate, who carries one or two torches).

Thus, the close proximity of a celestial *torch* to the figure of Boötes (who plays the role of Iolaus in this myth) is strong confirmation that our deciphering of the components of this story is correct. Iolaus, of course, uses a torch to burn the stumps of the Hydra's necks when Heracles cuts off their heads.

In the story, a crab of unusual size emerges from the swamp to grab Heracles by the heel. The constellation of Cancer the Crab, however, is nowhere near this region of the sky. Immediately adjacent to the extended foot and raised heel of the constellation Hercules, however, we do see the constellation Aquila the Eagle.

As I've noted before in this volume, Aquila appears to me like a great bat or even an enormous manta ray when I view the

Mighty battles with Serpents and Dragons

constellation in person, because there are no bright stars between the three stars of Aquila's head and the tips of the "wings" of the Eagle. We *can* imagine a line connecting each wingtip in horizontal fashion, and there *is* a very faint star along this imagined horizontal line to support such a configuration, and that is how I will usually depict Aquila in these star-charts, but on the chart on page 87 I've connected the sides of the three-star head of the constellation to its "wingtips."

Can you see how this depiction causes Aquila to look like a manta ray or a great bat? There are indeed mythical references to bats elsewhere which I have argued to be references to this same constellation. This way of looking at Aquila could also suggest the shape of a crab! The body of some crabs is shaped very much like the outline of Aquila when connecting the starry outline in this manner, and there is no denying the fact that the constellation itself is located immediately adjacent to the heel of the constellation Hercules. Ancient sources explicitly tell us that the crab emerges from the water to "bite" the foot of the hero Heracles as he battles the Hydra. The swampy river in this entire episode can thus be identified with the Milky Way band itself, as we've already noted (this identification of the crab in the story with Aquila serves as additional confirmation of that).

Another point to note is the fact that the nine-headed Hydra is almost universally described as the offspring of the half-woman, half-serpent mother -- Echidna -- and the monstrous giant whose legs are two great serpents, beginning at his thighs: Typhon.

I am convinced that one or both of these monstrous parents of the Hydra can be seen to be associated with the constellation Ophiuchus, *directly above* the constellation Scorpio which plays the nine-headed Hydra. Thus, the Hydra can be said to be *descended from* Typhon (Ophiuchus), because located beneath that constellation in the heavens. This pattern is very common in the world's Star Myths: a character associated with one constellation is described as being descended from a figure associated with a constellation directly above in the heavens.

Chapter Four

Note that the outline of the constellation Ophiuchus, which can be envisioned as a man or woman holding a huge serpent at waist level, can also be envisioned as a man or woman who has two enormous serpent "legs" issuing from the region of the hips -- which is just how Typhon and Echidna are described in some ancient accounts. The stars of the ordinary "legs" of Ophiuchus are rather faint: thus sometimes it becomes one-legged in other myths, and as Typhon the ordinary legs are not envisioned at all.

We are also beginning to see that the pattern in myth of battling a great serpent is a very widespread pattern, and that such serpent-battling myths are based on the constellations. In the case of the hero Heracles battling the Hydra, we can be quite confident that Heracles is associated with the constellation Hercules and the Hydra is associated with Scorpio. In the case of Zeus battling Typhon, we have already seen that Zeus can be confidently identified with the constellation Hercules as well, although Typhon is probably associated with Ophiuchus rather than with Scorpio. In the case of Apollo battling the great serpent-dragon Python, Apollo with his bow can be confidently associated with the constellation Sagittarius, and Python again corresponds to Scorpio, whom the god Apollo (seen in the figure of Sagittarius) drives out.

We have already seen evidence that the goddess Artemis, the twin sister of Apollo and also known for her use of the bow, is associated with the constellation Sagittarius (see the earlier discussion of the artwork on the bell-krater depicting Artemis in the act of slaying Actaeon). It is not surprising that her twin brother Apollo is also associated with the same constellation.

On the following page is an engraving from the 1500s which indicates that this connection between Apollo and the constellation Sagittarius was known -- and apparently preserved for centuries, with artists being taught to use specific artistic conventions when depicting certain characters and scenes, whether they knew that those conventions correspond to characteristics of constellations or not.

Mighty battles with Serpents and Dragons

The artist has clearly depicted the god Apollo in the posture and location of the constellation Sagittarius in the sky: note the level at which the bow is held, and the position of the other hand which has just released the arrow over the head, corresponding to the "plume" at the top of the constellation's head as well.

Just as in the ancient depiction of Artemis slaying Actaeon, the bow is targeting a figure associated with the constellation Scorpio, which is located next to Sagittarius just on the other side of the Milky Way's brightest portion. Indeed, we can see that the artist in this engraving has included a river in the correct location to represent the Milky Way, in between the god and the dragon.

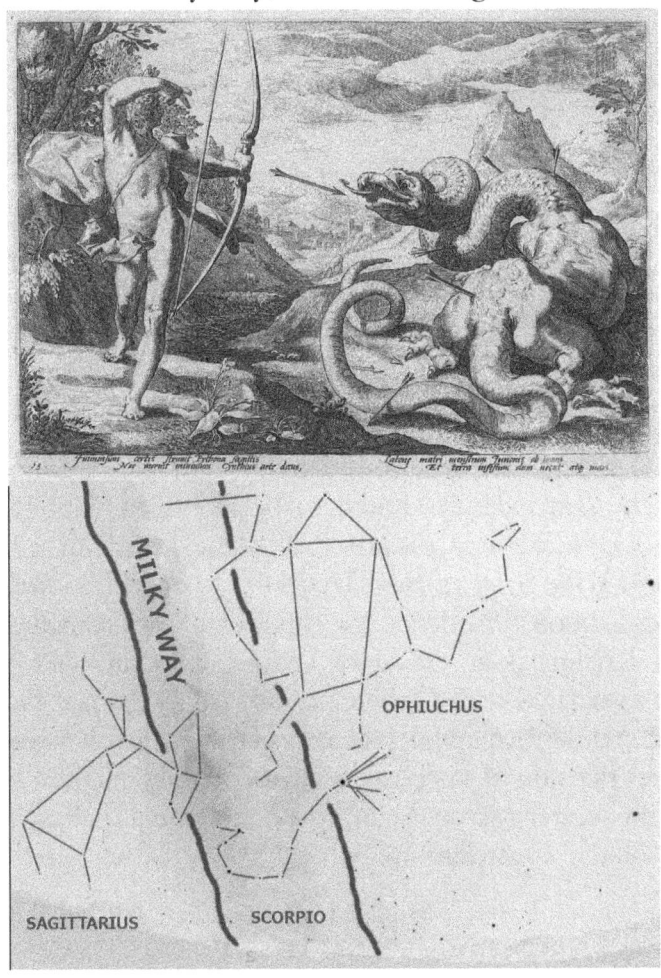

Chapter Four

An additional confirmatory detail in the artwork which reveals undeniable patterning of this scene upon the constellations is the mountain depicted directly above the dragon: this mountain corresponds to the constellation Ophiuchus, which (as we've noted already) is envisioned as a hill or mountain in ancient myths from many different cultures.

The parallels between the figures in the artistic rendition of Apollo battling Python and the constellations in the region of the sky we've been exploring should be self-evident, and should confirm that in ancient myth, figures corresponding to other major constellations surrounding Scorpio were envisioned as battling with serpents or dragons (in this case, Apollo is associated with Sagittarius, while in the case of Zeus versus Typhon or Heracles versus the Hydra, Zeus and Heracles both correspond to the constellation Hercules).

Having seen that figures associated with the constellations Hercules and Sagittarius were both described in ancient myth as battling with serpent-dragon figures associated with Scorpio, we might also surmise that figures associated with Ophiuchus, which is located directly above Scorpio, might also be envisioned as battling with dragons or serpents in myth as well, and indeed there are many examples which confirm that hypothesis.

In the Sanskrit texts of ancient India, for example, the god Krishna can be convincingly shown to be identified with the constellation Ophiuchus, as discussed at some length in *The Ancient World-Wide System: Star Myths of the World, Volume One* (Second Edition). Evidence for this identification include the fact that Krishna is an avatar of Vishnu, who can also be shown to be associated with Ophiuchus, as well as the fact that Krishna is often described and depicted as playing a flute held out horizontally to the side of his head, almost certainly inspired by the shape of the "eastern serpent-half" (the "serpent-tail" half) seen in the stars of the constellation Ophiuchus, as shown on the opposite page.[26]

Mighty battles with Serpents and Dragons

One of the most well-known of Lord Krishna's exploits involves his encounter with a great Naga serpent named Kaliya. This great serpent had multiple heads, each of them resembling a hooded cobra, emanating from a single tremendous serpent body. The ancient texts tell us he had taken up abode in the river Yamuna which flows from the mountain of Kalinda.[27]

This pattern recalls the abode of the Lernaean Hydra just described, and is of course patterned on the same region of the sky, with the river Yamuna being the Milky Way band, the mountain Kalinda being Ophiuchus, and the Kaliya Naga being Scorpio.

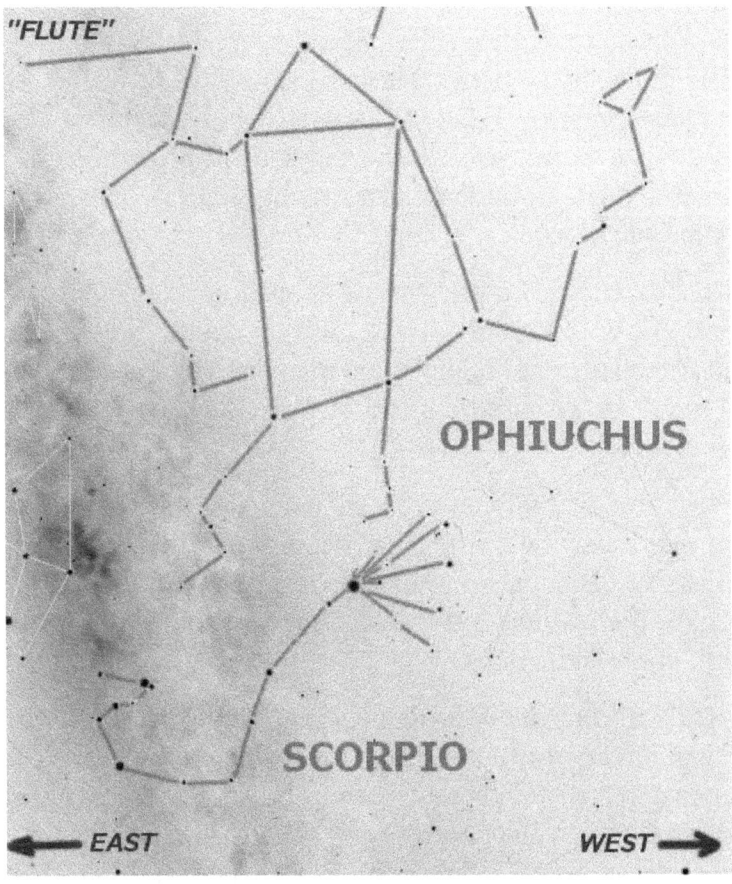

In the story of Krishna's encounter with the Kaliya Naga, the great poisonous serpent beneath the surface of the river causes

Chapter Four

the water to become toxic to animals and humans -- so toxic in fact that poisonous vapors wafting into the air cause birds flying above to fall dead into the river.

The young Lord Krishna (an avatar of Vishnu, although few people yet knew it) resolved to put an end to this problem and leapt into the contaminated river, whirling and agitating the waters as if playing. The great serpent, which had one hundred and one cobra-like heads according to the ancient text of the Bhagavata Purana, immediately rushed upon Krishna from the depths, furious that someone had intruded upon the river, which Kaliya considered to be his and his alone.

Biting Krishna in the chest, the great serpent began to throw coils around Krishna's body. Those looking on are fearful for Krishna's life -- but soon, the text tells us, Krishna decides to shed the illusion that he was a mere mortal, and his body begins to grow larger and larger, until even the mighty Kaliya Naga has to release him from his coils.

Then Krishna climbs on top of the many-headed serpent and begins to dance. As Krishna dances, all the celestial singers and musicians in the heavenly realm begin to express their joy in song and to send down showers of flowers and flower-petals, descending from the sky.

Whichever head of the Kaliya Naga refuses to bend down is trampled mercilessly by Krishna's dancing feet. The text tells us that Kaliya's heads begin vomiting blood and poison as Krishna dances upon the hooded cobra-heads, for Krishna has assumed the weight of the entire universe.

The Bhagavata Purana tells us that Kaliya realizes his danger and turns in his mind to Lord Narayana for shelter. Narayana is the special name for the aspect of Vishnu as the original being, meditating in yogic trance upon the primordial waters. At the same time, the wives of Kaliya approach Krishna and join their hands to plead with the god to have mercy upon their errant husband, the great serpent.

Mighty battles with Serpents and Dragons

This episode can be seen to be patterned upon the celestial region we have been discussing, and to represent yet another example of a god who defeats a great serpent-being, this time a god associated with the constellation Ophiuchus. The Kaliya Naga, with his multiple heads, is clearly associated with Scorpio. The Lord Krishna, who dances upon the multi-headed Kaliya, corresponds to the constellation Ophiuchus. Below is an illustration dating to 1718 from the region of Rajasthan, showing Krishna dancing upon the heads of the Kaliya Naga, while Kaliya's wives implore Krishna for mercy:

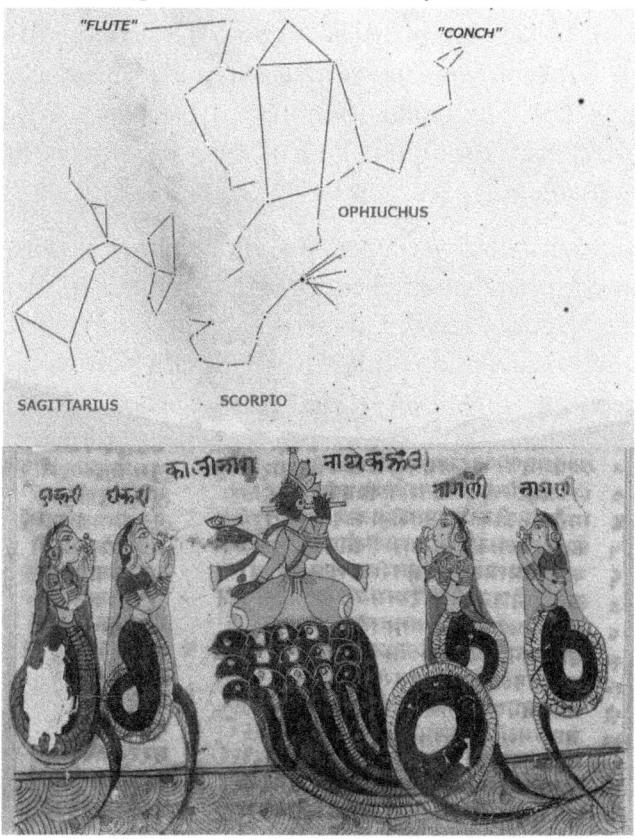

Ophiuchus is directly above Scorpio in the sky, and thus can be envisioned as "dancing upon the heads" of that constellation. Note that this depiction from 1718 shows Krishna holding his flute on one side of his head, but also holding up what appears to

Chapter Four

be a conch with another hand. In the star-chart above, I have added labels showing that this conch held by Krishna corresponds to the "serpent-head" feature of the constellation Ophiuchus, and the flute corresponds to the "serpent-tail."

Don't be confused by the fact that the artist of the 1718 illustration shown above has drawn the conch-shell to the left side of Krishna as we face the drawing, and the flute pointing to the right side of Krishna as we face the drawing. The 1718 artist has also depicted the heads of the Kaliya Naga as pointing to the left as we face the drawing: in other words, he has reversed everything from the way we see it in the sky. Nevertheless, from the iconography associated with Krishna, we can see that the god is associated with the constellation Ophiuchus (for more discussion of this association of Krishna with Ophiuchus, please see *The Ancient World-Wide System*).

The figure of the constellation Sagittarius can be envisioned as a man or woman with hands folded together as if in prayer, or in the *anjali mudra* (palms together, fingertips pointing upwards). The feature of the constellation often envisioned as a bow would, in such a case, be interpreted as "folded palms" instead. In this particular episode, I would suggest that Sagittarius forms the celestial basis for the wives of Kaliya who present themselves with hands folded and palms together to entreat Lord Krishna for mercy upon their husband.

According to the Bhagavata Purana, Lord Krishna does indeed grant mercy upon Kaliya, releasing the great serpent, who had been rendered nearly unconscious by the drumming of the god's dancing feet. He orders Kaliya to leave the river and go to the ocean and dwell there in peace, obeying the gods. Krishna purifies the River Yamuna of the poison, so that it can be enjoyed by mortal men and women, and their cattle.

Other examples from ancient texts involving an Ophiuchus-figure battling a many-headed serpent or dragon-figure associated with Scorpio include the conflict between Michael the Archangel and

Mighty battles with Serpents and Dragons

the dragon described in Revelation chapter 12, in the canonical Revelation of John (not to be confused with many other "revelation" or "apocalypse" texts from the same period, which were excluded from the canonical New Testament, some of them included in the Nag Hammadi corpus which was re-discovered in the twentieth century after being buried beneath the sands of Egypt for almost sixteen centuries).

Revelation 12 describes a dragon having "seven heads and ten horns" (Revelation 12: 3), which is opposed by "Michael and his angels" (Revelation 12: 7), the result of which battle, we are told, being that the dragon and his allied angels "prevailed not; neither was their place found any more in heaven" but instead the dragon was "cast out into the earth, and his angels were cast out with him" (Revelation 12: 8 - 9).

The defeat of the dragon by the Archangel Michael has been a popular subject of artwork for centuries, and that artwork consistently depicts the two main combatants with characteristics which point beyond any doubt to an identification with the constellations Ophiuchus (in the case of Michael) and Scorpio (in the case of the dragon, who is sometimes though not always depicted with multiple heads).

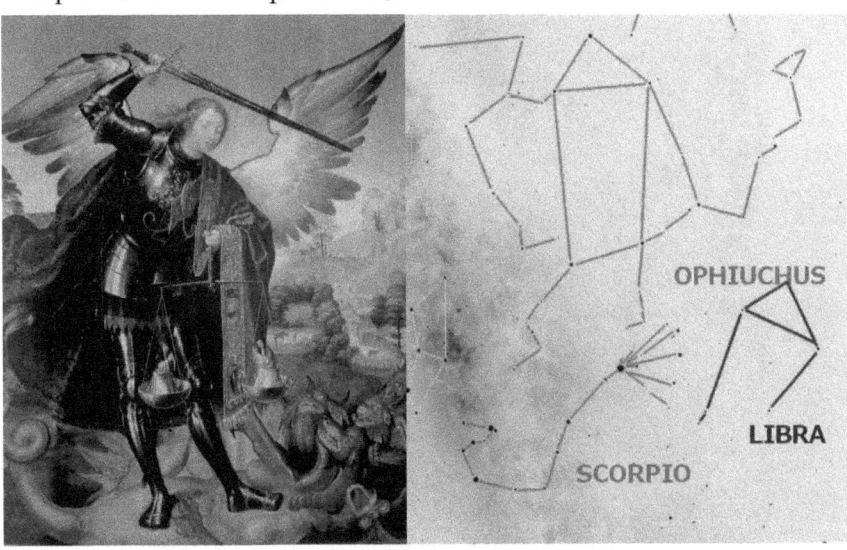

Chapter Four

In the image above, for example, we see a depiction of Michael the Archangel subduing the dragon, attributed to artist Garcia Fernandes of Portugal (c. 1514 - c. 1565), which observes many of the conventions commonly included in artistic renditions of this episode.

Important details include the fact that Michael is standing *directly upon* the supine dragon, and menacing the monster with a weapon in his upraised right hand (on the left as we face the image). The dragon in this artistic depiction has multiple heads, although it is not always depicted as having multiple heads despite the specificity in the text of Revelation 12: 3, probably because a later verse declares that the dragon is in fact "that old serpent, called the Devil, and Satan, which deceiveth the whole world" (Revelation 12: 9). Therefore other artists depict the "dragon" underfoot in much more anthropomorphic (if diabolical or satanic and thus still monstrous) form.

Other details to note include the fact that Michael is almost always depicted as having wings, and the fact that Michael is quite often depicted as holding a great set of scales or balances in the hand not holding the weapon (on the right as we face the image -- the same side as the heads of the great serpent underfoot).

Mighty battles with Serpents and Dragons

Above we see another depiction of Michael and the dragon, this by Pedro Garcia de Benavarre (1445 - 1485), this time showing Michael armed with the more typical spear. He is again shown winged, with his feet upon his fallen opponent, and holding a set of balances or scales in his lower or left hand (the spear is in his upraised right hand).

These details all point to the inescapable conclusion that this scene reflects the constellations Ophiuchus and Scorpio in the heavens. Ophiuchus can be thought to be "standing upon" Scorpio in the sky, and (as we have seen in many previous myths), figures associated with Ophiuchus very frequently favor the *spear* as their chosen weapon (and in some cases, *two spears*).

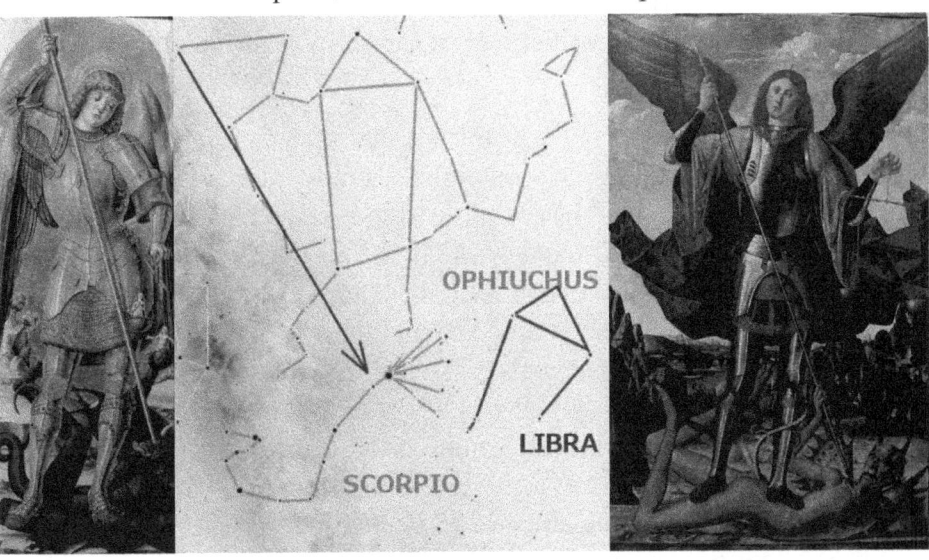

Above we see yet two more depictions of the same scene, along with a star-chart showing the constellations which form the foundation for this particular episode. On the left as we face the page we see the artwork of Bartolomeo Vivarini (1440 - 1499), and on the right the artwork of Francesco Pagano (d. 1506).

In both cases, as with the scene on the facing page, the angel holds a spear at almost the exact same angle in each depiction. In the star-chart accompanying the artistic depictions, I have added a line through the stars of the "eastern serpent-half" (the "tail-end"

Chapter Four

of the serpent held by Ophiuchus) which shows the way the stars could be connected in order to envision the constellation holding a great spear (showing the reason why Ophiuchus-figures in ancient myth often carry a spear as their chosen weapon, or at times a great rod or staff).

The angel is envisioned as having wings, which is also not uncommon for Ophiuchus-figures in myth: turn back to the depictions of Zeus battling Typhon on previous pages (see for instance the drawing on page 59 and the discussion on page 90), in which Typhon can be seen to be associated with Ophiuchus and in which the monster is depicted as having wings.

Directly below Ophiuchus we see Scorpio, depicted with multiple heads and playing the role of the dragon in Revelation chapter 12.

The detail which confirms beyond any reasonable doubt that these artistic depictions consistently identify the scene as corresponding to Ophiuchus above Scorpio is the set of *balances* or *scales* held in the lower hand of Michael the Archangel. These correspond to the constellation Libra, the Scales. Libra is directly adjacent to both Ophiuchus and Scorpio, and is shown in the star-chart on the preceding page -- in precisely the correct location to be imagined as being held by the Ophiuchus-figure (Michael in this case) in his left hand, on the right of the central body of Ophiuchus as we face the page, and rather lower than the upraised hand holding the spear on the other side of the central body of the constellation.

Thus we can see from the mythical episodes we've examined (and many others could be added if further evidence is needed) that many of the Star Myths involving gods or heroes who battle great serpents or serpent-like dragons have their foundation in the region of the sky containing Scorpio and surrounding constellations, with Scorpio playing the role of the serpent or dragon, opposed by figures associated with either the constellation Hercules (as in the myth of Heracles battling the

Mighty battles with Serpents and Dragons

Hydra), or with the constellation Sagittarius (as in the myth of Apollo battling Python), or with the constellation Ophiuchus (as in the story of Krishna dancing on the hooded cobra-heads of the many-headed Kaliya Naga, or in the conflict between Michael the Archangel and the dragon in Revelation chapter 12).

When we see this pattern in ancient myth, we should examine the details of the story closely in order to determine if correspondences to these constellations are present. Myths involving gods or heroes battling great serpents or dragons turn up in the sacred traditions of cultures around the globe. Other manifestations of this same pattern include Thor and the Midgard Serpent in Norse mythology (discussed at length in *Star Myths of the World, Volume Four*), Maui and the great eel Tuna in the myths of the cultures of the Pacific, and Bhima's encounter with a supernatural python in the ancient Sanskrit epic of Mahabharata from ancient India, in addition to those discussed in this chapter.

To this same pattern we could also add the battle between Marduk and Tiamat in the myths of ancient Mesopotamia, recounted in the Enuma Elish, and discussed at length in *The Ancient World-Wide System*.

In the scriptures included in the Old and New Testaments of the Bible, in addition to the story of Michael and the dragon in Revelation, we can also see the same pattern at work in the judgment pronounced upon the serpent in Genesis chapter 3, when God casts the serpent, the woman, and the man out of the Garden. There, God tells the serpent that he will place "enmity" the serpent and the woman, but also enmity between "thy seed and her seed," with the added detail that the seed of the serpent shall bruise the heel of the seed of the woman, but in turn the seed of the woman shall bruise the head of the serpent (Genesis 3: 15).

The reader should recognize that this description clearly evokes the relative locations of Scorpio and Ophiuchus in the night sky, with Ophiuchus standing atop the "head" (or multiple heads) of

Scorpio (thus "bruising" the head of Scorpio) while Scorpio simultaneously appears to be biting the heel of Ophiuchus. In this passage, Ophiuchus plays the role of the "seed" (or offspring) of the woman Eve (played by the constellation Virgo, as I discuss in *Star Myths of the World, Volume Three: Star Myths of the Bible*), while Scorpio plays the role of the "seed" (or offspring) of the serpent Hydra (the constellation Hydra, which is adjacent to Virgo and appears almost to be whispering in her ear).

Thus the promised enmity between the offspring of the woman and the offspring of the serpent, found in the very first chapters of the book of Genesis, fits this same worldwide pattern once again.

Indeed, there are verses in the texts of the Bible which indicate that the very God of the Bible also combats a great creature of the deep, very much paralleling the enmity between Thor and the Midgard Serpent or between Marduk and Tiamat, or between Heracles and the Hydra, or between Zeus and Typhon -- a connection of great significance, pointing to an identification of the God of the Bible with the figure of Hercules in the heavens.

What is going on here?

We are beginning to see beyond doubt that the ancient myths are celestial metaphor, and I would argue that this reveals that they are not about external (or historical) events but rather that they depict internal realities pertinent to the lives of each one of us -- indeed, not only pertinent but critically and vitally important.

All of this wrestling with and battling of monsters from the depths speak to subsurface monsters that we ourselves need to dredge up and confront -- monsters we probably suspect are lurking down within our own internal deep, but monsters whose very existence we may be afraid to admit, because we sense that they are far too powerful for us to handle.

But the ancient myths do not teach us that we have to face them alone. Rather, the myths point us towards a re-connection, through the depths, to one who holds the solution: one who connects us to the awesome power of the infinite realm. Read on!

Chapter 5
Gods of thunder and of wind

Augustine of Hippo (AD 354 to AD 430) remains one of the most influential theologians of literalist Christianity in history – and one of the most prolific, with over a hundred different works surviving to the present day.

Despite the generally congenial tone of his prose and the philosophically sophisticated level of his arguments, his opposition to the ancient gods and their ongoing veneration within the lands where they had been worshiped from time immemorial is unstinting, merciless, and launched with the full force of Augustine's redoubtable intellect and rhetorical power, holding nothing back.

The ancient myths and accompanying rites of the gods and goddesses and associated deities, including both those indigenous to the land of Rome and Italy and those of other cultures with whom the Romans had been brought into contact through economic and military expansion, had been under increasingly severe pressure during the century leading up to the birth of Augustine, a subject I explore at some length in my 2014 book, *The Undying Stars*. The first openly Christian emperor, Philip I, took the throne in AD 244, and when Constantine (often called Constantine the Great, who lived from AD 272 to AD 337) came to power in AD 313 (gaining undisputed control over the empire in AD 324), he made Christianity the official religion of Rome.

Later, the emperor Theodosius I, who lived between the years AD 347 and AD 395, and who ruled as emperor from AD 379 until his death, instituted laws and policies which prohibited non-Christian practice of all kinds. Theodosius closed temples, removed holidays associated with the ancient gods, and put an end to the annual tradition of the Eleusinian Mysteries, among other *mysteria*, whose observance went back many hundreds of

Chapter Five

years, if not further. Under Theodosius, the ancient Oracle at Delphi was also shut down, the Vestal Virgins were disbanded in Rome (where they had tended the sacred flame which was not allowed to go out), and the ancient Olympic games came to an end.

Given this history, we might wonder why the powerful bishop Augustine, who was born in 354 and would have been 25 years old when Theodosius became emperor, would waste time and energy writing against the worship and veneration of the ancient gods. But on August 24 of the year AD 410, well after the death of Theodosius, the king of the Germanic federation of the Visigoths (which at that time stretched across what is today Spain and France) marched upon and sacked Rome itself.

That king, Alaric I (c. AD 370 - AD 410), had himself served as a commander in charge of a unit of Germanic tribesmen fighting for Theodosius, helping the emperor defeat a western contender named Flavius Arbogastes (known as Arbogast) in a vicious battle at the river Frigidus in 394, during which the Goths had been used as the shock troops in a frontal assault. The battle itself has been seen as a defeat of the final major challenge mounted by supporters of the old gods, as Arbogast was an open proponent of the ancient traditions, and Theodosius framed his campaign to defeat the army of Arbogast as a holy war sanctioned by heaven.

Alaric apparently felt that the major contributions that he and his Visigoths had made to the victory were not properly recognized or rewarded, hence his decision to lead an army to sack Rome, which he finally accomplished in AD 410.

This was the first time the city had ever been successfully entered by a hostile army since the Gauls had done so in the early fourth century BC, long before the rise of imperial Rome. Even the most formidable opponents during the Punic Wars had never successfully reached the city, being defeated before reaching the capitol. There were many who blamed the catastrophe on the rise of Christianity and the abandonment of the old traditions, as philosopher and historian Étienne Henri Gilson (1884 - 1978) explains in a foreword to Augustine's most influential work, *The City of God*, which itself was written as a counter to these accusations following Alaric's successful march on the city:

> The capture of Rome by the barbarians made a deep impression upon the entire Empire. The endless polemics between Christians and pagans increased in violence and bittterness. To analyze all the arguments of both sides would be a task both long and detailed, and, like the polemics themselves, would not bring us to any goal. On the pagan side, there were two principal and simple arguments from which all the others directly or indirectly stemmed. First of all, Christian doctrine taught renouncement of the world; consequently it turned the citizen away from the service of the state, a fact which brought about the fall of Rome. Secondly, the destiny of Rome was always bound up with the worship of her gods. When the Christian religion began to spread, the pagans proclaimed that their betrayed gods would visit terrible punishments upon the Empire. No one would listen, but the turn of events finally had justified their prophecy, and to such an extent that it was no longer possible to refuse them a hearing. The Empire had become Christian and it was during the reign of a Christian emperor that Rome, for the first time in her long history, was conquered and sacked. How could anyone fail to understand a lesson so tragically clear?[28]

Augustine dedicated several of his works (including *City of God*) to Flavius Marcellinus of Carthage, a tribune who was interested in theology, who was friends with Augustine and who frequently asked him questions about Christian doctrine. It was in order to refute the accusations about the sack of Rome being due to the rise of Christianity and the abandonment of the old gods, accusations which were troubling Marcellinus, that Augustine wrote his *De civitate Dei contra paganos*, or "On the city of God against the pagans," commonly referred to in English simply as *The City of God*.

Chapter Five

Augustine unleashes the full force of his formidable intellectual and rhetorical arsenal in rebutting these accusations and in launching his own counterattack against the worship of the *deos gentium*, the "gods of the nations," the gods whom (as Augustine writes) *Christiana religio destruit* – "the Christian religion destroys."[29]

Augustine argues that the gods of the nations, particularly as they are celebrated by the poets (meaning, described in the myths and recounted in the plays featuring the adventures of the gods), are in fact unclean demons, in view of their various quarrels, feuds, and amorous affairs. Citing the earlier arguments of a Roman consul of the period of the Republic, Quintus Mucius Scaevola called Pontifex (d. 82 BC), Augustine writes in *City of God* that:

> Scaevola makes no secret of the reasons he had for rejecting the gods of the poets. It is because they so distort them that the gods cannot be compared even with decent men. One they turn into a thief, another into an adulterer, and otherwise make them talk and act like degenerates and fools, such as the three goddesses who fought amongst themselves for the prize of beauty, and destroyed Troy when two of them were bested by Venus. Jove himself is transformed into a bull or a swan in order to carry on amours with some wanton or other. A goddess marries a man. Saturn devours his children. In fine, no prodigy nor vice can be imagined which is not here, utterly irreconcilable with their divine nature.
>
> O Scaevola, pontifex, abolish those plays if you can. [. . .] But, they will not listen to you; they are demons, teachers of depravity, delighting in obscenity. They take it as no affront to have such things written about them.[30]

Augustine concludes this argument by declaring: "Gods of that sort, appeased, or rather dishonored, and thereby more vicious for taking delight in the filthy falsehoods ascribed to them than they would have taken if they were true, could never have extended and preserved the Roman Empire."[31]

Gods of thunder and of wind

Elsewhere he repeats many times his opinion that the gods of the nations are in fact demons, and that the stories about the gods are the inventions of demons -- and not, he says, the inventions of "good demons" either, but rather, he says, "to speak plainly, of unclean spirits and manifestly malign spirits." These unclean spirits, Augustine goes on to say, "work secretly and with incredible hatred to fill the minds of wicked people."[32]

Later Augustine writes:

> It was by means of the true religion alone that it could be made manifest that the gods of the pagans were nothing but unclean spirits who used the memory of people departed or the images of earthly creatures to get themselves reckoned as gods and who then rejoiced with proud impurity that divine honors should be paid to such disgusting and indecent things, all the while hating to see men's souls turn to the true God. [...]
>
> To this category of unclean spirits belong not only the lesser gods of which I have said so much, and many, many other gods of the same sort among the various peoples of the world, but likewise those gods who were selected to form a sort of Senate of the gods. From what I have just been reporting, they were obviously chosen more for the notoriety of their wickedness than for the nobility of their virtues.[33]

What Augustine appears not to have realized (unless he actually did know it, and deliberately taught otherwise, a level of treachery we need not impute to his character), is that the various adventures recounted in the myths, and preserved by the poets and the sacred reenactments in the theater involving the arguments and affairs of the gods, are all based upon a very ancient world-wide system of celestial metaphor -- and that this *same ancient system* forms the basis for all the characters and adventures recounted in the Biblical scriptures as well.

The main difference, which allows Augustine to impute "depravity" and "obscenity" and "wickedness" to the gods of the nations while believing that his own literalist religion is

107

Chapter Five

impervious to such accusations, is that the figures in the Bible who act out the drama of the celestial allegories are for the most part described as mortal men and women (such as Samson, or David, or Sarah, or Mary Magdalene, or Peter, and so on), rather than as gods.

But the divine figures in the scriptures of the Bible, including the God of the Old Testament as well as the Christ of the New Testament, can be shown to correspond to the same figures in the stars with which the gods of the world's other ancient traditions are also associated. And the supernatural beings described in the scriptures of the Bible, such as we have already seen in our brief examination of the celestial identity of Michael the Archangel, can be shown to be associated with constellations in very much the same way.

The same ancient world-wide system which underlies the stories of the gods of Rome against whom Augustine hurls his invective, as well as the stories of the "many, many other gods of the same sort among the various peoples of the world," also forms the foundation for the characters and events described in the scriptures of the Bible, from the beginning of Genesis all the way to the end of the Revelation of John. The evidence to back up this startling claim is so abundant as to be completely overwhelming, and (I would argue) conclusive.

And indeed, as we might suspect from his very name as recorded in the Biblical scriptures, the God of the Bible -- whose name is represented by the sacred tetragrammaton or "four letters" of YHWH which is sometimes articulated as Yahweh or Yahveh or (in previous centuries) as Jehovah -- can be shown to share many of the distinctive characteristics associated with the very same Jove of the ancient Latins, who is known also as Jupiter and who corresponds to the Greek god Zeus, and in fact to be connected with the very same constellation in the night sky.

Thus, if we find in the myths regarding the ancient gods of Greece and Rome stories involving infidelities and amorous

Gods of thunder and of wind

affairs, such as the amorous affair between Aphrodite and Ares recounted in the Odyssey (whose Latin names are Venus and Mars), to which affair Augustine refers as an example of the behavior he finds blameworthy in the poems and plays about the gods (in *City of God*, Book 4, chapter 10), it can be shown that the details of this affair are based upon the constellations of the night sky (as I discuss in *Star Myths of the World, Volume Two: Myths of Ancient Greece*).[34]

Meanwhile, there is certainly no lack of episodes involving infidelities, adulterous affairs, incest, rape, and similar behavior among the texts of the Biblical scriptures -- and these too can be shown to have their foundation in the celestial figures, upon which the stories in the Bible are likewise constructed.

Augustine spends a great deal of time in *City of God* berating the poets and stage players for reciting the same sexually transgressive behaviors described in the Greek and Roman myths, while ignoring the fact that the Biblical texts describe abundant examples of the same -- for example the adultery of David with Bathsheba (after David has Bathsheba's husband Uriah murdered, per instructions placed in a sealed letter which David gives to Uriah himself to deliver to those who will kill him).

It can be shown that this adulterous affair is celestial in its origins, as I explain in *Star Myths of the World, Volume Three: Star Myths of the Bible* -- and, what is more, the figure of David the notorious adulterer can be definitively identified with the very same constellation Hercules with which the god Jove (or Jupiter, or Zeus in the Greek myths) is also associated.[35] David sees Bathsheba from his position *on the roof* (because the constellation Hercules is positioned atop the constellation Ophiuchus in the heavens, and Ophiuchus can be seen as resembling a house), whereas Zeus or Jove dwells upon Mount Olympus (Ophiuchus also being envisioned as a great mountain, in numerous myths from around the globe) -- but in either case, the beautiful women they spy and with whom they carry on

Chapter Five

adulterous affairs can be confidently identified with the constellation Sagittarius, far below.

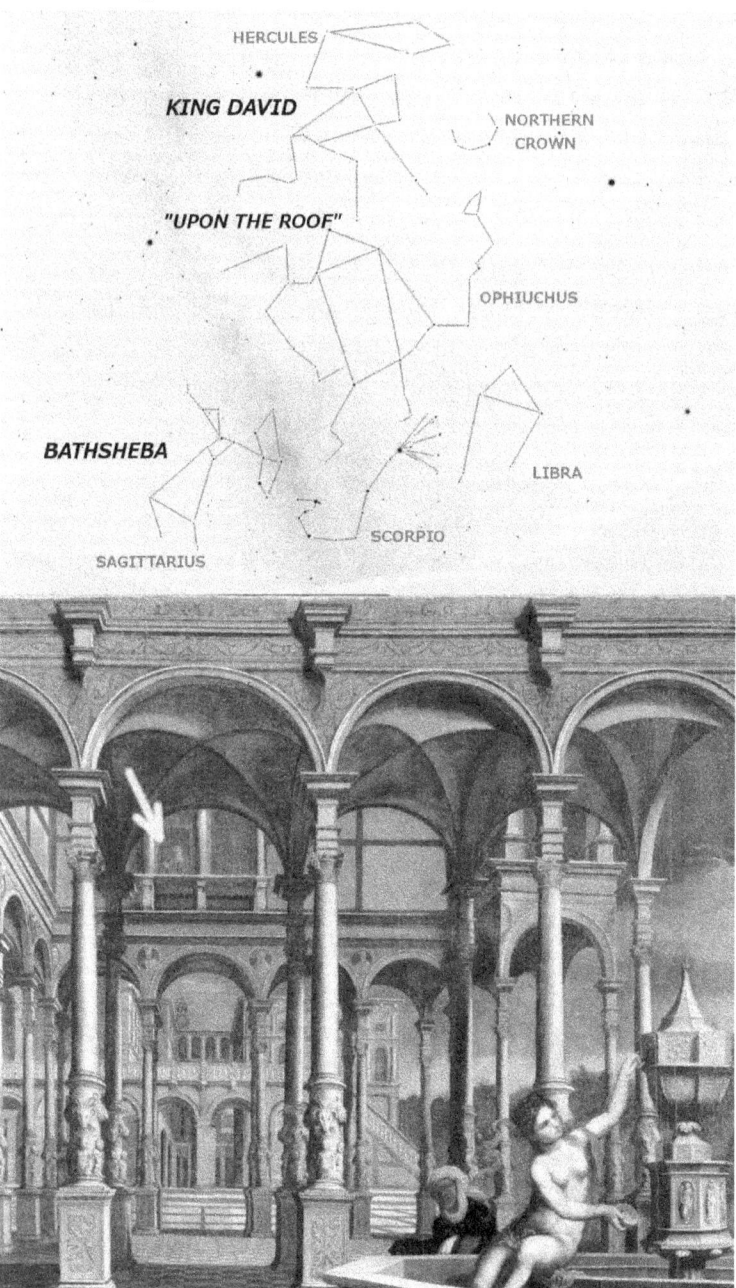

Gods of thunder and of wind

In the artwork on the opposite page, painted around 1540 - 1550, note the numerous "Ophiuchus-shapes." Observe also the similarity in posture between Bathsheba and Sagittarius. King David is indicated by an arrow that I have added. Note that he is depicted directly above an Ophiuchus-shaped arch, with two pillars on either side.

Can the proponents of literalist Christianity really argue (as Augustine does, at length, in *City of God*) that the recitation of such sexual liaisons is demonically inspired when they involve the "gods of the nations" but divinely blessed when recorded in the pages of Biblical scripture? The solution to the dilemma comes with the understanding that the events in either case are metaphorical dramatizations based on celestial characters, and that they can be shown to be parts of an extremely ancient system which is designed to convey profound practical and spiritual truth through esoteric metaphor, rather than being understood literally. The error only arises when the sacred stories in the scriptures of the Bible are viewed as being completely different from and unrelated to the myths and scriptures and sacred stories given to other cultures around the globe, virtually all of which can be shown to be built upon the very same world-wide system.

In the stories of the Bible, figures invested with overt divinity are much fewer than in the "myths of the nations" such as the numerous gods found in the myths of ancient Greece and Rome (as well as the "many, many other gods of the same sort among the various peoples of the world" referenced by Augustine in *City of God*), and yet the divine figures in the Bible can also be shown to correspond to constellations just as we find with all the other world myths.

The stories preserved in the Scriptures of the Bible are based on celestial metaphor, in common with the world's other ancient myths and sacred stories. In common with many other myth-systems, these texts "show" us aspects of the invisible and divine realm *through characters based upon the constellations* -- illustrating aspects of the most powerful divinity through the

Chapter Five

constellation Hercules, just as the myths of ancient Greece associate the god Zeus with the constellation Hercules, and just as the myths of ancient Mesopotamia associate the god Marduk with the constellation Hercules, and just as the myths of ancient Egypt associate the gods Ptah, Amun, Atum and Ra with the constellation Hercules.[36]

If the God of the Bible is associated with the constellation Hercules, then – like other figures associated with Hercules in other celestial myths – we might expect to find references to battles against great serpents or sea monsters, as we find with Thor versus the Midgard Serpent, with Marduk versus Tiamat, or with Heracles versus the Lernaean Hydra.

And indeed we do find such references in the Biblical texts, such as in reference to the creature known as "leviathan." In Psalm 74, which is explicitly addressed to God (beginning with the words "O God" and repeating that exclamation throughout the rest of the psalm), the scriptures declare of the LORD, "Thou brakest the heads of leviathan in pieces, *and* gavest him *to be* meat to the people inhabiting the wilderness" (Psalm 74: 14).

The fact that the text specifically says "the heads of leviathan" is extremely noteworthy, because leviathan is singular (and is later referred to using a singular pronoun) but multiple heads are clearly being specified: thus, a single creature called leviathan with multiple heads. We have already made the argument that the constellation Scorpio plays the role of the great serpent or dragon or sea-monster antagonist to Hercules-figures in other myths, and that this constellation Scorpio can clearly be envisioned as having multiple heads.

The enmity between God and leviathan is referenced again in Isaiah chapter 27, the first verse of which proclaims (referring to a future judgment day): "In that day the LORD with his sore and great and strong sword shall punish leviathan the piercing serpent, even leviathan that crooked serpent; and he shall slay the dragon that *is* in the sea" (Isaiah 27: 1).

Gods of thunder and of wind

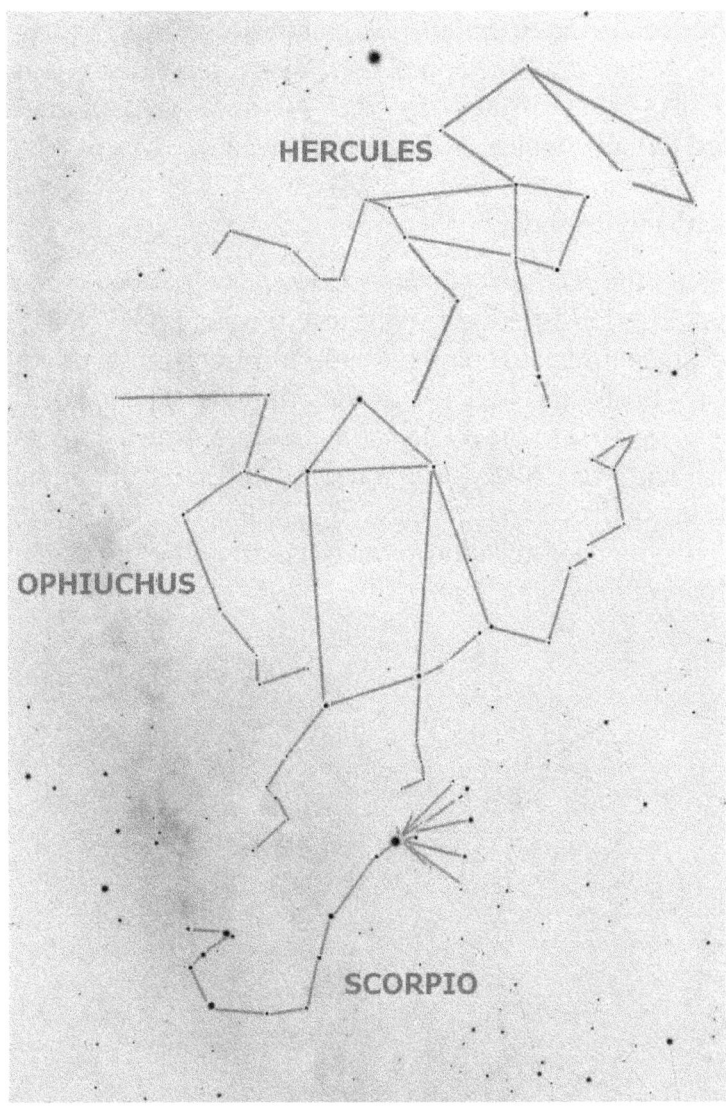

At this point, the reader should be able to recognize the reference to the "sore and great and strong sword" as a distinctive characteristic of the constellation Hercules. The description of leviathan as "that crooked serpent" can once again be seen as descriptive of the constellation Scorpio.

It is also interesting to note that the Hebrew word translated as "piercing" (in the description of leviathan as "the piercing serpent")

Chapter Five

is the adjective *bariyach*, designated as Strong's H1281 in the *Exhaustive Concordance of the Bible* compiled by James Strong (1822 - 1894) and published in 1890. There, this adjective is described as being related to the Hebrew verb *barach* (designated H1272), which is defined as meaning "to go, pass through, to flee, to hasten, to chase, drive way, put to flight," and also "to bolt" and "to shoot." [37]

According to the *Hebrew-Chaldee Lexicon* of professor and theologian Heinrich Friedrich Wilhelm Gesenius (1786 - 1842), this verb *barach* means "to pass through, to reach across, to cut through, to break through" -- all descriptions which could accurately be applied to the constellation Scorpio, which appears to be "piercing" the Milky Way (with the back half of the constellation) or "breaking through" the Milky Way (with the front half of the constellation, which is emerging from the brightest part of the Milky Way):

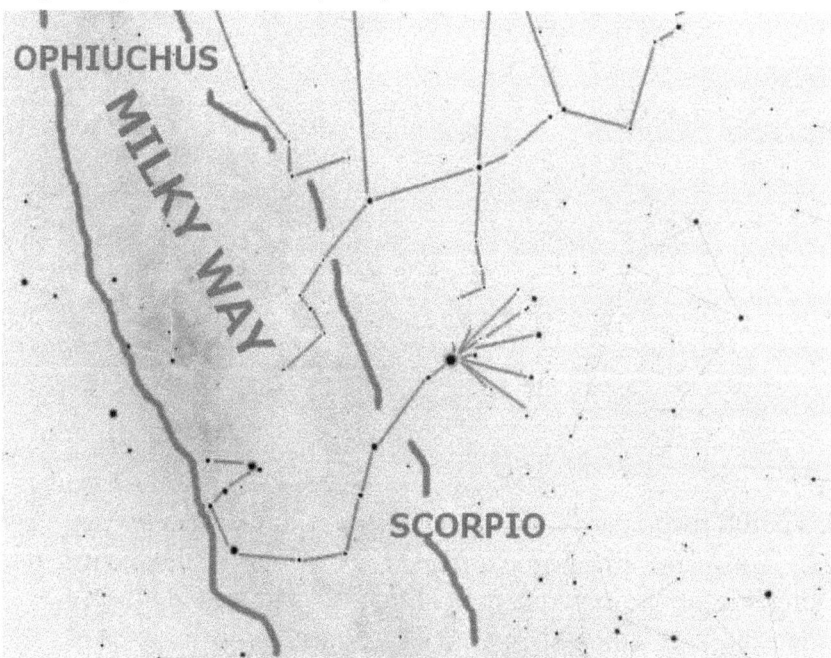

It is also very intriguing to note that Gesenius, in his *Hebrew-Chaldee Lexicon* for the adjective form *bariyach* (later designated Strong's H1281, the form of the word found in the text of Isaiah 27

Gods of thunder and of wind

to describe leviathan and translated "piercing" in the phrase "the piercing serpent), defines the word as "fleeing, an epithet of the serpent, both of the real creature, Isa. 27: 1, and of the constellation, Job 26: 13."[38]

Gesenius finds evidence that this description "fleeing" (*bariyach*) can be applied to a "crooked serpent" which is a *constellation*, because (as Gesenius points out in the above definition), this very same word *bariyach* is used in the book of Job, during Job's response to Bildad the Shuhite (in which Job is describing God's act of "garnishing the heavens"). Bildad is the shortest man in the Bible, according to an old joke popular among English-speaking preachers, which I heard in a sermon by Pastor David Jeremiah while I was still a believer in literalism (i.e. he is "*shoe-height*").

In a majestic passage in that chapter (Job 26), Job declares of the Almighty:

> 7 He stretcheth out the north over the empty place, *and* hangeth the earth upon nothing.
> 8 He bindeth up the waters in his thick clouds; and the cloud is not rent under them.
> 9 He holdeth back the face of his throne, *and* spreadeth his cloud upon it.
> 10 He hath compassed the waters with bounds, until the day and night come to an end.
> 11 The pillars of heaven tremble and are astonished at his reproof.
> 12 He divideth the sea with his power, and by his understanding he smiteth through the proud.
> 13 By his spirit he hath garnished the heavens; his hand hath formed the crooked serpent.
> 14 Lo, these *are* parts of his ways: but how little a portion is heard of him? but the thunder of his power who can understand?

As Professor Gesenius perceived, verse 13 in the above passage is describing the adorning or decorating of the heavens by the LORD, including the creation of a "crooked serpent" among the heavens -- in other words, the crooked serpent is obviously a constellation. The word translated as "crooked" in this verse is in fact the word *bariyach*, which could mean "fleeing" or "piercing" or "breaking through."

Thus we observe the very same adjective being applied to *leviathan* in Isaiah 27 as to the *constellational serpent* described in Job 26. I would argue that in both cases, the creature being referenced is celestial in nature, and associated with the constellation Scorpio, a constellation with a distinctive characteristic of "breaking through" or "piercing" (in reference to the Milky Way), and a constellation which could also be envisioned as "fleeing" (from the constellation Sagittarius, for example, or even from Ophiuchus -- and note that the later stories of St. Patrick chasing the snakes out of Ireland probably relate to Scorpio fleeing from Ophiuchus or from Sagittarius).

The fact that leviathan is associated with Scorpio (just as the Lernaean Hydra in the myth of the Labors of Heracles is associated with Scorpio) constitutes powerful evidence that the God of the Bible is associated with the constellation Hercules (as is Zeus in the Greek myths, as well as Thor in the Norse myths, and Indra in the myths of ancient India, and of course the hero Heracles himself, who battles the nine-headed Hydra).

In fact, other verses in the same passage from Job 26 hint at the same conclusion, such as the declaration in verse 11 that the "pillars of heaven tremble and are astonished at his reproof." The "pillars" which can be envisioned as being "reproved" by a figure associated with the constellation Hercules would of course be the two "pillars" on either side of the constellation Ophiuchus (the "serpent-head" and "serpent-tail" which flank the central body of the constellation).

These "pillars" can certainly be envisioned as "trembling" at the reproof of the figure of Hercules above, who appears to be bending down towards them in the sky:

Gods of thunder and of wind

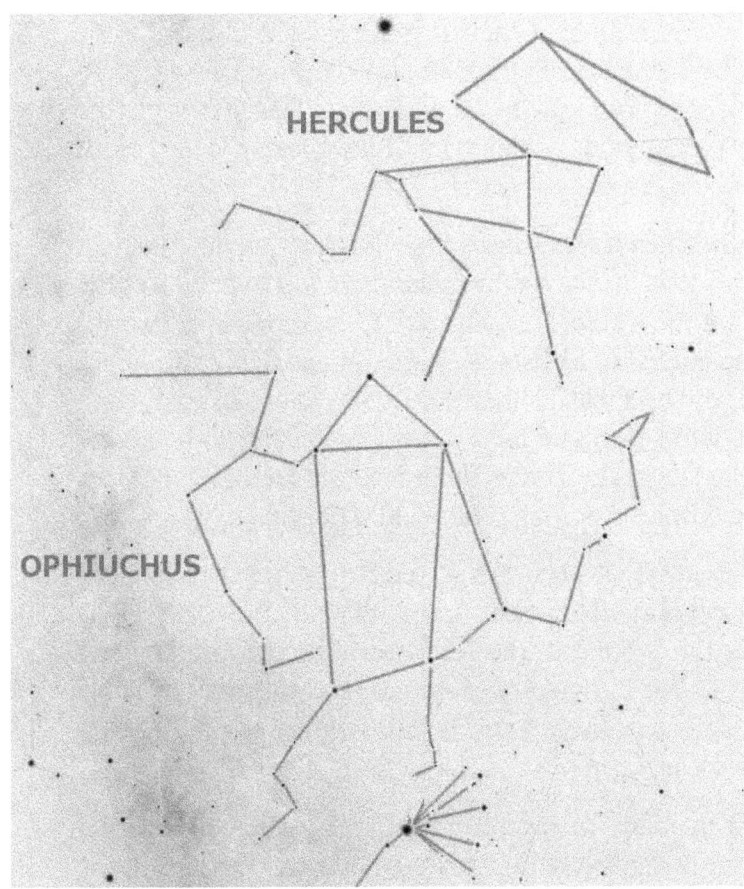

Based on such evidence, along with the connection to Hercules which we saw earlier in our examination of the story of Jacob's Ladder, the argument for an association between the constellation Hercules and the God of the Bible is quite compelling. But there is a plethora of other evidence in the Biblical texts to make the argument even more conclusive.

The texts themselves make it clear that the God of the Bible is associated with wind and even with the whirlwind, and this association with the wind or the whirlwind is a distinctive characteristic shared with many Hercules-connected figures in other cultures as well (including the god Marduk in the Enuma Elish of ancient Mesopotamia, who deploys winds against

Chapter Five

Tiamat in Tablet IV and lines 42 through 47, as well as the wind-god Vayu in the scriptures of ancient India, who is revealed to be the father of both the god Hanuman and the Heracles-like hero Bhima, both of whom can be confidently identified with the constellation Hercules, as explained in *The Ancient World-Wide System*).[39]

In Genesis 8, when God causes the flood to abate, the text explicitly states that he does so by making *a wind* to pass over the earth, such that the waters are assuaged (Genesis 8: 1). In Exodus 10, during the plague of locusts unleashed when Moses stretches forth his rod, the text tells us that the LORD made an east wind, and the east wind brought the locusts. When the LORD later takes away the locusts and casts them into the Red Sea, he does so by sending a "mighty strong west wind" (Exodus 10: 13 - 19).

Similarly, when the LORD parts the Red Sea, so that the children of Israel can cross the Red Sea on dry ground, the text tells us explicitly that the parting of the Red Sea is accomplished when Moses stretches out his hand over the sea, and the LORD causes the sea to be driven back by *a strong east wind* all night, dividing the waters (Exodus 14: 21).

As explained in many of my previous books, the constellation Hercules in the ancient system of myth could be envisioned in the outline of a powerful figure in a deep lunge, brandishing a weapon overhead, *but also* in an alternate outline consisting of the constellation's central distinctive square shape (which forms the "head" of the anthropomorphic Hercules-figure) from which spiralling lines emanate in four directions -- the "four winds" of ancient myth.

Below is a star-chart showing the constellation Hercules in this alternative outline, positioned above Ophiuchus (with which constellation, i.e. Ophiuchus, Moses stretching out rod or hand is undoubtedly associated in the Biblical passages cited above):

Gods of thunder and of wind

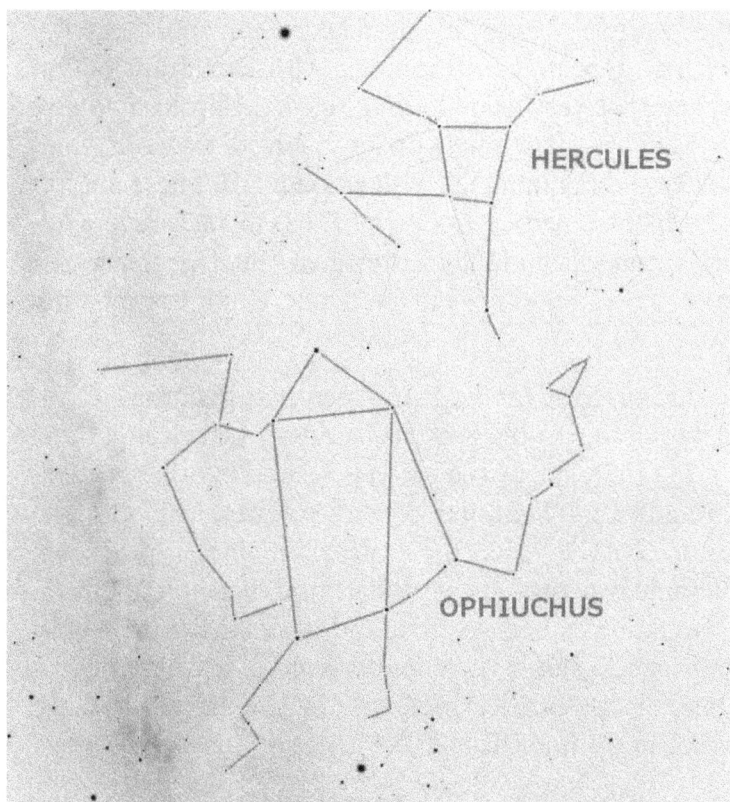

I sometimes refer to this as the "whirling form" of the constellation Hercules, and its importance in the world's ancient myth-system is discussed with numerous examples in *The Ancient World-Wide System: Star Myths of the World, Volume One (Second Edition)*, *Star Myths of the World, Volume Two: Myths of Ancient Greece*, and *Star Myths of the World, Volume Three: Star Myths of the Bible*, as well as in other previous books.

The constellation Hercules, when envisioned in this manner, can be said to resemble a whirlwind, with winds streaming in a spiral fashion around a central "eye of the hurricane." Indeed, our word "hurricane" appears to come from the name of a deity of the Maya civilization of Central America, as Giorgio de Santillana and Hertha von Dechend point out in *Hamlet's Mill*, a deity with parallels in the mythology of other cultures as well:

Chapter Five

> The One-Legged Being, in particular, can be followed through many appearances beginning with the Hunrakán of the Mayas, whose very name means "one-leg." From it comes our "hurricane," so there is no wonder that he disposes of wind, rain, thunder and lightning in lavish amounts. But he is not for all that a mere weather god, since he is one aspect of Tezcatlipoca himself, and the true original One-Leg that looks down from the starry sky -- but his name is not appropriate yet.[40]

Clearly the authors of *Hamlet's Mill* perceive that this "One-Legged" deity is found in the heavens, and they perceive that the deity known as Hunrakán by the Maya is related to other gods of wind, rain, thunder and lightning in other cultures, including the god Tezcatlipoca of the Aztec, the central deity in that pantheon in much the same way that Zeus is the central deity in the Greek pantheon. Tezcatlipoca is a sky god, and associated with winds and with hurricanes, and he is often depicted as having one leg made of bone, or else one leg made of a snake, having lost his right foot or leg in a primordial battle with a great earth monster.

In typical fashion, the authors of *Hamlet's Mill* in the above-quoted passage coyly avoid coming right out and declaring the celestial player with which they believe Tezcatlipoca (and, by extension, Hunrakán) to be associated. This kind of evasiveness can make *Hamlet's Mill* a singularly frustrating read. The authors obviously perceive the presence of a vast, unified, world-wide structure of myth -- and they perceive that it is unified via a connection of the characters to the celestial powers in the heavens above. For this we must be grateful to Giorgio de Santillana and Hertha von Dechend for their encyclopedic work.

However, they seem to have been groping without complete success for the keys that would help them make sense of this vast "echoing manifold," this ancient "edifice," this "huge framework of connections," this "great world-wide archaic construction," as they called it, using admirably evocative language.[41]

Gods of thunder and of wind

For the most part, the authors of *Hamlet's Mill* identify the heavenly originals of the figures in the myths with the visible planets. They write that:

> The real actors on the stage of the universe are very few, if their adventures are many. The most "ancient treasure" – in Aristotle's word – that was left to us by our predecessors of the High and Far-Off Times was the idea tht that gods are really stars, and that there are no others. The forces reside in the starry heavens, and all the stories, characters and adventures narrated by mythology concentrate on the active powers among the stars, who are the planets. A prodigious assignment it may seem for those few planets to account for all those stories and also to run the affairs of the whole universe. What, abstractly, might be for modern men the various motions of those pointers over the dial became, in times without writing, when all was entrusted to images and memory, the Great Game played over the aeons, a never-ending tale of positions and relations, starting from an assigned Time Zero, a complex web of encounters, drama, mating and conflict.[42]

Thus, Giorgio de Santillana and Hertha von Dechend come right out and state that the only "active powers among the stars" are the planets -- and these planets are the gods and all the other characters in the myths.

Elsewhere, they elaborate on their understanding of this concept somewhat, saying:

> The fixed stars are the essence of Being, their assembly stands for the hidden counsels and the unspoken laws that rule the Whole. The planets, seen as gods, represent the Forces and the Will: all the forces there are, each of them seen as one aspect of heavenly power, each of them one aspect of the ruthless necessity and precision expressed by heaven. One might also say that while the fixed stars represent the kingly power, silent and unmoving, the planets are the executive power.[43]

Chapter Five

I do not disagree that the power and personality of the gods and goddesses was anciently seen in and associated with specific planets. How could we disagree with that assertion, seeing that the planets themselves have been given the names of the various divine powers, such as Jupiter and Mars, Saturn, Venus and Mercury?

But to limit the understanding of the "active powers" in the myths to the planets alone is a grave misunderstanding, and results in the confusion that the authors of *Hamlet's Mill* obviously felt as they tried to decipher the connection between the myths and the heavenly actors, using the planets alone as the "executive power."

They do not *completely* miss the role of the constellations: there are many places in their book where de Santillana and von Dechend point out connections to constellations, such as their identification of the V-shaped Hyades playing the role of the jawbone of the ass in the story of Samson, or the constellations Sagittarius and Scorpio being related to the "strange locust demons of Revelation" (as they call them).[44]

But, for the most part, a comprehensive understanding of the "vocabulary" and "grammar" of the world-wide Star Myth language eludes de Santillana and von Dechend, because they do not perceive the role of the constellations in the stories of the gods and heroes of the ancients. I would attribute this tremendous oversight to the fact that the connections are *only* easy to perceive if one has access to the correct system of outlining and envisioning the constellations -- and without it, the connections will be nearly impossible to find.

By the time *Hamlet's Mill* was published in 1969, H. A. Rey had indeed made his outlining suggestions for the constellations public, with the publication of *The Stars: A New Way to See Them* in 1952. But, as we have already noted, H. A. Rey does not seem to have made any public proclamation about the usefulness of his constellational outlines in deciphering the celestial foundations of the world's ancient myths (and thus, whether Rey

Gods of thunder and of wind

himself knew of these connections can only be a matter of speculation).

In fact, the connections between Rey's outlines and the ancient depictions of gods and heroes, which seem so obvious once you begin to notice them, do not seem to have ever been publicly remarked-upon until I began to describe them in my books and my online blog and videos, beginning around the year 2012.

Giorgio de Santillana and Hertha von Dechend were both established professors and no longer young by the time they published *Hamlet's Mill* in 1969 (Giorgio de Santillana was born in 1901 and lived until 1975, and Hertha von Dechend was born in 1915 and lived until 2001). It is quite possible that they were not aware of the publication of *The Stars: A New Way to See Them* by the famous author of children's books. Certainly, none of the illustrations or star-charts included in *Hamlet's Mill* indicates any familiarity with Rey's method of outlining the constellations. On the contrary, the illustrations included between pages 142 and 143 of *Hamlet's Mill*, showing star-charts for the constellations around the north and south polar regions of the sky use outlines which are atrociously unhelpful and certainly non-H. A. Rey!

Thus, when the authors of *Hamlet's Mill* do venture to explain the celestial actor with whom the wind and hurricane gods Tezcatlipoca and Hunrakán might be associated, they implicate the planet Saturn, and argue a conjunction between Saturn and the north celestial pole-star, Polaris.[45] They also imply a connection between one aspect of Tezcatlipoca and the planet Mars (they appear to be arguing that the aspect of the god known as "Black Tezcatlipoca" is associated with Saturn, and the aspect known as "Red Tezcatlipoca" is associated with Mars).[46]

Again, I readily admit that planetary associations may indeed be present (although in this case, I might question whether Tezcatlipoca is associated with Saturn, since he can be shown to share characteristics with Zeus, who is of course associated with the planet Jupiter rather than with Saturn or Mars). But setting

123

Chapter Five

aside planetary associations, knowing what we know at this point from our examination of thunderbolt-wielding gods thus far, we can very easily see evidence pointing to the conclusion that Tezcatlipoca and Hunrakán are both associated with the constellation Hercules (in common with so many other sky-gods and stormweather-gods around the world, such as Zeus and Indra).

In the artwork below is a depiction of both the Red and Black aspects of Tezcatlipoca, from a codex thought to have been made either prior to or almost immediately after the European conquest, probably found in what is today central Mexico. This codex is today called the "Codex Borgia," because it was found in Italy among the effects of Cardinal Stefano Borgia (1731 - 1804) a year after his death. It is today housed in the Vatican library:

In the image above, from page 21 of the 76 pages of the Codex Borgia, Red Tezcatlipoca is on the left as we face the page, and Black Tezcatlipoca is on the far right. In the original, the images are full-color. In both figures, we see the characteristic depiction of Tezcatlipoca in a sort of "striding" or "large step-forward" posture, and in each case the forward leg is depicted as made of bone. Both figures have square-shaped heads, and both carry some type of a club-shaped instrument. We have seen all of these characteristics associated with figures relating to the constellation Hercules.

Additionally, we see a crested bird perched on the shoulder of the Red Tezcatlipoca figure on the left, reminiscent of the association

Gods of thunder and of wind

of the eagle with the god Zeus in the myths of ancient Greece, explained by the proximity of the constellation Aquila. We also see a branching tree-trunk directly in front of the Red Tezcatlipoca figure, which likely corresponds to the constellation Ophiuchus. One branch of this tree appears to be "torn off" and flying towards the right side of the scene -- it is possible that this branch corresponds to the location of Coma Berenices in the night sky, which appears in many other myths from around the world as a broken-off branch, or arm, or scalp with hair.

Note also that below this broken-off branch we see a spotted jaguar depicted, next to a serpent with a large head. If the broken branch corresponds to Coma Berenices, then the jaguar would be in a position corresponding to the constellation Virgo or Leo, which are located next to the long sinuous constellation of Hydra in the night sky (a constellation which appears to be a snake with either a very large head or a hood like a cobra, as this constellation is depicted in sacred artwork from India, where cobras are endemic, and where a cobra is associated with the goddess Durga, for example, who appears to have correspondances with the constellation Virgo).

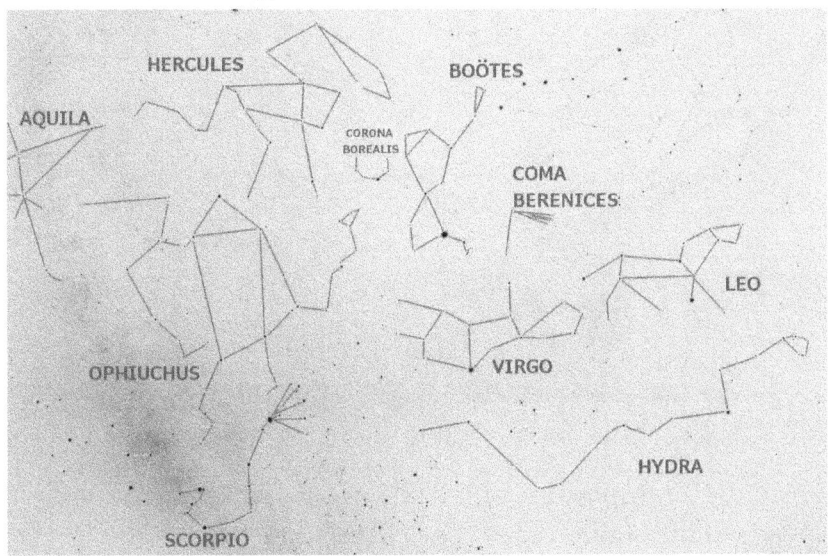

Chapter Five

Virgo, of course, is immediately adjacent to the constellation Leo the Lion in the heavens, and closely associated with this constellation in many myths -- thus the jaguar in this illustration could be related to the constellation Leo. In any case, the god Tezcatlipoca is associated with the jaguar and sometimes takes the form of a jaguar, which is interesting in light of the argued connection to the constellation Hercules (note that the hero Hercules is most-often depicted wearing the skin of a lion).

Below is another depiction of Black Tezcatlipoca, this time in the act of being speared by an eagle-headed deity. Tezcatlipoca and Quetzalcoatl are adversaries, and I have spent some time arguing for a correspondence between Quetzalcoatl and the constellation Ophiuchus, in *The Ancient World-Wide System* (and note that Ophiuchus-figures, in mythology around the world, most commonly use a spear as their distinctive weapon).[47]

Note that the body-posture of Tezcatlipoca in this depiction corresponds to the outline of the constellation Hercules, with the rear leg deeply bent. Even though the god is not depicted with a bone-leg or a serpent-leg, we can be fairly confident that the

Gods of thunder and of wind

figure in this posture is indeed Tezcatlipoca, based on his characteristic face-paint.

If the above analysis is not enough to establish the connection between Tezcatlipoca and the constellation Hercules beyond any doubt, we can also look to the very name of the god itself. *Tezcatlipoca* in the Nahuatl language of the Toltec and the Aztec signifies "Lord Smoking-Mirror deity."

I would argue that the image of the "smoking mirror" is seen in the heavens in the "whirling form" of the constellation Hercules, which resembles a central square with radiant lines emanating in four directions from the central hub. This same aspect of the constellation Hercules was shown beyond any doubt to be the basis for the winged solar disc of ancient Egypt and ancient Mesopotamia, in *The Ancient World-Wide System*, as well as for the swastika-shape depicted on artwork showing the Gorgons (themselves also associated with the constellation Hercules, as I have argued previously).[48]

Thus, the authors of *Hamlet's Mill* were indeed correct in their arguments that Hunrakán and Tezcatlipoca are related, although those scholars did not perceive that both are associated with the constellation Hercules, with which other storm-and-wind gods or thunder-and-lightning gods around the world can also be seen to be closely associated . . . including Zeus, Thor, and Indra -- and as we now see, the God of the Bible as well.

Indeed, the text of Snorri's Edda from Iceland, one of the two most important sources of our knowledge of the Norse myths, tells us that at the funeral of Baldr, when Baldr was placed upon a pyre on great ship to be pushed off into the water and then lit ablaze, the ship itself was so enormous that none of the Æsir could push it into the waves, and so the gods had to send for a giantess called Hyrrokkin to come and shove the ship into the sea for them, as I discuss in *Star Myths of the World, Volume Four: Norse Mythology*.[49] The similarity of this name to that of the god Hunrakán of the Maya is astonishing, and all the more so since

Chapter Five

Snorri's Edda was composed around the year AD 1200 based on source material that is almost certainly much more ancient than that date, and no conventional model of history has any way of explaining such a connection between the mythology of the Maya and the mythology of the ancient Norse.

The similarity is even more astonishing if, as I argue in *Star Myths of the World, Volume Four*, the giantess Hyrrokkin is associated with the constellation Hercules, as is the god Hunrakán of the Maya![50]

There are many other verses in the Bible which demonstrate an association of Jehovah with the wind, beyond those cited already. Among others, there is the proclamation in Psalm 48, "Thou breakest the ships of Tarshish with an east wind" (Psalm 48: 7), and when Elijah is commanded to stand on the mountain before the LORD, the text tells us: "And behold, the LORD passed by, and a great and strong wind rent the mountains, and brake in pieces the rocks before the LORD" (1 Kings 19: 11).

Additionally, as I point out in *Star Myths of the World, Volume Three: Star Myths of the Bible*, in the Genesis account of Adam and Eve in the garden of Eden, after the man and the woman have taken of the fruit of the tree, the text tells us in Genesis 3 that "they heard the voice of the LORD God walking in the garden in the cool of the day: and Adam and his wife hid themselves from the presence of the LORD God amongst the trees of the garden" (Genesis 3: 8). The word translated as "cool" in the phrase "cool of the day" is actually the Hebrew noun *ruwach* (Strong number H7307), meaning "wind." Thus, the text of Genesis 3: 8 should more accurately say "they heard the voice of the LORD God walking in the garden in the wind of the day."

The association between the God of the Bible and the constellation Hercules can really be established beyond any doubt. In addition to all the evidence presented thus far, there are many other episodes and examples which serve to corroborate this connection.

Gods of thunder and of wind

For example, in the famous episode of the "writing on the wall" described in Daniel chapter 5, we are told that the king Belshazzar made a great feast and commanded that the golden and silver vessels which his father Nebuchadnezzar had taken from the temple at Jerusalem be brought, so that the king and his princes, his wives and his concubines might drink out of them. And as they did so, the text tells us, "In the same hour came forth fingers of a man's hand, and wrote over against the candlestick upon the plaster of the wall of the king's palace" (Daniel 5: 5).

There are numerous other episodes in the scriptures of the Bible, as well as in myths from other cultures, in which the figure of the constellation Hercules is envisioned as leaning down to write upon something, usually something associated with the constellation Ophiuchus. Indeed, as I explain in *The Ancient World-Wide System*, the Egyptian god of writing, Thoth or Djeheuty, can be confidently argued to be associated with the constellation Hercules.[51]

In the case of the "writing on the wall" episode recounted in Daniel 5, the divine hand is described as writing "over against the candlestick" upon the plaster of the wall. I have presented evidence in previous volumes showing that the constellation Ophiuchus was definitely envisioned as a wall, such as in the Mesopotamian flood story recounted in the Atrahasis, when the god Enki (whose name in the later Babylonian versions is Ea) whispers through a chink in the wall to Atrahasis (one of the names of the Mesopotamian "Noah" figure, who survives the great Deluge in an ark) about the coming flood, Enki can be seen to be associated with the constellation Hercules, leaning down as if to speak through the chink in the wall of Ophiuchus.[52]

Additionally, the upraised part of the "serpent" held by Ophiuchus towards which the constellation Hercules appears to be leaning and extending a hand as if to write (the western half or "head-end" of the serpent, on the right side of the central body of Ophiuchus as we face the star-chart shown below), could be envisioned as a "candlestick." Indeed, the entire constellation

Chapter Five

Ophiuchus could itself be envisioned as a branching candlestick-holder, and thus the passage in Daniel 5 which tells us that the hand of God appeared and wrote upon the wall "over against the candlestick" could be added detail indicating Hercules writing upon Ophiuchus:

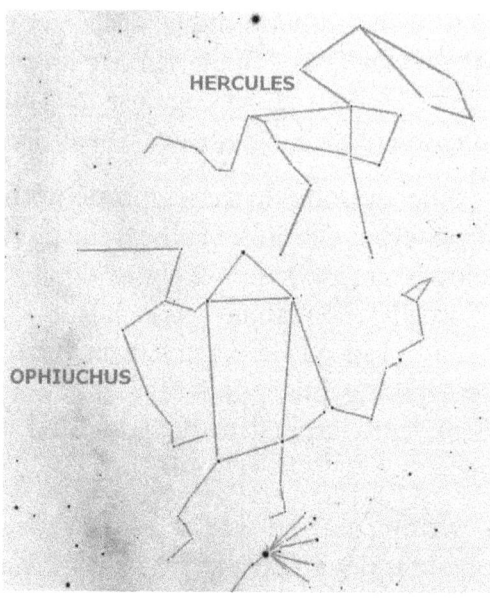

That the scriptures of the Bible sometimes envision Ophiuchus as a wall is evident from passages in which the character David, who can also be definitively shown to be associated with the constellation Hercules, sings a song of thanksgiving in 2 Samuel chapter 22, in which he addresses the LORD and declares, "For by thee I have run through a troop: by my God have I leaped over a wall" (2 Samuel 22: 30). A version of this same song of thanksgiving is repeated in Psalm 18, and the same declaration about leaping over a wall is found in verse 29 of that Psalm.

Note that in this song of thanksgiving, the LORD is also associated with *smoke*, such as when the song declares, "There went up a smoke out of his nostrils, and fire out of his mouth devoured: coals were kindled by it" (2 Samuel 22: 9, Psalm 18: 8). There are many other examples of similar proclamations throughout the scriptures of the Bible, such as in Job chapter 41 which declares, "Out of his nostrils goeth smoke, as *out* of a

Gods of thunder and of wind

seething pot or cauldron" (Job 41: 20), or Psalm 144 which proclaims, "Bow thy heavens, O LORD, and come down: touch the mountains and they shall smoke" (Psalm 144: 5). And in the famous vision of Isaiah described in Isaiah chapter 6, the place where Isaiah sees the LORD is described as being filled with smoke (Isaiah 6: 4).

These references show that, in addition to being associated with wind, the God of the Bible is also associated with smoke, another significant correspondence to the Central American tradition of Tezcatlipoca, whose name signifies "Smoking Mirror" and who also appears to be associated with the same constellation Hercules.

Just a few more examples should suffice to establish beyond any reasonable doubt that the scriptures of the Bible describe the supreme deity in terms associated with the constellation Hercules.

King Solomon is described as being the son of David -- and Solomon can be confidently shown to be associated with the constellation Ophiuchus (for one thing, Solomon is seated "between the pillars" of the temple, just as the central body of the constellation Ophiuchus is positioned between two "pillars" on either side).

It is very common for a figure associated with a constellation located *directly below* another constellation to be described as being "*descended* from" a figure associated with the constellation directly above it. In this case, for example, Solomon (associated with Ophiuchus) is described as being descended from David (associated with Hercules, directly above Ophiuchus).

There is an important episode recounted in 1 Kings 3, in which Solomon goes to the "great high place" at Gibeon to sacrifice and give burnt offerings, and the text tells us that "the LORD appeared to Solomon in a dream by night" and said to Solomon, "Ask what I shall give thee" (1 Kings 3: 4 - 5).

Solomon replies:

Chapter Five

> 7 And now, O LORD my God, thou hast made thy servant king instead of David my father: and I *am but* a little child: I know not *how* to go out or come in.
>
> 8 And thy servant *is* in the midst of thy people which thou hast chosen, a great people, that cannot be numbered nor counted for multitude.
>
> 9 Give therefore thy servant an understanding heart to judge thy people, that I may discern between good and bad: for who is able to judge this thy so great a people?

The text goes on to tell us that this speech pleased God, who says to Solomon that because he did not ask for long life, or riches, or power over the life of his enemies, but instead for understanding in order to discern judgment on behalf of the people, "Behold, I have done according to thy words: lo, I have given thee a wise and an understanding heart; so that there was none like thee before thee, neither after thee shall any arise like unto thee" -- and in addition he will give Solomon those things he did not ask for, including riches, and honor and long life (1 Kings 3: 10 - 14).

As I explain in *Star Myths of the World, Volume Three: Star Myths of the Bible*, we can actually behold God giving to Solomon the wise and understanding heart, just as the text proclaims, if we look to the heavens.[53]

There, we see the constellation Hercules reaching down towards the upraised part of the constellation Ophiuchus which is customarily envisioned as the "serpent head" on the western part of the "serpent" held by Ophiuchus, but which could also be envisioned as a *heart* rather than the head of a serpent!

Observe the now-familiar star-chart shown on the facing page, and imagine that Ophiuchus has just received in an outstretched hand the "wise and understanding heart" bestowed by the constellation Hercules, which similarly reaches towards that "heart" with the downward-reaching arm of Hercules, as if having just placed the heart in the upturned hand of Ophiuchus.

Gods of thunder and of wind

Note that the text of 1 Kings 3: 12 declares, "Behold, I *have done* according to thy words: lo, I *have given* thee a wise and an understanding heart." In other words, the text declares that these things have just been done -- and the scene in the heavens (which we are invited to "behold") shows this completed action in the outlines of the two constellations!

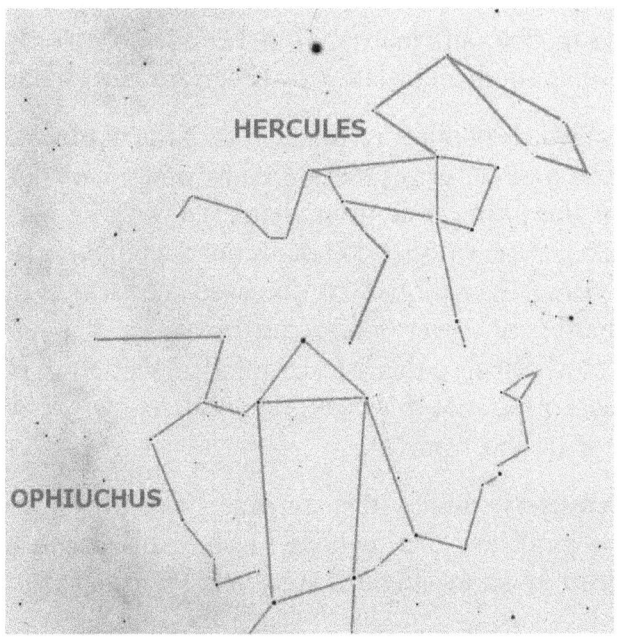

Lest any object that such an interpretation of Hercules and Ophiuchus is too far-fetched, and that the ancients would never have envisioned this interaction between the two constellations as depicting the *handing of a heart* from one to the other, those critics are invited to consult the ancient Sanskrit epic of India known as Mahabharata, the celestial foundations of which are discussed at great length in *The Ancient World-Wide System.*

There, we will find an extremely famous scene known as the "humiliation of Draupadi" during the disastrous dice-game of Yudhishthira (the eldest of the five Pandava brothers), in which the beautiful Draupadi (wife to all five of the Pandava brothers) is dragged by her hair into the great gaming-hall by the wicked

Chapter Five

Dushashana (one of the Kaurava princes, cousins to the Pandavas and their primary antagonists throughout the epic).

At this disgraceful treatment of Draupadi, the mighty warrior Bhima (the most physically powerful and imposing of the five Pandava brothers, and the one most likely to fly into a rage) can stand no more. Seeing Dushashana treating Draupadi in this way, Bhima utters a terrible oath in front of all the assembled lords and warriors, shouting (in the translation by Kisari Mohan Ganguli):

> "Hear these words of mine, ye Kshatriyas of the world. Words such as these were never before uttered by other men, nor will anybody in the future ever utter them. Ye lords of earth, if having spoken these words I do not accomplish them hereafter, let me not obtain the region of my deceased ancestors. Tearing open in battle, by sheer force, the breast of this wretch [meaning Dushashana], this wicked-minded scoundrel of the Bharata race, if I do not drink his life-blood, let me not obtain the region of my ancestors." [54]

Bhima subsequently fulfills this terrible vow by defeating Dushashana in battle and tearing open Dushashana's chest to rip out his very heart (as shown in the image on the opposite page).

And with which constellation do you suppose the mighty warrior Bhima might be associated?

The answer is beyond any doubt: Bhima, whose characteristics parallel those of the strongman Heracles very closely, even down to the strangling of two serpents as an infant, is undoubtedly associated with the constellation Hercules. This act of ripping open the chest of Dushashana in order to tear his heart out, described in the ancient epic of Mahabharata, is yet another example of the "serpent-head" of Ophiuchus being envisioned as a heart, towards which the constellation Hercules appears to be reaching.

Thus, we have strong confirmation that the interpretation of the Lord giving Solomon "a wise and an understanding heart" is

Gods of thunder and of wind

patterned upon the celestial figures of Hercules reaching down towards the constellation Ophiuchus -- constituting yet further evidence that the God of the Bible is associated with the constellation Hercules.

Finally, we can also look at the significant metaphor of God as the potter, which is found throughout the scriptures of the Bible, most notably in Jeremiah 18, and also in Isaiah 64 (among other places, including in the New Testament book of Romans, in chapter 9).

In Jeremiah 18, the prophet Jeremiah hears the word of the LORD commanding him: "Arise, and go down to the potter's house, and there I will cause thee to hear my words." Once there, Jeremiah sees the potter working on the potter's wheel, making vessels of clay. He sees the potter make a clay vessel, and -- being dissatisfied with it -- take up the lump of clay and start over with it, to make a new vessel which seems to him to be better.

Chapter Five

Then, the text tells us, the word of the LORD came to Jeremiah asking the prophet whether God could not do the same as the potter with the house of Israel, saying: "Behold, as the clay *is* in the potter's hand, so *are* ye in mine hand, O house of Israel" (Jeremiah 18: 6).

Once again, this metaphor has powerful resonance with Star Myths from other cultures, and can be seen to have a celestial foundation. As detailed at some length in *The Ancient World-Wide System*, the Star Myths of ancient Egypt also depict a powerful creator god in the role of a potter -- in this case, the ram-headed god Khnum -- and the artwork and associated myths demonstrate that Khnum in his role as potter is associated with the constellation Hercules, with the "serpent-head" feature of Ophiuchus playing the role as the potter's wheel, upon which the god shapes the clay.

The image above is an ancient wall-panel from Dendera in Egypt, and depicts Khnum and Heqet at the potter's wheel.

The potter's wheel is depicted as a small dish-shaped platform atop a narrow vertical axle. The small triangular-shaped "head" of

Gods of thunder and of wind

the western serpent-half of Ophiuchus corresponds to this potter's wheel, and the god Khnum corresponds to the constellation Hercules, bending forward and reaching out a hand to shape the clay upon the wheel (in this depiction, Khnum is shaping a mortal man or woman atop the potter's wheel).

The frog-headed goddess Heqet assists Khnum in the work at the potter's wheel in the artwork from Dendera in Egypt. As discussed in *The Ancient World-Wide System*, this goddess is almost certainly associated with the constellation Boötes.[55] The "potter's wheel" portrayed by the "serpent-head" section of the constellation Ophiuchus is positioned between the constellations Hercules and Boötes in the heavens:

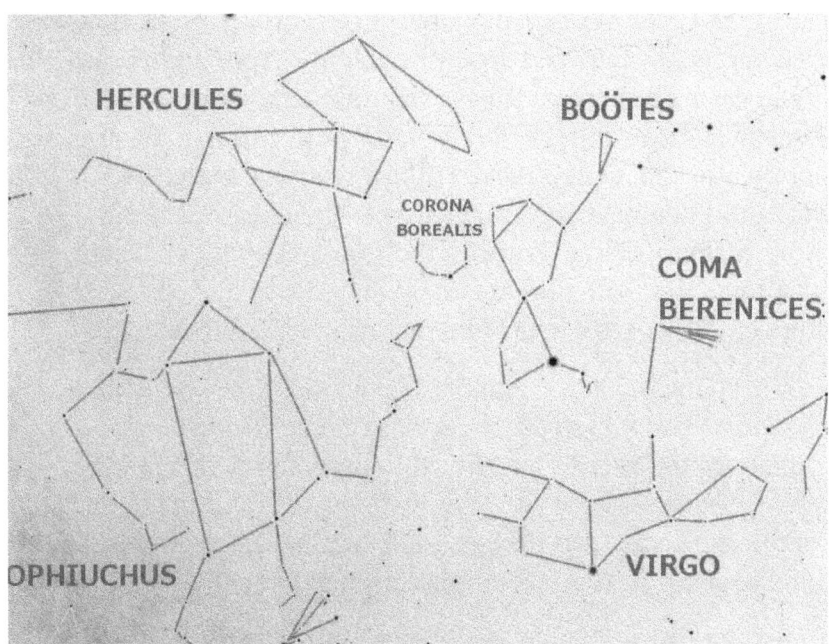

It is also possible that Heqet could be associated with the constellation Virgo, if Boötes actually plays the role of the mortal person being formed upon the potter's wheel of the serpent's head of Ophiuchus, although I believe the identification of Heqet with Boötes is more likely (the lantern-like object atop the staff in the hand of the goddess Heqet may find its inspiration in the "pipe-shaped" feature that is distinctive to the constellation

137

Chapter Five

Boötes in the heavens). However, in either case, the god Khnum at the potter's wheel can be confidently identified with the constellation Hercules, bending down with one arm outstretched towards the "potter's wheel" feature of the constellation Ophiuchus -- and the fact that the God of the Bible is repeatedly compared to a potter at the wheel provides still further confirmation of his association with the constellation Hercules in the night sky.

From the foregoing discussion, it should be established beyond controversy that the God of the Bible is associated with the constellation Hercules. He thus can be seen to share many characteristics with other powerful sky-gods from other cultures who are similarly associated with the same constellation, including the gods Zeus and Jove of ancient Greece and Rome (with whose names the names Jehovah and Yahweh are linguistically related), the god Thor of northern Europe, the god Indra of the ancient Vedas, the god Vayu who is revealed as the father of both Hanuman and Bhima in the Mahabharata, the god Xango or Shango of the Yoruba, the god Marduk of ancient Mesopotamia, the god Hunrakán of the Maya, and the god Tezcatlipoca of the Aztec and Toltec cultures of ancient Mexico.

Among the characteristics common to powerful gods associated with the constellation Hercules we can list possession of the most powerful weapon (such as the thunderbolt of Zeus, the unstoppable hammer of Thor, the dreaded axe of Xango, the Vajra of the god Indra, and the "sore and great and strong sword" belonging to Jehovah, described in Isaiah chapter 27).

Other characteristics include association with storms and with wind and rain (as well as with lightning, thunder, and smoke, in some cases).

Another characteristic of figures associated with the constellation Hercules is a tendency towards terrible wrath, with a countervailing propensity towards sudden reversal of that same wrath. We see this characteristic on display in many myths

Gods of thunder and of wind

involving Zeus as well as his son Heracles, for example, but it is also a personality trait which is prominent in Bhima and in many other mythical figures associated with the constellation Hercules.

The god Thor is a case in point. He is a jovial god who loves a good feast, and who possesses a prodigious appetite for beer and mead (the very word *jovial*, of course, comes from the name of the god Jove, indicating that this personality trait is prominent in Jove or Jupiter as well). However, Thor also possesses an extremely short temper, and can quickly fly into a murderous rage.

In the story of Thor's journey to the realm of the jotun Utgarda-Loki, recounted in the section of Snorri's Edda known as the *Gylfaginning*, Thor becomes enraged when he discovers that (contrary to his instructions) one of the leg-bones of his goats has been cracked.

As the Edda explains, Thor sets out for Útgardr in the realm of Jotunheim, accompanied by Loki and riding in his war-cart pulled by two billy-goats. Stopping for the night at the lodge of a simple husbandman or rancher, Thor slaughters his goats, flays off their hides, and proceeds to cook their meat, laying out their hides on the floor of the hut, away from the fire. He invites the husbandman and his wife, along with their son and daughter, to partake in the feast of goat-meat, instructing them to cast the bones upon the hides when finished with them.

The myth continues:

> Thjálfi, the husbandman's son, was holding a thigh-bone of the goat, and split it with his knife and broke it for the marrow. Thor tarried there overnight; and in the interval before day he rose up and clothed himself, took the hammer Mjöllnir, swung it up, and hallowed the goat-hides; straightway the he-goats rose up, and then one of them was lame in a hind leg. Thor discovered this, and declared that the husbandman or his household could not have dealt wisely with the bones of the goat: he knew that the thigh-bone was broken. There is no need to make a long story of it; all may know how frightened

Chapter Five

the husbandman must have been when he saw how Thor let his brows sink down before his eyes; but when he looked at the eyes, then it seemed to him that he must fall down before their glances alone. Thor clenched his hands on the hammer-shaft so that the knuckles whitened; and the husbandman and all his household did what was to be expected: they cried out lustily, prayed for peace, offered in recompense all that they had. But when he saw their terror, then the fury departed from him, and he became appeased, and took of them in atonement their children, Thjálfi and Röskva, who then became his bond-servants; and they follow him ever since.[56]

Notice that this pattern, of justifiable wrath and impending judgment, followed by a rapid change of heart and the extension of mercy and forgiveness, is demonstrated by the thunder-god Thor in the episode from Norse myth cited above, but it is a pattern which is very familiar to those who know the stories of the so-called Old Testament of the Bible as well.

What does all of this mean?

The ramifications are profound and far-reaching. We will explore some of them in the remaining chapters.

At the very least, the foregoing discussion should prove beyond any reasonable doubt that the scriptures collected into what has come to be called the Bible belong within a much larger, much more ancient system, a world-wide system, a celestial system, and an esoteric system: designed to convey profound truths through stories which cannot be fully grasped when approached at the surface level alone.

We are brought back to the lesson Jacob perceived, upon awakening in the middle of the desert, having experienced the glorious vision in the night of a ladder stretching from the earth up into heaven, with the angels ascending and descending, and the LORD standing above, speaking words of blessing.

Gods of thunder and of wind

When he awakens out of his sleep, Jacob declares: "Surely the LORD is in this place, and I knew *it* not" (Genesis 28: 16).

Jacob's epiphany conveys a powerful truth. The divine -- the infinite -- is present, irrespective of physical location. Jacob previously may have thought that the presence of the divine was connected to a specific location, such as a holy city, or to certain sacred architecture, such as a consecrated temple. He does not expect the LORD to be present in an empty desert wasteland, devoid of any human habitation, where amenities are so sparse that the lonely traveler must use stones as pillows.

Jacob experiences his vision of the infinite realm in *a dream*. The text is very clear that Jacob "lay down in that place to sleep" and that "he dreamed" (Genesis 28: 11 - 12). The infinite realm is not accessed through the pursuit or achievement of some outward circumstance, such as going to the right spot on the map or obtaining the favor of some holy person or group, some holy order.

Jacob gains access to the realm of the infinite, and the person of the divine, when he closes his eyes and goes to sleep, leaving the world of consciousness and the *persona* which dominates his daytime endeavors, the egoic mind which he has constructed throughout the course of his life: that calculating, sometimes conniving, mental construct that has learned how to navigate the fraught landscape of social structures and social norms, power relationships and familial tensions -- a construction which is not unique to the character of Jacob (who is, after all, a metaphorical figure based upon a celestial constellation rather than a literal, historical man) but which is present within every one of us.

Jacob's conscious mind goes to sleep, as ours does every night as well, but his conscious mind is not the entirety of who he is -- and the same is true for each one of us. The rest of the much larger entity of Jacob, including the subconscious which continues to inform him even when (*especially* when) his conscious mind is no longer tightly controlling his thinking, and filtering out threats in

Chapter Five

its endless campaign to "protect" and "defend" within what it perceives to be a hostile and unfriendly minefield of social pitfalls and obstacles, continues to exist and to operate all through the night -- and it is this part of Jacob (this more *authentic* part of Jacob) which receives the vision of the infinite, on the journey between Beersheba and Haran.

Jacob's declaration proclaims the truth that the infinite realm does indeed impact this seemingly-ordinary realm with which we are most commonly occupied and upon which we are most frequently focused. He declares: "the LORD is in this place." Jacob did not have to "go" somewhere else to experience the presence of the divine: it was already there, but (by his own admission) Jacob "knew it not."

The world's ancient myths employ the stars of the *infinite realm of the heavens* in order to show us truths pertaining to that invisible world -- a world which is very real, and which is in fact always accessible to us, but which we usually fail to "know," primarily because our conscious mind, our egoic mind, our *persona* which we have built up as a kind of mechanism to help us negotiate our course through this complicated world, filters it out (even though our wider self, including that aspect which has been called our "subconscious") is actually in touch with that invisible realm, if we would only listen to it.

The stars of the constellation Hercules are not themselves the God of the Bible, any more than they "are" the gods Zeus or Thor or Tezcatlipoca. But through the stars, the ancient myths show us truths which we would otherwise have difficulty seeing: truths which would be "filtered out" by our egoic mind. The myths use the infinite realm of the heavens in order to "show" us realities of an invisible realm which we could not otherwise see (it is, after all, the invisible realm, and thus hidden from our ordinary waking sight).

Jacob's vision points the way towards connecting with the power of that infinite realm, power which is sufficient to deal with the issues we face in this life we are leading, at this very moment. As we see in the myths of Hercules-linked figures battling with frightful monsters dwelling deep beneath dark waters, or in the dank recesses of poisonous swamps, it is a power which is more than capable of handling whatever we have lurking deep within the recesses of our own internal spaces.

The myths show that we do in fact have access to that power -- and the way we access it involves the recovery of who we are. And that means that we don't have to "go" anywhere external in order to find it -- as Jacob discovered.

These are truths we desperately need in our lives -- but for some reason, these are truths which have been suppressed by the forces of literalism, teaching the very opposite message from the epiphany depicted in the story of Jacob's vision.

The myths are not telling us about literal people, who lived outside of ourselves at some distant time in terrestrial history, or about external characters and events in whom and in which we must put our faith in order to somehow be changed. Because the literalist paradigm teaches that the myths describe events which literally happened in distant history, it naturally tends to *externalize* the meaning of the myths, because if they are about ancient literal persons and events, then they are about things external to us, and outside of our own experience (by definition).

The power of the invisible realm, the realm of the gods, seems at first blush to be external to us as well, but the ancient myths actually teach that the way we have access to that realm and its infinite potential is not external to ourselves at all: indeed, the connection lies through our own slumbering authentic self, from whom we have become disconnected but with whom we can always be reconciled, by a reconciliation which has little or nothing to do with external pursuits.

Thus the entire paradigm foisted upon the world by literalist Christianity, which from its inception has declared its stated mission to be the obliteration of the ancient sacred traditions given to the various cultures of the world can be seen to be in opposition to this ancient understanding.

Far from pointing us towards the recovery of our essence, literalist Christianity teaches that our essential nature is inherently sinful and alienated from the divine, and that to fix the problem we require an external savior and faith in the literal historicity of an external event.

It should be quite clear that these ancient myths are not retelling ancient literal events: they can be seen beyond doubt to be celestial metaphor -- and they are describing a solution which has to do with an *internal* path, but which is no less powerful, no less efficacious, and no less connected to the infinite realm of the gods, despite what we may think of "internal" solutions, conditioned as we are to always look outside of ourselves for fulfillment.

Indeed, the external and literal interpretations can be shown in most cases to be deliberately designed to mislead, and to make it more difficult for the true message of the ancient wisdom to point men and women towards the healing we need in these traumatic modern times.

The influence of more traditional forms of literalist interpretation of ancient scripture remains quite formidable around the globe, but as these have lost ground in more recent decades, new literalist distractions have been brought forward to keep us focused on external storylines -- such as Zecharia Sitchin's mistaken, or perhaps deliberately misleading, assertion that the Anunnaki of ancient Mesopotamian texts were literal space travelers arriving in rocket ships, or David Icke's assertion that the serpents and dragons described in the world's myths (including those we've examined in this chapter) represent literal reptilian beings who physically interbred with human women down through history.

So badly do these various forms of literalist error invert the original teaching of the ancient myths that many today conclude that the myths were intended for our enslavement rather than our empowerment, and they can certainly be forgiven for thinking so!

Chapter 6
Positive or Negative?

In the original 1984 film *Karate Kid*, the character of Daniel sneaks up on his nemesis Johnny at the Halloween dance at their southern California high school, while Johnny is rolling a joint in the boys' bathroom.

Taking a long hose, Daniel quietly hooks it over the wall of the bathroom stall where Johnny is carefully and attentively wrapping the cannabis inside the rolling paper, completely focused on the task at hand (and listening to headphones from what appears to be a Sony Walkman, which were extremely popular at that time). Once the hose is in position above Johnny's head, Daniel goes over to the spigot at a utility sink where the hose is connected and turns it fully on (dousing Johnny), then immediately runs as fast as he can, out of the bathroom and out of the school gymnasium.

On his way out of the bathroom with Johnny in hot pursuit, Daniel barrels through a group of Johnny's friends, dressed in skeleton costumes, who immediately join the chase.

Once outside of the gym where the dance was taking place, Daniel immediately runs in front of a car, which swerves and collides with another car, while Daniel keeps running and rapidly climbs over a chainlink fence into an empty field. As he runs across the field, Johnny and his four other friends (all football players) are clearly catching up to Daniel (who appears winded and running with some difficulty), and when Daniel tries to scale another chainlink fence on the other side of the field, they grab him by the waist and pull him down.

The five skeleton-costumed athletes, who also happen to train martial arts at the "Cobra Kai Dojo" in town, then proceed to "make Daniel pay" for "not leaving well-enough alone." The first of Johnny's friends pulls Daniel into a rising knee-strike, causing Daniel to bend over in pain, and then pushes him over to Johnny, who administers a forceful uppercut to Daniel's breadbasket,

145

Chapter Six

followed by a roundhouse kick and then a front kick and a reverse crescent kick that collectively leave Daniel unable to stand, and nearly unconscious.

While the five argue over whether Daniel has had enough (with only one of the five arguing to leave him alone, as the others repeat what they have been taught by their militaristic *sensei* at the Cobra Kai school: "an enemy deserves no mercy"), the figure of Mr. Miyagi appears, climbing over the fence, and jumps down just in time to thwart the next kick aimed at Daniel.

Mr. Miyagi then proceeds to defeat all five of the skeletal assailants, leaving them incapacitated on the ground, and then picks the unconscious Daniel up and puts him over his shoulder to carry him back to the apartment complex where they live.

As nearly everybody knows (the movie being very famous and widely watched), Mr. Miyagi agrees to teach Daniel (whom he always refers to as "Daniel-San") the martial art that Miyagi himself learned from his father -- and he does so through a training program that includes "wax the car," "sand the floor," and "paint the fence."

In a dramatic and memorable scene, Daniel-San finally confronts Mr. Miyagi about having to do all these chores, without ever actually learning karate -- to which Mr. Miyagi replies that he doesn't actually want Daniel to learn karate and he has been giving him these physically-demanding and time-consuming tasks just to keep Daniel from learning how to defend himself.

No -- of course that is not what actually happens in the movie! As everyone who has seen the film knows, Mr. Miyagi doesn't say very much at all in response to Daniel's complaint. Instead, he orders him to demonstrate "wax-on, wax-off" (correcting Daniel's form until he does it precisely, just as Mr. Miyagi has insisted the motion be performed), and then Mr. Miyagi proceeds to unexpectedly attack Daniel-San with punches, so that Daniel suddenly realizes that in performing these repetitive movements, he has actually been learning Mr. Miyagi's art (stopping each

Positive or Negative?

attack with the "wax-on, wax-off" motion), without perceiving the deeper meaning of what he has been doing.

This famous scene, as I have said many times in the past and written about in previous books, provides us with a powerful and very accessible illustration of the concept of "the esoteric" -- in which an *inner meaning* is not immediately apparent from the surface details (the word "esoteric" itself derives from the Greek word *esoterikos*, which is a compound containing the Greek word *eso*, meaning "within").

The word "esoteric" is often defined as meaning "hidden" or "secret," and there is certainly an element of that concept, even in the illustration from the *Karate Kid* given above, since the true import of the movements he was learning as he waxed the car or sanded the floor or painted the fence were not apparent to Daniel-San (they were "hidden within") until the moment of realization in the dramatic scene when he suddenly sees (and feels) the meaning of what he has been doing.

However, it should also be evident that Mr. Miyagi's primary purpose in assigning Daniel-San the time-consuming tasks of waxing the cars, sanding the floor, and painting the fence was *not* in order to "hide" karate from Daniel, or in order to keep it "secret" from Daniel. On the contrary, Mr. Miyagi employed those methods in order to *teach* Daniel-San, in order to actually *impart* his knowledge to Daniel-San.

Mr. Miyagi knew very well -- from first-hand observation -- that Daniel-San desperately *needed* to learn his martial art: Daniel had certainly antagonized Johnny, but the beating that Johnny and his friends administered to Daniel could have ended up killing him, had they continued to kick him mercilessly after he was already incapacitated, in line with the dictum of their aggressive Cobra Kai teacher.

Having seen this, Mr. Miyagi decided to teach Daniel his art. Therefore, his purpose in employing an esoteric teaching style

Chapter Six

was not in order to *hide* the deeper meaning, but rather to enable Daniel-San to grasp it.

This assertion echoes the declaration of René Adolphe Schwaller de Lubicz (1887 - 1961) that:

> Esoterism has no common measure with deliberate concealment of the truth, that is, with secrecy in the conventional sense of the term. [. . .]
>
> Esoterism can be neither written nor spoken, and hence cannot be betrayed. One must be prepared to grasp it, to see it, to hear it. [. . .]
>
> Spirit is found only with spirit, and esoterism is the spiritual aspect of the world, inaccessible to cerebral intelligence. [. . .]
>
> Thus esoteric teaching is strictly *evocation*, and can be nothing other than that. Initiation does not reside in any text whatsoever, but in the cultivation of intelligence-of-the-heart. Then there is no longer anything occult or secret, because the intention of the enlightened, the prophets, and the "messengers from above" is never to conceal -- quite the contrary.[57]

I return to this metaphor of Mr. Miyagi in the *Karate Kid*, despite having described it in previous books and writings and videos, because it is very pertinent to some of the subjects we will explore in the remainder of the book, and because I am convinced that this illustration answers so well the question of why the ancient myths employ the figures of the stars and constellations when conveying to us their teachings about the infinite world.

Readers, especially readers who may have a very deep personal investment in and attachment to the literalist teachings on the Biblical scriptures that have been propagated by religious authorities for the past seventeen centuries, may have a variety of reactions to the overwhelming evidence (only a small portion of which has been presented in the preceding chapters of this book) demonstrating beyond any doubt that the ancient texts of what are commonly referred to as the "Old Testament" and the "New Testament" are based on celestial metaphor basically from start to finish, and in common with virtually all of the world's other ancient myths, scriptures, and sacred stories.

One reaction (besides disbelief even in the face of overwhelming evidence, which is a not-uncommon reaction when presented with news which threatens to shake a paradigm around which one's egoic persona has been constructed) will often be to ask some version of the question: "But why?"

One answer which has been proposed by some researchers who have perceived at least some degree of the depth to which the world's ancient myths are built upon a foundation of celestial metaphor is the suggestion that, in essence: "It's all a psy-op," a popularly-used term deriving from military parlance and short for "psychological operation" -- a propaganda or public relations campaign designed to sway the opinion of the general public in the targeted country. In other words, one common argument which has gained fairly widespread traction in contemporary circles, particularly in contemporary "alternative" circles, is that the ancient myths are some kind of massive "psy-op" designed to fool the general populace, as a cover for enacting policies which the mass of the people would never otherwise tolerate.

Think, for example, of the level of oppression and immiseration imposed upon the general populace of men and women in Europe during the feudal period, during which the vast majority were reduced to serfdom while a small group of oligarchs (calling themselves "the nobility" and in cooperation with "the church") enjoyed the fruits of their labor and all the increase of the land.

An essential element to the maintenance of those inherently exploitive and deeply oppressive social and economic structures was the imposition of an intolerant literalist Christianity which taught that the oligarchs in charge were divinely chosen and inherently superior, that resistance to this order was resistance against heaven, and that questioning the dogmas propagated by the religious authorities should rightfully be punished by torture and death in this world, and eternal damnation in the next.

There are many researchers or public figures within "alternative" media circles who publicly expound some understanding of a connection between the myths and the stars and who appear to argue some version of the position that "this connection indicates that it's all a psy-op."

For example, David Icke (who, while I personally disagree with him, became for a time one of more prominent figures to publicly espouse "alternative" views of history during the past forty years) has publicly spoken about connections (observed by scholars beginning with the successful decoding of ancient cuneiform writing systems and the subsequent translation of ancient Mesopotamian texts) between the names of Babylonian deities and the names of characters in the Old Testament scriptures (particularly in the book of Esther, where Esther's name is cognate with the name of the Babylonian goddess Ishtar, and her uncle Mordecai's name is cognate with Marduk).

He does not necessarily perceive a connection between all the ancient myths *and the stars*, but he does speak openly about the connection *between* various ancient myths, asserting that the connection is likely a remnant of a pre-flood civilization.[58]

His conclusion, as stated in various forums down through the years, including a multi-hour-long presentation to a packed crowd in the O2 Academy Brixton in South London in 2008, is that: "All the religions come from basically the same source, and they are worshiping the same gods -- the same gods that the secret societies worship."[59]

David Icke argues that most of the stories are actually literal accounts of alien interbreeding with and genetic modification of human beings, pointing for instance to the oft-cited passages in Genesis 6 in which the text states that "the sons of God saw the daughters of men that they *were* fair; and they took them wives of all which they chose" (Genesis 6: 2). According to Icke, this verse should be interpreted literally, and records the creation of so-called "elite bloodlines" in cultures around the world.

In that 2008 talk, David Icke says:

> And another connection that you have between these areas, and many other areas in the world, is of an interbreeding between a non-human race / force / whatever, and humans -- creating a hybrid bloodline: a fusion of the two DNAs. Even in Genesis we have one version of this, but you find this all over the world, in every culture. As the Bible says in Genesis: "There were giants in the earth in those days; and also after that, when the sons of God came in unto the daughters of men, and they bare children to them, the same became mighty men which were of old, men of renown" [Genesis 6:4]. These hybrid bloodlines, this interbreeding, produced the kings and queens and the elite royal families of the ancient world, where they claim their right -- their genetic right -- to be the king or the queen or the leader because of their connection to the gods. And all over the world you find this. [. . .] The hybrid race became known as the demi-gods -- part-human, part-god -- because of this interbreeding connection. And from here they went out all over the world.[60]

David Icke argues that this interbreeding was literal, and that the non-human "interbreeders" (his term) were or are "reptilian" in nature -- and he backs up this assertion with examples from myths and from ancient images from around the world which contain images or descriptions of serpent-beings and human women, including images of the Eden story from Genesis (which obviously involves a woman and a serpent).[61]

Of course, as we have already seen, these myths and images can be convincingly shown to be *celestial* and *metaphorical* in nature, not literal and historical at all. The serpents in most of the stories and images correspond to the constellation Scorpio, although some undoubtedly correspond to other serpents in roughly the same region of the night sky, including the constellations Hydra

Chapter Six

and Draco, as well as the extremely important constellation Ophiuchus with its two "serpent-halves" on either side of the central body, often envisioned as a man or woman with a serpent wrapped around his or her waist or body, or even as a partly-human figure with serpents emanating from the waist in place of the legs (as is the case with some interpretations of the monster Typhon, as we've seen).

However, David Icke argues that these stories and images are describing actual, historical, literal interbreeding between certain humans and a class of non-human "reptilian" beings operating in a dimension "just outside" of the material frequencies we can perceive, and that the entire purpose of the interbreeding is to create "bloodlines" which are more receptive to being "taken over" or "possessed" by these trans-dimensional non-corporeal "reptilians." He says:

> It would appear from the endless research that I've done, and people I've talked to all over the world, and all the rest of it put together -- my own experiences, sometimes -- that what we're looking at are: these hybrid bloodlines, because of the hybrid nature of the DNA, the "software program" -- they have a vibrational sympathy with *that which interbred with them.* And this doesn't have to be physical interbreeding, either -- as I'll come to. And so these bloodlines can be, quote, "possessed" -- their emotional-mental faculties taken over much more easily than the general run-of-the-population [which] does not have that hybrid DNA, thus that vibrational sympathy-compatibility between the two energy fields. So what they're doing -- in effect -- is using the secret-society network they've set up to manipulate these *bodies* into power [he is referring to the actual men and women with the supposedly hybrid DNA as "bodies"], but in doing so they're putting *themselves* into power because they're controlling the mental and emotional processes of these vehicles [Icke here is referring again to the actual men and women with the supposedly hybrid DNA as "vehicles," and it is clear that the

pronoun "they" which is the subject of this particular sentence must refer to the non-corporeal "reptilians" who are supposedly able to "possess" or "take over" the mental and emotional "faculties" of the hybrid humans in the "elite bloodlines"].⁶²

I am presenting this extended set of quotations from a popular figure in contemporary "alternative" circles to illustrate one variant on the "ancient myths are negative" or the "ancient myths are a psy-op" argument -- an argument which alleges that, in general, the role of the ancient myths relates in some way to the oppression of the population as a whole. In Icke's paradigm, it is the oppression of the general population by a "part-human" elite which has distinctly different DNA, and which feels the need to keep everyone else in a "mental prison" because there are so many people with ordinary DNA compared to the tiny few with the "hybrid DNA" (never entirely explained is the question of why these reptilians would not simply choose to "interbreed" with the vast majority of the population, rather than just with an extremely tiny sub-segment -- since, as David Icke says later in the same presentation, "they want puppets").⁶³

It is difficult to argue that Icke does not present a negative interpretation of the purpose of even the most ancient known mythological systems from various cultures: he ultimately presents them as a vehicle for the control of individuals and the oppression of the individual will, and even for the turning over of that control to predatory inter-dimensional beings (whom he identifies as the "gods" of the ancient traditions).

In an extended discussion within the same 2008 Brixton presentation, he presents his view that all the ancient myths are basically variations of the same "reptilian religion" designed, ultimately, to "suck you dry," saying:

> To create this situation where people are locked in this vibrational prison, and are not decoding the vast range of frequencies they could, therefore opening their awareness: Sell

153

Chapter Six

them a religion, or sell them something to *believe*. Might not be an official religion, a "bricks-and-mortar religion" as my father used to call it, as long as it's a belief system, but the religions are of course the most obvious belief system. And once you take on a belief, that belief starts editing what you decode. And you start to enter a mind-prison, with the walls of the belief being the prison walls. This is a Neil Hague picture: these represent the different religions -- and what they're doing is all worshiping the same god -- or *gods*, in truth. The original religions of these ancient societies obviously went with the people as they located in other areas of the world: indeed it was a global society anyway. And it's based -- the reptilian religions, if you like -- are based on the moon and the sun: the moon goddess and the sun god, overwhelmingly. And they come in many and various forms [here Icke shows a slide with a picture of the god Krishna on the left, with a sunburst behind his head, and of a dancing goddess, possibly Freyja, on the right, with a full moon and starry sky behind her]. All these different religions are based on this same principle, while claiming to be different. And these religions came out of these areas of the world [here Icke shows a map with highlighted regions labeled "Egypt," "Mesopotamia," "Indus Valley" and "China"] that we have seen earlier: this is where the bloodlines came out of, to a very large extent. This area -- [here he shows a map of the eastern Mediterrannean with Greece and Egypt on the left, stretching eastward to the Bay of Bengal on the right, and labelling "Egypt," "Sumer," and the "Indus Valley Culture" most prominently] -- I've called "The Religion Factory," because that's where most of the major ones came from. Out of this same area came Judaism, came Christianity, came Islam, came Hinduism, and goodness knows how many in between. And these religions, *all based on sun and goddess worship*, and the reptilian gods (when you decode it) went with the bloodlines out across the world, taking this with them. And when they relocated in Rome, to form the Roman Empire and the Roman Church, the Roman Church (what we call

Positive or Negative?

Christianity) was merely the church of Babylon, relocated! That's why, when you take the names away, and all the rest of it, you find that Christianity in its structure and beliefs is a mirror of the Babylonian beliefs and religious structure. [. . .] In the end, they all lead into the same people, and they worship the same gods under different names without realizing it. And I have to say, it's the same with great chunks of what we call the "New Age," which is based on the Eastern religions. Now there's a lot of stuff in the Eastern religions about the nature of reality, and vibrations, and chakras and all this stuff, and it's very, very good. But still, the whole basis for a lot of it is the same story. And I was reading some articles recently by people who have researched this, and indeed directly experienced it, and a lot of these mantras that are chanted in Sanskrit -- the ancient knowledge of the Indian area -- they translate, some of them, as "giving yourself to the gods," or God. Giving yourself to the deity. And when you make that choice, that decision, to give yourself to the deity, you make a vibrational connection -- and the deity can *suck you dry*, and control and take over your thought-processes, because you've just given permission to -- you've opened yourself to it. And these are other-dimensional entities. [. . .] It's the *same gods* that we're feeding: they *set up* these religions, and their puppets did. At the highest, highest level in the religions, they know this -- so the rest of the pyramids don't [i.e., the rest of the people lower down in the hierarchy don't know that these beliefs are designed to oppress you]. The idea of religion is to lock people in a belief-system that locks out all other possibility.[64]

Note that in the above-cited passage, David Icke makes some moves in the direction of recognizing the celestial foundations of the ancient myths, asserting that the primary gods and goddesses are personifications of the sun and the moon. Later in the same lecture, he argues that "Nimrud or Baal" is a Babylonian sun god, and "Semiramis or Ishtar" is a Babylonian moon goddess, who have a divine child by virgin birth called Tammuz, corresponding to the similar versions of the same story in ancient Egypt (with

Chapter Six

Horus being the son of Osiris and Isis) and in the New Testament.

While I agree that celestial parallels are very much present in these different ancient mythologies, as well as in the myths of other cultures around the world (as David Icke asserts), and while I agree that the origin of this pattern is to be found in heavenly metaphor, I disagree with Icke's literalistic interpretations, and his analysis that the metaphor is as simple as "the male god represents the sun and the female goddess represents the moon." As we've already seen, and as evidence presented in my previously-published books has demonstrated, the gods and goddesses can be shown beyond any doubt to be closely associated with specific *constellations* (not just the sun and the moon). Even the goddess Artemis of ancient Greece (known as Diana to the Latins), who is most certainly a moon goddess, can be shown to have been associated with the constellation Sagittarius, as discussed in *Star Myths of the World, Volume Two: Myths of Ancient Greece*.

Why is this important? Because Icke, whether out of ignorance or because he is actually an agent of a system to be discussed more fully in a later chapter, is teaching a negative view of myth which has as its consequence the demoralization of the people (by elevating to superhuman status the supposedly "reptilian" and "interdimensional" beings involved in "secret societies," when in fact they are men and women like us) and an obscuration of the beneficial message that the ancient myths have for our lives.

In an earlier book, *Astrotheology for Life* (2017), I criticized such interpretations of ancient myth as "shallow astrotheology," citing the 2007 viral internet video *Zeitgeist* as an example of this shallow astrotheology, and voicing the concern that:

> shallow astrotheology that goes only as far as making connections to the cycles of the sun and the moon does not really provide enough structure to glimpse the purpose of the great esoteric system to most of those exposed to this type of popular astrotheological analysis.

Positive or Negative?

In other words, it goes far enough to undermine the foundations of the literal-historical interpretation (although not far enough to decisively refute the literal and historical approach), while not going far enough to reveal the incredible outlines of the esoteric system and its glorious purpose.

Shallow astrotheology thus serves a primarily *negative* purpose (casting doubt upon the framework of literalism) without a corresponding positive purpose to replace the decpit structure.[65]

While I was not referring to David Icke's 2008 presentation at the time I wrote those paragraphs, it should be clear from the portions cited that his interpretation of the ancient myths (which he perceives to have correspondences to heavenly bodies, in this case the sun and the moon) is primarily negative in its conclusions. While I do not disagree with David Icke's assertions that the ancient teachings encoded within the myths of the world have in fact been employed to oppress, enslave, and immiserate millions of men and women in recent centuries, I completely disagree that this oppression and enslavement and immiseration is the original and primary purpose of the ancient myths (as David Icke appears to be arguing in the passages cited above).

I think that based on the above quotations, we can categorize David Icke as representative of a position which argues that the world's myths serve a primarily negative purpose, but with whose interpretations I ultimately disagree. In contrast, let's look at the work of a very different analyst, one whose work and analysis I respect for its original and often extremely insightful and intriguing perspectives, and one who certainly shows that the ancient wisdom is today being used for negative purposes.

In my opinion, Christopher Knowles is one of the most important authors and researchers exploring the abundant signs of esoteric symbolism in pop culture and the media, and the evidence of the ongoing practice of ritual magic by certain groups wishing to influence events on the world stage -- and behind the scenes. In his work, he finds and unravels numerous interlocking

Chapter Six

threads which indicate very dark application (ongoing to this day) of ancient received wisdom, which he calls "star magic."

To summarize the amount of evidence of such ongoing ritual magic, which Knowles has documented in his long-running blog, *The Secret Sun Speaks*, would take an entire book in itself. The reader is advised to examine his writings there, as well as his published books and his numerous interviews on podcasts over the past several years. However, if I were to attempt to summarize what I see as the heart of what he has been exploring, it would involve the undeniable evidence that certain powerful groups and individuals have been deliberately practicing ritual magic (ongoing to this day) in order to invite powerful forces from the Other Realm to enact change in our reality -- and the even more disturbing evidence that the Other Realm is *answering* in response, in ways which appear to defy explanation by even the most "conspiratorial" human agency.

Some of the most compelling evidence that Chris Knowles has described can be referenced under the heading of the "Song to the Siren," in which he details evidence of a pattern of deaths which have connections to ancient myths involving Sirens (alluring mythical monsters encountered for example by Odysseus in Book 12 of the Odyssey: their irresistible song lures sailors to their death). Chris shows that these strange, water-related (and "Siren-related") deaths fit a frightening pattern which suggests ongoing occult ritual including human sacrifice to influence the unseen realm -- or perhaps caused by forces from the unseen realm. In an interview published in October 2017 (and recorded a few days before the Las Vegas shooting of October 01 of that year) on the *Higherside Chats* podcast, he walks through a web of connections related to death by drowning of at least one well-known young man connected by eerie links to a Siren-like singer with unworldly vocal abilities who herself appears to have been traumatized as a child, and connections to her songs (many of them released years before). Explaining the significance, he says:

So what, he drowns in a river? That happens.

Well, that's how these shepherd-boy consorts of these goddesses

Positive or Negative?

in the Siren lineage usually die. A classic example is Osiris. [. . .] Of course Venus has Adonis, her shepherd-boy lover who dies. This all probably sounds completely insane to a lot of your listeners but just take my word for it: every single *detail* in this story just lines up in ways that just, your head starts to spin. I could go on and on about all the songs that presage this. [. . .] Well, this means something to somebody. This is how these things become dominants: how they become archetypal dominants [*And, earlier in the same interview, discussing connections to intelligence agencies and to the heinous and traumatizing MK Ultra program of the 1950s and 1960s*]: I don't think that these people were just worried about mind control, and mind-controlled assassins, and interrogations. I think that their ambitions were far grander, and more disturbing, and just more all-encompassing than that, because we have the tie-ins to Stargate, and remote viewing, and on and on and on. I think that this was about the recreation of the world. Literally. Starting from the ground up: starting with the mind.[66]

Here, Christopher Knowles is clearly articulating an understanding, backed up with evidence, that ancient ways of contacting the other realm can be used for negative purposes, through forms of ritual magic or occultism. He also clearly shows that it is ritual magic very much linked to stars and constellations, as he outlines elsewhere in the above interview and in his writings (in a blog post published on December 03, 2017, he says "Any serious study of magic or occultism is going to eventually lead you to the stars").

And so the question: *are these ancient myths*, preserved in so many cultures around the world, and based upon an incredible system of celestial metaphor, *primarily positive or negative* in their purpose and intent?

My response to that question -- which is a very good question, and a very serious question, and a question we absolutely must ask ourselves -- is to ask another question, going back to the scene from the original *Karate Kid* movie recounted at the beginning of the chapter: in that film, is karate itself positive or negative?

Chapter Six

To ask the question is to answer it. Quite clearly, karate is used in *both positive and negative* ways, even within the single scene we re-lived at the chapter's opening. Johnny and his four companions, who have been taught by a ruthless and domineering sensei at the Cobra Kai dojo, are using their karate skills to "teach a lesson" to Daniel -- and they are quite prepared to go beyond beating him senseless, holding him up in order to allow Johnny to run at their victim full speed and launch a flying side-kick at Daniel, who has already been punished severely and is practically unconscious.

This flying kick is thwarted by the sudden appearance of Mr. Miyagi, who uses his own martial arts skill to protect the defenseless Daniel and incapacitate the merciless aggressors.

Thus, in the same scene, we see karate being used to bully and dominate others, and we see karate being used to protect and perhaps even save the life of others. Karate itself can thus, quite obviously, be used in *either* positive or negative ways.

The same can be argued for the world's ancient wisdom encoded within the myths. The position articulated by Christopher Knowles in the quoted passage above presents a view, an accurate view, that the ancient wisdom can be used to oppress, to abuse, and to traumatize -- and he shows evidence that it is being used in this way, right up to the present (often through film and through popular music, and note that both music and theater were understood in ancient cultures to be means of interfacing with the realm of the gods).

But I would counter that the use of this ancient wisdom to oppress and to brutalize is by no means its only possible application, any more than the use of karate strikes by five larger football players to beat a single smaller victim senseless is the sole possible application of martial arts skill and training (it's not).

Indeed, in the *Karate Kid*, the not-so-subtle message that is dramatized by the contrast between Mr. Miyagi (who learned his martial art from his father, in Okinawa) and the sensei of the Cobra Kai school (who acts like a domineering drill instructor and uses demeaning language when talking to his students and even to Mr. Miyagi himself) is that the Cobra Kai school has *twisted* something that was *originally intended to recognize the dignity of others and to protect the weak* into something that is quite the opposite of the original intent. And I would argue that something very similar is at work in the ancient wisdom preserved in the myths.

Please understand that I don't disagree with Chris Knowles in his observations regarding what he refers to as "star magic." He is describing the use of *some aspects* of this ancient knowledge for the purposes of oppression and traumatization of others, and his arguments are quoted here because it is undeniable that whatever the ancient myths *are* talking about *has indeed* been put to use for negative purposes down through the intervening centuries since the end of the ancient world -- and in fact continues to be put to use for negative purposes to this day.

His warning, that the power of the system encoded within the motions of the stars is very real and not to be taken lightly, should also be carefully heeded! The very fact that powerful actors on the world stage continue to observe specific calendar dates and number patterns associated with the heavenly cycles, as well as continuing to incorporate symbology taken directly from the ancient myths, would seem to indicate that the power that Christopher Knowles is warning about is indeed authentic, and that it is understood to be authentic by significant players operating at the highest levels of geopolitics and world affairs (and he provides evidence, with connections to songs published years earlier, that powers in the invisible realm are indeed responding to the ritual magic that he has discovered in action all around us).

Part of the misuse of the ancient system in these cases must be plainly admitted to have to do with inflicting *trauma*, as will be discussed in subsequent chapters. But I have found overwhelming evidence which argues that such use of the ancient myths is indeed misuse, and that the ancient wisdom was intended to serve a primarily *positive* purpose: one which has to

161

do with *overcoming* trauma and with *elevating*, rather than oppressing, the men and women in whom, the ancient myths teach, the gods themselves live and move.

Indeed, the figure of the Siren herself symbolizes the dark, alluring, destructive side of wisdom: a sort of antithesis to the goddess Athena who guides Odysseus throughout the Odyssey. Her tempting song explicitly promises wisdom, but leads to destruction: the Sirens tell Odysseus that they know all, and will share their knowledge with him, in Book 12, lines 200 through 207. In fact, Sirens and Mermaids (whether with one tail or two) can be shown to correspond to the figure of Ophiuchus in the heavens: a figure we will later see to be associated with wisdom (and with Athena), but in this case, the alluring *dark side* of wisdom – see the similarities in this drawing from the 1500s:

Indeed, the "shepherd-boy" who encounters the Mermaid beside the water clearly corresponds to Sagittarius, adjacent to the Milky Way (and to the Siren of Ophiuchus). So, the same constellations form the basis for frightening myths as well as uplifting ones. Based on this and other evidence, I would argue that the ancient wisdom itself was *intended* for positive purposes, but the possibility of its misuse for destructive purposes has always been present.

Let's explore the evidence to back up this assertion: evidence which shows that the myths themselves demonstrate that their *proper* purpose includes helping others, establishing justice and ending oppression and tyranny.

Chapter 7
The Divine Twin

Let's briefly revisit Solomon's dream at Gibeon, discussed in a previous chapter (beginning on page 131 in Chapter 5).

We travel swiftly over the surface of the globe until we come to the high place of Gibeon, the ostensible setting for this important episode. Scholars today argue that the modern town of El-Jib, on a hill just to the northwest of Jerusalem, is the location of the city of Gibeon featured in the Bible, but once again we will see that the ancient scriptures are describing a celestial location rather than a terrestrial.

The young king, Solomon the son of David, has completed a major sacrifice at the altar of the high place at Gibeon, as described in the book of 1 Kings chapter 3 (and also in a parallel passage in the book of 2 Chronicles chapter 1).

The text tells us that "a thousand burnt offerings did Solomon offer upon that altar" (1 Kings 3: 4), although this number causes some difficulty for those taking the text as literal, terrestrial history. Puritan theologian Matthew Henry, who lived from 1662 to 1714, offers some speculation in his famous commentary, saying: "It seems strange how so many beasts should be burnt upon one altar in one feast, though it continued seven days; but the fire on the altar is supposed to be more quick and devouring than common fire, for it represented that fierce and mighty wrath of God which fell upon the sacrifices, that the offerers might escape," and he notes the assertion of one "Bishop Patrick," referring to English theologian and Bible commentator Simon Patrick, who lived from 1626 to 1707, that "the smoke of the sacrifices ascended directly in a straight pillar and was not scattered, otherwise it would have choked those that attended when so many sacrifices were offered as were here."[67]

While Solomon is in Gibeon conducting this sacrifice in the high place, the text tells us, the LORD appears to him in a dream by

Chapter Seven

night, and says to Solomon: "Ask what I shall give thee" (1 Kings 3: 5). And, as we have already discussed, Solomon asks for wisdom -- and specifically, he requests that the LORD give him "an understanding heart" in order to judge rightly and discern between good and bad, for the benefit of the people of the kingdom, whom Solomon describes to God as "this thy so great a people" (1 Kings 3: 7 - 9).

God's reaction to this request of Solomon's is significant to our examination of the question of whether these ancient myths are intended to be used for positive or negative ends. The text tells us:

> 10 And the speech pleased the Lord, that Solomon had asked this thing.
> 11 And God said unto him, Because thou hast asked this thing, and hast not asked for thyself long life; neither hast thou asked riches for thyself, nor hast asked the life of thine enemies; but hast asked for thyself understanding to discern judgment;
> 12 Behold, I have done according to thy words: lo, I have given thee a wise and an understanding heart; so that there was none like thee before thee, neither after thee shall any arise like unto thee.

This response, to me, implies that the ancient text is acknowledging the fact that some will attempt to contact the divine realm for selfish and even malevolent purposes: to enhance their own wealth, or to bring harm (and perhaps even death) to their enemies. And yet, such selfish or malevolent ends constitute a perversion of the proper end we should be seeking, which Solomon demonstrates with his request (which pleased the Lord): wisdom, and specifically wisdom in order to help others, to administer justice rightly, and to elevate society as a whole.

In the episode of Solomon's dream at Gibeon, we see that the encounter with the Infinite results in a radical change in Solomon -- indeed, we are told that he is given an entirely new heart: a wise and an understanding heart. In other myths, the transformation will be dramatized differently -- often, as we will see, it will be dramatized as a reconciliation with a higher self, from whom we

The Divine Twin

are alienated and estranged: a divine self through whom we have access to the realm of the Infinite, the realm of the gods.

In this episode from Solomon's dream, as mentioned previously, we can actually *see* the God of the Bible reaching down to give Solomon a new heart, a wise and an understanding heart.

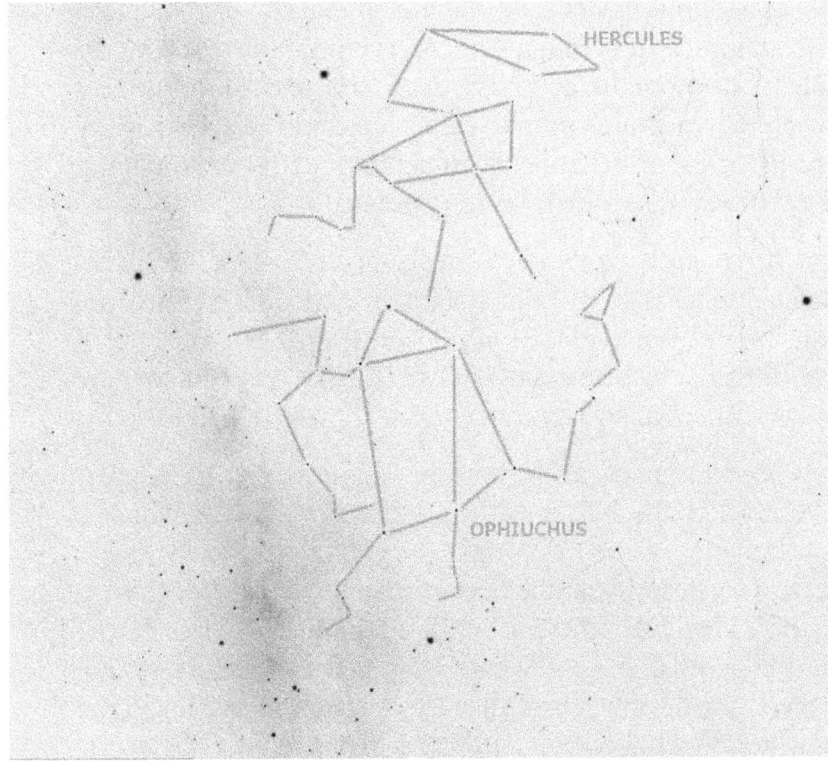

As we have already argued, the God of the Bible is most clearly associated with the constellation Hercules -- and in the above star-chart we see why the text tells us that the Lord delcares to Solomon: "lo, I have given thee a wise and an understanding heart" (1 Kings 3: 11). Solomon, associated with Ophiuchus, appears to be holding this "new heart" in the hand on the right side of the chart as we face it above, as if the Lord (associated with the constellation Hercules) has just given the heart to him.

Note that the "high place" of Gibeon itself is also almost certainly associated with the constellation Ophiuchus. The name "Gibeon"

Chapter Seven

means "a hill" or "a hill-city," and as we have seen in this volume already (and as we see even more extensively in earlier books, such as *The Ancient World-Wide System*), the constellation Ophiuchus was undoubtedly envisioned as a hill or as a mountain in many ancient Star Myths from cultures around the globe.

In fact, although scholars (and Biblical literalists) like to assert that the scriptures describing Gibeon are primarily referring to the hill-city at modern-day El-Jib, there are reasons to suspect that when the scriptures refer to events around Gibeon, they are referencing the constellation Ophiuchus and its surrounding region of the sky, rather than the terrestrial city.

I strongly suspect that the Gibeon in the Bible refers to Ophiuchus rather than to a literal and terrestrial hill-city because the texts in other books of the Old Testament refer to "the pool of Gibeon" (in 2 Samuel 2: 13) and later to "the great waters that *are* in Gibeon" (in Jeremiah 41: 12).

There is in fact a "pool" at the bottom of a deep circular hole cut into the rock of the hill at El-Jib, down the sides of which a circular stairway of rock descends in a spiraling path with no railing, to a small spring at the bottom, over 80 feet below the top of the pit. However, there is nothing in the area to fit the description of "great waters" whatsoever (just a trickle of a stream) – and therefore it is much more likely that both the "pool" and the "great waters" mentioned in the scriptures actually refer to the great column of the Milky Way band itself, which rises past the constellation Ophiuchus like a mighty coursing river, with the widest and brightest part of the Milky Way (the region of the Galactic Core) being described as a great pool (a role this part of the Milky Way band plays in numerous other Star Myths, including many myths from ancient Greece which are described in *Star Myths of the World, Volume Two*).

On the facing page we see the same star-chart presented on the previous page, but this time the outline of the Milky Way band is indicated and labeled. Remember that this region of the Milky

The Divine Twin

Way, beside Ophiuchus and rising up between the constellations Scorpio and Sagittarius, is the brightest part of the glorious Galaxy in our night sky.

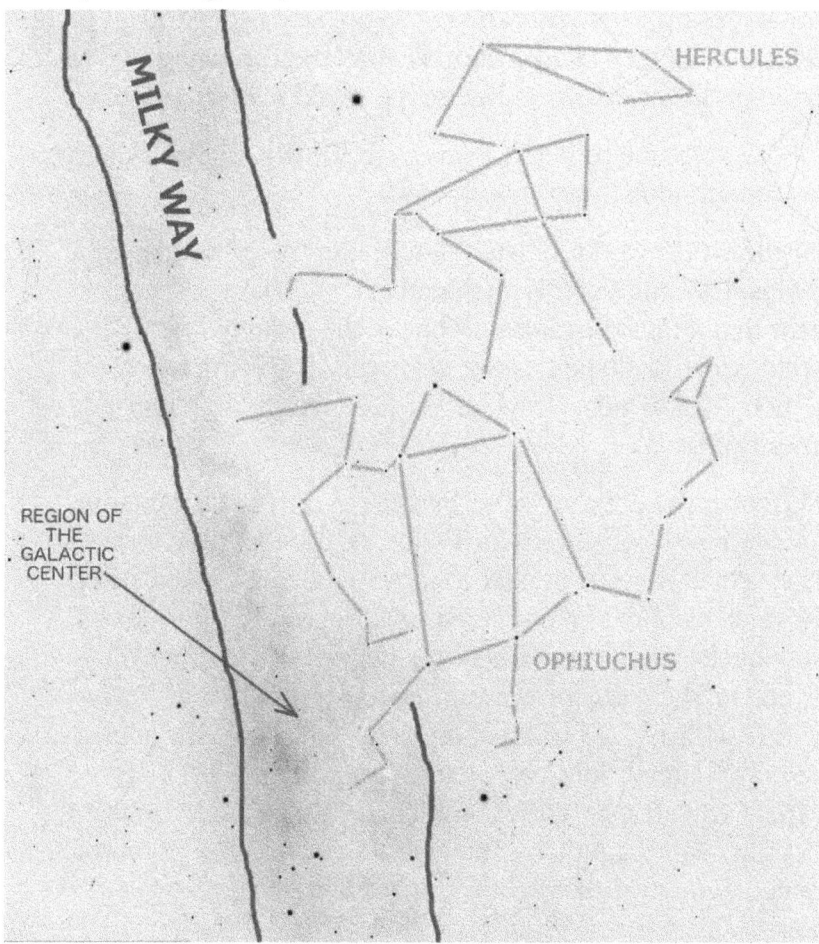

Note too that in the Norse myths, the High Seat of the god Odin, known as the *Hlidskjálf*, can be shown to be associated with the constellation Ophiuchus in the night sky, suggesting that the "high place of Gibeon" is associated with Ophiuchus as well.[68]

In any case, we can see in this episode strong evidence suggesting that the ancient myths themselves tell us that their purpose is benign, involving the conveying of wisdom, the regeneration of hearts, and ultimately the benefit of the entire society. But in this

Chapter Seven

episode we also see the text informing us in no uncertain terms that the power of the invisible realm *can* be used wrongly, to pursue selfish or even malevolent purposes, and to harm others. Such ends are explicitly criticized in the episode of the dream of Solomon at Gibeon -- which argues that these pursuits are a perversion of the intended purpose of the world's ancient wisdom.

Let's look at some other evidence from the myths which demonstrates a similarly positive intent.

Around the world we find myths describing the adventures of a set of twins. Examples of this myth-pattern (or "oicotype")[69] are so abundant that it must be ranked as one of the most widespread of all mythological oicotypes, along with the myth-pattern of the "dying god" (to which, I would argue, the twins-pattern is thematically related).

In the Greek myths, of course, we find the example of the Gemini twins, Castor and Polydeuces (or Pollux, to use the Latin form of his name, which is more familiar to most of us today). According to most versions of the myth, these heroic twins were born to the beautiful queen of Sparta, whose name was Leda, after Zeus visited her in the form of a swan, seducing Leda and having intercourse with her -- but later on the same night, her mortal husband Tyndareus, king of Sparta, also slept with his wife (unaware of what had transpired earlier), and thus the twins were born of the same mother, but one of them was immortal (Polydeuces) and the other twin was mortal (Castor).

We might suspect that the seduction of Leda by the god Zeus in the form of a swan has a celestial foundation, and indeed the evidence is very strong to argue that it does (along with the other famous seductions of mortal women by the god in various disguises). The constellation Cygnus, the Swan, is located within the Milky Way band not far from the constellation Hercules (with which constellation Zeus can without any doubt be seen to be associated, as we have seen in previous chapters and as is established with additional evidence in *Star Myths of the World*,

The Divine Twin

Volume Two). The outline of Cygnus appears to be flying downward along the Milky Way band, for observers in the northern hemisphere, and thus fits very well the narrative that the god took on the shape of a swan and descended to earth in order to seduce the gorgeous queen whose beauty had captured his attention.

Some ancient sources tell us that the seduction took place "near the river Eurotas," by which assertion we have another clue that this celestial interpretation of the swan in the myth being the constellation Cygnus, with the Milky Way of course being envisioned as the river.[70]

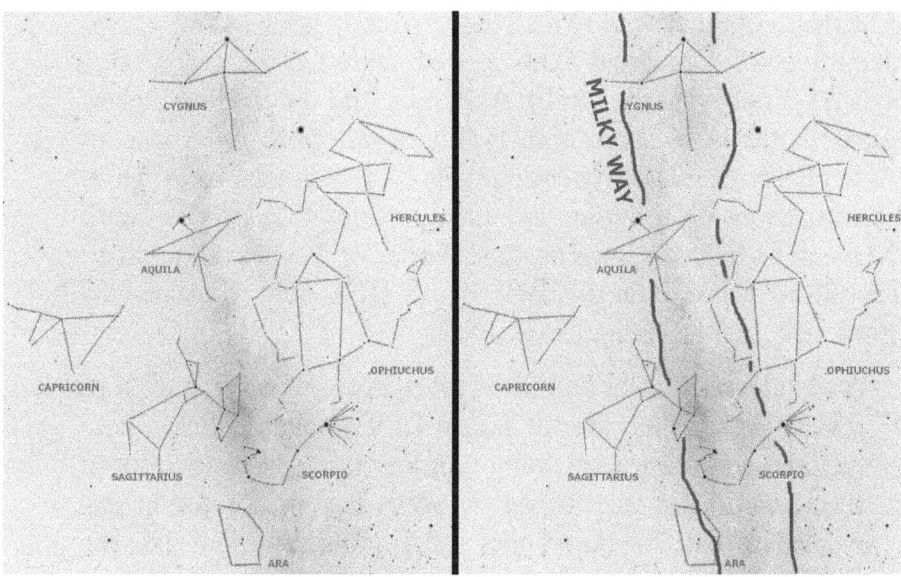

From the ancient accounts telling us that the seduction of Leda by Zeus took place beside the river Eurotas, we can deduce that Leda in this episode is most likely played by the constellation Sagittarius, a constellation which plays the role of a beautiful woman or a beautiful goddess beside a pool or a river in many ancient myths. Above is a star-chart showing the pertinent region of the sky, with Hercules (associated with Zeus) and Cygnus the Swan near the top, and Sagittarius near the bottom. The outline of the Milky Way is indicated in the version on the right.

Chapter Seven

Because of their descent from the god Zeus, these famous twins were known as the *Dioscuri* in ancient Greece, meaning "the youths of Zeus" (the word *Dios* itself being a form of the name of the god Zeus, as also in the name of the god Dionysus, whose name literally signifies "Zeus of Nysos," from the name of the mountain where Dionysus was born). They were known as tremendous horsemen, an association which should not surprise us, given the fact that the constellation Sagittarius is associated with the horse (it is also notable that the twins Nakula and Sahadeva in the Mahabharata of ancient India are described as consummate horsemen).

The death of the mortal twin, Castor, over an issue involving two daughters of Leucippas who eloped with Castor and Pollux instead of marrying the sons of Aphareus, and the ensuing theft of some cattle by Castor and Pollux from these two sons of Aphareus to send as a wedding gift to Leucippas, in order to taunt the sons of Aphareus still further, is described in the Tenth Nemean Ode of the ancient poet Pindar of Thebes (thought to have lived from about 518 BC to 438 BC), here translated by Frederick Apthorp Paley (1815 - 1888):

> And indeeed, Castor and his brother Polydeuces once went to receive hospitality at the house of Pamphäes [Paley here includes a footnote explaining that Pamphäes is an ancestor of the victor of the race whose victory is commemorated in this particular ode], 'tis no wonder if it is inborn in them [i.e., the family of Pamphäes], to be good athletes. For as lords of Sparta's wide plains they [i.e., Castor and Polydeuces], with Hermes and with Hercules, assign success in contests and festivals, showing a great concern for honest men; and trusty indeed is the race of gods. And now, by changing places in turn, they enjoy one day with their loved sire Zeus, and the next they pass under the dark recesses of earth in the vales of Therapnae, and so fulfil one and the same destiny. For after the death of Castor in war, Polydeuces chose this existence rather than the being altogether a god, and living always in heaven. It had chanced that Idas, in a passion about some oxen,

The Divine Twin

had wounded Castor with the point of a bronze spear; for Lynceus, on the lookout (for the robbers) from Mount Taÿgetus, had seen them crouching under the stump of an oak; for he of all mortal men had the sharpest eye-sight. So with nimble feet they came [that is, the brothers Lynceus and Idas, who are the sons of Aphareus, as Paley clarifies in his footnote] at once to the spot, and a bold attack they made forthwith. But terrible too was the vengeance the sons of Aphareus suffered by the designs of Zeus; for at once the son of Leda arrived in pursuit; and they stood to face him hard by the tomb of their father (Aphareus). From it they caught up a carved stone that adorned the grave, and threw it at the breast of Polydeuces. Yet they crushed him not, nor even made him step back; but he rushed at Lynceus with his ready dart and drove the brass into his side. Then Zeus hurled at Idas his scorching bolt; and far away from their friends the two brothers were burned on one pyre; for a quarrel with mightier beings is hard for mortal men to engage in. And now quickly to his (wounded) brother returned the son of Tyndareus, and found him not yet dead, but gasping hard for breath [literally, "with hard gasping roughly-sounding in his breathing," Paley informs us]. Whereupon, shedding hot tears, he cried aloud, "Father, son of Cronus, what then is to be the end of our griefs? Bid me too to die with him, O king; for his honour hath departed from a man when he is bereft of his friends. Few mortals in a time of trouble can be trusted to take part in one's toil." So he spoke; and Zeus came at once before him and uttered these words: "You are my son [thus, Paley explains, cannot die along with Castor]; but your brother here was begotten afterwards by mortal seed in the union of the hero her husband with your mother. But come, I nevertheless offer you a choice of this or that; if you wish to escape death and hateful old age, and to dwell in Olympus with me and Athena and Ares with the sable spear, you have the chance even of this: but if you make a stand for your brother, and have a mind to take an equal share with him in everything, why, then you may live half your time

Chapter Seven

remaining beneath the earth, and half in the golden abodes of heaven." When he had said thus, Polydeuces doubted not in his mind which counsel he should follow [literally, Paley tells us, the text says that the immortal twin "did not set in his mind a double resolve" or "propose to himself in his mind a two-fold plan"]. So Zeus unclosed the sealed eye, and next loosed the tongue, of the brazen-mailed Castor.[71]

Thus, Polydeuces chose to join his brother in death, and the two spend alternating days, one day lying in the tomb beneath the earth under the folds of the hills and valleys of Therapnae (and sojourning on that day in the realm of the dead, the vale of Hades), and the other day enjoying the halls of Olympus as immortal gods.

Translator Frederick A. Paley, in his 1868 English edition of this ancient poem by Pindar, includes his gloss in a footnote to this story about the Dioscuri: "As elemental gods, they typified the alternate appearance and obscuration of the heavenly bodies,"[72] and this interpretation is accurate, as far as it goes.

The statement is perceptive in that Paley here discerns the truth that the world's ancient myths are based on celestial metaphor, encoding the great heavenly cycles and the movement of the celestial bodies, including the sun, moon and visible planets but also the stars and constellations. The daily cycle of our earth's turning upon its axis does indeed cause all of these heavenly bodies to appear at one horizon, cross the sky above, and then sink down into the opposite horizon: the "alternate appearance and obscuration of the heavenly bodies" described in Paley's footnote.

For example, we are all familiar with the sun's apparent motion through the sky each day. As our earth turns upon its axis, the spin of the globe is towards the east. If you were to look "down" upon the spinning earth from a point above the north pole, the motion of the planet would be counterclockwise from this observation point: thus, the east coast of the North American continent would be seen to be leading the body of the continent, with the west coast of the same continent trailing behind it (which is why the time zone on the east coast is three hours ahead of the time zone on the west coast, in the United States).

Because the earth is spinning in that direction, the rotation of our globe towards the east will cause the sun to "rise" each morning above the eastern horizon. The sun, in fact, is not actually "rising," but rather the globe upon which we are standing is spinning inexorably towards the east, which eventually brings the sun into view as the eastern horizon continues to plunge forward, and then causes the sun to cross the sky (appearing to move from the east to the west) as the globe continues its daily rotation. Eventually, the same turning of the earth will cause the sun to sink down behind the western horizon, as the part of the globe upon which we are standing turns away from the sun, such that our view of our sun is obscured due to the fact that we are now facing out into space, while the other side of the earth is turned towards the sun.

In identical fashion, this same daily rotation causes the rising and setting of the other heavenly bodies as well: the rising and setting of the moon, as well as all the visible planets, and the stars and constellations. Note that those stars and constellations closest to the north celestial pole (for observers in the northern hemisphere, and closest to the south celestial pole for viewers in the southern) will not actually "set" behind the western horizon, but instead will turn in a constant circle around the central axis-point of the night sky (these are the so-called "undying stars" discussed in the texts of ancient Egypt).

So, the daily turning of the earth causes the sun, moon, visible planets and stars to be obscured from our view for about half of each rotation, and visible for the other half – which is why the interpretation offered by Frederick A. Paley in his 1868 translation, that the myth of the Dioscuri spending half their time below the earth and half their time among the glorious immortals in Olympus, makes sense at a basic level.

Chapter Seven

But the question remains: why this exercise of personifying the motions of the heavenly bodies, and the cycles of the celestial mechanics, in the first place? Academics are fond of asserting that myths evincing some connection to the annual cycle, such as the disappearance of the goddess Persephone for some portion of the year during which she must make her abode in the realm of the dead and during which nothing can grow upon the surface of the earth, must have had something to do with the knowledge of when to plant crops in early agrarian societies (a somewhat ludicrous assertion but one that has been repeated so often it is rarely examined critically: it is inane to suggest that people would not have known when it was favorable to plant crops and when conditions were unfavorable for planting them). But to suggest that the ancients needed myths to help them know the difference between night and day is even more ridiculous.

There must be some deeper purpose. The great cycles, even the familiar cycle of day and night, are ripe with spiritual symbolism: when we hear of a goddess of night, for instance, we can be fairly certain that she is associated with far more than the phenomenon of the world being plunged into darkness each evening, as the sun disappears below the horizon and the temperature drops, and mortal men and women must seek the shelter of their homes or at least of a fire if outside. Night and its accompanying darkness carry with them symbolic meanings which go far beyond the physical, often having connotations related to the realms of death and the underworld, for example.

Additionally, we know that the Dioscuri were in fact extremely important gods in the ancient world, even though they have not received the level of popular awareness which is accorded to the other gods and goddesses of ancient Greece. As discussed at some length in my 2014 book *The Undying Stars*, the ancient *mysteria* celebrated at Eleusis each year honored the goddess Demeter and her search for (and eventual recovery of) her daughter Persephone (who is also known, especially in

The Divine Twin

conjunction with the ancient *mysteria*, as Kore or "the Maiden"). But there were also *mysteria* held in other parts of the ancient world, associated with other deities, including the Mysteries of Samothrace, of Lemnos, and of Boeotia, dedicated to "the Nameless Gods" or *Kabeiroi*. Some scholars point to evidence suggesting that these Nameless Gods can in fact be identified with the Dioscuri.

In his 2010 book *Mystery Cults of the Ancient World*, for example, author Hugh Bowden (a professor of ancient history at King's College London) points to an inscription in an ancient sanctuary on the island of Delos, a building which in ancient times was known both as the Kabeireion and the Samothrakeion, calling the priests of that place: "priests of the Great Gods of Samothrace, the Dioscuri, the Kabeiroi."[73] He also notes the inscription on an ancient coin, from the island of Syros in the Aegean Sea, bearing the image of two young men, each with a star on his head (typical iconography when depicting the twins Castor and Polydeuces, as Professor Bowden points out), which declares: "The Divine Kabeiroi of Syros."[74]

Clearly, then, the Dioscuri were figures of profound importance in the ancient world. Further evidence to support this contention is found in a fragment of the poet Alcman, who lived and wrote during the period we call the seventh century BC. In one of his surviving poems, he calls the Dioscuri "most worthy of reverence from all gods and men."[75]

Why are the Dioscuri so worthy of reverence? Perhaps it is because their story symbolizes more than simply the daily obscuration and revelation of the heavenly bodies caused by the turning of the earth upon its axis – or, to put it more precisely, *because their story points us towards the deeper meaning with which the myths imbue the turning of the heavens throughout the daily cycle and all the other great celestial cycles.*

The great sacrifice of Polydeuces, recounted above in Pindar's Tenth Nemean Ode, is to choose to descend into the underworld

Chapter Seven

for half of his time in order to be alongside his mortal brother, whom he loves, and from whom he refuses to be separated – and in doing so, sharing his divine nature with Castor, who otherwise would have been doomed to spend eternity in the realm of Hades. The meaning and significance of this great myth-pattern becomes most clearly understood when we consider the singular insight of Alvin Boyd Kuhn (1880 – 1963), who perceived that when the ancient myths talk about "death" and the "underworld," they are not describing the world that comes after this life: rather, the ancient myths around the globe describe *this very incarnate existence*, when the soul is plunged down into the material realm and encased in a body of flesh and blood, as the realm of death and darkness, and as the veritable "underworld"!

Kuhn establishes this radical new and extremely helpful perspective in his 1940 masterpiece, *Lost Light: An Interpretation of Ancient Scriptures*, weighing in at over 600 pages and filled with supporting evidence to advance his case beyond and reasonable doubt. There, he declares:

> For everywhere throughout antiquity *earthly life was depicted as our death*! [. . .] The fact stands that they did call our life here death, and that when they spoke of "the dead" in sacred books, it is indubitable that they meant the living humans. The words "death" and "the dead" are used in the old scriptures to refer to living humanity in earthly embodiment. [. . .] The astonishing point, of revolutionary significance for all religion, will receive textual treatment in the present chapter, and a later one will further vindicate the correctness of the thesis. It is perhaps the cardinal item of the whole theological corpus, the real "lost key" to a correct reading of subterranean meaning in esoteric literature. In ancient theology "death" means our life here on earth. [. . .]
>
> To be sure, it is death in a sense to be understood as dramatic and relative only. And it pertains to the soul in man, not to the body. Life and death are ever as two end seats on a "see-saw." As the one end goes to death the other rises to life. The death

The Divine Twin

of the body releases the soul to a higher life; conversely the "death" of the soul as it sinks in body opens the day of life to that body. The theological death of the soul in incarnation is a death that does not kill it in any final sense. It is a death from which it rises again at the cycle's end into a grander rebirth. It is a death that ends in resurrection.[76]

In other words, Kuhn is arguing that when the ancient myths picture this incarnate life as "death and the underworld," they mean "from the perspective of the soul, buried alive within a physical body." He later makes this argument explicitly clear, saying:

> The incarnation, for the soul, was its death and burial. But it was a living death and a burial alive. It was an entombment that carried life on, but under conditions that could be poetically dramatized as "death."[77]

Having grasped this essential point of Kuhn's argument, we are in better position to understand the deep message of the Dioscuri. The sacrifice of Polydeuces, who cries aloud to his father Zeus at the death of his mortal counterpart Castor that he would rather join his brother in death than to live without him, involves *the descent of the soul into this mortal life*, this incarnate existence. Castor the mortal twin is doomed to go down into the underworld – this life we are each of us now experiencing, as perceived by Alvin Boyd Kuhn and articulated in *Lost Light* – but he is not abandoned to undergo this fate all alone: his divine twin will go with him!

The divine twin, filled with love, voluntarily goes down to the underworld (this mortal life) to accompany his brother – and in doing so, also lifts him up to enjoy the heights of Olympus. We now begin to perceive the outlines of the truly profound message of the Dioscuri myth (and its many, many counterparts in Star Myths around the world). For we ourselves are *both* twins: condemned to dwell for a time in this underworld of the incarnate life – but (as the ancient myths show us, through one powerful

177

Chapter Seven

esoteric metaphor after another) we are not alone during this earthly sojourn: there is one who has pledged to "take an equal share with us in everything," to paraphrase the words of Zeus when hearing the request of Polydeuces.

This is the one "who sticketh closer than a brother," to quote the words of Proverbs 18: 24 -- the divine twin, the higher self, seen in so many of the world's ancient myths and scriptures.

Now we begin to understand why this ancient system, which underlies the sacred traditions of virtually every culture on our planet, employs this system of celestial allegory, in which the figures of the "elemental gods" can be seen to "typify the alternate appearance and obscuration of the heavenly bodies," in the words of Frederick A. Paley in his footnote to the story of the Dioscuri. The awesome cycles of the celestial machinery, which alternately raise up and cast down the heavenly actors through the successive motions of the daily rotation, the annual orbit, and the even longer motions of the precessional clockwork, can be seen to exemplify *our own condition* and our own soul's journey, being plunged down into the living burial within a human body (like Castor and Pollux when they must go down to the tomb beneath the hills and valleys of Therapnae's landscape) and then raised up again to the undying realm, perhaps doing so over and over and over again (just as the celestial bodies themselves repeat the cycle over and over, rising up into the clear heavenly sphere above only to plunge back down into the western horizon to "toil below" for a time during their earthly sojourn).

And, as we have already noted, the pattern of the Dioscuri twins is a myth-pattern or oicotype which is extremely widespread throughout the world's myths. We see it other times within the Greek myths, as well as in other cultures. As we have already briefly noted when visiting the battle against the Lernaean Hydra during the Twelve Labors of Heracles (Hercules), that hero is also a "divine twin" with a mortal twin brother, in a pattern very similar to that of the Dioscuri.

The Divine Twin

In the story of the birth of Heracles, the god Zeus becomes enamored of the mortal woman Alcmene (or Alcmena), daughter of Electryon king of Mycenae and himself the son of Perseus (father of Electryon) and Andromeda (Electryon's mother).

The ancient poem called "Shield of Heracles," attributed to Hesiod (thought to have lived in the eighth century BC), describes Alcmene as surpassing all other women in beauty, wisdom, and physical stature. She had been married to a great warrior, Amphitryon, but refused to let him sleep with her until he had avenged her brothers (who had been killed in a feud with strong parallels to the feud between the Dioscuri and the sons of Aphareus, even to the point of including a dispute over a herd of cattle).

Electryon's cattle had been stolen by the six sons of a rival king and relative of Electryon's brother, Pterelaos of the Taphian Isles, who had sailed to Mycenae along with Taphian (also called Teleboan) warriors and demanded part (or, in some versions, all) of the kingdom of Mycenae based on their familial relation, only to be rejected by Electryon. These six sons and their warriors then drove off the cattle belonging to Electryon, and killed Electryon's sons (eight in number) when they tried to stop the Taphian raiders (all except the youngest son of Electryon, who had been too young to go out and do battle).

Electryon, in giving his daughter to Amphitryon, made the groom swear not to sleep with Alcmene until Amphitryon had avenged himself upon Pterelaos and the men who had killed Electryon's sons.

Hesiod (or whoever wrote the ancient poem "Shield of Heracles") explains how this vow led to the seduction of the beautiful Alcmene by the god Zeus, describing how Amphitryon and Alcmene settled in Thebes after getting married:

> There he dwelt with his modest wife without the joys of love, nor might he go in unto the neat-ankled daughter of Electryon until he had avenged the death of his wife's great-hearted

Chapter Seven

brothers and utterly burned with blazing fire the villages of the heroes, the Taphians and Teleboans; for this thing was laid upon him, and the gods were witnesses to it. And he feared their anger, and hastened to perform the great task to which Zeus had bound him. With him went the horse-driving Boeotians, breathing above their shields, and the Locrians who fight hand to hand, and the gallant Phocians eager for war and battle. And the noble son of Alcaeus led them, rejoicing in his host.

But the father of men and gods was forming another scheme in his heart, to beget one to defend against destruction gods and men who eat bread. So he arose from Olympus by night pondering guile in the deep of his heart, and yearned for the love of the well-girded woman. Quickly he came to Typhaonium, and from there again wise Zeus went on and trod the highest peak of Phicium: there he sat and planned marvellous things in his heart. So in one night Zeus shared the bed and love of the neat-ankled daughter of Electryon and fulfilled his desire; and in the same night Amphitryon, gatherer of the people, the glorious hero, came to his house when he had ended his great task. He hastened not to go to his bondmen and shepherds afield, but first went in unto his wife: such desire took hold on the shepherd of the people. And as a man who has escaped joyfully from misery, whether of sore disease or cruel bondage, so then did Amphitryon, when he had wound up all his heavy task, come glad and welcome to his home. And all night long he lay with his modest wife, delighting in the gifts of golden Aphrodite. And she, being subject in love to a god and to a man exceeding goodly, brought forth twin sons in seven-gated Thebe. Though they were brothers, these were not of one spirit; for one was weaker but the other a far better man, one terrible and strong, the mighty Heracles. Him she bare through the embrace of the son of Cronus lord of dark clouds and the other, Iphicles, of Amphitryon the spear-wielder -- offspring distinct, this one of

The Divine Twin

union with a mortal man, but that other of union with Zeus, leader of all the gods.[78]

Thus the translation into English by Hugh G. Evelyn-White, published in 1914. Notice the nearly identical pattern seen in this myth to that seen in the myth of the Dioscuri, in which one child is the son of Zeus by a mortal mother. Once again, as will be explained in greater depth momentarily, the myth-pattern of the twins can be seen to dramatize a profound truth regarding our own condition in this incarnate life -- for the two "twins" in each case do not actually represent two different individuals but rather two different aspects of our own self, whom we can refer to as the "egoic self" (represented by the weaker of the two brothers -- in this case, Iphicles) and the "higher self" or the "authentic self" or even the "divine self" (represented by the divine brother, descended from the god, generated by a supernatural rather than a natural birth).

In presenting us with these sets of twins, the world's ancient myths are telling us something about our own situation -- something of profound importance to our lives, even in this very present moment. These twins are not two different people -- any more than are Gandalf the Grey and Gandalf the White in the *Lord of the Rings* stories created by J. R. R. Tolkien (1892 - 1973), who himself knew a thing or two about the world's ancient myths, having been an Oxford Fellow and Professor of English Language and Literature, and a scholar of Beowulf and of the Eddas, among other mythology. One of the twins in the pattern is usually mortal -- and often goes down to death, as in the case of Castor in the story of Castor and Polydeuces (and in the case of Gandalf the Grey, in the world of Tolkien).

Other twin-patterns found among the myths of the world include, but are by no means limited to, the figures of Gilgamesh and Enkidu in the Gilgamesh cycle of ancient Mesopotamia (perhaps the oldest extant mythical narratives known at this time), the figures of Jacob and Esau in the Old Testament scriptures, the Hero Twins of the Maya Popol Vuh whose names are Hunahpu

Chapter Seven

and Xbalanque, the Pandava twins Nakula and Sahadeva mentioned before and found in the Mahabharata of ancient India (who are also known as the Ashvineya), and even the pairing of Arjuna and Krishna in the same epic, in a partnership in which the Lord Krishna plays the role of the divine twin.

What are the ancient myths around the world trying to dramatize for our understanding in this recurring pattern of the twins?

I am convinced that through this pattern, they are conveying a powerful and healing message for our benefit in this incarnate life, one that can be described in modern terminology as the recovery of the self: the authentic self, from which (or indeed *from whom*) we risk become estranged and alienated during the encounter with human society and its entangling rules, restrictions, regulations, and complicated power relationships.

Over the past few decades (beginning in the mid-1970s) a group of respected psychologists and medical doctors have begun describing this separation from the authentic self using the term *trauma*, a word which has long been used to describe physical injury but which more recently has been applied to psychological and emotional injury resulting in long-term damage.[81]

Dr. Peter Levine, a pioneering clinical psychologist and the originator of the "Somatic Experiencing" approach to dealing with psychological trauma, writes that:

> Trauma is the most avoided, ignored, denied, misunderstood and untreated cause of human suffering. When I use the word trauma, I am talking here about the often debilitating symptoms that many people suffer from in the aftermath of perceived life-threatening or overwhelming experiences. Recently, trauma has been used as a buzzword to replace everyday stress, as in, "I had a traumatic day at work." However, this use is completely misleading. While it is true that all traumatic events are stressful, all stressful events are not traumatic.
>
> [. . .]

The Divine Twin

> Perhaps the most important thing I have learned about trauma is that people, especially children, can be overwhelmed by what we usually think of as common everyday events. Until recently, our understanding of trauma was limited to "shell-shocked" soldiers who have been devastated by war, victims of severe abuse or violence, and those who have suffered catastrophic accidents and injuries. This narrow view could not be further from the truth.
>
> [. . .] For now, I will simply say that almost all of us have experienced some form of trauma, either directly or indirectly.[82]

To understand the connection between this definition of trauma and the prevalent oicotype in ancient myth of the twins (one of whom is often divine), we must understand that the leading specialists in the field of trauma describe its effect on the individual as a *separation from the self.*

Dr. Gabor Maté, who has written several bestselling books on the relationship between trauma and addiction and also between trauma and chronic physical illness, describes this separation from the self in a talk given at the 2017 Psychedelic Science Conference in Oakland, California in these words:

> So trauma is not these terrible things that happen to people. What trauma actually is, fundamentally, is a disconnect from the self: a disconnect from the body and a disconnect from the essential self. Why do people disconnect? Because it's too painful to be connected. So the disconnection is not a mistake -- it's not an accident: it's actually a coping mechanism. When you're being hurt, and you have no recourse to help or escape or fight, then in order to endure the hurt, you're going to have to just adapt somehow. And how do you adapt? You adapt -- one way to adapt is to disconnect from the self. Now you no longer are in touch with your feelings -- I mean your gut feelings, or with your emotions. And that means that you start living life inauthentically. Now, coping mechanisms that in the short-term help the child endure, can become the source of pathology later on. In fact, invariably they do. And this is

recognized, actually, in scientific research, in medical research. It's just not recognized in medical practice.[79]

Dr. Peter Levine gives a very similar assessment in his 2008 book *Healing Trauma: A Pioneering Program for Restoring the Wisdom of Your Body* when he writes:

> In short, trauma is about loss of connection -- to ourselves, to our bodies, to our families, to others, and to the world around us. This loss of connection is often hard to recognize, because it doesn't happen all at once. It can happen slowly, over time, and we adapt to these subtle changes without even noticing them. These are the hidden effects of trauma, the ones most of us keep to ourselves. We may simply sense that we do not feel quite right, without ever becoming fully aware of what is taking place; that is, the gradual undermining of our self-esteem, self-confidence, feelings of well-being, and connection to life.[80]

A *loss of connection* -- to ourselves, to our bodies, to our families, to others, and to the world around us: this list describes the devastating effect of trauma, and although they do not use the word "trauma" itself, the ancient myths can be seen to be singularly focused upon this disconnection, and its remedy.

The Genesis account of the expulsion from the Garden of Eden clearly dramatizes the kind of alienation described in the above quotations from Dr. Levine and Dr. Maté. After they eat from the fruit of the tree of the knowledge of good and evil, Adam and Eve hide from the LORD, as we read in the text of Genesis 3: 8.

They have become disconnected from the divine realm, and soon we see that they have also become alienated from one another, from nature, and even from themselves. In Genesis 2: 25, before they eat from the tree, the text tells us of Adam and Eve that "they were both naked, the man and his wife, and were not ashamed." However, immediately after they eat of the fruit, their attitude about their own nakedness changes dramatically, and the text tells us that they sew fig leaves together in order to hide their

The Divine Twin

nakedness. They are no longer comfortable *in their own skin*. A more concise way of dramatizing their alienation from themselves would be hard to find.

Please note that, lest any reader misunderstand me as taking this story literally, it can be shown beyond any doubt to be based on celestial metaphor, as I have explained in many previous books and videos (see for example the dicussion in *Star Myths of the World, Volume Three*).

The famous verse in Genesis 3 in which the serpent is told that there will be "enmity between thee and the woman, and between thy seed and her seed; it shall bruise thy head, and thou shalt bruise his heel" demonstrates beyond any doubt that the events described in the expulsion from the Garden are based on *celestial metaphor*. Ophiuchus is the "seed of the woman," and is positioned in the heavens in such a way that the constellation can be seen to be standing upon the "head" or multiple heads of the constellation Scorpio, which is the "seed of the serpent," such that Ophiuchus is bruising the head of Scorpio, while Scorpio is "bruising the heel" of Ophiuchus (as mentioned earlier).

Thus, we can confidently conclude that this story is *not* about some ancient literal event at all, but rather that it is a powerful esoteric metaphor, and it applies to each one of us in this incarnate life.

When the LORD casts out the man, the woman, and the serpent from the Garden in the text of Genesis 3, he does so in the order that the figures of the serpent (the constellation Hydra), the woman (the constellation Virgo), and the man (the constellation Boötes) sink down out of the heavens and disappear into the western horizon: first the serpent (in Genesis 3: 14 - 15), then the woman (in verse 16), and then the man (in verses 17 - 19). We can conclude from this observation that the "Paradise" from which they are expelled is in fact the *heavens above*, and the application of this fact is the realization that it applies to us in our descent from the infinite realm of spirit (represented by the figures in the

Chapter Seven

infinite realm of heaven above, the realm of the upper elements of fire and air) to the realm of matter and physical incarnation (dramatized by the motion of the constellations sinking down into the western horizon, where they plunge into the lower realm of earth and water).

The implication we can draw from this foundational story includes the realization that our plunge into this realm of matter and physical existence involves trauma -- it involves separation from the divine, from nature, from the world around us, from our families (notice how Adam and Eve, previously so close that they are described as becoming "one flesh" in Genesis 2: 24, become alienated from one another immediately following the fall, with Adam blaming Eve for the episode with the fruit in Genesis 3: 13 in what might be described as a very early example of "throwing under the bus"), from other men and women in society beyond our immediate family, and ultimately from ourselves.

This brief examination of one of the foundational stories of the entire Bible (and one with echoes in the traditions of other cultures) should establish beyond much doubt that the dramatization of the alienating impact of psychological trauma (which Dr. Peter Levine says *almost all of us* have experienced in some form) plays a central role in the world's ancient myths.

Not only do the ancient myths dramatize this traumatic alienation from our own self, but they also show us the path towards the recovery of the self, and one of the ways they demonstrate this path to recovery is through the ubiquitous oicotype of the twins.

One of the very earliest myth-cycles preserved for our examination in the modern day, if not the earliest of them all in terms of a fairly complete narrative, is the Gilgamesh cycle, preserved in the clay tablets of Mesopotamia recovered during the first half of the nineteenth century and decoded over the course of the ensuing hundred years.

The earliest versions of the Gilgamesh texts (or Bilgameš, as the hero is called in the more ancient Sumerian versions of the myth),

The Divine Twin

are thought to date back as far as the Third Dynasty of Ur, around 2200 BC, although oral versions of the myths are thought to have existed for some centuries before that.[83]

As discussed at some length in my 2019 book *The Ancient World-Wide System*, the central characters in this ancient myth-cycle are explicitly described as being alike, even though they are not born of the same mother. The gods specifically make Enkidu, the counterpart to Gilgamesh, very closely matched with him in nearly every aspect of stature and strength, but covered in hair:

> All his body is matted with hair,
> he bears long tresses like those of a woman:
> the hair of his head grows thickly as barley,
> he knows not a people, nor even a country.
>
> Coated in hair like the god of the animals,
> with the gazelles he grazes on grasses,
> joining the throng with the game at the water-hole,
> his heart delighting with the beasts in the water.[84]

Note the pattern of hairiness in this "twin" of Gilgamesh who is associated with the beasts of the field and with living a life in the wild, a pattern which appears again in the description of the twins Jacob and Esau in the book of Genesis, where Esau is described as being hairy, covered all over as if with a "hairy garment" (Genesis 25: 25), and as being "a man of the field" (Genesis 25: 27).

And yet, despite their differences, the ancient Mesopotamian texts make it clear that Gilgamesh and Enkidu are nearly identical, as nearly everyone who encounters Enkidu remarks aloud upon seeing him for the first time, such as the first shepherds he meets ("how like in build he is to Gilgamesh," they exclaim to one another)[85] and the people of the great city of Uruk, who call him "the image of Gilgamesh" albeit somewhat shorter in stature but larger in bone.[86]

Like the Genesis account of Adam and Eve's expulsion from the Garden, and subsequent alienation from the divine, from nature,

Chapter Seven

from one another, and from themselves, the Gilgamesh cycle also contains a "fall" and subsequent disconnection, and one of the most poignant in ancient myth. This disconnection is dramatized through the person of Enkidu, the hairy twin, who originally lives in harmony and communion with nature and with the wild beasts, but who is seduced by the beautiful temple prostitute Shamhat (or Shamkatum), and after having sexual relations with her for six days and seven nights, discovers that the beasts of the field no longer tolerate his presence but shy away from him in fear, and that he himself can no longer run with them with the speed of a wild gazelle, the way he could before.[87]

Like Adam and Eve after eating from the tree of the knowledge of good and evil, Enkidu has lost something but also gained something. The ancient Mesopotamian texts explain:

Enkidu was weakened, could not run as before,
but now he had *reason*, and wide understanding.[88]

The text goes on to relate the increasing acculturation and "domestication" of Enkidu, including his introduction to bread and wine (or to bread and beer), his introduction to a group of shepherds (who put him to work driving away wolves and lions in order to protect the flocks of sheep), and his first haircut at the hands of a barber among the shepherds, who grooms his hair, anoints Enkidu with oil, and gives him a garment appropriate to a warrior.[89]

From all of this textual description (and from the fact that the episodes in this poem, like virtually all of the world's other ancient myths, can be shown to be built upon celestial metaphor, and thus not to be describing literal and historical figures but rather to be profound metaphor, applicable to all of us even to this very day), I argue that the ancient text of the Gilgamesh cycle is dramatizing something about our human condition, and our loss of connection to nature and the wild, through our entanglement with the norms, mores, and trappings of civilization -- customs and conventions which are indeed necessary in order to enable us to live together in a society, but which at the same time create as a byproduct the very alienation that we have been discussing, an alienation which separates us from who we are at the most basic level, and thus separates us from our selves.

In other words, I would argue that in some of the very oldest-known mythical narratives preserved in original texts anywhere on the planet, we find a sophisticated depiction of the modern understanding of psychological trauma and alienation from the self, beginning with Enkidu's loss of innocence and loss of connection to the natural world. And this focus on disconnection and alienation is by no means limited to the myths of ancient Mesopotamia or to the stories of the Bible: it is a central theme in ancient myths around the globe.

But the myths not only dramatize our state of disconnection and alienation: they point us towards the recovery of the authentic self. In the case of Enkidu, it is clear that he cannot simply go back to the way he was before. He has lost his connection to nature and the innocence of his days among the beasts of the wild, but he can seek out and find (and wrestle with) his semi-divine twin, Gilgamesh – and this twinning relationship, as can be convincingly shown from many examples in myths of many cultures, helps picture our recovery of our own connection to the essential self, and how this recovery can be effected.

The argument that the twin-pattern in ancient myth dramatizes the restoration of connection with the essential self is perhaps most easily illustrated with an example that is probably very familiar to many readers, although not usually recognized as one of the consummate examples of the twinning oicotype in ancient myth: the episode in the New Testament which has come to be known as the story of Doubting Thomas.

Although Thomas is mentioned in all four of the canonical gospels, the "Doubting Thomas" episode is found only in the Gospel according to John (as indeed are any other details about Thomas beyond simply his name included in the list of the

Chapter Seven

disciples, which is all that we find about Thomas in the three "synoptic" Gospels according to Matthew, Mark and Luke).

In the Gospel according to John, however, we are told that when the risen Christ visits the disciples on the evening of the first day of the week (the evening of the day of resurrection), "Thomas, one of the twelve, called Didymus, was not with them when Jesus came" (John 20: 24).

This absence of Thomas from the episode in which the risen Christ first appears to the disciples sets the scene for the next verse in the text, which says that when the other disciples proclaim to Thomas that they have seen the risen Lord, Thomas famously replies: "Except I shall see in his hands the print of the nails, and put my finger into the print of the nails, and thrust my hand into his side, I will not believe" (John 20: 25).

The narrative continues:

> 26 And after eight days again his disciples were within, and Thomas with them: *then* came Jesus, the doors being shut, and stood in the midst, and said, Peace *be* unto you.
> 27 Then saith he to Thomas, Reach hither thy finger, and behold my hands; and reach hither thy hand, and thrust *it* into my side: and be not faithless, but believing.
> 28 And Thomas answered and said unto him, My Lord and my God.

Because of this episode, Thomas is often referred to as "Doubting Thomas." It is an extremely significant episode, and one containing a powerful illustration of the path towards the recovery of our essential self, from whom we become alienated by the trauma described by Dr. Peter Levine and Dr. Gabor Maté, an alienation which the world's ancient myths understand and address.

In order to perceive this episode's esoteric message, however, we should note a very important hint provided for us in the text cited

The Divine Twin

above, when verse 24 tells us that on that first day of the week, "Thomas, one of the twelve, called Didymus, was not with them."

What does this appellation "Didymus" signify? What does it mean that the text calls this disciple *Thomas Didymus*?

As I have written in some detail in my 2016 book *Star Myths of the World, Volume Three: Star Myths of the Bible* (as well as in previous blog posts), this second name of Thomas provides a key for understanding this episode, because the word "Didymus" signifies "the Twin." The prefix *di-* is still found in many English words, carrying the meaning of "two" or "twin" or "twinned," such as "diode" or a "dipole" or a "dichotomy" or a "diplodocus" or even a "diploma" (diplomas apparently being given this name because originally they were folded in *two*, or *doubled*, rather than being rolled up and stuffed into a tube the way they are today).

Indeed, the very name *Thomas* itself signifies "a twin" in Aramaic, just as Didymus (or Didymos) is derived from Greek.

But if Thomas is called Didymus, then who is the twin of Thomas? We are never told in any of the canonical gospel accounts (in fact, we are never told much of anything about Thomas in three of the canonical gospels, and we are not told very much about this figure even in the Gospel according to John, which at least tells us that he is called *Didymus* but does not tell us who his twin might be).

However, Thomas is an extremely important figure in ancient gospel accounts which were excluded from the canon (by the authorities who were imposing a literalist religion and who selected texts to deem "canonical" based on their specific agenda), including in the texts discovered during the mid-twentieth century near Nag Hammadi in Egypt, texts now called the Nag Hammadi Corpus or the Nag Hammadi Library, texts which can be broadly categorized as Gnostic in paradigm (some of them being more specifically Sethian, some Valentinian, some

Hermetic, and some Gnostic in nature but falling outside the characteristics of those streams).[90]

The figure of Thomas is so important that one sub-group of the Nag Hammadi Corpus is categorized as "Thomas texts," consisting (according to Nag Hammadi scholar Marvin Meyer) of "the Gospel of Thomas, the Book of Thomas, and probably the Dialogue of the Savior."[91]

The second of those mentioned, the Book of Thomas (not to be confused with the Gospel of Thomas), reveals the identity of the twin of Thomas. Below is a translation of the relevant passage, as translated by Professor John D. Turner (1938 - 2019) of the University of Nebraska and posted on the website *gnosis.org*:

> The savior said, "Brother Thomas, while you have time in the world, listen to me, and I will reveal to you the things you have pondered in your mind.
>
> "Now, since it has been said that you are my twin and true companion, examine yourself, and learn who you are, in what way you exist, and how you will come to be. Since you will be called my brother, it is not fitting that you be ignorant of yourself. And I know that you have understood, because you had already understood that I am the knowledge of the truth. So while you accompany me, although you are uncomprehending, you have (in fact) already come to know, and you will be called 'the one who knows himself.' For he who has not known himself has known nothing, but he who has known himself has at the same time already achieved knowledge about the depth of the all. So then, you, my brother Thomas, have beheld what is obscure to me, that is, what they ignorantly stumble against."[92]

What does this ancient text tell us that the savior calls Thomas? He calls Thomas "my twin and true companion."

In other words, the Book of Thomas reveals to us the identity of the twin of Thomas Didymus -- and his twin is Jesus himself.

The Divine Twin

No wonder the literalizers left such information about Thomas Didymus out of the "canonical" gospels! If we take the scriptures of the New Testament as recording literal, historical, terrestrial events, then we would have a serious problem with a text which has Jesus declaring that Thomas is his own twin and true companion.

For one thing, other New Testament texts provide a birth account of the baby Jesus, laid in a manger, and there is no mention in that account of a twin (as nearly everyone knows, since the Nativity story is one of the most famous New Testament accounts, being re-enacted every year at Christmas time and commemorated in manger-scenes which feature Joseph and Mary giving adoration to one newborn baby, not two). Thus, if we want to take the New Testament texts as recording literal, terrestrial history, then an account in another text in which Jesus calls Thomas his "twin" poses problems. But if we realize that these ancient accounts, in common with the world's other Star Myths, are actually intended to be profound esoteric metaphor, then we should have no problem with the understanding that Doubting Thomas is in fact the "twin" of the Christ.

Indeed, the understanding that Thomas is the twin of Jesus fits the pattern we have already observed regarding the Dioscuri (the "youths of Zeus") as well as the twins Heracles and Iphicles: one twin is divine, the son of a divine father, and the other is mortal, the son of a mortal father. Jesus is the son of a mortal woman and a divine father, just as we see in the case of Polydeuces (but not Castor) in the case of the Dioscuri, and just as we see in the case of Heracles (but not Iphicles) in the story of the seduction of Alcmene (wife of Amphitryon) by Zeus in the birth of the divine Heracles.

And, as I have already asserted, these two "twins" are not two separate people, any more than Gandalf the Grey and Gandalf the White are two separate people. Instead, they dramatize our alienation from our true self -- our essential self -- just as the text of the Book of Thomas tells us (in the words attributed to Jesus

Chapter Seven

himself). These myths are intended to point us towards the discovery of the essential self, from whom we have become alienated (and of whose existence we are often hardly even aware): to point us towards our reconciliation and reintegration with our essential self -- our authentic and true self.

We can quite clearly see, in the passage cited above from the Book of Thomas, that this recognition and reconciliation with the true self is very much the focus of the ancient text as it is written. Jesus tells Thomas in no uncertain terms that Thomas is his twin, and because of this fact, it is not fitting for Thomas to remain (as Jesus tells him) "ignorant of yourself." The implication is that Thomas is indeed ignorant of his own self. But Jesus tells Thomas that Thomas will be called, "the one who knows himself." Going further, Jesus explains to Thomas the consummate importance of this knowing of himself, declaring: "he who has not known himself has known nothing."

It does not take any deep analysis to interpret this passage as having to do with the state of alienation from one's own self: the text explicitly tells us that it is not fitting for Thomas to be ignorant of himself (indicating that it is *very easy* and *very common* to be ignorant of our own self). Nor does it take any special insight to realize that the text has to do with recovering our relationship with our true self: Jesus tells Thomas that Thomas will come to be known as "the one who knows himself," indicating that although it is easy to be estranged from one's self, it is also possible to recover our self, and that Thomas will do so.

But notice that the text implies that it is possible to not even realize that we are alienated from our essential self. Jesus says to Thomas, "Since you will be called my brother, it is not fitting for you to be ignorant of yourself." How can we possibly be ignorant of our self?

Peter Levine asserts that the byproduct of trauma is "loss of connection," including first and foremost loss of connection to ourself.

Gabor Maté asserts that, "What trauma actually is, fundamentally, is a disconnect from the self: a disconnect from the body and a disconnect from the essential self. Why do people disconnect? Because it's too painful to be connected. So the disconnection is not a mistake -- it's not an accident: it's actually a coping mechanism."

What does Dr. Maté mean when he says "the essential self"? The *essence* of something means what it really is at the deepest level. Our essential self is who we really are, at the deepest level. How could we become disconnected from that? As Dr. Levine and Dr. Maté explain, we disconnect from who we truly are, from our essential self, as a *defense mechanism*, because it's *too painful* to be connected.

In his 2011 book, *When the Body Says No: Exploring the Stress-Disease Connection*, Dr. Maté explains this defense mechanism, which typically arises from trauma experienced in childhood, even when we are too young to consciously understand the source of the distress. Speaking of a child (Ronald Reagan) whose father was routinely arrested for public drunkenness, Dr. Maté writes:

> While a young child may not be *cognitively* aware of family disgrace, *emotionally* he is absorbing all the negative psychic vibrations of the stressed family system. An emotional shutdown, a tuning-out of reality, is his brain's most readily available defence.[93]

This "emotional shutdown" and "tuning-out of reality" includes the tuning-out of the full spectrum of information we receive from our body's incredibly rich array of sensors, including our gut, and from the wider awareness beyond our conscious mind. It also includes a disconnection from aspects of who we really are but which make us feel vulnerable, and the creation of a "second self," a *persona*, which will shield us from being hurt again.

The word *persona* actually comes from an ancient Etruscan word which means a "mask" -- putting on an outward face which the world sees, which is a helpful image to enable us to understand

Chapter Seven

what is going on: we create a persona, an outward-facing mask, in order to shield ourselves from being hurt. And this process is how we become alienated from our essential self, and create instead a persona, a mask, a kind of "mechanism" that will protect us and help get us through this threatening and traumatic world.

It is as if we are driving along a dangerous road, perhaps a cliff-side road with a sheer drop onto sharp rocks hundreds of feet below, and this *persona* we create takes over the wheel in order to "get us through" this dangerous stretch of road -- thinking that it is the only thing between us and terrible pain and even destruction.

The problem is that this persona never wants to let go of the steering wheel. We identify with it so completely that we lose touch with our essential self -- who we really are, in our core -- with the very essence that this persona: this defense mechanism, this "ego," was constructed to protect and shield in the first place!

For this reason, we have a tendency to think that our egoic mind, the "ego" we create in order to navigate the complex maze of rules and social norms and power structures we encounter as we are indoctrinated into society, is actually who we are -- to the point that we become ignorant of our true self, our authentic self, our essential self.

This is why the figure of Jesus in the Book of Thomas tells Thomas, "it is not fitting for you to be ignorant of yourself." This line informs us that, although it is not a desirable condition, we are typically so disconnected from our essential self that we are actually in ignorance (or even in denial) of its very presence, of its very existence.

Having examined the ancient passage in the Book of Thomas which illuminates for us the identity of the twin of Thomas Didymus, and which at the same time indicates quite overtly that this twin relationship has everything to do with revealing our alienation from our essential self, and also with the repairing of that broken relationship with our essential self, let us now return to the episode of Doubting Thomas presented in the Gospel according to John, interpreting it in light of this understanding.

If Jesus and Thomas are twins in this episode, and if twins in ancient myth do not actually represent two different individuals but rather two aspects of each and every man and woman going through this life, then which of these two twins do we suspect must represent the essential self, and which of the two twins represents the "defense mechanism" described above: the persona we fashion in the face of the trauma we experience in this world, in order to shield ourself from getting hurt?

The answer should be obvious.

Jesus, the divine twin in the pair, is the essential self, the authentic self, the higher self. Thomas, who is filled with doubt, represents the egoic mind, the one who is in fact "ignorant" of the true self (in this dramatic episode, he is indeed ignorant of the existence of his divine twin, and refuses to believe the accounts of the other disciples who tell him that they have seen the Lord).

When the other disciples tell Thomas that they have seen Jesus, he refuses to believe them. Why is Thomas so skeptical? Thomas is skeptical because he does not want to be burned. His doubts are a defense mechanism. He has been wounded in the past, and his attitude is a way of shielding himself from being hurt again.

Note of course that the above description is not intended to pertain to some historical ancient figure named Thomas, but rather to our own egoic mind, our own persona or mask, crafted over time as a "coping mechanism" against psychic trauma. In each of our cases, these were different experiences and different hurts, but having very much the same result: alienation from our self. It is a condition of alienation which the ancient myths dramatize over and over, with breathtaking accuracy and perception, and one which continues to play itself out in the lives of men and women to this very day, right up to this very moment.

Chapter Seven

How does the egoic mind respond when the true self, the essential self, the self which has in fact been "buried" (as Jesus has been buried in the story, before his return and appearance to the disciples), makes an appearance? Does the "coping mechanism" of the egoic self, who has taken over the steering wheel, and who thinks that it is the only one who "gets us through" this dangerous and traumatic world, exclaim: "Oh, I'm so happy to see you! Here, take the wheel! After all, *you* are the essential self"?

Of course not.

The egoic mind, the "Thomas mind," responds to revelations of the existence and power of the essential self in very much the same manner that Thomas responds when the other disciples tell him that they have seen the Lord. Thomas replies, in essence: "That's nonsense! I don't believe it."

The egoic mind wants to invalidate the very existence of the essential self, the authentic self. And that is just what Thomas tries to do in this episode from John chapter 20.

The egoic mind is full of doubts because it is a defense mechanism, a "coping mechanism" as Dr. Maté puts it in the passage from his book quoted above. Thomas (the "Thomas mind") has developed these doubts in order to not get hurt. His doubts are a means of responding to wounds experienced in the past, and of trying to avoid similar pain in the future.

The egoic mind reacts this way because it developed over a long period of time, beginning in infancy and then continuing on into our childhood, in response to the hurts of this world, and to the rules that we are taught or that we absorb, or even that we make up for ourselves. And it separates us from who we really are. But this egoic mind, this mechanism we craft for ourselves in order to cope, has the effect of becoming so familiar that we think this egoic mind is who we really are. And the mind gets very defensive, perhaps even very frightened, when we begin to remember who we really are, or take steps to reconnect with our essential self –

and it will absolutely resist any attempt to take the steering wheel away from the egoic self and let the essential self take over.

As part of a different talk, given in 2015 at the California Institute of Integral Studies in San Francisco, Dr. Gabor Maté said some very enlightening things about this relationship between the egoic mind and our essential self. Although he was not citing the episode of Doubting Thomas, the words he says in the passage below sound as though they could be describing the reaction of Thomas in the New Testament story.

Part of the quotation discusses psychedelics, because Dr. Maté's talk involved the role that psychedelic plant medicines can play in relaxing that artificial coping mechanism of the mind in order to reveal the authentic self -- the authentic self that our egoic mind wants to bury and hide. Dr. Maté says:

> We live in a world that rewards us for being inauthentic, and punishes us for being authentic. And we live in a world, and a culture, that seduces us from our true selves with every possible blandishment, reward, and promise of fulfillment through artificial means. [. . .] The other problem, as Alma says, is that your mind, your egoic mind, always wants to invalidate your essence. Because the egoic mind develops as a replacement for the essence. When essence shows up, the mind is threatened: the ego is threatened. So it wants to fight back. When the psychedelic substance really reveals the mind -- what's underneath the mind -- and puts the ego onto the sidelines, as soon as the effect is gone, the mind wants to come in and reclaim its territory. And it does that by making nonsense of the experience you just had.[94]

Look how closely dramatizations in ancient myth match the experience and teachings of some of today's most respected voices in the field of dealing with psychological trauma, such as Dr. Gabor Maté and Dr. Peter Levine! The episode of Doubting Thomas illustrates, very powerfully, the attempt to invalidate the revelation of the essential self, the higher self that Dr. Maté describes above -- seen in this story of Thomas trying to invalidate the accounts of the return of the risen Lord.

But the ancient myths also dramatize the path we can take towards reconciliation between egoic mind and essential self.

At first, Thomas is estranged from the risen Christ -- kept apart by his doubt, and by his instinctual desire to invalidate the essential self (the essential self for whom, as Dr. Maté tells us in the quotation above, the egoic mind attempts to substitute and whose role the egoic mind attempts to usurp).

If we look closely at this text, and at other ancient myths which follow a similar pattern, we will see that these esoteric stories are showing us how to recover the right relationship with our essential self.

We will explore the ways that the world's ancient Star Myths can point us towards recovering our own self in the next chapter, but before moving on we should pause to consider the fact that if the myths can be shown to be guiding us towards such a recovery, as they clearly can be shown to be doing, then we have gone a long way towards establishing that they seem to have been intended to serve a very positive purpose indeed.

This ache for the recovery of our own self can be said to be at the center of our deepest longings, and the disconnection from our own self at the heart of our greatest sufferings -- even if we generally don't realize that this reconnection is what we are longing for, and that this disconnection is what is causing our suffering (we typically don't even realize that the essential self even exists, let alone that we have become alienated from who we are). Remember that Dr. Peter Levine declared, in a quotation cited above, that "Trauma is the most avoided, ignored, denied, misunderstood and untreated cause of human suffering." If the myths exist in part to remedy *the most untreated* (and the most overlooked, and even the most denied) cause of human suffering, then their purpose is positive indeed. Let's look at how they help us with this very ancient, but very modern, affliction.

Chapter 8
"Reach hither thy finger . . ."

Let's begin this chapter by repeating an important assertion made by Dr. Gabor Maté in one of the quotations cited in the previous chapter, regarding the definition of *trauma*. He said:

> So trauma is not these terrible things that happen to people. What trauma actually is, fundamentally, is a disconnect from the self.[95]

He is careful to distinguish between the painful experiences themselves, which happened in the past, and the alienation from the essential self, which continues to the present. The reason this distinction is so important is that we cannot go back and undo painful events which happened in the past -- but we *can* repair the disconnection which resulted from that pain (and which is what causes problems in our present lives).

In another part of the talk delivered in 2015 at the Psychedelic Science Conference in Oakland, Dr. Maté explains:

> So if you look at the essence of trauma, it is actually -- as I said before -- that disconnection from the self. And that is expressed very well by two spiritual teachers, one of them is Eckhart Tolle, who says, "Basically all emotions are modifications of one primordial, undifferentiated emotion that has its origin in a loss of awareness of who you are beyond name and form" -- in other words, the loss of the true self. "Because of its undifferentiated nature, it is hard to find a name that precisely describes this emotion. *Fear* comes close, but apart from a continuous sense of threat, it also includes a deep sense of abandonment and incompleteness. It may be best to use a term that is as undifferentiated as the basic emotion and simply call it *pain*." And another teacher, A. H. Almaas, says -- talking about childhood -- that: "the fundamental thing that happened, and the greatest calamity, is not that there was no love or support. The greater calamity, which was caused by that first

calamity, is that you lost the connection to your essence. That is much more important than whether your mother or father loved you or not." Well, that's really good news. Because if the trauma was that you were sexually abused, or that your parents were too depressed to really connect with you, or too stressed to be emotionally available to you, or if they hit you, or emotionally stressed you -- if that was the trauma, then unfortunately, it's over, because that happened decades ago. But if the trauma is actually the loss of self, loss of connection to self, then that self can be reconnected with at any time. And when we talk about, say, the healing of addiction, what's the word for that? We call it *recovery*. And recovery of course very specifically means, "the finding of something -- the finding *again* of something." Well, what is it that's recovered, or found again, in the recovery from addiction? When we ask people, "Just what did you find when you recovered" -- invariably, the answer is: "I found myself." So what happens in recovery is that remembering of the self -- which means that it's always available.[96]

The essential self is actually always available, and we can reconnect with our self at any time. And that, as Dr. Maté says, "is really good news."

Let's turn to the ancient myths and see how they dramatize our reconnection with the essential self, and how they point us towards the path to finding ourself again.

In the story of Doubting Thomas which we have been examining, we see Thomas (representative of the egoic mind) alienated from Jesus (representative of the essential self), and we see Thomas alienated by his *doubts* -- doubts which function as a defense mechanism, doubts which are there in order to "keep from getting burned."

The words and actions of Thomas illustrate very well the observation cited by Dr. Gabor Maté and quoted in the previous chapter that, when the *essence* is revealed (for example, through

"Reach hither thy finger . . . "

the agency of plant medicines which relax the grip of the doubting mind, revealing the essence "underneath the mind"), the mind immediately wants to regain control, deny the essence, and invalidate the experience. The disciples tell Thomas that they have seen the risen Lord (the formerly buried essence), and Thomas immediately seeks to *invalidate* that revelation.

At the core of this suppression of the appearance of the essential self is the principle of *doubt*. Doubt is so central to this episode that it has come to be known as the story of "Doubting Thomas," a phrase which serves as a shorthand for the entire sequence of events described in John chapter 20. The egoic mind is characterized by doubt -- can almost be said to be *constructed* of doubt.

Doubt characterizes other characters in Star Myths from other cultures who are representative of the egoic mind as well, such as Arjuna in the Bhagavad Gita, consumed with doubt prior to the start of the great Battle of Kurukshetra (in which text, i.e. the Bhagavad Gita, the figure of the Lord Krishna himself acts as the essential self, the divine self), or such as Psyche in the story of Eros and Psyche, consumed with doubt to the point that she temporarily loses her relationship with the divine Eros.

Why is the egoic mind characterized by doubt, even to the point of being virtually constructed of doubt?

It is because the detachment from the self which led to the creation of the ego in the first place arose from the experience of trauma which could not be handled except by detachment -- as Dr. Maté wrote in the passage cited above (referring specifically to the situation of the young Ronald Reagan, whose father was repeatedly arrested for public drunkenness). In response to severe psychic stress, the most readily-available defense is a "tuning-out of reality" in order to reduce the pain, an "emotional shutdown" in order to reduce the hurt.

At the core of this detachment are defense mechanisms which seek to escape from the pain of the *present moment*, and this

Chapter Eight

detachment from the present moment leads the mind to seek solace and escape somewhere else -- by flinging itself forward into the future or backwards into the past: anywhere but the present moment, which is too painful to endure.

And, if we think about it carefully, we will see that the essence of doubt is projection forward into the future ("what might happen if I do this," for instance) or backwards into the past ("remember what happened the last time I tried to do this," for example, or "remember how we got burned the last time we put our trust in someone else").

Indeed, returning again to the lectures of Dr. Maté, who was not referencing the Doubting Thomas episode in this talk at all (and yet whose remarks so perfectly articulate the powerful messages conveyed by the world's ancient myths that I was astonished the first time I heard his message), in a passage just following the passage quoted above in this chapter, the extended quotation about trauma and the ability to *recover* at any time (due to the availability of the essential self, which is still present and thus available to us, because the essential self is our *essence*, it's who we actually are, and thus can never go away), Dr. Maté declares:

> Now the other aspect of trauma is that once it happens, you can no longer be comfortable in the present moment. When the present moment hurt you so much that you became afraid of it, then your whole mind will be oriented towards escaping the present moment -- escaping it by any means possible. And, what kind of a culture do we live in? We live in a culture that is predicated, and economically based on, escape from the present.[97]

No wonder the egoic mind is characterized by doubt! It is practically composed of various rules it has collected and assembled in order to avoid pain, and it is always scanning forward into the future in order to try to avoid pain, or looking back to the past in order to extract lessons (again, to avoid pain), all of which is perfectly understandable because that is its job.

"Reach hither thy finger . . . "

The egoic mind is a defense mechanism, a "coping mechanism" as Dr. Maté calls it, developed in order to shield us from the pain we experience as a function of our interaction with the world (and primarily as a function of our entanglement in the complexities of human society, as we saw with the story of Enkidu in the ancient epic of Gilgamesh).

The creation of the egoic mind, the "doubting mind" we might call it, is in fact a necessary development in one sense. We actually need to have doubts which can protect us from pain, or from making mistakes which can hurt us (we need an egoic mind which can remember mistakes we made in the past and caution us against making them again). The ability to cast our mind forward into the future and backwards into the past is not, in and of itself, a bad thing!

However, the problem with this doubting mind is that it tends to take over and refuse to relinquish the steering wheel of our life, and in doing so our doubts run away with us, to the point of self-sabotage. The experience of having our mind "run away with us" to the point that we fail to achieve what we are perfectly capable of achieving is in fact so familiar that it hardly needs any examples to be provided here -- each reader can (no doubt!) furnish abundant examples from his or her own life experience.

So, we don't actually need to *extinguish* the "Thomas mind" -- we need to recover our connection with our essence, and place the two in a proper relationship, such that the essential self regains the primacy and the egoic mind *serves* the essential self (rather than trying to bury the essential self and keep it suppressed and hidden away).

Well then, how do we recover our essential self, and restore that proper relationship? Let's first touch upon how we *don't* do it, by examining another illustration from the fertile imagination of J.R.R. Tolkien and his masterpiece, the *Lord of the Rings*.

In addition to giving us one "twinned pair" who are actually two aspects of the same figure, in the person of Gandalf (Gandalf the

Chapter Eight

Grey and Gandalf the White), Tolkien provides another example of a character who personifies a kind of "twinned pair," this time dramatizing the creation over long years of suffering of an extremely negative "egoic self," in the person of Gollum, a persona which is a kind of "coping mechanism" created by the originally hobbit-like Sméagol, and one that basically takes over and dominates Sméagol to the point that Sméagol is entirely subsumed in the *persona* of Gollum.

The division of the personality in the case of Sméagol - Gollum is so complete that when talking to himself or about himself, he uses the first-person plural pronouns "we" and "us." At one memorable point in the story, Tolkien even has Sméagol and Gollum hold a debate or an argument, while leading Sam and Frodo through the Dead Marshes. Sam awakens in the middle of the night and sees Gollum beside the sleeping Frodo:

> For a moment Sam thought that he was trying to rouse Frodo; then he saw that it was not so. Gollum was talking to himself. Sméagol was holding a debate with some other thought that used the same voice but made it squeak and hiss. A pale light and a green light alternated in his eyes as he spoke.
>
> 'Sméagol promised,' said the first thought.
>
> 'Yes, yes, my precious,' came the answer, 'we promised: to save our Precious, not to let Him have it -- never. But it's going to Him, yes, nearer every step. What's the hobbit going to do with it, we wonders, yes we wonders.'
>
> 'I don't know. I can't help it. Master's got it. Sméagol promised to help the master.'[98]

This debate between the "two thoughts" who speak in the same voice (but with actual physical alterations when speaking in the person of Gollum) dramatizes the creation of a "doubting mind" (or, in the case of Gollum, perhaps we could term it a "scheming mind") which arises as a coping mechanism and takes over the steering wheel, so to speak, to the point that the original Sméagol is totally dominated by the persona that has been created.

"Reach hither thy finger..."

Later, on the stairs of Cirith Ungol, Tolkien portrays another internal debate, this one not dramatized in dialogue, but showing the "other side" of Sméagol when the Gollum persona temporarily relaxes its grip on him, when the young hobbits Sam and Frodo are asleep, eliciting a moment of tenderness when the "Sméagol who could have been" comes to the surface:

> And so Gollum found them hours later, when he returned, crawling and creeping down the path out of the gloom ahead. Sam sat propped against the stone, his head dropping sideways and his breathing heavy. In his lap lay Frodo's head, drowned deep in sleep; upon his white forehead lay one of Sam's brown hands, and the other lay softly upon his master's breast. Peace was in both their faces.
>
> Gollum looked at them. A strange expression passed over his lean hungry face. The gleam faded from his eyes, and they went dim and grey, old and tired. A spasm of pain seemed to twist him, and he turned away, peering back towards the pass, shaking his head, as if engaged in some interior debate. Then he came back, and slowly putting out a trembling hand, very cautiously he touched Frodo's knee -- but almost the touch was a caress. For a fleeting moment, could one of the sleepers have seen him, they would have thought they beheld an old weary hobbit, shrunken by the years that had carried him far beyond his time, beyond friends and kin, and the fields and streams of youth, an old starved pitiable thing.
>
> But at that touch Frodo stirred and cried out softly in his sleep, and immediately Sam was wide awake. The first thing he saw was Gollum -- 'pawing at master,' as he thought.
>
> 'Hey you!' he said roughly. 'What are you up to?'
>
> 'Nothing, nothing,' said Gollum softly. 'Nice Master!'
>
> 'I daresay,' said Sam. 'But where have you been to -- sneaking off and sneaking back, you old villain?'
>
> Gollum withdrew himself, and a green glint flickered under his heavy lids. Almost spider-like he looked now, crouched back

Chapter Eight

on bent limbs, with his protruding eyes. The fleeting moment had passed, beyond recall. 'Sneaking, sneaking!' he hissed.[99]

At the first sign of conflict, and at Sam's harsh words of approbation, the "defense mechanism" persona of Gollum returns, like a barking dog that believes everything is a threat.

Thus the internal debate of Sméagol vs. Gollum as it is portrayed in the original books by J.R.R. Tolkien: in the blockbuster movie adaptation by Peter Jackson, the conflict of the internal debate is heightened even further.

In the movie version of the audible debate that Sméagol - Gollum is having with himself in the Dead Marshes, which Sam awakens and overhears, Sméagol actually tries to banish his Gollum persona -- and originally believes that he has done so.

Although the movie adaptation adds lines that are not found in the original books, the scene is extremely memorable -- and eerily familiar to any of us who have ever wished we could simply tell our constructed "egoic mind" (along with any of the addictive or self-sabotaging behaviors that arise from our loss of the essential self) to stop tormenting us.

Here is how that scene unfolds in the movie:

> Sméagol: Master's my friend.
>
> Gollum: You don't *have* any friends. Nobody likes *you*.
>
> Sméagol: Go away -- go away! I hate you!
>
> Gollum: Where would you be without me, [involuntary hacking noise] *gollum*? I saved us! It was *me*: we survived because of *me*.
>
> Sméagol: Not anymore.
>
> Gollum: What did you say?
>
> Sméagol: Master looks after us now. We don't need you!
>
> Gollum: What?
>
> Sméagol: Leave now, and never come back![100]

"Reach hither thy finger..."

This well-known scene illustrates the tenacity of the egoic mind, which believes it is the only one "getting us through" whatever painful experiences this life throws at us, and which clings fiercely to the steering wheel, unwilling to give it up for even a moment (believing that maintaining control is a matter of survival).

Additionally, as those who have seen the movie realize, Sméagol is mistaken to think that he can simply order the egoic mind to "leave now, and never come back." Simply attempting to "banish" the egoic mind is futile, and the ancient myths never imply that we can ever restore our relationship with our essential self simply by telling the egoic mind, this "coping mechanism" we have created in response to the exigencies of society and this world, to "go away." Neither does Tolkien in the *Lord of the Rings*, for that matter: in the books and in the movies, the "Gollum persona" returns the moment Sméagol feels threatened or hurt (as we saw in the episode on the stairs of Cirith Ungol).

Returning now to the episode of the encounter between Doubting Thomas and the risen Christ, note that we do not see Christ say to Thomas, "Ah, Thomas -- you are the worst of my disciples! So filled with doubt all the time! Leave now, and never come back!"

That's not what we see at all. Instead, we see Christ (representative of the essential self in the story) act with *compassion* towards Thomas (representative of the egoic mind).

The essential self understands the situation -- understands what has led to the creation of the egoic mind -- understands why the egoic mind is so afraid of letting go of the wheel -- understands the egoic mind's lack of trust.

The egoic mind became that way because of trauma. It is like a frightened dog, filled with fear and anxiety, barking at every sound, going beyond the boundaries of what it should rightfully protect and barking at things going on in areas completely outside of its responsibility, because it has been deeply scarred. Yelling at it will not solve the problem: it will only make it worse.

Chapter Eight

So how do we see Jesus interact with Thomas in this crucial episode?

First, note that when Jesus appears, he says the same thing to the disciples who were within the locked room that he said the first time he appeared, on the first day of the resurrection: "Peace *be* unto you" (again, the reason the translation italicizes the word "be" is that this verb is not found in the original text but was inserted by the translators in the early sixteen hundreds in order to be more syntactically familiar to readers of that day -- the original text itself would translate more directly and literally as "Peace unto you").

This salutation itself reveals a great deal about the message of this entire episode in ancient scripture: it has to do with bringing peace. And why is it necessary to greet someone with a wish that they would have peace? If Jesus is pronouncing a benediction of "peace" then what does that blessing imply? It implies that there is a state of division somewhere, a conflict which should be reconciled and healed (*warring parties* need peace). And the division and the conflict which needs to be healed and reconciled is found within each of his listeners -- it is the division *within us.*

We have already seen, in our examination of the Genesis episode of the expulsion from the Garden, that the ancient texts recognize and dramatize our *division* against ourself, resulting in our "discomfort in our own skin" -- our inability to be in harmony with our own essence, to "be ourself" and not be ashamed. As the quotation cited earlier from Dr. Peter Levine tells us: "In short, trauma is about loss of connection -- to ourselves, to our bodies, to our families, to others, and to the world around us."[101]

If we have experienced loss of connection to ourselves, to our bodies, to our families, to others, and to the world around us, then we are divided: we are not in a state of peace but in a state of division and conflict, conflicted even against ourselves (against our self).

"Reach hither thy finger . . . "

This episode in the John Gospel is about healing that division, reconciling that conflict, and regaining a status of peace. Thus, when Jesus appears (both times) in this particular story, the first thing he says each time is: "Peace unto you."

The second time he appears, on the eighth day (as the text of John 20: 25 tells us), the disciples are again within, and this time Thomas is with them. Jesus again greets them by saying "Peace unto you," and then he addresses Thomas directly:

> 27 Then saith he to Thomas, Reach hither thy finger, and behold my hands; and reach hither thy hand, and thrust it into my side: and be not faithless, but believing.

This encounter has been interpreted by literalists, those maintaining that the text is describing a literal and historical encounter between two historical persons, as teaching the importance of "faith" or "believing," specifically the importance of believing or accepting a literal account of the death and resurrection of a literal person named Jesus, external to ourselves. But as we have been seeing from the context of the passage itself, as well as the wider context of the twins-pattern in world myth (in which one twin has a divine father and represents the higher self), this story is likely not intended to teach that lesson at all: it is not teaching a lesson of literalistic acceptance of the resurrection as an external, literal, historical event.

Instead, it appears to be very well supported by the clues in the text itself that this episode is showing us the way towards recovery of our own self, and towards the repair of that split, repair of that disconnection, that alienation which took place deep in our past, and which is often buried so deeply that we ourselves can remain completely ignorant of its impact on our lives (as Jesus says to Thomas his twin in the Book of Thomas: "it is not fitting that you be ignorant of yourself").

And the way that the higher self in this dramatic illustration (Jesus) brings Thomas back into the recognition of and reconciliation with the divine self (who has always been present

Chapter Eight

and available to him, but separated because of the doubting nature of the egoic mind) is by directing Thomas to "reach hither thy finger . . . and reach hither thy hand."

We have seen that the primary characteristic of *doubt* is a restless flitting of the mind, forward into the future and backwards into the past, and an inability to remain in the present moment, because the present moment is too uncomfortable and threatening (as Dr. Gabor Maté explains in the passage cited earlier in this chapter: "When the present moment hurt you so much that you became afraid of it, then your whole mind will be oriented towards escaping the present moment -- escaping it by any means possible").

The words Jesus addresses to Thomas in this dramatic illustration of the reconciliation of the egoic mind to the essential self are the antidote to the restless flitting backwards and forwards: a command to touch, to experience, and to know.

Jesus brings Thomas out of the "everywhere else but the present" and into the *immediate moment*. This is a very difficult place for the Thomas mind to be -- but it is where we come into contact with the essential self, as Thomas does in this story.

And notice how the essential self treats the egoic mind in this ancient illustration: Jesus treats Thomas with patience, and with compassion, and indeed with love. Our essential self is who we really are, just as the "essence" of something is what it really is at its deepest, purest core. Our essence does not change, and thus is not threatened by the lack of trust displayed by the egoic mind, and it does not become impatient with the endless machinations of this *persona* that has sprung up as a result of the world's relentless pressures and entanglements. Our true self, our authentic self, is always there, ready for us to get back in touch.

Just to add further evidence that this episode is not about a literal, historical, and terrestrial event (and therefore is not teaching as its primary lesson the importance of literalistic belief in a literal resurrection of a person external to ourselves), below are artistic

"Reach hither thy finger . . . "

depictions of the famous "Incredulity of Thomas" episode, which consistently depict the scene with undeniably constellational imagery (whether the artists themselves knew that these conventions were based on constellational characteristics or not):

As I have discussed in previous books and writings, these paintings (and others showing the same scene) typically employ imagery which specifically evokes the constellation Capricorn, which itself has horns, two triangular shapes, and a little bob-tail:

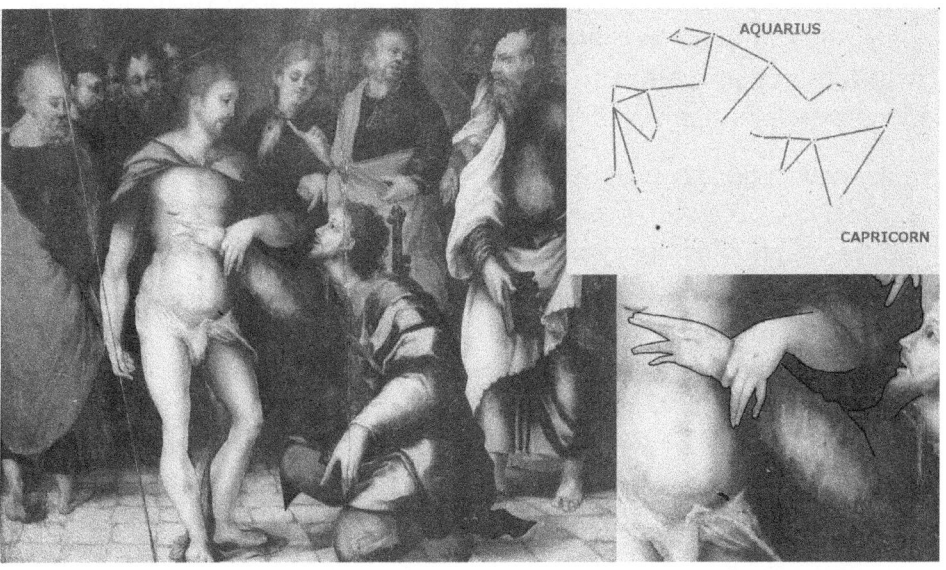

Chapter Eight

The horns of Capricorn in the heavens are pointing directly towards the outstretched "forward leg" of the constellation Aquarius -- which could also be envisioned, instead of a leg, as a spear going into the side of the constellation Aquarius (and indeed, as I explain in some detail in *Star Myths of the World, Volume Two: Myths of Ancient Greece*, figures in the Iliad described as being a "swift runner" or a "headlong runner" will often meet their demise with a spear to the bowels, or by being speared through the lower back such that the spear goes all the way through and comes out through the bowels in front).[102]

Jesus is undoubtedly associated in some of the gospel texts with the sign of Aquarius, such as when he describes himself as being associated with the "sign of the Son of man in the heaven" (in Matthew 24: 30) and says "he shall set the sheep on his right hand, but the goats on the left" (Matthew 25: 33), which certainly describes Aquarius, situated between the signs of Aries (a ram or sheep) and of Capricorn (a goat).

However, I have also found abundant evidence which argues that Christ is frequently associated with the constellation Ophiuchus (and this brings up the fact that there appears to have been a definite connection between Aquarius figures and Ophiuchus figures in the ancient system of Star Myths, because there are other figures such as Dionysus who also have characteristics which associate them with both Aquarius and Ophiuchus, as I demonstrate in *Star Myths of the World, Volume Two*).

The connection between Christ and *Ophiuchus* should not surprise us, because we spent a great deal of analysis during the earlier chapters of this book establishing the argument that the God of the Bible can be seen to be closely associated with the constellation Hercules, as can so many of the most powerful gods in other mythologies from other cultures. In the ancient system of celestial metaphor which underlies the world's myths, a character who is *the son of* (or *descended from*) another figure will often be associated with the constellation *directly below* the constellation which corresponds to the father. We have already mentioned that

"Reach hither thy finger . . . "

the figure of Solomon the son of David is associated with the constellation Ophiuchus, and Ophiuchus is positioned directly below the constellation Hercules, with which constellation his father David is associated (thus Solomon can be seen as being *descended from* David).

Thus, in the New Testament, if the figure of Jesus is described as being the *son of God*, then it would not be at all surprising to discover that he is most closely associated with the constellation Ophiuchus (directly below and thus "descended from" the constellation Hercules, the constellation with which Jehovah can very clearly be seen to be closely associated).

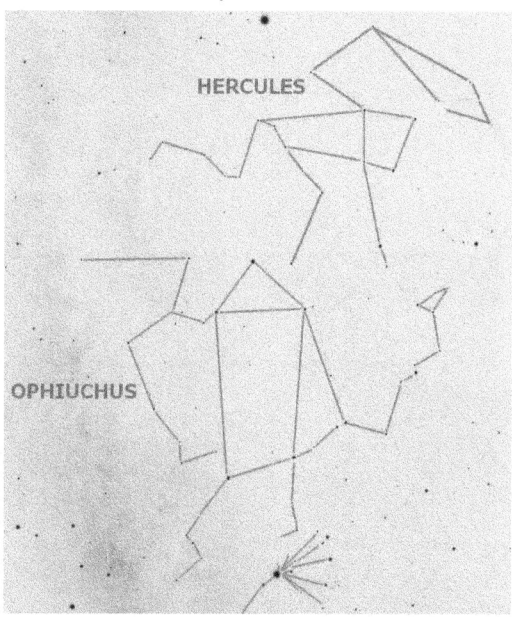

As demonstrated in *Star Myths of the World, Volume Three: Star Myths of the Bible*, the outline of Ophiuchus can confidently be seen as furnishing the framework for the cross upon which Christ is crucified between two thieves. The stars forming the central body of the constellation Ophiuchus can be connected to create a cross that matches the traditional shape of the cross of the crucifixion perfectly, and the two "serpent-halves" on either side of the central body correspond to the two thieves, as shown in the illustration on the following page:

Chapter Eight

216

"Reach hither thy finger . . . "

This powerful painting, done in the form of a triptych, was completed between 1545 and 1550 by Maarten van Heemskerck, and depicts the cross of Christ in traditional proportions, which can be seen to mirror the "cross" created by the stars which frame the central body of Ophiuchus, while the two thieves crucified on either side of Jesus are depicted in extremely contorted positions, reminiscent of the two "serpent-halves" which flank the central body of Ophiuchus on either side.

Instead of traditional cross-shapes, the two thieves are depicted as nailed to twisted tree-trunks -- and there are numerous examples in the world's Star Myths in which the two "serpent-halves" on either side of the central body of Ophiuchus play the role of a branching tree or twisting vine, growing to either side.

And this painting by Maarten van Heemskerck is by no means an isolated example of a painting in which the central cross flanked by the two crucified thieves evokes the distinctive features of the constellation Ophiuchus -- many other examples could be offered which bolster the argument for associating the scene of the crucifixion with the figure of Ophiuchus and the other constellations in its immediate vicinity.

If we look closely at the painting, we will notice that the artist has placed the soldier (who is using a long spear to pierce the side of Christ) *on horseback*, and in the correct location to correspond to the constellation Sagittarius. There are actually stars which lead from Sagittarius to the region of Ophiuchus where Christ is usually envisioned as being pierced by the lance, as shown in the star-chart on the upcoming pages (page 219).

Before turning to that illustration, however, note also that the artist has included some soldiers casting lots for Christ's garment at the base of the cross, and to the right of the foot of the cross as we face it. One of these figures is depicted as naked, and in a prone position, highly suggestive of the posture of Scorpio in the heavens (beneath Ophiuchus, and opposite Sagittarius, just as the artist has indicated in the composition of the painting itself).

Chapter Eight

There is even a skull depicted in the painting, at the base of the cross and near the feet of the horse upon which the cavalier who is spearing Christ is seated. The inclusion of a skull near the foot of the cross is a common element in sacred art depicting the crucifixion (and the place where Christ is crucified is of course called Golgotha or Calvary, both of which words refer to a *skull*). Sometimes the skull is half-buried in the earth, such that only its dome-like crown and gaping eye-sockets are visible.

I have suggested that it is possible that this skull corresponds to the arc-shaped Southern Crown (or Corona Australis) which is located in the heavens near the feet of the constellation Sagittarius and in between Sagittarius and Scorpio -- just as the skull in the painting above by Maarten van Heemskerck is positioned at the feet of the horse of the Sagittarius-figure, and in between the Sagittarius-figure and the Scorpio-figure in the artwork.

On the page facing this one is a close-up view of the stars leading from Sagittarius to Ophiuchus, stars which can be (and evidently were) envisioned -- if connected in a line -- as forming the lance or spear with which the soldier in the gospel accounts pierces the side of Christ on the cross.

Although more evidence could be offered, this discussion should establish the very solid case for understanding the figure of Jesus as being closely connected to the constellation Ophiuchus. This association with Ophiuchus in no way invalidates the argument that Jesus is sometimes associated with Aquarius as well (such as in passages in which he refers to himself as the "son of Man" and describes separating the "sheep from the goats").

But it is very important to establish the correspondence between the figure of Jesus and the constellation Ophiuchus in the heavens, because as we will see, the constellation Ophiuchus plays an absolutely central role in the system of ancient myths when it comes to pointing us towards the recovery of our self and when it comes to bringing the "Thomas mind" under control.

"Reach hither thy finger . . . "

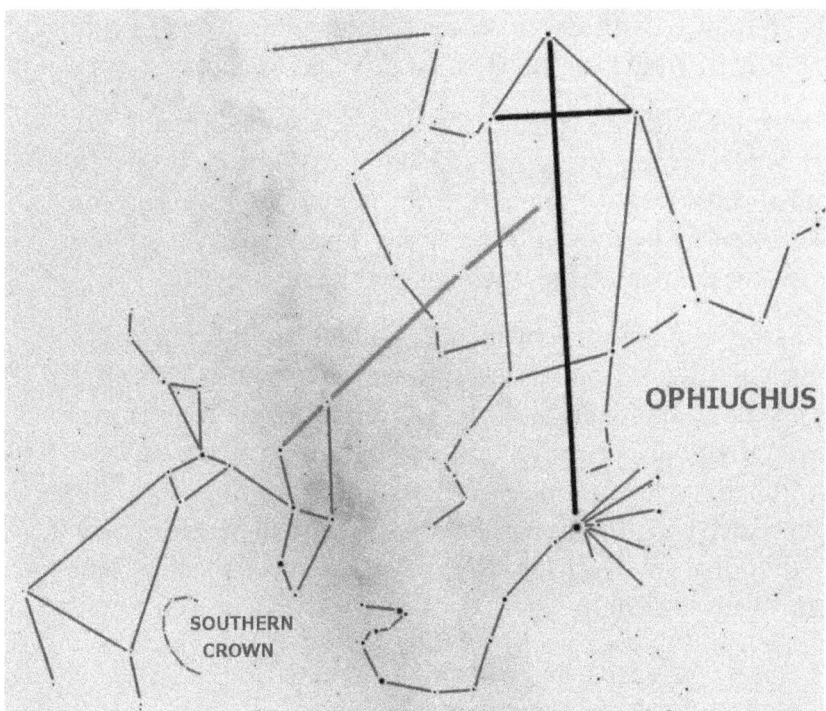

At the conclusion of the episode of Doubting Thomas, the text has Thomas exclaim, "My Lord and my God" (John 20: 28).

I would argue that what the text is illustrating is the restoration of the right relationship between the essential self and the egoic mind, in which the egoic mind is no longer trying to retain control (frantically gripping the steering wheel and refusing to let go) but has instead relinquished control and acknowledged the authentic self.

That acknowledgment was facilitated by bringing the focus to the very present moment ("reach hither thy finger . . . reach hither thy hand"), and by dealing with the egoic mind (the Thomas mind) in a patient and loving manner.

As we have already noted, we don't want to obliterate the egoic mind, or even its capacity to doubt and to look forward into the future and backward into the past -- but we also don't want it to take over the steering wheel and refuse to let go, while letting doubts "run away with us" (in effect driving the car over a cliff, which is exactly what runaway doubts can cause to happen).

The Doubting Thomas episode can thus be seen to contain very powerful and very positive lessons for our lives -- lessons having to do with the recovery of our self, from whom we have become divided (often without even realizing it). The deeper we go into this story, the deeper are the teachings that it offers.

But the story of Thomas is by no means unique in this regard. In fact, ancient myths from other cultures also convey powerful truths related to this same vital topic of repairing the trauma that divides us from our authentic self -- and because this subject is so vital to our lives today (trauma being, as Dr. Levine says, "the most untreated cause of human suffering"), we will briefly explore some additional myths in order to glean more of their ancient wisdom regarding the path to recovering our relationship with our higher self.

Chapter 9
The Master of the Chariot

As the sun rose on a certain morning in the days of ancient India, the approaching light was greeted by the sound of the drums and blowing conch-shells of the largest assembly of men-at-arms that the world had ever seen. The increasing light of day brought into view the golden armor of two enormous armies of warriors, facing one another across the field of Kurukshetra.

Facing towards the west was the Karauva army of Duryodhana the son of the ruling king Dhritarashtra, and on the other side of the battlefield and facing towards the east was assembled the Pandava army assembled and led by the five sons of Dhritarashtra's brother Pandu -- each vast host consisting of many hundreds of thousands of warriors, although the Kaurava army was larger and outnumbered the Pandava army by a ratio of eleven to seven, according to the Sanskrit texts of the ancient epic Mahabharata.[103]

The ancient text describes the sight of all the assembled ranks and their weapons -- lances, bows, swords, maces -- as the first rays of the sun and the great war-cars topped with umbrellas and pulled by teams of horses in which the kings and leaders of each division fought (though some of the leaders chose to ride into battle upon the necks of mighty elephants standing out like hills amid the sea of warriors) and clad in mail like great fish-nets, their trumpeting adding to the din of the beating drums and clanging of cymbals and weapons and the sounding of conch-shells.

The Mahabharata relates the scene through the words of Sanjaya, who travels back to describe to the acting king Dhritarashtra what takes place upon the battlefield: Dhritarashtra is blind, and his continued indulgence of his wicked son Duryodhana's repeated and ever-increasing injustices against the Pandava brothers is directly responsible for the approach of this cataclysmic battle at the field of Kurukshetra, which will bring

Chapter Nine

about the end of the lives of many on both sides, including some of the king's wisest and bravest counselors who have been warning Dhritarashtra that Duryodhana's arrogance and greed will inevitably lead to disaster.

Sanjaya says to Dhritarashtra (addressing him as "Bharata," the ancient name of the continent and ruling dynasty of India):

> When the night had passed away, loud became the noise made by the kings, all exclaiming 'Array! Array!' With the blare of conches and the sound of drums that resembled leonine roars, O Bharata, with the neigh of steeds, and the clatter of car-wheels, with the noise of obstreperous elephants and the shouts, clapping of arm-pits, and cries of roaring combatants, the din caused everywhere was very great. The large armies of the Kurus and the Pandavas, O king, rising at sunrise, completed all their arrangements. Then when the Sun rose, the fierce weapons of attack and defence and the coats of mail of both thy sons and the Pandavas, and the large and splendid armies of both sides, became fully visible. There elephants and cars, adorned with gold, looked resplendent like clouds mingled with lightning. The ranks of cars, standing in profusion, looked like cities. And thy father [referring to Bhishma, the most virtuous warrior of his generation, of unsurpassed prowess and moral character], stationed there, shone brilliantly, like the full moon. And the warriors armed with bows and swords and scimitars and maces, javelins and lances and bright weapons of diverse kinds, took up their positions in their respective ranks. And resplendent standards were seen, set up by thousands, of diverse forms, belonging to both ourselves and the foe. And made of gold and decked with gems and blazing like fire, those banners in thousands endued with great effulgence, looked beautiful like heroic combatants cased in mail [. . .].[104]

As the two armies begin to rumble towards one another, their leaders sounding great blasts on their conch-shells (some of these shells being so large and legendary that they have their own

The Master of the Chariot

names), arrows begin to fly through the air -- and suddenly, the great hero Arjuna, one of the five Pandava brothers and the most accomplished with all sorts of weapons -- requests of his charioteer to drive him out to the open field in between the two mighty armies.

Arjuna's charioteer is none other than the Lord Krishna himself, who (because of his love for both sides in the upcoming conflict) promised to participate in the battle for one side as a non-combatant charioteer, and to give a host of his invincible warriors to the other side. Krishna allowed Arjuna to choose whether he would prefer to have Krishna as a non-combatant on his side, or whether he would prefer the army of Krishna's warriors -- and Arjuna unhesitatingly chose Krishna himself (to the delight of his cousin Duryodhana, who preferred the host of warriors and would have chosen them had he been allowed to pick first).

Krishna complies with Arjuna's request and drives their war-car to the space in between the armies, where he can see the faces of those arrayed in battle on the other side (in Duryodhana's army), and at the sight of so many of his kinsmen and respected elders and teachers among the ranks of his adversaries, the text tells us that Arjuna is overcome with pity and grows despondent, and declares that he no longer wishes to fight, saying in part:

> "Beholding these kinsmen, O Krishna, assembled together and eager for the fight, my limbs become languid, and my mouth becomes dry. My body trembles, and my hair stands on end. Gandiva [the invincible bow of heaven, loaned to Arjuna for this battle] slips from my hand, and my skin burns. I am unable to stand; my mind seems to wander. [. . .] I do not desire victory, O Krishna, not sovereignty, nor pleasures. Of what use would sovereignty be to us, O Govinda, or enjoyments, or even life, since they, for whose sake sovereignty, enjoyments and pleasures are desired by us, are here arrayed for battle ready to give up life and wealth, *viz.* preceptors, sires, sons and grandsires, maternal uncles, father-in-laws, grandsons, brother-in-laws, and kinsmen. I wish not to slay these though

Chapter Nine

they slay me, O slayer of Madhu, even for the sake of the three worlds, what then for the sake of this earth? [. . .] Better would it be for me if the sons of Dhritarashtra, weapon in hand, should in battle slay me (myself) unavenging unarmed."[105]

Thus begins the section of the Mahabharata known as the Bhagavad Gita, the Song of the Lord (that is, the Song of the *Lord Krishna*), in which Krishna counsels Arjuna about how to act rightly in this world.

Before examining what Krishna has to say to Arjuna, let us note at the outset that we here have another case of a character in myth who is overcome by *doubt*.

It is not that Arjuna does not believe that his side can prevail in the upcoming battle: he has only recently been counseling his elder brother Yudhishthira on the fact that, just because the Pandavas have a smaller army than that of the Kauravas, this by no means indicates that their side will be defeated.

In that exchange, Arjuna tells Yudhishthira that "soldiers that are few in number may vanquish the many" and that victory actually belongs to the righteous, and to those with truth and compassion on their side, which describes the Pandavas as opposed to their wicked and unrighteous cousins. Arjuna ends by telling Yudhishthira:

> "For this know, O king, that to us victory is certain in (this) battle. Indeed, as Narada said, – There is victory where Krishna is. – Victory is inherent to Krishna."[106]

And, even more recently, the goddess Durga has appeared to Arjuna and Krishna, and has told Arjuna in so many words that:

> "Within a short time thou shalt conquer thy foes, O Pandava. O invincible one, thou hast Narayana [that is, Vishnu – and Krishna is himself an avatar of Vishnu] for aiding thee. Thou art incapable of being defeated by foes, even by the wielder of the thunderbolt himself."[107]

The Master of the Chariot

Thus, Arjuna is not despondent because of fear for his own life or fear for the outcome of the battle. Rather, he is in a state of doubt and despair because he is not sure if what he is doing is the right course of action, and because he is anticipating the negative results that will come about when he and his companions are victorious in the upcoming fight.

From this starting point, Krishna proceeds to counsel the doubting Arjuna in a long dialogue filled with various illustrations and principles, having at its core a concept which preeminent scholar of East Asian languages and literature, Professor Victor H. Mair of the University of Pennsylvania, regards as being present at the heart of the Tao Te Ching as well. Professor Mair writes:

> When the two armies draw up their ranks and face off, Arjuna becomes depressed at the thought of having to fight against many of his acquaintances and relatives who are in the opposing camp. He questions whether he should throw away his weapons and submit to a sure death or participate in a war that, no matter how just, is certain to result in much slaughter. Krishna reminds him that it is his duty to be a warrior and embarks upon a long discourse on action.
>
> The chief lesson Krishna has to offer Arjuna is that altruistic or disinterested action (*niṣkāma karma*) leads to realization of Brahma. That is to say, one should act without regard or desire for the fruits (*phala*) of one's action. This idea is repeated over and over again in countless different formulations. These passages are of great importance for understanding the enigmatic concept of "nonaction" that is so prominent in the *Tao Te Ching*. "The person of superior integrity takes no action," says the Old Master, "nor has he a purpose for acting." We are told straightaway to "act through nonaction" and that "through nonaction, no action is left undone." [108]

Chapter Nine

Note carefully the language of the Tao Te Ching itself, translated and quoted here by Professor Mair: "the person of *superior integrity*."

The word *integrity* implies a lack of division: a unity, a wholeness. In English, an *integer* is a whole number, one that is not fractionated.

As we have been discussing, trauma *divides* us -- from nature, from other men and women, and most importantly from ourselves. If we are divided against ourselves, we cannot be described as being whole -- rather, we are fragmented, like a fraction in mathematics.

In the Doubting Thomas account from the Gospel according to John we examined previously, when Jesus appears, the first thing he says (both times) is: "Peace unto you." The story is clearly about healing the division within ourselves: this salutation spoken by the figure of Jesus in the story reveals that the story is about repairing that fractionated state in which we find ourselves when we are divided from who we are.

The Tao Te Ching places a great deal of importance upon this state of wholeness and lack of division: Professor Mair argues that the concept of integrity is so central to the Tao Te Ching that the title of the text itself should rightly be translated as *The Classic Book of Integrity and the Way* (with the word *Tao* or *Dao* meaning "way" or "road," the word *Te* or *De* [pronounced "duh"] properly understood as signifying "integrity," and the word *Ching* or *Jing* signifying a "classic book").[109]

In the quotation cited above, Professor Mair argues that the central message of Krishna to Arjuna during Arjuna's moment of crisis and doubt at the start of the battle of Kurukshetra is very much the same message as that given in the first chapter of the Tao Te Ching (as arranged in the most ancient Ma Wang Dui silk manuscripts, uncovered in an ancient tomb in central China in 1973, an arrangement that differs from later texts of the Tao Te Ching, such that the first chapter in the Ma Wang Dui

The Master of the Chariot

manuscripts is the chapter normally numbered 38 in later arrangements). Krishna informs Arjuna that he should perform what is his duty with absolutely no regard for the outcome of the action -- and in doing so, he will act as if he is not even acting, and thus he will be without division (and thus, he will be integrated, whole, and single in unity). Krishna says:

> Regarding pleasure and pain, gain and loss, victory and defeat as equal, do battle for battle's sake and sin will not be thine. This knowledge, that hath been communicated to thee, is (taught) in the *Sankhya* (system). Listen now to that (inculcated) in the *Yoga* (system). Possessed of that knowledge, thou, O Partha, wilt cast off the bonds of action. In this (the *Yoga* system) there is no waste of even the first attempt. There are no impediments. Even a little of this piety delivers from great fear. Here in this path, O son of Kuru, there is only one state of mind, consisting in firm devotion. The minds of those, however, that are not firmly devoted are many-branched and attached to endless pursuits. [. . .] Thy concern is with work only, but not with the fruit (of work). Let not the fruit be thy motive for work; nor let thy inclination be for inaction. Staying in devotion, apply thyself to work, casting off attachment, O Dhananjaya, and being the same in success or unsuccess. This equanimity is called *Yoga*.[110]

By acting without attachment, Krishna advises Arjuna, one actually casts off or escapes "the bonds of action." One with such detachment acts as though he is not even acting, with an equanimity that is unconcerned with success or unsuccess. Thus, he is not wracked with doubt!

Since doubt is a casting forward of the mind in order to try to weigh the relative chances of success or failure, detachment from the outcome enables us to escape from doubt and self-division, remaining in the present moment (as Krishna says: "Staying in devotion, *apply thyself* to work, casting off attachment," implying that the focus is on the work of the moment and not attachment to the future outcome).

Chapter Nine

In this state, Krishna explains, "there is only one state of mind" -- instead of being divided against ourselves, we are unified! In contrast, however, Krishna says that those who do not have this condition are "many-branched" (a condition all of us probably recognize, if we are possessed of a Thomas mind, a doubting mind, an egoic mind). They are "attached to endless pursuits" (one way of interpreting this description might be: their mind pursues endless possible outcomes).

In other words, both the Tao Te Ching and the Bhagavad Gita are showing us that the remedy for the "many-branched" and divided state in which we find ourselves is *integrity*, and that this integrity comes from *detachment* to the outcome (detachment from the "endless pursuits" which the egoic mind always chases). Then, we act as if not acting at all -- action and non-action become identical.

So the texts clearly support Professor Mair in his assertion of a deep connection between the message of the Tao Te Ching and the Bhagavad Gita -- an assertion which comes from one who is intimately familiar with both ancient texts. Professor Mair writes: "Having read both of them in their original languages repeatedly and attentively over the past two decades, I have come to believe that they are connected in an essential way." [III]

I would add that there appears to be a connection to the message of the Doubting Thomas episode as well -- a connection having to do with healing the schism which we find within ourselves (if we are disconnected from our essential self). The Bhagavad Gita is pointing us towards the way to become whole again.

It is not a story about something that happened to someone else, far removed from us, on a battlefield far away in a distant century that has now receded far into the past: this story is about us, each one of us. And we can be quite certain that this is a metaphorical story which is not about some literal ancient event but which is intended to illustrate profound truths about our own situation right now, because as with every other myth we have examined in

The Master of the Chariot

this volume, this critical episode in the Mahabharata of ancient India can be seen to be based on the constellations of the night sky.

As I demonstrate at some length in my 2019 book *The Ancient World-Wide System: Star Myths of the World, Volume One (Second Edition)*, the Lord Krishna is one of the avatars of the god Vishnu, and can be conclusively shown by an abundance of evidence to be most closely associated with the constellation Ophiuchus in the night sky -- as can Vishnu himself.

The god Vishnu is often described as reclining upon a great many-headed cobra, and as having a lotus-flower growing from his navel, and those who have read all of the analysis in the previous chapters should immediately be able to see how these characteristics describe the constellation Ophiuchus, which "rests upon" Scorpio in the heavens:

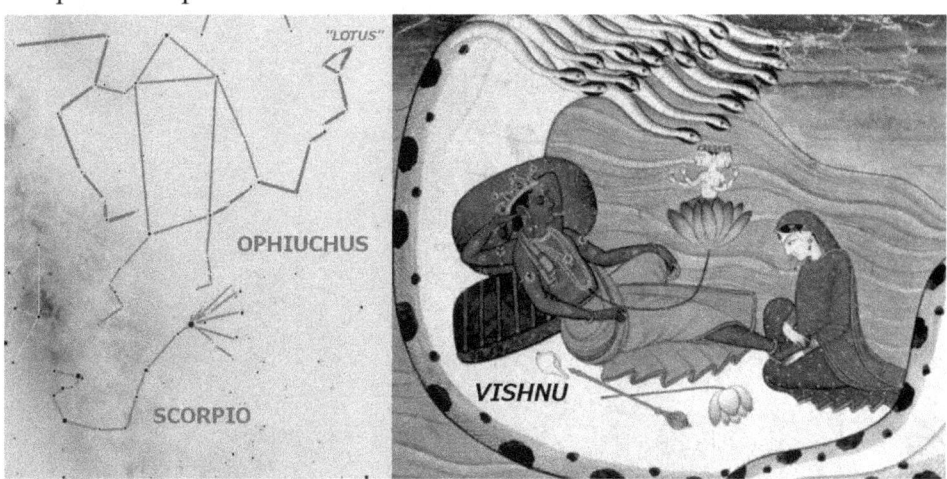

The "lotus" that grows from the navel of Vishnu is the "serpent-half" on the right of the central body of Ophiuchus as we face the star-chart above, and Scorpio plays the many-headed cobra (who is known as the Shesha Naga in the ancient Sanskrit texts).

Krishna, who (as mentioned) is an avatar of Vishnu, is primarily associated with the same constellation Ophiuchus in the night sky (the celestial identity of other avatars of Vishnu is explored in

Chapter Nine

more detail in *The Ancient World-Wide System*). The celestial feature that becomes the lotus growing from the navel of Vishnu (when Ophiuchus is envisioned as Vishnu) becomes the great conch-shell which Krishna blows when he acts as the charioteer of Arjuna before the great battle of Kurukshetra. The other "serpent-half" of the constellation Ophiuchus (on the opposite side of the central body of the constellation from the "head-end" of the serpent which plays the role of the lotus) becomes the distinctive flute of the Lord Krishna, which is one of his most well-known characteristics in artistic representation:

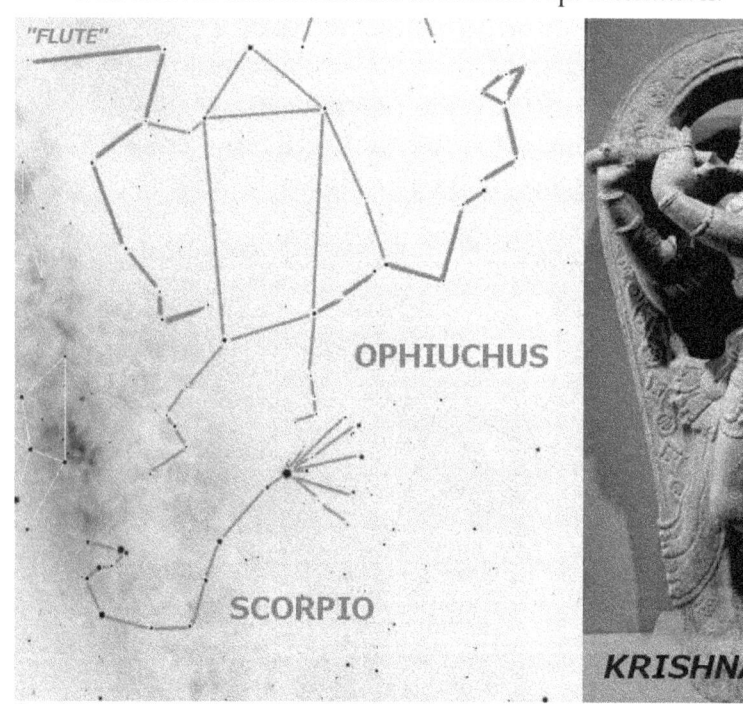

In the tremendous battle of Kurukshetra, the Lord Krishna volunteers to act as Arjuna's noncombatant charioteer during the conflict. As we have already seen, the most prominent leaders on either side generally ride into battle in their "war-cars" -- which consist of a kind of wagon with four wheels, drawn by a team of horses, and usually with a kind of canopy or "umbrella" over the top, as shown in many artistic depictions such as in the image to the right.

The Master of the Chariot

The above scene is actually a depiction of the war-car of Arjuna and Krishna in the scene we have been discussing. Arjuna has dismounted and is standing in front of the team of horses, facing the charioteer who is the Lord Krishna, with his hands in the *anjali mudra* position (the hand mudra which is customarily used with the *namaskaram* and which indicates a recognition of divinity).

Note that Arjuna's bow and arrows can be seen on the ground beside him in the above illustration. Arjuna's characteristic weapon is the bow, and for this battle he has been given the illustrious bow named Gandiva -- but in his despondency before the battle he says he wants to just put his weapons on the ground and wait for death, rather than slay his friends, relatives, and respected teachers.

The team of four horses is harnessed to the war-car, which is depicted as a four-wheeled wagon with a canopy above. At the front of this canopy, we see the god Hanuman holding the banner of the war-car: the text of the Mahabharata informs us that the banner on Arjuna's war-car depicts Hanuman, and that in fact the

Chapter Nine

god Hanuman himself is present above the war-car, and roars forth when Krishna sounds his conch.

Note that Hanuman in the above illustration is holding his customary weapon over one shoulder -- his great mace. From this favored weapon, and from other characteristics of Hanuman, we can see that this god can be confidently associated with the constellation Hercules. Arjuna's brother Bhima, who also carries a mace and who has many of the same characteristics as the hero Heracles (such as tremendous strength, and a propensity to uproot trees and use them as a club), is also clearly associated with the constellation Hercules -- and at one point in the epic of the Mahabharata, we learn that Bhima and Hanuman are actually half-brothers, which adds further confirmation for our identification of Hanuman and the constellation Hercules.

The fact that Hanuman (associated with the constellation Hercules) appears at the top of the war-car of Arjuna and Krishna is a clue which helps us understand that this war-car is in fact associated with the constellation Ophiuchus. Note the shape of the central body of Ophiuchus: this shape, I have argued in previous writings, inspires the characterstic war-cars of ancient Indian myth, complete with their distinctive canopies or "umbrellas" above the cart itself.

Note that we have already seen the constellations in this part of the sky playing the role of a chariot, in the artwork on a vase from ancient Greece depicting Achilles dragging the body of the slain hero Hector of Troy, on page 62.

In this famous episode from the Mahabharata (which sets the scene for the Bhagavad Gita), I believe that Ophiuchus (which is also associated with the Lord Krishna himself) plays the role of the war-car of Arjuna, and the god Hanuman (above the war-car) corresponds to the constellation Hercules. Arjuna almost certainly corresponds to the constellation Sagittarius, which can be seen in the heavens to carry a massive bow.

The Master of the Chariot

Much more could be said about the celestial correspondences of this particular scene, but the most important points to note for our discussion here regarding the recovery of the relationship with the higher self is the fact that Krishna can clearly be seen to be associated with the constellation Ophiuchus, and that the image of a war-car or chariot pulled by horses functions in ancient Sanskrit sacred texts as a metaphor for the mind-body connection.

For example, in the text of the Katha Upanishad (also referred to as the *Kathopanishad*), we find the following teaching -- given by the person of the god Yama, lord of death, himself:

> Many there are who do not even hear of Atman; though hearing of Him, many do not comprehend. Wonderful is the expounder and rare the hearer; rare indeed is the experiencer of Atman taught by an able preceptor.
>
> Atman, when taught by an inferior person, is not easily comprehended, because It is diversely regarded by disputants. But when It is taught by him who has become one with Atman, there can remain no more doubt about it. Atman is subtler than the subtlest and not to be known through argument.

Chapter Nine

> This Knowledge cannot be attained by reasoning. [...]
>
> Atman, smaller than the small, greater than the great, is hidden in the hearts of all living creatures. A man who is free from desires beholds the majesty of the Self through tranquility of the senses and the mind and becomes free from grief.
>
> Though sitting still, It travels far; though lying down, It goes everywhere. [...]
>
> Know the atman to be the master of the chariot; the body, the chariot; the intellect, the charioteer; and the mind, the reins.
>
> The senses, they say, are the horses; the objects, the roads. The wise call the atman -- united with the body, the senses and the mind – the enjoyer.
>
> If the buddhi, being related to a mind that is always distracted, loses its determinations, then the senses become uncontrolled, like the vicious horses of a charioteer.
>
> But if the buddhi, being related to a mind that is always restrained, possesses discrimination, then the senses come under control, like the good horses of a charioteer.
>
> If the buddhi, being related to a distracted mind, loses its discrimination and therefore always remains impure, then the embodied soul never attains the goal, but enters into the round of births.
>
> But if the buddhi, being related to a mind that is restrained, possesses discrimination and therefore always remains pure, then the embodied soul attains that goal from which he is not born again.[112]

This passage from the Katha Upanishad contains profound truths for our understanding of the reconnection with our authentic self – and for our understanding of the message of the Bhagavad Gita.

First, we see once again the assertion that many are not even aware of the existence of the higher self: Yama explains that "many there are who do not even hear of Atman." When we hear someone talking about the authentic self, the higher self, the divine self, we are initially doubtful as to the existence of such a concept. We are so disconnected from our authentic self, and we identify so completely with our egoic mind, that we actually believe our egoic mind is who we are, and are skeptical of the very existence of our authentic self!

Flip back to the earlier definition of trauma (a loss of connection to ourselves) given by Dr. Peter Levine in his book *Healing Trauma*, quoted on page 184 of this volume, and note that he says: "This loss of connection is often hard to recognize, because it doesn't happen all at once. It can happen slowly, over time, and we adapt to these subtle changes without even noticing them." We adapt to the gradual loss of our connection with our essential, authentic self and in the end we *do not even notice* what we have lost!

It is a horrifying assertion -- but one which Dr. Gabor Maté also confirms from his extensive personal experience working with adults who have experienced severe trauma. Our egoic mind, which functions as a coping mechanism, does not even want us to be aware of the self from whom we have become alienated (this lack of awareness, this willful forgetting, being another aspect of the coping mechanism). In fact, it does its best to suppress the full import of the rejection (or perceived rejection) that led to the psychic wounding that caused the disconnection from the self.

In an interview with Dr. Maté conducted by Dr. Rangan Chatterjee of the *Feel Better Live More* podcast published on November 21, 2018, discussing a woman who attended one of Dr. Maté's lectures and who publicly objected to his assertion that *all* those with addictions must have suffered from trauma during childhood (because she had suffered from addiction but had had a "perfectly happy" childhood), Dr. Maté says:

> Well, that confidence itself is a giveaway, because it's an assumed stance to protect herself from the pain that she doesn't want to feel, or she's afraid to feel. So she says, "Well,

Chapter Nine

maybe I felt I was intruding on my parents." In other words, really what she felt was that she wasn't accepted and loved for who she was, and when she felt unhappy, there was nobody for her to talk to. And all you have to do is ask that person, "If your own child did the same thing, how would you understand it?" And they totally get it. So, what's going on there -- she's not lying. But believing that she had a happy childhood was her way of dealing with her pain. Because if she dropped that idea, she'd have to realize that she suffered, and she actually, as much as her parents did their best and loved her -- we're not blaming the parents -- but she herself got the impression that she was alone and unsupported and unloved for who she was. Well, that's very painful. So, we defend against the pain by suppressing those emotions, and developing this ideology of the happy childhood. And so that's just another form of self-defense. And then, given her ideology that she had a happy childhood, she can't understand why she turned to an addiction. But once she gets that, "Yeah, OK, that belief that I was happy denies the fact that I was feeling isolated and alone, and I felt myself as an intrusion on my parents," now she can understand what her pain was. But not feeling that pain was how she survived her childhood -- because as a child, how would she survive if she believed that she wasn't loved for who she was? Life would be intolerable for her. So she has to deny and suppress that. [. . .] So that suppression of her pain, and denial of it, is a completely appropriate defensive response. These are not "mistakes" that we make: these are essential survival adaptations. The problem is -- then, because we learned how to ignore our feelings as children, now we learn to ignore them for the rest of our lives, and *that* then creates problems for us. So, again, it's that whole idea of an early adaptation -- essential adaptation, brilliant adaptation -- but because it's subconscious, it stays with us, and now it limits our lives. So we become imprisoned with our own adaptations. Our childhood patterns become the prison through which we live our lives."[113]

The Master of the Chariot

This powerful and lucid explanation by Dr. Maté demonstrates the mechanism by which our egoic mind (which itself is a defense response, a survival adaptation) tends to suppress and deny the very trauma and sense of betrayal and rejection which led to the disconnection from the essential self. We often reject the very idea of the existence of an essential self, because we wish to protect ourselves from the admission of the import of the trauma we experienced that caused us to disconnect from the essential self in the first place.

Thus, the god Yama in the Katha Upanishad declares: "Many there are who do not even hear of Atman; though hearing of Him, many do not comprehend." The majority of us, even having experienced trauma and the loss of our essential self, do not know it -- and if we do hear about it, we don't understand.

This assertion by the god Yama echoes an assertion by Jesus in the passage from the Book of Thomas the Contender, cited earlier, in which Jesus says to Thomas: "Since you will be called my brother, it is not fitting that you be ignorant of yourself." We should not be ignorant of our authentic self -- it is not fitting for us to deny and suppress our own self -- and yet this self-imposed ignorance is an extremely common and completely understandable by-product of the trauma that caused us to sever communications with our essential self in the first place (completely understandable in light of the chain of reasoning elucidated by Dr. Gabor Maté in the quotation given above).

The Katha Upanishad in the above passage as translated does not use the word "self" but rather the Sanskrit word *atman*, which literally means "self" but which is employed in the ancient Sanskrit texts including the Upanishads to convey a deeper concept which cannot be easily defined in a few words but which is closely related to the same concept that this book is trying to convey using the terms *essence* or *higher self* or *divine nature*.

A different translation of the passage cited above has the god of death expressing it this way:

Chapter Nine

> Concealed in the heart of all beings is the Atman, the Spirit, the Self; smaller than the smallest atom, greater than the vast spaces.[114]

This divine nature concealed in the heart of all beings is connected to -- is in fact part of -- the infinite divine, or the Brahman, as we are told in the Mandukya Upanishad, which declares: "Brahman is all and Atman is Brahman."[115]

In a lecture entitled "Psychedelics and Unlocking the Unconscious: from Cancer to Addiction," given on April 20, 2013 in Oakland, California, Dr. Gabor Maté made a very similar assertion regarding the connection (and ultimately the *identity* or the *unity*) between the essential self and the wider world around us, saying:

> What if, furthermore, we understood something in the West, which has been the underlying core insight of Eastern spiritual pathways and Aboriginal shamanic pathways around the world, which is that human beings are not their personalities, we're not our thoughts, we're not our emotions, we are not our dysfunctional -- or functional -- dynamics: but at the core there is a *true self* that's somehow connected to, in fact not *connected to* but *part of,* nature and creation? And that illness, from that perspective, represents a loss of that connection: a loss of that unity, a loss of that *belonging to* a much larger entity? And that therefore to treat the illness, or the symptom, as *the problem,* is actually to ignore the real possibility that the symptom or the illness are themselves symptoms rather than the fundamental problems?[116]

This teaching of a deep connection or even unity between the true self and the wider realm of nature and creation is astonishing, because we are taught through years and years of schooling and related indoctrination, that such connection is impossible and unscientific, and that those who give any credence to such an idea are either naïve, gullible, superstitious, misguided, ignorant, or otherwise wrong. But there can be little disagreement that the

The Master of the Chariot

ancient myths and scriptures of humanity, including the Upanishads quoted above, teach just such a profound connectedness between higher self and wider cosmos, and we shall have more to say on this subject in a later chapter.

Clearly, the passage in the Katha Upanishad spoken by the god Yama and quoted above has to do with the essential self -- with the Atman who resides, concealed, in the heart of all beings, and who is both smaller than the smallest atom and greater than the vast spaces, and who is part of the undifferentiated spirit of the entire universe itself.

And the illustration that the god Yama provides to help us to understand the Atman is the illustration of the "master of the chariot."

We are told that the body itself in this illustration is the chariot, and that the powerful horses are the senses, which pull the body towards its desired object.

In this illustration, the mind is identified with the reins which are supposed to steer and control these horses.

This identification of the mind with the reins is extremely significant, because if we think about this metaphor at all, we immediately realize that the ancient scriptures are here informing us that there must be *something else* behind the mind (because reins don't hold themselves).

In other words, the mind is *part* of the picture (an important part of the picture), but by no means the totality of "who we are." And yet we typically identify so strongly with the mind that most of us are unaware of the existence of the one who is identified as the proper "master of the chariot."

There is much more to learn from the Katha Upanishad, but we will point out just one other notable aspect relative to the subject of trauma, and that is the fact that the speech given by the dreaded god Yama cited above is given to a youth named Nachiketa (also sometimes spelled *Naciketa* or *Naciketas*),

Chapter Nine

whose father at the beginning of the story is diligently performing a complicated *yaaga* ritual, which includes conducting fire sacrifices and oblations to different gods, and the giving of certain gifts to members of the community. During his father's performance of this ritual, Nachiketa keeps asking to whom his father wants to give *him* as a gift, seeing as he is giving away a great many cows and other items of value.

Frustrated and concerned that he might perform an error during the *yaaga*, and annoyed at his son's continued repetition of the same question, Nachiketa's father exclaims, "I will give you to Yama!" And so, Nachiketa makes his way to the realm of the dreaded god of death.

When he arrives at the home of Yama, however, the god is not at home, and so Nachiketa waits there for Yama's return, and he waits for three days without tasting so much as a grain of food for sustenance. When the god of death finally returns home, he is shocked to find the young Nachiketa waiting there, having had no food for three days (a serious breach of hospitality), and he apologizes to Nachiketa, offering to grant the youth three boons (three wishes).

For his very first boon, Nachiketa asks Yama to cause his father's anger with Nachiketa to be assuaged, along with any distress regarding Nachiketa's absence and sojourn within the realm of the god of death, and asks that when Nachiketa returns home his father would receive him with joy.

Is it not significant that this Upanishad, containing the profound teaching regarding the nature of the higher self (particularly in the form of this metaphor of the chariot and the master of the chariot, to which we shall return momentarily), begins with a story of a father's unthinking curse of his son, in a moment of anger and frustration, and that the first wish of that son is for reconciliation with his father, and that his father would receive him back?

Is it too much of a stretch to ask if this ancient text (one of the most well-known of all the Upanishads) is not here dramatizing

The Master of the Chariot

the very same pattern of childhood trauma that Dr. Gabor Maté described in the conversation he had with Dr. Rangan Chatterjee, regarding a woman who upon reflection realizes that as a child she felt she was an intrusion into the lives of her parents?

It's not that Nachiketa's father doesn't love his son -- but he is too busy to address his son's concern that maybe he too will be given away along with the cows. Nachiketa's father is too caught up in the external duties of the *yaaga* ritual, and he explodes in anger at Nachiketa instead of addressing the boy's concern.

The narrative frame of the story certainly suggests that the ancients understood the phenomenon we today are calling psychological trauma -- and that the ancient myths are addressing that problem and teaching us the way to repair the disconnection that results from trauma.

And, as we have seen, the teaching in the Katha Upanishad on this subject, as related by the god Yama to Nachiketa, involves (first) becoming aware of the very existence of the essence or Atman, of which we are often unaware, due to our identification with the egoic mind (the very egoic mind which, as part of its coping strategy, wants to suppress even the awareness of the fact that we have suffered trauma and have severed our connection to our true self).

Then, Yama offers the powerful metaphor of the chariot, in which the horses are the senses, and the mind is the reins, and the Atman is the "master of the chariot."

Turning now once again to the Bhagavad Gita (one of the most beloved and widely-read of the world's surviving ancient scriptures), we can now apply our understanding of the metaphor of the chariot and perceive some new insights regarding the teaching of the ancient myths on the subject of the healing of trauma.

In the preceding discussion of the encounter between Jesus and Doubting Thomas in the gospel story, I argued that Jesus in that

Chapter Nine

episode represents the essence, the higher self, and Thomas represents the egoic mind. I supported this argument, in part, by pointing to the fact that Thomas is specifically "called Didymus" ("the twin") and that elsewhere (in the Book of Thomas, for example) Jesus refers to Thomas as *his* twin -- matching a pattern we see in many other examples from myths around the world in which one twin is divine and the other twin is mortal (such as the story of Castor and Polydeuces, in which Zeus is the father of Polydeuces but not of Castor).

Based on that analysis of the Thomas story, we can see some very strong parallels in the story of "doubting Arjuna" at the beginning of the Bhagavad Gita -- and I believe a very compelling case can be argued that in this episode from ancient myth, the god Krishna is representative of the essence or higher self, and Arjuna represents the egoic mind.

Based on this understanding, we can now perceive the profound teaching that the ancient myths are dramatizing when they make Krishna the noncombatant charioteer for Arjuna in the great battle of Kurukshetra: we are here seeing an illustration of giving the reins to the essential and authentic self!

The typical arrangement is for the egoic mind to refuse to give up control -- to resist, in fact, any suggestion of the existence of the authentic self (let alone any suggestion that the authentic self should be driving). Like Denethor in Tolkien's *Lord of the Rings*, who is only the temporary *steward* of Gondor but who over time grows so used to power that he refuses to acknowledge the return of the true king, the egoic mind grows so enamored with the job it is doing of "protecting us" that it doesn't want to relinquish control to the real master of the chariot.

But in the Doubting Thomas story, at the conclusion of the episode we witness the recognition by the egoic self of the return of the one who has been buried and presumed lost forever -- and the exclamation by Thomas to Jesus, "My Lord and my God."

The Master of the Chariot

Similarly, in the depictions of the scene of Arjuna and Krishna in the Bhagavad Gita, Krishna is almost invariably depicted as holding the reins of the chariot, and Arjuna is almost invariably depicted performing the *anjali mudra*, acknowledging the divinity of Krishna.

Below is the same illustration of the chariot presented earlier, but this time with labels added corresponding to the metaphorical interpretation given in the Katha Upanishad:

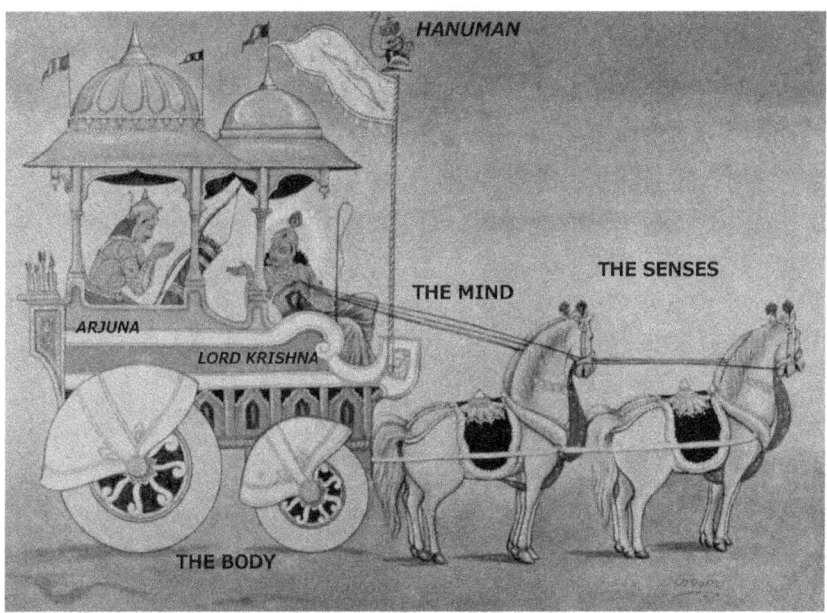

In the illustration, we see Arjuna acknowledging the divinity of Krishna (as indicated by his palms folded in the *anjali mudra*), just as Thomas finally acknowledges the divinity of Christ in the episode from the Gospel according to John. The higher self, the authentic self, the divine self -- represented by the Lord Krishna in the Bhagavad Gita and by the risen Jesus in the episode of Doubting Thomas -- is our connection to the divine realm. Indeed, as the Mandukya Upanishad teaches us in the verse quoted earlier, "Brahman is all and Atman is Brahman."

This picture dramatizes the right relationship between our egoic self and our authentic self: the higher self is holding the reins.

Chapter Nine

As the god Yama explains in the Katha Upanishad, "If the buddhi [the seeker after enlightenment], being related to a mind that is always distracted, loses its determinations, then the senses become uncontrolled, like the vicious horses of a charioteer."

The egoic mind is basically *always distracted*: as Dr. Maté asserts in the speech cited earlier, just about anything is more tolerable to the egoic mind than is the prospect of *remaining in the present moment*. Recall his explanation: "When the present moment hurt you so much that you became afraid of it, then your whole mind will be oriented towards escaping the present moment -- escaping it by any means possible."

Thus, if we understand that the egoic mind arises as a coping mechanism for dealing with trauma, and that part of its defense strategy involves disconnecting from the present moment, then we understand that if we let the egoic mind "steer the chariot," we are handing the reins to the "mind that is always distracted" (the condition of being distracted, by definition, refers to *lack of presence* in the moment). Permitting the reins to stay with the egoic mind, which is always distracted, results in the horses being uncontrolled, "like the vicious horses of a charioteer."

The solution is to acknowledge the essential self (dramataized by Arjuna's recognition of Krishna's divinity, shown in his posture and folded palms) and let our essence, our authentic self, take the reins. Doing so does not imply the obliteration of the mind (we do not see Krishna banishing or destroying Arjuna for his doubts, any more than we saw Christ banishing or destroying Thomas for his): the goal is to restore the right relationship between the mind (with its propensity to cast forward into the future or back into the past -- a necessary capability, but one that can crash our chariot if we let this ability "run away with us") and the authentic self.

On the contrary, rather than banishing or obliterating the egoic mind, the essential self treats the mind with patience, with compassion, and with love. We see this important lesson being dramatized in both the Doubting Thomas episode and the Doubting Arjuna episode from the sacred texts of two very different cultures. And we see the importance of this approach being emphasized in the teaching of Dr. Maté and other contemporary healers and psychologists.

In an interview with Eric Zimmer, host of a podcast entitled *The One You Feed*, published on October 16, 2018, Dr. Maté says the following regarding the importance of compassion, and of understanding that the essential self has compassion towards the egoic mind, within the larger context of the relationship between the egoic mind and the essential self in our day-to-day (and even minute-to-minute) life:

> People who are not conscious simply have no freedom. They may *believe* they do, but they don't make decisions. The decisions are made for them by automatic, emotional reactions that are the result of early experiences.

> So, as an Austrian-Swiss, or German-Swiss, writer and psychologist called Alice Miller, who was one of the first ones who wrote about the impact of childhood trauma on adult dysfunction -- and her most famous book is called *The Drama of the Gifted Child*, but the original title, or the German title, of that book is actually much better: it was called *Prisoners of Childhood*. And what she was implying was that, until we are aware and create some gap between our emotional reactions and our behavior, we're actually held prisoner by what happened to us in childhood.

> And I find myself, at age 72, still very often reacting like I was a two-year-old child, unless I create that gap of consciousness, in which I have a moment to reflect upon and make a conscious decision. And in our society, which makes us unconscious in so many ways, that's constant work -- for most of us, I would say -- that's significant *work*. And that's why I think so many people are increasingly drawn to practices that support mindful

Chapter Nine

awareness – because they just want to be free! They don't want to be automatons.

And even for me, as a middle-class successful person, I cannot claim freedom as long as my reactions and behaviors and preferences are governed by unconscious factors that come out of a childhood sense of insufficiency that goes back to my first year of life. [. . .]

So this constant question of "Who do I think I am?" – it needs to come up at every moment, almost. Where am I coming from at this particular moment? And just because I answer the question appropriately one time, it doesn't mean that five minutes later the same question does not arise again in a different way.

So that awareness -- and ultimately, I think, whatever people have to do to overcome their addiction, I would say, first of all: Get in touch with your pain – don't run away from your pain. Your whole addiction is an attempt to run away from pain. And it just creates more pain. So don't be afraid of it.

And if you're one of these people that you think you had a really happy childhood? If you're addicted, that tells me you didn't. Which doesn't mean that happy things didn't happen. It just means that you've repressed, you haven't dealt with, you haven't allowed yourself to experience, the child's feelings that you distanced yourself from, as a way of surviving it.

So be aware of your pain, and get some help with it. And have compassion for yourself. Don't judge yourself. Metaphorically, it's fine to talk about the "bad wolf" -- but don't reject the "bad wolf" part of you: have compassion for it. Understand that it came along, really, to meet needs that otherwise were not being met.

And then, create that gap of awareness, of mindfulness, that you and I were talking about, in which you can make *free* choices to feed that "good wolf." [117]

The Master of the Chariot

This incredibly important and helpful segment from that interview published in 2018 sheds a great deal of light upon the profound message (or at least, upon one particular aspect of the profound message, and an aspect with tremendous importance to our lives in the world in which we find ourselves living) of the scene from the Bhagavad Gita that we have been exploring.

Taking the liberty to rephrase some of the powerful assertions which Dr. Maté makes in the quoted passage into the metaphor of the myth episode, in which (using the metaphor provided by Lord Yama in the Katha Upanishad) we understand the chariot to represent the body and the horses to represent the senses and emotions, and in which (using our understanding of the similar episode in the Gospel according to John examined previously) we understand "Doubting Arjuna" to be dramatizing our egoic mind while the Lord Krishna represents the essential self, the authentic self, and the divine self, we might say:

> People who are not conscious -- whose egoic mind refuses to let go of the reins -- simply have no freedom. They may *believe* that they do -- they may believe that they are making decisions, but they don't make decisions: their egoic mind, which arose as a defense mechanism or a coping mechanism due to early childhood experiences, is making emotional, automatic reactions based on a kind of "security program" that was written decades earlier. If the egoic mind is driving the chariot, then the horses are actually "uncontrolled, like the vicious horses of a charioteer," to quote the Katha Upanishad -- because the egoic mind is more of a mechanism, a kind of computer program, an algorithm.
>
> So this question which we should constantly ask ourselves, the question of "Who do I think I am?" could be rephrased in terms of the ancient metaphor as a different question: the question of, "Who is driving the chariot right now?"
>
> Is the egoic mind, the doubting mind, gripping the reins with a death-like grip, in the belief that it is the only one who can

save us? Or can we, like Arjuna in the illustration, hand the reins over to the higher self, while making the gesture of the *anjali mudra* in recognition of Krishna? Wouldn't we really prefer to have our essential self steering the chariot and guiding our decisions of who we want to be, rather than trusting our journey to some decades-old algorithm that was developed and coded during our childhood trauma, a long-obsolete defense program from an almost-forgotten past?

And, just because we answer those questions appropriately one time, it doesn't mean that five minutes later the same question doesn't arise again in a different way. Just because our egoic mind, our doubting mind, is able to turn over the reins to our higher self one moment, like Arjuna giving the reins to Krishna, doesn't mean that the next moment the egoic mind won't grab the reins again and start to implement the old algorithms.

So the path to defusing that old defense mechanism is to recognize and become aware of the pain that created it, so that when it breaks in and tries to grab the reins, we can understand what long-ago traumatic feelings it is reacting to, and which are causing it to leap into action.

So we have to get in touch with our pain, rather than trying to run away from that pain, trying to suppress that pain, trying to tell ourselves that it never happened, because if we do that then it will be much more difficult to recognize what is causing the egoic mind to want to grab the reins whenever it thinks it is seeing the same conditions that led to its creation in the first place. Because, again, people who are not conscious simply have no freedom.

So be aware of your pain, and get some help with it. And have compassion on your egoic mind: have some compassion for your "Arjuna mind," for your "Thomas mind," in the same way that Krishna and Jesus demonstrated compassion for Arjuna and for Thomas.

The Master of the Chariot

But don't reject the "Doubting Thomas" or the "Doubting Arjuna" part of yourself: understand that it came along, really, to meet the needs that were not being met.

And then, create that gap of awareness, that mindfulness, that allows you to hand the reins to Krishna, to turn over your chariot to your higher self, your essential self, as a free choice, instead of always letting that automaton grab the reins every time that it thinks it is seeing the same conditions that caused you pain when you were very young, conditions which bring up those same feelings of being overwhelmed and afraid and filled with doubt (just as Arjuna was overwhelmed with doubt at the beginning of the great battle of Kurukshetra).

The advice and observations given by Dr. Maté, who is one of the leading-edge thinkers on the subject of trauma and recovery from trauma of the present-day, can be seen to parallel very closely the teaching embedded within the world's ancient myths.

Dr. Maté's advice in the quoted passage is extremely practical and extremely helpful, and involves creating "a gap between our emotional reactions and our behavior," a space in which we can detach from the programatic response and in which we can observe the situation without letting the egoic mind reflexively respond outside of our conscious control.

How do we create this gap, this space, in which we can guard ourselves against the unthinking reaction -- in which we can give the reins to our authentic self instead of allowing the horses to bolt as if they are "vicious" and "uncontrolled"?

The myths have more to show us on that front, and we will pursue the subject a bit further in the next chapter -- but for now we can conclude this chapter by observing that the evidence from the myths themselves demonstrates that one of their central themes involves the acknowledgement of the existence of our essential self, from whom we become alienated due to trauma. Although the ancient myths and ancient texts may well have been twisted and distorted by those who want to use them to oppress and even to traumatize, the foregoing analysis strongly suggests that oppression and traumatization was not the original intent of the myths – indeed, quite the contrary. They are illustrating a path towards the recovery of the essential self, and that is a theme that is undeniably positive, uplifting, and empowering.

We should also be able to see from the preceding analysis that an understanding of the myths *as metaphor* helps us to understand that they are talking about struggles we ourselves must face in our own lives. If we interpret the myths as literal, terrestrial history, then we are much less likely to perceive the teachings we have been uncovering in the myths examined in this chapter and the previous chapter (for example, if we take the episode of Doubting Thomas literally, we are much more likely to extract all kinds of different messages from the story, and much less likely to perceive that this story actually conveys profound truths about our reconciliation with our essential self, from whom we have become alienated and who has actually been suppressed and "buried" and denied by our egoic mind).

When we begin to perceive the overwhelming volume of evidence showing these ancient myths to have their foundations in the stars and heavenly cycles, then the conclusion that they are metaphorical becomes virtually irresistible.

But that is not all that the understanding of the connection between the myths and the stars can reveal to us. As we begin to understand the significance with which this ancient system imbues specific constellations and specific points aspects of the interlocking heavenly cycles, then these stars and cycles become a kind of "code" or "language" which conveys still further teaching for our benefit in this life and in this present moment.

We will soon discover that one of the most important of the constellations, particularly for this question of creating that "gap" of which Dr. Maté speaks, is the constellation Ophiuchus.

Chapter 10
Ophiuchus

The Pali Canon is considered to be the most complete surviving body of scripture from the early Buddhism, and is thought to have been transmitted orally for some centuries before being written in its original form in the year 29 BC (or BCE), although various revisions have been made since that time. It is written in the Pāli language and its teachings have been preserved among the Theravada school of Buddhism, the name *Theravada* in translation signifying "School of the Elders."

Most of us are familiar with the story of how the Buddha-to-be sat in deep austerity beneath the famous Bodhi tree until he reached Awakening. This tree is usually said to have been a sacred fig tree (*ficus religiosa*), known as a *pippal* or an *ashvattha* tree in India. Many sacred temples to this day have a majestic sacred fig growing nearby, said to have been descended from that original pippal tree under which the Buddha reached Awakening.

There are many indications, however, that the tree under which the Buddha sits is not literal or terrestrial at all, but rather celestial. Indeed, some of the ancient texts themselves describe different species of tree -- and use language which strongly suggests that this well-known scene must be located in the heavens.

The Pali Canon tells us that when the Buddha (sometimes referred to as "the Blessed One") was newly Self-awakened, "the Blessed One was staying at Uruvelā on the bank of the Nerañjarā River, at the root of the Bodhi tree -- the tree of awakening."[118]

Another translation calls this tree at the bank of the Nerañjarā River "the Goatherd's Banyan Tree."[119]

Elsewhere in the accounts of the life of the Buddha, the Pali Canon also describes the Blessed One meditating in solitude in a mountainous place, within the cleft of a rock. The texts tell us:

Chapter Ten

> Then he, the Buddha, went to Rajagaha,
> the mountain fortress of the Magadhans,
>   and wandered for alms,
> endowed with all the foremost marks.
> King Bimbisara, standing in his palace, saw him,
> and on seeing him, consummate in marks,
> said: "Look at this one, sirs.
> How handsome, stately, pure!
> How consummate his demeanor!
> Mindful, his eyes downcast,
> looking only a plow-length before him,
> as one who's not from a lowly lineage:
> Send the royal messengers at once
> to see where this monk will go."
> They -- the messengers dispatched --
> followed behind him.
> "Where will this monk go?
> Where will his dwelling place be?"
> As he went from house to house --
> well-restrained, his sense-doors guarded,
>   mindful, alert --
> his bowl filled quickly.
> Then he, the sage, completing his alms round,
> left the city, headed for Mount Pandava.
> "That's where his dwelling will be."
> Seeing him go to his dwelling place,
> three messengers sat down,
> while one returned to tell the king.
> "That monk, your majesty,
> on the flank of Pandava,
> sits like a tiger, a bull,
> a lion in a mountain cleft." [120]

We have already seen evidence which strongly points to the conclusion that Jesus and Krishna are both closely associated with the constellation Ophiuchus, as is that paragon of wisdom in the Biblical texts, King Solomon. The above passages from the

Ophiuchus

Pali Canon, describing the life of the Buddha, provide reasons to conclude that the Buddha, the Blessed One, is likewise associated with the same pivotal constellation Ophiuchus.

Those familiar with some of my previous books, particularly *The Ancient World-Wide System*, will know that the "cleft of a rock" or the "mountain cleft" in which the Buddha sits in contemplation can be identified with the outline of the constellation Ophiuchus, the two flanking "serpent-halves" of which constellation can be envisioned as the steep cliff-like sides of a canyon, rising up on either side of the central body of Ophiuchus:

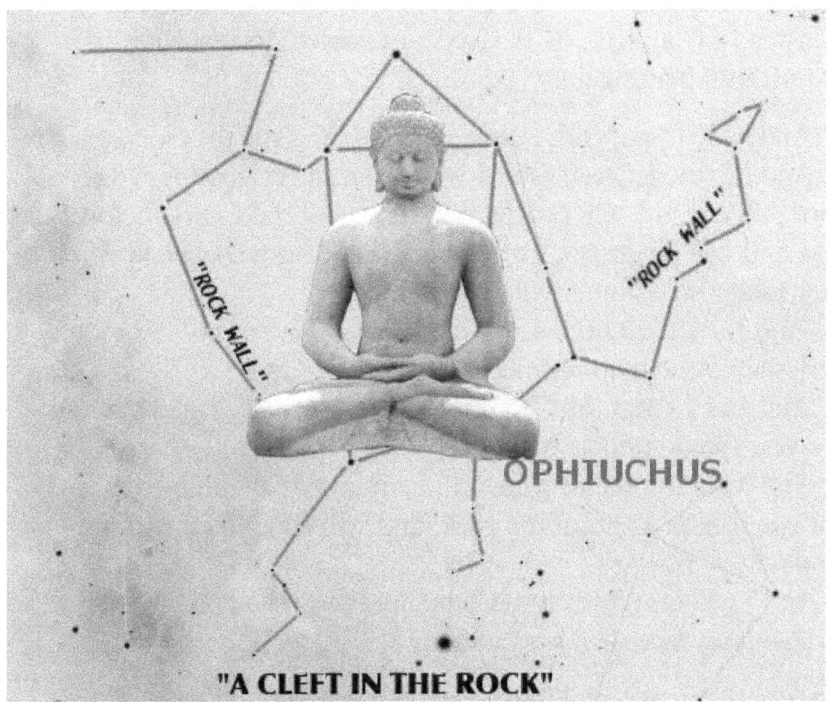

If this is your first time encountering this assertion, it may initially seem like something of a stretch – but there is abundant evidence from myths found in many different cultures which shows that the ancient system did indeed envision Ophiuchus in this way, with its flanking "serpent-halves" seen as two sides of a cliff, and that figures associated with Ophiuchus will, in certain mythical

Chapter Ten

episodes, be described as retreating within the very same kind of cleft in the rock.

The most familiar example, perhaps, especially to readers from cultures whose history is heavily intertwined with the Biblical scriptures, is of course the story of Moses, when he asks to see the glory of the Almighty himself.

In Exodus 33, we are told that when Moses asks the LORD to show Moses his glory, a special arrangement involving a *cleft of the rock* (the original but now-obsolete spelling used in the Authorized Version of 1611, aka the "King James Version," says "a clift" instead of "a cleft") is devised to enable Moses to see the LORD without being slain:

> 18 And he [Moses] said, I beseech thee, shew me thy glory.
> 19 And he [the LORD] said, I will make all my goodness pass before thee, and I will proclaim the name of the LORD before thee; and will be gracious to whom I will be gracious, and will shew mercy on whom I will shew mercy.
> 20 And he [the LORD] said, Thou canst not see my face: for there shall be no man see me, and live.
> 21 And the LORD said, Behold, *there is* a place by me, and thou shalt stand upon a rock:
> 22 And it shall come to pass, while my glory passeth by, that I will put thee in a clift of the rock, and will cover thee with my hand while I pass by:
> 23 And I will take away mine hand, and thou shalt see my back parts: but my face shall not be seen.

I must admit that as a child, this episode caused me quite a bit of confusion when it was described (but never illustrated) in my "Bible for Children" book, which did include many other very lively illustrations including an illustration of the gaping, lifeless, severed head of John the Baptist being carried on a platter by the daughter of Herodias (see the episode described in Matthew 14). What did it mean that Moses had been allowed to see God's back but not his front, I used to wonder.

Ophiuchus

What is this verse telling us? What does the text mean when it has the LORD telling Moses that Moses shall "see my back parts" but not his face? It all seems extremely difficult to understand, especially because earlier in the very same chapter of Exodus, we have been told: "And the LORD spake unto Moses face to face, as a man speaketh unto his friend" (Exodus 33: 11).

The solution becomes very straightforward, however, when we realize that the scenes described in the ancient scriptures of the Bible are *celestial* in nature -- and that (as we have already seen) the LORD is associated with the constellation Hercules and Moses with the constellation Ophiuchus:

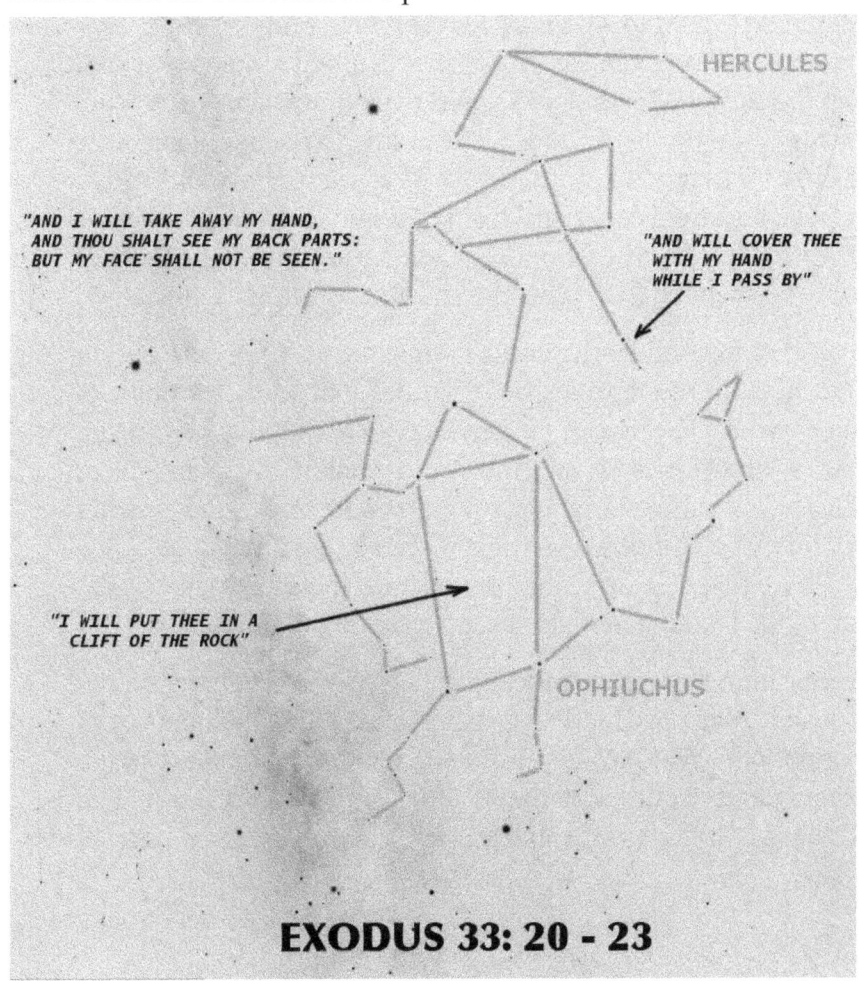

Chapter Ten

Note that we have already mentioned, back on page 118, some evidence which supports the identification of Moses with the constellation Ophiuchus. Figures associated with the constellation Ophiuchus are often envisioned as carrying a long spear or a long staff (the eastern "serpent-half" can be envisioned as a staff or spear, and because there are two serpent-halves in this constellation, sometimes Ophiuchus-figures carry *two* spears instead of just one, as does Hector in the Iliad of ancient Greece). Moses, of course, is frequently described as carrying a rod, and when he lifts up this rod (as commanded by the LORD in Exodus 14: 16), then the LORD parts the Red Sea (i.e. the Milky Way).

As discussed in *Star Myths of the World, Volume Three: Star Myths of the Bible*, the eastern serpent-half of Ophiuchus which forms the rod of Moses does indeed extend into the Milky Way (which plays the role of the Red Sea in the Exodus 14 episode), and in fact it extends into the Milky Way right above the "Dark Rift" which forms a "dry path" from one side of the Milky Way to the other: the dry ground upon which Moses and the Israelites can cross, when the LORD divides the Red Sea in Exodus 14.[121]

Thus, we can confidently identify Moses with the constellation Ophiuchus in the Exodus 14 episode, and can be similarly confident that Moses can be identified with Ophiuchus in the "clift of the rock" episode in Exodus 33 as well. By the same token, when we encounter an ancient scripture from the Pali Canon describing the Buddha as sitting within a "mountain cleft," we can be sure that this is one important clue which suggests that the figure of the Buddha may also be associated with Ophiuchus

There is abundant other evidence which points inexorably to the conclusion that the Buddha is associated with Ophiuchus. On the opposite page, for example, we see an image showing a statue of the seated Buddha dating to the first century AD. The Buddha is holding an egg-shaped object in the uplifted palm of his hand.

Ophiuchus

This upraised hand with egg-shaped object corresponds to the western "serpent-half" of the constellation Ophiuchus, as do other egg-shaped (or pinecone-shaped) objects seen in other ancient artwork, including from ancient Mesopotamia, as discussed extensively in *The Ancient World-Wide System*.

Behind the seated figure of the Buddha in this artwork we can see the figure known as Vajrapani, grasping an upraised mace-like weapon, which is in fact a Vajra. We have previously discussed the Vajra and its association with mythical figures corresponding to the constellation Hercules (see pages 67 - 70, for instance), and indeed we can see that Vajrapani is depicted with characteristics we can immediately recognize as Hercules-like.

Chapter Ten

The name *Vajrapani* itself signifies "Vajra-in-hand" in Sanskrit, and there can be little doubt that this character is associated with the constellation Hercules in the heavens -- and that the ancient artwork shown on the previous page indicates an awareness that the Buddha (seated, holding up an egg-shaped object) is associated with Ophiuchus, confirmed by the looming figure of Vajrapani behind and above the seated Buddha.

This evidence confirms the identification of the figure of the Buddha with the constellation Ophiuchus, but if additional confirmation is needed, we can also note the previously mentioned fact that the constellation Hercules, directly above Ophiuchus, is sometimes envisioned in the Star Myth system with a different outline which I refer to as the "whirling form" of the constellation Hercules (see page 119 in this volume, as well as extensive discussion in *The Ancient World-Wide System*, and also *Star Myths of the World, Volume Two* and *Volume Three*). In this way of envisioning Hercules, the square-shaped "head" of the constellation becomes a central hub, from which arms radiate outwards in four directions:

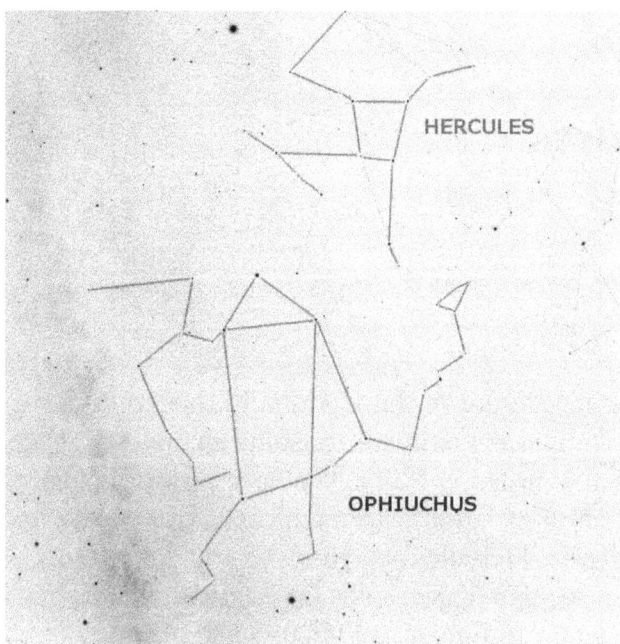

Ophiuchus

As can be demonstrated with abundant evidence from myths found in numerous different ancient cultures, this whirling form of the constellation Hercules is sometimes envisioned as a branching tree -- often a fig tree, such as when Odysseus grasps a convenient fig tree growing on a lonely rock near the dreaded whirlpool of Charybdis, in the Odyssey of ancient Greece, or when Jesus tells Nathanael that he saw Nathanael while Nathanael was still sitting under the fig tree, in the Gospel according to John, chapter 1 and verses 48 and following.

When envisioned as a tree, an additional "connecting line" can be envisioned to connect the whirling form of the constellation Hercules to the western serpent-half held by Ophiuchus (the "head-end" of the serpent), as shown in the diagram below (the added line is thicker than the others, for ease of identification):

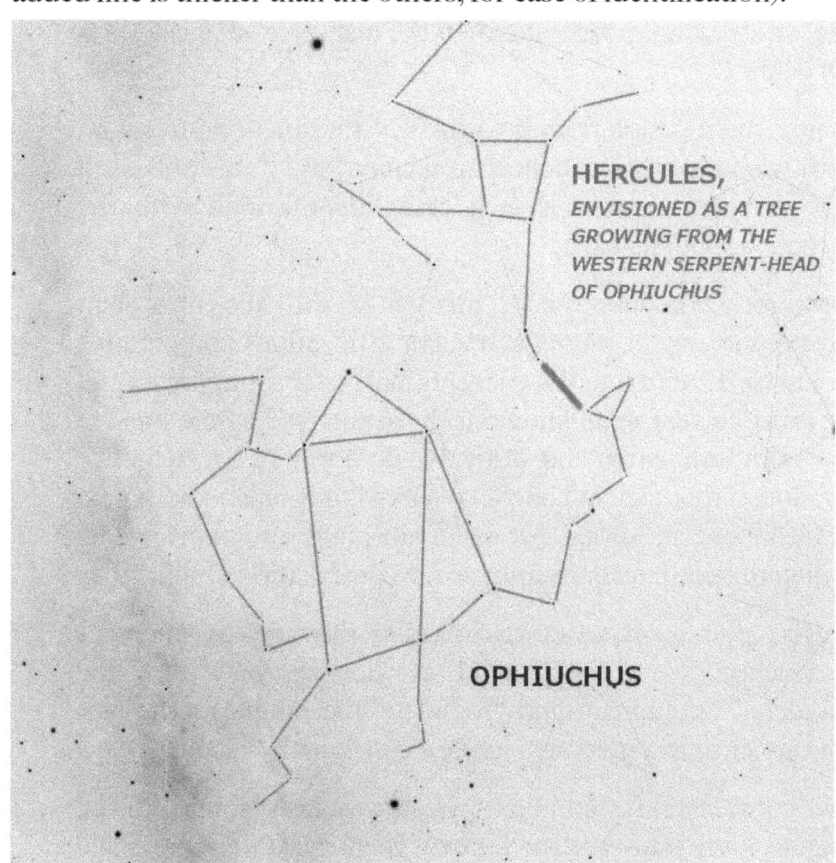

Chapter Ten

Hence, the description of the Buddha meditating patiently beneath the sacred fig tree: the Buddha is associated with the constellation Ophiuchus, and the constellation Hercules overhead plays the role of the spreading tree.

We thus have a variety of celestial evidence which points towards an identification of the Buddha with this important constellation Ophiuchus.

Is there any significance to the fact that we have now found associations between figures such as the Buddha, the Christ, Krishna, Solomon and this specific constellation?

If the ancient world-wide system which forms the foundation for the Star Myths of virtually every culture is using these constellations as a kind of "language" or "code" through which to convey their teaching message, then the answer to that question is: "Of course!"

Of course there is significance to the fact that these figures who embody wisdom, transcendence, awakening, and the essential self can be demonstrated to have a close identification with the constellation Ophiuchus.

Unfortunately, because the originators of this ancient system clearly predate any of the most ancient civilizations and cultures known to (or admitted to) by conventional history, and predate all of the most ancient texts known to have survived to the present day for our examination and study, we do not have any definitive explication of this ancient code -- no surviving "guidebook" which we can follow in order to make absolute pronouncements regarding the deeper significance of the constellation Ophiuchus.

However, after many years of exploring this ancient system, I have reached some fairly solid conclusions regarding the "vocabulary," "grammar" and "logic" of the language through which this ancient system of metaphor conveys its meaning.

If the constellation Ophiuchus is consistently found to be associated with transcendent figures, then there must be some

Ophiuchus

aspect or aspects of the constellation itself which would suggest some kind of transcendent qualities. And indeed when we consider Ophiuchus and its positioning both in the starry heavens and within the zodiac band of constellations through which the sun, moon, and visible planets make their various inter-related cycles, we can posit some of the reasons why the incredible ancient system might employ Ophiuchus to embody the lessons which point us towards recovery of our higher self.

In its position in the heavens, Ophiuchus is positioned alongside the Milky Way near the brightest and widest part of the galactic band. We've already discussed the fact that this brightest and widest region, located between Sagittarius and Scorpio (with Ophiuchus directly above Scorpio and indeed appearing to "stand upon" the multiple heads of Scorpio) is identified as the Galactic Core or Galactic Center by modern astronomy -- akin to the *yolk* of a fried egg, if the galaxy in which we are located is envisioned as a tremendous fried egg, whirling slowly through space.

When we look towards the region of Sagittarius, Scorpio, and Ophiuchus, we are gazing towards the very core of our galaxy, the place where (it is thought) the stars of our local system were formed. Of course, we don't see our own galaxy as a tremendous "fried egg" of stars with a bulging yolk at its center, because we are not observing from a vantage point *outside* of the galaxy but rather *within* it: accompanying a star (our sun) located within the "white" of that fried-egg shape in space.

Therefore, we see our own galaxy as a great ring or band, flipping around us endlessly, once per day (a function of our earth's rotation on its axis), with one side of that band distinctly brighter and more impressive than the other side (the side of the band we see when looking towards the Galactic Core). Thus, the Milky Way appears to us like a beautiful starry road, or a beautiful starry river, crossing the night sky from one horizon to the other, its brightest region being the part of the band which passes between Sagittarius and Scorpio and continues upwards past Ophiuchus

Chapter Ten

and on past Hercules, becoming less bright and less dazzling as it proceeds past Hercules towards the Great Square of Pegasus and the head of Perseus and on towards Gemini and Cancer on the opposite side of the sky from Scorpio and Sagittarius.

I have found abundant evidence, particularly in my celestial analysis of the Odyssey of ancient Greece explored in six pairs of chapters in *Star Myths of the World, Volume Two*, that the path of the Milky Way itself was envisioned in the ancient system of celestial metaphor as the path of escape from the imprisoning and enslaving aspects of the lower self, the path of awakening and transcendence, and the path of reconnection and reconciliation with the higher self -- and through that reconnection and reconciliation, reconnection with the divine realm, the realm of the infinite: the realm of the gods.

The figure of Ophiuchus, standing alongside this brightest portion of the Milky Way (and indeed with one foot within the bright band), is located in such as way as to appear to be ascending along that heavenly road.

The Milky Way band ascends and crosses the sky as a ring (only half of which we can see at one time) in a way that is *perpendicular to* the band of the zodiac constellations.

We can think of the example of an armillary sphere, which is composed of rings, one of which represents the ecliptic band -- although traditional armillary spheres do not typically include the Milky Way band. However, they do typically include vertical rings which cross perpindicularly to the ecliptic band -- such as in the armillary sphere shown on the opposite page, in which the ecliptic band is marked by the letter "B." In that diagram, the rings which run through the axis of earth's rotation -- the rings which go through the little "point" sticking out of the top of the armillary sphere marked with the letter "N" at the upper-right part of the drawing, at roughly the "two o'clock" position on the circle as we face the page -- can be said to be roughly perpendicular to the band of the ecliptic:

Ophiuchus

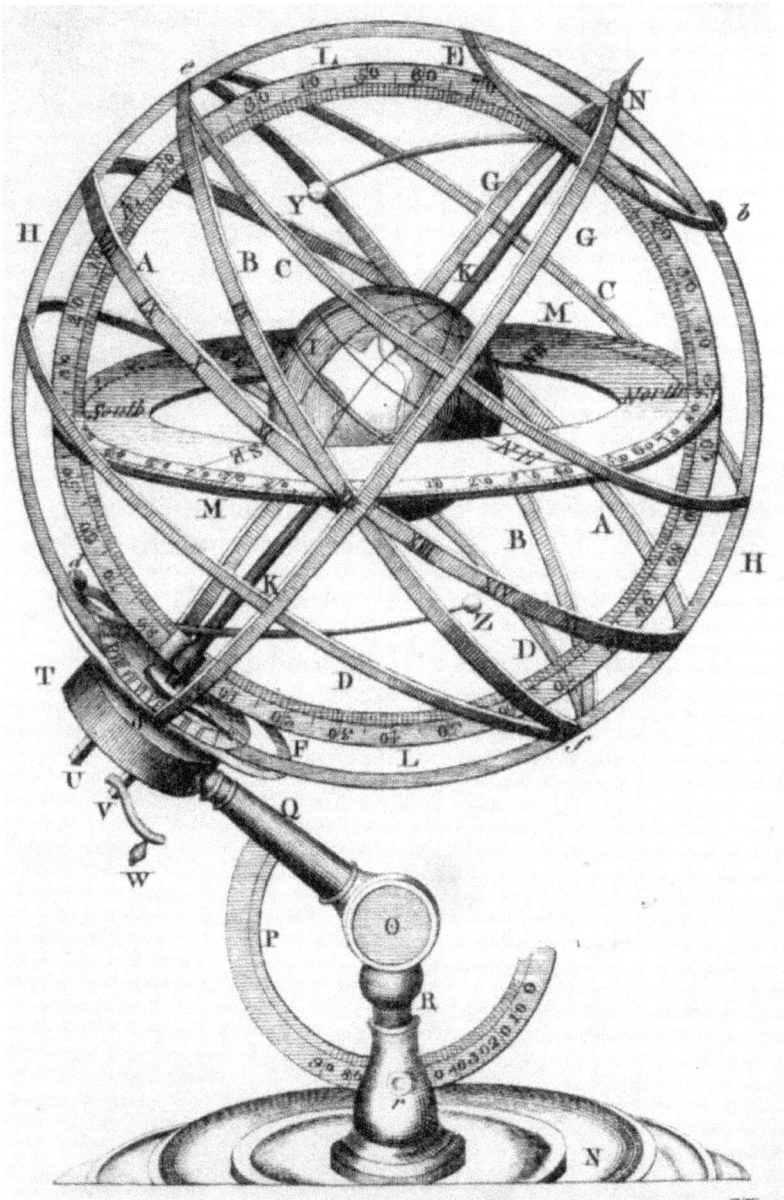

The ring on the above drawing marked "H" forms the outer circle as we face the page, "perpendicular" to the ecliptic ring "B."

The Milky Way in the sky does not cross over the north and south celestial poles, and thus is not in the exact same position as the ring in the armillary sphere marked "H" (or any of the other rings

Chapter Ten

on a traditional armillary sphere), but it does rise roughly perpendicular to the band of the ecliptic along which the sun, moon, and visible planets travel, through the background stars of the zodiac constellations.

To illustrate, below is an image from Stellarium showing the view from the northern hemisphere facing towards the south, which is the direction an observer in the northern hemisphere will look in order to see the path of the sun crossing the sky during the day, as well as the path of the visible planets crossing the sky during the night. The plane of earth's relationship with the sun is known as the "plane of the ecliptic" (because when the moon intercepts this plane, an *eclipse* can take place, if the moon intersects the ecliptic plane at either a new moon or full moon). Thus, the ecliptic can be seen in the sky as the path traced out by the sun, and the planets and our moon trace their wheeling paths very close to this same ecliptic line. Their paths are shown in the diagram below as faint lines within the horizontal ecliptic band:

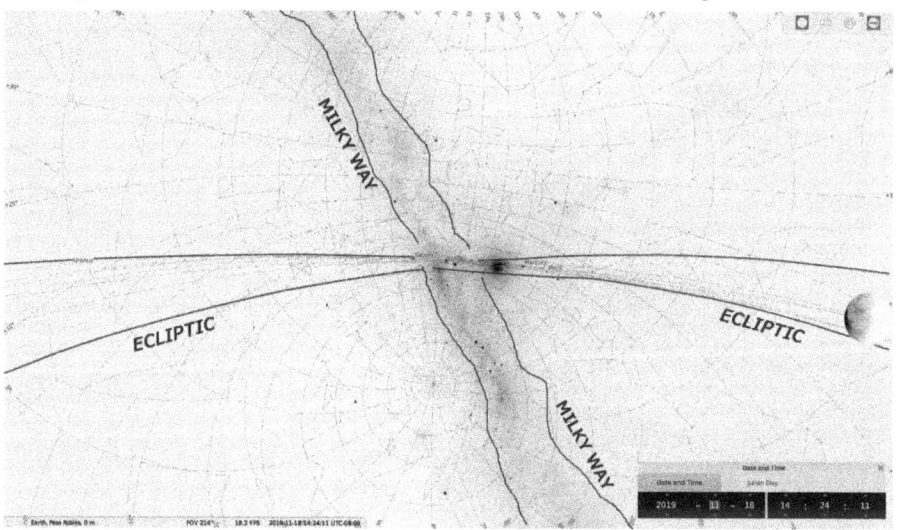

If you look closely, you can see that the zodiac constellations are transected by the ecliptic path (see diagram on the next page).

To understand what I am trying to show in these diagrams, think of the ecliptic as a ring (like the rings of Saturn) which runs all the way around the viewer and connects behind us as we are facing

Ophiuchus

towards the south. Now, look at the Milky Way, which is also a complete ring but one which is roughly perpendicular to the ring of the ecliptic path. It arcs up overhead and forms a complete circle as well, coming down behind our backs to join up with the part of the Milky Way which descends to the bottom of the picture shown. It is as if we are inside an enormous armillary sphere, and we see the sun, moon and visible planets wheeling around us along the ecliptic band (you can see the enormous form of the moon on the right edge of the image), and we see the Milky Way as a huge ring which is roughly perpendicular to the ecliptic.

Below is another version of the same diagram, but this time with the outlines of the zodiac constellations drawn in with connecting lines, and labeled, and the outlines of the constellations Ophiuchus and Hercules as well:

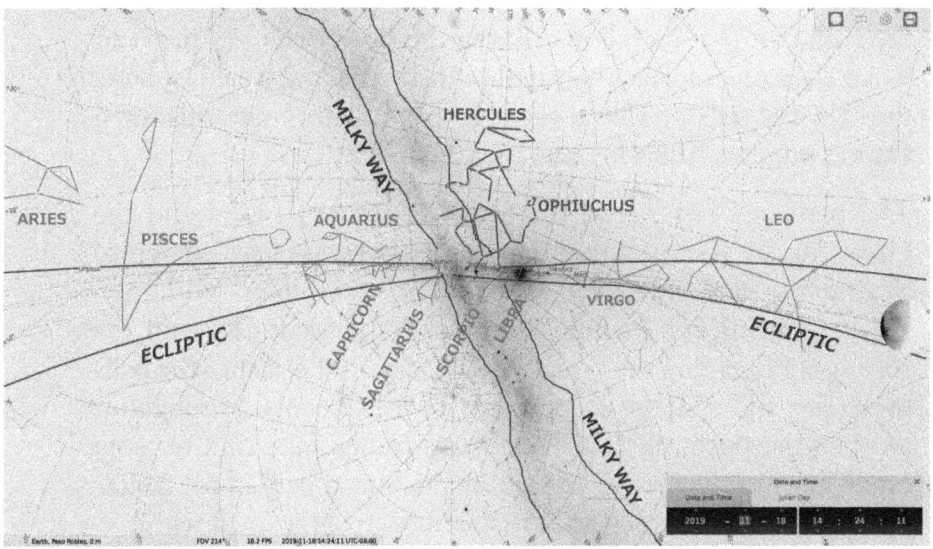

Note that this image is taken from the free open-source planetarium app Stellarium, which simulates three-dimensionality by making the constellations appear larger as they approach the left and right edges of the screen, which is why the constellation Scorpio looks so much smaller than Leo, for example (even though Scorpio is actually a very large and impressive-looking constellation when seen in the night sky).

265

Chapter Ten

Note also that the ecliptic band is represented by everything between the two roughly parallel lines, through which the sun, moon and visible planets travel.

Finally, and this is the main point of the two diagrams on the preceding pages, note that if we were to travel "up" the Milky Way path, ascending alongside Ophiuchus and on up towards Hercules, we would be leaving the ecliptic path and traveling in a new direction, roughly perpendicular to and away from the band of the ecliptic.

A celestial analysis of the action of the Odyssey of ancient Greece, such as the analysis presented in *Star Myths of the World, Volume Two*, reveals that Odysseus and his ill-fated crew constantly travel along the path of the zodiac between Virgo and Pisces by way of Sagittarius and Scorpio (in other words, along the path that the sun follows during the "lower half" of the year, when days are shorter than nights in the northern hemisphere, through the sign of Libra, then Scorpio, then Sagittarius, then Capricorn, then Aquarius, and then Pisces).

The path of Odysseus in the Odyssey reaches Pisces and the Great Square several times, only to be "bounced back" down to Sagittarius and Scorpio again. The encounter with the Laestrygonians, for example, can clearly be identified with the region of Pisces and the Great Square, as can the visit to the halls of Aeolus, and even the encounter with the Cyclops. Throughout most of the poem, in fact, Odysseus is stuck in a kind of "spin cycle" in which he reaches the end of the "lower half" of the zodiac journey only to be hurled back to the bottom of the great wheel.

It is only when he begins to travel in a new direction -- which is *upwards* along the Milky Way itself – that Odysseus is finally able to break free from the whirl of the zodiac's lower half, and reconnect with his true identity as the husband of Penelope, the father of Telemachus, and the king of Ithaca.

Indeed, the entire reconciliation scene with Penelope involves the famous bed of Odysseus, which he shaped from the trunk of a great olive tree, still rooted in the ground -- and as the analysis in *Star Myths of the World, Volume Two* demonstrates, this bed itself can be confidently identified with the constellation Ophiuchus.[122]

Thus, the position of Ophiuchus along the Milky Way band -- and along the Milky Way's brightest and widest section, near the very center of the galaxy itself -- carries esoteric significance within the ancient system of metaphor underlying and informing the world's myths and sacred stories. Not only is Ophiuchus positioned alongside the Milky Way, but the constellation is positioned along the Milky Way *where the galactic pathway intesrsects with the ecliptic path* of the zodiac constellations -- and, more significant yet, near the zodiac constellations of Scorpio and Sagittarius, at the lowest point on the zodiac wheel, marking the winter solstice for the northern hemisphere.

The evidence I have encountered during my exploration of the world's ancient Star Myths so far indicates that the lower half of the zodiac wheel (the half during which days are shorter than nights, beginning with the fall equinox between Virgo and Libra, and continuing downwards along Scorpio and Sagittarius towards the winter solstice, then turning back upwards through Capricorn and Aquarius towards Pisces and the spring equinox, which marks the transition back to the upper part of the year) was seen as representative of our path through this incarnate life -- and representative of all of the entanglements which enslave us to our passions and impulses and reactions, all of which are demonstrated in the Odyssey as Odysseus and his crew get bounced back and forth along the lower path of the zodiac band.

We heard Dr. Gabor Maté assert in the quotation cited in the previous chapter, "People who are not conscious simply have no freedom," because they are reacting automatically, just like a pre-programmed algorithm, based on defensive or coping responses which arose due to situations which may have happened decades earlier, usually during childhood.

Chapter Ten

These pre-programmed reactions can lead us into disaster -- just as the impulsive crew in the Odyssey find themselves rushing into one disaster after another, when they follow their appetites and devour the cattle of the Sun-god, or follow their lusts and end up being turned into swine in the house of Circe, and just as Odysseus himself sometimes "forgets himself" and invites disaster through his own rash and impulsive actions, usually when his pride takes over (most notably during the extended encounter with the Cyclops, Polyphemus).

The way to transcend this imprisonment within the algorithms of the egoic mind, the myths appear to be telling us, lies along a different path -- the ascending path of the Milky Way itself, indicated by the position of the constellation Ophiuchus, with which constellation so many transcendent figures in myth can be seen to be associated, including Krishna, and the Buddha, and the Christ, and many others as well.

To reiterate the point and to ensure that it is clear to all readers, below is a diagram from *Star Myths of the World, Volume Two*, showing a zodiac wheel (which is a kind of "shorthand way" of representing the actual path of the sun, moon, and visible planets through the background constellations, as seen from our vantage point on earth: a shorthand way of depicting what was shown in the preceding two diagrams, and to do it for the full year's cycle).

This zodiac wheel is arranged such that the progress through the year is depicted in clockwise fashion around the circle, and such that the points of equinox are situated at the nine o'clock and three o'clock positions on the circle. Thus, if the progress around the dial is clockwise in this depiction, that means that the nine o'clock position (at the left of the diagram as we face the page) represents the equinox where the sun ascends towards summer, meaning that from this point around the "top half" of the wheel the hours of daylight will be longer than the hours of darkness.

Likewise, as the year progresses in a clockwise fashion, the equinox located at the three o'clock position (on the right of the dial as we face the page) must represent the fall equinox, after which the hours of daylight are shorter than the hours of darkness, on the way down to the winter solstice, which is situated at the very bottom of the wheel (the six o'clock position).

This zodiac diagram, originally published in *Star Myths of the World, Volume Two* as part of the discussion of the trials of long-suffering Odysseus, shows that his journey during that epic progresses along the lower half of the zodiac wheel -- the half "beneath the line" of the two equinoxes, the half which stretches from the fall equinox downwards to the winter solstice and then back up to the spring equinoxes: the "lower half" of the year, when days are shorter than nights.

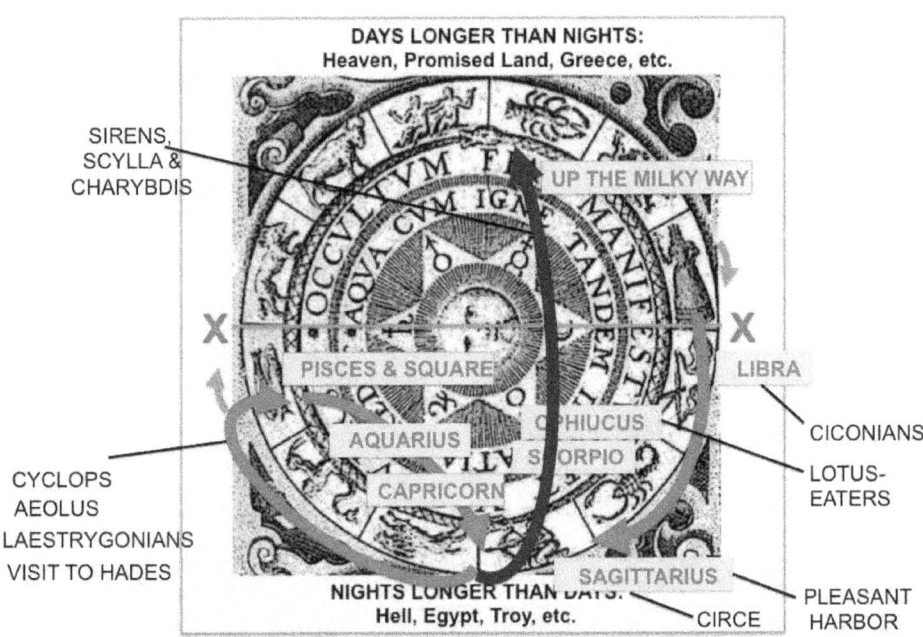

THE "UNDERWORLD PASSAGE" IN THE ODYSSEY

The arrows in the diagram follow the path of Odysseus and his ill-fated crew, along the path of the zodiac through the "lower half" of the wheel, continually rebuffed each time they reach Pisces (at the end of the lower journey), stuck in a kind of "spin cycle" with seemingly no escape from the endless loop -- until

Chapter Ten

finally Odysseus ascends along the "upward path" of the Milky Way, out of the "repeating algorithm" of the cycle.

This path of escape -- up the Milky Way -- leads past Ophiuchus and upwards towards Hercules: the very constellations we have been examining in depth throughout this volume. It appears to me to be very likely, based on an abundance of evidence found in myths I have analyzed from cultures around the world, that the figure of Ophiuchus was used as a transcendent figure, a pivotal figure, because of its location along the upward path of the Milky Way -- the path of escape from the cycle of the zodiac band, transcending the zodiac track which represents our cyclical descent into incarnation and "imprisonment" not only in the body but also in the entanglement of the "egoic self" (the egoic self which becomes "programmed" as a coping mechanism, but which makes us less than free, and which separates us from our essence).

Let's summarize some of the characteristics of Ophiuchus which we have touched upon so far, before introducing what is perhaps the most significant aspect of them all:

- ➢ Ophiuchus is positioned alongside the Milky Way band, just above Scorpio. *The Milky Way represents a path that ascends upwards and perpendicular to (away from) the "spin cycle" of the zodiac.*

- ➢ Ophiuchus is positioned just beneath the constellation Hercules. *We have seen that Hercules is frequently associated with the most powerful god in many myth-systems: Ophiuchus thus functions as an "intermediary" between the mortal realm (and our ordinary path along the zodiac's lower arc) and the infinite realm of the gods.*

- ➢ Ophiuchus is positioned besides the widest and brightest portion of the Milky Way band. *This widest and brightest zone represents the Galactic Center, thought to be the birthplace of the stars, and thus represents a place of "rebirth" or "second birth" -- and this region is also*

> *associated with rebirth because it roughly corresponds to the lowest point on the zodiac cycle, at the winter equinox: this point represents kind of a "birth" because the sun has been declining steadily, getting lower and lower in the sky as days get shorter and shorter, but at the point of winter sosltice the sun makes its great turn and begins to travel higher and higher in the sky each day, as days begin to grow longer again instead of shorter.*

All of these aspects of the location of Ophiuchus help to explain why this constellation is such a pivotal figure in the heavens, located as it is at the juncture of the lower zodiac band and the ascending column of the Milky Way, and located in such a way as to form a kind of linch-pin between that same "lower path" and the constellation Hercules, who often plays the role of the supreme divinity.

But there is yet another significant characteristic of the constellation Ophiuchus upon which I have remarked in previous volumes and which would seem to be extremely significant to this volume's discussion of the role of myth in overcoming trauma and breaking free from the "algorithmic pre-programming" of the egoic mind, which acts to separate us from our own authentic self.

That significant characteristic is the fact that the constellation Ophiuchus is actually positioned in such a way as to intersect the plane of the ecliptic and the path of the sun through the heavens -- which would seem to qualify Ophiuchus for inclusion in the zodiac band of constellations (through each of which the ecliptic also passes). And yet Ophiuchus is quite clearly *not* included in the twelve constellations of the zodiac.

As can be seen in the star-charts on pages 264 and 265, showing the ecliptic band intersecting with the Milky Way, the ecliptic plane of earth's relationship to the sun (which defines the path our sun appears to take as it crosses the daytime sky, and which also roughly defines the path along which the visible planets travel as they cross the night sky) cuts through the extended leg of

Chapter Ten

the constellation Ophiuchus, which protrudes into the space between the zodiac constellations Sagittarius and Scorpio.

Below is a close-up of the same star-chart shown on page 265, which shows the ecliptic path along which the sun and visible planets (as well as the moon, although with greater deviation) travel through the sky (and through the background stars of the zodiac constellations):

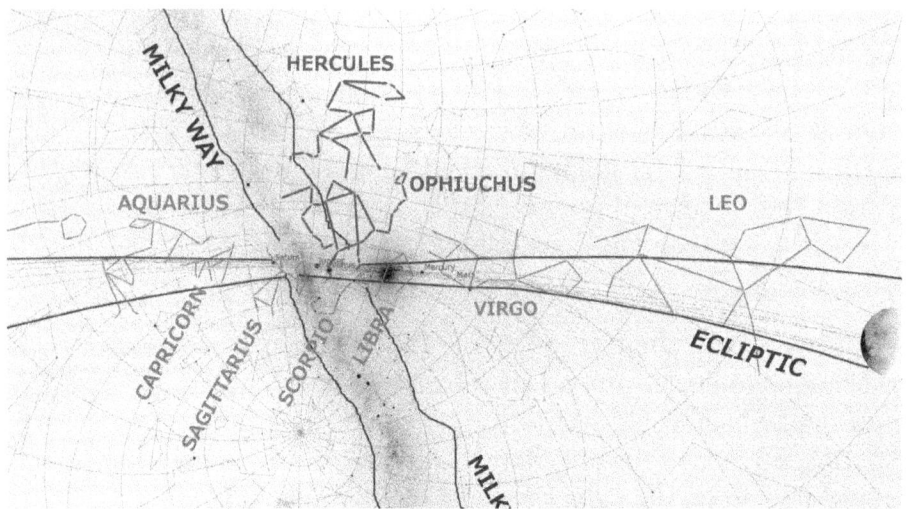

It should be evident from the illustration that the feet of the constellation Ophiuchus protrude into the band of the ecliptic, particularly the foot on the left side as we face the image above (the eastern side of the constellation, because we are facing south, which means east is to our left and west is to our right).

If the ecliptic path upon which the sun travels crosses through the constellation Ophiuchus, then it would seem appropriate to argue that Ophiuchus should be considered a "zodiac constellation," if by the term *zodiac constellation* we mean those constellations arranged along the path of the ecliptic, such that they form the backdrop of stars through which the sun (as well as the moon and other planets) can be seen to travel, from the point of view of an observer on earth.

Ophiuchus

And yet the constellation Ophiuchus *is not included* in the zodiac, which consists of the twelve constellations Aries, Taurus, Gemini, Cancer, Leo, Virgo, Libra, Scorpio, Sagittarius, Capricorn, Aquarius, and Pisces. Because of this omission, Ophiuchus is sometimes referred to as the "thirteenth zodiac sign," and there are some who argue that during an earlier, more matriarchal ancient age, Ophiuchus was recognized and included in a system of thirteen zodiac constellations, but was excluded when a later patriarchy usurped power and reduced the zodiac to twelve signs, in order to privilege the sun and the annual cycle over the moon and the more feminine lunar cycle.

Whether there is enough evidence to back up such a hypothesis, I cannot say -- but the evidence which shows that the ecliptic path does indeed cross through the stars of the constellation Ophiuchus is quite indisputable, even though Ophiuchus has obvioiusly been excluded from the zodiac system.

Based on the number of figures in myth such as the Buddha and the Christ and the Lord Krishna, figures whose teachings have to do with being in some way *detached from* the world while still remaining in the world, I am of the opinion that this curious "dual status" of the constellation Ophiuchus (a constellation which is simultaneously *part of* the zodiac by virtue of having the ecliptic pass through its stars, but at the same time *not part* of the zodiac) is actually an *original feature* of the ancient system (not a mistake introduced later by malevolent patriarchal misogynists) -- and that this ambiguous status of the constellation Ophiuchus is used by that system to convey one of its central messages.

That message is one of *detachment.*

Ophiuchus is simultaneously part of the zodiac -- and yet detached from it, not included in it, and thus not part of it.

Thus, figures personifying the constellation Ophiuchus, such as the figure of the Buddha, illustrate a certain type of detachment from the various external stimuli which would normally trigger a kind of automatic response or reflex. When the Buddha is

Chapter Ten

meditating under the Bodhi tree, for example, he is beset by the demon Mara (sometimes spelled "Maara"), the Tempter.

Various traditional texts describe Mara attempting to dissuade the Boddhisatva from his ascetic pursuit of Awakening beneath the Bodhi tree. At first, Mara approaches with feigned kindness, voicing concern for the health of the Buddha-to-be, observing how thin and pale he looks, saying that this path is too difficult for him to bear, and urging him to choose a life of worldly merit and community approval instead of this self-imposed deprivation and withdrawal.

When that approach fails to turn the Boddhisatva from his motionless meditation at the foot of the Bodhi tree, Mara tries a variety of other ways to elicit a reaction, including loud noises, breaking things, and even charging at the Buddha-to-be as if on the battlefield, threatening his life in an attempt to force the Boddhisatva to react.

Note that all of the efforts of the Tempter in this famous episode can be seen as illustrative of the truth articulated by Dr. Gabor Maté in the quotation cited on page 247, in which he declares that:

> People who are not conscious simply have no freedom. They may *believe* they do, but they don't make decisions. The decisions are made for them by automatic, emotional reactions that are the result of early experiences.

If someone else can elicit an "automatic, emotional reaction" from us, then we are basically their puppet at that particular moment, responding automatically to the buttons they are pushing. Mara tries a number of different ways to make the Buddha-to-be react to the buttons that Mara is pushing, but to no avail.

Finally, in some versions of the story, Mara sends his three voluptuous daughters to try and distract the Boddhisatva from his ascetic meditation beneath the Bodhi tree. The daughters dance suggestively and try to coax the motionless young man to respond to their temptations, but even this fails to cause him to lose control.

The ancient myth illustrates the achievement of what Dr. Gabor Maté calls a "gap" between the stimulus and the normally automatic response of the egoic mind. In that quotation (cited on page 245), he says that unless we can find a "gap between our emotional reactions and our behavior, we're actually held prisoner by what happened to us in childhood."

Dr. Maté goes on to say: "I find myself, at age 72, still very often reacting like I was a two-year-old child, unless I create that gap of consciousness, in which I have a moment to reflect upon and make a conscious decision."

Dr. Maté appears to be conceiving of this "gap" as the ability to mentally disconnect from the pre-programmed response, and instead to step back and view the impulse of the egoic mind with compassion and with curiosity, asking the question of what is behind or beneath that impulsive response: what insecurity, or what decades-old coping mechanism is driving that unthinking reaction?

I would argue that the fact that the world's ancient myths illustrate this ability to detach from the automatic response using figures (such as the Buddha) who are associated with the constellation Ophiuchus, that constellation which is *part of the zodiac* and yet at the same time *detached from the zodiac*, demonstrates the subtlety of this ancient system. When we begin to grasp the depth of this metaphorical language the ancient myths employ, we open up insights we can apply in our own life.

The pathway to reconnection to, and reconciliation with, our essential self involves detachment from the impulses -- the unthinking reactions -- of the egoic mind, because when the egoic mind is reacting based on algorithms written in decades earlier (as a response to trauma), we are like a programmed robot: a puppet, a mechanism.

Chapter Ten

As Krishna explains to Arjuna in the Bhagavad Gita, this understanding does *not* mean that we are supposed to take no action at all -- but rather that we are to *act in a detached way*: doing what is right, without attachment.

In the Odyssey, it is only when Odysseus begins to travel along the path up the Milky Way that he can return home (when, if we understand the celestial metaphor, we see that he has primarily journeyed along the zodiac path for most of the story). Odysseus is a character who exhibits tremendous self-control over his instincts, reactions, and doubts -- and yet even he gives in at times to impulsive reaction, always with disastrous consequences, such as when he taunts Polyphemus the Cyclops as Odysseus and his surviving crew-members are rowing their ship away from the island of the monster.

Is there an "Ophiuchus figure" in the Odyssey who helps Odysseus to overcome his occasional tendency to let his doubts and insecurities run away with him?

Indeed there is: the person of the goddess Athena.

The goddess Athena is the one who repeatedly rescues Odysseus from impulses which, if not checked, would lead to the hero's certain ruin. One very overt example is found in Book Five of the epic, when Odysseus has finally built a raft to begin his journey home, and has left the island of Calypso behind and is making his way across the open sea, only to be spied by the god Poseidon, who flies into a rage (the enmity of Poseidon is a consequence of Odysseus' encounter with the Cyclops Polyphemus, who is a son of Poseidon).

Poseidon destroys the raft of Odysseus and whips up a raging storm upon the ocean, and Odysseus has to be convinced by a visit from a different goddess, Leucothea (who herself was once a mortal, a woman named Ino the daughter of Cadmus, and who later became a deity) to abandon the wreckage of his raft. Even in that exchange, the text gives us a window into the thoughts running through the protagonist's head, as he says to himself that he fears this advice from the goddess Leucothea might be some kind of trap, thinking: "Woe is me! does not some one of the immortals contrive again a deceit against me, since she orders me to go from the raft?"[123]

As the long-suffering wanderer is debating against himself in his mind, Poseidon the earth-shaker raises a wave so steep and lofty that it overshadows the sky like a roof before crashing down upon the wreckage of the raft, and Odysseus eventually has to trust the advice of the goddess, strip off his clothes, secure the sash she has given to him around his waist as an amulet of divine protection, and swim through the mountainous swells for three days and three nights -- until at last he sees a shoreline in the distance.

Here again, however, Odysseus is filled with doubts, and the poem provides us insight into his thoughts as he beholds a shoreline made up of steep cliffs and jagged rocks, against which the mighty waves are crashing with terrific force. We hear him saying to himself that if a mighty wave snatches him and throws him against the stony cliff, he will be dashed to pieces, and he calculates that the water is so deep below the rocks that he will be unable to stand up on his legs and battle the storm surge, so he thinks ruefully that the gods have granted him an unexpected view of the land only to get his hopes up before the inevitable end.

Then we see the mind of Odysseus begin to consider other alternatives, such as swimming further along the shoreline in hopes of locating a better point to try and make landfall, but even as he weighs this option, his mind is filled with fear and doubt and he says to himself that if he tries to swim further, the currents of the storm might snatch him back again into the deep ocean, teeming with fish, and we see his thoughts literally "running away with him" as he thinks to himself that Amphitrite, queen of the sea and consort of Poseidon, will no doubt send a great sea monster to seize him.

It is at this moment, when the interior dialogue we are shown indicates that Odysseus is allowing his mind to run away with

Chapter Ten

him in a kind of panic, that the text tells us that the goddess Athena inspires him. A terrific wave lifts Odysseus up and propels him towards the jagged rocks, but with the clarity of mind that the goddess has just inspired, he is able to avoid being smashed to pieces and instead clings like an octopus to the rock until the returning surge drags him back out to the depths again, leaving shreds of skin behind.

Then, the poem tells us, he would certainly have perished, had not the goddess Athena inspired Odysseus yet again -- and with a renewed burst of strength he swims free from the waves pulling him towards the looming cliffs and instead begins to swim along the shoreline until he finds a place where a broad river is flowing out from the interior of the land to the sea, making a wide cove free from rocks, with a sandy beach.

At this point, Odysseus senses the presence of the river's god (according to the superlative translation of Robert Fagles) and prays to that god – "whoever thou art" -- to show mercy to the desperate traveler and allow Odysseus to land safely.[124]

This extended episode from the Odyssey of ancient Greece is extremely revealing in our investigation of the ways that the world's myths point us towards the recovery of our higher self.

We are given unusual insight into the thoughts running through the mind of Odysseus, and the doubts that almost bring him to an untimely end. First, he is wary of Leucothea's offered assistance, fearing that it is just another trap sent from the gods to ensnare him. Then, when he finally spies land, he tells himself it must just be a trick of the divine powers, to get his hopes up (for just a moment) before he concludes that his situation is hopeless.

However, the goddess Athena provides him needed inspiration not once but twice during the ordeal – and Odysseus acts on that inspiration.

Notice that the goddess does not actually physically rescue him herself: rather, she provides him with inspiration when his thoughts threaten to run away with him, interrupting his runaway chain of thoughts leading to imagined sea-monsters sent by Amphitrite, and then he takes the appropriate action which (it would seem) his runaway doubts were previously preventing him from taking.

Then, when Odysseus does successfully swim downshore until he finds an inviting place to land, he is attuned to the presence of the god of the river -- and this sensitivity to the presence of the gods would appear to be an important characteristic of the hero throughout the epic. Time and time again (we see), Odysseus would have wandered into certain catastrophe, had he not listened to the gods who offer him direction -- such as the time when Odysseus is confidently striding towards the palace of the bewitching goddess Circe of Aeaea, thinking to bring back his crew, and he is intercepted by the god Hermes, who warns Odysseus that he will never return if he does not take appropriate precautions against her magic, and specifically her power to turn men into swine and other beasts.

It is through our higher self that we have access to messages from the gods and the wider universe, and it is the "incessant scurrying of the superficial mind" which keeps us from hearing their voice or perceiving their presence, to quote the words of Alvin Boyd Kuhn, who declares:

> Deity for man is at home, not afield in distant skies. The kingdom of heaven and the hope of glory are within. They lurk within the unfathomed depths of consciousness. Divinity lies buried under the heavier motions of the sensual nature and the incessant scurrying of the superficieal mind. It is the still small voice, drowned out mostly by the raucous clamor of fleshly, material, and mental interests. It is a pure, mild Presence, awaiting the day when the outer man will give more heed to its quiet speech.[125]

Kuhn's reference to the "still small voice," of course, comes from the Biblical account of the prophet Elijah, in which the prophet

Chapter Ten

goes up to Mount Horeb and fasts for forty days and forty nights, and the text tells us that the word of the LORD came to Elijah and asked what he was doing there, and Elijah replied that he was in despair and felt that he was the last remaining one who sought after God, and that the whole world was against him and pursuing him to take his life.

Then the word of the LORD tells Elijah: "Go forth, and stand upon the mount before the LORD." And the text goes on to say:

> And behold, the LORD passed by, and a great and strong wind rent the mountains, and brake in pieces the rocks before the LORD; *but* the LORD *was* not in the wind: and after the wind an earthquake; *but* the LORD *was* not in the earthquake: And after the earthquake a fire; *but* the LORD *was* not in the fire: and after the fire a still small voice. 1 Kings 19: 11 - 12.

That this passage can be observed, based upon many examples we have already seen in this book, to be patterned upon the constellation Ophiuchus (a mountain that is "rent" or "cleft") and above it the constellation Hercules (representative of the Most High), indicates that it is not intended to be understood as applying to one particular historical person in the distant past, but rather to be conveying something of profound importance to the lives of each and every one of us. We too have access to that "still small voice" – but in order to perceive its presence we must quiet the raging of the egoic mind, under whose "incessant scurrying" the essential self is patiently waiting.

Here once again the importance of the pivotal figure of Ophiuchus becomes evident. Ophiuchus illustrates for us that "cleft within the rock" in which the Buddha meditates, and within which Elijah has access to the "still small voice."

Ophiuchus is the figure in the heavens who is both part of the zodiac and yet strangely detached from it as well. And it is in this *simultaneous presence and detachment* that the ancient myths tell us that wisdom is found.

Ophiuchus

The goddess Athena can be confidently understood to be associated with the same starry figure of Ophiuchus. We see, for instance, that:

- ➢ she is born from the head of her father, Zeus (Zeus being seen, of course, in the constellation Hercules just above Ophiuchus);
- ➢ she wears a crested helmet and carries a long spear (both of which are distinctive characteristics associated with Ophiuchus-figures, as explored in previous books: the spear-bearing aspect of Ophiuchus being easily seen if we imagine a straight line connecting the stars of the eastern "serpent-half" of the constellation, and the helmet and crest being suggested by both the triangular top of the constellation and by the nearby arc of the Corona Borealis, which can be shown to form the crest of helmets in artwork, particularly artwork in which Heracles is grasping a helmet-crest, as we saw on pages 53 - 55 of this book);
- ➢ and she wears the Aegis breastplate fringed with serpents (the long central body of the constellation Ophiuchus being often depicted in ancient artwork as a long tunic, coat of mail, or a tall shield, and the multiple heads of Scorpio just beneath suggesting the serpent-fringe of the invincible Aegis).

Chapter Ten

Note that in the ancient artwork on the preceding page, Athena is depicted in "mirror image" to the outline of Ophiuchus in the sky. In other words, the ancient artist has depicted her crested helmet on the left of the artwork as we face the image, even though this helmet corresponds to "serpent head" feature of the western serpent-half of the constellation Ophiuchus in the sky, which is on the right as we look at the star-chart. Similarly, the tip of the spear of the goddess in the artwork is on the right as we look at the image, and it corresponds to the eastern serpent-half of Ophiuchus, which is on the left as we face the accompanying star-chart. This kind of "mirror-imaging" is common in artwork -- but the correspondences to the constellation in question are unmistakeable.

What is extremely noteworthy is the fact that other figures associated with the quality of wisdom, in the sacred traditions of other cultures, can be shown to be associated with the constellation Ophiuchus as well. For instance, we have already mentioned in several places in this present volume the evidence which leads to the conclusion that the figure of Solomon in the texts of the Hebrew scriptures of the Old Testament corresponds to the constellation Ophiuchus. My 2016 book *Star Myths of the World, Volume Three: Star Myths of the Bible* spends more time exploring additional evidence for concluding that Solomon can be confidently associated with the constellation Ophiuchus in the heavens.

Some of the more compelling details which support this conclusion include the fact that Solomon is descended from David (and David can be very confidently associated with the constellation Hercules), and the fact that Solomon is "given a wise and understanding heart" by the Almighty (we have discussed this episode on pages 132 and 133 of this volume). Solomon is also frequently depicted as being seated "between the pillars" of the Temple -- and this description applies very directly to the constellation Ophiuchus in the heavens, a constellation which consists of a central body flanked by two "pillars" in the sky.

Thus, we can see a consistent pattern in the world's ancient myths associating the constellation Ophiuchus with *detachment from the whirl of the zodiac* (and, by my interpretation of the metaphor, detachment from the "automatic" or "pre-programmed" responses of the egoic self); with becoming *attuned to* the messages from the divine realm; and with *wisdom*.

It would not be too much of a stretch to say, based upon abundant evidence, that the world's ancient myths teach us that wisdom involves detachment from the impulsive reactions of the egoic mind, and, through detachment from the "auto-pilot" of the egoic mind, a reconnection with the essential self. And through the essential self, we achieve reconnection with the infinite realm, and with the messages sent by the gods.

Many other wisdom-bearing figures in world myth can also be shown to be associated with the pivotal figure of Ophiuchus, including the deity known as Sovereign Plumed Serpent in the Popol Vuh of the Quiché Maya (a god likely known in other cultures of the Americas as Quetzalcoatl, Viracocha, Kukulkan, Gucumatz, Con, Kon Tiki, Tupaca, and by other names as well), and the figure of Bodhidharma (also called Da Mo and Daruma in different cultures) in the traditions of China and surrounding cultures, and the figure of Odin in the Norse myths (and this list could go on and on). Many of these identifications are explored in previous volumes, including *The Ancient World-Wide System* and *Star Myths of the World, Volume Four: Norse Mythology*.

It is also worth pointing out that when Odysseus puts on the sash given to him by the goddess Leucothea during the sea-trial described in Book Five of the Odyssey discussed earlier, he himself almost certainly becomes associated with the figure of Ophiuchus, at least during this particular episode of the epic.

The outline of the constellation Ophiuchus can be envisioned as a figure clothed only in a sash or cloth (or winding-sheet), wrapped about the waist (the two "serpent-halves" on either side of the central body of the constellation being envisioned as the sash).

Chapter Ten

Thus, this myth-pattern or oicotype of a woman or goddess giving a sash or girdle to a male character to wear about his waist for protection can be confidently interpreted as having its original inspiration in the contstellation Ophiuchus (the female figure in these episodes likely associated with Sagittarius, or with the descending bird of the Milky Way, the constellation Cygnus the Swan).

As discussed in passing in *The Ancient World-Wide System*, we can easily detect strong parallels between the gift of a sash from the goddess Leucothea to the hero Odysseus, a sash which he must wear about his waist in order to gain protection, and the gift of a girdle from the beautiful queen Bertilak to the knight Gawaine in the medieval romance of *Gawaine and the Green Knight*.[126] In that romance, Gawaine (wearing the girdle of the queen) can be identified with the constellation Ophiuchus, and the mysterious figure of the Green Knight can be identified with the constellation Hercules, looming over the top of Ophiuchus, brandishing a powerful weapon menacingly overhead (the weapon of the constellation Hercules being envisioned in various myths as a club, a mace, or a giant sword, but also as a great hammer, and as a thunderbolt, and also as an axe -- an axe being the chosen weapon of the Green Knight in the Gawaine romance).

Finally, although much more could be explored regarding the significance of the constellation Ophiuchus and the meaning conveyed by this pivotal figure in the ancient Star Myth system, it is also worth noting as well that the constellation Ophiuchus, in addition to all its other associations, also plays the role of a *door* or *portal* or *gate* in numerous myths from multiple cultures.

The outline of the constellation can easily be seen to resemble a tall doorway or gateway, and can be shown to act as a portal in myths, depicting the gates to the underworld in the myths of ancient Greece,[127] and the gate to the underworld in the Norse myths, described during the episode in which Hermod the son of

Ophiuchus

Odin travels to the realm of Hel in order to try to retrieve Baldr from the land of the dead.[128]

One reason offered in *Star Myths of the World, Volume Four* to explain the role of Ophiuchus as the gates to the underworld is the constellation's location at one end of the "pathway" or "bridge" across the Milky Way made by the Dark Rift in the band of the galaxy. This Dark Rift pathway is the same passage across the Red Sea which is opened for Moses when he extends his rod in Exodus 14: 21, where the figure of Moses is associated with the constellation Ophiuchus. In other mythologies, during journeys to the underworld, the constellation is envisioned as a gate, guarding one end of the passageway across a gloomy river (the Milky Way again):

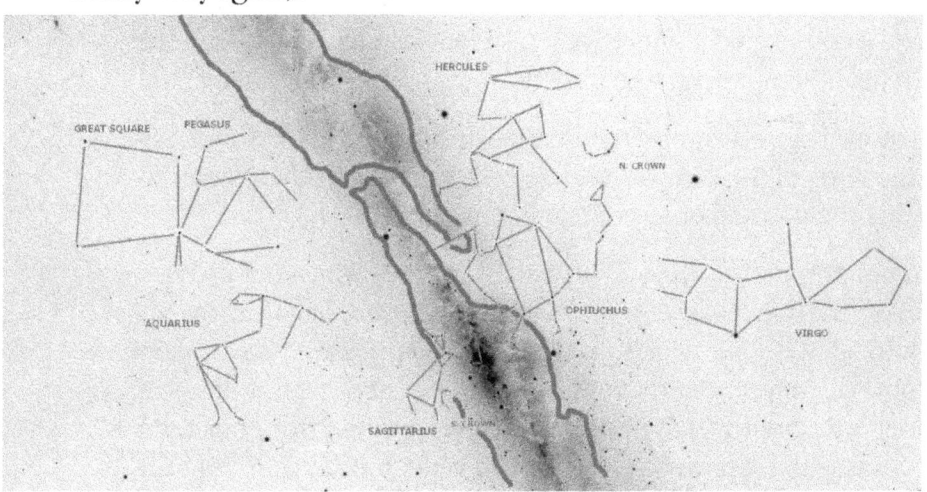

In the star-chart above, the general contours of the Milky Way band have been outlined in bold, and the pathway which forms the "dry land" over the Red Sea -- the Dark Rift path -- is clearly visible, crossing the galaxy from a point near the feet of Pegasus on the east (on the left as we face the star-chart above) down to an opening guarded by Ophiuchus on the west (to the right of the Milky Way as we face the chart).

Hence the role of the constellation Ophiuchus as a gateway between one realm and the next, adding yet another dimension to all the other aspects of this crucial constellation which we have examined so far. Ophiuchus is the gateway through which we have access to our higher self, and -- through that connection -- access to the infinite realm: the realm of the gods.

Note that in the scriptures of the New Testament, the figure of Jesus (whom we have already seen to be closely associated with the constellation Ophiuchus) says at one point: "I am the door" (repeating this declaration twice, in John 10: 7 and also John 10: 9).

Through these Ophiuchus connections, the ancient myths present us with powerful illustrations relating to the path of reconciliation with our essential self. The way of recovery involves *detachment* -- opening up a "gap" within which we can disconnect from the automatic, programmatic response of the superficial self, within which we may observe "from a distance" how the egoic mind wants to react, so that we can choose to "give the reins" to our essential self instead.

When we begin to unpry the death-grip that the egoic mind has on the reins of the chariot, we can only then begin to be open to hearing the *wisdom* of our higher self.

And not only do we begin to hear the messages which our essence has for us, but through our essence we can have access to additional wisdom which is difficult or impossible to explain within the conventional paradigm of physics and the five physical senses -- wisdom which appears to come not just from our own subconscious (suppressed by the "coping mechanism" of our egoic mind) but also from the subconscious of other people, even if separated from us by great distances (and thus inexplicable through the mechanism of the "physical senses").

In other words, our higher self appears to act in some way as a *gateway* or *portal* to wisdom which is difficult to explain within the conventional paradigm -- wisdom which appears to originate in another realm, a realm which the ancient myths would describe as the realm of the gods.

Chapter 11

A still small voice

An AP story published in the *New York Times* and dated February 20, 1979 recounts the outline of the grueling ordeal:

> An 11 year-old boy with a broken hand trudged two miles to safety through waist-deep snow and ice after surviving a plane crash in the rugged San Gabriel Mountains.
>
> Two men, including the boy's father, were killed in the crash yesterday and a woman died trying to walk from the crash site with the boy.
>
> The boy, Norman Ollestad, Jr. of Santa Monica, California, sitting in a wheelchair with his mother at his side after his release from a hospital, told of how he and Sandra Cressman, 30, survived the crash of the single-engine Cessna 172 at about 8 a.m. yesterday.
>
> He said they huddled for warmth under a wing for about seven hours. Fearing they would freeze, they decided to try to make it down the mountain.
>
> "I was just sliding down on my butt and every time I got going too fast, I stuck a stick in the snow."
>
> But Miss Cressman slipped on the ice and could not go on, Norman said. "Her eyes were open, but she couldn't talk." By the time rescuers arrived, she was dead.
>
> Norman covered about half of the two miles from the crash site to the ranch house by stop-and-go sliding, said Lieutenant Richard Smith of the San Bernardino County Sheriff's Department. Norman said he then came to a meadow and followed a creek to the house where people called for help. It took him two hours, he said.

Chapter Eleven

> The plane crashed about 50 miles northeast of Los Angeles. The wreckage was discovered today after clouds that had covered the mountains cleared. A rescue party was flown to the site by helicopter.
>
> The body of Miss Cressman was found about 100 yards from the plane. The police recovered the bodies of Norman Ollestad, Sr., a lawyer, and Bob Arnold, 27 years old, a flying instructor, of Mar Vista, at the crash site. Mr. Ollestad, a student pilot, was a former agent of the Federal Bureau of Investigation and wrote a book critical of the bureau. [. . .]

Thirty years later, Norman Ollestad -- the eleven-year-old boy in the article above -- wrote a bestselling book entitled *Crazy for the Storm: A Memoir of Survival* (2009) in which he describes the ordeal of surviving the crash that killed his father, his father's girlfriend Sandra, and the pilot, and of making his way down the steep, snow-covered mountain face from the crash site, interspersed with flashbacks to personal memories of growing up between his divorced parents and his mother's abusive boyfriend, and of the lessons his father taught him which helped young Norman make it through the harrowing situation.

I believe Norman Ollestad's book is an important work on many levels. Those who have not read it may wish to stop and do so before reading further here, since this chapter will touch upon one aspect of his escape from the dangerous situation in the snowy mountains which deserves to be read in Mr. Ollestad's own words and which might give away one of the surprising details that he discovered when he returned to the scene of his ordeal decades later.

Obviously, it is not a "spoiler" to reveal here that the young eleven-year-old Norman survived the planecrash into the sheer face of the 8,600-foot high mountain and the dangerous journey down the steep ice-chutes below the crash site and the deep snow along the rugged forested terrain further down, and was

A still small voice

eventually rescued. The very fact that he was able to write a book about the experience thirty years later removes that suspense.

However, and this is the part where readers may want to go read *Crazy for the Storm* first before returning to this chapter, Norman Ollestad distinctly remembers making his way towards a meadow which, when he later went back to the scene itself, he determined that he could not actually have seen until he was much further down the mountain than he remembers seeing it and making his way towards it that day.

Above, to give a sense of the steepness and mass of the mountain range into which the little single-engine Cessna 172 crashed on that stormy, foggy February morning, and down the face of which young Norman Ollestad had to make his way through the snow and ice, is a photograph showing Ontario Peak on the far right as we face the page (marked with a black arrow).

This is the peak, elevation 8,696 feet at the summit (just over 2,650 meters), into which the small plane slammed in the poor visibility, hitting the side that the camera is facing in the above photograph. The eleven-year-old boy, who had just witnessed the death of his father, had to descend from a point near that summit on the sheer face of the mountain, down and towards the right of the photgraph above.

Chapter Eleven

Norman Ollestad's memoir of the event explains that, far below, a young mother named Patricia Chapman was awakened on the morning of the crash by what she describes as a loud thud. "Her first thought was that it sounded like a plane crashing," she explains.[129] She also describes having heard a strange beeping sound and a coyote who wouldn't stop howling. The text continues:

> Later that morning, nagged by a remote yet unshakable feeling that something bad had happened on the mountain, she led her two sons on a miserable hike to the meadow. They called out toward Ontario Peak, above the crown of rock, into the long apron that she called Gooseberry Canyon. Although the canyon was several thousand feet away, their voices echoed off the canyon walls. The wind and heavy fog buffered their voices that day. When no one answered, she figured that her hunch was wrong.[130]

As it turns out, young Norman was trying to make his way towards this very same meadow, into which Pat Chapman had led her two sons "on a miserable hike" based on her unshakable feeling that something bad had happened on the mountain.

Norman thought he had seen this meadow from the steep cliffs near the top of the mountain, and he steered towards it after he made his way down through the terrifying ice-chutes and funnels formed by the rock faces of the mountainside below the crash site.

When he finally did make it to that meadow, it was only because he saw Pat's bootprints in the snow and followed them that he was able to trace his way through the forested areas surrounding the meadow back to a dirt road where he was eventually found by another person who followed a hunch that day, a teenager named Glenn Farmer.

When Norman later returned to the mountain twenty-seven years later (during the warmer months this time), he was astonished to discover that there was no way to see the meadow at all from the

A still small voice

part of the mountain that he had traversed -- it was hidden by another ridgeline the entire way!

And yet, if he had not navigated towards that meadow, and then followed the bootprints left in the snow by Pat Chapman and her two children, young Norman Ollestad might not have found anyone to help him in that remote location.

Below is a screenshot of a topo map from Google Maps, showing Ontario Peak and my estimation of the approximate route Norman probably took down the north face of the mountain, based on my reading of the book and my knowledge of terrain:

The contour lines on this map each represent forty feet of elevation. The closer they are together, the steeper is the terrain (and there are several extremely steep areas in the path that young Norman would have had to negotiate on his way off the mountain). Those familiar with reading topo maps may be able to observe the fact that there is indeed what we used to call in the U.S. Army an "intervisibility line" (or "i.v. line") which forms a kind of "mini-horizon" blocking visibility of whatever is on the other side of the i.v. line. This i.v. line formed by the terrain would have blocked Norman's ability to physically see the meadow towards which he eventually made his way.

Chapter Eleven

An intervisibility line is created by the bulge of terrain which masks whatever is on the other side of that bulge, and the i.v. line itself runs along the "false horizon" created by the curve of the terrain. You can think of your own experience driving along a road or highway in order to get a feel for the concept of intervisibility lines: where the road goes over a rise (sometimes referred to as a "donkey-back" in earlier generations) such that you cannot see the road on the other side, you would be ill-advised to try to pass a car ahead of you by going into the opposite lane belonging to oncoming traffic, because there could be a car (or even an eighteen-wheeler) coming up the road just behind the donkey-back, but you can't see it.

The line of the "false horizon" created by that rise in the terrain, beyond which you cannot see, is designated as an "intervisibility line," and this line's location will actually change depending on your location (the false horizon will shift as the location of the observer changes).

On the page opposite, we see a close-up of the same contour map from the preceding page, this time with the intervisibility line indicated, based on my reading of the terrain and my estimation of the route. The intervisibility line means that an observer located along the north face in the vicinity of the plane crash, and all the way down the route indicated, would not be able to see over the ridgeline along which I have drawn a thick line (and which I have labeled with the words "intervisibility line").

In other words, a person to the right of this intervisibility line (to the east of it, since north is up in the orientation of this map) would not be able to see terrain to the left or west of that line, unless that terrain was higher in elevation than the ridgeline of the intervisibility line itself. Thus, in the map shown below, the terrain beneath the label containing the words "intervisibility line" (for example) would be masked by the intervening ridgeline and thus not visible to an observer located any distance to the right of that line (to the east of the line).

A still small voice

What this means for the story of Norman Ollestad is that he could not have seen the region labeled "meadow area" from any point along his route (beginning at the crash site near the peak), until he reached the part of the route that crosses over to the "left" (west) of the indicated intervisibility line.

In his memoir, he recounts his surprise when, after reaching the site of the crash twenty-seven years later (an extremely moving and emotional description), he turns his gaze towards searching for the meadow which had been his "true north" during his journey down the mountain so many years before, and realizes that: "I could not see it over the massive ridgeline rising from the gulch and blocking anything to the left of the gulch. I was perplexed."[131]

He notes that in his audiotape recording of the interview he gave on the day after the crash, his eleven-year-old self clearly states that, "There was a meadow and I tried to go toward that every time because I knew there was a house near there."[132]

Chapter Eleven

But during his 2006 return to the site he realizes that even from his highest vantage point and on a clear day (unlike the day of the disastrous crash), there was no way to see the meadow from the crash site or any point along the route of his descent until near the very end: "It was eclipsed by the ridgeline and only visible once I made it through the gulch."[133]

This discovery creates a dilemma for Norman, because he has a very clear memory of steering towards that meadow during his difficult descent, and yet his on-the-ground obvservations as an adult show beyond doubt that the meadow could not have been seen from the crash site or his route down the mountain, until he was already very close to his destination.

To reconcile this dilemma, Norman Ollestad notes in his book that animals sometimes appear to "navigate by instinct" in such a way that they seem to be guided by knowledge beyond what can be attributed to the five physical senses. Reflecting on his perplexing later discovery that runs counter to his own memory of the ordeal, he writes:

> And even in the face of insurmountable contradictory evidence I still have a vivid memory of heading toward that meadow, compelled to reach it, believing that it would guide me to safety.
>
> Bears and wolves navigate wilderness by instinct, and migratory birds are guided by an internal compass, so maybe the notion that I had to see the meadow in order for me to perceive it is an artificial concept.
>
> Maybe I sensed a place where I could rest from the steep ice and broken terrain -- a place where other humans like Pat were compelled to go -- just as a wolf or bear can sense such places. Maybe the footprints of Pat and her boys, those human markings, called to me, and because I was cut off from civilization I was able to access my animal instinct and hang on to life.[134]

A still small voice

Think back to the Star Myth episode described in the very opening illustration of this book, when a lonely traveler was in the wilderness and suddenly had a vision which he did not expect: a vision of a ladder or stairway stretching to heaven, with angels ascending and descending. The astonished traveler declared aloud that the divine was in that place, even though he did not at first perceive it. He thought he was alone in the wilderness, and was surprised to find that he was connected to the infinite, even there.

Our higher self, our essential self, is aware of so much more than our conscious mind, our "superficial mind" (in the words of Alvin Boyd Kuhn), typically perceives. Our body has an array of sensors which gather data about the world around us in an abundance far too great for our conscious mind to assimilate at any given time. We could almost say that our body itself is a multifarious array of subtle and sophisticated sensors, sensing all the time, even though we are not usually listening (with our conscious mind).

Animals, not divided against themselves by the artificial construct of the egoic mind, are aware on a level that we generally are not, as Norman Ollestad observes in the passage above, in which he tries to reconcile his memory of navigating towards the meadow with the observation that he could not have seen the meadow at any point after the crash until he was almost on top of it.

I myself distinctly remember one day in the ninth grade, when I was walking into my high school (Aragon High School in San Mateo, California) up a long asphalt walkway past the outdoor basketball courts below the main gymnasium, and going past some low juniper bushes that served as ground-cover along the pathway, when a large rodent of some kind popped its head out of the bushes and looked right at me while chattering excitedly, as if it was trying to tell me something.

I continued walking to school, somewhat surprised by the encounter, as I had never seen anything like that before. There was no one else with me at the time.

Chapter Eleven

Later that day, while in Ms Bailey's trigonometry class, the entire school began to shake – not violently but rather in an undulating manner, as if the ground underneath the buildings had suddenly turned to water, and we were on a ship in the sea, with rolling swells causing the floors of the classrooms to roll rapidly themselves, with us inside. It was the 1984 earthquake of April 24th, a 6.2-magnitude event with its epicenter along the Calaveras Fault just northwest of Anderson Lake on the edges of the city of Morgan Hill, only a couple miles south of San Jose and less than fifty miles south of our high school.

Not long after the rolling concluded, I thought back to that encounter with the "rat in the bushes," and realized that the little animal must have somehow been aware of the impending earthquake, and that it had popped its head out of the plants in order to warn me about it as I was walking up the pathway towards the school buildings that morning, several hours before the quake actually hit (the Morgan Hill earthquake took place at 1:15 pm local time that day).

I had previously heard that animals are able to sense an earthquake long before it actually occurs, and here it seemed was an example of it happening, right at my high school!

It is interesting to stop and consider exactly how animals might possibly be able to perceive in advance the approach of a significant earthquake. A 6.2-magnitude quake is a fairly significant event: there were no other earthquakes over 5.0 recorded anywhere in California during 1984, and the next one with a magnitude over 5.0 in the state would not occur until 1986. The Morgan Hill earthquake of April 24, 1984, had a surface-wave magnitude (M_s) of 6.1 and a body-wave magnitude (m_b) of 5.7, according to the U.S. National Earthquake Information Service in Golden, Colorado.[135]

The report published by the U.S. Geological Survey (USGS) on the Morgan Hill Earthquake states that:

A still small voice

No clear changes in the pattern of seismicity immediately before the Morgan Hill earthquake have been identified that would have permitted prediction of the earthquake. The Morgan Hill earthquake rupture zone lies within a dense network of seismographic stations operated by the U.S. Geological Survey (USGS) in central California, so that all earthquakes of M_L greater than or equal to 1.5 in the vicinity are recorded and located [note that M_L stands for "local magnitude" and is measured with the Richter magnitude scale developed in 1935 by Charles F. Richter based upon the logarithm of the amplitude of the waves on a seismograph; because it is a log-based scale, each whole number increase in magnitude represents a tenfold increase in amplitude, such that a 6.0 quake produces waves ten times greater in amplitude than a 5.0 quake, and represents approximately 31 times more energy released]. During the 24 hours before the main shock, only two small earthquakes occurred on April 24, at 0341:37.0 GMT (coda-duration magnitude, 0.7) and 1811:37.7 GMT (coda-duration magnitude, 0.4), both located at the main-shock epicenter (Bakun and others, 1984).[136]

Those small earthquakes, each measuring less than 1.0 on the Richter scale, occurred at 10:11 am local time (1811 hours Greenwich Mean Time) that morning, which is after I had already had the encounter with the rodent in the bushes on my way in to school that day, and at 7:41 pm local time the night before (0341 hours Greenwich Mean Time).

Based on this information, it is very difficult to explain how animals are able to detect an approaching earthquake several hours ahead of time, as the rodent in the bushes at Aragon High School apparently did that day. Clearly, animals tend to be much more highly attuned to their surroundings and to the signals that the complex array of body sensors is constantly receiving from the universe around them. It is interesting to wonder if we ourselves are actually receiving the same level of data from our own sophisticated bodily grid of sensing equipment (including the

Chapter Eleven

sense organs that comprise what we refer to as "our gut"), which we too could hear, if only our conscious mind would allow that information to get through.

In the passage quoted above, Norman Ollestad contemplates the fact that he vividly remembers working his way down the mountain with a plan to head for the meadow, and that his audio recording of the interview taken the very day after the ordeal contains his own statement that he was making his way to the meadow because he "knew there was a house near there," while considering at the same time the fact that the physical layout would have prevented his seeing that meadow until near the very end of his long and harrowing journey. He wonders if perhaps his own senses and animal instincts were able to reach him more clearly in that intense situation, "cut off from civilization" as he says, and struggling for survival.

I agree that this is a very possible explanation. As we will see, the wider awareness of our entire being, which is much wider than the narrow stream of information which our egoic mind allows into our conscious awareness, is truly amazing in its abilities, and it appears to "break through" the filter of the egoic mind and unexpectedly "take over" when survival is at stake.

In some of my previously-published blog posts (now numbering more than 1,200 since 2011), I have linked to videos posted on YouTube showing "dad saves" -- in which some amazing rescues, primarily of infants or very young children, are caught on video. In one of these videos, a father lying full-length on his back on a couch and apparently asleep (or at least dozing off) suddenly shoots out his hand to catch an infant about to fall head-first off the same couch to the floor.[137] The man was not even looking at the child, and indeed appeared to be quite oblivious to his surroundings, when his arm extends *seemingly on its own* and unerringly grasps the baby, saving it from potentially serious injury.

A still small voice

Clearly, the man whose arm shoots out and saves the child is not directing this action with his conscious mind – but by now we should be well aware that the conscious mind does not at all represent the sum total of "who we are," but rather only a small subset. It is quite apparent that in some situations, often situations involving the need for immediate and precise action to save a child from serious injury, the body and the "wider" or "deeper" subconscious can perceive danger and perform inspired action without direction from the conscious mind.

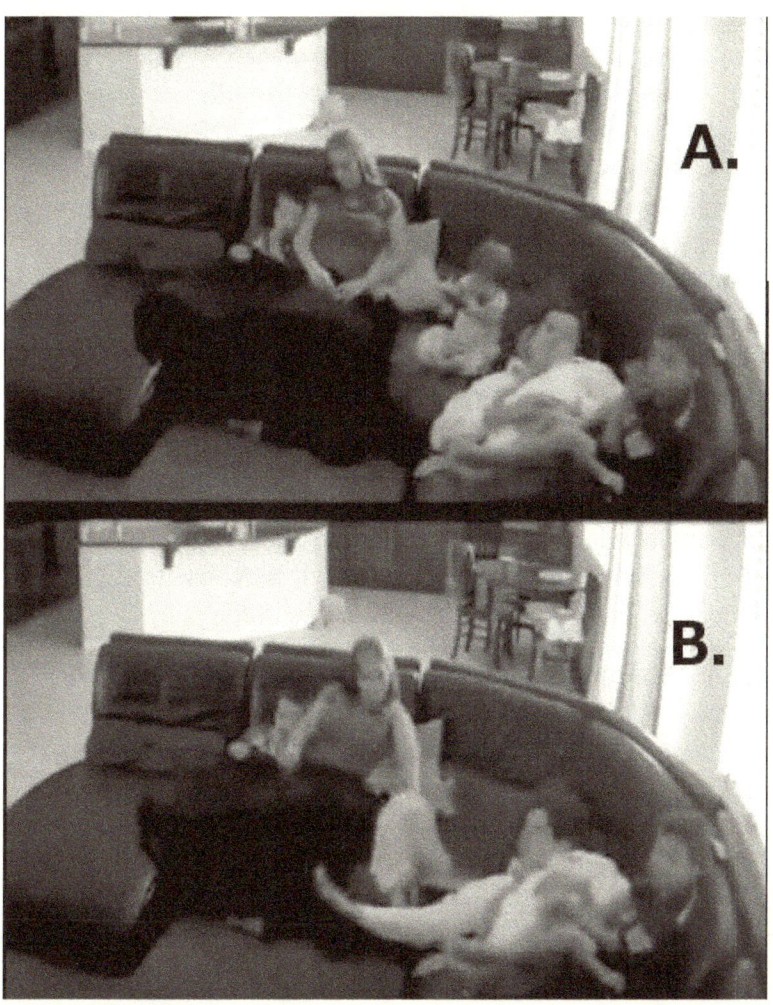

Chapter Eleven

It is possible that the man's subconscious self or higher self could perceive, by the minute changes in the cushions of the sofa transmitted through his skin and even the hair on his head, the roll of the child towards the edge, resulting in the seemingly miraculous last-second rescue, by "instinct."

Our subconscious can obviously perceive and absorb a much wider range of information than our conscious mind allows itself to be aware of most of the time.

Based on this fact, one possible explanation for Norman Ollestad's vivid memory of steering towards a meadow where he "knew" there was a house nearby, even though he later determined that it was impossible to see the meadow from the site of the crash or the route that he took down the mountain, is the thought that Norman might have seen the meadow and the nearby house *from the air*, prior to the crash -- even though at the time he was not consciously aware that the plane was going to crash. His subconscious might have absorbed this important information and then provided it to him during the ordeal that followed the plane's collision with the face of Ontario Peak.

Of course, this explanation is only speculation: it is also quite possible that Norman was not looking out the window at all when the meadown was in view, or that the fog and clouds which obscured the ridgeline and led to the crash itself also obscured the view of the meadow (and house nearby) to those in the plane.

The reason for mentioning this speculative possibility is that such an explanation would fit within the "materialist" paradigm, by avoiding any suggestion of extrasensory perception of any kind. This explanation would still be amazing and extraordinary, and show just how wide and deep the perception of the subconscious can be, far beyond the narrow band of the conscious mind -- and how information from the subconscious (or whatever we want to call this "wider" perception of information) can provide help in time of need that seems truly miraculous and inexplicable.

A still small voice

However, even if proponents of a strict materialist paradigm were to offer such an explanation as that proposed above (that Norman may have seen the meadow while still airborne in the plane, prior to the crash, and that this information bubbled up to his conscious mind after the crash, when he needed to make his way down the mountain and find someone who could give him shelter and get him back to civilization), thinking that this explanation solves the dilemma without having to resort to any awareness beyond what can be explained within the confines of materialism, there still remain other difficult to explain "synchronicities" or "coincidences" which enabled Norman to be rescued that day, and without which he might yet have died of exposure before finding help.

As has already been mentioned, there is also the case of the young mother named Pat Chapman, who was awakened on the morning of February 19, 1979 by what she described as a "loud thud." After that, she heard a coyote howling incessantly, as well as a beeping noise. Norman Ollestad was able to meet with her on his return to the scene in 2006, and she told him that she hadn't awakened her husband Bob because she was not certain of what she had heard, but she was unable to shake a feeling that something bad had happened on the mountain -- and this led her to take that fateful hike out to the meadow with her two young sons later that morning. Had she not done so, young Norman might not have been able to find his way to the road (he followed their bootprints in the snow when he got to the meadow).[138]

During that reunion in 2006, Pat told Norman that not long after Norman had been rescued, a sheriff's deputy came to her house for a statement. When she told him about the noise that had awakened her, "the sheriff's deputy informed her that she could not have heard a plane and that it must have been the snowplow clearing the highway."[139]

This fact is very curious, and appears to indicate that Pat Chapman's subconscious was somehow able to perceive the fact

Chapter Eleven

that "something bad had happened on the mountain" even though it had been too far away for her to have heard it.

The coyote who would not stop howling is also an aspect of the story worth pondering, and the fact that Pat Chapman noted the coyote's howling in her statement to the sheriff's deputy the day of the incident and to Norman Ollestad all those years later indicates that this howling may well have contributed to her unshakable sense that something was wrong. Was the coyote, like the rodent in the bushes on the day of the earthquake in 1984, aware of something that it was trying to communicate?

Again, if Patricia Chapman had not followed her "hunch" that something was wrong, and had not gone out into the meadow with her two boys, leaving fresh bootprints in the snow, young Norman Ollestad might not have found his way to the road where he was eventually discovered. But even after he did find the bootprints, he describes in his memoir how he was becoming nearly delirious at that point -- and was forcing himself to hold on and concentrate, when he heard a voice calling out into the wind, yelling, "Hello! Anybody there!"[40]

At first, Norman relates, he thought it was a trick of the wind, and that it wasn't real. Then, however, he yelled back, crying for help. And that is how he made his way to the dirt road, where a teenager named Glenn Farmer found him, and carried him to the Chapman family's nearby place, where he was able to warm up in front of a potbelly stove and sip a mug of hot chocolate.

Twenty-seven years later, when Norman Ollestad went back to the mountain, he was able to meet with Glenn Farmer as well – and he learned that Glenn had spoken with members of the sherriff's search & rescue team in the early afternoon on the day of the crash, and that they had pointed towards the direction of Ontario Peak but because of the fog, he had mistaken what they were pointing at for a closer terrain feature, north of the area I've labeled as "meadow area" on the topo map on page 293.

A still small voice

Glenn explained to Norman that after the search & rescue team members had left,

> Glenn decided to hike up toward that lower crown of rock and see what he could find. He was never able to get close to the crown because the buckthorn was too thick. Glenn said he yelled many times and, having given up, was walking back down the dirt road when he decided to give it one more shot.[41]

Once again, a strict materialist might ascribe all these decisions, which led directly to Norman's survival of the terrible ordeal, to "mere coincidence" -- but it is worth considering the question of what might have prompted Glenn Farmer to yell out one more time while he was walking back along the dirt road? Had he not done so, the plane crash might have had no survivors, instead of only one.

As we've noted, it is possible to speculate that young Norman might have seen, and subconsciously noted, the meadow and the buildings while still airborne, not knowing (at least not consciously knowing) that he would need that information in the near future. Such an explanation would at least allow diehard supporters of the materialist paradigm to explain Norman's vivid memory of trying to make his way towards a meadow that he *could not have seen* from the part of Ontario Peak where he was situated following the plane crash.

However, evidence such as Pat Chapman's memory of being awakened by something that sounded like a crash (even though too far away to have heard it) and of having a kind of premonition that something bad had happened, causing her to go out to the meadow, is more difficult to explain within the materialist paradigm which dogmatically asserts that nothing exists beyond the material universe, and that consciousness arises from strictly chemical processes in the material organ of the brain, and cannot extend beyond the physical senses. So is Glenn Farmer's decision to "give it one more shot" while walking back along the dirt road

Chapter Eleven

near the meadow where young Norman Ollestad was desperately trying to find his way to someone who could help him.

Certainly the wider sensitivity of our body's incredible array of information-gathering organs, including the skin and the gut, and the deeper capacity of the subconscious to know far more than the conscious mind perceives, can explain many incredible and seemingly miraculous incidences. As healers such as Dr. Peter Levine and Dr. Gabor Maté explain, trauma separates us from ourselves and even from our own body, and causes us to shut off the information coming from our gut and our subconscious and our wider and deeper self. Healing that alienation from our self enables us to begin to open up to that seemingly miraculous source of assistance and wisdom that the interference of our egoic mind typically keeps us from experiencing.

But I would argue that even beyond the awareness that can be attributed to the subconscious and the wider sensitivity of the whole body including the gut, there appears to be abundant evidence that our higher self (or, if materialists prefer, our subconscious) has access to information and awareness that cannot be explained by the material senses: that somehow, our higher self (or our subconscious) sometimes has access to information and awareness which comes from a connection with the higher self of other men and women, and indeed from a connection with the wider universe, or the realm of the gods (please note that this assertion is one that I myself am making, and I do not at all intend to imply that others such as Norman Ollestad, Peter Levine, or Gabor Maté would necessarily agree with me, or – even if they did – if they would phrase their opinions on the subject in quite the same way).

Into this category we might tentatively put the subconscious "hunches" described by both Pat Chapman and Glenn Farmer, which were instrumental in Norman Ollestad's ultimate rescue. We might also put Norman's own perception to steer towards a meadow that he could not have seen (although it *might* be possible to explain this awareness of the meadow without

A still small voice

resorting to any agency beyond what can be explained by the physical senses within the materialist paradigm).

And certainly these remarkable examples from the dramatic ordeal of eleven-year-old Norman Ollestad, Jr. in 1979 are not alone: in fact, there are volumes of evidence which suggest that the higher self (or, if some prefer, the subconscious) can at times "tap in" to information or awareness that defies easy explanation within the materialist paradigm -- awareness which can best be described as originating in the wider world beyond the reach of the physical senses, or even as originating in the infinite realm: the realm of the gods (just as the ancient myths, such as the Odyssey, appear to be trying to show us).

For example, while I was in the U.S. Army for eleven years on active duty, I had occasion to hear stories ("anecdotal evidence," perhaps -- except that I suspect there are many hundreds of such stories which could provide the basis for a rigorous academic study) of families during wartime (usually stories from veterans who had been in the military during the Vietnam War) in which a mother would wake up in the middle of the night with a dreadful premonition, only to later learn to her horror that her son who was halfway across the globe in Vietnam had been killed in action on that same day. These kinds of premonitions cannot be explained by recourse to the five physical senses, but appear to indicate examples of the subconscious somehow tapping-in to an awareness that does not fit within the materialist paradigm.

In the book *An American Town and the Vietnam War: Stories of Service from Stamford, Connecticut* (2018), by Tony Pavia and Matt Pavia, a heart-wrenching story along these lines is recounted surrounding the death of William B. Mitchell, a combat engineer in the Marine Corps who was killed in action less than two months after his nineteenth birthday, on the 3rd of November, 1965.

Chapter Eleven

The seventh of ten children, Billy Mitchell was particularly close to his younger sister Marjorie, who was the youngest of the ten children.

The book by Tony and Matt Pavia explains that on the day he was killed, Mitchell expressed concern to a friend that something bad was going to happen to him, because he could not find his St. Christopher medal which he always wore around his neck. The authors write:

> Tragically, the premonition was realized moments later when Mitchell was killed by an enemy explosive.
>
> That same morning back at home, his sister Marjorie also had a premonition. "That morning, for some reason I began to cry uncontrollably," she said. "I just knew something terrible had happened to Billy." Later that morning, she received the news that she had dreaded.[142]

This tragic example is very difficult to explain within the materialist paradigm. How could Marjorie's subconscious have experienced an overwhelming sense of grief, before the news was actually delivered to the family? And yet, this does not appear to be an isolated example.

The fact that she somehow had the premonition that something terrible had happened specifically to her brother Billy, to whom she was particularly close, is especially difficult to explain from a materialistic perspective, because at the time of Billy's death, the family actually had three sons on active duty in the military out of the seven total boys, and yet Marjorie describes somehow knowing that something terrible had happened to Billy specifically.[143]

Skeptics argue that because incidents like these are not repeatable in the same way that a laboratory experiment is repeatable, they must be disqualified as evidence upon which to base any conclusions one way or another -- and thus cannot be used to cast doubt upon the prevailing materialist ideology, which declares out of hand that direct extrasensory awareness beyond the physical senses is impossible and that any incidents such as those described above must have materialistic explanations (including the fallback "mere coincidence").

There is also the problem of verifying incidents of premonition or similar non-sensory awareness which rely on subjective testimony that is difficult or impossible to prove or disprove. However, the sheer number of such incidents, and the fact that some examples appear to be backed up with strong supporting evidence (such as the ordeal of Norman Ollestad described above, in which testimony from a recorded interview conducted the day after the actual incident can be consulted even now) argues against trying to explain away all of these examples as "mere coincidence."

Another problem is the troubling record of close association between intelligence agencies and research into psychic phenomenon, particularly since the putative end of World War II, which tends to call into question some of what has been published and popularized on this subject, since intelligence agencies during the past seventy-five years have a documented record of deliberately spreading disinformation on a variety of subjects for a variety of reasons. The undeniable activity of numerous individuals in this field who are clearly associated with various intelligence services is documented, for example, in Annie Jacobsen's 2018 book *Phenomena: The Secret History of the U.S. Government's Investigations into Extrasensory Perception and Psychokinesis* (among other places).

However, there are so many examples which can be offered from the lives of individuals who are not associated with intelligence agencies that, although the intelligence activity in this area undoubtedly muddies the water, it is inadvisable to completely disregard the weight of evidence suggesting that men and women sometimes tap into levels of awareness which defy the materialist paradigm, a paradigm which has been so aggressively pushed onto the populace during the past one hundred years.

Chapter Eleven

Researcher Chris Carter, who has written numerous books in which he exhaustively documents evidence for the existence of "psychic phenomena" as well as presenting and confronting the strongest arguments of skeptics who seek to "debunk" the possibility of extra-sensory awareness, cites numerous instances of precognition in his 2007 book *Science and Psychic Phenomena: The Fall of the House of Skeptics.*

One example, published by pioneering parapsychologist Louisa Rhine in a 1954 article in the *Journal of Parapsychology,* involves a premonition that appears to have led a mother to save her baby from a falling chandelier. Of this incident, Louisa Rhine writes:

> It concerns a mother who dreamed that two hours later a violent storm would loosen a heavy chandelier to fall directly on her baby's head lying in a crib below it; in the dream she saw her baby killed dead. She awoke her husband who said it was a silly dream and that she should go back to sleep. [. . .] The weather was so calm the dream did appear ridiculous and she could have gone back to sleep. But she did not. She went and brought the baby back to her own bed. Two hours later just at the time specified, a storm caused the heavy light fixture to fall right on where the baby's head had been -- but the baby was not there to be killed by it.[144]

This same example is also cited by physician Larry Dossey in his multiple books examining the subject of premonitions, as well as in an interview transcript entitled "The Power of Premonitions: How Knowing the Future Can Shape Our Lives," which is posted on his website.

In that interview, Dr. Dossey cites tests devised to try to objectively measure "ability to predict the future," such as a test which asked subjects to try to predict a string of randomly-generated numbers which they would only be shown later (and which would in fact only be generated after the subject made his or her prediction). He also cites a "presentiment" experiment devised by consciousness researcher Dean Radin of the Institute

A still small voice

of Noetic Sciences in Petaluma, California, which Dr. Dossey describes as follows:

> Briefly, a person sits in front of a computer, which will make a random selection from a large collection of images that are of two types -- calming or violent. Calming images may be a lovely scene from nature; violent images deal with death, carnage, grisly autopsies, and so on. The subject has some physiological function being measured, such as the electrical conductivity of the skin or the diameter of the pupil. The bodily function begins to change several seconds before the image is randomly selected by the computer and shown on the screen. Here's the shocker: the physiological change occurs to a greater degree if the image to be shown is violent in nature. How is this possible? How does the body know which image is going to be shown *in the future?*
>
> Dozens of these studies have been done by various researchers. They show that we have a built-in, unconscious ability to know the future. Somehow the body knows before our awareness kicks in.[145]

Many other examples documented over the years appearing to demonstrate "wider awareness" beyond what should be able to be known based upon the physical senses could be offered, but as these are written about quite thoroughly in many books devoted exclusively to this subject, the examples cited thus far will have to suffice to support the contention that our higher self (by whatever term we decide to refer to it) has access to far wider levels of awareness than our conscious mind knows, and the possibility that when we become more integrated with this essence (from whom we become alienated during our indoctrination into society), we may at times actually tap into awareness which goes beyond even our own subconscious -- awareness which is connected to the subconscious of others around us, and also to that realm which the ancient myths describe as the realm of the gods.

Chapter Eleven

While not nearly as dramatic as some of the other incidents described in this chapter and recorded by other researchers who focus more intensely on this particular subject, I myself can report that on more than one occasion over the past several years of examining the connection between the stars and the myths, "answers" have seemed to come to me from a source beyond my conscious mind.

For example, I have had the experience of trying to uncover the celestial foundations for a specific episode in ancient myth or scripture, and staying up late into the night trying to work it out, only to go to sleep without the answer. The next morning, not immediately upon waking up but within the first half hour, I suddenly realized that the solution to the question of the night before had come into my thoughts, even though my conscious mind had obviously been out of the picture all night while I slept.

Clearly, my subconscious had not been asleep, and it presented the answer to my waking mind within a short time after awakening, all unbidden. I distinctly remember this happening with regard to the celestial foundations of the Genesis story of Noah's drunkenness after the flood, when Noah plants a vineyard and drinks of the wine, and passes out, and his sons Shem and Japheth walk backwards with a sheet between their shoulders in order to cover their father's nakedness, while Ham mocks and ridicules his father's compromised condition.

I was unable to put my finger on the celestial basis for this famous episode in Genesis 9 when I first tried to work it out, and I went to bed pondering what the solution could possibly be. The next morning, I woke up and was not thinking about it at all, but went about my morning routine without giving any conscious thought to the problem that I had been working on the night before.

It was actually while I was in the shower that I suddenly realized that I knew the answer to the puzzle (the drunken Noah is associated with the constellation Aquarius, and the sheet his two sons Japheth and Shem place over him by walking backwards with the sheet between their shoulders can be seen in the figure of the Great Square of Pegasus, "carried" as it were between the two Fishes of Pisces). This incident from Genesis 9 is discussed in more detail in my 2016 book *Star Myths of the World, Volume Three: Star Myths of the Bible*.[46]

This answer did not come to me in the form of a dramatic dream or through a mysterious voice – it was more like a feeling that I had already known the answer, and I was just "remembering it" the next morning, some time after I had woken up (not too long after waking up). It was as though the answer had been placed in my awareness, but it had obviously not been placed there by virtue of any effort on the part of my conscious mind. It was actually a very "organic" experience, and not like something from "another world" at all.

And I have had similar experiences, often relating to connections between the myths and the stars, since that time as well.

Stepping back from "help" seeing specific connections between individual myth-episodes and the underlying pattern of the stars, I can also detect, in the path which led me to the entire star-myth connection in the first place, a guiding direction which was absolutely outside of my conscious intention.

A biblical literalist for nearly twenty years, I was certainly not consciously looking for evidence which would show that the characters and stories in the scriptures of the Bible were based on a system of celestial metaphor, and a system that could be shown to be worldwide and to form the foundation of myths from cultures as seemingly far-removed as the ancient Sumerians, ancient Egyptians, ancient Greeks, or the cultures of Africa, Australia, the Americas, the Pacific, the Norse, ancient China and Japan, and ancient India.

This realization, which took place over a period of years between 2011 and 2014, completely changed my entire life in numerous significant ways, as well as my outlook on many issues including political and economic issues, and nearly every aspect of the way I see the world.

Looking back now, I can see that this process of discovery began in 2009 with the direction of ideas that I was exploring regarding the myths and the world's ancient history, a line of investigation which would lead to the realizations which followed after a few years, but the outcome of which I could never have guessed at the time -- an outcome which was completely antithetical to the "framework" which my egoic mind had constructed for my outlook on life, and which I had built as an attempt to sort out various experiences and to understand the world around me.

With the benefit of hindsight, I can also perceive that my childhood love of the myths and of the stars (and of the books written by H. A. Rey about the constellations) all contributed to the unexpected direction into which I would later be led, without consciously knowing it (a direction filled with revelations sufficient to obliterate that framework to which I had previously been holding on rather tightly).

There is also the fact that a rodent in the bushes of my high school tried to warn me about an impending earthquake in 1984!

While my own personal experiences do not involve premonitions that demonstrate phenomena which in and of themselves demolish the materialist paradigm, I believe that a strong case can be made for understanding that our essential self (so often buried beneath the "protective" mechanism of our egoic mind) is in a very profound and very real sense connected to and indeed *part of* the wider cosmos, and that the more we are able to relax the iron grip of our egoic mind, the more we open ourselves up to connecting with our own essence and what it has to tell us -- and through that reconnection, the more we become receptive to the messages from the realm of the gods.

Our essential self is always present: it never left. No one else can recover it for us, but the myths point us towards the way we ourselves can recover who we are. But the message of the ancient myths has been hijacked and used *against* the men and women of the world, and it is to this sad story that we must now attend . . .

Chapter 12

Collaborators against the gods

According to the Anxiety and Depression Association of America's statistics, anxiety disorders are the most common mental illness in the United States, impacting approximately forty million adults (defined as those eighteen years of age and older), out of a total national population estimated at about 327 million in 2018 and a population of adults of 221 million -- an astonishing 18.1% of the adult population, or nearly two out of every ten adults in the country.[147]

According to the National Health and Nutrition Examination Survey for the period 2011 to 2014, a survey which has been conducted by the Department of Health and Human Services in the United States starting in the period from 1960 to 1962 (the same department was formerly known as the Department of Health, Education, and Welfare), approximately 12.7% of all those surveyed ages twelve years and up had taken an anti-depressant medication in the past month prior to answering the survey, and approximately 25% of those who were taking antidepressants said they had been taking anti-depressant medications for ten or more years.[148]

That survey noted that the percentage of those who had taken antidepressant medication in the past month was even higher for females: 16.5% among females ages twelve and up, as opposed to 8.6% of males, and found that "females were approximately twice as likely as males to have taken antidepressant medication at all time points" (meaning at all age groupings studied by the survey).[149] The survey noted a significant increasing trend in antidepressant use from the survey covering the years 1999 to 2002 (when about 7.7% of both sexes said they had taken antidepressant medication in the past thirty days) to the periods 2003 to 2006 and 2007 to 2010 (when about 10.2% and 10.3%, respectively, said they had done so).[150]

Chapter Twelve

The same survey also determined that approximately 17.3 million adults (defined as men and women ages eighteen or older) said they had experienced a major depressive episode at some time, with a "major depressive episode" defined as lasting for at least two weeks and exhibiting a majority of specified symptoms including problems with sleep, eating, energy, concentration, and self-worth.[151]

This represents approximately 7.1% of the adult population. Disturbingly, the prevalence of those having experienced a major depressive episode increased by 64% over that which was indicated by the results of the same survey for the period of 1999 to 2002. Equally disturbingly, an estimated 3.2 million adolescents ages 12 to 17, or 13.3% of the total population of adolescents in the country, reported having experienced at least one major depressive episode, and 2.3 million adolescents or about 9.4% of the total adolescent population reported at least one major depressive episode with severe impairment.[152]

These numbers for adolescents who have experienced depression show an increase of 59% from the previous national survey (for the period of 2007 to 2010), another shocking development.[153]

Of course, all surveys are imperfect. The "caveats" page of the National Survey on Drug Use and Health notes that 32.9% of those selected to take the survey did not complete the interview based on either "refusal to participate" (23.1%), "unavailable or no one at home" (5.0%), or "physical/mental incompetence or language barriers" (4.8%).[154] Thus the actual numbers could be either higher or lower than what the survey was able to determine.

Nevertheless, the statistics show that there is a significant incidence of depression and anxiety among the population of the United States, and that the incidence is growing at alarming rates.

For those who want to cavalierly dismiss or "pooh-pooh" these statistics by telling themselves some form of the rationalization that "people are just getting softer / more self-absorbed / more

Collaborators against the gods

likely to complain" and that "things aren't any different than they've ever been -- in fact they're probably easier now," note first that this kind of cavalier dismissal of increased suffering by our fellow men, women and children around us *is itself* a form of reflexive defense mechanism developed as a way of trying to insulate oneself from trauma, one which fits Dr. Peter Levine's definition of trauma found in the quotation cited earlier (on page 184 of this volume) which says that: "trauma is about loss of connection -- to ourselves, to our bodies, to our families, to others, and to the world around us."[155]

Secondly, it is important to note that the incidence of anxiety and depression certainly reflects the levels of stress produced by the external environment, but more important than the external stress level is *the individual's level of preparation for and ability to handle the stresses* which will always be present in this material world and in a human society. It is quite possible to argue that "kids today" or "adults today" are exhibiting higher levels of depression and anxiety even though forms of external stress in the environment have not increased (although one could debate forever whether the external environment is more or less stressful today than at some selected period in the past) -- but that's not the point.

The more valuable point to examine is why more and more of us are experiencing anxiety and depression, as the statistics clearly illustrate -- and the answer to that question almost certainly has to do with higher levels of disconnection from the self, which will result in anxiety and depression even if external conditions are seemingly benign. In fact, as Dr. Gabor Maté explains, anxiety and depression *themselves* are signs of disconnection from who we are:

> If our environment cannot support our gut feelings and our emotions, then the child, in order to "belong" and "fit in" will automatically, unwittingly and unconsciously, suppress their emotions and their connections to themselves, for the sake of staying connected to the nurturing environment, without

> which the child cannot survive. [. . .] Automatically we disconnect from ourselves, in order to continue to be looked after. It's a tragic choice. It's not even a choice -- the child's not aware of making a choice. It's an automatic process. Then we get into adulthood, and all of a sudden we say, "I don't know who I am." Especially people in mid-life -- they realise that they've been living lives that were not their own lives at all. They did it all because they got disconnected.[156]

There should be little doubt, based on the statistics shown above (and many other statistics that could be offered, not only from the United States but also from other countries), that something is creating higher levels of *internal* disconnection, which would result in anxiety and depression even if external pressures became less. At the same time, however, Dr. Maté observes that the level of external stress has also increased and continues to increase, and that the external factors lead directly to greater incidence of trauma in a culture:

> This is a highly stressed and traumatising society. And you can't separate that from social-economic factors. With neoliberalism and loss of peoples' meaningful and secure employment, austerity, loss of communities -- not only are more people stressed and traumatised, they're also less resilient because resilience requires connection and communal support.[157]

The more difficult it is to obtain and provide for the necessities of life within an economy without going into debt, the more difficult it is for parents of young children to be present and available for those children during the critical formative years and the more likely that children will be exposed to stresses they cannot deal with, resulting in alienation and potentially lifelong psychological trauma.

It should not be hard to see that the United States, despite having the largest GDP of any country in known history and thus being able to claim the title of "wealthiest country in the history of the world," fits the above description -- and based upon the statistics, the situation is growing worse. And the same can be said for many other nations around the world.

Obviously, if the ancient myths are talking about recovering our authentic self, and if alienation from the self is a result of trauma, then psychological trauma and alienation are not unique to modern society. By now, I hope that the foregoing examples from ancient myth have established that the recovery of the self is a major central theme running through the world's ancient myths, scriptures, and sacred stories. We can and should take comfort in the fact that this situation of disconnection appears to have been known to the ancient wisdom of virtually every culture, and that the sacred myths preserved by our distant ancestors point us towards ways to repair that terrible schism that separated us from our self.

That being said, we can also recognize the reality that some environments can be more conducive to producing healthy individuals who are more capable of thriving, more resilient in the face of inevitable stress and difficulty, and (if separated from their essence, as nearly all of us are) more capable of repairing the split with the authentic self and restoring the proper harmonious relationship (as dramatized in myths such as those we've examined -- Jesus and Thomas, Krishna and Arjuna, Eros and Psyche – and many others we have not examined in this volume but which await within the world's myths for our heart's instruction).

Conversely, we can also acknowledge the reality that some environments can be more trauma-inducing than others -- more likely to induce trauma in men, women, and children: toxic cultures which produce individuals who are less capable of thriving, less resilient in the face of inevitable stress and difficulty, and so deeply alienated from their essence that the defense mechanism of their egoic mind refuses to even countenance the idea that such a thing as the "essential self" even exists, let alone entertaining the possibility of repairing the schism that caused the mind to suppress that self.

Chapter Twelve

Acknowledging that some environments can be more conducive to producing healthy, thriving individuals in whom the egoic mind and the authentic self can become reconciled and integrated while other environments can be highly dysfunctional, creating greater incidence of trauma and alienation and higher numbers of men and women who carry the effects of that trauma and alienation throughout their lives, in whom healing and restoration will be even more challenging, most men and women would naturally want to do whatever we can to foster the *first* kind of environment, in which we ourselves as well as those around us (and especially our children and the members of the younger generation) experience *less* trauma and less alienation from who they are, and in which we and others have a greater ability to thrive and to become who we are capable of being, in tune with and guided by our most authentic nature.

One would think that, given the two societal choices, *everyone* would naturally want to foster a society with less trauma and more ability for everyone to thrive -- and that the more that the negative impact of trauma is understood, the more we would want to create societies that reduce its deleterious effects on the lives of men and women and especially on children and adolescents.

The sad fact, however, is that there have been those throughout history, and there continue to be those today, who understand the debilitating impact of trauma on men and women, and who seek to use that knowledge to enhance their ability to oppress, enslave, and deprive their fellow men and women of the gifts bestowed by the gods upon the world (some readers may prefer to say that these gifts are bestowed by "the divine realm" rather than saying that they are bestowed "by the gods," and some may prefer to go even further and say that these gifts are bestowed by "nature" -- whatever terminology you prefer is of course up to you, but it can be demonstrated beyond any doubt that the world's ancient wisdom, even including the Tao Te Ching which is discussed in my 2019 second edition of *Star Myths of the World, Volume One,*

Collaborators against the gods

describe the gifts of nature as coming from the divine realm, and most often as being gifts of the gods themselves).

In doing so, those who deliberately employ trauma in order to oppress other men and women are essentially *stealing from the gods*.

We can easily establish the fact that the ancient myths describe the gifts bestowed upon the earth as originating in the divine realm by examining the well-known episode in which Athena and Poseidon compete to prove who of the two could be the greater benefactor of the ancient polis of Athens in Greece.

The contest between the two deities is described in numerous surviving ancient accounts, including references in the works of Plato and Ovid. I am particular to the retelling found in the wonderful 1962 edition of *Ingri and Edgar Parin D'Aulaire's Book of Greek Myths*, which I had as a child and which was a major influence on me growing up. That book describes the contest this way:

> Athena was very fond of a certain city in Greece, and so was her uncle, Poseidon. Both of them claimed the city, and after a long quarrel they decided that the one who could give it the finest gift should have it.
>
> Leading a procession of citizens, the two gods mounted the Acropolis, the flat-topped rock that crowned the city. Poseidon struck the cliff with his trident, and a spring welled up. The people marveled, but the water was as salty as the sea that Poseidon ruled, and not very useful. Then Athena gave the city her gift. She planted an olive tree in a crevice on the rock. It was the first olive tree the people had ever seen. Athena's gift was judged the better of the two, for it gave food, oil, and wood, and the city was hers. From her beautiful temple on top of the Acropolis, Athena watched over Athens, her city, with the wise owl, her bird, on her shoulder, and under her leadership the Athenians grew famous for their arts and crafts.[158]

Chapter Twelve

This contest, the reader might have already perceived, can be seen to be celestial in nature, and also to have parallels in myths of other cultures around the world (for example, Moses also causes water to gush from a rock, as described in Exodus chapter 17 and Numbers chapter 20).

Moses can be convincingly demonstrated to be a figure associated primarily with Ophiuchus: the "staff" or "rod" of Ophiuchus, seen in the eastern or "left-side" serpent-half of Ophiuchus extends into the Milky Way pointing to the "Dark Rift" that creates what can be envisioned as a "dry path" through the "Red Sea" of the Milky Way, as has already been mentioned on page 256 of this volume. The striking of a rock to produce water may have to do with envisioning the same eastern or "left-side" serpent-half of Ophiuchus as a flat-topped cliff or precipice, which is one way that this half of the constellation Ophiuchus is indeed envisioned in some myths, and the water flowing out of it would again be the Milky Way galaxy:

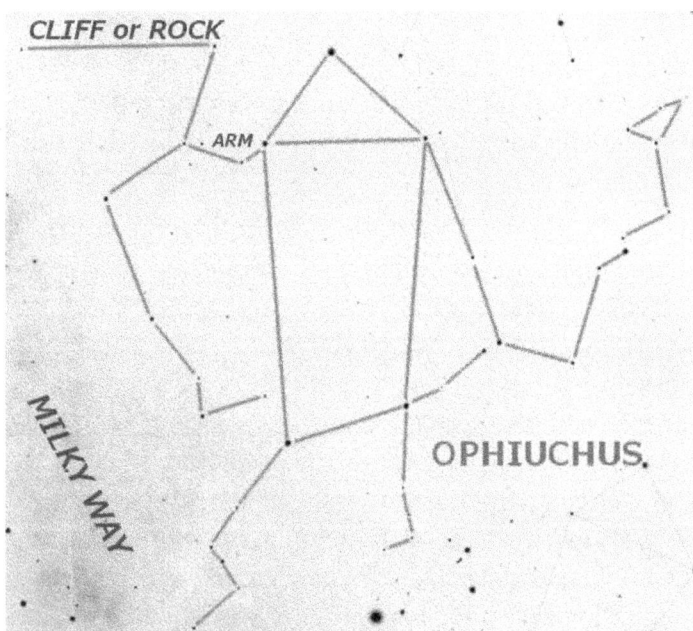

If that left-side (east-side) serpent-half is envisioned as a cliff or overhanging rock, then Ophiuchus can be envisioned as striking at it with his arm (labeled in the illustration). The same serpent-half, as mentioned, also plays the role of the rod or staff of Moses when he parts the Red Sea.

In the case of the contest between Poseidon and Athena, it is possible that Poseidon is envisioned as being associated with Ophiuchus, in which case the other serpent-half (the western or "head-end" of the serpent, on the right of the central body of the constellation as shown) could be envisioned as a trident (it does have three stars across the top, and I do argue that this feature plays the role of the trident of the god Shiva of ancient India, who can be confidently shown to be closely associated with the constellation Ophiuchus).

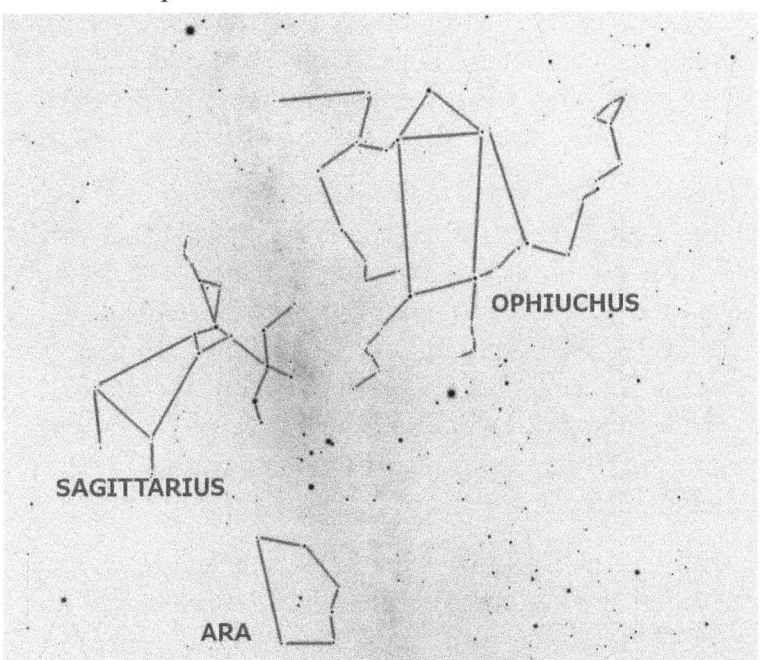

However, as I argue in *Star Myths of the World, Volume Two*, the god Poseidon can also be shown to be associated with the constellation Sagittarius -- and figures associated with that constellation are often found in juxtaposition with figures associated with Ophiuchus in various myths around the world. Sagittarius can also be seen as wielding a trident (the bow of Sagittarius can be envisioned as having three prongs), and

Chapter Twelve

Sagittarius of course is also positioned next to the Milky Way and thus can be seen as causing water to gush forth from a rock (possibly from Ara the Altar, located not far "below" -- to the south of -- Sagittarius). See the illustration in the star-chart on the previous page.

Athena can be confidently shown to be most closely associated with the constellation Ophiuchus, as we've already seen, which makes an identification of Poseidon with Sagittarius for this confrontation more likely. Many previous volumes have presented abundant evidence to show that the constellation Hercules, when envisioned in its "whirling" form, plays the role of a tree growing up above Ophiuchus (see the discussion of the Buddha meditating beneath the Bodhi tree as well as the diagram on page 259 of this volume, for example). Thus the olive tree growing atop the Acropolis in the story – like the rest of this well-known and foundational myth of ancient Athens -- can be shown to be celestial in its original.

Like the rest of the world's myths, however, showing that they are *celestial* does not mean that they are "not true" -- quite the contrary. As I feel compelled to repeat in many different venues, the myths are using the vast theater of the heavens (itself a truly infinite realm) in order to "show" us truths about the invisible realm which we cannot ordinarily see: the myths use the "visible infinite realm" of the stars to convey truths about the "invisible infinite realm" of the gods.

Likewise with this myth of the contest of Athena and Poseidon, which teaches us (among other lessons) that the resources of a land are given to the people by the gods. The gifts of the olive tree, and of access to the mighty sea and all its blessings, as well as of the horse (another gift of Poseidon, and an animal also associated with Sagittarius in the ancient Star Myth system, which is often envisioned as a horseman or as a centaur), were rightfully seen as *gifts from the gods* by the ancient cultures of the earth, and by the ancient myths which these various cultures preserved from remotest antiquity.

Collaborators against the gods

The same understanding can be found in the world's other sacred traditions, which declare that the blessings of sunshine and rain and fertile soil and harvest and wood-bearing forests and mighty rolling oceans and even the treasures of gold and silver and other mineral wealth hidden deep in the earth were all gifts from the gods.

But by far the most important resource bestowed upon any land are *the people themselves*, whom the gods allow to be born into that nation. Men and women are endowed with gifts essential to the survival of the community, each individual receiving a unique combination of gifts.

The birth of every single child was expressly declared to be a gift from the gods: for example, in the Orphic Hymn dedicated to the goddess Artemis, it is acknowledged that this goddess presides over every woman in labor, and brings delivery from the travail of childbirth, each birth taking place by her permission.[159]

The talent-gifts in which various men and women excel were also clearly understood to be given specifically by the gods, and failure to recognize and acknowledge this fact frequently leads to disaster in various ancient myths. Turning again to ancient Greece (although myths from other cultures convey the same message), there are numerous examples of a mortal failing to recognize that his or her gifts were given by the divine realm -- such as the story of Arachne, whose skill at weaving was world-renowned, but who met with swift punishment when Arachne's pride and arrogance led her to declare that her skill at the art was greater than that of the goddess Athena herself, from whom such gifts are given to mortals.

This understanding, that all the resources given to a land come from the gods, and that the most important of all the resources are the people of that land and the gifts given to those men and women (gifts which also come from the gods), is absolutely central to the understanding that all forms of oppression by which the people of a land are deprived (by those who want the resources for themselves) of the resources given to the people of that land constitutes a form of stealing the gifts of the gods.

Likewise, but even more significant, economic and political oppression which prevents men and women who have been given specific gifts and talents by the divine realm from actually using those gifts and talents and realizing the potential which those men and women might otherwise have been able to achieve (absent deliberate economic and political oppression) constitutes a wasting of the gifts bestowed by heaven and thus another and even more egregious form of stealing from the gods.

But why on earth would anyone want to do something as egregious and unnatural as depriving men and women of their opportunity to realize their full potential and express the gifts given to them by the gods? A variety of reasons suggest themselves, many having as their lowest common denominator a motive shared with the suitors in the Odyssey: freeloading off the wealth and work of others, through the collection of what can broadly be categorized as "rent" -- which economists define as "essentially a private tax."[160]

We can see a fairly stark illustration if we look at the forms of feudalism that arose in western Europe following the division of the Roman Empire into an eastern and a western imperial court in the fifth century AD and the subsequent dismantling of the western empire towards the end of that century (particularly after the forced abdication of the western emperor in AD 476). As discussed in my 2014 book, *The Undying Stars*, the dissolution of the empire and rise of feudalism can be directly traced to a deliberate campaign to install literalist Christianity as the central religious authority. Citing the analysis of Italian researcher Flavio Barbiero, I wrote in 2014 of this transition to feudalism:

> After the split of the empire in two, with two emperors east and west, Barbiero notes that in light of the conditions just described, the west had devolved into a bloodbath of successive battles over who would occupy the imperial throne.

Collaborators against the gods

The leaders of the Roman church and the Roman senate in the west came up with a novel solution: they decided to abolish the imperial office in the west, and grant the senate in the East the right to appoint the sole emperor themselves, without the previously-required ratification of the western senate as well. This would put an end to the nonstop battles to appoint short-lived and ineffectual emperors, and leave the clergy and the wealthy landowners to consolidate their power in peace. Without an imperial office to fight over, the barbarian armies became a source of stability, instead of a threat.

This means, Barbiero points out, that "the so-called fall of the Western Empire should be wholly attributed to the Western priestly family, and not to the barbarians." [161] The priestly families were happy to free themselves of the emperor, and later to let the west disintegrate into a patchwork of local barbarian sovereigns at the head of their own armies of professional warriors. Under this arrangement, the great landowners, civil servants, and the Catholic church itself all came from the wealthy and powerful priestly families. The landowners supplied the food that kept the barbarian kings and their warriors alive, and the barbarians provided the defense. The hierarchy of the Church called the shots when necessary, able to exert its influence over the local leaders at least as effectively as it had been able to do so over the centralized emperor in the past.

"Thus in practice the West, although administratively divided, was more united than ever under the church of Rome," Flavio Barbiero writes. "None of the new states saw themselves as independent political and territorial entities. Instead, they continued for centuries to consider themselves as autonomous entities within a single Christian empire." All these kingdoms in the west paid a tax to Rome, while the lands of the church wherever they were located remained exempt from any local taxation (significantly, one of the privileges which Josephus

Chapter Twelve

boasted of receiving from the imperial family was that of tax-exemption on his lands).[162]

Under the system of feudalism that arose after this series of changes in what had formerly been the western empire, the "noble" families and the institution of the church (working together) claimed exclusive right to own the land and all its natural resources, including the increase of the fields and the fruits of the labor of those working that land, beyond what was required for the laborers' modest sustenance.

Rather than having to work themselves, in other words, those who claimed the riches of the lands as their domain could enjoy the yield of everything over and above what was required to keep the laboring serfs alive and producing. This system was enforced in the minds of the people by the church's teaching that the entire arrangement was God's will.

Those fields and their soil, and the rain and the sunshine that fell upon them and caused the crops to grow, and the grass in the pasture that caused the sheep and the cows to grow fat, were given by the divine realm for the benefit of all those whom heaven allowed to be born in that land -- and under the ancient system the function of the rulers in conjunction with the priests was to administer those riches for the benefit of the entire land (this is why the taxation function and the coining of money were associated with the temple, and the coins had images of the gods stamped into them). Those who replaced the ancient worship with literalist Christianity and dissolved the Roman Empire instituted a new arrangement whereby the wealth of the land was said to belong by God's decree only to a privileged few, the "landlords" and self-styled "nobility" -- a form of privatization (one might even accurately say a "monopolization") by a *very few* of the gifts poured out freely by the gods for the benefit of *all the people* of the land.

As feudalism transitioned into capitalism, those benefiting from an arrangement of charging rents ("private taxation") sought ways to preserve (and extend) their monopoly privileges over the gifts of nature, and to beat back attempts to reform or abolish those *rentier* privileges -- *rentier* privileges which continue right up to the present day, not only through the continuation of "aristocratic" land monopolies (such as in some nations of Europe) but also through private control over other gifts of nature and resources properly belonging to the entire nation.

Indeed, as Professor Michael Hudson, Distinguished Research Professor of Economics at the University of Missouri, Kansas City and Professor of Economics at Peking University in China explains in his numerous books and essays on this subject, the central focus of classical economics was to free nations from the "rent grabbing, financialization and kleptocracy" that characterized the feudal period, freeing economies from the "legacy of feudal privileges."[163] Hudson refers to this as:

> the great fight of classical free market economists, from the French Physiocrats to Adam Smith, John Stuart Mill, Henry George and their contemporaries to tax land and natural resource rents as the fiscal base. Their aim was to replace the vested aristocracy of rent recipients with public taxation or ownership of what was a gift of nature -- the sun that the Physiocrats cited as the source of agriculture's productive powers, ineherent soil fertility according to Ricardo, or simply the rent of location as urbanization increased the value of residential and commercial sites.
>
> Classical value and price theory was refined primarily to measure this land rent as not reflecting an expenditure of labor or enterprise (in contrast to buildings and other capital improvements), but as a gift of nature and hence national patrimony.[164]

Professor Hudson describes how these efforts at reform gained steady ground throughout the eighteenth and nineteenth centuries, to the point that they caused serious enough concern among the beneficiaries of the rent-seeking arrangement to

Chapter Twelve

spark a counterattack – such that beginning in the late nineteenth and accelerating throughout the twentieth century, such efforts at reform were largely beaten back and reversed. Today's neoliberalism, characterized by the privatization of virtually every area which the classical economists argued was "a gift of nature and hence national patrimony" represents an updated and even more virulent form of the feudal system that was imposed following the dissolution of the Roman Empire.

Those benefiting from this system have shown willingness to employ physical force to preserve it, as well as the subtler arts of mind manipulation, and even the manipulation of the invisible realm to the extent that they are able do so.

At this point some may object -- or at least wonder silently to themselves -- whether it does not go too far to conflate an understandable self-interest by those who are benefiting from a certain system (and who thus wish to see that system perpetuated) with a willingness to deliberately impose both physical and psychological trauma on others in order to prevent changes to the system.

We do not have to go very far back in history to see that this objection, unfortunately, does not withstand close scrutiny.

Is it only a coincidence that, after a century and a half of increasing pressure to reform the oligarchic *rentier* system, initiated by the American Revolution in 1776 and the French Revolution in 1789 and developing into an even more serious threat as socialism began to gain significant traction in the second half of the 1800s, two devastating world wars were unleashed on the populations of Europe and Russia (and other parts of Asia and Africa as well), resulting in wholesale slaughter of massive numbers of working class and middle class young men? All of these countries had the potential to embrace socialism -- but killing off huge numbers of their young men while they were still in their late teens and early twenties might be seen as an expedient means of preventing such a development.

Collaborators against the gods

It may seem outrageous to suggest that the catastrophe of World War I was engineered in order to divert and ultimately to dissipate the rising stream of dissatisfaction with the *rentier* systems that remained from the feudal era, although I am certainly not the first to suggest this possibility.

In *The great class war: 1914 - 1918*, Belgian-Canadian historian Jacques R. Pauwels has documented in abundant detail the evidence which argues that:

> the Great War was wanted and unleashed by a European elite that was essentially a "symbiosis" of the nobility, that is, the large landowners, and the haute bourgeoisie or "upper middle class," the latter consisting above all of industrialists and bankers. The nobility -- not only in France, but everywhere in the Europe of the *ancien régime* -- was counterrevolutionary from the very moment when, in 1789, the "great" revolution broke out in France. [. . .] The working class loomed more and more menacing because it had discovered a potent emancipatory strategy in Marxist socialism. Moreover, it had developed forms of organization, especially workers' parties and trade unions, and had thus managed to obtain more and more political and social reforms, such as a widening of the electoral franchise. The fear of revolution and even of a seemingly irresistible democratization -- the "rise of the masses" -- convinced the elite that Nietzsche and the apostles of Social Darwinism were right; these intellectuals propounded that only war could eliminate the grave risks associated with democritization and above all the mortal danger of revolution.[165]

It is a fact of history that just as that war was coming to an end, a socialist revolution took place in Russia, resulting in the expulsion or execution of nearly all of the "nobility" of that nation. The spirit of revolution threatened in western Europe as well, including in Bavaria, in Belgium, and in the British Isles. Pauwels notes that:

Chapter Twelve

the Great War would turn out very differently from what the elite had hoped for and expected in 1914. It is one of the great ironies of history that the war gave birth, at least in Russia, to precisely the kind of revolution that it was supposed to have prevented. The war was also supposed to have halted, and even to have "rolled back" the democratization process; but when it ended, the elite was forced to introduce even more political and social reforms in order to forestall revolutions *à la russe* in countries such as Great Britain and Belgium.[166]

It does not take much analysis to realize that the nobles and other beneficiaries of the *rentier* system in Europe (and elsewhere) would have taken notice of the threatening development of revolution in Russia, and that some of them might not have been above resorting to rather extreme measures to prevent a repeat of anything similar in other countries further west. It has even been suggested that certain parties might not have been above re-arming Germany in the decades following the Great War in order to point its formidable fighting force at Russia. Such activity would of course be indisputably treasonous when viewed from the perspective of national boundaries (certain "elites" in the United States or Great Britain aiding Nazi Germany) -- but if we understand that some (by no means all) "elites" and "nobles" view their allegiance to social class, or to trans-national "aristocracy," or to some other group transcending national boundaries (including to religious orders which also see themselves as mortally threatened by the rise of socialism), then this treasonous behavior can be "justified" by the perpetrators as honoring a different loyalty. And evidence suggests that such aid did occur.

After the defeat of Germany and the other fascist powers allied with Germany (including fascist Italy and Imperial Japan) in 1945, the fear of socialism did not abate at all. Criminal acts of extreme treachery, including acts of brutal violence against innocent civilians which would be blamed on "the left," were carried out in order to terrorize the populace and drive them away from voting for reformers who might threaten the *rentier* vestiges of the feudal

Collaborators against the gods

system, particularly in Europe: see for example the evidence presented by historian Daniele Ganser in *NATO's Secret Armies: Operation Gladio and Terrorism in Western Europe* (2005).

In the United States, the concern that the large and assertive Baby Boom generation with its willingness to question the status quo might pose a threat to the economic and political structures of the establishment and the support of the United States for policies favored by Europe's imperialist and colonialist powers led directly to the assassination of President John F. Kennedy in 1963, followed by the assassinations of Malcolm X in 1965 and of Martin Luther King, Jr. and Robert F. Kennedy in 1968. All of these assassinations have been conclusively shown by subsequent researchers to have been treacherously *initiated, organized, executed,* and then *covered up* by the very establishment forces that felt threatened by these charismatic leaders.

These were trauma-inducing events, carried out in public in a trauma-inducing manner. The evidence that murders such as the assassination of President Kennedy were not committed by a "lone nut" the way the official story insists that they were committed is so overwhelming that this evidence simply cannot be ignored -- which means that our higher self, aware of so much more than what the conscious mind allows itself to perceive, cannot fail to realize that the official story is a lie.

The reason that the egoic mind of so many men and women simply refuses to accept the truth -- the truth which we already know deep down, "in our gut" as we say -- is that the truth in this instance is so jarring to the artificial reality which the "defense mechanism" of the egoic mind constructs for us that the egoic mind simply refuses to allow itself to see what is staring us right in the face.

The same can be said for the unsolved crimes committed on September 11, 2001, in which not two but *three* massive steel-framed skyscrapers collapsed into their own footprints, demolition-style, supposedly (according to the official narrative)

Chapter Twelve

due to fires. The evidence, which should be plain to everyone who lived through that trauma-inducing day in history, overwhelmingly demonstrates that the official story is a bald-faced lie. The implications, however, are so threatening to the rules by which we order our world that most of us suppress and refuse to see the evidence which is staring us in the face -- resulting in internal division, alienation, and a pervasive sense of background angst.

That the official story is a lie can be explained in four simple words: "*Building 7, freefall speed.*"

Building 7, of course, refers to World Trade Center 7, which was a 47-story steel-frame building which was not struck by any airplanes and which suddenly collapsed into its own footprint, at a speed indistinguishable from freefall speed, on the afternoon of September 11, 2001, well after the collapse of World Trade Center Buildings 1 and 2 (the North and South Towers, also known as the Twin Towers).

Supposedly this collapse of Building 7 at freefall speed, into its own footprint, was due to fires started from debris which fell from the other towers. That explanation is so ludicrous that it simply cannot be believed, and I would argue that our deeper self (buried by our egoic mind in most cases) already knows that it is false. The reason our egoic mind refuses to allow itself to see that the official narrative cannot possibly be true is that the implications of that fact -- that the official story is a bald-faced lie -- obliterate the facade of what we believe to be true about the world around us.

There are many other aspects of the events of that day which demonstrate, almost as blatantly as the collapse of Building 7 at freefall speed, that the official story about the crimes perpetrated on September 11 is a criminal lie.

These include, but are not limited to, the complete failure of the military to scramble fighter-jets to intercept the other hijacked airplanes which continued to fly around for over an hour even after the Twin Towers had been hit, and the failure of any air defense weapons to stop (or even attempt to stop) a jet from hitting the Pentagon (if indeed a jet did hit the Pentagon), as well as the fact that numerous military drills involving aircraft were taking place on that same day by "astonishing coincidence," and also the fact that the crime scene of the collapsed towers of the World Trade Center was not investigated but instead was deliberately and rapidly destroyed and the steel carted away in short order, never to be subjected to rigorous forensic analysis.

All of these trauma-inducing events fall into the same broad pattern -- the same pattern we have been examining. The central feature of this pattern is the seizure of more and more of the gifts of heaven and of nature for the benefit of a privileged few at the expense of the many, coupled with the willingness to *impose trauma* as one of the tools available to enable that seizure and to prevent it from being corrected by men and women who would normally see what is going on and take action to apprehend and bring to justice those responsible, and to protect what belongs to the people from being monopolized by a privileged minority.

Many, many other examples from recent history could be offered: these are simply some of the most obvious and egregious. When bringing up the topic of the trauma that was deliberately inflicted on the Baby Boom generation in order to prevent that large and rambunctious demographic from carrying through with some of the changes that they initially seemed ready and eager to initiate in society, we must not overlook the catastrophe of the Vietnam War, the escalation of which took place in a short span of time immediately following the assassination of President Kennedy (the extent to which Kennedy was reducing military engagement in Vietnam before he was killed, and the extent to which that policy was completely reversed after his death, has been ably established by the research and analysis of Professor Peter Dale Scott, as well as by other researchers).

Chapter Twelve

Not quite five years later, Martin Luther King, Jr. would be murdered. He was killed exactly one year to the day after speaking out publicly and eloquently against the Vietnam War.

It is difficult to argue that the examples cited here (among many others which could be offered to support these selected examples) do not demonstrate the willingness of certain groups to deliberately inflict trauma on other men, women and children in order to seize the gifts of the gods -- the natural resources of the earth -- for their own enrichment rather than allowing those gifts to benefit all the men and women whom heaven has allowed to be born into a given land or nation.

It is important to see that the underlying pattern relates to the feudal system which arose after the triumph of literalist Christianity in the Roman Empire: central to this pattern is the seizure of the gifts of nature for the benefit of a privileged few at the expense of the rest of the men and women born into a given land or nation.

This pattern can be captured in the word "privatization," which derives from a Latin word meaning "to restrict" and which is applied in an economic sense to the granting of monopoly ownership over gifts provided by nature -- gifts which the ancient myths (such as the story of the contest between Athena and Poseidon) describe as gifts of the gods for the benefit of the land and the people in it, and which thus should be seen as gifts to the *public* (the entire people of a land, as opposed to a privileged few).

As economist Michael P. Hudson explains in his outstanding 2017 book *J is for Junk Economics: A Guide to Reality in an Age of Deception*,

> The word "private" derives from Latin *privatus*, meaning restricted, as in *privilege*, and *privare*, "to deprive" and indeed, "to rob," as in *prevaricate*. Starting with the enclosure of the commons -- the fencing in of communal graing land and forests in Britain -- the enclosures of the 16th through 18th centuries deprived peasants of their land rights and means of subsistence,

Collaborators against the gods

driving them into the cities as "loom-fodder." [. . .] The prime assets being privatized are natural monopolies able to extract economic rent by raising prices for hitherto public services.[167]

In other words, Professor Hudson writes, the goal is to "deprive host economies of a public return on their land and natural resource patrimony"[168] -- to siphon the wealth rightfully given to the entire nation as a kind of inheritance (the word *patrimony* signifying an inheritance, or a legacy -- in this case, the inheritance of the bounty bestowed upon the land by nature, and I would add "by nature and the gods").

Throughout that book, Michael Hudson provides numerous descriptions of the gifts which are properly seen as the inheritance of the land, given by nature to all the people, and thus rightly belonging to the *public domain*. These include "land, water and natural resources,"[169] as well as "mineral rights, airwaves and other public infrastructure."[170]

The pattern involves the attempt to deprive the people of the bounty of nature by claiming private ownership rights over the natural resources which properly belong in the public domain -- and this pattern continues to this day, with the main difference being that the extent of the public domain which the privileged few want to "make private" and claim for their own has expanded much further than it did even during the dark ages of overt feudalism.

It is immensely profitable for a privileged few to gain ownership over the natural resources bestowed upon a land for the benefit of all the people. The inheritance bestowed by the gods in the riches of the land and soil, forests, rivers, ports, sunshine, rain, and minerals do not carry the same costs of production as other goods and services (because these blessings are given by nature -- given by the gods). Professor Hudson explains that the classical economists recognized this distinction and applied the term "rent" (or, more precisely, "economic rent") to profits derived from the sale of what is supplied by nature:

Chapter Twelve

> Rent was the classical term for income that has no counterpart in necessary costs of production. Rent recipients have no out-of-pocket costs for supplying land or monopoly "services" for what basically are transfer payments.[171]

Elsewhere, he writes:

> The classical meaning of "rent seeking" refers to landlords, natural resource owners or monopolists who extract economic rent by special privilege, without their own labor or enterprise.[172]

Note that once again the word "privilege" itself derives from the same Latin root which gives us the word "privatization," and the same root which is found in the words "deprive" and "privation," words whose meanings have to do with *taking away*, with *restricting*, and with a resulting level of *lack*, *want* and *hardship*.

If the reader is wondering why I spend so much time underscoring and reiterating this point, it is because I am arguing that this central pattern of a privileged few wrongfully claiming ownership over gifts bestowed by nature and the gods upon the land and upon all the people that heaven has allowed to be born into that land constitutes a rebellion against the gods and the motivation behind a war being waged to suppress the ancient wisdom which was imparted to all the peoples of the earth in their earliest myths and sacred traditions.

I emphasize this concept of *privatization* and *economic rent* because it is at the heart of the system by which a privileged few extracted all the benefits of the wealth of the land without labor or enterprise, at the expense of the rest of the people -- a system of exploitation and oppression which was sustained and excused and wrongfully "justified" by the teachings of a literalist Christian clergy (who similarly benefited from the arrangement) for centuries on end.

And I emphasize the importance of this understanding because once we perceive this pattern, we can more readily appreciate that *it is in order to preserve and advance this same system of privatizing the gifts of the gods* that the *collaborators against the gods* continue to this day to carry out the obfuscation of the world's ancient wisdom, the promotion of various forms of literalist interpretation of ancient myth, the violent overthrow of any world leaders who seek to prevent the privatization of their nation's natural resources which rightfully belong to the public domain for the benefit of all the people of their country, and the deliberate traumatization of vast numbers of men, women and children in order to disrupt their ability to stand in the way of this catastrophic centuries-long campaign.

As we have seen from abundant evidence, one of the core messages of the world's ancient myths concerns the reconnection with the authentic self, the essential self, the higher self -- and as we have also seen, the higher self appears to have an inexplicable connection with others and with the infinite realm (inexplicable, that is, from the point of view of materialist science).

When someone wakes up in the middle of the night with a terrible sense of unease, and then receives a phone call some minutes later or a visit the following morning conveying the news that someone very close to them has died, that awakening cannot be explained within the conventional materialist paradigm -- but incidences such as these (abundantly documented to the point that we cannot dismiss them out of hand or deny that something is going on which materialist science cannot explain) indicate that the higher self, beyond the boundaries of the egoic mind, is mysteriously connected to other men and women, and to a realm beyond the material realm -- which the ancient myths describe as the realm of the gods.

The goal of literalism (and of literalist Christianity in particular, for approximately the past seventeen centuries) has consistently been to obfuscate the teaching of the world's ancient wisdom on this subject, by insisting that the dramatic illustrations in the sacred stories were intended to be understood as literal history, rather than as profound esoteric metaphor pointing to the truth regarding our authentic self, and the importance of reconnecting with the authentic self from whom we have become estranged.

Chapter Twelve

Is it any wonder that the relatively small percentage of the population who are the collaborators against the gods, who actively conspire to steal the bountiful gifts and benefits bestowed upon the land by nature and the divine realm, and who have demonstrated that they are willing to oppress and traumatize large numbers of men, women and children in order to do so, would seek to obscure and confuse this clear and central message of the world's ancient myths: the message that we are all actually mystically connected in a way which we still do not fully understand, and that we are also connected to the wider cosmos and indeed to the invisible realm itself (a message which would, of course, argue very strongly against the kind of *exploitation and oppression of others*, and against the *trashing of nature and of nature's resources*, which are the consistent hallmark of these conspirators down through the centuries)?

In the modern-day land of Greece, where the myths tell us that the goddess of wisdom contended with the great sea-god over the question of who could bestow the more blessed gifts upon the people of what would become Athens, the ancient port of that city -- the famed Piraeus -- has now had its "ownership" sold off to a private corporation, the China COSCO Shipping Corporation, as of the month of April in the year 2016: the privatization of Greece's biggest port, and one whose storied history stretches back to ancient times.

The port, which is quite obviously a part of the patrimony or inheritance of the land of Greece, belonging to the people and bestowed by the bounty of nature and the gods, was sold to a foreign corporation for €280.5 million -- in exchange for which sum the COSCO Shipping Corporation received 51% ownership of the Piraeus. As part of the deal, the new corporate owners promised to make investments of another €350 million over the subsequent ten years, in exchange for which they will also be entitled to purchase another 16% of the ownership of the port for an additional €88 million in the year 2021, giving them 66% ownership of the Piraeus.[173]

Collaborators against the gods

At the time of the privatization, a port worker named Constantinos Tsourakis complained, "This is not a concession: it's a giveaway of property belonging to the Greek people."[174]

Constantinos is exactly correct in this declaration.

His complaint reveals that the sons and daughters of Greece perceive very clearly the inherent injustice of the privatization of the natural resources, given by nature to the people of the land -- a pattern of privatization which is taking place all over the world, and at an accelerated pace in recent decades.

This trend can be seen as a direct continuation of the very same feudal pattern described in this chapter, a feudal system instituted by those who overthrew the worship of the ancient gods, those under whom the ancient Oracle at Delphi was closed down during the reign of the emperor Theodosius I (AD 347 - 394).

Theodosius was born about ten years after the death of Constantine (AD 272 - 337), the first emperor to openly declare his adherence to the literalist Christian faith and to proclaim that Christianity would now be tolerated in the Roman Empire. Theodosius would be the last emperor to rule over a united empire prior to the division into eastern and western imperial courts.

It was Theodosius who outlawed paganism in the empire, instituting the death penalty for augury and for the performance of many other traditional Roman sacred traditions, and ordering the cessation of the *mysteria* of Eleusis (the Eleusinian Mysteries) -- which had been observed near Athens for centuries prior to the advent of literalist Christianity.

The outlawing of the Eleusinian Mysteries and the shuttering of the Oracle at Delphi can be seen as symbolic of the desire by the proponents of literalist Christianity to silence the voice of the gods and their message preserved in the myths, a message we have been examining in this book, and a message which proclaims the inner divinity of all men and women, their inherent

Chapter Twelve

connection to one another and to the realm of the infinite, and the importance of remembering that the ultimate source of the gifts given to men and women (both the gifts of nature's bounty in the resources of the land, and the gifts given to individual men and women in their skills and talents and individual genius) is the divine realm, among the blessed gods themselves.

If the *natural resources* are given as a blessing from the gods to all the people they allow to be born in that land, then it stands to reason that these cannot properly be "sold off" or awarded to some private entity, whether a corporation or a wealthy individual or family who claims ownership over what rightly belongs as a patrimony or inheritance to *all* the men and women of the land.

The idea that a nation can be forced into selling off this patrimony in order to "pay its debts" is ludicrous on the face of it: a sovereign government can create money to pay those debts, or it can declare those debts to be null and void if some foreign entity demands the impoverishment of the people in order to pay those debts. The government representing the people has an *obligation to those people* before it has an obligation to foreign creditors who demand the sale of what cannot be properly or rightfully sold in order to service their debts.

And yet under this pretense, the supposed government of Greece (which has actually been hijacked by the collaborators with the foreign creditors, much as hijackers might take over the controls of an airplane from its rightful captain and crew) has in recent years sold off not only the port of Piraeus but also the port of Thessaloniki, as well as Greece's fourteen regional airports, the Greek public train company TRAINOSE, the water system (the new private owners of which immediately imposed a 50% hike in the rates charged to residences for their water), and many other resources over which corporations and private investors salivate due to their production of what the classical economists called "economic rents" and "monopoly services."

Collaborators against the gods

Well-informed readers might take exception to the assertion that a sovereign government need not sell off its assets because it can issue currency at will to pay its debts, noting that Greece voluntarily entered into the eurozone and thus gave up its right to issue its own currency, and that even if it had not done so, if it owed money to foreign bondholders for bonds payable in a currency other than the currency of Greece, the government of Greece could not issue *foreign* currency to pay those foreign-currency bonds.

However, this objection ignores the fact that these supposed limitations are all self-imposed limitations: the government of Greece (representing the people of the land) can declare at any time that it has decided to reverse the process by which it entered into the eurozone, and go back to issuing its own currency -- and it can also inform its foreign bondholders that it will henceforth be paying its debts in its own sovereign currency, which they can choose to either accept or get nothing.

What it cannot rightfully do is sell off the gifts of the gods belonging to the people.

These self-imposed limitations are all completely illusory, and they are all contrary to the ancient wisdom preserved in the world's myths, scriptures and sacred stories around the world. The illusion is maintained and reinforced by the efforts of the collaborators against the gods -- those who stand to gain by obtaining the supposed "rights" to "ownership" over the public domain (which actually cannot be properly sold off).

The same illusion is imposed upon the minds of the populace in many other parts of the world besides Greece, including in the United States which is neither a part of the eurozone (and which thus may issue its own currency) nor a party to foreign-denominated bonds, and which yet acts as though it is under these same illusory constraints and must sell off the patrimony of the people in order to "make ends meet."

Chapter Twelve

Countless examples could be offered, such as the self-imposed stripping of the national postal service in order to enable privatized shippers such as FedEx and UPS to make money by essentially privatizing what could very easily be done by the postal system. The federal postal service in the United States constantly raises its prices and reduces its level of service, and we are told that it must increase its rates in order to "keep from going out of business," which is ludicrous.

In fact, the US Postal Service would be in no danger of going out of business even if it decided to deliver packages and letters for a penny each, or even for free. The reason that it does not (and this reason is actually encoded in laws which the interested reader can research and read for himself or herself) is that it is *prohibited* from delivering mail at rates which would be too difficult for the privatized companies such as UPS or FedEx to compete against.

These are self-imposed limitations which benefit a privileged few (in this case, those who make enormous amounts of money by privatizing a formerly public service) at the expense of the general populace, who are left with an artificially impoverished federal postal system which once was the envy of the world but which has been deliberately starved of resources and forced to raise its rates to levels which make it unattractive to use.

Even more damaging examples could be offered, such as a very similar pattern of raising rates at public universities in order to enrich banks making government-backed student loans to families who cannot possibly afford the cost of tuition at universities that just one generation ago (when I and my peers were going to college) charged only a few hundred dollars tuition per semeseter for a full load of courses. This policy has indebted an entire generation with decades of debt unknown to previous generations, with disastrous and wide-ranging consequences.

The privatization of the credit function may be the most significant area to be discussed, which (as Professor Hudson argues in another of his books) was anciently considered to be a

Collaborators against the gods

function proper to the public sphere (the sovereign and the temple) rather than the private sphere.[175] Just as a robust postal service would counter private courier companies such as UPS, a robust public panking option could serve as a counterbalance to the "rule by banks" which obtains today in the western world[176] -- but the idea is so vehemently opposed by the privatizers of the public domain that it is never seriously discussed by lawmakers.

How do those whose goal is the privatization of everything that properly belongs within the public domain manage to impose the illusions which sustain these populace-impoverishing policies?

Without doubt, those in position to reap enormous benefits by squatting atop the monopoly chokepoints within an economy have every incentive to spend tremendous sums of money to maintain their *rentier* privileges and to fend off any challenges to the economic structures which sustain the system as it is (and even to expand the scope of privatization over time as well).

They use money to influence elections and legislation, as well as to influence media coverage in all kinds of ways (even to influence movies and other forms of popular entertainment when possible). They also use money to influence education, particularly at the college level, which are chokepoints through which anyone wishing to enter many industries must pass in order to gain credentials.

They will also use all kinds of pressure when challenges to their activities become more serious, such as the intense pressure that was leveled against the elected members of the Syriza Party in Greece following the victory of that party in the 2014 elections and the initial resolve of its leaders to oppose the austerity (and sale of public domain) demanded by foreign creditors. The leaders of Syriza eventually buckled under this pressure and accepted the demands of the foreign bondholders in 2015, betraying the people who had voted for rejection of the creditors' demands.

Chapter Twelve

In the ancient epic of the Odyssey, the concept of living off of the wealth of another without providing any labor or enterprise (the very definition of *rentier* behavior according to the classical economists cited by Professor Hudson) is dramatically pictured for us in the illustration of the suitors who camp out in the house of the absent hero Odysseus, devouring his food while they hatch schemes to marry his beautiful wife Penelope.

Indeed, the epic makes clear that the suitors are not at all above resorting to treachery and underhanded violence in order to secure their position: when Telemachus, the son of Penelope and Odysseus, reaches young manhood and begins to signal that he would like nothing better than to rid his household of the suitors who are bleeding it dry of its resources, the suitors come up with a plot to murder him.

Meanwhile, Odysseus is trapped on the island of the goddess Calypso in the middle of a trackless sea, far from home. He is one of the heroes who sailed for Troy during the Trojan War described in the epic of the Iliad, but his return home with the other fighting men of the Greek island of Ithaca has been delayed by a series of misadventures and obstacles. Meanwhile, the suitors scheme to sleep with his wife, murder his son and heir, and take everything he owns for themselves.

Many times, the text of the epic describes the behavior of the suitors as morally reprehensible to both men and the gods.

When the goddess Athena first visits the home of the absent hero, taking on the guise of an older warrior named Mentor, and finds young Telemachus obsessed with grief for his absent father and complaining about the more than one hundred young men who are lounging about his household, feasting on the fat of the land, the goddess uses these phrases to describe the suitors (in the superlative translation of the great Robert Fagles, whom I had the opportunity to meet when I was teaching the Odyssey to cadets in the Department of English and Philosophy at the United States Military Academy at West Point):

> "What's this banqueting, this crowd carousing here?
> And what part do you play yourself? Some wedding-feast,
> some festival? Hardly a potluck supper, I would say.
> How obscenely they lounge and swagger here, look,
> gorging in your house. Why, any man of sense
> who chanced among them would be outraged,
> seeing such behavior." [177]

The suitors are a perfect illustration of the outrageous behavior of those who violate the laws of heaven by using schemes and even underhanded violence in order to plunder the wealth of nations without contributing any labor or enterprise of their own, at the expense of others.

And note that the entire epic itself dramatizes displacement and alienation: Odysseus is displaced from his proper role as husband to his wife Penelope and father to their son Telemachus, leading to the reprehensible situation just described (as well as to serious confidence issues for Telemachus, who appears to have grown up in a traumatizing environment, without his father present, and in a house that has been invaded by violent bullies who have no concern for his well-being or his safety).

Where there is trauma and dislocation and disconnection, the ancient epic clearly appears to be saying, the suitors can move in.

And this is what we see taking place in the world around us today. These modern-day "suitors," like those depicted in the Odyssey, feel entitled to take what belongs to other men and women -- after all, there is a long history of their predecessors doing the same thing, stretching back to the earliest days of feudalism which descended upon Europe following the rise of literalist Christianity, the closure of the Oracle at Delphi, and the cessation of the Eleusinian rites.

The imperialist and colonialist powers of western Europe, led by those same "noble" families whose predecessors claimed the increase of the land for themselves during the feudal times, *then proceeded to plunder the world* during the subsequent centuries, always being sure to impose their literalist Christian faith whenever they did so, and to stamp out as much as possible of the original sacred traditions of whatever culture they found in the lands whose resources they desired -- reaching as far as the lands of Australia and Aotearoa (New Zealand) and everything in between there and Europe, wreaking havoc and imposing greater misery and poverty wherever they went while enriching themselves in the process.

They employed schemes, cunning, outright violence, and the deliberate imposition of trauma in order to impose and expand and perpetuate their *rentier* privilege -- and they were not above *inflicting psychological trauma* in order to make resistance to their efforts much more difficult. When men and women are displaced and alienated even within their own selves, effective resistance to the exploitation of the suitors is much less likely.

All of these forms of influence, as disgusting as they are and as outrageous to the sensibility of the gods as Athena describes them to be in the ancient epic of the Odyssey, can easily be understood as tools that fit within the conventional materialist paradigm: these are all activities which take place within what we might call ordinary space and time, and in compliance with the laws of physics as commonly understood.

However, in addition to these more "mundane" methods of advancing their agenda to usurp the gifts of heaven to the earth and its people, the collaborators against the gods also commonly and routinely (and in fact openly) also resort to what might be described as *occult ritual* or *ritual magic* -- practices intended to evoke the influence of the unseen realm, to which (as we have seen) we are all somehow already connected, even though most of us don't even realize it.

Just who are these collaborators against the gods? Towards an answer to that question, and towards a better understanding of their attempts to employ the ancient system for the purpose of exploitation rather than empowerment of their fellow men and women, we will now turn . . .

Chapter 13

The Cult of Mithras

The young man hovers in the air over the wide sandy beach, gazing intently at the shield strapped to his left forearm, which he holds extended away from his body and rotated downwards as if looking at a wristwatch, so that he is able to see the curved outer surface of the large polished disc, in which is reflected with mirror-like accuracy the image of the Gorgons below.

In his right hand, the youth holds a gleaming hooked blade, curved-over at the top like a long sickle, and sharpened on both edges to a razor finish. It is made of marvelous adamantine, the hardest substance in the cosmos, and by some ancient accounts was originally forged by Hephaestus, the god of smiths and fire, known to the Latins as Vulcan, after whom volcanoes are named. This special hooked sword is known as the *harpe* sword.

He floats in the air by virtue of having strapped to his feet the winged sandals (known as the *talaria*) of the god Hermes, in some ancient accounts given to him by the god himself, and in other accounts by nymphs whom the young man had to find by tricking the ominous Gray Sisters (the *Graiai* or *Graeae*) into leading him to their secret home. Upon his head he wears a cap of invisibility and darkness, also supernatural in origin and by most accounts belonging to the Unseen God.

Thus, Perseus is able to gaze upon the figure of Medusa (as well as her two sisters, Stheno and Euryale) without being turned to stone, for he has been directed by the goddess Athena to look only at their reflection in the shield, and not directly at them. On the beach below, reflected in the shield's gleaming surface, he can see the petrified remains of those who have previously reached these forbidding shores, in hopes of slaying the Gorgons, and who have instead been turned to stone by them, there to remain until the end of time.

Chapter Thirteen

But the young man's eye is drawn irresistibly to Medusa herself, lying in blissful sleep upon this beach at the end of the world.

Even in her altered state, Perseus admires her beauty.[178] Her body is now covered in smooth, scaly skin, like a serpent, but it is a body of such perfect proportion that it is easy to see why the great god of the sea, Poseidon, had previously been overcome with lust at the sight of the maiden and had ravished her within the sacred boundaries of a temple dedicated to the goddess Athena -- for which desecration Athena had punished the young woman by transforming her into a monster with the ability of turning men into stone.

As he hangs in the air above the remote shoreline, held aloft by the miraculous sandals, Perseus cannot help admiring her awe-inspiring beauty, even now when her flowing hair has been changed into a mass of writhing venomous serpents, and her blood-red lips -- slightly parted as she dreams -- reveal pointed fangs where once were seen a row of perfect teeth. The ancient poet Pindar of Thebes, writing in the fifth century BC (he is thought to have died in 438 BC), describes her in this encounter as "fair-cheeked Medousa," despite her having been transformed by the goddess into a fierce monster with the horrendous power of petrifaction.[179]

Perseus himself is clean-limbed and well-muscled, as befits a son of Zeus, who is his true father. When Acrisius (or Akrisios), king of Argos, the father of the beautiful maiden Danaë, had been warned by a prophecy that his daughter's son would someday bring about the death of Acrisius, the king determined that Danaë would never marry, and locked her in a bronze chamber built beneath the earth (some accounts call it a stone chamber).

But the god Zeus, seeing the incredible beauty of the maiden, descended in the form of a shower of gold into the cell in which Danaë was imprisoned, and made love to her. Perseus was the son born of that union -- but when his grandfather Acrisius learned of the birth of the child, he had Danaë and the baby placed into an ark and cast into the sea, which is a myth-pattern or oicotype which appears in the Star Myths of cultures around the world, from the story of King Sargon of Akkad (in ancient Mesopotamia), to the story of Karna son of the maiden Kunti by the sun god Surya (in ancient India), to the story of Moses cast adrift in an ark made of bulrushes (in the Hebrew Scriptures), to the story of Hiruko son of Izanagi and Izanami in the Kojiki of ancient Japan, to the story of baby Maui cast into the sea-foam by his mother in the myths of the cultures of the Pacific.

All of these myths, of course, can be seen to be celestial in nature, and in fact to invoke the same crucial region of the night sky in which we find the constellations Sagittarius, Scorpio, Ara the Altar, and Ophiuchus (which plays the role of the ark, adrift in the water), as well as of course the glorious band of the Milky Way itself (which represents the water into which the infant is cast in all these traditions, as well as playing role of the shower of gold through which the god Zeus descends in his liaison with Danaë).

The ark containing Perseus and his mother makes its way to the island of Serifos (sometimes spelled Seriphos), located in the Aegean Sea to the southeast of the tip of the Attic peninsula, where a kindly fisherman named Dictys drags the seaweed-encrusted ark to shore in his nets, and is astonished to discover the beautiful Danaë and her baby within.

The fisherman cares for Danaë and raises Perseus, but the king of the island, whose name is Polydectys and who in some accounts is the brother of the fisherman, eventually learns of the presence of the boy and his mother, and when he sees her, he becomes enamored with Danaë and wants to make her his queen. Perseus, now grown into a brave and upright young man, stands in the way of the desire of Polydectes, and so the wicked king of the island tricks Perseus into embarking on a journey to the ends of the earth, to find the Gorgons and bring back the head of Medusa.

Chapter Thirteen

For all his physical strength and courage, the young son of Zeus would undoubtedly have perished on this seemingly-impossible quest, had it not been for the fact that he was attuned to detect the help offered by the gods who dwell in the unseen realm, and willing to listen to their advice.

As he sets out on his mission to find the Gorgons and slay Medusa, Perseus is visited by the goddess Athena and the god Hermes, and they explain to him that he must take necessary precautions in order to avoid being turned to stone himself, as have so many worthy heroes who have gone before Perseus with the same goal in mind. They point him towards the steps he must follow in order to gain the tools he will need on his quest: the winged sandals, the cap of invisibility, the *harpe* sword which can cut through the scales of the Gorgon's skin, the *kibisis* bag which can safely hold the severed head of the monster without allowing her poisonous blood to slay Perseus, and of course the mirror-like shield belonging to the goddess herself, in the reflection of which the hero can safely observe Medusa without being turned to stone.

Thus it is that we find the young hero, hanging in the air above Medusa, averting his gaze as he prepares to slice off her head with his hooked sword. I have already written in other places about the indisputable celestial foundation for this scene, but will elaborate here upon some of its aspects: Perseus, of course, is found in the heaven in the figure which bears his name, a bright constellation with a peaked cap, and one hand which can be seen as holding a curving sword very much suggestive of the distinctive *harpe* used by the hero in this episode.

The other arm of the constellation Perseus (the one not holding the hooked sword) is reaching out in the direction of the body of the gorgeous figure of the constellation Andromeda, which (I am now fairly well convinced) plays the role of the headless corpse of Medusa, who herself was once among the most beautiful of maidens. As can be seen from the star-chart on the opposite page, Andromeda can be envisioned as lacking a head.

The Cult of Mithras

When Perseus cuts off the head of the unfortunate Medusa, the ancient accounts inform us that the great winged horse, Pegasus, springs upwards from her neck -- and this is exactly what we see in the heavens: the constellation Pegasus, its mighty wings associated with the Great Square of Pegasus itself, emerging from the neck of the constellation Andromeda (her neck terminates at one corner of the Great Square):

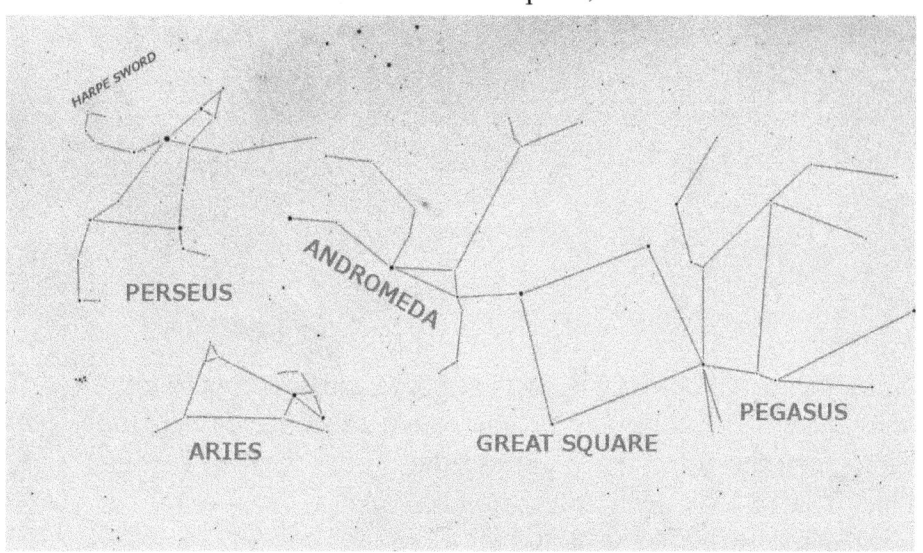

The feature of the constellation corresponding to the *harpe* sword (with which Perseus beheads Medusa) is seen on the left (the east) side of Perseus and is labeled. Note that the outline of Perseus in the sky can be envisioned as turning its head to "look away" from the direction of Andromeda -- and we find confirmation of this celestial connection in the Odyssey, when Odysseus goes down to the underworld and is told he must slay a black ram while turning his face in the other direction.[180]

Indeed, in the text of the Odyssey itself, Circe instructs Odysseus to *turn his head away from the ram* when he slays it, and "towards the Ocean River."[181] This textual evidence could not be more conclusive: it describes the constellation Perseus, with its head envisioned as *turned away* from Andromeda and from Aries (the Ram) and *towards* the stream of the Milky Way: the Ocean River mentioned in that scene from the Odyssey chapter 10.

351

Chapter Thirteen

Below is the same star-chart, this time showing the path of the Milky Way as it arches over the head of the constellation Perseus:

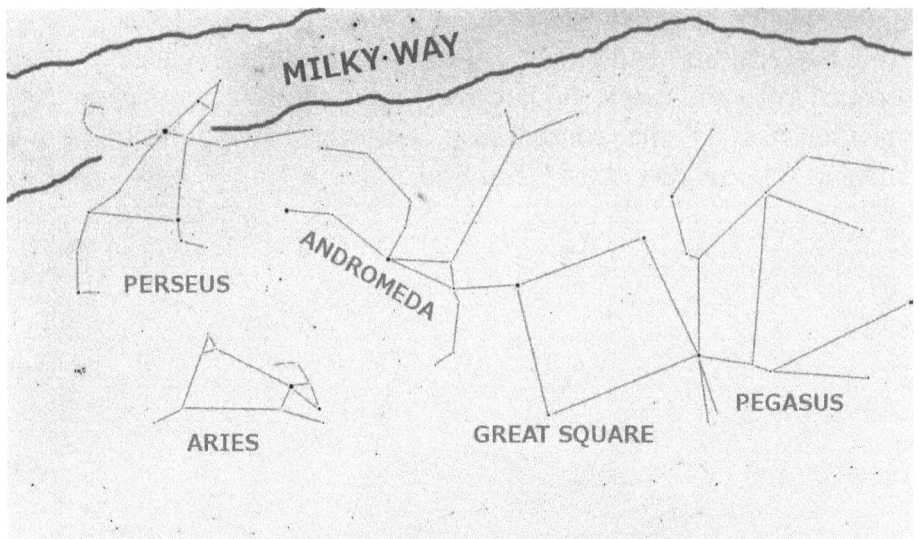

Thus, the text of Odyssey Book 10 offers conclusive proof that the constellation Perseus could be (and was) envisioned as "looking away" from the direction of Andromeda -- just as the hero Perseus himself must look away from Medusa, even as he cuts off her head, in the myth of Perseus and the Gorgons.

As I discuss in *Star Myths of the World, Volume Two*, the other Gorgon sisters then awaken and pursue Perseus, although due to his cap of invisibility they are not successful in catching him. These Gorgon sisters are likely associated with the same important constellation Hercules we have examined earlier (see discussion earlier in this present volume, pages 62 and following).

Later in the same Perseus cycle, of course, the young hero rescues the beautiful maiden Andromeda, chained to a rock. All of these adventures can be conclusively demonstrated to be celestial in nature, and to convey profound truths which we need in this very present moment (including the truth that even the most seemingly-impossible tasks can be successfully accomplished, if we avail ourselves of the help offered to us from the realm of the

The Cult of Mithras

gods, just as we saw in the earlier discussion of the ordeal of young Norman Ollestad).

But the primary reason for reiterating here the undeniable evidence that the myth of Perseus is based upon celestial metaphor concerns the existence of an ancient esoteric society of tremendous importance to world history which appears to have centered its entire secret mythical arcanum upon this heavenly figure. That powerful secret society consisted of the initiates into the mysteries of *Sol Invictus* (the Unconquered or the Unconquerable Sun), better known today as Mithraism -- but known to contemporaries in the days of ancient Rome, and also among themselves, simply as the "Persians."[182]

As even the most-recently published studies of the ancient Mysteries of Mithras readily admit, we still must rely on conjecture and detective work regarding the cult of Mithras, because its actual adherents left us almost no written clues whatsoever regarding their secretive meetings. In his 2019 doctoral thesis, scholar Dr. David Walsh of the University of Kent's School of European Culture and Languages explains that:

> Nearly all of what we know regarding the cult comes from a script for a Mithraic initiation ceremony. As such, all surviving written accounts describing the cult emanated from outsiders. This means that, while we can piece together what appears to be a relatively accurate model based on the available evidence, it is important to remember there is much that we do not know. Furthermore, given that many of the outsiders who wrote about the cult probably never witnessed a Mithraic ritual, some of their descriptions are certainly distortions of the reality.[183]

Writing in the late 1980s, Professor Manfred Clauss of the Free University of Berlin describes the problem this way:

> One can hardly do better, with regard to the problem of the sources for the cult of Mithras, than to cite A. D. Nock's vivid comparison. Imagine a historian attempting at some distant

353

Chapter Thirteen

date in the future to write about contemporary twentieth-century Christianity. He has at his disposal the following:
- a few chance allusions in Jewish religious texts,
- the ground-plans and structure of a few churches, stripped for the most part of their ornaments,
- some altars and carvings, together with some fragments of stained glass,
- a few pages from baptismal registers.

We should add that our imaginary historian also has available around 700 diverse representations of the crucifixion from many different sites, some of them including other scenes from the Passion. It would be hard indeed to describe Christianity on such a basis; and it is likewise extremely hard for us to give an account of the cult of Mithras. The material is quite simply ruinously incomplete.[184]

The point being made in the above quotation is that we have no scriptures and virtually no written documents from the actual participants in the Mysteries of Mithras (unlike the case with ancient Christianity) -- and thus what we know of this ancient sub-group within the Roman Empire is primarily derived from the distinctive gathering places of the sect: the so-called "Mithraic temples" (which are actually completely unlike other temples from the ancient period, which is why some scholars refer to them as Mithraic "cult rooms" instead of as "temples") known as *mithraea*, including their floor-plans and general pattern (over 420 of which have been found to date, and more continue to be discovered), as well as their decoration and iconography (sometimes including large artistic murals), the dedicatory inscriptions which remain for many of these structures (approximately 1,000 of which have been recovered), as well as a very small amount of written material thought to involve the questions and answers required for those initiates trying to move from one grade to another within the secret order (in other words, fragments of a catechism). The most central iconography of each mithraeum was a scene

The Cult of Mithras

known as the *tauroctony*, discussed below: over 700 of these have been found.[185]

Although the individual "Mithraic temple" is known to modern scholars as a *mithraeum*, the plural form being *mithraea*, these terms were only applied in modern times and the ancient inscriptions refer to them by other terms such as "cave" (*speleum* or *antrum*) or "crypt" (*crypta*), or "sacred place" (*fanum*), or "temple" (*templum*).[186]

As Dr. Jonas Bjørnebye writes in his 2007 dissertation on the cult of Mithras in fourth century Rome, "Almost all mithraea seem more or less to follow the same general architectural plan, though practical considerations, such as for example structural changes in the buildings housing mithraea, can change the proportions of the cult rooms somewhat."[187]

David Walsh describes the design of the mithraea found around the Roman world (while noting that some variations do occur, particularly in the mithraea of the fourth century, AD 300 - 399):

> The general plan though was of a small rectangular room containing a central nave, flanked by parallel benches, leading to a niche or altar. [. . .] Mithraea usually had no windows and were entirely artificially lit, although some mithraea have been found to contain shafts in their roofs that allowed light to shine on the altar or niche on certain days of the year when opened. The reason for this lack of natural light appears to have been to create a cave-like atmosphere (some mithraea were actually installed in caves) so as to replicate the setting of Mithras' most important act. Indeed, in Italy mithraea are often referred to in inscriptions as *spelaea*. Furthermore, evidence has even been found indicating that the *cella* was decorated, so as to add to the cave-like efect, such as at Gross-Krotzenburg where rough basalt covered the ceiling. In contrast, there is no evidence that mithraea had any form of external decoration, although occasionally the entrance way was covered by a portico.[188]

Chapter Thirteen

What does the author of the above quotation mean when he suggests that the creation of the "cave-like atmosphere" was sought after in order (perhaps) to "replicate the setting of Mithras' most important act"?

No doubt he is referring to the slaying of the bull, depicted in the ubiquitous tauroctony ("bull-slaying") scene dominating the wall opposite the entrance of the cave (or mithraeum), a scene in which Mithras -- a flowing cape (which is sometimes decorated with stars) billowing above his shoulders, and wearing a distinctive Phrygian cap -- plunges a long knife or short sword into the shoulder region of a powerful bull, upon the back of which the triumphant god has placed one knee, while with his other hand he pulls the head of the bull upwards by the nostril of the animal. Mithras is depicted in these scenes beneath a vaulted or arching ceiling in some cases, leading to the interpretation by some that he has carried the bull into a cave in order to slay it, and leading to the suggestion cited above that the mithraea themselves replicate a cave in a symbolic attempt (perhaps) to re-create the scene of this famous bull-slaying by Mithras.

David Walsh also points out, however, that Mithraic scholar Roger Beck, emeritus professor at the University of Toronto, has suggested that the cave-like setting of the mithraea might also have been understood as replicating the cosmos, and to convey thereby esoteric meaning regarding the descent of the soul itself into incarnation.

In an article entitled "If So, How? Representing 'Coming Back to Life' in the Mysteries of Mithras," Professor Beck explains that the Neoplatonic philosopher Porphyry of Tyre (c. AD 234 - 305) left us an essay entitled *On the Cave of the Nymphs in the Thirteenth Book of the Odyssey* in which he tells us that "the Persians" (by which term he designates the members of the cult of Mithras) "perfect their initiate by inducting him into a mystery of the descent of souls and their exit back out again, calling the place a 'cave.' This cave bore for him the image of the cosmos which Mithras had created, and the things which the cave contained, by their proportionate arrangement, provided him with symbols of the elements and climates of the cosmos."[189]

Beck explains:
> A natural cave is an inside without a clearly defined outside; so is the apparent universe. And so, usually, are mithraea. Frequently they are rooms or suites of rooms within larger buildings. And when they are self-contained buildings, in dramatic contrast to the standard temples of classical antiquity, they seem to have had no exterior decoration at all. A mithraeum, literally, is all interior.[190]

Professor Beck's essay then proceeds -- using the architectural plan and iconography of the Mithraeum of the Seven Spheres (also known today as the *Mitreo delle Sette Sfere*), located in Ostia (the port closest to Rome, by which trade goods from all over the empire, as well as the fresh harvest of the bounty of the sea, were brought to the capitol) and discovered in the modern era in the year 1885 -- to analyze the Mithraic cave as a replica of the cosmos and a model delineating the soul's descent from the point of summer solstice down to winter solstice, and ultimate re-

Chapter Thirteen

ascent in the other direction begining at winter solstice and moving towards summer solstice.

His inspired deciphering of the arrangement of the mithraeum deserves to be read in its entirety, and is only summarized here. Beck demonstrates that the layout of the cult space of the cave, as described by Porphyry and as evidenced by the remains of the Mithraeum of the Seven Spheres at Ostia, "instantiates the macrocosm" and the cycles of the heavens above.

On the facing page is an image of the remains of the Mithraeum of the Seven Spheres, below which I have created a diagram based on that drawn by Roger Beck and F. S. Tappenden accompanying the article referenced.[191]

Noting the positions of the *mosaic representations of the zodiac* signs along the benches flanking the long axis of the central aisle of the cave (a feature so far found only at this mithraeum), Professor Beck argues that the cave's layout replicates the annual cycle of the sun, beginning at the entry-way (at the bottom of the diagram) corresponding to the fall equinox, and proceeding counter-clockwise around the space of the mithraeum, along the bench on the right side of the image -- starting with Libra, then Scorpio, Sagittarius, Capricorn, Aquarius, and finally Pisces before reaching the far wall with the tauroctony depiction.

Noting that the tauroctony wall is situated between Pisces (at the top-right of the floor-plan as we face the image on the opposite page) and Aries (at the top-left as we face the diagram), Beck explains that the tauroctony panel (located in what scholars call the "cult-niche" of the mithraeum) corresponds to the position of spring equinox, and that the entrance side of the mithraeum (at the bottom of the diagram at right, through an opening in the wall opposite the cult-niche) represents the fall equinox (in between Virgo, on the bottom-left, and Libra on the bottom-right of the diagram).

Further strengthening his argument, Professor Beck notes that there are in fact small, "non-functional" niches built-in to the

The Cult of Mithras

benches on either side of the aisle in between the mosaic representations of Sagittarius and Capricorn (on the right-hand bench) and between Gemini and Cancer (on the left-hand bench) exactly where, according to his argument, we should imagine the "solstitial diameter" as Beck calls it, indicated by a line (below):

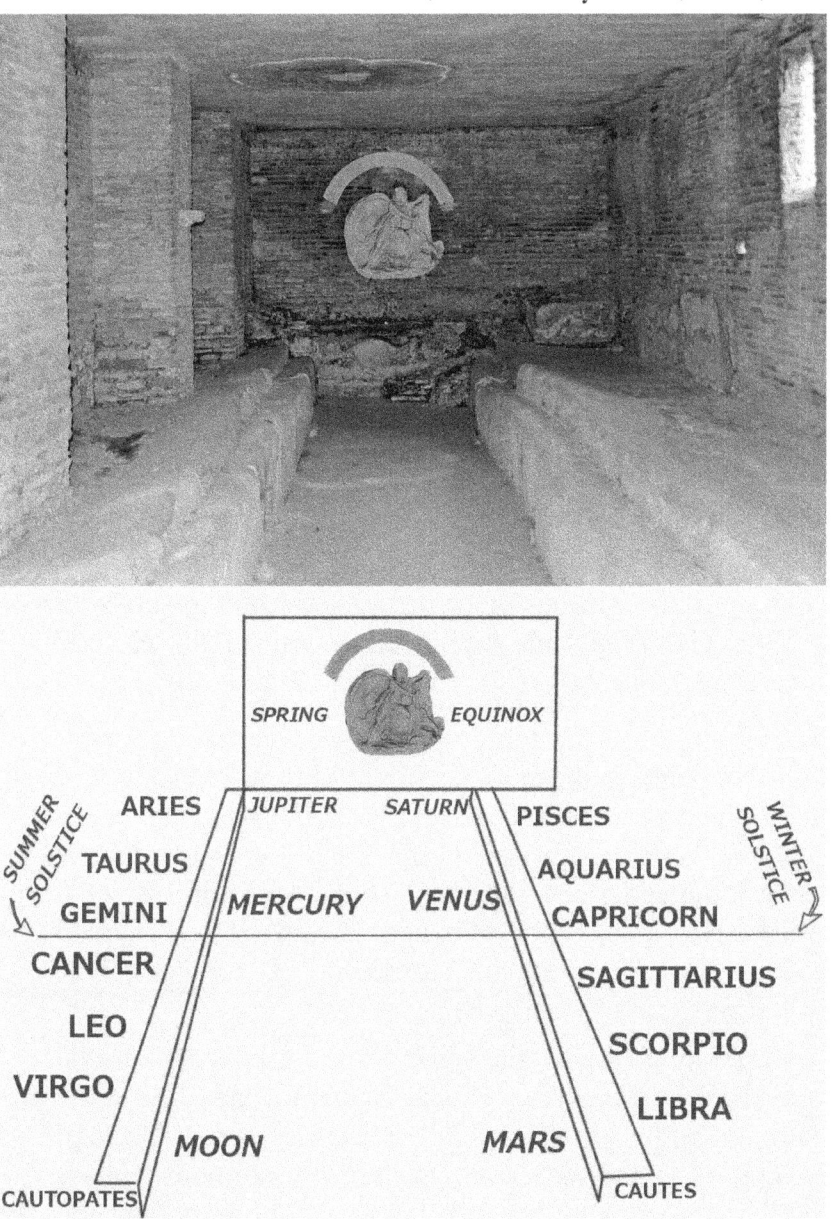

Chapter Thirteen

In addition to mosaics representing each of the zodiac signs, this mithraeum also features anthropomorphic representations of each of the gods or goddesses associated with the five visible planets plus the moon (this aspect of the layout is not unique to the Seven Spheres cave, although the method of representing these heavenly bodies varies -- other mithraea appear to have used statues). The location of these deities in the Mithraeum of the Seven Spheres is also indicated on the diagram on the preceding page. Professor Beck observes that because mithraea, including this one from Ostia, represent the gods associated with all the visible planets (Mercury, Venus, Mars, Saturn, and Jupiter) as well as the moon, the absence of a figure representing the sun leads us to the logical conclusion that *the figure of Mithras in the tauroctony scene* is associated with the deified sun itself.

Significantly, this particular mithraeum in Ostia also included in its original decoration seven "undifferentiated mosaic arcs" set into the floor of the aisle of the cave, and "understood by all to represent the seven planetary spheres -- hence of course the mithraeum's name."[192]

Drawing upon the writings of ancient philosophers in surviving texts, Roger Beck explains his understanding of the esoteric meaning of this replication of the cosmos within the mithraea:

> The solstices, from a Mithraist's perspective, are the most important points in the universe. For in Mithraic thinking they are the points at which the soul-journey, intimated by Porphyry in *On the Cave* (the "mystery of the descent of souls and their exit back out again"), starts and finishes. The Mithraists were not alone in this belief. We find it also in Neoplatonic speculation, where Proclus attributes it to Numenius explicating Plato's "Myth of Er":
>
>> By 'heaven' he means the sphere of the fixed stars, and he says there are two chasms in this, Capricorn and Cancer, the latter a path down into genesis, the former a path of ascent . . . and introduces a further enormous fantasy (τερατολογιαν) with leapings (πηδησεις) of souls from the

tropics to the equinoxes and returns from these back to the tropics, leapings that are all his own and that he transfers to these matters, stitching the Platonic utterances together with astrological concerns and these with the mysteries (συρραπτων τα Πλατωνικα ρηματα τοις γενεθλιαλογικοις και ταυτα τοις, τελεστικοις).[193]

Beck adds a quotation from Porphyry to make the esoteric connection between the heavenly cycles and the soul's journey perfectly clear:

> Taking the cave as an image and symbol of the cosmos, Numenius and his pupil Cronius assert that there are two extremities in the heavens: the winter tropic than which nothing is more southern and the summer tropic than which nothing is more northern. The summer tropic is in Cancer, the winter tropic is in Capricorn. . . . Two of these [i.e. signs of the zodiac], Cancer and Capricorn, the theologians treated as gates. . . .Numenius and Cronius say that the gate through which souls descend is Cancer and the gate through which they ascend is Capricorn. Cancer is northern and suited for descent, Capricorn southerly and suitable for ascent.[194]

Professor Beck then adds his analysis of the purpose of the mithraeum, based on their connection to the pattern of the cosmos and the esoteric understanding of the journey of the soul's descent and return:

> It is noteworthy that neither Proclus nor Porphyry in *On the Cave* speaks of teaching the initiates anything about "the descent of souls and their exit back out again" through these solstitial gates. The mithraeum was indeed an instrument, but it was not a teaching aid. It was an instrument for getting the initiates down from heaven and back out again *in a mystery*. How precisely the mystery was effected must wait until further pieces of the picture are in place.[195]

The seven arches representing the seven spheres of the five visible planets plus the sun and the moon which give the Mithraeum of

Chapter Thirteen

the Seven Spheres its name add another layer of esoteric meaning, as Roger Beck argues, bolstering his case with a quotation from the ancient philosopher Origen (whose name signifies "Horus-born" or "Horus-generated," c. AD 185 - 253). In his treatise *Contra Celsum* or *Against Celsus*, thought to have been written in the year AD 248, Origen says:

> These things ["i.e., the celestial ascent of souls," Professor Beck explains] the λοϒος of the Persians ["i.e., the Mithraists, as in Porphyry," Professor Beck interjects] and the τελετη of Mithras intimate. . . . for there is therein a certain συμβολον of the two celestial revolutions (περιοδων), that of the fixed stars and that assigned to the planets, and of the route of the soul through and out (διξοδου) of them. Such is the συμβολον: a seven-gated ladder and an eighth gate on top (κλιμαξ επαπυλος, επι δ'αυτη πυλη ογδοη).[196]

Incorporating this information from Origen, Professor Beck explains the esoteric meaning of the mithraeum:

> In sum, then, the soul descends into mortal genesis through the summer solstice in Cancer, located in the mithraeum at the midpoint of the bench on the left, marked at Sette Sfere (and in some other mithraea in the area of Ostia, Rome, and vicinity) by a small niche; it departs back out again in apogenesis through the winter solstice in Capricorn, likewise marked by a niche in the bench opposite. From the gate of entry in the sphere of the fixed stars at the summer solstice the soul descends sequentially through the spheres of the planets, represented at Sette Sfere -- and at Sette Sfere only -- by the seven mosaic arcs in the floor of the aisle; and through the same seven spheres, in reverse order of course, it ascends again to the gate of exit at the winter solstice.[197]

One other important detail to note is that, in the diagram on page 359, the locations of two figures found at the Mithraeum of the Seven Spheres (and in other mithraea as well, although by no means in all of them) are indicated towards the bottom of the

The Cult of Mithras

illustration: the figures known as Cautes and Cautopates. As we see indicated in the diagram, Cautes is located on the right as we face the tauroctony (the tauroctony on the far wall). Cautes is at the near end of the bench containing the zodiac signs that we have previously designated as making up the "lower half" of the annual cycle -- that half of the year containing the winter solstice.

Cautopates is located at the near end of the opposite bench, the bench on the left as we enter the mithraeum and face the tauroctony scene on the far wall -- the bench containing the zodiac signs of the "upper half" of the annual cycle, those flanking the the summer solstice in between Gemini and Cancer.

Note that each wears a Phrygian cap (which "flops over" at the top), each carries a lighted torch (one pointing upwards, and one pointing downwards), and each stands with his legs crossed.

Chapter Thirteen

In the essay we have been citing, Professor Beck describes these two supernatural figures in this way:

> Cautes and Cautopates are deities of the Mithras cult -- and of no other. In appearance they are small clones of Mithras and they are present in representations of his adventures, notably the bull-killing scene. They are twins, differentiated solely by the fact that one of them, Cautes, carries a raised torch, the other, Cautopates, a lowered torch. Cautes thus represents, among other things, ascent and Cautopates descent. In our present context, then, the descent of the soul into mortal genesis through the gate of the summer solstice (Cancer) would be represented by Cautopates, and the soul's ascent back out again into immortality through the gate of the winter solstice (Capricorn) by Cautes. And this is precisely what we find both in Sette Sfere and in the texts of Porphyry quoted above. Mosaic images of the torchbearers are found on the bench ends closest to the entrance. Cautopates is set on the end of the bench carrying the northern signs (Aries to Virgo) and is thus to the right of Mithras in the cult-niche; Cautes is set on the end of the bench carrying the southern signs (Libra to Pisces) and is thus to the left of Mithras in the cult-niche. This is not only so at Sette Sfere, but also at every other mithraeum -- admittedly rather few -- where the torchbearers are represented as an opposed pair elsewhere than in the composition of the principal cult icon. Once again cosmic symbols are found appropriately positioned.[198]

Thus we see that the originators of the cult of Mithras appear to have been extremely well-versed in the very symbology we have been discussing throughout this volume -- the ancient system underlying and informing the world's ancient myths from virtually every culture around the globe. It is a celestial system, and an esoteric system -- and there can be little doubt that iconography underlying the symbols which have survived from the ancient Mysteries of Mithras were based upon this celestial and esoteric system as well.

In his extremely insightful and helpful article cited above, Professor Roger Beck notes that the valuable information regarding the meaning of the Persian initiations given by Porphyry seems to have been pointedly ignored by Mithraic scholars of the past hundred years. He writes:

> Strangely, however, what appears at first sight to be germane information from a contemporaneous source [i.e., Porphyry] about the design and function of the mithraeum is generally either ignored or dismissed offhandedly by modern scholars. For example, Jan Bremmer, in an otherwise exhaustive book entitled *Initiation into the Mysteries of the Ancient World*, even though at one point he cites this very passage from *On the Cave*, fails to mention its assertion that "induction into a mystery" was precisely the intent behind the mithraeum's design! The only modern scholar of Mithraism to engage with this issue in a substantial way -- the present author excepted -- has been Robert Turcan.[199]

This fact is remarkable and extremely noteworthy. Beck then notes that Turcan, the only other scholar to take up the contemporary perspective authored by Porphyry (certainly an important, intelligent, and philosophically formidable ancient source, and one we would not expect a century or more of Mithraic scholars to ignore), basically dismisses the testimony of Porphyry as dishonest, telling us nothing about ancient Mithraism itself but only a picture of Mithraism as imagined by a Neoplatonist -- "a *Neoplatonic construction* of Mithraism."[200]

Professor Beck notes that he disagrees with this view and elsewhere gives his reasons for assessing Porphyry to be a reliable source.[199] This information from Porphyry, along with Professor Beck's placing it in context of the mithraea as "three-dimensional models" of the space in which this descent and ascent takes place, is extremely significant, particularly in relation to my thesis that the *descent and re-ascent* also has to do with the "burial" (suppression) of the higher self (trauma and alienation from our essence) and the recovery of that lost connection (the "re-ascent")!

Chapter Thirteen

Note in particular the presence of the widespread pattern of *twins* (in the figures of Cautes and Cautopates), one indicating descent and one re-ascent: we have seen that this pattern of twins relates directly to the "estranged twins" of our lower self (egoic mind) and our higher self (the essential and authentic self).

The baffling refusal by *some of the most prominent and prolific scholars in the field of Mithraic studies* to consider the available evidence is noteworthy, and brings us to the revolutionary interpretation of the Mithraic iconography made by David Ulansey, Professor Emeritus of Philosophy and Religion at the California Institute of Integral Studies in San Francisco.

In 1989, Professor Ulansey published a book which changed Mithraic studies forever, by presenting a conclusive argument supported by overwhelming evidence demonstrating that the scenes of the tauroctony, along with other aspects of Mithraic iconography and cult practice, are celestial in nature -- and that the figure of Mithras slaying the bull corresponds to the constellation Perseus in the heavens.

In that book, entitled *The Origins of the Mithraic Mysteries: Cosmology and Salvation in the Ancient World*, he makes a very noteworthy observation near the very beginning of his argument. In his first chapter, Ulansey explains that:

> Attempts by modern scholars to unravel the secret of this bull-slaying scene -- and Mithraism in general -- have taken a path almost as strange as the religion itself, in that for most of this century they have been dominated by the work of a single man: the Belgian scholar Franz Cumont, who in 1896 and 1899 published the two volumes of his magisterial *Textes et monuments figurés relatifs aux mystères de Mithra*. In one of the volumes Cumont gathered together and made available for the first time the primary evidence relating to Mithraism, while in the other he presented his interpretation of the evidence. The fact that Cumont's interpretation was presented as an accompaniment to his vast catalogue of the evidence

concerning Mithraism, in which the texts and monuments of the cult were made easily accessible to scholars, lent to his ideas a sense of imposing authority which persists to this day.[201]

The central thesis of Franz-Valéry-Marie Cumont (1868 - 1947) was that Mithraism was descended from an Iranian antecedant called Mazdaism (where there is a god named Mithra, although Mithra himself does not slay a bull), and his voluminous work was built around arguments that everything in the cult -- including the iconography of the bull-slaying scene (the tauroctony) -- had its origins in the ancient mythology of Persia.

Despite major problems with Cumont's theory, it held sway for nearly a hundred years, although scholars eventually began to find evidence that the Persian-origin theory was irreparably flawed. The situation came to a head in 1971 at the First International Congress of Mithraic Studies held at the University of Manchester in England, in which papers critical of Cumont's theory were presented by two of the scholars in attendance: John Hinnells of the University of London (1941 - 2018, and the organizer of that First International Congress of Mithraic Studies) and Richard L. Gordon, currently a professor at Universität Erfurt in Germany.

At that conference, Professor Hinnells presented a paper which raised the possibility that "the Roman Mithras was the Mithra of Iran in name only" (although he did not go so far as to fully embrace this possibility, Ulansey notes).[202]

"Of more importance in the long run, however," David Ulansey writes, "was the more radical paper presented by R. L. Gordon, who argued that Cumont's interpretations of Mithraism were virtually useless and that Mithraic studies essentially had to start over from scratch."[203]

After presenting some examples of the convoluted arguments about the tauroctony used by those trying to tie its figures back to an ancient Iranian precedent, and why those arguments were

Chapter Thirteen

basically absurd, David Ulansey drops a bomb when he says, at the beginning of chapter two of his text:

> In 1869 a German scholar named K. B. Stark proposed an explanantion for the symbolism of the tauroctony which was ignored by scholars for most of this century. However, in the wake of the attack on Cumont at the First International Congress, Stark's hypothesis was rediscovered and in the past decade has come to form the basis of an entirely new and rapidly growing school of thought regarding the essential nature of Mithraism.
>
> It would be difficult to imagine a more radical alternative to Cumont's interpretation of the tauroctony than the explanation offered by Stark. For according to Stark, the figures in the tauroctony represented not characters out of Iranian mythology but rather a series of stars and constellations. The Mithraic tauroctony, therefore, was not a pictorial representation of an Iranian myth -- as Cumont and his followers claimed it was -- but a star map![204]

Here once again we have a startling case of extremely important information which would help unlock some of the mystery surrounding the ancient cult of Mithras being pointedly ignored by scholars for *over a century* -- just as Professor Roger Beck demonstrates regarding the insights to be gleaned from the contemporary accounts left to us by Porphyry of Tyre in the section above, also largely ignored by conventional Mithraists (it should be noted that David Ulansey in advancing his thesis definitely does *not* ignore the evidence from Porphyry).

Curious! We have the case of Stark's theory being ignored, Cumont's deeply flawed theory being carried along for a hundred years unchallenged, and Porphyry's significant contemporary testimony about the meaning of the Mithraic initiations being largely ignored and occasionally disparaged. What could be going on here? We should not discount the possibility that this emerging pattern indicates something more than "coincidence."

The Cult of Mithras

Karl Bernhard Stark (1824 - 1879), a professor of archaeology at the University of Heidelberg and the founder of the Archaeological Institute of the University of Heidelberg wrote a paper entitled "Die Mithrassteine von Dormagen" (about the "Mithras-stone" or tauroctony from Dormagen, a town along the Rhine in what was once known as Germania Inferior or "Lower Germania" during the Roman Empire, where a mithraeum was discovered in 1821, containing not one but two limestone monuments depicting Mithras slaying the bull), which was actually published in 1868 (according to the title page of the volume in which this paper can still be found to this day, in its original German), a book entitled *Jahrbücher des Vereins von Alterthumsfreunden im Rheinlande, Heft XLIV und XLV*.

This paper by Professor Stark identified the tauroctony scene as celestial in nature -- an argument that would lie dormant for over a hundred years before being picked up by scholars in the wake of the 1971 First International Congress of Mithraic Studies described above.

Ulansey gives credit to other researchers who, in the wake of the 1971 conference mentioned, rediscovered the long-neglected argument of K. B. Stark -- beginning with Roger Beck, whose decoding of the Mithraeum of the Seven Spheres we have just been exploring. Ulansey explains that at the 1973 meeting of the American Philological Association, "the Canadian classicist Roger Beck read a paper in which he rejuvenated K. B. Stark's long-fogotten hypothesis concerning the astronomical significance of the tauroctony." [205]

Beck's work was followed by arguments from other Mithraic scholars also advancing some aspect of the celestial argument, including Stanley Insler (1937 - 2019), Alessandro Bausani (1921 - 1988), and Michael P. Speidel (professor at the University of Hawaii, born 1937). However, as David Ulansey argues in his 1989 book, although all these scholars agree that the tauroctony is celestial in nature, the first three do not address the celestial identity of Mithras himself. Michael Speidel does address the

Chapter Thirteen

identity of Mithras, arguing that he is associated with Orion (in his 1980 book *Mithras-Orion: Greek Hero and Roman Army God*).

Professor Ulansey, while acknowledging the important contributions of these scholars and the importance of the fact that they all present abundant evidence for seeing that the tauroctony scene is celestial in nature, advances a different hypothesis: that Mithras is associated with the constellation Perseus -- and the argument to support such an identification is simply beyond question.

Noting that the tauroctony scene features the slaying of a bull, and that in this scene the figure of Mithras is invariably depicted *above the bull*, Ulansey writes: "It thus cannot be without a certain amount of astonishment that one looks at the region of the sky directly above Taurus the Bull -- that is, the region of the sky exactly analogous to the position of Mithras in the tauroctony -- and sees the constellation figure of a young hero, carrying a dagger, and wearing a Phrygian cap!" [206]

Professor Ulansey does not avail himself of the constellational outlines suggested by H. A. Rey, but he does reproduce a star-chart upon which the constellation Perseus is depicted (in "flowery" artwork) wearing just such a Phrygian cap, identical to that worn by Mithras in the tauroctony scenes, as well as artwork from ancient Greek pottery showing the hero Perseus in the same type of headgear. [207]

On the page opposite I have placed a star-chart showing the region of the constellation Perseus above Taurus in the sky, with Perseus outlined as suggested by H. A. Rey (I tend to outline the constellation Taurus in a manner which differs from Rey, but the differences are not important for this argument). We can see that Perseus is indeed situated directly above Taurus in the heavens, from the perspective of an observer in the northern hemisphere.

The Cult of Mithras

I myself would add the following important details to the analysis offered by Professor Ulansey, bolstering his arguments:

- The knee on the right side of Mithras as we face the scene is bent, so that all we see is the thigh of Mithras and not his lower leg on that side: this detail can be seen to correspond to the leg on the right side of the constellation Perseus as we face the chart (this leg is noticeably shorter in the outline of the constellation).
- Mithras is wearing the distinctive Phrygian cap, which is also associated with the hero Perseus: in addition, the constellation itself appears to be wearing a "peaked cap" and this triangular cap can even be envisioned as having

"ear-flaps" dropping down on either side of the face, which are also characteristic of the Phrygian cap design as depicted in some ancient artwork, although not always, and not in the tauroctony scenes featuring Mithras.

- Mithras has his head *turned away* from the place he is stabbing the bull: this aspect of the tauroctony is noted by Ulansey, and he correctly connects this turned-away head of Mithras to the turned-away gaze of Perseus when slaying the Gorgon, which he illustrates using a scene from an Attic vase dating to the sixth century BC or BCE[208] -- and we can also add that Odysseus in the text of the Odyssey (chapter ten) is also instructed to turn his face away from the ram when he slays it as an offering in the underworld, as we have already discussed earlier in this chapter, on pages 351 and following (the constellation Perseus, in other words, can be shown to have been associated with "looking away" in other ancient myths besides the Gorgon myth and besides the tauroctony).

- Mithras is consistently depicted in the tauroctony scene wearing a cape which is flying in the breeze, extended out to the side of the god in the same direction that he is turning his head: look back at the star-chart presented on the previous page featuring the constellation outline as suggested by H. A. Rey and see if you can identify the feature which plays the role of the billowing, curling cape of the god Mithras. It is the "arm" on the left side of the constellation, which ends in the distinctive curved-up hook: the same arm which also forms the inspiration for the *harpe* sword of Perseus (as well as forming the inspiration for the "flaming sword which turned every way," that is to say, *in all directions*, described in Genesis 3: 24).

Based on these abundant clues, we can be absolutely confident that Professor Ulansey is correct in identifying the god Mithras with the constellation Perseus in the tauroctony scene. Even *further* supporting evidence could be offered from other myths from other cultures, such as the fact that figures associated with

The Cult of Mithras

Perseus are often described as *riding upon a donkey or an ass* -- the ass with its long ears being Taurus again, this time with the long horns of the bull envisioned as the long ears of a donkey instead.

The god Hephaestus, for example, rides upon a donkey -- and we can be fairly confident that Hephaestus is associated with the constellation Perseus, because Perseus-figures are often described in myth as having "twisted legs" or a "twisted leg," for reasons that should be obvious from the star-chart on page 371, in which the outline of the constellation can be seen to have a twisted leg or legs.

Further confirmation for this assertion comes from the figure of Balaam in the book of Numbers (chapters 22 through 24), who also rides upon a donkey or ass, and who has his foot crushed or twisted during the episode in which the ass would not go forward because she perceives the presence of an angel blocking their way (the angel in this case corresponds to the constellation Andromeda, as I have argued elsewhere).

These mythical episodes in which a figure with a crushed or twisted foot or feet (clearly corresponding to the constellation Perseus) rides upon an ass (a long-eared animal corresponding to Taurus, which is sometimes envisioned as an ass rather than as a bull -- including in the story of Samson when Samson reaches out his hand to grasp the "jawbone of an ass" in Judges 15: 15) provide yet further support (as if any further support is needed) to conclusively prove beyond any reasonable objection that David Ulansey is correct in his identification of Mithras with Perseus in the tauroctony scene.

And there is yet further evidence which must be mentioned. The god Mithras in the tauroctony scene is frequently depicted beneath an arch, sometimes an arch which could be the mouth of a great cave, or perhaps the arch of a vaulted ceiling. As we have already noted, the band of the Milky Way passes above the head

Chapter Thirteen

of the constellation Perseus in the heavens, suggesting just such an arch:

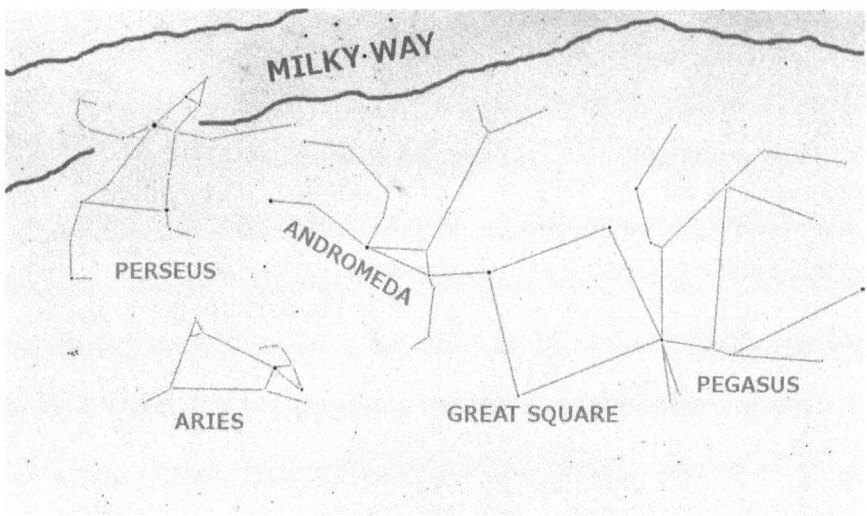

Indeed, there is an important myth in which a figure who also wears a Phrygian cap is ordered by a god to dip his head in a river: the foolish King Midas, who asked for the ability to turn whatever he touched into gold (in marked contrast to King Solomon, who, when God asked him what gift Solomon might desire, instead asked for wisdom rather than for riches or for long life or for power over his enemies). The fact that Midas wears a Phrygian cap and dunks his head in a river (the River Pactolus) shows once again that the Phrygian cap is associated with the constellation Perseus.

On the page opposite we see a tauroctony scene in which a distinctive arch is depicted above the head of Mithras as he slays the bull. This tauroctony is catalogued in the *Corpus Inscriptionum et Monumentorum Religionis Mithraiacae* (the "Corpus of Inscriptions and Monuments of the Mithraic Religion," or CIMRM, compiled by Dutch Mithraic scholar Josef Vermaseren beginning in the 1950s) as CIMRM 546, and the dedicatory inscription beneath the bull-slaying scene is catalogued as CIMRM 547. The inscription is important: the first line of it clearly says "SOL INVICTO DEO," which translates as "The Unconquered (or Unconquerable) Sun God."

The Cult of Mithras

Other arches over the tauroctony scene sometimes contain the symbols for the twelve signs of the zodiac, such the famous tauroctony from Heddernheim, CIMRM 1083:

Chapter Thirteen

The presence of distinctive arches above the head of Mithras in many surviving ancient tauroctonies provide still further evidence, I would argue, that the god Mithras was consciously understood to be connected with the figure of Perseus in the heavens. These arches correspond to the arching band of the Milky Way above the head of Perseus in the night sky.

Finally, there is the evidence from antiquity, noted by Ulansey, that the initiates of the cult of Mithras appear to have referred to themselves and to have been referred to by others as "Persians." This terminology is significant, because it may well indicate a connection not to the geographic region of Persia, but rather to the figure of Perseus!

The two possibilities (the geographic region and the heroic son of Zeus) are not mutually exclusive -- as Professor Ulansey points out, ancient sources demonstrate that even though the actual origin of the name "Persia" is now believed to have nothing to do with Perseus, a connection was perceived in ancient times, including in the writings of Herodotus.[209]

But why such importance invested in Perseus? Professor Ulansey advances a truly inspired thesis in answer to that question. He argues that the solution has to do with the phenomenon of *precession*, which we have already mentioned (briefly) in this volume and which acts to slowly "delay" the background of stars expected on any specific day of the year, such as the date of spring or fall equinox, or the date of summer or winter solstice.

The inexorable motion of precession delays the background of stars by only a single degree every 72 years (actually, every 71.6 years), such that the stars on a specific day of the year (such as spring equinox) will be seen to be "held back" by only a single degree on spring equinox after 72 years. Thus, the action of precession is extremely subtle -- one can barely perceive its effects in a human lifetime.

However, over a great deal of time, approximately 2,160 years, this motion of precession will delay the rising of the background

The Cult of Mithras

of stars to such a degree that an entirely different zodiac constellation will be seen to be rising above the eastern horizon on the expected day. The period of 2,160 years is determined by observing that if there are twelve constellations in the zodiac, each can be seen to occupy approximately 30 degrees of the total 360 degree cycle of the year, which means that if the background of stars is delayed by one degree every 72 years, it will take approximately 2,160 years, or 72 years per degree multiplied by 30 degrees per zodiac sign, to delay the background enough to have a different zodiac constellation rising on a specific day of the year, such as on the morning of spring equinox.

This delaying action of precession means that if, in a previous age of human history, the sun was observed to be rising in the background stars of the constellation of Taurus, after approximately 2,160 years (in which the background of stars is delayed by a single degree every 72 years), the rising of Taurus will be delayed to the point that it is not seen to rise in its anticipated position on the morning of spring equinox. Instead, due to the delaying action of precession, the sun will occupy the *preceding* zodiac constellation on the anticipated day.

The subtle action of precession will cause us to move from the Age of Taurus (when the sun rises in Taurus every spring equinox) to the Age of Aries (when the sun is now in the preceding constellation on spring equinox, Aries, instead of Taurus, due to the fact that the background stars have been "delayed").

As David Ulansey argues in *The Origins of the Mithraic Mysteries*, through its focus upon the tauroctony scene in which Mithras is slaying a bull (a bull which is associated, beyond any doubt, with the constellation Taurus) the cult of Mithras appears to be commemorating the transition of precessional ages from the Age of Taurus to the Age of Aries. The slaying of the bull represents in graphic detail the precessional motion which eventually caused the sun to rise in the constellation of Aries on the spring equinox, when in the previous age the sun had been

Chapter Thirteen

located in the constellation Taurus on the same significant day of spring equinox.

The slaying of the bull represents the termination of the Age of Taurus. The brilliant insight David Ulansey offers in his 1989 book on the celestial foundations of the Mithraic Mysteries (in addition to his insight that the god Mithras is associated with Perseus, positioned above Taurus and in fact slaying Taurus) is his perception that because the inexorable action of precession moves the sun's rising point from one zodiac constellation to another through the various ages, this *displacement of the sun* was perceived as indicating that the sun itself (associated with the god Helios) was subject to a higher power!

That is to say, precession demonstrates that the sun itself is subordinate to a higher power -- a higher power which forces it to move from one zodiac constellation to the preceding zodiac constellation. The tauroctony, then, represents Mithras (associated with Perseus) as that higher power who drives the sun from one constellation to the next, through the inexorable motion of precession (in this case, Mithras is ending the Age of Taurus and driving the sun into the preceding sign, thus initiating the Age of Aries).

With this understanding, we can now address the fact that Mithras appears to have been referred to in some inscriptions, including the inscription shown in the upper image on page 375, as the *Unconquered* Sun. As Professor Ulansey shows in his 1989 book, the ancient mithraea furnish us with many pieces of artwork in which Mithras is shown alongside the sun-god, who is depicted with different iconography from the figure of Mithras himself (such as wearing the seven-pointed halo of the sun-god, associated with Helios). In most of these ancient images, Mithras and Helios (the sun-god) are depicted as co-equals – but in some of them, Helios is represented as kneeling before Mithras.

Once we understand the ages-long action of precession, and once we understand that Mithras (associated with Perseus) is to be

The Cult of Mithras

seen as the power who ends one precessional age and ushers in another, then we are in a position to understand why Helios is sometimes depicted in ancient Mithraic iconography as kneeling in a subordinate position to Mithras himself, and why Mithras is described as the *Unconquered* Sun God (in contrast with another sun-god, who *has* been conquered: in this case, Helios -- conquered by precession). Professor Ulansey explains:

> We may now carry the argument one final step further by focusing on the word *invictus* (unconquered) in the title *Mithras sol invictus*. When Mithras is referred to as the *un*conquered sun, one naturally becomes curious as to whether or not there is also a *conquered* sun. And here, of course, Mithraic iconography gives us an absolutely explicit answer: all of those scenes depicting the sun god kneeling before Mithras or otherwise submitting to him make it abundantly clear that it is the sun itself who is actually the conquered sun. Mithras, therefore, becomes the unconquered sun by conquering the sun. He accomplishes this deed, as we saw earlier, by means of the power represented by the symbol of the celestial pole which he holds in his hand in the "investment" scenes, a power which consists in his ability to shift the position of the celstial pole by moving the cosmic structure and which clearly makes him more powerful than the sun. And so we may say that Mithras is entitled to be called "sun" insofar as he has taken over the role of *kosmokrator* formerly exercised by the sun itself.
>
> Thus the entire relationship between Mithras and Helios becomes fully explicable: Helios sometimes submits to Mithras in recognition of Mithras's superior ability to shift the entire cosmic structure. Mithras and Helios are sometimes portrayed as equals (in the banquet and chariot scenes, for example) in recognition of the fact that they are both *kosmokrators* (like the situation with the two *kosmokrators* in Cicero's *Dream of Scipio*) and thus are in a sense sympathetic allies sharing a common bond. And Mithras is called

Chapter Thirteen

"unconquered sun" as an acknowledgement of the fact that he has taken over the role of *kosmokrator* which formerly was the sole prerogative of the now-conquered sun.[210]

In the dedicatory inscription found on the first tauroctony scene on page 375, we saw that the dedicator of the marble plaque, one Atimetus -- who calls himself the servant or slave "Augustorum" (in other words, "of the emperors") -- has dedicated this artwork to the Unconquered Sun God, *Sol Invicto Deo*. Those *not* familiar with Ulansey's thesis (and his explanation quoted above) may find this ancient inscription confusing, as the image in the marble tauroctony upon which the inscription is placed is clearly an image of Mithras, not of the sun-god Helios.

Ulansey's brilliant explication clears up the difficulty: the action of precession in effect "conquers" the ordinary sun. The action of precession forces the sun to move successively from one zodiac constellation to another, over the course of thousands of years. The figure of Mithras is depicted in the tauroctony as the power who ends one celestial age and ushers in another. Thus, Mithras is associated with the mysterious power of the motion of precession -- a power which is above the power of the sun itself.

The personification of the sun (Helios) represents the *conquered* sun. The figure of Mithras, who initiates the age-changing cycle of precession, represents the Unconquered Sun. Thus, Mithras is properly addressed as *Sol Invicto Deo*: the *Unconquered* Sun God. He is associated with the inexorable power of precession (because he is seen to be slaying the Bull of Taurus: ending the Age of Taurus) -- and thus commands the power which conquers the sun and forces it into a new zodiac sign every successive Age.

From David Ulansey's brilliant decoding of the celestial significance of the tauroctony, as well as Roger Beck's inspired deconstruction of the iconography of the Mithraeum of the Seven Spheres at Ostia, we can see that the originators of the Mithraic Mysteries must have been possessed of a deep and sophisticated understanding of the esoteric system through which the

The Cult of Mithras

constellations and heavenly cycles relate to teachings regarding the descent of the soul and its subsequent re-ascent.

They clearly had masterful fluency in the symbolic "language" wherein the great annual cycle (running from summer solstice, on down to the autumnal equinox and eventually to the winter solstice, and then back upwards through the spring equinox on the way back to the summer solstice) takes on esoteric meaning relating to the soul's journey – and they clearly understood the deep significance of the inexorable motion of precession by which the entire cosmos seems to be "displaced."

All of these cycles can be demonstrated to have to do with our larger theme of trauma.

The annual cycle demarcated by the zodiac wheel, as we have seen, can be conclusively shown to be employed in ancient myth to illustrate the trauma of the buried god and the alienation from our authentic self, which is dramatized in the myths using the zodiac constellations, and using in particular the "lower half" of the zodiac constellations following Virgo and the "plunge" down into the half of the year when hours of darkness dominate over hours of daylight.

The awe-inspiring cycle of precession, by which the entire sky is "displaced" every 2,160 years (approximately), can also be conclusively shown to be related to the concept of displacement and alienation in the ancient myths, for example in the Odyssey. There, the central figure Odysseus is displaced and alienated: his proper role of husband to his wife Penelope, father to his son Telemachus, and king to the people of his native island of Ithaca is being *usurped* by the rowdy gang of suitors who have occupied his house and are devouring his wealth, while scheming to marry Penelope, murder Telemachus, and become king *in his place.*

When we understand that the motion of precession causes a new zodiac constellation to "usurp" the place of the previous "rightful" ruler of the "house" in which the sun rises on the specific day (such as the morning of the spring equinox), we can readily

Chapter Thirteen

perceive how the situation depicted in the Odyssey could serve as a metaphorical dramatization of the action of precession.

And, just to provide us with positive confirmation that this interpretation is correct, and that we are not just imagining a possible parallel between the motion of precession (by which one zodiac constellation "takes over" or "usurps" the role and in fact even the "house" of another) and the plot of the Odyssey (in which a scheming mob of hopeful suitors take over the house of Odysseus, hoping to usurp not only his throne but also his marriage bed), the text of the ancient poem itself provides us with an unmistakable clue in the total count of the suitors themselves.

As I have already discussed in *Star Myths of the World, Volume Two*, the text of Book 16 of the Odyssey tells us the number of suitors, albeit without actually blurting out the total (we have to do the math to add up the count of suitors from each part of Ithaca and the surrounding lands).[211] Telemachus counts off the totals to his father as the two are discussing their plan to slay the violent usurpers: fifty-two from Dulichion, twenty four from Same, twenty from Zacynthus, and twelve from Ithaca itself.[212]

That count adds up to 108 suitors -- a distinctive precessional number found in myth and in ancient architecture around the globe! If anyone was skeptical of the argument that the "displacement" of Odysseus by the suitors dramatizes the displacement of the sky due to the ages-long motion of precession, the fact that *the poem itself* tells us that the suitors number 108 does away with all objections.

As I write in *Star Myths of the World, Volume Two*, the return of Odysseus dramatizes an *undoing* of the dislocating power of precession: if precession is used by the world's ancient myth to convey the displacement which keeps us from our true self, our true identity, our true potential (even as Odysseus in exile is alienated from *his* true place), then the return of Odysseus and the slaying of the suitors represents a *repair* of that alienation.[213] It is noteworthy that in this return -- and in the successful defeat of the suitors -- Odysseus is aided by the goddess Athena, without whose help and inspiration he would never have survived.

The testimony of the ancient philosopher Porphyry demonstrates that the cult of Mithras was designed with the purpose of "inducting the initiate into a mystery of the descent of souls and their exit back out again." He also declares that the layout of their cave-like temples form a microcosmic prism of the cosmos in what Porphyry calls "proportionate arrangement." Beck shows that the mithraea functioned as models of the cosmos, demarcated by the stations of the zodiac and the four great waypoints of the annual cycle in the two solstices and two equinoxes, and Ulansey shows that their distinctive iconography (particularly the focal tauroctony scene) all reflect a deep understanding of the ancient esoteric system which underlies the world's myths and sacred stories, and an understanding of the power of that system to point us towards the path of overcoming of the trauma, division, and alienation we face in this incarnate life.

And yet the cult of Mithras did not share their esoteric understanding widely. This fact can be clearly seen by a number of pieces of evidence, most obviously by the size of the mithraea themselves, which are "for the most part small meeting-places for small congregations consisting of a handful of people,"[214] typically with seating sufficient for only fifteen or twenty men, and if (as some think) there were also those in attendance who stood in addition to those who sat, then the total present at any given time could have been about forty, but no more.[215]

Clearly this was not a "religion" with any intention of winning over the masses, despite the way it is typically portrayed by history books, which depict Mithraism as some kind of early rival to Christianity. Indeed, Professor Ulansey himself (whose thesis and analysis regarding the celestial foundations of the Mithraic Mysteries I regard as revolutionary and inspired) goes so far as to call Mithraism "'the road not taken' by Western civilization nearly two thousand years ago"[216] and cites French historian Ernest Renan (1823 - 1892) who wrote that "if Christianity had been stopped at its birth by some mortal illness, the world would have become Mithraic."[217]

And yet there is absolutely nothing about the cult of Mithras that indicates that it was vying with Christianity to "take over the world" (and Ulansey notes when citing Renan that this assertion by the nineteenth-century historian is clearly "somewhat exaggerated").[218] On the contrary, everything about the cult strongly indicates *exclusivity*, rather than inclusivity, beginning with the size of the mithraea, which remain small wherever they are found, despite spanning the geographical breadth of the Empire (all the way from Syria and Egypt to the British Isles near Hadrian's Wall) and despite continuing to be built for a period of more than two hundred years.

Manfred Clauss describes the initiates who met in the outwardly unobtrusive structures as seeking "a place where one could withdraw from the outer world for a limited period among a familiar and exclusive group."[219] He also points out that:

> In this context it is moreover relevant that the cult of Mithras had no public ceremonial of its own. The festival of *natalis Invicti*, 25 December, was a public festival of the Sun and thus by no means limited to the mysteries of Mithras. There was nothing in the cult comparable to the great festivals and celebrations of other cults, such as the 'Discovery' of Osiris or the 'Voyage' of Isis, spectacular occasions which attracted great crowds of people. Nor did it possess buildings famous all over the Empire, such as the Serapeum at Alexandria or the Iseum in the Campus Martius at Rome. Unlike the well-known mysteries of Eleusis, for example, which according to Herodotus had 30,000 initiates (8. 65), and attracted 3,000 of them to its festivals, Mithraic congregations were esoteric groups.[220]

Another sign of the exclusive rather than inclusive nature of the cult of Mithras is the fact that its membership was composed only of men and did not admit women. Further, there are strong

The Cult of Mithras

indications that its structure was strictly hierarchical in nature, even though composed of such small groups in each community in which it operated.

This structure consisted of seven initiatory grades or ranks, which are known from evidence including a mosaic design on the floor of another mithraeum in Ostia, the *Mithraeum of Felicissimus* [221] (not the Mithraeum of the Seven Spheres – although the fact that there are seven grades within the Mithraic system strongly suggests an esoteric connection to the seven spheres themselves, one sphere for each of the five visible planets plus one more each for the sun and the moon: down through each of these successive spheres the soul was thought to descend into incarnation in this world, and back up through these aetheric levels the soul had to ascend once again in order to transcend this incarnation).

The seven grades of the Mithraic order, beginning with the initial and lowest grade and proceeding to the highest, are: the Raven (or *corax*), the Bridgroom (or *nymphus*), the Soldier (or *miles*), the Lion (or *leo*), the Persian (or *perses*), the Sun-Runner (or *heliodromus*), and the Father (or *pater*).[222]

If one thinks carefully about the possible reasons for creating such a steep vertical hierarchy, even in a group numbering no more than forty members, one suggestion would be for the careful maintenance of strict secrecy. By limiting the information which is given to new initiates and only revealing additional details as successive ranks are attained, the more senior and trusted members of the community have plenty of time to observe and assess the worthiness of new candidates vying for entry into the successively more exclusive inner circles.[223] Such structures, as with the ranks of the military in most armies and navies around the world today, are also useful for filtering out persons with undesireable traits, or limiting their advancement to lower or middling levels within the organization (see endnote 223).

In sum, everything about the cult of Mithras indicates that it was designed quite intently for the dual purposes of *exclusivity* and

Chapter Thirteen

secrecy -- rather than for mass appeal and inclusion (very much the opposite of literalist Christianity).

The cult of Mithras, in other words, is not a "religion" (as it is often portrayed) so much as it is a *secret society*.

Researcher (and retired Admiral of the Navy of Italy) Flavio Barbiero has put forth an audacious theory regarding the importance of this secret society in world history, in a 2010 book entitled *The Secret Society of Moses: The Mosaic Bloodline and a Conspiracy Spanning Three Millennia*, in which he argues that the ancient cult of Mithras represented a powerful underground society which necessarily operated in strict secrecy, because its aims were nothing less than the gradual but inexorable *acquisition of increasing influence over the nodes of control of the Roman Empire* -- and that in this ambitious goal it was eventually successful.

I have discussed his theory at some length in my 2014 book *The Undying Stars*. As I made clear in my 2014 book, while I *do not agree* with some central aspects of Barbiero's theory[224] -- most importantly, the idea that the figure of Moses and others described in the scriptures of the Old Testament reflect literal, terrestrial, historical figures (I believe they can be shown to be entirely celestial metaphor) -- I *do agree* that Admiral Barbiero presents compelling evidence to support his argument that the cult of Mithras Sol Invictus was no "competing religion" to the emerging faith of Christianity, but rather that it very likely represented the "cadre" or "backbone" of an *underground movement* executing a masterful long-term plan to take over the Empire, and that it actually co-opted the early forms of Christianity as part of that strategy, deploying literalist Christianity as a kind of visible "shield" or "cover" (one that was public, inclusive, and had mass appeal: one which welcomed even the most marginalized members of society) to help camoflage its secretive plotting.

The Cult of Mithras

In other words, Christianity and Mithraism were not rivals at all (as Barbiero explains in detail) but rather were two columns of a kind of "pincer maneuver" to outflank the Roman establishment (represented primarily by the old patrician families) and ultimately place their own candidates on the throne of the Empire.

How could such a nearly-unbelievable goal have possibly been achieved? The skeptical reader is invited to examine the evidence and narrative presented by Flavio Barbiero in his 500-page book. However, within the scope of this present volume, it is instructive to focus on a few specific aspects of his thesis, beginning with his analysis of the spread of the mithraea themselves, which give an indication that there was a specific purpose in mind from the very beginning of Mithraism.

Citing German historian Reinhold Merkelbach (1918 - 2006), Admiral Barbiero notes that the first mithraeum we know of was built in Rome at the time of the emperor Domitian (the third Flavian emperor, following the reigns of his father Vespasian and of Domitian's older brother Titus; Domitian ruled from AD 81, when he took the throne at the age of 30, until his death in AD 96).[225]

Barbiero notes that this mithraeum appears to have been attended by those close to the imperial family -- and that it was "dedicated by a certain Titus Flavius Hyginus Ephebianus" who appears to have been a freedman of the emperor Titus Flavius, the predecessor of Domitian.[226]

Barbiero speculates that this name indicates the strong possibility that Ephebianus was one of those captured by Vespasian and Titus in the wars of Judea -- along with Flavius Josephus, who also took the name of the emperor who freed him after the conquest of Jerusalem (i.e. the name of *Flavius*, the family name by which the Flavian emperors Vespasian, Titus and Domitian were known). As I explain in some detail in *The Undying Stars*, and as Admiral Barbiero outlines in depth in his book, there is evidence which strongly suggests that Josephus may have betrayed his people by giving the location of the buried and

387

Chapter Thirteen

hidden treasure of the Temple at Jerusalem to the Romans, treasure which is listed on the Copper Scroll found among the Dead Sea Scrolls in the middle of the twentieth century: treasure which Vespasian used to buy the continued loyalty of his armies and ultimately to secure his pathway to the throne of the Empire.

For this betrayal of the location of the hidden treasure, Vespasian and Titus appear to have rewarded Josephus handsomely, bringing him back with them to Rome and giving him a villa once occupied by Vespasian himself, along with significant privileges, including a rich annuity, as well as exemption from taxes (Josephus attests to these rewards in his own writings, although of course he says nothing about betraying the location of the treasures of the temple to Vespasian and Titus).

From the first-known mithraeum, built during the time of Domitian, Barbiero moves to the second-oldest archaeological evidence related to Mithraism, "a statue dedicated to Mithras by a certain Alcimus, a farmer in the service of Tiberius Claudius Livianus, the prefect of the praetorium under Trajan (the successor to Domitian)."[227]

This evidence foreshadows the strong affiliation between the Praetorian Guard and the cult of Mithras in the subsequent centuries. "From that moment on," Flavio Barbiero writes, "Sol Invictus was a constant presence in the Praetorian Guard. The greatest concentration of mithraea in Rome, in fact, is in the vicinity of the Praetorian barracks."[228]

Barbiero then traces the spread of the mithraea outwards from Rome, to nearby Ostia, "the port with the greatest volume of trading in the world in that period. There, goods and foodstuffs from every part of the Empire arrived to delight the insatiable appetite of the capitol."[229]

Dedicatory inscriptions also indicate that civil servants in charge of the customs, not only in Ostia but also along the lower Danube and up into all the Danubian provinces to the Black Sea, became active and important members of the secret society.[230] Barbiero writes that the followers of the cult of Mithras within a few years were installed in positions of control over the customs and tax-collection offices, over transport and the postal services (the *cursus publicus*), and over the aministrative machinery of many aspects of the civil service including finances and mining, particularly in the provinces of Mesia and Pannonia, but also in Rome itself, where "followers of the cult of Mithras occupied positions of great importance at the court and in the imperial administration." [231]

It is as though the secret society was deliberately moving to gain control over the administrative nerve centers of the Empire. Barbiero writes that, within 100 years of that first Mithraic inscription from the time of Domitian (towards the end of the first century AD), "Already, at the end of the second century, practically all public money -- or at least a large slice of it -- passed through the hands of the followers of the cult of Mithras [. . .]." [232]

The significance of the above statement simply cannot be overemphasized. The evidence we have been exploring and the argument we have been assembling regarding the "collaborators against the gods" suggests that the overthrowers of whatever remained of the ancient wisdom given to humanity in the myths had as their goal the severance of the understanding that the resources of the natural world, and the gifts and talents given to individual men and women, are gifts from the gods to the people of the land -- and, once this understanding has been obscured, the related goal is the *privatization* of these resources, such that they no longer benefit the public but only a small subset of the people (the oligarchs, the "elite").

The thesis of Flavio Barbiero, then, argues that a talented and dedicated group, acting in secret but from a position of imperial favor and privilege (having helped Vespasian to secure the throne following his conquest of Judea), used literalist Christianity -- along with the much more secretive vehicle of the cult of Mithras Sol Invictus -- to effect a major paradigm shift that would obliterate the knowledge of the ancient wisdom for all but a select

Chapter Thirteen

few, and that this secret group also patiently and deliberately worked to gain positions of control over the administration of public services and the collection of taxes and customs.

As Barbiero states once again, "we have definitive proof that by the end of the second century they controlled the main levers of economic and financial power, together with the public administration of the Roman Empire." [233]

And, equally if not more importantly, the cult of Mithras had another major target for its expansion, besides the levers of civil administration: the Roman Army, which Barbiero calls "the other great power structure of the Roman Empire." [234]

The close affiliation of the cult of Mithras with the army is well-known to conventional scholarship, and beyond any dispute. Barbiero explains:

> Soon, mithraea sprang up in all the places where Roman garrisons were stationed. The first that we know of was built at the garrison of Carnuntum, in Pannonia, practically at the same time as the mithraeum of the nearby customs center of Poetovium: between AD 100 and 110. Subsequently, mithraea multiplied all over the region -- besides Carnuntum, they can be found in Vindobona (Vienna), Brigetium and Aquincum (Budapest), in Dacia, and in the area of the lower Danube: all places where military garrisons were situated. At the same time, mithraea were erected along the border with Germany, in particular at Wiesbaden, Heddernheim, Mainz, Treviri, Gross-Krotzenburg, Lorsch, and numerous other places in the Palatinate and in Alsace. In Britannia, at least fifteen mithraea have been discovered; eight are scattered along Hadrian's Wall and the others can be found in the territory around the main military garrisons (London, York, St. Albans, Segontium, etc.). In Spain, at least twenty-five sites dedicated to Mithras have been found. They have also been found in Africa, mainly at Lambesis, and in Tunisia, at the post of the only legion stationed on that continent. [235]

The Cult of Mithras

Barbiero speculates that Josephus Flavius, having observed that control over the army can facilitate accession to the throne (as in the case of his patrons Vespasian and Titus), well understood the importance of gaining control over the military leadership not just at the highest levels but also among the centurions who commanded the actual units of the line, and that the vehicle through which they could be directed would be the secret organization of Sol Invictus.

"This was his winning move," Barbiero opines.[236]

By gaining a subtle lever of control within the Praetorian Guard, who were charged with the personal protection of the emperor and the Capitol City, as well as within the upper leadership and the actual unit commanders of the far-flung military legions, the secret society of Mithras Sol Invictus was able, within about one hundred years, to maneuver a member of that organization to the highest position in the Roman world -- the imperial throne.

According to Flavio Barbiero's analysis, the first emperor who was an actual initiate of the cult of Mithras was the emperor Commodus (AD 161 - 192),[237] who became co-emperor with his father Marcus Aurelius in AD 177 (when Commodus was sixteen) and became the full emperor three years later, in AD 180 when Marcus Aurelius died at the age of fifty-eight in Vindobona (modern-day Vienna -- and as has already been noted, a military city and one where the remains of a mithraeum have been found).

Those familiar with the movie *Gladiator* (2000), starring Russell Crowe, may recall that Commodus was the megalomaniac character played by Joaquin Phoenix in that film, and that the movie implies that Commodus had something to do with the death of his father.

Whether or not Commodus (or the secret society of Mithras) had something to do with the death of Marcus Aurelius, it is an undeniable fact of history that Commodus took for himself the name "Invictus," which is just one of many pieces of evidence

Chapter Thirteen

supporting Barbiero's theory that Commodus was the first emperor supported by the Sol Invictus cult.

How was this initiatory network able to maneuver with such effectiveness that it gained the throne by AD 180? It is true that this capture of the throne was not permanent: after Commodus there followed another century of struggle which did not end until the rise of the emperor Constantine in AD 306, at which point the secret society of Sol Invictus gained full control.

But despite numerous setbacks and changes of tactics between Commodus and Constantine, Barbiero explains that the strategy exercised through the organization of the Sol Invictus network enabled those at the upper levels of that organization to steadily gain greater and greater control over the critical functions of the public sphere -- and eventually, to dissolve the government altogether, carving up the remains of the western empire among themselves as their fiefdoms, aided by the literalist Christian church which was the more public emanation of the Mithraic cult.

The strategy consisted of a few major concepts -- all of them extremely illuminating for the political and economic landscape of the entire twentieth and early twenty-first century, during which a very similar playbook is being followed in order to beat back the democratic and progressive challenges to the old oppressive feudal structures (challenges that arose with the rise of national governments able to check the power of the *rentier* classes).

During the capture of the public administrative machinery of the Roman Empire, we see a pattern which should be eerily familiar to those of us who have lived through the second half of the twentieth century. First of these was the formation of a new class in opposition to the longstanding senatorial aristocracy -- the class known as the *equites* or "equestrian" class. Barbiero explains (speaking of the equestrian class):

> This was the backbone of the imperial administration, and it consisted mostly of new families that had emerged in the course of the second century. Almost all of these families were

The Cult of Mithras

initiates of Sol Invictus, which, as we have seen, had seized possession of the administrative bureacracy and the army.[238]

Another critically important aspect of the strategy was the rank system of the secret society itself, which as we have seen was organized into a strictly hierarchical structure of seven initiatory grades. Based on the texts left to us by Porphyry, Flavio Barbiero deduces that outsiders to the networked families who were running the Mithraic system would only be allowed to work their way up through the bottom three initiatory grades, whereas the levels from four through seven were reserved for those who were actually pulling the strings.[239]

This system would make it easy for those in the upper levels of the Sol Invictus organization to wield tremendous control over those whom they allowed to come in and be initiated at the lower degrees, while retaining access to the true inner workings of the secret society for those they knew (beyond any doubt) that they could trust.

A third tool of the collaborators was the use of assassination. Whether or not Marcus Aurelius himself was assassinated, Barbiero argues that the erratic and unpredictable emperor Commodus was targeted for elimination by the leaders of Sol Invictus, which they accomplished through the efforts of Marcia Aurelia Ceionia Demetrias, the Christian concubine they had assigned to Commodus as an additional means of influencing him, and also the efforts of "Quintus Aemilius Laetus, prefect of the Praetorian Guard, which, by then, was completely under the control of Sol Invictus."[240]

Admiral Barbiero then gives a chronology of the emperors who reigned in the years after the assassination of Commodus, many of whom meet a similar fate, often being assassinated by the Praetorians (such as the emperors Caracalla and Elagabulus) or by members of the army itself (such as the emperors Severus Alexander and Gordian III).[241]

Chapter Thirteen

Many of the emperors whom Barbiero judges to have been killed on the orders of the leadership of the Sol Invictus network had themselves been selected and advanced to the throne by that same Sol Invictus network, only to run afoul of them while governing (some of them apparently deciding that now that they were the emperor, they could do whatever they wanted). This pattern should be very familiar to those who have studied the history of the twentieth century following the purported end of World War II.

One of the consistent agendas pursued by the various emperors advanced by the Sol Invictus network (even by emperors who were later terminated for one reason or another) was that of deliberate confrontation with the traditional patricians of the Senate and old Italic families, and incessant efforts to diminish their power and to humiliate them. This agenda, of course, aroused a pushback from the Senators and long-entrenched Roman elites -- but yet another brilliant aspect of the strategy of the secret society, Barbiero argues, was the use of literalist Christianity as the visible, public side of the plot, and it was against the Christians that the beleaguered Senate and other aristocratic defenders of the old order turned their wrath, thus overlooking the more virulent branch of the conspiracy that opposed them, which was found within the secret society of Mithras.

Flavio Barbiero explains (describing the rise of Philip I, the first openly Christian emperor, known also as "Philip the Arab" because he was born in the city of Bosra, who gained the throne following the assassination in AD 244 of the emperor Gordian III by the army):

> Sol Invictus had complete control over the army, the Praetorian Guard, and the imperial administration -- but given the absolute secrecy of its meetings and of the decisions it made, nobody at the time was able to perceive or understand the role it had in the management of pubic matters.
>
> [. . .]

The Cult of Mithras

It would appear, however, that the senate and the pagan world in general never identified Sol Invictus as being responsible for their misfortunes. The public profession of Christianity flaunted by Philip the Arab offered them, finally, a well-identified target against which they could work out their frustrations. It was then that the senate found the strength to react and attempt a restoration. In 249, Philip was assassinated by Quintus Traianus Decius, a general from Pannonia who bore the name of an ancient Roman senatorial family. It was Philip who had put him in charge of the Syrian troops who then made him emperor. Once in Rome, Decius unleashed a violent persecution of the Christians, whom he may have perceived as being responsible for the assault on the Empire. He did not cause any serious harm, because the Christians were the wrong target, and also because he immediately had to go to the Danube to deal with a barbarian invasion. He died after just two years of his reign, in 251, killed in battle with the Goths. [A footnote here explains: "Other emperors disliked by the Christians died in battle (or were captured by the enemy). The battlefield was the ideal place for getting rid of inconvenient leaders without being accused of assassination."][242]

In other words, Barbiero argues that the growth of literalist Christianity, which was growing at the very same time that Mithraism was also spreading, was not a "rivalry" at all, but rather can be understood as "two sides of the same coin" (or two aspects of the same strategy).[243] He believes that the leadership of the secret society of Mithras was connected to the leadership of literalist Christianity, and that the more visible Christians were used as a kind of "heat shield" to draw the attention and ire of the old Roman aristocracy who could understand that they were under attack, but who never completely figured out who was attacking them.

Barbiero does not use the term "heat shield" -- that is a slang-term used in the US Army when I was in the infantry, to denote some

Chapter Thirteen

unfortunate fellow-soldier or fellow-officer who draws the ire of a higher-ranking officer, allowing everyone else to breathe a sigh of relief because their own faults will probably be overlooked while the "heat shield" is being attacked for his more obvious or more egregious mistakes. This parallel serves as a helpful illustration for seeing the way that the secret society of Sol Invictus used Christianity during its long campaign to gain control of the empire: Sol Invictus went unnoticed while all counter-attacks were focused on the more visible early Christians.

Barbiero provides a number of very strong arguments which demonstrate that Christianity and Mithraism were not rivals at all, but rather that one was a more public and more inclusive arm of the other. For example, he notes that a great number of mithraea have been found underneath ancient Christian basilica or churches, indicating that there may well have been some kind of symbiotic connection between the leadership of the cult of Sol Invictus Mithras and that of the Christian church.[244]

Of course, some might try to explain away this evidence of cooperation by arguing that the Christian church must have triumphantly taken over the old worship sites of its supposedly "defeated" rival and built its Christian churches on top of the old Mithraic grottoes (as it later did with sacred sites from other cultures as it expanded around the globe).

However, there is evidence that this suggested explanation does not hold up for the relationship between Christianity and Mithraism. Specifically, Flavio Barbiero observes that the very Basilica of St. Peter itself, on Vatican Hill in Rome, the heart of Roman Christianity even to this day, was built above the mithraeum known as the *Phrygianum*, the most central mithraeum in Mithraism. Indeed, the Phrygianum was the location where the highest-ranking of all the members of the order of Sol Invictus held sway. His title was not just *pater* ("father"), which we have seen to have been the title of the top grade of the Mithraic ladder of seven ranks: rather, he was styled

The Cult of Mithras

the *pater patrum*, a phrase which means "father of fathers" in Latin.

Most significantly, not only was the Basilica of St. Peter built above the Phrygianum of the pater patrum of Mithras, but as Flavio Barbiero explains, Constantine ordered the construction of the Basilica in AD 322, but the last "father of fathers" (*pater patrum*) of the Sol Invictus cult did not die until AD 384 -- and he continued to use the mithraeum in the Phrygianum in the grotto on Vatican Hill for all those years in between!²⁴⁵

It would certainly be remarkable, if Christianity and Mithraism were truly rival faiths, for the headquarters of the two cults to have been co-located for even *two* years -- but the actual dates indicate that this coexistance went on for a full *sixty-two* years.

Barbiero writes:

> In this light, we are forced to conclude that Sol Invictus Mithras and Christianity were not two religions in competition, as we often read, but were two institutions of a different nature that were closely connected. Rather than being a simple hypothesis, this is practically a certainty. It is unthinkable that the Roman church continued to extend hospitality to the head of a rival pagan religion for more than half a century and at the heart of its most exclusive property, dedicated to the prince of apostles. The Mithraic pater patrum and the bishop of Rome must necessarily have been closely linked.²⁴⁶

Even more remarkable, and even more difficult to explain from the perspective of the conventional view of Mithraism and Christianity, is the fact that the supreme *pater* in the cult of Sol Invictus was known by the title of *pater patrum*. It is most significant, then, to note (as Flavio Barbiero notes) that after the death of the last *pater patrum* of Mithras in AD 384, "the cult of Mithras was officially abolished and the cave was occupied by Syricius [Siricius] (the successor of the bishop of Rome, Damasus)

Chapter Thirteen

who adopted the name of the head of the Mithraic sect, pater patrum, or pope, for the first time in the history of the church."[247]

This is truly astonishing information: the term "pope" (or *papa*) is a contraction or an abbreviation of the words *pater patrum* -- the title of the highest pater in the cult of Sol Invictus. As we know, that title continues to be used to this day by the bishop of Rome (aka "the pope").

Barbiero goes on to note that, in addition to taking over the grotto on Vatican Hill which had been the Phrygianum of Mithraism, and in addition to taking over the title of *pater patrum*, the bishop of Rome "also adopted the same clothing and sat on the same chair, which became the throne of St. Peter of Rome. Mithraic designs were -- and still are -- engraved on this throne."[248] Among the accoutrements of Mithraism that the high Christian clergy would adopt was the distinctive headgear of the Christian bishops, still known to this day as the bishop's *mitre* (a word with linguistic connections to *Mithras*).

Given this remarkable information, can anyone still argue that Mithraism and Christianity were actually "rival faiths" rather than two heads of the same great constrictor-serpent that had as its purpose and unshakable goal the slow envelopment and suffocation of the ancient "pagan" faiths and (at the same time) the infiltration of the administrative bureaucracy in charge of the public functions of the Roman state in order to take over the resources of the empire, and the lands of western Europe (with all their many blessings bestowed by nature and the gods)?

Barbiero explains that, based on his analysis, the leaders of the Sol Invictus society finally decided to make Christianity the official religion of the empire in response to an "insurance policy against assassination" devised by the emperor Diocletian, who preceded Constantine and who came up with a scheme to prevent being murdered the way so many of the previous emperors who had fallen out of favor with the "power behind the throne" had been murdered before him.

The Cult of Mithras

Diocletian, a successful army officer, became the emperor in the year AD 286, and created a novel power structure known as the "tetrarchy," or "rule of four," by which he appointed a co-emperor (a fellow officer named Maximian), and then each of them appointed a "caesar" -- almost as if a US president were to appoint a co-president, and then each of them were to choose a vice-president.

Barbiero explains that Diocletian was almost certainly a member of Sol Invictus (although probably not allowed past the third rank), and that his decisions while in office were not, strictly speaking, antagonistic to the Sol Invictus organization (although his "caesar," Galerius, instituted a brutal persecution of Christians). However, Barbiero argues that Diocletian's true purpose in creating the unwieldy system of the tetrarchy "must have been that of ensuring his own position and personal safety by removing from Sol Invictus -- at least, within his own lifetime -- the initiative to create rival emperors."[249]

This innovation by Diocletian was eminently successful in making it very difficult or even impossible for a secret society, operating in the shadows, to replace the emperor the way they had been accustomed to doing in the preceding hundred years. Because of this temporary setback, Flavio Barbiero argues, the Sol Invictus deep state decided on a change in tactics: they would come out much more into the open by having their next emperor adopt Christianity, after which the leadership of the literalistic Christian church (which was part of the same Sol Invictus operation) could openly "advise" and influence the emperor and operate the other levers of power within the empire.[250]

Following Diocletian and the aggressive and violent persecution and indeed massacre of Christians unleashed by Diocletian and Galerius, Barbiero believes that the Sol Invictus organization immediately began casting about for candidates to elevate to the position of emperor: "candidates who would put an end to this madness."[251]

399

Chapter Thirteen

Among the candidates they selected, Flavius Licinius and Flavius Constantinus (better known to us today as Constantine) eliminated their various rivals (Constantine doing so at the famous Battle of Milvian Bridge in AD 312, prior to which he claimed to have seen the Christian *chi-rho* symbol in the heavens, along with the inscription *In Hoc Signo Vinces*, which he took to mean that he should place the *chi-rho* symbol upon the shields of his army in order to conquer his opponent).

Constantine's victory at Milvian made him the master of the western half of the empire, and Licinius had gained sole command over the eastern half. Flavio Barbiero explains:

> Directly afterward, at the beginning of 313, Constantine and Licinius met in Milan. There, they fraternally acknowledged each other's respective spheres of influence and sealed their agreement with the marriage of Licinius to Constantine's sister, Flavia Constans. They also agreed to eliminate the last enemy of the Christians, Maximinus Daia, which they did soon afterward.[252]

Their alliance gradually began to crumble in the ensuing years, however, and by AD 324 the tensions erupted into full-on war between the two, a war which Constantine's forces decisively won in a series of successive victories against the armies of Licinius. Constantine had Licinius and his wife (Constantine's half-sister) hanged. Constantine became the sole emperor and ruled until his death in AD 337 at the age of 65.

During his reign, as we have all been taught, Constantine declared Christianity to be the official faith of the Roman Empire. He did not make Christianity the only allowable faith -- although it would not be many years after Constantine that the emperor Theodosius (who ruled from AD 379 until his death in AD 395) would effectively do so.

The conventional narrative says that Constantine promoted Christianity as a shrewd political move, but Flavio Barbiero finds that argument to border on the ridiculous:

This was political opportunism, say the historians, according to whom Constantine decided to straddle Christianity because he saw it as a secure basis for his power. Yet it is difficult (indeed impossible) to accept this explanation if we consider the numbers involved. Out of a population estimated at fity million inhabitants in the whole of the Roman Empire, there were no more than seven million, or at the very most ten million, Christians. They were therefore a negligible minority that hardly made up 20 percent of the whole population and that was faced with an overwhelming majority of pagans. It was certainly not for political gain that Constantine married the Christian cause in such an open and decisive way, but rather because it was the mission of the family of which he was a member -- the mission that he openly proclaimed to have been given by God, declaring himself "universal bishop." [253]

In other words, he was promoting Christianity in order to advance a different agenda, and not because Christians were all that powerful in the Roman Empire at the time of his declaration. According to the theory we have been examining, that agenda was the installation of the infrastructure of the secret society (of those I have been calling the "collaborators against the gods") in a position of public power.

It only makes logical and strategic sense that when the time finally came for formally elevating the representatives of that secret society to positions of supreme power within the empire, they would choose to elevate the *public-facing* side of their organization (that is to say, Christianity), rather than the much smaller and inherently exclusive cult of Mithras. Since the same people controlled both Sol Invictus and Christianity, the elevation of Christianity would enable them to steer the course of events through the structure of the that visible and outward-facing wing quite well (and, as Barbiero demonstrates, most of the powerful early bishops were also actual members of Sol Invictus, or the sons of men who were members of Sol Invictus).[254]

Chapter Thirteen

Indeed, Constantine himself employed Sol Invictus imagery in conjunction with Christian imagery, such as on some of the coins minted during his reign. In their commentary on their translation of the text of the *Life of Constantine* by Constantine's contemporary and early Christian bishop, Eusebius (AD 263 - 339), editors Averil Cameron and Stuart G. Hall note that Constantine is described by Eusebius as having seen the *chi-rho* "resting over the sun," and then they write that Constantine "continued to commemorate [this chi-rho symbol] on his coins as Sol Invictus."[255]

Such numismatic evidence indicates that Constantine conflated the vision of the cross over the sun with the concept of Sol Invictus, and that coins during his reign bore both the *chi-rho* symbol and the words Sol Invictus -- an extremely revealing juxtaposition!

If Flavio Barbiero is correct, and I believe that the evidence overwhelmingly supports his thesis as describing the machinations which led up to the otherwise extremely improbable takeover of the Roman Empire by the numerically small, occasionally persecuted, and generally obscure cult of literalist Christianity, then the cult of Sol Invictus Mithras is absolutely crucial to our understanding of world history -- and to our understanding of the silencing of the voice of the ancient world (the voice of the myths, and the voice of the gods), first in the territories controlled by the Roman Empire, and subsequently in other parts of the globe by the colonial powers that would later grow out of the feudal project of western Europe following the dissolution of the empire.

Let's consider the significance of some aspects of this transition which might be easy to overlook but which have tremendous bearing on the argument being put forward in this volume.

> ➢ First, recall the evidence presented by Porphyry, and expanded upon by the redoubtable Roger Beck, which demonstrates that the design of the cult of Mithras indicates a deep understanding of the "mystery of the

The Cult of Mithras

descent of souls and their exit back out again" (in Porphyry's own words) and that their initiatory practices as well as the very layout and decoration of their mithraea was designed to facilitate the experience of this "descent and exit back out" within their initiates.

➢ I would argue that, although this "descent of souls and their exit back out again" is usually interpreted as being primarily associated with the *descent of the soul into incarnation* and eventual re-ascent to the realm of spirit, it is not hard to defend the argument that this "descent and exit back out" also describes the descent of the *essential self* (into suppression and alienation, which happens to virtually all of us in this life, and which in fact is closely connected to the concept of the soul's descent and imprisonment during incarnation) and its eventual recovery. The dramatization is not only about the soul's descent into physical life, but also (perhaps even more significantly) about the loss of connection with the essential self, and how this situation can be repaired.

➢ The symbology of the Mithraic space also evinces an understanding of the concept of precession, which can be shown to have been employed in ancient myth as an illustration of this same concept of alienation, disconnection and displacement (such as in the Odyssey).

➢ The Mithraic tauroctony scene can be demonstrated beyond any doubt to be celestial in its pattern, evidence which strongly suggests an understanding of the ancient system of Star Myth metaphor and symbology which we have been exploring throughout this book.

➢ And yet, the cult of Sol Invictus Mithras can also be definitively linked to the rise of literalist Christianity, and shown to be allied with it (St. Peter's Basilica on the Vatican Hill being built atop an active mithraeum, and not just any mithraeum but the Phrygianum itself). If, as Flavio Barbiero argues (supported by voluminous amounts of evidence) literalist Christianity was deeply

Chapter Thirteen

connected to the society of Sol Invictus, this means that the cult of Mithras supported the very Christian leaders (and Christian emperors, including Flavius Theodosius) who were actively shutting down and eventually outlawing the traditional gods. In other words, as we have just noted, the originators of the cult of Mithras appear to have understood the ancient system of celestial metaphor, as well as its profound esoteric meaning with regards to the loss of communion with the essential self, and the path to the recovery of the essential self -- and at the same time the cult of Mithras was advancing literalist Christianity which as a system was vehemently opposed to the gods and to the ancient myths, and whose leaders were saying that the myths were the work of demons, and arguing that the stories of the Bible were of a completely different character than the character of the world's other myths (even though the stories of the Bible are of course based upon the very same system of celestial metaphor which underlies the myths of other cultures).

➢ The mithraea of Sol Invictus frequently feature statues and other representations of the gods, indicating that at the same time the Christian emperors (installed by the Sol Invictus network) were denying access to the worship of the gods to the people and shuttering their temples, along with the Oracle of Delphi and the *mysteria* of Eleusis, aspects of the ancient system were being retained in private by an exclusive group who wanted the benefits of that knowledge for themselves, but not for others.

➢ The location of the mithraea around Rome and throughout the empire, along with other clues, indicates that the top leadership of the Sol Invictus organization had a well-defined long-term strategy targeting control over the beuraucratic apparatus of the public adminstration of the Roman Empire – a very significant detail when we understand that the privatization of that which is properly a gift of the gods to the public is one of

The Cult of Mithras

the hallmarks of the feudal system which was clamped in place following the deliberate dismantling of the Roman state (the state being the most natural and most powerful potential check on the power of oligarchs who want to seize control of public resources for themselves) -- and that we see the same tension continuing to this day. In addition to gaining decisive influence over the nodes of public administration, the strategy of these collaborators against the gods also included the acquisition of a deep network of control within the legions and leadership of the Roman army, and of the Praetorian Guard.

The fact that the actual members of the cult of Mithras were known among themselves and to those who wrote about them at the time (including Porphyry) as "Persians" suggests the strong possibility that the connection between Mithras in the tauroctony scene and the constellation Perseus (a connection that was not rediscovered until the 1980s, through the efforts of Professor David Ulansey) was understood by at least someone within the ancient organization. It is also noteworthy that Mithras was known as "the rock-born god,"[256] and shown in ancient artwork in mithraea as being born from a rock: and as we have seen, the hero Perseus was miraculously born as the son of Danaë from an underground chamber made of bronze or, in some versions, of stone (yet another parallel between Perseus and Mithras).

The mythical hero Perseus faced a seemingly-impossible task: bringing back the head of Medusa. When the wicked king Polydectes tricks Perseus into agreeing to face the Gorgons, the king knows that the young man is doomed for certain -- no mortal can face the power of being turned to stone and survive. The only way that Perseus is able to succeed in this impossible mission is through the help of the gods: because Perseus heeds the guidance which is given to him by the goddess Athena and the god Hermes, and employs the tools they provide, he returns with the head of Medusa and defeats the wicked king.

The Mithraic followers of Perseus seem to have succeeded in their own seemingly-impossible quest: the takeover of the empire.

Chapter Thirteen

We all face the same impossible mission that Perseus faces in the myth. The myth can be shown to be celestial metaphor, designed to convey profound truths about a realm we cannot perceive with our physical vision, but which is nonetheless very real. The dynamic of the egoic mind suppressing the authentic self that we have been discussing in this volume is a very real phenomenon, but the egoic mind typically keeps us from even being aware of the reality that we have buried our essential self.

Additionally, as we have seen in this book and discussed at some length, the egoic mind is reactive, akin to an algorithm or computer program. It can turn us into a puppet, responding almost like an automaton whenever certain of our "buttons are pushed" (buttons which tend to have something to do with whatever childhood trauma our egoic mind is trying to defend us from experiencing and being wounded by again).

When we are acting (or rather *re*-acting) based on deep programming, as if we are a puppet or a computerized robot, we are not acting as a subject (someone with our own agency): we become an object (something that is acted *upon*). When someone or some circumstance can cause us to respond in a completely pre-programmed way, then we are actually being controlled -- we are objectified -- we have given up our agency.

This danger of being "turned into an object" is the very danger that the hero Perseus faces when he confidently heads off to the island of the Gorgons in order to fulfill the mission that Polydectes tricks the young hero into accepting (Polydectes in the story appears to know a thing or two about "pushing someone's buttons," in order to get them to react in a certain way).

And, had Perseus not been attuned to the realm of the gods, he most certainly would have been turned to stone.

The myths teach us that the way to avoid the fate of being turned into an object, the fate of losing our true agency, is to loosen the grip of the reactive, defensive, deeply pre-programmed egoic mind so that we can hear the deeper voice of our essential self: our

The Cult of Mithras

authentic self, which also turns out to be the conduit through which we can receive the messages which come to us from the divine realm (just as Perseus does, and just as young Norman Ollestad appears to have received guidance which cannot be easily explained during his ordeal of making his way down the mountain after the deadly plane crash in February of 1979).

The message of the myth of Perseus is an absolutely vital message, an absolutely essential message for our lives.

It appears that the mysterious and secretive society of Sol Invictus was a vehicle created by those who understood these concepts, and who used their understanding to great effect.

The evidence also strongly suggests that, although the cult of Sol Invictus appears to have been created by those with an understanding of these profound concepts, its mission involves the suppression of the ancient myths and the ancient gods and the installation of literalist Christianity as a control mechanism to take over the Roman Empire and dissolve it, removing any government that could stand against the monopolization of the natural resources of Europe (monopolization by a small privileged group of families and the church during the long feudal era which ensued following the dissolution of the empire).

These collaborators against the gods want to sever the connection to the ancient wisdom among everyone but themselves. They want to get rid of the knowledge of the gods and replace it with a literalist institution that actually *inflicts* trauma (through both its teachings and its actions). Although they ostensibly follow a Perseus figure, it appears that they want to turn others "to stone" (taking away their agency, traumatizing them on purpose) while retaining agency for themselves.

We can discern a consistent pattern beginning to emerge: a pattern in which a privileged few take the gifts of the divine realm (gifts bestowed by the gods to benefit all men and women) for themselves, while denying these gifts and their benefits to others.

Chapter Thirteen

The pattern is the same whether this privileged few is stamping out the ancient myths given to the various cultures of the world while keeping their ancient wisdom for themselves, or whether this privileged few is seizing for themselves the riches of the land bestowed by the gods for the benefit of the people, while keeping the vast majority of the benefits of those natural resources for themselves and denying them to the rest of the men and women of the land.

Indeed, the two emanations of this same pattern are connected. The seizure of the gifts of the gods in the form of the natural resources is facilitated by the destruction of the knowledge of the gods contained within the ancient myths and sacred traditions of a people.

The ancient myths clearly teach that the resources of nature are provided at the good pleasure of the divine realm. In the sacred traditions of ancient Greece, for example, it is clear that the gifts of the sea are provided at the pleasure of Poseidon, and the gifts of the fields are given by Demeter. The gift of wine is a blessing from the god Dionysus, while the riches of mineral wealth found under the earth come from the god of the dark underworld, whose name the ancients were very careful not to speak except under certain circumstances and with respect.

The assault upon the worship of the gods can be seen as a precursor to the seizure and monopolization by a privileged few of the resources of nature, resources belonging to and bestowed by the gods as a sacred trust. The collaborators against the gods intend to violate that trust, and in order to do so with greater impunity, they wish to abolish the ancient knowledge describing the terms of that trust.

In preparation for doing so in western Europe (in the lands that were under the administration of the western Roman Empire prior to its intentional dissolution), the collaborators against the gods first desired to stamp out the worship and knowledge of the gods of ancient Greece and Rome, as well as the sacred

The Cult of Mithras

knowledge preserved in cultures in other parts of the Mediterranean (including Egypt and Anatolia and the Levant), and also the sacred knowledge preserved in more distant parts of Europe including ancient Gaul and Spain, ancient Germania, and ancient Britain.

Later, the descendants of these collaborators against the gods, who installed themselves as lords of Europe (in conjunction with the control mechanism of the literalist Christian faith and its militant church) expanded further north and brutally eliminated the worship and knowledge of the Norse gods, records of whose sacred traditions only survive because of a few manuscripts preserved in Iceland.

The feudal powers of western Europe later evolved into the colonial powers of western Europe, which commenced a centuries-long campaign of seizing the natural resources given by the gods to the people of other lands and nations around the globe -- and wherever they went, the process of appropriating those gifts of nature and the gods went hand-in-hand with the brutal suppression and elimination of the ancient sacred traditions and myths given to the cultures of those various lands, and the imposition in their place of literalist Christianity.

The campaign involves obscuring the teachings of the ancient myths, because the ancient myths point the way to repairing the trauma that alienates us from our higher self, through whom we have access to the help of the gods. It stands to reason that a privileged *few* will have a very difficult time stealing the resources and blessings given to *the entirety* of the people, especially if the majority of the people are strong, confident, and attuned to their own authentic nature and to the assistance of the divine realm. If a small privileged group wants to seize the gifts given to the majority of the people, gifts which are absolutely essential to the health and well-being of those other people, then such a bamboozle will be much easier to pull off if the majority of men and women can be kept in a state of disconnection, of alienation, of doubt and axiety.

Chapter Thirteen

In short, it is far easier for the few to rob the many if the many are traumatized -- and if they are also kept from the teachings that could help them to repair and overcome that trauma.

I would suggest that this scenario is exactly what has taken place.

The details of the cult of Mithras that we have examined in this chapter, then, are of tremendous significance when it comes to understanding the present state of affairs we find around us in the world today. These details about this mysterious ancient group remain quite unknown and misunderstood even to this day, several decades after the groundbreaking work of scholars such as Roger Beck and David Ulansey.

The history of scholarship in the field of Mithraism itself indicates the strong possibility that misinformation may have been deliberately introduced as the mithraea were beginning to be studied in earnest during the late nineteenth century, and that false leads were maintained for almost a hundred years after that, in order to try to steer people away from the kinds of conclusions that a clear understanding of this ancient society might generate.

If Flavio Barbiero is correct in his thesis, and the evidence he presents in his book along with other evidence we have examined in this volume strongly suggests that he is, then the success of the cult of Sol Invictus in taking over the empire is breathtaking, and speaks to the power available when we open the channels to assistance from the other realm.

In the myth of Perseus and the Gorgons, Athena and Hermes did not slay Medusa for Perseus: he had to act with skill and courage, but he also could not have been successful without listening to the gods and without their help. In the history of the Roman Empire we have just examined, the men behind the secret society of Sol Invictus had to execute their plan with great vision and care over the course of a very long time -- and it may be that their astonishing success also had something to do with the knowledge of "the descent of souls and their exit back out again."

The Cult of Mithras

When our buried authentic self is recovered (when it "exits back out again" from its place of exile), we can regain connection with who we are -- but also, mysteriously, with the wider cosmos, with which the higher self is connected and of which in fact it is a fractal part (recall that the scriptures of India teach that Atman is not only *connected to* Brahman but actually somehow an aspect *of* Brahman: "Brahman is all and Atman is Brahman," says the Mandukya Upanishad, as we saw on page 238).

The knowledge of how to gain access to the assistance of the divine realm may well be part of the story of the incredible success of the men behind the cult of Mithras and their plan to gain access to the throne of the Roman Empire, and later to the resources of the world.

It is quite clear that the ancient myths teach that the power of the invisible realm can be employed for beneficial purposes but also for malevolent ones. When God asks Solomon what he would ask of him, Solomon asks for wisdom in order to help others, and the LORD tells Solomon he is pleased with Solomon's choice, while noting that Solomon could have asked for "the life of thine enemies" (I Kings 3:11). From this and other ancient stories it is evident that access to the invisible realm can be used to help us reach our full potential, and to help others as well -- and that this is in fact what we are intended to use this power to do.

It is also indicated in the very same verse that our connection to the divine realm *can* be used to harm others (implied when God says, "Because thou hast asked this thing [i.e. wisdom to serve the people and to promote justice throughout the land], and hast not asked for thyself long life; neither hast asked riches for thyself, nor hast asked *the life of thine enemies . . .*" [my italics]).

Using the power of the invisible realm to enhance one's own agency, especially in order to help others (by increasing justice and opposing injustice, as the context of Solomon's request implies) is framed in a positive manner: using it to diminish someone else's agency is not.

Because of this potential for misuse or abuse, one could argue that limiting the distribution of this powerful information might be justified, by those entrusted to work for the good of others, and prevent use of such knowledge by those working to harm others. However, what we appear to find in the history of the rise of literalist Christianity (and its underground twin, Sol Invictus) is a plot to limit the availablity of the ancient wisdom to those desiring to enrich themselves, at the expense of others.

It's as if the Cobra Kai school from the *Karate Kid* movie decided to stamp out knowledge of karate and kung fu everywhere else (outside of their own closed circle of in-crowd, popular kids and families), so that they could more easily bully and beat down the rest of the populace. In such a situation, keeping this knowledge a secret would be immoral: sharing this knowledge is necessitated by the fact that a malevolent organization has been using it for centuries to traumatize and oppress others, and continues to do so to this day.

The story of the cult of Mithras we've explored in this chapter is not only ancient history: it is quite evident that the story continues right up to our own present time. The power of the literalist Christian church obviously did not end with the dissolution of the empire: indeed, it only became exponentially *more* powerful with the dissolution of the structures of the civil state and the rise of the feudal patchwork of fiefdoms across Europe (continuing right up to the present).

Once literalist Christian clergy rose to such heights of power, the need for aggressive action by the secret underground branch receded -- but the concept of the secret network was far too valuable to discard altogether. It could be re-activated, wherever or whenever it was needed. And as the church, and literalist belief, came under more and more serious opposition in the eighteenth, nineteenth and early twentieth centuries, the old playbook would be brought back with a vengeance.

Chapter 14

The path of Perseus and the path of Midas

The King of Phrygia was among the wealthiest of men, if not the wisest. It is said that as a very young boy, ants had carried ears of wheat to his mouth, signifying that one day he would be the wealthiest on earth. He was also said to be the son of the Great Goddess, Cybele, who taught him many wonderful things, including the secret of catching a satyr.

Following her advice, the king (now grown to adulthood) once captured the old satyr Silenus, companion and tutor to the god Dionysus himself, when Dionysus and his army were traveling through the land of Phrygia on their way to India.

Dionysus has a mysterious ancient connection to the land of India: there, the ascetic *sadhus* allow their hair to grow long and matted (the god Dionysus is called in ancient verses, such as *Phaedra* by the playwright and philosopher Seneca the Younger: "thou, Bacchus, from thyrsus-bearing India, of unshorn locks, perpetually young"[257]), and *sadhus* also frequently sit upon a leopard skin -- just as the god Dionysus (called Bacchus or Liber by the Romans) is often depicted in ancient artwork wearing a leopard skin about his shoulders or waist.

Thus, given his connection with India, it happened one time that Dionysus was traveling to India and passing through Phrygia. Ancient Phrygia occupied western and central Anatolia, the massive peninsula between the Black Sea in the north, the Mediterranean Sea in the south, and the Bosporus and Dardanelles and Aegean Sea to the west -- the westernmost land of the continent of Asia, adjacent to Greece. Ancient Phrygia (and the Anatolian peninsula) contains within its boundaries the city of Ankara, which is the capitol of modern Turkey.

Old Silenus had wandered away from the train and had been captured by the Phrygians, or by the king himself, who knew that

Chapter Fourteen

a satyr who is overcome by wine falls asleep, and therefore had mixed wine in with the waters of a bubbling spring, from which Silenus drank deeply, which is how Silenus became the captive of Midas of Phrygia: that king whose great wealth had been foretold when Midas was still just a child.

Midas had great affinity for the satyrs, and in fact some ancient accounts tell us that Midas had some blood relation to the satyrs himself, and thus when old Silenus finally slept off his wine, Midas entertained him famously for ten straight days, providing the wise satyr with sumptuous feasts and listening to his discourses on many subjects.

Finally, the king brought Silenus back to the army of Dionysus, and the young god was overjoyed to see the old satyr, who had been missing without a trace. When he heard how King Midas had entertained Silenus with such generous hospitality, Dionysus turned to Midas and said that, as a reward for entertaining the old satyr so graciously, the god would grant the king the privilege of asking Dionysus for whatever he wanted.

As we've already seen, King Midas was tremendously wealthy, and yet this wealth was evidently not enough for him. As most readers already know, given this tremendous offer from the god Dionysus, Midas responded by asking that whatever he touched should become gold (thus giving rise to the phrase, used even to this day, of having the "Midas touch").

The Roman poet Ovid (43 BC - c. AD 17) describes the outcome of this "ill-advised reply"[258] in this way (as translated by Brookes More in 1922):

> Bacchus agreed to his unfortunate request, with grief that Midas chose for harm and not for good. The Berecynthian hero, king of Phrygia, with joy at his misfortune went away, and instantly began to test the worth of Bacchus' word by touching everything. Doubtful himself of his new power, he pulled a twig down from a holm-oak, growing on a low hung branch. The twig was turned to gold. He lifted up a dark stone

The path of Perseus and the path of Midas

from the ground and it turned pale with gold. He touched a clod and by his potent touch the clod became a mass of shining gold. He plucked some ripe, dry spears of grain, and all that wheat he touched was golden. Then he held an apple which he gathered from a tree, and you would think that the Hesperides had given it. If he but touched a lofty door, at once each doorpost seemed to glisten. When he washed his hands in liquid streams, the lustrous drops upon his hands might have been those which once astonished Danaë. He could not now conceive his large hopes in his grasping mind, as he imagined everything of gold. And, while he was rejoicing in great wealth, his servants set a table for his meal, with many dainties and with needful bread: but when he touched the gift of Ceres with his right hand, instantly the gift of Ceres stiffened to gold; or if he tried to bite with hungry teeth a tender bit of meat, the dainty, as his teeth but touched it, shone at once with yellow shreds and flakes of gold. And wine, another gift of Bacchus, when he mixed it in pure water, can be seen in his astonished mouth as liquid gold.[259]

The foolish wish of King Midas, now that it has been granted by the god, turns out to be a certain death sentence. Unable to eat or drink, Midas is cut off by his request from any future.

As if to underscore this point, the most famous aspect of this story, of course, is the terrible scene in which the king's daughter rushes towards Midas to embrace her father, and before he can warn her away she too is transformed into lifeless gold. Now his future has been completely ruined, to include his legacy and continued existence of his family line through the person of his innocent daughter, all because of his insatiable appetite for more wealth.

We have, of course, seen this pattern before, in which a king is granted a request of anything he wishes to ask of the divine realm. It is the same favor granted to King Solomon in the Bible. But instead of asking for wisdom (wisdom to help others), Midas foolishly asks for unlimited riches, in the form of having anything he touches turn into lifeless gold.

Chapter Fourteen

Too late, the horrified king realizes he has made an awful mistake, and he lifts his arms to heaven and cries out in anguish to the god for pity. Midas admits that he was wrong to make the request he did, and prays that Dionysus will save him from the curse which had at first seemed so desirable.

The god has mercy upon the king, seeing that Midas has admitted his folly, and gives Midas a chance to take back his disastrous request, by plunging "head and body" into the snowy foam of the river Pactolus, which flows past the great city of Sardis.[260] Midas does so, undoing the curse and turning everything back to the way it was before (including his daughter).

Here once again, the ancient myth can be shown beyond doubt to be celestial metaphor. Midas in this story is played by the very same constellation Perseus which we examined in the previous chapter as playing a leading role in a different myth involving the themes of petrification and objectification.

The constellation Perseus in the heavens appears to be reaching out towards the constellation Andromeda -- giving rise to the episode in which Midas turns his own daughter into gold.

Midas, as King of Phrygia, was specifically described as wearing a Phrygian cap, in order to hide the ass's ears which the god Apollo gave to the king as a result of another of the foolish choices of King Midas (in that story, it was the bad judgment of Midas in judging a musical contest between Apollo and a satyr named Marsyas). We have already seen that the constellation Perseus is associated with the Phrygian cap.

But perhaps the most decisive clue found in the ancient myths which confirms the association of Midas with the constellation Perseus is the fact that he is told he must wash his head in the upper reaches of the stream of Pactolus, which the king obediently does in order to undo the curse.

As the reader can easily verify, the band of the Milky Way arches over the Great Square of Pegasus and on past Perseus (we have

The path of Perseus and the path of Midas

already discussed this important feature in the examination of the imagery of the tauroctony of the cult of Mithras). The head of the constellation Perseus actually protrudes into the Milky Way at this point, as if plunging its head into the stream:

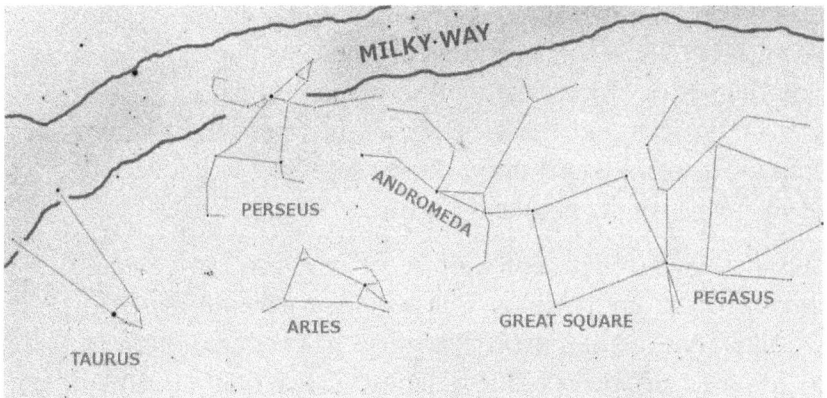

Once again, as we begin to realize that this ancient myth is unarguably a metaphor, we can perceive that this myth is actually about us. We all have moments in which we make choices worthy of the foolish King Midas. What kind of insecurity drives such behavior? If we are honest with ourselves, we realize that his choice and its motivations are sadly familiar.

We might ask ourselves this question: what could possibly be wrong with this king? Presumably, as the powerful King of Phrygia, and one who was destined even as a child to be known as the wealthiest man alive, Midas already had access to plenty of gold, likely more than anyone he knew. And yet, when given a boon by the god Dionysus, the king asked for more gold -- infinitely more gold -- the ability to continually turn things into gold, because there was apparently no amount of gold that would ever be enough, no amount that would ever satisfy him.

What is Midas lacking that causes this kind of insecurity? It is obviously a lack that is not external but rather internal, and thus cannot be satisfied by any amount of gold, no matter how abundant.

This pattern of behavior exemplifies the condition of addiction.

Chapter Fourteen

The king's ill-advised pursuit of gold only leads to his own self-inflicted anguish, when he finds that he cannot even nourish himself and is in grave danger of losing his very life because of his addiction to the lifeless metal. In his obsessive pursuit, he ends up turning those around him into commodities -- literally, in the case of his daughter. The myth of Midas obviously explores some of the same themes of objectification and agency which we saw in the story of Perseus and the Gorgons, a myth which was also (intriguingly enough) based upon these very same constellations in the same region of the night sky.

Although he may not have consciously realized it when he made his request of the god, Midas was willing to commoditize or objectify those around him in order to get whatever he thought he needed in order to be secure or happy. This dramatic myth provides a powerful insight into our own condition, when separated from our authentic self: searching desperately to fill a void which external substitutes can never fill, sometimes even harming others in the process, including those we love (and also including ourselves).

Scholar, author, philosopher and teacher Peter Kingsley, in a remarkable 1999 book entitled *In the Dark Places of Wisdom*, tells us that:

> What's missing is more powerful than what's there in front of our eyes. We all know that. The only trouble is that the missingness is too hard to bear, so we invent things to miss in our desperation. They are all only temporary substitutes. The world fills us with substitute after substitute and tries to convince us that nothing is missing. But nothing has the power to fill the hollowness we feel inside, so we have to keep replacing and modifying the things we invent as our emptiness throws its shadow over our life.
>
> [. . .]
>
> And there's a great secret: we all have that vast missingness deep inside us. The only difference between us and the mystics

is that they learn to face what we find ways of running away from.[261]

In the ancient myth, Midas in his insatiable desire for gold ended up harming his daughter, turning her into a commodity. Midas was not setting out with the conscious decision to rob others of their human agency in his lust for more and more wealth. But his answer to the offer of the divine Dionysus came from an internal emptiness that was bound to have self-destructive consequences, and to harm those closest to himself at the same time.

Unfortunately, there are also those who, unlike Midas, are in fact *consciously* willing to do harm to others in their pursuit of wealth and power, and to use any leverage they can get from the occult or hidden realm in order to do so -- those who, in the words of the passage in 1 Kings chapter 3, are quite ready to approach the invisible realm and ask for "the life of their enemies," or to otherwise seek any edge available (including the supernatural or the occult) in their quest to oppress others while enriching themselves.

In the previous chapter, we examined the abundant evidence supporting Flavio Barbiero's theory that the ancient order of Sol Invictus Mithras was an *instrument of subversion*, designed to gain influence within the critical institutions of public administration and power of the Roman Empire: the offices responsible for the collection of taxes, the checkpoints of customs and import-export, the Praetorian Guard, and the legions of the army itself.

The cult of Mithras was exclusive and secretive, employing a hierarchical rank structure which enabled careful screening and filtering of members -- restricting who would be given access to the most important aspects of planning and policy -- while also enabling the organization to invite important members of the community into its secret circle (keeping them at the lower ranks within the system) in order to direct their actions when necessary.

Chapter Fourteen

Flavio Barbiero's thesis also posits that this exclusive and secretive network had a twin: the inclusive and public branch of the operation, which was equally necessary. Indeed, once this public-facing organization -- the institution of the literalist Christian church -- was elevated to the sufficient level of power (by Constantine and the emperors who followed him), the network of Sol Invictus could fade to the background.

This is the critical point for an understanding of the situation in more modern times: if (as Flavio Barbiero argues and as I believe the evidence supports) the cult of Mithras is by its very design an *instrument of subversion*, capable of wrapping its tendrils around the sensitive nodes of the state and *squeezing*, capable even of "flipping" the state altogether, then *once its masters have succeeded* in publicly seizing control of the levers of power (as happened with the accession of Constantine to the throne and the public declaration of Christianity as the religion of the empire), that instrument of subversion needs to be placed on "safe," just like a powerful firearm.

When your people have achieved the goal of controling the levers of power, then this type of power-undermining cult is not something you want to leave lying around in your country with the selector switch set to "semi-automatic" -- it's far too dangerous!

And turning the selector switch from "semi" to "safe" is precisely what we see taking place in the Roman Empire after the rise of Constantine, where (as even the conventional modern Mithraic scholars admit), the cult of Mithras faded into near invisibility by the end of the fourth century. Indeed, as we have already seen, the mithraeum known as the Phrygianum, located in a grotto on Vatican Hill, peacefully shut down upon the death of the ultimate *pater patrum* of the cult of Mithras in AD 384 -- and the Vatican Hill then became the sole possession of the literalist Christians and the center of the Roman church.[262]

However, as Flavio Barbiero explains, this useful instrument of political warfare (the underground secret society) did not

The path of Perseus and the path of Midas

disappear altogether. It continues to this day, in what he refers to as a "fossilized" form: the institution of Freemasonry, the origins of which are shrouded in mystery but which almost certainly stretch back centuries before the conventionally-recognized year of 1717, and even perhaps many centuries prior to the Cooke Manuscript of the early 1400s and the Regius or Halliwell Manuscript of AD 1390, the earliest known documents to speak of Freemasonry according to Barbiero.[263]

According to Flavio Barbiero's hypothesis, the institution of Freemasonry was created in western Europe following the dissolution of the western Roman Empire as a means of preserving a Sol Invictus style instrument within the ranks of the self-styled aristocratic "noble families" who had gained monopolistic control of the land and who represented the dominant military power capable of keeping the majority from taking it back. Just as in the cult of Sol Invictus, which came to dominate the army of the empire, the institution of Freemasonry was only open to men, and its initiatory and hierarchical structure made it ideally suited to observe and select promising candidates for the upper levers of power within the organization, while exercising control over those deemed less capable of being given too much authority or allowed into the "steering committee" of the upper echelons.

Of the parallels between the two institutions, Barbiero writes:

> It is not by chance that modern Freemasonry seems to a large extent to be a tributary of the cult of Mithras. The points of similarity are numerous and substantial, not only in initiatory structure, but also in ritualistic content: continuous reference to the sun; the most significant anniversaries; the constant link to the solar cycle; the architecture and decoration of the Masonic Temple itself, which has maintained the shapes and dispositions of the mithraeum. If we enter a Masonic Temple today, we will see on the wall opposite the entrance the sun on the left and the waxing moon on the right. On the right-hand and left-hand walls are the signs of the zodiac, six on each side,

421

Chapter Fourteen

which begin with Aries on the left, and finish with Pisces on the right. Alternating with the signs of the zodiac are the statues of Minerva, Hercules, Venus, and Saturn. On the ceiling there is a starry sky. Along the sides are benches where the followers take their seats. On the back wall is the throne where the venerable master sits, and at his side are the chairs of the important people of the lodge. All is exactly as was in a mithraeum. The substantial difference is that behind the throne there is no image of Mithras with the bull, but instead there is a triangle with an eye at the center (and normally the sun in the background).[264]

The reader is invited to flip back to page 359 to compare elements in the above description to the outline of the ancient Mithraeum of the Seven Spheres from Ostia depicted in the diagram there.

Barbiero further notes that surviving depictions of initiatory ceremonies of the ancient cult, in artwork discovered within some mithraea, bear striking resemblance to Masonic initiations.[265] He also notes that the continuation of bone-chilling "blood oaths" within Freemasonry, by which the initiate is sworn to secrecy and calls down harrowing and violent punishments upon himself if he violates his oath, indicate that keeping secret the proceedings within the lodge (at least at one point in time) was likely a matter of absolute life and death (as it would have been for members of a subversive organization within the Roman Empire, if their business involved taking over the power of the state).[266]

Finally, among other pieces of evidence too extensive to list exhaustively here, he notes evidence that in earlier centuries, the institution of Freemasonry was for sons of the nobility and the ecclesiastical elite – and not at all for common workers (contrary to what the ordinary meaning of the terms "mason" and "masonry" might seem to imply). He points out that the Regius Manuscript of 1390 mentions among the members of the York Lodge "dukes, earls, and barons also, knights, squires, and many more, and the great burgesses of that city."[267]

"All the historical evidence," he writes, "indicates that members of the Masonic confraternities were always and exclusively members of the ecclesiastical world, the nobility -- including sovereigns -- and the cultural elite. There is not the slightest mention of simple workers." [268]

The records indicate plainly that the Emperor Maximilian I (who lived from 1459 to 1519 and ruled as Holy Roman Emperor from 1508 until his death) "took part in the congress of stonemasons held at Regensburg in 1459 and in the following one held at Speyer (1464) -- not as an observer, but as a member of the confraternity." [269]

In other words, the institution of Freemasonry, at least in the centuries prior to the modern era, appears to have been the domain of men from the same oligarch families who controlled the lands of Europe as their exclusive monopoly -- those descended, according to Barbiero's theory, from the families who took over and later dissolved the Roman Empire.

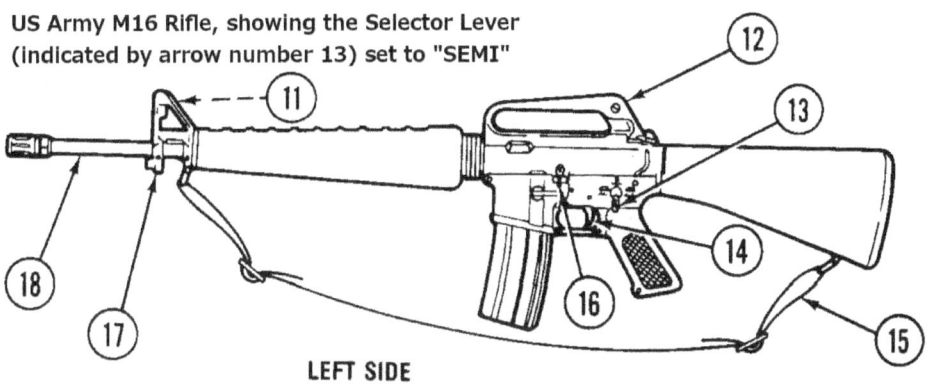

US Army M16 Rifle, showing the Selector Lever (indicated by arrow number 13) set to "SEMI"

LEFT SIDE

It is as though this powerful weapon -- a secret society that could be used to overthrow a government, even an empire -- had to be kept around, but kept around *in safe mode*. All modern weapons, such as the US M16 rifle pictured above, have a safety switch of some sort (in the M16, this switch is a lever, numbered "13" in the diagram, by which the weapon's operator can easily switch from "safe," to "semi-automatic," to "full auto" -- newer versions replace full auto with a "three-round burst" mode).

Chapter Fourteen

When the secret society of Sol Invictus was maneuvering to actually take over the Roman Empire, it was fully operational, functioning as a live weapon to seize control of the nodes of power. Once its operators had achieved that aim, however, and once it became clear that their victory was complete and would not be reversed, they turned that dangerous weapon back to the "safe" setting. The institution of Mithraism was peacefully discontinued, but a remnant of it would continue to be passed down from one generation to the next, within the elite families who had now gained complete control over Europe. That remnant institution would become what we call Masonry, and it preserved the same important hierarchical structure, and the critical and very serious oaths of secrecy, that the original institution had employed -- because in times or in regions where the aristocracy and the church might not have full control, for one reason or another, then it could it be "weaponized" as necessary.

In support of this theory, Flavio Barbiero notes that Freemasonry itself contains the terms "operative" and "speculative," which he believes may distinguish between the mode in which the organization primarily serves to pass along ancient traditions and preserve a sense of identity among the sons of the oligarchy (such activity is termed "speculative") and the more active mode in which the leadership of the network actually makes political decisions and takes decisive action (the "operative" mode).[270]

It is possible that this finely-crafted instrument is usually kept in "safe" mode (corresponding perhaps to the "speculative" mode) but in certain circumstances the selection lever can be switched to "fire" ("operative").

Because the powerful literalist Christian church and the oligarch families who took control of western Europe over the centuries following the success of Sol Invictus had nearly total power over the subsequent millennium in almost all areas, it is quite likely that the institution of Freemasonry was primarily kept in "safe" mode, initiating the sons of noble families in order to maintain certain traditions and knowledge and to use the initiatory

The path of Perseus and the path of Midas

hierarchy as a "filtering" or "sifting" function to observe and select promising potential leaders and strategists from the rising generation as the decades and centuries rolled along.

However, in certain circumstances, the selection lever could be rotated off of the "safe" setting and the mechanism could be weaponized for any of various levels of action. This transition would have been used in countries where the absolute power of the church was challenged or diminished in some way. For example, we know that Freemasonry appears to have become much more active and virulent within England and Scotland during the centuries following the defiance by Henry VIII of the authority of Rome, as well as in France and other hotbeds of Protestantism following the Reformation and the turbulent struggles and conflicts that it unleashed.

And, while it may be a controversial hypothesis, I would suggest that the evidence also supports the possibility that following the Russian Revolution of 1917 -- which featured the abolition of the monarchy and the slaughter of the "royals" and "nobles" in that nation (who were of course blood relations of the oligarchic families of Europe as well), an event which absolutely terrified the church and ruling families of western Europe who saw clear indications that such revolutions could take place in their centuries-long strongholds further west (including Germany, France, Italy, Spain, Belgium and the United Kingdom) -- the same hidden instrument of control was activated and weaponized in an astonishing manner in order to neutralize the threat.

By this suggestion I mean that the selector switch appears to have been flipped from "safe" to "rock-and-roll" in Germany, in response to the abortive attempt to declare a new Socialist Republic in Munich, Bavaria on November 7, 1918 (following the Russian Revolution).

Peter Levenda's groundbreaking book *Unholy Alliance: A History of Nazi Involvement with the Occult*, first published in 1995 (all quotations here from the Third Revised and Expanded

Chapter Fourteen

Edition published in 2019) provides extensive and compelling evidence and analysis showing beyond any doubt that the Nazi Party in general and the SS in particular functioned as a cult: a cult patterned upon existing secret societies and initiatic orders.[271]

Indeed, Levenda quotes Hitler himself in an epigraph at the start of Chapter 6 of *Unholy Alliance*, a chapter entitled "The Dangerous Element: The Ahnenerbe and the Cult of the SS," in which Hitler says (in a quotation first published in a 1939 book by Hermann Rauschning entitled *Hitler Speaks*):

> The hierarchical organization and the initiation through symbolic rites, that is to say, without bothering the brain but by working on the imagination through magic and the symbols of a cult, all this is the dangerous element, and the element I have taken over.[272]

This quotation is very revealing. It demonstrates that Hitler and the Nazis knew exactly what they were doing when they deliberately "took over" the powerful instrument of hierarchical organization and the initiation through symbolic rites.

The quotation also reveals that Hitler and the Nazis understood such initiatory rites and hierarchical cults as being capable of being weaponized (perhaps even designed for it): Hitler says quite plainly that "all this is *the dangerous element*."

It is dangerous because it is a weapon -- or at least because it is capable of being used as a weapon. And no one would argue that Hitler, and in particular the SS led by Heinrich Himmler, did *not* intend to deliberately use the combination "hierarchical organization and initiation through symbolic rites" as a weapon -- and what an extremely sharp and devastating weapon it would prove to be.

In describing the SS as an occult secret society, Peter Levenda traces the influence of esoteric societies in Germany beginning in the late nineteenth century, focusing initially upon the *Thule Gesellschaft* (or "Thule Society") of Munich, which had been founded and led by one Adam Alfred Rudolf Glauer, who would later call himself Baron Rudolf von Sebottendorff (1875 - 1945). Young Adam Glauer left home as a young man of 22 (his father was a locomotive driver) and made his way to Australia, then Egypt, and then Turkey, "becoming initiated into Freemasonry there in 1901," before founding "his own mystical lodge in Constantinople in 1910" and finally making his way back to Germany in 1913 at the age of 38.[273]

Levenda explains that the *Thule Gesellschaft*, while portraying itself as a "literary-cultural group," was actually created in part as a cover or front for Hermann Pohl's *Germanenorden*, a rapidly growing group "identified with the type of right-wing extremism and virulent anti-Semitism that the various German republican and socialist groups were seeking to weed out and destroy."[274]

Significantly, Peter Levenda notes that the *Germanenorden* could be described as a "magic-oriented, occult society with its secret initiation rituals patterned after Masonic ceremony and its Theosophical-style philosophy encompassing everything from Eastern mysticism to runic lore to a rabid, pseudoscientific racism."[275]

As it turns out, these esoteric initiatory secret societies, patterned upon Freemasonry, functioned as the nerve center and the cadre that mobilized an organized armed resistance against the "godless Communists" of the socialist *Volksstaat Bayern* ("Bavarian People's-state") that Kurt Eisner tried to establish in Munich in November of 1918 -- armed resistance that ended in violent clashes in the streets, the execution of seven members of the Thule Society by the socialists, and ultimately the obliteration of the socialist experiment and the assassination of Eisner.[276]

In *Unholy Alliance*, Peter Levenda provides abundant evidence to demonstrate the channels through which the influence of turn-of-the-century occultists including Sebottendorff and others, and secret societies such as the *Thule Gesellschaft*, flowed into the formulation of the Third Reich, the selection of Adolf Hitler as

Chapter Fourteen

Führer to lead it, and the creation of the murderous and fanatical SS under Heinrich Himmler. Through it all, Levenda asserts that:

> The Nazis were not simply a political party. As has been mentioned before, they were a *cult*, and as such had every trapping of the typical cult, from a spiritual Master to a brotherhood of identically clad disciples, secret rituals performed in remote castles, and a sign -- a totem -- that summed up their ideology as effectively as the Cross and the Star.[277]

Levenda explains that following the defeat of the socialists and communists in Munich (which was completed by May of 1919), the threat of socialist or communist revolution did not disappear in the rest of Germany -- that threat was very real and very frightening to the nobility and the large industrialists, and included even the mutiny of units in the Navy who hoisted the red flag over German battleships.

To counter this looming threat, some members of Germany's right wing favored a unified Greater Germany (absorbing Bavaria) under a new kind of leader, "a leader with vision."[278] And the *Thule Gesellschaft* instituted a two-pronged strategy to find such a leader -- itself searching among Munich's rich and powerful, "the society figures, the wealthy capitalists, the inteligentsia," but also creating a new entity called the German Workers Party (abbreviated as the DAP and later as the NSDAP, for National Socialist German Worker's Party, knowing that there was a strong and growing sympathy towards the idea of socialism among the working class, which was exactly what the right wing was trying to defuse), both to organize allies among "the working people, the lower- and middle-class citizens who have been hit hardest by the civil wars, the enormous rates of inflation, the chaos and confusion," and to see if a gifted leader might be found by looking in that direction instead.[279]

The path of Perseus and the path of Midas

Even though the Thule Society was involved with coordinating both halves of this effort, they kept their connection with the DAP (aka the NSDAP, which eventually morphed into the Nazi Party) hidden from view. Thus, decisive evidence linking the two is difficult to find, but Peter Levenda argues the circumstantial evidence is compelling:

> So, while we cannot show a document stating that the DAP and NSDAP were subsidiaries of the Thule Gesellschaft or the *Germanenorden*, the author believes it is safe to say that the DAP (and, by extension, the Nazi Party) was originally a creature of both the Thule Society and Sebottendorff (as claimed by Sebottendorff and as admitted by Toland), and, certainly, the wildest, most extreme aims of the Thule Society would all eventually become official policy of the Third Reich, while its metaphysical and occult characteristics were adopted wholeheartedly by the SS.[280]

The above understanding, and the voluminous evidence Levenda provides in his book to support his hypothesis, also argues in favor of the suggestion that the phenomenon of Nazi Germany represents the weaponization of pre-existing traditions preserved through the centuries in the form of secret initiatory societies, patterned upon the ancient cult of Mithras. These esoteric societies typically remain dormant, existing in the shadows of society, devoted to the study of arcane esoteric subjects and ancient traditions, but in times a significant threat to the control system by oligarchic families and the church that has held most of Europe in its grip since the triumph of Constantine, they can be awakened and turned loose.[281]

And that is precisely what appears to have taken place with the creation of the Nazi war machine, which ended any thought of socialist revolution within Germany and (once it began attacking the rest of Europe) within other European nations further west -- and which, once it had done what was necessary to remove the threat of socialist revolution in western Europe, would almost

Chapter Fourteen

immediately launch an invasion of unparalleled ferocity against the Soviet Union (their primary target of the Second World War).

It should be beyond dispute to observe that the Nazi Party in general, and the SS in particular, deliberately incorporated structures and traditions associated with the secret societies of the European elites, including both the initiatory Masonic lodges and the militant knightly orders (including those of the Knights Templar and of the Teutonic Knights), traditions which Barbiero sees as yet another aspect of the same Mithraic heritage.[282]

The atrocities committed by the Nazis in general and the SS in particular need not be catalogued here in exhaustive detail. They include the objectification and deliberate dehumanization of other men and women, the violation of the innate and inalienable rights of their victims, through imprisonment, rape, torture, vile medical experimentation, and mass murder. The pertinent observations for the thesis being advanced include the direct link to the esoteric initiatory societies, and the undeniable evidence that the upper echelons of Nazi leadership sought the influence of the invisible realm to help influence a favorable outcome for the actions they were taking and the larger goal they were pursuing.

This appeal to the realm of the occult illustrates the central theme of this book: that although the ancient myths can be shown beyond any doubt to be designed for the repair of human trauma and the healing of our alienation from the higher self (and thus are clearly designed for the *uplift* and *empowerment* of men and women: all men and women from all the many cultures and nations on the planet because the ancient myths are given in various forms to every people and nation in every inhabited part of our globe), they can and have been twisted and inverted by those who seek to use them for the *oppression* and *enslavement* of other men and women, in order to enrich a privileged "elite" at the expense of everyone else.

The examples of conscious, deliberate attempts by the Nazis to appeal to the realm of the occult and the supernatural (in order to

The path of Perseus and the path of Midas

tip the scales in their own favor) are numerous and undeniable, even if they were largely ignored by most contemporary historians until the publication of Peter Levenda's groundbreaking work.

These efforts by the Nazis are explored in *Unholy Alliance*, and they include the consultation of astrologers (including Himmler's personal astrologer, Wilhelm Wulff),[283] the eployment of psychics and "pendulum readers" to locate Allied warships in the Atlantic Ocean and to determine the secret location to which Mussolini had been taken when he was arrested and imprisoned on orders of the king of Italy in 1943,[284] as well as the organization by the SS of extended expeditions to both the mountains of Tibet and to the northern stronghold of Iceland in order to search for original texts related to ancient sacred traditions (purportedly "Aryan" sacred traditions), which were carefully shipped back to Germany and studied in minute detail.[285]

Some well-informed readers, however, might object to the suggestion that the undeniable evidence of Nazi involvement with occult practices necessarily indicates any continuity with the institution of Freemasonry which (according to Barbiero's theory) was preserved among the oligarchic families of Europe during the centuries following the dissolution of the Roman Empire, as a kind of "insurance policy" to be used when the primary control mechanism of the authority of the entrenched noble families, reinforced by the formidable power of the Christian church was thrown aside, as it was with the Russian Revolution of 1917 - 1918, and as it was to a lesser degree by the actions of Henry VIII of England in the 1500s and in other parts of western Europe during the Protestant Reformation and the wars between the Protestants and Rome -- a kind of "break glass in case of emergency" situation, with the Russian Revolution (and the possibility that this spirit of revolution might spread to western Europe) representing an emergency of the first order, necessitating the creation of a truly ferocious military initiatory cult in response (necessity, that is, from the perspective of the "collaborators against the gods" who had taken over the lands of

Chapter Fourteen

Europe centuries before and were accustomed to living off the blessings bestowed by nature and the divine realm, to the detriment of everyone else).

These readers might object to the suggestion that the Nazis and the SS represented any kind of continuity with the secret societies of previous centuries (secret societies which were all variations of Freemasonry, which itself descends directly from the cult of Sol Invictus Mithras) on the grounds that the Nazis absolutely banned and aggressively persecuted any traces of Freemasonry within the Third Reich, viewing it as subversive, Jewish, and tainted by association with revolution and especially with the despised concept of democracy.[286]

This objection seems reasonable, on its face. But remember the point which was stressed earlier in this chapter, regarding the very logical conclusion that once absolute control over the levers of power within a society have been secured, the need for the incredibly effective instrument of subversion represented by secret societies fades away -- and in fact it becomes necessary to "turn off" the weapons of subversion which were previously so valuable during the campaign to take control away from whomever had it before.

In the case of the secret society of Mithras, once the throne of the Roman Empire had been decisively secured by Constantine, and once Constantine had elevated the literalist Christian church to a position of great power within the empire itself, the instrument of Sol Invictus could be dialed down, and could eventually retire into the background as a "speculative" organization (morphing into Freemasonry in the subsequent centuries, ready to be used again as necessary in any country where the church of Rome somehow lost its grip on the levers of power).

In the case of Germany, the very esoteric societies which had given rise to the National Socialist Workers Party were no longer necessary once Hitler and the Nazis assumed complete and total control over the state and all its levers of absolute power -- and the

The path of Perseus and the path of Midas

decision by the Nazis in 1939 to ban all "Freemasonlodge-like Organizations" (including the Theosophical Society, the Anthroposophical Society, the Golden Dawn, the OTO, the Brotherhood of Saturn, the Odd Fellows, the Ancient Order of Druids, the Christian Scientists, and the Independent Order of Owls)[287] makes complete sense and fits the playbook that has been used in prior centuries, going all the way back to the fourth century AD. The "open power" and the "secret order" never wish to appear to be working together or even connected in any way.

It is a playbook which was employed in ancient times in order to take over and destroy the power of the government of Rome which, although certainly open to criticism on many levels, provided public infrastructure and a means of checking unrestrained accumulation of private wealth and power -- and preventing unrestrained seizure of the natural resources which were understood to have been given by the gods for the public good. Governments in general have the potential to stand in the way of unrestrained privatization and *rentier* activity, "rents" as we have seen being a form of *private* taxation.

The successful placement of their man (Constantine) upon the throne led directly to the obliteration of the worship of the old gods (and the obliteration of the teachings that the resources of nature each belonged to a specific god) and to the dissolution of the government which acted as a check upon the monopolization of the resources by various private oligarchs -- and this dissolution of the government led to the rise of what were basically "warlords" who had no restraint on their power and privilege whatsoever and who, in cooperation with the literalist Christian church, provided virtually no public infrastructure and reduced the standard of living for everyone else to subsistence poverty. We see the same pattern of the rise of warlords repeating itself today, when a state is dissolved and the people are unable to form a government strong enough to restrain rapacious oligarchs.

The various powerful families who carved up Europe amongst themselves following the fall of the empire set in place a system of

Chapter Fourteen

self-enrichment and exploitation (sanctioned and defended by the church) that would not be challenged until the rise of modern states powerful enough to check the power of the clergy and the "nobility" -- and even then it was not until widespread acceptance of literalist Christian dogma began to come under increasingly intense scrutiny (beginning in the eighteenth century) that the old system which had prevailed since the fall of Rome began to experience severe strain. It should be considered no coincidence, then, to find that this time period (the eighteenth century) witnessed the re-emergence of more aggressive Freemasonry and the proliferation of new secret societies and esoteric groups patterned upon the same model.

In general, these esoteric societies should be viewed as conservative in nature, despite what we might conclude at first glance -- "conservative" in that they are by no means dedicated to the overthrow of the aristocracy of Europe, but rather to the preservation of the same system of privilege which benefited the members of these societies. They are basically "elitist" in their philosophy and, despite embracing worldviews which appear radically different from those held by wider society, they reinforce the idea that some men and women are inherently superior to others, destined to rule and keep down the majority of other men and women within a nation -- and around the globe.[288]

The ancient wisdom had been suppressed, and those aspects of the ancient wisdom which *were* preserved (among those families who had suppressed it everywhere else) would primarily be employed to help maintain their system of control and monopoly.

This paradigm helps explain the prevalence of elitist, racist, and in some cases viciously anti-Semitic sentiments running through the teachings of many branches of esotericism in the nineteenth and twentieth centuries. These objectionable and repellant doctrines should not be misconstrued as inherent aspects of esoteric pursuits, although one could easily arrive at that mistaken conclusion by surveying the teachings of various esoteric and secret societies including those whose streams eventually flowed into the emergence of Nazism in Germany (as well as by noting that many of the prominent twentieth century esoterists displayed sympathies which were clearly aligned with fascism in one form or another).

I argue that the ancient wisdom preserved among all the various cultures found around the globe is clearly and demonstrably designed for the uplift and empowerment of men and women, and that the use of such knowledge to oppress and exploit and debase other men and women (and to privatize the resources given to the people) is an *inversion* of that original purpose: an inversion that can be traced back to the rise of literalist Christianity and its secret underground institution, the cult of Sol Invictus. I trust that the previous chapters detailing the extent to which the myths point us towards the recovery of our suppressed authentic self have established that position beyond reasonable doubt, and have established that the myths demonstrate quite plainly that their intended use is to foster justice and not exploitation and oppression.

The collaborators against the gods who sought to take the precious resource of the ancient wisdom of the myths from the men and women for whom it was intended, and to monopolize it and its benefits for themselves alone, have distorted the reputation of this esoteric lore to the point that many today mistakenly believe that the original purpose of the knowledge of the gods must *always* have been the oppression and enslavement of the majority by the elite, when in fact oppresssion and enslavement is an inversion of the ancient wisdom's intended purpose.

If esoteric knowledge and occult ritual magic have primarily been employed by the oligarchic elites themselves (or those working for them) in order to protect their oligarchical system of exploitation and oppression, then it is no wonder that many think this exploitation and oppression is what esoteric knowledge was originally designed to further.

Chapter Fourteen

The crimes against humanity perpetrated by the Nazis demonstrate the depths of depravity to which defenders of the "aristocracy" (and opponents of those who seek to overturn that oligarchical system) can sink in their willingness to inflict mass trauma upon humanity while preserving the institutions of elite privilege -- bolstered by the lie of innate racial superiority.

However, without in any way seeking to equivocate or diminish the heinousness of the atrocities which were routinely committed by the Third Reich upon men and women within Germany's own boundaries and within those countries the Nazis invaded during their war of aggression (crimes in which Nazi collaborators outside of Germany also participated), it should be acknowledged that the atrocities committed by the *colonial powers of Europe* against men and women in colonized continents of Africa, Asia, Australia and the Americas (as well as in the islands of the Pacific) during the foregoing centuries were also unspeakably heinous and inexcusable -- and yet the teachings of the literalist Christian church and the racist and elitist beliefs of the so-called European "nobility" were used to try and falsely "justify" and condone these depredations and to assuage the consciences of those who committed those heinous crimes and the consciences of those who benefitted from them.

All of these atrocities and crimes against humanity share a common root and heritage: the racism and violence of the Nazis did not simply appear out of nowhere.

Just as there was no *actual* conflict between the leadership of the cult of Sol Invictus and the hierarchy of the literal Christian church during the waning days of the Roman Empire (although conventional scholars continue to propagate this misleading trope), there is also no real enmity between the reactionary literalist Christian church of the modern era and the right-leaning esoteric secret societies of the eighteenth, nineteenth, and twentieth centuries (and some of the more freewheeling descendents of these secret societies who have appeared in the decades following World War II). These apparently opposing

The path of Perseus and the path of Midas

forces are once again merely the two seemingly-independent heads of the same two-headed monster, just as we saw to be the case with the cult of Mithras and the hierarchy of Roman Christianity in the second through fourth centuries.

Peter Levenda (and other authors and scholars) have detailed that, just as the leadership of the Nazi apparatus publicly condemned and ridiculed occultism and magic in speeches and official policy while secretly consulting astrologers and psychics and participating in occult rituals,[289] they also publicly attacked and belittled Christianity and the church, and yet we find irrefutable evidence that the highest echelons of the Catholic Church actively conspired to enable literally thousands of unrepentant Nazis (including many members of the SS) to escape to South America, Tibet, and Indonesia after the defeat of Germany in 1945.[290]

It is very difficult to make sense of this undeniable fact of high-ranking Catholic Church collaboration in an elaborate effort to help Nazis escape justice after the war -- unless we understand that the literalist Christian church is inextricably intertwined with the oligarchical system instituted in Europe following the fall of Rome, and committed to the preservation and expansion of that oppressive and exploitative system (indeed, to the *world-wide* expansion of that system), and unless we understand that the fanatical, initiatory *cult* of Nazism is actually a weaponized form of the more secretive and underground "shadow control mechanism" that has always existed as the hidden "other half" of the public control mechanism of organized Christian religion.

Once we understand that, we understand that the secret societies and the conventional, open, public (and "legitimate") institutions of control (such as the aristocracy and the church itself) are actually allies -- even though they often *pretend* to be antagonists, in a kind of large-scale "good cop, bad cop" routine.

They are no more antagonists in the modern era than were the cult of Mithras and the ancient literalist church -- and recall the

Chapter Fourteen

fact that the central Phrygianum of the cult of Mithras and the basilica of St. Peter's were co-located on the Vatican Hill in Rome, indicating in the most undeniable manner that the two institutions were actually intimately interconnected.

After the putative end of the Second World War, rather than completely dismantling the deadly instrument that had been *switched on* in Germany in response to the Russian Revolution and the threat of socialist uprising in other parts of Europe, high ranking leaders of the Nazi Party and the SS were deliberately transported out of Germany and provided with hiding places and new identities.

In her thoroughly-researched 2014 book *Operation Paperclip: the secret intelligence program that brought Nazi scientists to America*, Annie Jacobsen details how over sixteen hundred Nazis were secretly employed by the US Department of Defense and other agencies in order to participate in weapons programs, the space program, and a host of intelligence programs after the cessation of open wartime hostilities. These were not merely "nominal" members of the Nazi Party: some had been members of the SS, some had worked directly with either Hitler, Himmler, or Hermann Göring during the war, some had worn the Golden Party Badge, "indicating favor bestowed by the Führer," some had stood trial at the Nuremberg war crimes tribunal, and some had been released "without trial under mysterious circumstances." [291]

In addition to scientists who were brought to the United States, Army Intelligence brought Hitler's former senior intelligence officer for the eastern front, Lieutenant General Reinhard Gehlen, to the US Military Intelligence Service Center at Camp King in Oberursel (eleven miles northwest of Frankfurt), in 1946.[292]
Annie Jacobsen explains:

> Army Intelligence decided to make Gehlen head of its entire "anti-Communist intelligence organization," under the code name Operation Rusty. Eventually the organization would

The path of Perseus and the path of Midas

become known simply as the Gehlen Organization. A network of former Nazi intelligence agents, the majority of whom were members of the SS, began working out of offices at Camp King side by side with army intelligence officers. Colonel Philp was in charge of overall supervision. By late 1947, the Gehlen Organization had gotten so large it required its own headquarters. Army intelligence moved the organization to a self-contained facility outside Munich, in a village called Pullach. This compound was the former estate of Martin Bormann and had large grounds, sculpture gardens, and a pool. The two facilities, at Oberursel and Pullach, worked together. Gehlen and Baun claimed to have six hundred intelligence agents, all former Nazis, in the Soviet zone of occupied Germany alone.[293]

Jacobsen notes that Gehlen was rumored to have received a salary of a million dollars a year (an extraordinary sum today, but an absolutely astronomical sum in 1947).[294] She also notes that in 1948, the director of the CIA and the heads of military intelligence agreed to transfer the Gehlen Organization into the fledgling Central Intelligence Agency; thus on July 1, 1949, Reinhard Gehlen and his vast network of agents were officially absorbed into the CIA.[295]

Researchers including Paul Manning, Curt Riess, Mae Brussell, Dave Emory and others have documented the evidence that the Nazis "went underground" after the cessation of open hostilities, submerging into secrecy while continuing to carry out operations designed to advance a reactionary political agenda. Some of their work suggests that intelligence agencies in the United States and western Europe were heavily influenced by the absorption of the Nazi intelligence apparatus and the Gehlen Organization in particular.

The deliberate incorporation of tremendous numbers of high-ranking members of the SS and the Nazi Party into positions of influence within military and intelligence organizations in the United States and other western nations following World War II

Chapter Fourteen

becomes much more understandable within the framework of the suggested hypothesis regarding the role of secret societies descended from the ancient order of Sol Invictus.

If, as we have argued, the elevation of literalist Christianity and the dissolution of the Roman Empire were accomplished through the secret society of Sol Invictus in order to impose an oppressive, monopolistic and exploitative feudal system dominated by what were basically warlords who later became the aristocratic landed families of Europe, supported by the church . . .

And if, as we have argued, that same system (dominated by the European aristocracy, supported by the church, and bolstered by their many collaborators) managed to remain relatively intact down through the centuries, evolving into the European nations which in later centuries became the colonialist and imperialist powers that would export their system of exploitation, oppression, and monopolization of natural resources around the globe . . .

And if, as the evidence regarding parallels between initiatory societies such as Freemasonry and the original secret society of Sol Invictus suggests, that "aristocratic" system was kept in power in part through the two-pronged efforts of the openly powerful institution of the literalist Christian church and the more secretive instrument of the initiatory secret societies (which could be weaponized when necessary) . . .

Then it is very reasonable to conclude that the Nazi Party, which most resembles a cult and which can be shown to have had deep roots in initiatory secret societies, was a weaponized aspect of the more secretive, occult instrument, activated in order to defeat the mortal threat posed to the aristocratic system by the rise of popular progressive, socialist, and communist movements and especially by the Russian Revolution and the potential for socialism (and its enmity to both clergy and aristocracy) to spread.

Within the framework of this hypothesis, the astonishing fact of a deliberate, coordinated campaign to rescue thousands of important Nazi officials and SS officers and to place them in

The path of Perseus and the path of Midas

positions conducive to the continuation of their efforts, albeit "underground" and in secret, becomes perfectly understandable -- and is in fact exactly what we would expect if the hypothesis is correct.

The execution of this effort to preserve certain functional elements of the Nazi machine was not known to *the people* of the various nations who had given so much in the fight to defeat Nazi Germany and the other fascist powers during the war -- in fact it is still widely unknown to the general populace of the United States, for example (and largely unremarked-upon by the controlled media organs of the western nations). The campaign appears to have been coordinated by reactionary institutions controlled by certain members of the ruling elite of Europe and the US (including the wartime intelligence agencies), as well as by men within the upper echelons of the Vatican.

It also appears quite likely that there has long been an affiliation between *espionage and intelligence operations* on the one hand, and *both aspects* of the two-headed entity we are discussing (on the other hand): both the underground secret network and the more "above-ground" elements of the literalist Christian church. Cooperating with the church on intelligence operations is only logical: for starters, the church has always been closely aligned with the governing powers in the west (indeed, for centuries the ecclesiastical and political leaders were co-dependent upon one another, because the teaching that the existing oppressive oligarchical system was "God's will" acted as a potent obstacle to popular revolt, a co-dependency that lasted until the Enlightenment).

Additionally, the church sends "missionaries" all over the world in order to try to spread the adoption of literalist Christianity, an ideal cover for gathering intelligence. Within any nation where it operates, the church by virtue of its local networks can gather enormous amounts of "actionable intelligence." The enormous intelligence potential inherent in the institution of regular weekly confession should also not be overlooked.

Chapter Fourteen

If the overt and open side of the two-headed institution is well-suited for intelligence operations, how much more so the secretive "head" of the same serpent? Based on what we have already observed regarding this secretive network's activities during the Roman Empire and down through the ensuing centuries, its pattern of operations also appear to be similar if not identical to what are termed "intelligence operations" today.

During the twentieth century (and now the twenty-first), we would naturally expect to see the more secretive and underground side of this ancient control mechanism assume a more and more active role in the defense of the old order, because the power of the literalist Christian church has diminished somewhat, at least in comparison to the power that it wielded over the minds of the general population in previous centuries (its power remains quite formidable -- but certainly diminished beginning in the nineteenth century and onwards).

It is due to this diminished hold over the minds of the overall population exercised by literalist Christianity, in my analysis, that we would expect to see a corresponding intensification of the activity of intelligence agencies and also of underground occult and initiatory organizations during the twentieth century (and now the twenty-first). The decline in power of the *overt* institution (the literalist Christian church) requires the more *covert* instrument to shoulder more of the load.

The threat became so severe during the years following the Russian Revolution that the *covert institution* had to explode into full view in a gleaming, weaponized, mechanized form: the Nazi cult. After exploding onto the world stage quite publicly for a brief and violent period of time -- a period of time sufficient to beat down the threat of widespread worker uprising and even socialist revolution in Germany and western Europe, and a period of time which was almost, but not quite, sufficient to conquer the Soviet Union -- this deadly, weaponized cult disappeared back into secrecy. It should be no surprise that in

The path of Perseus and the path of Midas

doing so, an important chunk of the Nazi machine grafted itself into the intelligence network of the western powers, since intelligence organizations by their very nature are designed to operate in the shadows.

The connections between secret initiatory societies and espionage did not originate in the twentieth century – Peter Levenda and other researchers have found evidence for such a connection going back centuries. Speaking of the fin-de-siècle esoteric society known as the Hermetic Order of the Golden Dawn, itself an important influence on the *Thule Gesellschaft*, and referencing as well the figure of Aleister Crowley (1875 - 1947) who himself was also almost certainly an intelligence operative, Levenda writes:

> Another element of the Golden Dawn which is relevant to our case is that the structure of many of its rituals, the peculiar language in which its invocations are made, and the odd designs of many of the magic seals and insignia are all based on a system of occult correspondences known as Enochian, and codified within the writings of Elizabethan mathematician, philosopher, and spy, Dr. John Dee.

> Crowley would become so conversant with the "Enochian" language that he would translate medieval spirit conjurations into that tongue for use by his own cult members. Having its own alphabet and its own rules of grammar, its very existence is a technical impossibility: an artificially created language developed by one (or at most two) men in the sixteenth century, John Dee and his assistant Edward Kelley. According to their story, it was given to them by an angel who communicated the language, the alphabet, and all the magic squares, invocations, etc. by means of a laborious process that took months of "scrying" in the equivalent of a crystal ball. The massive amount of manuscript that resulted from these bizarre efforts has been largely ignored by historians of the Elizabethan period, or cited as evidence of Dee's emotional instability. In fact, the existence of these writings was used for many years to

discredit Dee's genius altogether. (This is a pattern of thought that exists to this day: occult practices are evidence of either insanity, emotional instability, or simple credulousness).

However, recent research into the Elizabethan period and particularly concering Dee's relationship to Sir Francis Walsingham (1530? - 1590), Queen Elizabeth's secretary of state, suggests that Dee was on a secret mission for the British government at the time of the revelations (which took place in Prague). Further, as the pseudonymous historian Richard Deacon has pointed out, the Angelic language itself may have been devised as a particularly effective code -- based on the work of famed German cryptographer Johannes Trithemius (1462 - 1516) -- for communication between Dee in Prague and Walsingham in England.

In other words, the entire basis of the famous occult order known as the Golden Dawn may well have had its origins in espionage work, from the coded language of Elizabethan spy and mystic John Dee to the "Cypher manuscript" of a nonexistant German lodge.[296]

This passage contains an absolute gold mine of evidence supporting the theory being advanced in this chapter regarding the covert and overt branches of the control system of feudal land monopoly imposed on Europe following the fall of Rome.

We see evidence for a connection between occult activity and espionage: espionage (it should be emphasized) conducted in support of the existing order.

We also see evidence that the famous occultist and astrologer John Dee (1527 - 1608), who served the Queen of England, was involved in espionage: evidence which reinforces the argument that espionage and attempts to access the invisible realm for assistance in intelligence projects have a long and distinguished history.

The path of Perseus and the path of Midas

We see evidence that the language created by Dee and Kelley (which they attributed to supernatural revelation) was used for the encryption of intelligence-related communications across great distances, and we see evidence that this very same coded language wound up forming the basis for rituals in the nineteenth century esoteric Hermetic Order of the Golden Dawn – strong support for the argument that the secret societies descended from the ancient cult of Sol Invictus Mithras have close ties to espionage and intelligence work.

Additionally, and notably, we also see Peter Levenda pointing out the strange reluctance of conventional historians to engage with what we would consider to be extremely significant evidence (in this case, the evidence that Dee's occult interests might have overlapped with Dee's espionage operations). We have observed this same pattern of what we might call "willful blindness" or "looking the other way" among historians in other related subjects, as if important evidence is being deliberately and pointedly ignored and obvious implications are being papered over with cover stories (or dismissed altogether, along with a healthy dose of ridicule in order to discourage anyone else from picking up the trail).

In the decades since the ostensible end of World War II, intelligence agencies have increased their prominence in world affairs -- and the prominence of occult ritual in connection with intelligence operations has increased apace.

As mentioned above, Aleister Crowley -- perhaps the most important and influential occult figure of the twentieth century -- can be shown to have moved in intelligence circles, although which nation he was working for has been a subject of contention (even during his own lifetime).

Perhaps the reason it is difficult to pin down whether he was in the employ of the intelligence services of Great Britain, or those of the United States, or even those of Germany, stems from the mistaken tendency to focus upon individual nations as the most

Chapter Fourteen

important actors upon the world stage, when it may be more appropriate to understand that just as the literalist Christian church has acted as an institution which transcends national boundaries (and which historically has been absolutely fundamental to maintaining the oligopoly imposed on Europe following the dissolution of the Roman Empire), so too does the less visible "underground" reflection of that more overt institution, the secret network that is heir to the cult of Sol Invictus.

Crowley himself is a figure well worthy of careful consideration. Born in 1875 and named Edward Alexander Crowley by his parents, he was raised in a strict literalist Christian household by parents who were members of a movement called by outsiders the "Brethren from Plymouth" or "the Plymouth Brethren," a fundamentalist network of worshipers rejecting existing hierarchical church authority and seeking to base their lives and conduct and worship on the principle of *sola scriptura*, or "the Bible alone."

In the introduction to the collection of academic essays on Crowley edited by Henrik Bogdan and Martin P. Starr, these editors write:

> [. . .] Crowley as a proponent of a new religious movement does not fit neatly into a generalized construct of a charismatic revelator. Rather, it was a position into which he grew without seemingly abandoning his prior worldview. Before he assumed the role of a prophet of a new age and promulgator of a scripture, *The Book of the Law* (1904), that could not be changed "so much as the style of a letter," as a university student he sought to understand philosophy and empirical science. His reaction against the fundamentalist faith of his childhood predicated on biblical inerrancy led him to seek for religious truths that could be justified in terms of the science and philosophy to which he was first exposed while at Cambridge. Crowley's signal contribution to Western esotericism was his attempt to legitimate his essentially religious approach to reality through appeals to elements of

The path of Perseus and the path of Midas

philosophical and empirical skepticism. His first critical interpreter, J. F. C. Fuller, described Crowley's philosophical positiona as "Crowleyanity: or in other words, according to the mind of the reader: -- Pyrrhonic-Zoroastrianism, Pyrrhonic-Mysticism, Sceptical Transcendentalism, Sceptical Theurgy, Sceptical-Energy, Scientific-Illuminism, or what you will; for in short it is the conscious communion with God on the part of an Atheist, a transcending of reason by scepticism of the instrument, and the limitation of scepticism by direct consciousness of the Absolute." In Crowley's view, contemporary science and revealed religion had failed to answer their own questions because of their inherent methodological limitations; the ultimate truths were to be found only in a union of their epistemological strengths. Crowley chose as the motto of his occult journal, *The Equinox*, "The Method of Science; the Aim of Religion." Magick was the third way.[297]

Crowley was clearly deeply traumatized by his upbringing within an extraordinarily confining literalist Christian cult (one which, because interpreting the ancient scriptures of the Bible literally, when they are manifestly not literal at all, was bound to run into all kinds of profound contradictions and errors when trying to apply its doctrines of "inerrancy" as a guide for human life). Crowley himself characterized his upbringing as "a childhood in hell."[298]

In the first essay in the collection edited by Bogdan and Starr, a study entitled "The Sorcerer and His Apprentice: Aleister Crowley and the Magical Exploration of Edwardian Subjectivity," Professor Alex Owen of Northwestern University describes Crowley's quest to free himself of his egoic self (which Crowley in his own writings referred to as "the I" and also as "the Ego") and unleash his higher self, his magical self.

Professor Owen explores the significance of a transformative ritual which Crowley performed in December of 1909 in the desert outside of Bou Saada (in modern-day Algeria, at that time

Chapter Fourteen

under French colonial administration following France's 1830 invasion and bloody conquest which involved forty-five years of fighting and the decimation of Algeria's indigenous population), during which Crowley had to summon and defeat a being he himself later described when writing about the incident as "Choronzon, the mighty devil that inhabiteth the outermost Abyss." In her penetrating analysis of this significant event, Professor Owen writes:

> It was magical practice rather than psychoanalytic theory that taught Crowley that the apparent coherence of human selfhood is illusory. Although Crowley held to the idea of a hidden essential "Self," a unique core at the heart of the man, magic taught him that the "I" of Aleister Crowley was only one possible self among many. The most terrible lesson that Crowley had to learn, however, and he learned it in the desert, was that it is precisely this "I" -- that which apparently secures one's place in the worldly order of things -- that must undergo dissolution in the ordeal of the Abyss. Crowley understood the Abyss to be a great gulf fixed between "intelligible intuition" and "the intellect." Other commentators have seen it as "an imaginary gulf" between the real and the ideal, or "the gulf existing between individual and cosmic consciousness." As in all magical practice, however, the Abyss can manifest in physical form, the plastic representation of its assumed qualities. But whether understood in symbolic or literal terms, crossing the Abyss involves the final and irrevocable abandonment of the "I" along with its accompanying claim to sole rational authority.

> The preamble to confronting the Abyss, and its demonic guardian, Choronzon, is a mental crisis, a "terrible pinnacle of the mind;" to cross the Abyss, "one must abandon utterly and for ever all that one has and is." As Crowley recognized, this is represented in the language of mysticism "as the complete surrender of the self to God" -- mystical death as the prerequisite of mystical union; in secular terms, it is "the

The path of Perseus and the path of Midas

silencing of the human intellect." Crowley, schooled in the magical tradition, conceptualized both Choronzon and the Abyss as having an external reality, and he made no subsequent attempt to amend this view. In psychoanalytical terms, however, terms that Crowley was later to embrace, it can be said that Choronzon is equally a manifestation of the dark, repressed components of the psyche. In this reading, Choronzon's great resistant cry, "I am I," is simultaneously the magician's last cry of horror and terror as he plunges headlong into the Abyss and the emergent voice of the unknown and unpatrolled unconscious. Characterized by Disintegration, Dispersion, and Chaos, qualities suggestive of the fracturing experience of modernity, the Abyss is both symbolic and real. It is emblematic of breakdown -- the breakdown of the personal self as manifested by the ego, the uncoupling of the body from the "I," and the dissolution of everyday consciousness. It marks the formal erasure of the boundary between the conscious and the unconscious, an erasure that the future magus must invoke at will. Successful negotiation of the Abyss represents the ultimate test of high adeptship. The magus is one who can establish a harmonious relationship with the unconscious, working with it to achieve "change in conformity with the Will." [299]

Those familiar with the work of Mircea Eliade (1907 - 1986), and his encyclopedic 1951 study *Shamanism: Archaic Techniques of Ecstasy*, will recognize in this ordeal of dissolution and uncoupling the consistent pattern of the initiatory ordeal of shamanic technique worldwide -- a pattern which Giorgio de Santillana and Hertha von Dechend remark upon in *Hamlet's Mill* as being deeply connected to the ancient celestial myths found in all cultures around the globe.

Writing of this initiatory ordeal found in shamanic cultures across many continents, the authors of *Hamlet's Mill* write:

> The real shamanistic initiation of the soul happens in the world of spirits -- while his body lies unconscious in his tent for days --

Chapter Fourteen

who dismember the candidate in the most thorough and drastic manner and sew him together afterwards with iron wire, or reforge him, so that he becomes a new being capable of feats which go beyond the human. The duties of a shaman are to heal diseases which are caused by hostile spirits who have entered the body of the patient, or which occur because the soul has left the body and cannot find the way back. Often the shaman is responsible for guiding the souls of the deceased to the abode of the dead, as he also escorts the souls of sacrificed animals to the sky. His help is needed, too, when the hunting season is bad; he must find out where the game is. In order to find out all the things which he is expected to know, the shaman has to ascend to the highest sky to get the information from his god -- or go into the underworld. On his way he has to fight hostile spirits, and/or rival shamans, and tremendous duels are fought. Both combatants have with them their helping spirits in animal form, and much shape-shifting takes place. In fact, these fantastic duels form the bulk of shamanistic stories. The last echoes are the so-called "magic-flights" in fairy tales. The shaman's soul ascends to the sky when he is in a state of ecstasy; in order to get into this state, he needs his drum which serves him as a "horse," the drumstick as a "whip." Now the "frame" within the shaman proper acts, that is, the world conception [. . .] with its three "domains," with seven or nine skies, one above the other, and with corresponding "underworlds," with the "world-pillar" running through the center of the whole system, crowned by the "north Nail" or "World Nail" (Polaris), goes farther back than Indian and Iranian culture, namely to the most ancient Near East, whence India and Iran derived their idea of a "cosmos" -- a cosmos being in itself by no means an obvious assumption. The shaman climbing the "stairs" or notches of his post or tree, pretending that his soul ascends at the same time to the highest sky, does the very same thing as the Mesopotamian priest did when mounting to the top of his seven-storied pyramid, the ziqqurat, representing the planetary spheres.[300]

The path of Perseus and the path of Midas

Note of course that the shaman can be male or female, as Mircea Eliade discusses extensively in his comprehensive examination of shamanism around the globe, undertaken at a time when the first-hand memory of the undisturbed institution of shamanism was still largely intact in many cultures, prior to the sweeping tide of onrushing modernity which later washed over nearly every corner of the world.

Indeed, Eliade notes a pattern, not present in all shamanic societies but consistent enough to manifest in multiple cultures on different continents around the world, of shamans who transcend the understood boundaries of their society's gender norms, assuming the clothing and identity normative for persons of the opposite sex.[301] It seems reasonable to consider this widespread pattern as being related to the concept that Alex Owen is articulating when she writes of "the final and irrevocable abandonment of the 'I' along with its accompanying claim to sole rational authority" which the magician undergoes during the dissolutive encounter with the Abyss.

The discerning reader will also have noted in the quotation from *Hamlet's Mill* cited above the reference to the ascension of the shaman through "seven or nine skies," which Santillana and Von Dechend equate with the seven planetary spheres (in a footnote they opine that the number nine may result from the addition of the two lunar "nodes" to the traditional seven) -- and will have recalled the seven initiatory grades of the ancient cult of Sol Invictus. Indeed, these grades are depicted in the form of a ladder in an important mosaic found running along the axis of the floor of the remains of the ancient Mithraeum of Felicissimus in Ostia, shown on the following page.

Indeed, as Professor Roger Beck points out in his essay "If So, How? Representing 'Coming Back to Life' in the Mysteries of Mithras," which we examined in connection with the layout of the Mithraeum of the Seven Spheres at Ostia, the ancient philosopher Origen in *Contra Celsum* describes the Mithras initiate as following the route of the soul "through and out" of the

Chapter Fourteen

celestial revolutions of the fixed stars and the planets (implying seven spheres for the planets plus an eighth for the fixed stars) along a path which is symbolized in Mithraism by "a seven-gated ladder with an eighth on top."[302]

In other words, we have here ancient evidence that the seven grades of Mithraism correspond to a ladder to be climbed, even as the shaman in cultures around the world climbs a tree with seven branches or a pole with seven notches as part of his or her ecstatic journey, understood to be directly related to the seven layers in the celestial realm corresponding to the motions of the heavenly spheres.

It has been remarked upon by many observers that when Gilgamesh and Enkidu travel to the celestial forest to find the great cedar whose top pierces the heavens and to confront the dreaded Humbaba (I would add: much as Crowley confronted Choronzon), they travel across seven hills as they make their way to the appointed place. This pattern, then, is found in texts that are among the most ancient surviving texts in the world (at least of those that are known to us at this time).

It is also notable that in the system propounded by John Nelson Darby (1800 - 1882), one of the three founders of the original Plymouth Brethren, the radical literalist sect of which Crowley's parents were devout followers, there are seven "dispensations" (or Seven Ages) -- a system known as Dispensationalism and still widely accepted among fundamentalists to this day, including throughout the US "Bible Belt" and within influential literalist Protestant Christian seminaries.

As Henrik Bogdan of the University of Gothenburg remarks in his essay "Envisioning the Birth of a New Aeon: Dispensationalism and Millenarianism in the Thelemic Tradition," the system of *Thelema* (from a Greek word meaning "will") that Crowley designed (or received) retains some of the core aspects of the same dispensationalist fundamentalism that alienated him as a child.

Bogdan writes, "Although Crowley rebelled against the religious views of his parents when still in his teens -- and continued this revolt throughout his life -- it is striking that two characterstic aspects of the religious worldview of the Plymouth Brethren, the importance placed on the study of the Holy Scripture and the notion of dispensationalism, are echoed in the religious system of Thelema."[303]

Chapter Fourteen

And, returning full circle to the vision of Jacob's dream in Genesis chapter 28, we find the pattern of the ladder which reaches up to heaven dramatized there as well, just as we find it in the ecstatic ascent undertaken by shamanic initiates in numerous traditional cultures, and just as we find it in the initiatory grades of the cult of Mithras, and in the architecture of ancient seven-story ziggurats noted by the authors of *Hamlet's Mill*.

It is one of the ways that the world's ancient wisdom points us towards the recovery of our disconnected essential self, and it should be abundantly clear that Crowley himself was engaged in the very serious quest of recovering his own essential self through his Thelema.

We come back then to the question of what this reconnection to the higher self -- and through the recovered higher self, connection to the awe-inducing higher realm, the invisible realm, the realm of the very gods themselves -- gives us, or allows us.

And, as the many examples of "judgment myths" from cultures around the world clearly demonstrate (such as the myth of the choice given to Solomon, and the myth of the choice given to Midas, and the myth of the famous Judgment of Paris in which three goddesses each offer Paris a different divine reward if he will pronounce her the most beautiful), the answer given by the world's ancient wisdom appears to be that we can obtain from the divine realm gifts that bless or gifts that curse -- gifts that elevate ourselves and others, and gifts that objectify and even destroy ourselves and others.

This answer makes clear why many contemporary analysts who examine the world of the occult come to the conclusions that they do, such as the observations of Christopher Knowles and David Icke cited earlier as examples of the view that the gods are "inter-dimensional entities" whose purpose is to "lock people in a belief-system" and to "suck you dry" (as stated by David Icke), and that contact with the world of the gods can get "really dark and heavy" and all boil down to "raping thirteen year-old girls when you really get to the core of the symbolism" (as Chris Knowles observes about modern dark applications of the ancient system).

Aleister Crowley, for example, clearly achieved some success in recovering his essential self, from whom his egoic mind had been alienated due to traumatic childhood – and (it seems clear) he achieved significant levels of personal empowerment from that process. But if we wonder what Crowley might have answered when given the offer that we see extended in the ancient myths to figures such as Midas and Solomon and Paris, we find a revealing glimpse in a letter he wrote in 1905 at the age of nineteen or twenty, to his friend Gerald Festus Kelly (with whose sister Crowley soon eloped): "I want blasphemy, murder, rape, revolution, anything good or bad, but strong."[304]

The power of the hidden realm is by no means exlusively a power for helping others -- it can also be tapped in order to aggrandize and enrich oneself and also to harm and oppress others. We see this dramatized in other myths, such as the ancient Sanskrit epic of Ramayana, in which the most powerful of all the Rakshasas, a class of supernatural beings described in the Vedas who oppose the Vedic gods and who thus are sometimes described in western translation as *demons* or *titans*, is given whatever he might ask for from the great god Brahma. This mighty Rakshasa, named Ravana, becomes the primary antogonist in the epic of Ramayana.

Ravana's main pasttimes appear to be wreaking havoc: flying through the cosmos in his aerial chariot Pushpaka, accompanied by his army of fellow evil supernaturals, slaying anyone unable to withstand his martial prowess, and abducting beautiful women.

The gods and other benevolent supernatural beings are unable to stop Ravana. The blessed Lord Brahma has awarded a boon to Ravana, as explained by the assembled gods when speaking to Vishnu in the text of the Ramayana:

> "Ravana has long practiced austerities, by means of which he has won the favour of the world-renowned Brahma. That deity has granted him a boon, by which he is rendered invulnerable

Chapter Fourteen

> to all but man. Considering man of no account, he does not fear him. The boon bestowed on him by Shri Brahma has made him arrogant and he is bringing destruction to the three worlds and carrying off women in violence."[305]

In the same epic, the god Brahma explains that when he granted a boon to Ravana as a reward for Ravana's practice of austerities, Ravana could have asked for whatever he wanted, but the demon asked only for invulnerability to supernatural beings. Brahma explains:

> "It was granted to Ravana that no gandharva, yaksha or deva should be able to slay him, but thinking man to be of no account, he did not ask to be made invulnerable in regard to man; therefore, none but man can destroy him."[306]

Upon hearing this explanation, the celestials implore the god Vishnu to incarnate once more among the children of men in order to restore balance to the cosmos, since Ravana's power has unbalanced things so egregiously. Vishnu incarnates in the person of four sons of King Dasaratha of Ayodhya, the eldest and most powerful of them being Rama, the central protagonist of the Ramayana, which tells the story of Rama's struggle against Ravana.

The Ramayana tells us that when Vishnu heard of Ravana's answer to the offer of Brahma to bestow any boon for which Ravana might ask, Vishnu told the assembled gods to relax: he would take care of the situation and slay Ravana and usher in a period of great peace and blessing on earth.[307] From this episode we see that even though the gods will sometimes grant boons which are used by the evil to do evil, these wicked requests will come to wicked ends. The gods themselves will see to it, bringing about their desired purpose by acting *through* men and women.

Ravana was given access to the boon of Brahma, just as Solomon was given access to a boon from Jehovah, but Ravana's choice was more like Crowley's stated desire: "blasphemy, murder, rape, revolution, anything good or bad, but strong."

From examples such as this one, we can see that the employment of the power of the celestial realm for the purpose of wreaking violence and harm upon other men and women, of enriching and empowering oneself at the expense of others, is far from the intended purpose of the gods, according to the ancient myths.

And yet it is also abundantly evident that, with the decline of the power of literalist Christianity over the population (compared with that exercised by the church in previous centuries), those accustomed to living (like the suitors in the Odyssey) off of the labor and wealth of others and at their expense now must increasingly employ the more secretive and occult instrument, the underground twin of the more overt institution – and that in doing so they think nothing of inflicting violence and trauma upon innocent men and women and children in their quest to continue enriching themselves.

Examples abound and could easily fill an entire series of books, but the two clearest would probably be two of the most significant traumatic events inflicted upon the people of the United States during the post-World War II period (and, in their aftermath, unleashing trauma and misery on people around the world as well): the murder of President John F. Kennedy in Dallas in 1963, and the crimes of September 11, 2001.

These traumatic events, each of which resulted in almost immediate escalation of military wars of aggression upon the men and women of other nations, can be shown to have incorporated undeniable aspects of occult ritual, indicating a desire by the criminal perpetrators to tap into the power of the unseen realm in order to help further their wicked designs.

Researcher Michael Joseph has published a video entitled "33 Occult Ritual Aspects of the JFK Assassination" on his YouTube channel entitled *Schism206*.

The video's original publication date is October 31, 2016 and it can be viewed by going to his YouTube channel rather than by searching for it (since it is published under "unlisted" status).

Chapter Fourteen

That video demonstrates that the layout of Dealey Plaza and the streets leading to the "Triple Underpass" beneath the railroad overpass which crosses above Elm Street, Main Street, and Commerce Street forms an unmistakable parallel to the Kabbalistic "Tree of Life" pattern, as shown in the diagrams below:

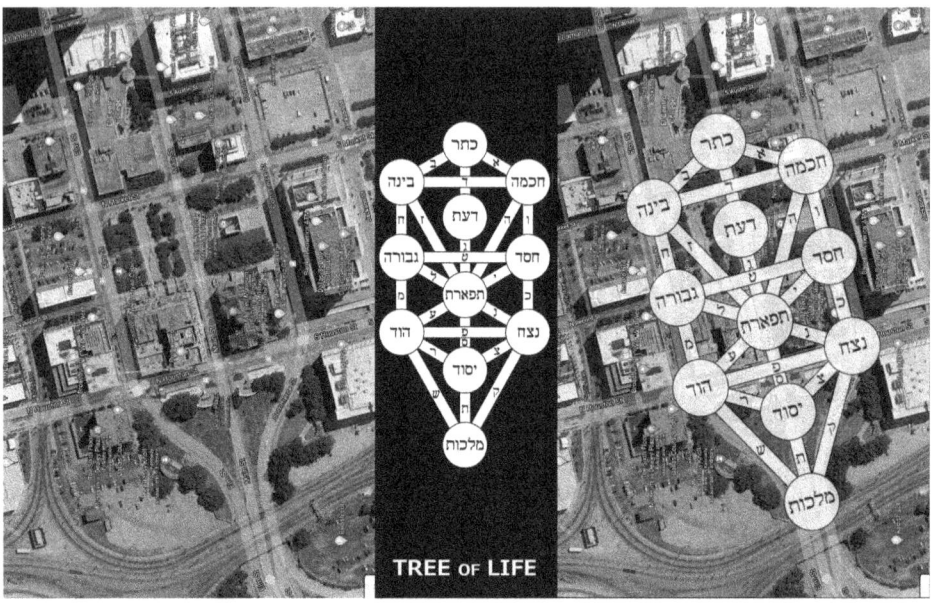

The Tree of Life diagram shown above plays a central role in western mysticism, including in Jewish Kabbalah and in Hermetic tradition (including the form of mysticism practiced by the Hermetic Order of the Golden Dawn).

The pattern consists of three vertical lines, often called "columns" or "pillars," and three horizontal crossbars, creating a series of "emanations," or "illuminations," or "nodes" as indicated above (by circles, each with a name and different spiritual aspects), traditionally understood to be ten in number due to the fact that the top two nodes of the cenral column are considered to be two aspects of the same emanation (one conscious, one unconscious).

As Michael Joseph explains in the video referenced above, Elm Street would correspond to the North Pillar (on the left side of

The path of Perseus and the path of Midas

the Tree of Life schematic), and Commerce Street would correspond to the South Pillar (on the right side of the Tree of Life), with Main Street of course as the Central Pillar. According to occult traditions going back many centuries (if not millennia), these pillars have specific characteristics and esoteric significance, as do all of the nodes or eminences as well as each of the twenty-two connecting paths in between them.

The Left Pillar of the Tree of Life is traditionally known as the *Pillar of Severity*, as explained in the video -- and it is towards this portion of the pattern that the presidential motorcade turned on the fateful day on November 22, 1963 when the President of the United States was murdered in broad daylight in Dealey Plaza.

On the next page, we see a closeup of a contemporary photograph of the scene of the murder, included in the Warren Commission cover-up report which falsely upheld the ridiculous proposition that a lone assassin was responsible for the murder of President Kennedy. To the original photograph (from Warren Commission Exhibit 359) I have added labels giving the names of most of the significant buildings and streets, as well as a wide arrow showing the route of the motorcade, and a starburst or explosion symbol showing the area where the president was shot.

In the interest of keeping the image from being too cluttered, I did not add a label showing the infamous "grassy knoll" or the location of Abraham Zapruder, who captured the only film footage of the shooting to have been released to the public to this day. However, for those not familiar with the scene of this event (an event with which every single citizen of the United States should see it as his or her duty to study and understand: the duty, in fact, of every other man and woman on the planet as well, since it is an event which changed the course of the history of the world, leading directly to changes in the foreign and domestic policy of the United States which would have an exponentially increasing negative impact on world events for the following fifty-seven years thus far, with no sign at this point that the negative changes will be slowing down), the region which has come to be known as the "grassy knoll" can be found in this photograph just within the

Chapter Fourteen

lower-left corner of the area enclosed by the "starburst" or "explosion" that I've drawn on the Exhibit 359 photograph. Alternately, you can find it by looking at the area to the left of the first car you see on Elm Street below the outline of the "starburst explosion." There was a picket fence where the four white cars are parked side-by-side to the left of that car and below the starburst: this is known as the "stockade picket fence" and would have run along the line formed by the front of the four parked cars. It is thought that shooters were likely positioned just behind this fence and just above the location of these four cars.

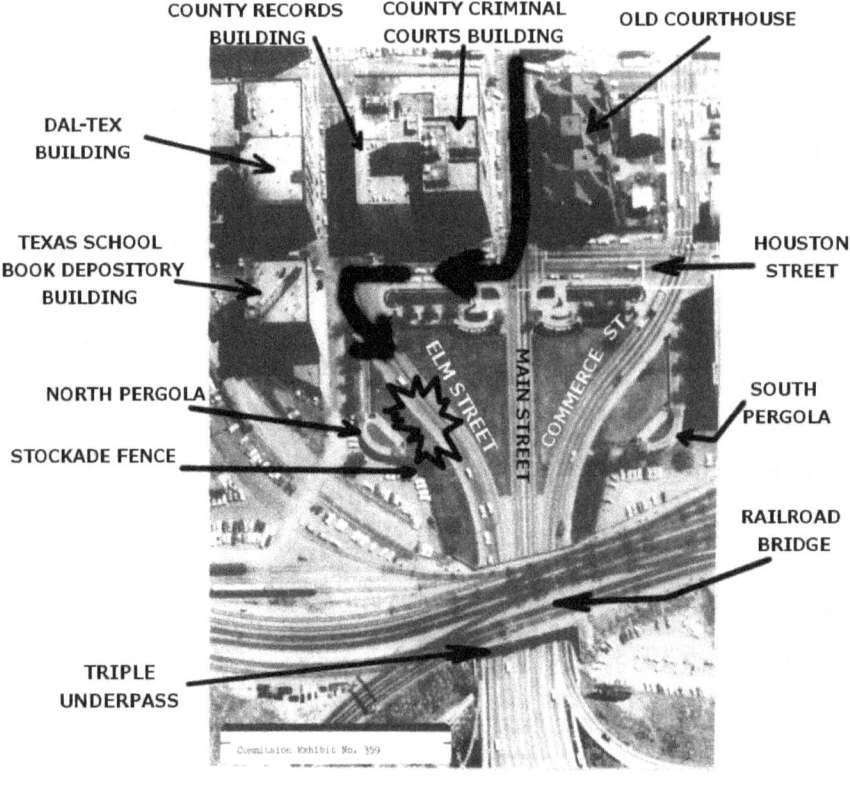

COMMISSION EXHIBIT 359

The location of Abraham Zapruder and his Bell & Howell Zoomatic movie camera would have been at the lower-right corner of the "D-shaped" or "half-moon-shaped" feature known as the "north pergola" which is just left of the "starburst explosion" that I've drawn on the photo (it is also sometimes called "Bryan's

460

The path of Perseus and the path of Midas

pergola" -- you can see that there is another pergola opposite it on the right of Commerce Street, which was called the "south pergola" or "Cocktrell's pergola").

The route of the motorcade, then, can be seen to have esoteric and occult significance, as each node and each path and each pillar in the Tree of Life pattern is imbued with specific associations in the various occult systems that have been preserved through the centuries. Each of the paths along the Tree of Life is also traditionally associated with a specific card in the tarot deck.

According to Joseph's analysis in the video, there is occult ritual significance in the presidential motorcade's turning from Main Street (corresponding to the Central Pillar) towards Elm Street (the North Pillar, associated with darkness and strength) along Houston Street (corresponding to the 27th path -- associated with the Tower card, associated with the direction of darkness and the north, and a number associated with the death of many famous musicians later in the twentieth century) and then onto Elm Street towards the triple underpass (this part of Elm Street being associated with the 31st path, associated with the Judgement card in the tarot).

As Michael Joseph also explains in his video, the pillars feature prominently in the symbology of Freemasonry down through the centuries, with the left pillar typically identified as Boaz and associated with strength and with the north, and the right pillar typically identified as Jachin and associated with beauty and with the south, just as we see in the layout of Dealey Plaza in Dallas where the president was assassinated.

Freemasonic drawings in the public record, such as the illustration shown below, published in a book entitled *Masonic Emblems* by the publishing house of George Kenning of London, Liverpool and Glasgow in 1874, show two pillars at the left and right of the drawing, with a sun emblem near the left pillar and a moon emblem near the right pillar, which is typical of Masonic

Chapter Fourteen

illustrations in the public record (and is found in the Masonic tracing-board Michael Joseph includes in his video during the discussion that begins at approximately 0:02:58 in the video).

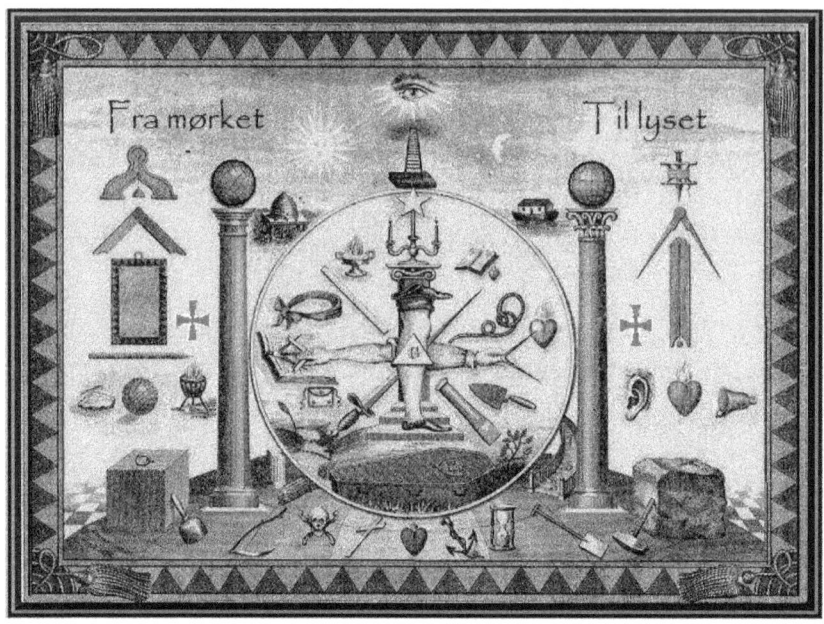

Note that the above diagram includes a third pillar, in the center of the diagrams, in between the pillars on the left and right. This central pillar is above the other two, and immediately below the symbol of the all-seeing eye. Based on even a very superficial familiarity with the three pillars of the Tree of Life, it is not difficult to detect correspondences between the Tree of Life symbol and the pattern of Masonic illustration in the diagram shown above (as well as in the tracing-board included in the Michael Joseph video).

One need not accept all of Michael Joseph's proposed conclusions, nor agree with him on every point of his argument, in order to concede the presence of abundant evidence which suggests the strong possibility that the assassination of President John F. Kennedy contained elements of occult ritual.

The information in the Michael Joseph video, abundant as it is, might perhaps be dismissed as only an astonishing collection of

The path of Perseus and the path of Midas

coincidence, were it not for the fact that an overwhelming amount of research has been conducted in the years following that murderous day in 1963 which argues beyond any possible doubt that the story presented to the world regarding the assassination of President Kennedy cannot be anything other than a complete lie: that Lee Harvey Oswald could not have been responsible for the shooting (and in fact probably never fired a weapon that day at all), and that a carefully-planned coup d'etat had been carried out in broad daylight in Dallas on November 22, after which the real details of the killing were assiduously covered up by the Warren Commission and by the controlled media.

There is no need to recite that evidence here: this chapter has focused only on the added evidence which suggests that not only was the murder of John F. Kennedy in Dallas that day the product of a cabal of treasonous conspirators operating at the highest levels within the government -- with enough clout to put together the Warren Commission cover-up, led by the Chief Justice of the Supreme Court and composed of Warren Commission members who included the head of the CIA, two US Senators and two members of the US House of Representatives (one of whom, Gerald Ford, later became an unelected president), and a former president of the World Bank (John J. McCloy, who had previously also been instrumental in the creation of the OSS, the forerunner organization to the CIA, as well as in the internment of Japanese-American citizens in prison camps throughout the Second World War).

Anyone who still believes after more than fifty years of evidence to the contrary that the assassination of President Kennedy was the work of a "lone nut" is believing that because the defense mechanism of the egoic mind is desperately deflecting the undeniable weight of the evidence, in order to avoid having to confront the overwhelming fact that the nation was overthrown in 1963 and has been run ever since by those who perpetrated that criminal act.

Chapter Fourteen

We now have evidence, added to all that previous evidence compiled by diligent and serious researchers over the past fifty-seven years, which strongly suggests that not only was it a criminal act committed by a highly-placed cabal of conspirators, but it was also carefully designed to function as an occult ritual.

But the next question which immediately springs to mind, of course, is: "Why?"

Why, if some individual or some group wanted to murder the president and seize control of the nodes of power within the United States, would they do so in such a public manner -- especially if they wanted to keep the coup d'etat largely hidden from the public, allowing them to continue voting and joining political parties just as if nothing had happened? Why not quietly poison the president in private, in a manner that would be very difficult to detect (for example) instead of murdering him in the middle of Dealey Plaza in the middle of the day?

And, even beyond those questions, why in the world would whatever secret organization was responsible for this grave crime do so in the form of an occult ritual, one with clear connections to esoteric symbology such as the Tree of Life and one which insightful investigators who knew something about the symbols of Freemasonry and its related esoteric organizations might recognize as having parallels to the symbology of the pillars depicted in Masonic illustrations and symbology?

Channelling Sherlock Holmes in order to try and list all the potential answers, there are several different possibilities:

One possibility might be that someone is trying to frame the Freemasons or other occult secret societies, but that possibility seems pretty remote, since the connection to the Tree of Life is so obscure that decades of dedicated JFK researchers did not even notice it (the fact is that the Tree of Life symbol is not widely known among the general populace -- even among dedicated JFK researchers: it is a symbol that is very familiar to those interested in western occultism, but not to many others).

The path of Perseus and the path of Midas

If perpetrators were trying to frame an esoteric group (by selecting an assassination site shaped like the Tree of Life symbol), we would expect those perpetrators to drop some hints in order to help point out the connection, in the event that their "frame job" was too subtle and nobody picked up on the connection. We wouldn't expect them to take fifty years to drop those hints!

An alternative possibility which must be considered is that, far from being a frame-up, the selection of a site with clear parallels to the Tree of Life diagram was made because this site and this symbology was judged by the perpetrators to be necessary in order to set up resonances in the unseen realm. In other words, the murder of President Kennedy was intended as an occult ritual and one with actual "operational effects" to shape some outcome or achieve some desired result.

Regardless of what the individual reader thinks of the reality of the power of occult rituals, and regardless of what the majority of the members of the general public thinks of the reality of the power of occult rituals, we have already demonstrated that there are those who believe in the use of specific practices, including ritual magic, to tap into the power of the occult realm: Peter Levenda has filled an entire 425-page volume with evidence that high-ranking Nazis during the war, including members of Hitler's entourage, members of the SS, and the head of the SS himself (and probably Hitler as well), believed in the power of the occult realm and actively sought access to it (and Levenda also documents incidents in which the Allies did so as well).

It is very likely that such a desire to tap into the influence of the unseen realm is at least *part* of the explanation for the occult aspects of the assassination including the chosen location in Dealey Plaza. Not only do I suspect that those who organized the murder hold the belief that the invisible realm can have an influence on events and outcomes in the physical realm, but I also strongly suspect that such a belief is grounded in reality. Another

Chapter Fourteen

term sometimes used for the invisible realm or the unseen realm is the phrase "non-ordinary reality" -- and I do not think it is unreasonable to believe that non-ordinary reality can have an impact or an influence on events which take place in what we would recognize as "ordinary reality."

Indeed, we have already examined at some length one such event: the experience of eleven-year-old Norman Ollestad during the ordeal in February of 1979, and the possibility that his very survival hinged on certain "hunches" that two other people received, and (importantly) hunches that those other people decided to *follow*, as well as on his own inexplicable vision of a meadow with human habitation towards which he tried to navigate -- a meadow which did indeed exist but which he could not have seen from where he was on the mountainside.

As discussed earlier in the examination of the episode in the Odyssey in which Odysseus is trying to swim to shore, and also in the examination of the quest of Perseus to slay the Gorgons, the gods do not actually pick Odysseus up and bring him to shore, nor do they actually slay Medusa for Perseus -- the myths appear to teach that help from the divine world often works in the form of *inspiration*, and *influence*, and *assistance*, but that even with this help, we still need to take action ourselves.

Certainly this pattern is what we see in the account of the ordeal of young Norman Ollestad: Pat Chapman received a "hunch" (or we might say she received some kind of inexplicable *inspiration*) to go investigate the meadow that day -- but she still had to take action herself and go do it. Later that same day, Glenn Farmer had a "hunch" to "give it one more shot" while searching for the plane crash and any survivors, but he still had to follow that hunch and start yelling into the seemingly-empty wilderness to see if anyone could hear him.

In a similar way, Norman Ollestad had a vision of a meadow that he decided to try to steer towards during his long descent off the mountain, but he still had to take action with courage and skill

The path of Perseus and the path of Midas

and intelligence (not to mention all the lessons that his father had taught him) in order to actually get down that mountain and make his way towards the meadow that he "saw" (even if we cannot explain how he could have seen it).

Even if access to the invisible realm, the realm of non-ordinary reality, does not in and of itself *guarantee* success, if it may in some inexplicable way help to increase the likelihood of success, then that subtle increase will be sought after, especially in situations where the outcome is seen as highly uncertain and where the consequences of failure are particularly severe (such as in cases of war -- or, one might add, in the case of an attempt to illegally seize control of a country by murdering its elected leader).

In the 2002 preface to his second edition of *Unholy Alliance*, Peter Levenda writes the following of those who dismiss occultism, ritual and magic as unscientific or as "pseudo-science":

> One might as well call Roman Catholicism, the paintings of Picasso, or the films of Marilyn Monroe pseudo-science, if one wishes to devalue them speedily and does not have the intellectual gifts to do so on their own terms. One might as well complain about the unnecessary complexity of Rube Goldberg machinery: confusing form with function is often a characteristic of the cultural critic as it is of the devout scientist, a case of wondering why roses are red and violets are blue. And as much as the scientist scoffs at magic, in equal terms does the politician, military commander, and terrorist mastermind employ magic as one of a specialized arsenal of the arcane, alongside psychological warfare, disinformation, Vietnamization, and assassination. War is the ultimate proof of utility: if a weapon works, it stays in the arsenal. Magic has been part of the arsenal of politics and of war (the continuation, after all, of politics by other means) for millennia, alongside the club, the seige engine, gunpowder, advertising campaigns, and dirty tricks.[308]

Chapter Fourteen

Thus, one explanation which must be considered in seeking to explain the evidence of occult ritual aspects in the assassination of John F. Kennedy is the explanation that those who planned that murder believed that "if a weapon works, it stays in the arsenal," and that they had reason to believe that occult ritual (to put it bluntly) "works."

Towards what ends might this occult ritual murder have been carried out? What corresponding conditions did its planners hope to establish in the realm of non-ordinary reality? What events did its planners hope to set in motion (or, what events did they hope to carry out afterwards, events whose success they hoped to make even slightly more likely through the performance of this ritual in this particular way)?

We cannot know for certain, but one outcome they likely desired would have been the same outcome we have seen in our examination of the deliberate dissolution of the Roman Empire: the removal of obstacles to the elitist system, the system of exploiting the labor and natural resources of others which was instituted after the fall of Rome in the form of European feudalism, and which later expanded into European colonialism and imperialism.

John F. Kennedy was openly supportive of independent national leaders in exploited nations ("Third World" nations, today called "developing nations") such as Patrice Lumumba (1925 - 1961), the first prime minister of an independent Republic of the Congo, a nation which had been absolutely brutalized by Belgian imperialism lasting from the late nineteenth century until 1960, when Congo achieved its independence from Belgium.

Kennedy was also supportive of the first president of Indonesia, Sukarno (1901 - 1970), who had been an important leader in the independence movement against Dutch colonial rule of Indonesia, and one of the leaders who declared Indonesia independent in 1945 (and led the resistance against efforts to re-impose colonial rule, until the Netherlands recognized the

Republic of Indonesia in 1949). Kennedy had a trip planned to visit Sukarno but was murdered before it could take place.

And of course, Kennedy opposed further escalation in Vietnam and actually had a plan in place to withdraw US military forces from Vietnam, a plan which was immediately overturned just days after his murder. This intention to withdraw from Vietnam is often covered over (or denied outright) by defenders of US policy after the death of Kennedy, but has been established by author John Newman in *JFK and Vietnam* (1992), which builds on the research and analysis of professor and poet Peter Dale Scott in *The War Conspiracy* (1972).

Thus one (rather mundane) aim may well have been the continued exploitation of former colonies and the removal of those who stood in the way of that exploitation (Lumumba and Sukarno were both later deposed, and Lumumba was executed, and their replacements were *happy* to allow western corporations to continue the privatization of the tremendous natural resources bestowed by nature upon both lands, Indonesia and the Congo).

But another more ambitious aim might have been the reversal of the rising tide of political sentiment which rejected the injustices of exploitation and oppression of men and women throughout the developing world, and opposed the seizure of natural resources by private corporations for the enrichment of the owners of those corporations and at the expense of everyone else. That rising tide, we have already observed, was frightening enough to serve as a possible explanation for the creation of the Nazis during the first half of the twentieth century, as a weapon to stamp out socialist unrest in Germany (and elsewhere in western Europe) and as a weapon to be turned towards Russia.

If the ritual murder of John F. Kennedy and the subsequent murders of Malcolm X, Martin Luther King, Jr., and Robert F. Kennedy were intended to stem this tide, and to begin to turn it back, and to usher in a new era in which private interests would increasingly win out against popular and governmental

Chapter Fourteen

restrictions on their ability to monopolize the commons and the natural resources bestowed upon the nation by nature and the gods, then perhaps the ritual was successful, from the perspective of those who desire such a scenario.

And, if the aim of the planners and perpetrators of this crime involved unleashing other forces of evil, or influences of evil, upon the world . . . perhaps they succeeded in that aim as well.

And there is yet another possibility in our search for an explanation for the presence of the clearly-discernable occult aspects present in the slaying of JFK, an explanation which is by no means mutually exclusive with the possibility just discussed -- and that is that by killing the president in a way which can be seen to be tied to knowledge of esoteric matters (even though doing so might indicate that the perpetrators included those with knowledge of such matters), the planners of the killing were *sending a message.*

Leaving clues at the scene of the crime which point to your identity does not ordinarily seem like something that you would want to do, when planning a crime -- unless, by leaving those clues, you are trying to send a message.

What kind of message might the planners of the murder of JFK have been sending, and to whom might they have been trying to send that message?

Again, we don't know for certain, but we can make some deductions based on the abundance of evidence, and also based on the perspective provided by the larger framework we have been exploring, regarding the "visible" instrument of the literalist Christian church and the more "invisible" instrument of the underground secret societies descended from the cult of Sol Invictus (primarily Freemasonry down through the centuries, but branching into various related societies and networks as well).

The decline in the ability of the defenders of the old order (that oligarchical socio-political order imposed during feudalism and

The path of Perseus and the path of Midas

the ensuing centuries) to command assent through literalist Christian doctrine over larger and larger wedges of the population has necessitated a concomitant rise in activity of the secret branch of control, the branch which in ordinary circumstances is generally kept on "safe" but which is switched to "fire" when other control measures begin to lose their grip.

As that segment of the mechanism of control rises to greater prominence on the world stage, it appears likely (based on the evidence) that it often sends cryptic messages identifying itself as the one acting, the one exercising agency, and that it does so using the ancient language of symbology and numerology preserved among the descendants of those who worked to eliminate the ancient system while preserving aspects of its knowledge for their own use.

These messages can take the form of esoteric symbols and patterns, and of specific significant numbers (including the precessional numbers of 72 and 108, as well as 216, 432, and other multiples of 108), and also the number 33 (associated with the number of vertebrae in the spinal column of the human skeleton -- seven cervical vertebrae, twelve thoracic vertebrae, five lumbar vertebrae, five fused vertebrae in the sacrum, and four fused vertebrae in the coccyx -- as well as with the number of initiatory grades in many branches of Freemasonry), among others.

One reason for sending these messages may be to inform other members of these far-reaching networks (particularly the high-ranking members: the extent to which all participants in secret societies are aware of the deep history of these groups and their operational purpose is not known, but logically we would expect it to be limited), so that they can recognize the handiwork of their fellows.

One would expect, for example, that when the location at which John F. Kennedy is murdered is examined for its latitude, and found to be very close to the thirty-third parallel, this information would be recognized as a possible coded sign by members of

Chapter Fourteen

secret organizations which ascribe tremendous significance to the number thirty-three. If those same observers within occult networks were to then observe that the streets of Dealey Plaza form a pattern having unmistakable parallels to the Tree of Life, this would act as a coded confirmation that their network (or a related network) had a hand in the plan to murder the President of the United States, and would perhaps inform them that this momentous event was part of a deep occult ritual as well.

Thus, one answer to the question of *for whom this message might be intended* would be, "For the initiates of the secret network, descended from that original secret society of Sol Invictus Mithras -- and in particular for the higher-ranking members of the inner circle who would be expected to be privy to such secrets, even if the general membership is not let in on such secrets -- so that wherever they happen to be at the time, they can immediately recognize the actions of their own organization."

But perhaps the more important *additional* answer to that question would be to recognize that the other intended recipients of that coded message is . . . we ourselves.

As strange as it may seem at first blush, to assert that the perpetrators of these heinous crimes (including the crime of the murder of an elected president, a crime which should by rights be categorized as treason) would deliberately leave their calling card at the scene of the crime, not merely to inform other members of their secret cabal but also to make manifest, to any who care to take the trouble to really investigate, who was responsible for such brazen violence, we can actually see that these perpetrators might have excellent reasons for doing so.

Why?

The old order, the oppressive order of feudalism, by which the gifts of the land and the blessings of nature are appropriated by a privileged few, with the rest of the men and women of the land given the equivalent of the scraps, was held in place by the threat of military force: the "nobles," that is to say the warlords, had the horses and the armor and the time to train at skill-at-arms. But even more importantly, that exploitative world-system was upheld by the *awe and dread* induced by the fear of God and his angels in the minds of the deprived majority of the population, awe and dread which was engendered by the institution of the literalist Christian church and its teachings.

Without this awe and dread, which included the threat of eternal damnation and unending torment in the pit of hell for those who opposed the will of God as taught by the clergy, even the superior weaponry and mobility and armor and military training of the warlords could not have prevailed over an organized and angry majority (especially since that majority was also responsible for providing the food that the warlords depended upon for their continued survival).

Even today, in its greatly diminished capacity, that nagging doubt regarding the possibility of being consigned to eternal punishment in hellfire commands a powerful level of influence upon a subset of the population (although by no means close to the level of influence it once carried as a tool for inducing obedience and acquiescence to the exploitative arrangement of the feudal system).

Having watched that awe and dread diminish at an ever-increasing rate over the past century and a half, the beneficiaries of the exploitative systems of aristocratic privilege, and the beneficiaries of the privatization of the resources given by nature, and of colonialism in all its ongoing forms, must realize that (because they are vastly outnumbered by the oppressed and exploited) they need to replicate that essential control mechanism (awe and dread) another way.

That "other way" of inducing awe and dread, among those who no longer believe in the omnipotence of the clergy, is to inculcate a different illusion of omnipotence: the illusion of the omnipotence of the secret societies.

Chapter Fourteen

In other words, they must nurture the illusion of the omnipotence of the mysterious "*they*" (as in: "Look at what *they* are doing! *They* are everywhere!").

The implication is that *they* are not just "everywhere" but also that *they* are all-powerful.

We have seen that the secret branch of the two-headed serpent transitioned from the society of Mithras to the institution of Freemasonry, which appears to remain like a weapon on "safe" within societies where things are already "in control," but which can also be switched into various levels of "fire" mode (the orders of the Templars and Teutonic Knights, mentioned earlier, may represent examples of this weaponization).

We have also seen that the occult initiatory model of Freemasonry propagated various other branches during the eighteenth and nineteenth centuries (as challenges to the authority and omnipotence of the church grew more and more threatening). Some of these variations on Freemasonry include the Rosicrucians, the Bavarian Illuminati, the Hermetic Order of the Golden Dawn, and the *Thule Gesellschaft*, among others.

There is a demonstrable connection between these (and other) esoteric and occult societies and the official agencies of espionage and intelligence, as we saw earlier. All of these organs and agencies can be seen to be primarily "conservative" in nature, in that they are institutions employed by the aristocratic interests (the representatives of that "old order" imposed upon the western world following the fall of Rome) in defense of the system.

Following the end of World War II, we see an exponential increase in the activity and lethality of intelligence agencies, and a corresponding awareness among an increasing percentage of the population (those who are paying attention) that intelligence agencies are increasingly seen "pulling the strings" on the international stage, including in assassinations of leaders (such as those of John F. Kennedy and Patrice Lumumba).

We also see a corresponding increase in overt occult activity, such as in the frightening explosion of serial killers and mass murderers during the 1960s through the 1980s (including the intelligence operation that was the Manson Family that led to the Tate-LaBianca murders, and the Peoples Temple that led to the Jonestown massacre, and the Son of Sam murders, and the Zodiac murders, and so on).

These traumatic events had an effect on every single member of the population, no matter how old or how young. The majority of the people, in the classic pattern of trauma described earlier, suppress the significance of what they are seeing taking place in the world around them, denying the evidence that indicates that criminal outfits such as the Manson Family or the Symbionese Liberation Army could not possibly have stayed in operation without law enforcement looking the other way at some level. This is true of all organized crime, but in the case of the Manson Family and the Symbionese Liberation Army, both of whose leaders were released from prison and furnished with whatever they needed to run their respective organizations, the evidence is particularly obvious. They were being *allowed* (by the very government agencies whose primary charter is to protect the people) to terrorize the population on purpose, for social and political ends.

Such suppression has a splintering effect upon the psyche, as we have already seen. It leads us to suppress and deny that part of us which knows better, which sees through the lie -- but we suppress that truth because the truth is too painful, and we do it without even realizing we are doing it (and, in doing so, we suppress the voice inside that is telling us that something doesn't add up).

A small percentage of the population (an increasing percentage, as the years go on) have faced the truth instead of suppressing that voice inside -- and it is towards this percentage of the population that the repetition of occult symbology and numerology may well be largely directed.

Chapter Fourteen

Why? Because the purpose of these trauma-inducing crimes is to *induce in the population a feeling of awe and dread*, either through splintering the psyche and leading to the suppression of the essential self (the *traumatization* of a large percentage of the people), or through the repetition of esoteric symbology, leading to the increasing impression of omnipotence in the intelligence agencies and / or occult networks perpetrating these heinous crimes.

In other words, these rituals may function essentially as a type of *initiation* of those who learn to look for these symbols, and who then begin to ascribe power to the hierarchy which is employing those symbols, almost as if becoming a low-ranking member of the secret society itself!

The awe and dread formerly induced by the church, and inculcated within the men, women, and children of the populace through the symbolism and rituals of the weekly liturgy presented in the overt and above-ground institution of literalist Christianity has (of necessity, due to the diminished impact of the overt institution) increasingly been replaced by the awe and dread induced by the apparent omnipotence of the covert and underground branches of the same group (a group employing a centuries-old playbook).

As Christopher Knowles, with much of whose analysis I agree, explains in his work, the invisible realm is real, and the forces therein do indeed have power, and dark occultists down through the centuries have accessed that realm to enhance their efforts to control others, magnify their own power, and harm their enemies.

The idea that they would stop seeking to do so in the twentieth (and now the twenty-first) century simply does not make any sense, and does not match the evidence that we see.

On the other hand, as I've already emphasized many times, the evidence should be equally clear that the attempt to access the hidden realm in order to harm and oppress others and to enrich oneself regardless of the collateral damage caused along the way is not the path towards which the ancient myths point us -- quite the contrary. This use of the power of the unseen realm can be shown to be an inversion of the intended purpose as described in the myths.

As well, the myths also teach that access to the divine realm does not make anyone omnipotent. Such access undoubtedly provides inspiration (inspiration beyond what we ourselves might ordinarily be able to see or to conceive), and empowerment, and even the tools we need in order to achieve our full potential. But it does not guarantee success, either for ourselves or for those who are using the ancient knowledge for oppressing others.

Thus, whether David Icke actually believes everything he espouses or not (and I have no reason to believe that he doesn't), it is a mistake to teach that the privileged few who have been oppressing humanity are super-human reptilian beings who are qualitatively different than the rest of humanity.

I'm sure, based on my awe and dread hypothesis, that those oligarchs are quite happy to have someone spreading around the idea that they are not men and women like the rest of us but rather that they are inter-dimensional reptilian entities.

But I would counter by pointing out that, if the vast "non-elite" majority composed of all the men and women of this planet (with all their gifts and talents and raw power) were not in fact *vastly more powerful* than the tiny number of so-called "elites" who are the primary beneficiaries and primary defenders of the oligarchical *rentier* system, then we would not see the urgent need by those beneficiaries and upholders of that system to deceive the people, to traumatize the people, and to induce awe and dread within the people.

If they were truly that much more powerful than we are, then they would not have to trick us at all.

And yet we can clearly see their need to deceive, to traumatize, and to induce awe and dread: we see it in their repeated use of occult ritual designed to traumatize the people, increasing in

Chapter Fourteen

frequency as the old means of control (including literalist religion) lose their power. We see it in the details of the JFK assassination, and we see it again in the more-recent occult ritual of the September 11 crimes, which has already been mentioned in a previous chapter and which should, now almost nineteen years after that trauma-inducing event in 2001, reveal beyond any doubt the callousness with which these criminal conspirators will murder innocent men and women, will start wars of aggression based upon false pretenses, and will shamelessly lie about what they are doing.

The "official story" of the events of that day is plainly a complete lie. This official story, it must be recognized, was immediately used in order to falsely "justify" an entire series of illegal wars of aggression which continue to this day, over eighteen years later (having killed hundreds of thousands or even some millions of men, women and children so far).

Having looked at some length at the evidence of occult symbology present in the assassination of President Kennedy, we can also plainly see in the destruction of the Twin Towers along with the destruction of a Third Tower evidence of an occult ritual being enacted (one which included violent and deliberate murder of innocent men and women). Indeed, the towers of WTC One and WTC Two were actually nicknamed the "North Tower" and the "South Tower," recalling the North and South Pillars discussed in the earlier examination of Dealey Plaza and the Tree of Life pattern, and depicted in the Masonic diagrams and symbology presented in that discussion (see pages 458 and 462).

Many other researchers have compiled lists of details which support the conclusion that aspects of the 9/11 attacks point to occult symbology and numerology. Once again, one need not agree with every conclusion (or even with the overall conclusion) of each of these researchers to agree that the sheer abundance of the correspondences point to the likelihood that the planners of that murderous event in 2001 intended it to be an occult ritual.

The path of Perseus and the path of Midas

In a 2012 book entitled *The Most Dangerous Book in the World: 9/11 as Mass Ritual*, author S. K. Bain points out that WTC 7 (or "Building Seven"), which collapsed after the fall of the Twin Towers, was known as the Salomon Brothers Building, a name which obviously evokes the figure of King Solomon, who presided over the building of the Temple described in the book of 1 Kings chapter 7, a chapter which describes the famous two pillars of the house of God: the right pillar called Jachin and the left pillar called Boaz.[309]

The destruction of two twin pillars (the Twin Towers) plus a third building named the Salomon Brothers Building evokes the symbology of Solomon and the Temple so overtly and so precisely that it is difficult to attribute to "sheer coincidence." It is even more difficult to attribute these correspondences to coincidence when we consider the fact that WTC 7, the Salomon Brothers Building, was never struck by any airplane, and thus its extraordinary collapse is nearly impossible to explain within the official narrative (and its collapse certainly could not have been part of the supposed plan of the official narrative's supposed hijackers, since no one could possibly have predicted the freefall collapse of a nearby forty-seven story steel building that was not targeted by any aircraft).

However, if the collapse of the three modern steel-frame skyscrapers was in fact caused by pre-planned and pre-positioned demolitions (as the evidence suggests), then it seems clear that the selection of those three buildings was intended to send a specific message -- an esoteric message, with deep connections to Freemasonic symbology and tradition having to do with the construction of the Temple.

Other occult correspondences S. K. Bain finds among the details of the events surrounding the "mega-ritual" of September 11, 2001 include the fact that the Salomon Brothers Building is trapezoidal in shape (he notes that US Army Lieutenant Colonel Anton LaVey, founder of the Church of Satan, named the governing body of his organization "The Order of the

479

Chapter Fourteen

Trapezoid"),[310] as well as possible occult connections in the flight numbers given in the official report for the planes which ostensibly hit the Twin Towers and the Pentagon, as well as of the plane which is said to have crashed into a field in Shanksville, Pennsylvania.

Many of these flight numbers are numbers which featured prominently in the writings of Aleister Crowley, including the number 11 (the flight number of American Airlines Flight 11, purported to have struck the North Tower or WTC Building One),[311] the number 175 (the flight number of United Airlines Flight 175, purported to have struck the South Tower or WTC Building Two),[312] the number 77 (the flight number of American Airlines Flight 77, purported to have struck the Pentagon, a building which is situated at longitude 77 degrees west),[313] and the number 93 (the flight number of United Airlines Flight 93, purported to have crashed into a field in Somerset County, Pennsylvania).[314]

He also points out that at the moment of the attacks, George W. Bush was in a second-grade classroom in Sarasota, Florida, where a room full of children were listening to a reading of *The Pet Goat*, or *My Pet Goat*, by Siegfried Engelmann (1931 - 2019). Bain points out that the goat is associated with the god Pan, as well as with imagery of the Devil in literalist Christianity, and with the occult figure of Baphomet.[315] It is noteworthy that, according to Professor Alex Owen in "The Sorceror and His Apprentice," the god Pan "had a particular significance" for Aleister Crowley, who "revered him as the diabolic god of lust and magic" and who, in his transformative ritual in the desert outside of Bou Saada "probably 'called down' or invoked the god Pan."[316]

These are just some examples of the compelling and abundant evidence which points to the conclusion that the criminal mass-murder perpetrated on September 11, 2001 was also a carefully-planned occult ritual. S. K. Bain argues that it included specific cryptic references to Aleister Crowley and his teachings, which is

The path of Perseus and the path of Midas

certainly a possible conclusion. But regardless of whether or not one agrees with all of the analysis of Bain or other researchers who point out the numerous occult elements surrounding the despicable events of that day, it should be abundantly clear that the events of September 11 display the unmistakable hallmarks of an occult ritual, and that this massive occult ritual set in motion a chain of far-reaching and disastrous events, a chain of events which continues to play out to the present.

Note that the "official story" of September 11, 2001 can be seen by anyone who investigates the evidence to be a blatant and unsustainable lie, just as the official story of the murder of President John F. Kennedy can be seen by anyone who investigates the evidence to be a blatant and unsustainable lie.

The lie regarding those responsible for the attacks of 9/11 was used to falsely "justify" and excuse a series of unending wars (and the institution of increased citizen surveillance under the "Patriot Act"), just as the murder of President Kennedy led to a reversal of Kennedy's withdrawal plans and the rapid escalation of troop deployments to Vietnam in what would become an extremely unpopular war lasting over eleven years (and by some accounts, for over twenty years).

The fact that massive lies (and massive occult rituals) are seen to be necessary in order to stampede the public into support for decades-long wars to protect the colonialist structures of exploitation should indicate that *the majority of the people are actually more powerful* than the "elite" few who stand to benefit from the privatization and monopolization of those natural and national resources: were this not the true situation, then there would be no need to deceive, traumatize, and cow the general public prior to launching these multi-year military adventures.

Whether there are other, even more sinister aims behind these and many other dark occult rituals perpetrated upon the people and upon democratic governance, the brief foregoing examination of the John Kennedy assassination and the

Chapter Fourteen

September 11 attacks should demonstrate beyond any doubt the existence of a powerful, well-connected network (or networks) which thinks nothing of murdering innocent men, women and children and of unleashing illegal wars of aggression based on false pretenses, in order to enrich its own members, at the expense of "non-elite" men and women and children around the world -- a network which repeatedly appeals to the power of the invisible realm in order to try to tilt the scales in its favor.

Our study of the ancient myths themselves indicates that these are not the intended purposes of the ancient wisdom bestowed upon humanity: one of its core purposes, as we have seen, involves *recovery from trauma* and reconciliation with the higher self (whereas the collaborators against the gods seek to *deliberately inflict trauma*, as part of a plan to prevent the men and women of the world from realizing that they can easily stand up to these criminals and stop their wrongful seizure of the resources that were given for the benefit of all).

We began this chapter with an examination of the myth of King Midas, who -- given the opportunity to ask of the divine realm anything he chose -- impulsively asked for the ability to turn everything he touched into gold.

Midas could have used this opportunity to ask for wisdom to help others, as King Solomon did when presented with a similar choice, but Midas chose to ask for riches, endless riches: riches far in excess of whatever vast wealth he already possessed as king of Phrygia.

The occultists who seek to tap into the power of the invisible realm through their rituals appear to share the insatiable desire of Midas -- the need for ever-increasing wealth, no matter the consequences, no matter the damage it does to innocent bystanders, and (ultimately) no matter the damage it does to themselves in the process (for even King Midas learned that his insatiable lust for gold turned out to be self-destructive: a curse rather than a blessing).

The path of Perseus and the path of Midas

Their desire to seize the commodities of the earth, and to rob other men and women of agency and dignity as part of their quest to seize the world's natural wealth, ends up objectifying others and eventually ends up objectifying themselves as well.

The opening chapter of this entire book examined the episode of Jacob's Ladder in the text of Genesis, and the evidence that in the celestial foundations for that story, Jacob asleep on the rock might correspond to the constellation Scorpio, at the base of the brightest and widest portion of the Milky Way (Jacob may at times correspond to nearby Sagittarius: both constellations are at the "base" of the Milky Way's brightest section).

We saw that the ladder itself, whose top reaches to heaven, likely corresponds to the Milky Way itself. Intriguingly, if we follow the Milky Way path (the "ladder") upwards from Scorpio and Sagittarius, we will eventually reach the constellation Perseus. And the highest grades in the initiatory hierarchy of the ancient cult of Sol Invictus Mithras, included the rank of *perses* (Persian) and *pater* (Father), whose symbols as seen in surviving mithraea (image on page 452), include the *harpe* sword of Perseus (among the symbols at the level of *perses*) and the Phrygian cap (among the symbols at the level of *pater*).

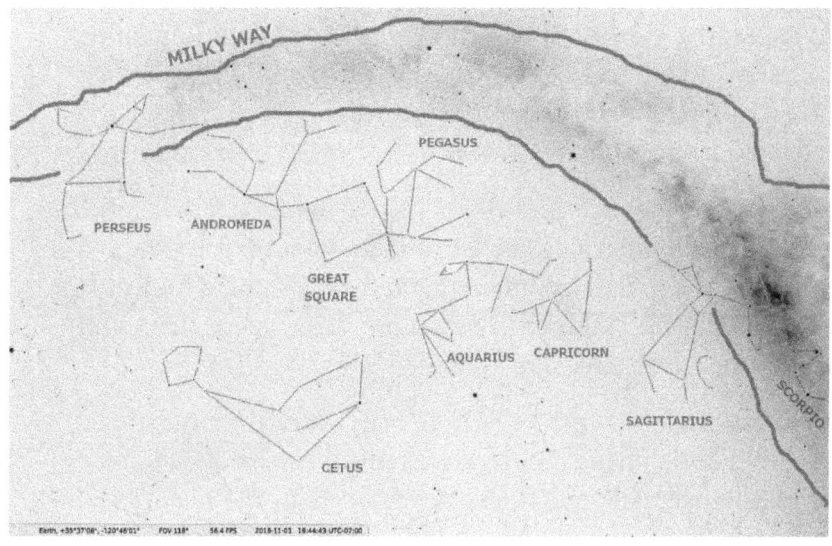

Chapter Fourteen

In other words, the elevation of the soul through the seven levels was understood by the cult of Mithras to involve *ascension to the region of the constellation Perseus* -- the very constellation which we have found to be the heavenly foundation for the story of the hero Perseus (who overcomes the threat of objectification posed by the Gorgons) and also for the story of the foolish King Midas (who dramatizes the insatiable addiction of the traumatized soul for more and more external substitutes, never satisfied no matter how much is obtained: a form of addiction which leads directly to the objectification of others and ultimately to self-destruction, unless the situation is repaired by an appeal to the divine realm, as we see in the story of Midas).

We see that in this ancient myth-pattern of the ladder which reaches to heaven, the myths depict a rather stark choice once we actually achieve that connection with the infinite realm.

When we connect with the realm of the divine, and can ask whatever we want, we have a choice between the path of Perseus and the path of Midas.

We can oppose tyranny and oppression and the objectification of ourselves and others (as demonstrated in the myth of Perseus), or we can pursue our own enrichment at the expense of those around us, even at the expense of robbing them of their humanity, their agency, their ability to reach their own full potential: commoditizing and objectifying those around us, and (ultimately) objectifying ourselves in the process.

It should be self-evident that those responsible for staging the deception of September 11, in order to launch murderous wars of aggression, seek their own enrichment and are willing to objectify, oppress, traumatize, and eliminate countless other men and women in order to achieve that end.

If it is true that the tiny privileged minority who unlawfully seize for their own enrichment the resources given by the gods for the benefit of all is actually much less powerful than the majority of the men and women of any nation, let alone the majority of the

The path of Perseus and the path of Midas

men and women of the world (and this assessment of the situation is undoubtedly true), then to some degree we are all complicit in allowing them to continue to do what they are doing -- to objectify us, and to oppress us, and to over-awe us with their rituals, and even to literally sacrifice some of us in the pursuit of their wicked goals.

To the extent that we allow ourselves to be mystified by their spectacles, their September 11ths, we are partly complicit in the objectification of the population and of the world -- and thus we are also guilty of the choice of Midas. The Midas story is about us as well.

To the extent that we ourselves have suffered trauma, we have also suppressed our authentic self and developed that reflexive "defense mechanism" of the egoic mind, that instinctive survival-seeking response that urges us to grasp after external bread-crumbs, and thus to tolerate and to look the other way, or even to collude to varying degrees, with these collaborators against the gods when they seize for themselves the riches of the world (objectifying other human beings as they do so, and even sacrificing other human beings as they do so).

If some of the crumbs of the blessings they have seized fall to us (even though we know deep down that something is wrong), then the defense-mechanism of our egoic mind will tell us that it is better to go along with the objectification, because we are afraid of getting burned again, we are afraid of getting wounded again, we are still scarred by deep hurts we experienced at some point in our childhood and which we may not even realize we are avoiding.

In doing so, we assent (like Midas) to the objectification of others (perhaps rationalizing it as unavoidable "collateral damage") in order to try to fill an internal lack which will never be filled that way. And in doing so, we assent to the objectification of ourselves, as well. In our traumatized condition, we fail to realize that we have the power to stop the injustice, the oppression, the commoditization, the sacrifice of innocents, and the unlawful

Chapter Fourteen

seizing of the gifts of the gods -- that in fact, these collaborators pursue their rituals because they need us to remain in awe of them, knowing that if we ever wake up to the true situation, those plotters will be finished.

But in the ancient myth of the foolish choices of King Midas, the gods had mercy upon the king and upon those he had harmed. Midas was given an opportunity to undo his wish and repair the damage caused by his greed.

One would hope that all those who have used the power of the gods to enrich themselves or to harm their enemies would similarly repent of their decision and seek to undo the harm that they have done to others by their decisions.

As with the example given by the story of Midas, it may be that such restoration is only possible by seeking the power of the divine realm, and admitting our errors, and asking for the blessing of the gods to point the way to the River Pactolus, where we can, like Midas, immerse ourselves in that celestial stream, and be restored in the places (the traumas) that led us to seek after such self-destructive and unsatisfying addictions to begin with.

As long as we are alienated and disconnected from our own true self, then this usurping algorithm of the egoic mind, which arose in order to defend us from deep hurt, will continue to reflexively act out its program, and we will be prone to manipulation by those sorcerers who know how to push our buttons. That's why we won't stop acting like foolish King Midas until we, like the repentant king in the story, come to that place where we are ready to seek the restorative power of the divine realm.

In the story, we see it when Midas admits to Dionysus that he has been foolish, and that he wants to repair his egregious mistake. We see this surrender to the god dramatized in action when Dionysus tells Midas to travel all the way to the remote source of the pure river, and to dunk his head in it -- and Midas complies with the directive of the god.

It is the same principle that is dramatized in the Mahabharata, when Arjuna hands the reins of the chariot over to Krishna, and in the story of Doubting Thomas, when Thomas finally surrenders to Christ and exclaims, "My Lord and my God!"

When our egoic mind, controlled by its childhood hurts and fears, refuses to let go of the reins, we are easy for the criminal manipulators to play like a marionette.

But when, like Perseus listening to the counsel of Athena and of Hermes, we are in touch with the divine realm -- and enflamed with the desire to stand up to oppressors even as Perseus stood up to the wicked Polydectes -- then we can accomplish what seems impossible, and undo the curse of objectification which trauma (and the reactive, pre-programmed, egoic mind) seeks to impose upon us during our journey through this incarnate realm.

Concluding Thoughts

In the ancient Sumerian myth of the descent of the goddess Inanna into the underworld, we encounter a myth-pattern which surfaces in many other myths in other cultures around the world.

The goddess Inanna is the Sumerian goddess of love and beauty and sexual desire. The later Mesopotamian cultures of Akkad and Babylon would call her by the name Ishtar.

In preparing to undertake the harrowing journey to the underworld, the goddess puts on her most alluring garments, and lines her eyes with mascara that inflames desire, mascara which is called, "Let a man come, let him come," according to the ancient texts.[317]

She wore a turban on her head, and a necklace of finely-shaped beads of lapis lazuli around her neck. She wore twin egg-shaped beads upon her breast, and a glorious pectoral as well. Upon one finger she wore a golden ring, and in her hand she carried a measuring rod, also made of lapis lazuli, with a measuring line. Finally, over her body the goddess wore the *pala* dress, which the texts refer to as "the garment of ladyship."[318]

Then, clothed in her glorious power, Inanna "set her mind on the great below" -- the underworld. But before descending, Inanna gives specific instructions to her minister or handmaiden, Ninshubur, telling her:

> Come my faithful minister of E-ana, my minister who speaks fair words, my escort who speaks trustworthy words: I am going to give you instructions: my instructions must be followed; I am going to say something to you: it must be observed. On this day I will descend to the underworld. When I have arrived in the underworld, make a lament for me in the ruin mounds. Beat the drum for me in the sanctuary. Make the rounds of the houses of the gods for me. Lacerate your eyes for me, lacerate your nose for me: lacerate your ears for me, in public. In private, lacerate your buttocks for me. Like a pauper,

clothe yourself in a single garment and all alone set your foot in the E-kur, the house of Enlil. When you have entered the E-kur, the house of Enlil, lament before Enlil: "Father Enlil, don't let anyone kill your daughter in the underworld. Don't let your precious metal be alloyed there in the dirt of the underworld. Dont let your precious lapus lazuli be split there with the mason's stone. Don't let your boxwood be chopped up there with the carpenter's wood. Don't let young lady Inanna be killed in the underworld."[319]

In addition to instructing her to publicly and privately mourn when Inanna descends to the underworld, the goddess tells Ninshuber to wait three days and if Inanna does not return at that point, to carry out a backup plan to rescue the goddess from the dreaded underworld.

When the goddess arrives at the gate of the underworld, she demands that Neti, the gatekeeper, open the door and allow her to enter. Neti seeks permission from the goddess of the underworld, Erishkegal, who is Inanna's sister. Erishkegal directs Neti to lock and bolt the seven gates of the underworld, and only to allow Inanna to pass through each one when she has given up one of her seven divine powers, each associated with one of the accoutrements of Inanna's glorious attire.

Neti obeys the directive given by Erishkegal, and bolts the seven gates of the underworld. He opens them successively, one at a time, but before Inanna can pass through each gate, she is stripped of one of her seven divine powers -- first the turban, then the beaded necklace of lapis lazuli, then the twin egg-shaped beads from her breast, then the gorgeous pectoral, then the golden ring from her finger, and the lapis lazuli measuring rod and measuring line.

Finally, at the last gate, the *pala* dress -- the garment of ladyship -- is removed from her body, leaving the goddess Inanna naked.

Inanna approaches the throne of her sister Ereshkigal, and makes Ereshkigal rise from the throne and let Inanna have it instead.

Concluding Thoughts

But then the text tells us that the seven Anunna appear, and they render judgment against Inanna:

> They looked at her -- it was the look of death. They spoke to her -- it was the speech of anger. They shouted at her -- it was the shout of heavy guilt. The afflicted woman was turned into a corpse. And the corpse was hung on a hook.[320]

When Inanna does not return, her minister Ninshuber puts the backup plan into action, mourning and lacerating herself and then making the rounds to the houses of the gods to see who would help Inanna. She goes to Enlil, but he does not help her. She goes to Urim, and then to Nanna, but they will not help her.

Finally, she goes to Enki, and Enki declares that he too has been concerned for Inanna -- and he agrees to help her.

Enki creates two spirit-like helpers to travel with Ninshuber to the underworld, and gives them instructions to be followed carefully. They are to slip through the pivots of the door to the underworld, and hold council with Ereshkigal. When the goddess of the dead offers them food or drink, they are not to accept it (this too is a myth-pattern or oicotype we find around the globe, from the myths of ancient Greece to those of the Indigenous First Nations of North America).

Instead, they are to ask for the corpse, hanging on the hook. When they are brought to the corpse, they are to sprinkle it with life-giving water and a life-giving plant.

All this takes place just as Enki directs -- and Inanna is revived. She is just about to depart from the underworld and return to the realm of the living, when the Anunna seize her and declare that she must bring them a substitute, if she is going to leave the land of the dead.

And so, when Inanna returns to the land of the living, she is accompanied by demons who are ready to seize a substitute to take Inanna's place in the realm of the dead. But each time they encounter someone, and the demons exclaim that this man or that woman will make a perfect substitute, Inanna stops them -- for each one is sitting in the dust, beating upon a drum, lacerating themselves in grief, clothing themselves in filthy garments of mourning.

It is only when Inanna comes to the great apple tree in the plain of Kubala, and she finds her consort Dumuzid the shepherd dressed in a magnificent garment, seated in luxury upon a throne, that the goddess becomes enraged. She looks at Dumuzid with the look of death, and informs the demons that they can take Dumuzid to the underworld. Later, Dumuzid will be allowed to return to the land of the living for half the year, and spend the other half of each year in the realm of the dead.

What does this ancient myth, from ancient Sumerian texts of tremendous antiquity, want to tell us? Why this emphasis on mourning and grieving the god or goddess who goes down into the underworld, a pattern we find as well in the Norse myth of the death of Baldr, and in the tradition of the observation of Ash Wednesday and the season of Lent which is still performed every year in association with the death and descent into the underworld of the Christ?

These are ancient patterns, and they must have deep significance, even if no longer clearly understood.

One layer of meaning conveyed by this ancient story of Inanna's Descent becomes more apparent when we begin to decode the likely celestial foundation underlying this myth, and realize that when she is "turned into a corpse" and "hung on a hook," the goddess Inanna is almost certainly associated with the constellation Ophiuchus, which can without much difficulty be envisioned as "hanging from a hook," the hook being formed by the "eastern serpent-half" (the "tail-half") of the serpent held by that constellation.[321]

Below we see the now-familiar outline of the pivotal figure of the constellation Ophiuchus – with a large arrow indicating the "hook-shaped" section of the eastern (tail-side) serpent-half:

Concluding Thoughts

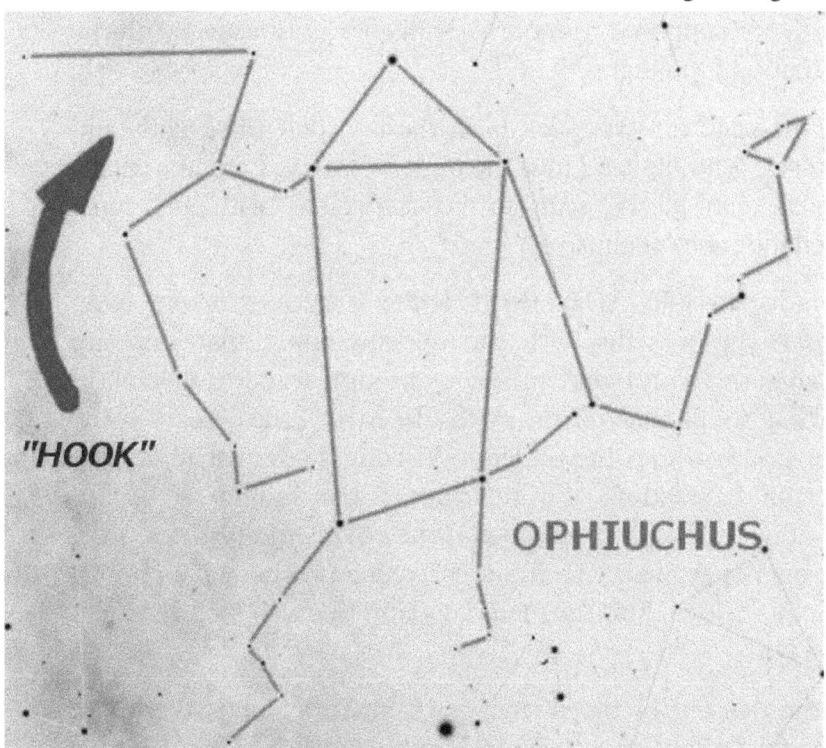

The tremendous significance of this identification of the goddess Inanna, *hanging* upon a hook as a corpse in the underworld for *three days* is brought home to us when we understand that the figure of Christ, hanging upon the cross before descending into the realm of the dead for three days, is likewise associated with the constellation Ophiuchus, as we have already demonstrated in a previous chapter of this volume (see for instance page 216).

Additionally, *The Ancient World-Wide System: Star Myths of the World, Volume One (Second Edition)* provides abundant evidence to conclude that when the god Osiris is slain and placed into a narrow coffin or sarcophagus and wrapped in a linen shroud, he too is associated with the constellation Ophiuchus (another example of the god or goddess who descends to the underworld).[322] And *Star Myths of the World, Volume Four: Norse Mythology* presents evidence that the slain god Baldr, who also descends into the underworld (and for whom all beings

Myth and Trauma

on earth are supposed to mourn), is likewise associated with the constellation Ophiuchus.[323]

What message can we glean from the fact that these gods and goddesses, who descend into the underworld and are universally mourned, can all be seen to be associated with the same constellation, Ophiuchus?

The indispensable Alvin Boyd Kuhn argues that we must approach these myths with the understanding that they are conveying their profound message through esoteric metaphor. According to his analysis, the myths describing the descent of the god or goddess into the underworld actually dramatize for our deeper understanding the descent of the human soul into incarnation -- the process which occurs with the birth of every single man or woman who has ever lived, a process which brings divine spirit down into the material realm to dwell for a time in a human body.

It is the descent of the divine spark into the "underworld" of matter, the "tomb" of the physical body, which is being depicted in these myths, Kuhn argues. In *Lost Light*, Kuhn writes:

> The incarnation, for the soul, was its death and burial. But it was a living death and a burial alive. It was an entombment that carried life on, but under conditions that could be poetically dramatized as "death." Our inability to comprehend any but the physical sense of the word "burial" has left us easy victims of ancient poetic fancy, and led to the foisting upon ourselves perhaps the most degraded interpretation of the crucifixion, death and resurrection of deity in mortal life ever to be held by any religious group.[324]

Elsewhere, he writes: "In the esoteric doctrine which regarded the present life as death, and the living body as the soul's tomb, we have the necessary background for adequate elucidation of the matter."[325]

While I agree with Alvin Boyd Kuhn that the ancient myths regarding the descent of a god or goddess into the underworld

Concluding Thoughts

evoke the pattern of our own soul's descent into this incarnate life, in light of all the evidence we've examined in the preceding chapters, I would hazard to propose that this ancient pattern expresses an additional and closely related subject of vital importance: these myths are dramatizing (in a manner designed to jolt us into awareness) the importance of perceiving the situation in which we find ourselves when, due to trauma, we *bury and suppress* our essential self, our divine or higher self: our authentic self.

Note well that Inanna is turned into a corpse and hung upon a hook in the underworld after being *shouted at* by the seven accusers of the Anunna (dramatizing accusation, humiliation, shaming: in short, trauma). This ancient myth, inscribed upon some of the very earliest tablets which have survived for examination into the modern day, is brilliantly and poignantly depicting the kind of shaming and humiliation which drives our essential self, our authentic self, underground -- where it remains suppressed, kept there by our egoic mind which above all things seeks to avoid dredging up old psychic trauma.

Note too that we see the same pattern in the gospel stories surrounding the crucifixion of the Christ, who is accused, slandered, reviled, beaten, and mocked prior to being hung up on a cross.

And in the story of Baldr, in the Norse myths, we see a similar kind of mocking game when the gods all undertake to attack gentle Baldr with weapons and stones in a kind of good-hearted game, thinking that nothing on earth can hurt the benevolent god -- a game that turns dark and dreadful when Loki directs the blind Hod to shoot a dart made of mistletoe at Baldr, killing Baldr and sending the god of light down to the realm of death.

The echoes to the mocking and beating of Christ before the crucifixion are here somewhat faint, but we can still make them out. I would argue that in this ancient oicotype we have, preserved for our elucidation, a teaching about the way that our

495

essential self is suppressed and sent down to the land of shadows: sometimes through harsh and accusatory criticism, censure and deliberate shaming, and other times through thoughtless jesting and carelessness, which nevertheless bring about tragic consequences.

Most important to observe in the pattern running through these ancient myths is the emphasis on mourning, found in myths literally around the globe and usually related to this oicotype of the god or goddess who descends into the underworld. Its significance should now be plain enough for us to decipher: the ancient myths are here showing us the tremendous importance of perceiving our disconnection from our essential self, our alienation from our essential self, and of *lamenting that situation* (rather than simply ignoring it, as Dumuzid does in the story of Inanna's Descent).

We should grieve over the separation and burial of our authentic self -- because becoming aware of what has happened, and seeking to remedy and repair the disconnection, must be ranked as one of the most important missions of our life. In the myth of Osiris, the goddess Isis will stop at nothing to find her lost, murdered lover. In the myth of Persephone's abduction into the realm of the dead, her mother Demeter will search to the ends of the earth for anything that could lead her to the recovery of her beloved daughter.

But the sad fact is that a great many men and women who are alienated from themselves do not even know it! They do not even realize that they have been disconnected from their own essence (or, if their egoic mind does realize it, the ego suppresses that painful knowledge and tries to keep the very *existence* of the authentic self a secret -- going even so far as to mock the idea of a higher or essential self). Thus, if we are unaware of our own loss, we neither mourn the burial of the divine essence, nor seek like Isis to find and recover it.

Concluding Thoughts

In this sense, in our ignorance, we act like Dumuzid in the myth of the descent of Inanna -- carrying on as though nothing at all is wrong, completely oblivious to the true situation.

The world's ancient myths, however, are here to wake us up to the catastrophe of this profound alienation. And the myths are here to show us the way to recover our own buried self.

As we've already seen, the constellation Ophiuchus plays a pivotal role in the recovery. The figures of the Buddha, the Christ, the god Osiris, the wise King Solomon, the god Baldr of the Norse myths, the goddess Athena, the gods Vishnu and Shiva and Krishna and Yama, the god Quetzalcoatl or Kukulcan or Q'ukumatz or Viracocha, the figure of Bodhidharma or Da Mo or Daruma -- all of these can be conclusively shown to have close correspondence with the constellation Ophiuchus, and all are transcendent figures, closely associated (I would argue) with the concept of our own recovery of the higher self.

And, as we've now just seen, the goddess Inanna can also be shown to be associated with the constellation Ophiuchus, in her descent into the underworld, where she must be turned into a corpse and hung on a hook for three days before being revived. And once again we see that this myth may be interpreted as dramatizing the suppression and burial of the essential self and with its recovery.

Why is Ophiuchus such a pivotal figure, and why does Ophiuchus feature so prominently in ancient myths about the recovery of the higher self?

We've seen and discussed a number of reasons in this book, including the important aspect of Ophiuchus being a so-called "thirteenth sign" of the zodiac, simultaneously *part of* the zodiac band and also *detached from* that band's endless revolutions.

And we've also seen that the figure of the constellation Hercules, positioned directly above Ophiuchus, is the constellation with which the supreme deity in any pantheon in most of the Star

Myth and Trauma

Myths of the world is associated. These preeminent deities associated with the constellation Hercules include Father Zeus, Father Jupiter (Jove Pater), Thor the Thunderer, Brahma and Indra of the Vedas, Atum-Ra and Amun-Ra and Ptah and Khnum of ancient Egypt (and the Aten as well), the Maya god Heart of Sky or Huracan, and also of course the God of the Bible, or Jehovah.

Thus, the position of Ophiuchus in the sky positions this constellation as the intermediator between the revolving signs of the zodiac (through which we move while we are in this earthly sojourn, metaphorically speaking) and the supreme divinity. In the same way (this book has argued) our higher self acts as our own interface and connection with the divine.

In addition, Ophiuchus stands beside the glorious Milky Way, just above Scorpio, and adjacent to the widest and brightest region of that galactic band. We have now seen evidence which suggests that this galactic path was envisioned as the ladder connecting the earth to the heavens, the ladder Jacob saw in his dream, the stairway which the soul descends and ascends.

We have seen evidence that the seven levels of the ancient cult of Mithras were also envisioned as a ladder, and that this ladder too was associated with the Milky Way, having symbols related to the constellation Perseus at the top stations on that ladder. That ladder of the ancient Mithraic order had seven steps -- and the reader has undoubtedly noted that in the story of Inanna's descent into the underworld, she must pass through seven successive gates (losing part of her glory with each step) before being turned into a corpse.

Thus, we can ascertain that the ancient "stairway to heaven" (a stairway which, according to Porphyry, was a stairway that the soul *descends* before it later ascends, just as Inanna had to do), was the Milky Way galaxy itself, forming a stairway which was understood to have Sagittarius and Scorpio and Ophiuchus near its base, with Perseus at or near its top:

Concluding Thoughts

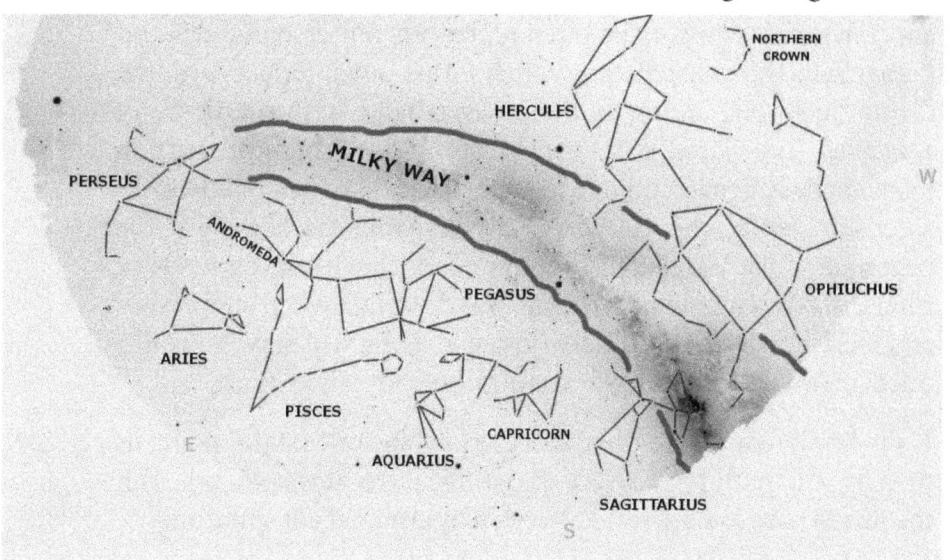

While it may be difficult to perceive from the above diagram, the Milky Way does grow so thin and faint as it reaches Perseus that it appears to fade out there -- as if this is the top of the shining band. That the region of the Milky Way near Perseus was sometimes envisioned as the fount from which the galactic river originates, and from which it pours down in an ever-widening stream, is confirmed by versions of the Midas myth in which the king is told to follow the river all the way until he reaches its source, and there plunge head and body into the snowy stream.[326]

If Midas (associated with the constellation Perseus) is envisioned as plunging into the stream (associated with the Milky Way) at *its source*, then it can be confirmed that the ancient myths sometimes envisioned the Milky Way band as flowing out from this very region, growing wider and thicker as it flows down towards Ophiuchus and Sagittarius and Scorpio. Thus, the argument that this region near Perseus was sometimes envisioned as the "top" of the ladder can be established with strong supporting evidence.

All this to say that the constellation Ophiuchus occupies an absolutely crucial location in the heavenly canvas upon which the ancient myths paint their esoteric figures. It is the constellation, I

499

am convinced, which most often represents our essential self, our higher self: the constellation which forms our interface with the divine (including acting as the intermediator with the figure of Hercules, associated with the Most High or highest deity in many myth-systems) and it is the constellation which pictures our ascension along the celestial path reaching to heaven – the beautiful Milky Way band forming a ladder with seven levels or rungs, down which our authentic self descends when suppressed and locked away in the underworld, and along which we too must travel in order to recover our connection with our essence.

I am firmly convinced that the world's ancient myths point us towards the path to recovery of our alienated authentic self. But the myths have been wrested from us by criminal conspirators.

With the elevation of literalist Christianity to its position of authority during the Roman Empire in the years of Constantine and his successors, and in the oligarchy that arose following the dissolution of Rome in the west, the teachings of the ancient gods and goddesses have been labeled the "doctrines of devils" by the proponents of literalist faith (as we read in 1 Timothy 4: 1, which may well be a spurious epistle added by literalizers long after epistles such as Galatians or Ephesians were written by the author calling himself Paul).[327]

Augustine in *City of God* says of the gods: "they are demons, teachers of depravity, delighting in obscenity" (in a passage cited earlier in this book, on page 106). This despite the overwhelming and indisputable evidence which can now be presented to show that the figures and events described in the Bible are built upon the same foundation of celestial metaphor underlying the world's other myths, and that they are all thus more closely related than has ever previously been taught.

The pathway back to our essential self -- which appears to be closely connected to that same "stairway to heaven" or celestial ladder we examined at the very outset of this book -- is given to all men and women in the myths, and those who want to keep it to

Concluding Thoughts

themselves and deny it to others (claiming it as their own private driveway), for the benefit of their own enrichment and the privatization of earth's resources, can only be described as enemies of humanity.

The myths belong to all men and women: they are given to every culture on earth, living in every inhabited land on our planet. Their wisdom cannot be claimed to be the property or private domain of any privileged, limited group. And they cannot be legitimately taken away from those to whom they are given: us.

The secret networks who want to claim the world's ancient wisdom as their own private property, their own private playground, are fond of incorporating ancient mythical references into their occult rituals and symbology -- leading some to believe that the ancient gods and their message to us are somehow intrinsically related to oppression, exploitation, and abuse. After all, says one analyst in a recent article: "Jeffrey Epstein constructed an elaborate Greek polytheistic temple on his island hideaway."[328]

But the expropriation by the agents of the kleptocracy (this kleptocracy which seeks to steal the gifts of the gods for its own private enrichment) of the ancient wisdom given to all mankind should not in any way lead to the mistaken conclusion that just because criminals steal something, it therefore follows that whatever they stole naturally belongs to them!

Just because assassins, exploiters, molesters, and oppressors appropriate the symbols of the ancient gods, this does not mean that the ancient wisdom is properly theirs.

These criminals are the enemies of the ancient wisdom, because they seek to impoverish the very men and women in whom the gods have their dwelling-place, and through whom the gods work their will.

The ancient myths teach that every single child that is born within any nation is *allowed to be born* by the will of the gods.

Myth and Trauma

Thus *every* child born in every land is a gift from the divine realm: a gift from the gods.

And the ancient wisdom declares unequivocally that the gods live in and act *through* human beings: the Egyptian Book of the Dead, for example (the ancient title of which is more accurately translated as the *Book of Going Forth by Day*) declares, in the scroll buried with the scribe Ani around the year 1250 BC, in the 42nd chapter (as translated by E. A. Wallis Budge in 1901, with occasional clarification by Raymond O. Faulkner added in brackets) the identification of Ani with Osiris and other gods:

> The hair of Osiris Ani, triumphant, is the hair of Nu [or Nun]
> The face of Osiris Ani, triumphant, is the face of Ra
> The eyes of Osiris Ani, triumphant, are the eyes of Hathor
> The ears of Osiris Ani, triumphant, are the ears of Ap-uat [or Wepwawet]
> The lips of Osiris Ani, triumphant, are the lips of Anpu [or Anubis]
> The teeth [or molars] of Osiris Ani, triumphant, are the teeth of Serqet [or Selket]
> The neck of Osiris Ani, triumphant, is the neck of Isis
> The hands of Osiris Ani, triumphant, are the hands of Ba-neb-Tattu
> The shoulder of Osiris Ani, triumphant, is the shoulder of Uatchet
> The throat of Osiris Ani, triumphant, is the throat of Mert
> The forearms of Osiris Ani, triumphant, are the forearms of the Lady of Sais
> The backbone of Osiris Ani, triumphant, is the backbone of Set
> The chest of Osiris Ani, triumphant, is the chest of the lords of Kher-aha
> The flesh [or chest] of Osiris Ani, triumphant, is the flesh of the Mighty One of Terror [or, He who is Greatly Majestic]
> The reins and back [or belly and spine] of Osiris Ani, triumphant, are the reins and back of Sekhet [or Sekhmet]

> The buttocks of Osiris Ani, triumphant, are the buttocks of the Eye of Horus
> The phallus of Osiris Ani, triumphant, is the phallus of Osiris
> The legs [or thighs and calves] of Osiris Ani, triumphant, are the legs of Nut
> The feet of Osiris Ani, triumphant, are the feet of Ptah
> The fingers of Osiris Ani, triumphant, are the fingers of Orion
> The leg-bones [or toes] of Osiris Ani, triumphant, are the leg-bones of the living uraei [the rearing cobras of the goddess Wadjet]
> There is no member of my body which is not the member of some god ["There is no member of mine devoid of a god"]
> The god Thoth shieldeth my body altogether ["And Thoth is the protection of all my flesh"], and I am Ra day by day.[329]

Literalist Christianity has waged a centuries-long campaign to divorce men and women from the ancient gods, as well as from the rhythms of the earth and of the heavens, from the power of the invisible realm, from the realm of nature and the wider universe, and even from our own selves.

But, as we have seen, it would be a mistake to focus exclusively on literalist Christianity as the exclusive source of this campaign: this mistake was the same one that the ancient Roman emperors such as Marcus Aurelius made, and the same mistake that the ancient Roman senatorial families made. The brilliant (if nefarious) tactic which appears to have been employed in past centuries -- and which appears to still be employed to this day -- involves the use of a two-pronged instrument, one more secret and esoteric and one more open and overt. These two wings will frequently pretend to be at odds with one another, even violent enemies, because this tactic necessarily involves deception.

In fact, it is very likely that the great majority of those who volutarily enter into various institutions associated with either the overt or covert sides of this network -- including the clergy of various literalist church bodies, and even including members of various esoteric societies including Freemasonry and all its related organizations, as well as members of various intelligence agencies -- do so with honorable intentions, and it is only certain select individuals who are permitted to see more sinister activities, and only after they are in too deep to easily extricate themselves (even if they wanted to).

Author Douglas Valentine, who has spent decades researching the operations of covert intelligence agencies, describes this process (as he understands it, based on first-hand accounts which have been related to him over the course of many hundreds of interviews and personal contacts) in these words:

> The young and the innocent are getting sucked into these things, just like they're getting sucked into everything all the time, by the old farts who run this country. And when you get into the military, you're expendable. You sign up, and you think – well, they're going to teach me how to repair a helicopter. Or, they're going to teach me how to be a communications person -- and then the next day you find yourself in the midst of a battle. And then horrible things happen.[330]

As Jacques Pauwels emphasizes in his analysis of the Great War (World War I), "vertical" dividing lines can be distractions or red herrings which take us off track: the more significant lines are often "horizontal."[331] The real collaborators against the gods are undoubtedly located within the upper echelons of a variety of *ostensibly different* organizations and institutions and religious groups, groups which might *appear* to be separated from one another by various "vertical" lines – but the more important lines are horizontal (separating the levels or strata in a hierarchy).

In other words, those at the lower levels of *all* of these various organizations might be largely innocent, honorable, decent individuals, and it is primarily within the inner circles at the top of some of these seemingly separate (and even seemingly antagonistic) groups where we find more nefarious actors, working *across groups* for purposes that involve exploitation and

Concluding Thoughts

oppression, and whose tactics include violence, terror, and the deliberate infliction of psychic trauma in order to achieve their ends.

The hanging of a corpse upon a hook, described in the ancient Sumerian myth of Inanna's descent, dramatizes in the starkest possible manner the condition of *objectification*. In this grim image, we see that when the essential self is suppressed and buried, we ourselves become an object: recall again the quotation cited earlier on page 247 in which Dr. Gabor Maté declares:

> People who are not conscious simply have no freedom. They may *believe* they do, but they don't make decisions. The decisions are made for them by automatic, emotional reactions that are the result of early experiences.

If our egoic mind largely reacts in a programmatic way, and if our authentic self is buried so deeply that we have no idea that we've been isolated from our own self, then we are easily controlled, like a puppet or a robot.

One of the central purposes of the ancient wisdom given to humanity in the myths (if not *the* central purpose) is to awaken us to this terrible calamity of the loss of the essential self, and to help us to repair the disconnection. The path of reconnection actually leads *down*: down into the darkness of our own interior space, where the authentic self lies buried, waiting for the egoic mind to relax its grip and allow us to remember who we are.

Ancient disciplines such as meditation, drumming, chanting, and the use of a variety of other techniques (including at times the use of substances such as mushrooms, ayahuasca, and other psychedelics which can reveal what lies beneath the egoic mind) have been used for centuries to facilitate the reawakening of the awareness of the essence that lies sleeping beneath the dark waters within. Down in those dark waters is where we must look for the slumbering essence, like Thor trying to fish up the Midgard Serpent.

Myth and Trauma

The portal of ascension, then, is actually a descent -- just as Inanna herself demonstrates in the ancient myth.

The ancient originators of the society of Mithras may have understood this truth: certainly Porphyry says that their initiations dramatize the mystery of "the descent of souls and their exit back out again," implying awareness of the understanding that the "route" necessarily involves a descent.

But the collaborators against the gods demonstrate by their actions that they are not interested in helping men and women with this repair of trauma and recovery of the self: in fact, they seek to inflict trauma.

We can observe that the institutions on both sides of the two-pronged strategy (the overt and the covert) employ trauma. The institution on the *overt* side of the trauma operation (the literalist Christian church and the doctrines it imposes on people after their original sacred traditions are obliterated) primarily works on the level of the individual. Through teachings such as original sin, eternal torment in hell, the use of "the rod" in the raising of children, the subordinate status of women, and many other doctrines, it works to impose trauma on an individual level. The operations of the secret branches (beginning with the cult of Sol Invictus) are more focused on *inflicting trauma at a societal level*, for political ends (through the use of assassinations, occult ritual, and various types of intelligence operations).

In his 1990 book *The Phoenix Program*, Douglas Valentine describes the operations of the CIA in Vietnam in these terms: "The subliminal purpose of terror tactics was to drive people into a state of infantile dependence."[332]

The staging of massive, trauma-inducing events such as the assassination of President Kennedy in public and in broad daylight, and the occult ritual of September 11, 2001 in which three symbolic towers were brought down into their own footprints at freefall speed, serve to further alienate the people and reduce them to "infantile dependence" in two different ways.

Concluding Thoughts

One way is for people to suppress the implications of what they saw take place, and to continue going about their lives (now for decades) as if the murder and subsequent cover-up of a president, or the destruction of those three towers at freefall speeds, does not indicate the hijacking of their government by criminals. To continue on as though nothing has happened requires a certain amount of disconnection from what one knows deep down to be true – but psychologists and those who have studied trauma can testify that we are absolutely capable of doing this very thing, and that it is in fact a survival mechanism which typically takes place without our even being aware that we are doing it.

In fact, this is exactly how disconnection from the self always takes place, and why it happens without our knowing that it happens. Recall a quotation from Dr. Maté cited earlier (on pages 315 - 316):

> If our environment cannot support our gut feelings and our emotions, then the child, in order to "belong" and "fit in" will automatically, unwittingly and unconsciously, suppress their emotions and their connections to themselves, for the sake of staying connected to the nurturing environment, without which the child cannot survive. [. . .]
>
> Furthermore, if the parents themselves are not in touch with their feelings, they can't tolerate the child's feelings because they threaten them. The parent reacts against the child for having anger -- and the child learns, I mustn't express what I feel, because I have to belong to my parents. If I don't, who will protect me and nurture me? Automatically we disconnect from ourselves, in order to be looked after. It's a tragic choice. It's not even a choice -- the child's not aware of making a choice. It's an automatic process.[333]

As with all the other authors and researchers I cite in this book, I have no idea if Dr. Maté would agree with *anything* that I write, let alone with my analysis that the very same kind of automatic process of suppressing is taking place within men and women regarding the assassination of President Kennedy and with the events of September 11, 2001. However, I am convinced that this suppression is one way in which these events are designed to traumatize a population, and to reduce them (in Douglas Valentine's words) to "infantile dependence."

On the other hand, as mentioned previously, there will be some men and women who do not suppress the implications altogether, but who investigate further -- and the discovery of symbology such as the fact that President Kennedy was murdered near the 33rd latitude line, in a plaza with clear parallels to the Tree of Life pattern, and that the destruction of the Twin Towers as well as of the nearby Salomon Brothers Building has esoteric connections to the pattern of the Temple of Solomon in the Bible (which is also connected to the Tree of Life pattern, and which -- as my analysis in this and other books has demonstrated -- is also connected to the constellation of Ophiuchus in the heavens) will function as a kind of "initiation" as they work through the esoteric symbolism.

But it is not an initiation intended to elevate anyone's consciousness: rather, it is an initiation intended to induce awe, in very much the same way that boot camp or basic training is intended to induce awe of the drill instructors or drill sergeants within the recruit, or the way that West Point's initial "Beast Barracks" is intended to induce awe of the cadre in the new cadets.

If the evidence presented in this book regarding the assassination of President Kennedy and the events of September 11, 2001 is not enough to convince you that this intentional traumatization is part of a nefarious strategy, then I suggest you spend some time examining the history of Operation Gladio in Italy and the rest of Europe during previous decades, the creation of the Red Brigades, the Manson Family and similar modern cults, the Patti Hearst kidnapping and the Symbionese Liberation Army, the Jonestown massacre, the Oklahoma City bombing, and the Las Vegas shooting of October 2017 (among many other operations

Concluding Thoughts

which fit into the same larger pattern and which could also be mentioned -- all pointing to the same conclusion). See also the abundant analysis and research by Christopher Knowles on more recent operations, which incorporate undeniable occult elements.

These violent criminal operations are deliberately designed to inflict trauma on the men and women who refuse to see what is going on, and to act as an "initiatory" process for those who do look into them, intended to instill a feeling of awe, as if those behind such despicable acts are superior to the rest of us in some way.

But the fact is that they are not superior. They do not have any greater right to access the ancient wisdom of the myths than you do. They do not have any greater inherent access to the real of the infinite than you do, either.

The way to overcome trauma is given in the ancient myths. The way involves the recovery of the buried divinity. And the myths point us towards a descent to the underworld, just like the one undertaken by Inanna in the myth, as well as the voyage to the underworld undertaken by Odysseus in the Odyssey, and by Hunahpu and Xbalanque in the Popol Vuh, and by Osiris in the ancient texts of Egypt, and by Jesus in the gospels, and by Parmenides (or Parmeneides) in the ancient poem discussed in Peter Kingsley's *In the Dark Places of Wisdom*.

That descent into darkness teaches us that the reconnection we are looking for is not found anywhere outside of ourselves, but rather within.

Those who have been involved in the centuries-long campaign to privatize the resources of nature for their own self-enrichment, at the expense of others, show by their very goals and actions that they are pursuing solutions external to themselves. Amassing assets into the billions of dollars exemplifies this pattern. It is certainly very possible to become a billionaire, if through political connections you are able to privatize the telephone company of a nation, or the oil deposits of a country, or the ports or roads or water supply of a country.

Myth and Trauma

We have been conditioned to view those controlling accounts with billions in asset value as being somehow different than everyone else – and it is true that these assets (although they are simply entries in a spreadsheet) do give those who control them access to real resources not available to everyone else. But that does not make those who have higher numbers entered in spreadsheets under their name any more worthy of awe than any other man or woman: it does not make them gods, it does not make them inter-dimensional beings, it does not indicate that they are reptilian in origin, and it does not give them greater access to the invisible realm than anyone else. In fact, as we see in the story of King Midas, the insatiable need for external riches is often indicative of an internal trauma, a lack which cannot actually be filled by external substitutes, no matter how hard anyone tries.

The entire project of those who overthrew the ancient wisdom betrays a lack of understanding of the deepest teaching of those ancient myths and ancient gods whose wisdom and purpose they consistently oppose.

Their billions do not make them happy: those riches cannot satisfy the longing that actually results from the loss of the authentic self. Neither numbers in a spreadsheet nor any other external thing can replace the deepest longing of our divided souls, which is the recovery of who we actually are. And all this is foretold in the ancient myth of Midas, and in a thousand other sacred stories preserved in the wisdom entrusted to humanity.

While denying the ancient teachings to everybody else, the collaborators against the gods attempt to appropriate the world's ancient wisdom for themselves. But the ancient wisdom does not belong to them, any more than the gifts given by nature and the gods to the people of a nation belong to corporations such as ExxonMobil or Rio Tinto. And the continued Midas-like behavior of these deceivers reveals that they have themselves failed to see what the myths teach at a deeper level.

Concluding Thoughts

Those who are truly willing to harm millions of other men and women for their own self-enrichment show themselves to be enemies of the gods, and enemies of humanity.

They themselves are not gods. They are not superhuman beings. They are in fact very afraid: very afraid of men and women waking up, very afraid of losing their improper ability to impose "private taxes" upon other men and women, very afraid that the numbers in the asset side of their spreadsheet might be reduced, with a corresponding reduction in their ability to command resources and impose their will on other men and women around them.

And those who have through their actions perpetrated murder are also very afraid of being brought to justice for those crimes.

If we have been fooled into following their lies, if we have been entranced by their spells, if we have been played like a marionette by those who know how to "push our buttons" (because our egoic self, like a pre-programmed algorithm, reacts automatically when certain ancient fears are triggered) then -- like Midas -- we can repent of our foolish choices.

The solution lies in the path of repairing our trauma (so that we give the reins to our higher self, and stop being played like a puppet), and in recovering our inborn connection to the realm of the gods. When we reconnect with ourself, we reconnect as well with the wider universe and with the invisible realm -- and this reconnection reveals the truth that we are in fact also inseparably connected with each other.

Those who want to steal the gifts of the gods given to all nations, and to all humanity, would much prefer us to be divided against one another, and divided against our selves.

But the gods are not on their side, as much as those enemies of humanity want to portray themselves as the sole proprietors and representatives of the ancient ways. In Ramayana, the gods permit the depredations of Ravana for a time, but in the end, they bring about the wicked one's destruction -- and they do so by *manifesting in mortal human beings*, and by working out their divine will *through* the courageous actions of mortal men and women.

Manifesting the power of the gods is the very opposite of the enslavement to the fearful pre-programmed reflexes which characterize the egoic self.

We overcome that lamentable condition by tapping into the divine realm, where we can find the strength to look with compassion upon the unhappy egoic mind, recognizing that it has been deeply hurt, and that it is deeply fearful and deeply enslaved by its own doubts -- just as Jesus demonstrates compassion in the famous reconciliation scene with Thomas.

The power to transcend the fearful doubt of the egoic self is always shown to have its origin in the divine realm. It certainly cannot originate with the egoic mind itself, but rather from the higher self and its connection to the higher realm. The antidote to the petty tyranny of the egoic mind is *reunion with the essence*, and it is through the essential self that we recover our connection with the infinite, and can hear the voice of the gods.

As Ovid says of the repentance of Midas, after he realizes he has made a terrible mistake:

> How patient are the gods! Bacchus forthwith,
> Because King Midas had confessed his fault,
> Restored him and annulled the promise given,
> Annulled the favor granted, and he said:

> "That you may not be always cased in gold,
> Which you unhappily desired, depart
> To the stream that flows by that great town of Sardis
> And upward trace its waters, as they glide
> Past Lydian heights, until you find their source.
> Then, where the spring leaps out from mountain rock,
> Plunge head and body in the snowy foam.
> At once the flood will take away your curse." [334]

Your higher self is always there . . . even when you "know it not."

You are already connected to the Infinite . . . and always will be.

Notes

1. Gabor Maté, "From Jungle to 'Civilization': How Plant Medicines Can Promote Health in a Toxic Culture," available in *MAPS Podcast*, Episode 37.
2. Genesis 28: 13b - 15.
3. The Milky Way, as explained on pages 7 - 10, does not "rise up" only from the southern horizon, but forms a ring which (from our perspective on earth) stretches from horizon to horizon, generally from the southern to the northern horizons. It appears to "rise up" from the southern horizon if we are situated in the northern hemisphere and imagine the widest and brightest portion of the galactic band to be the "base" of the shining column. Most descriptions throughout this book of "up" and "down" in the heavens are given from the perspective of a viewer in the northern hemisphere, with apologies to the readers in the southern hemisphere who will have to invert some descriptions (but they are probably used to that already).
4. *Star Myths of the World, Volume Three*, 377 - 378.
5. *Ibid*, 375.
6. "About H. A. and Margret Rey."
7. *Ibid*.
8. Rothstein, "Monkey Business in a World of Evil."
9. *Ibid*.
10. "About H. A. and Margret Rey."
11. "Monkey Business in a World of Evil."
12. "About H. A. and Margret Rey."
13. *Ibid*.
14. *Ibid*.
15. Rey, 9.
16. *Ibid*, 10.
17. *Ibid*.
18. *Ibid*, 12.
19. *Ibid*, x.
20. Orwell, 246.
21. Rey, 16.
22. *Ibid*.
23. *Ancient World-Wide System*, 85.
24. Orwell, 246 - 247.
25. *Star Myths of the World, Volume Two*, 432 - 433.
26. The constellation Ophiuchus can be envisioned as having three components: a central body and two "serpent-halves" flanking the central body on either side. If we orient the constellation such that its triangular head is upwards and fainter legs and feet are downwards, then we can describe the serpent-halves as a "left serpent-half" and a "right serpent-half." The diagram below shows the constellation, with the serpent-halves labeled. The left

515

Notes

serpent-half can more precisely be called the "east serpent-half" and the right half can be called the "west serpent-half" (because when we look towards Ophiuchus and the zodiac constellations near it, we face south if we are in the northern hemisphere, and west will be to the right when we face south, and east to the left; in the southern hemisphere, Ophiuchus will be upside-down from the way it is pictured here but we will look towards the north to see it and the zodiac constellations near it). The west serpent-half, on the right of the central body, is surmounted by a small circlet of stars, and thus is typically envisioned as the head of the serpent that the Ophiuchus figure is holding, and thus we can also call the west half the "head-end" of the serpent, and we can call the east half the "tail-end." These serpent-halves of Ophiuchus take on many other roles in various myths: one or both can be envisioned as spears, pillars, vines, branches of an olive tree, sides of a cliff, or other figures.

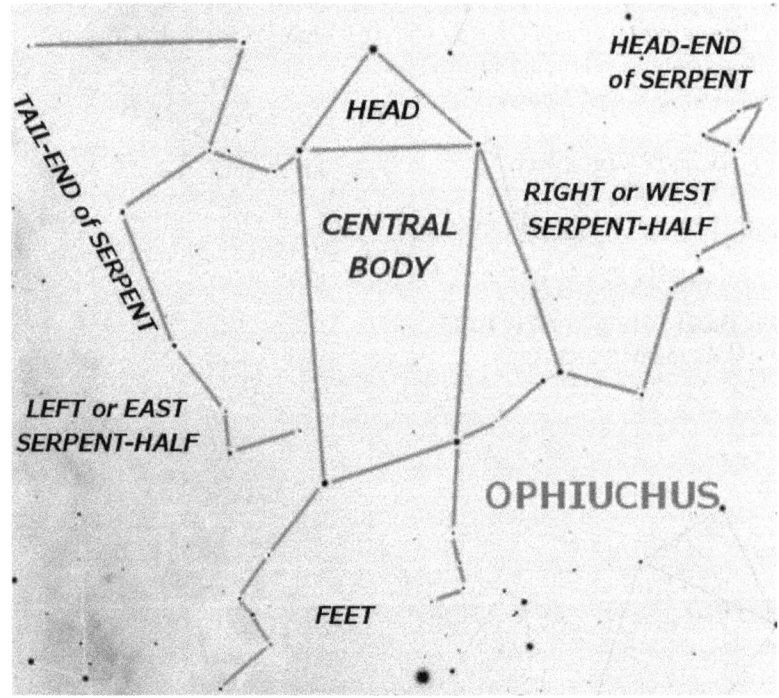

27. See the Bhagavata Purana, canto 10, chapters 15 and 16, which can be found online at bhagavata.org.
28. From Étienne Henri Gilson's Foreword to *City of God*, 16.
29. *City of God*, Book 6, chapter 1 (this passage is found on page 120 of the edition listed in the Bibliography).
30. *Ibid*, Book 4, chapter 27, pages 96 - 97.
31. *Ibid*, Book 4, chapter 28, page 97.
32. *Ibid*, Book 6, chapter 4, page 126.
33. *Ibid*, Book 7, chapter 33, page 142.

Notes

34. *Star Myths of the World, Volume Two*, 484 - 500.
35. *Star Myths of the World, Volume Three*, 525 - 537.
36. For evidence of the connections of Marduk, Ptah, Amun, Atum, and Ra with the constellation Hercules, see *The Ancient World-Wide System*.
37. From the "Hebrew and Chaldee Dictionary" section of James Strong's *Exhaustive Concordance of the Bible* (listed in the Bibliography) for the entries *barach* (H1272) and *bariyach* (H1281), found on page 24. An online scanned edition of the 1890 Strong's *Exhaustive Concordance* (including the "Hebrew and Chaldee Dictionary" section following the English concordance) can be accessed at:
https://archive.org/details/exhaustiveconcor1890stro/page/n11/mode/2up
The definitions given for H1272 and H1281 can also be found online at the *Blue Letter Bible* website at www.blueletterbible.org -- see:
https://www.blueletterbible.org/lang/lexicon/lexicon.cfm?strongs=H1272&t=KJV
and:
https://www.blueletterbible.org/lang/lexicon/lexicon.cfm?Strongs=H1281&t=KJV
sfdg
38. From the *Hebrew and Chaldee Lexicon* of Wilhelm Gesenius, page 141.
39. *Ancient World-Wide System*, 408, 708.
40. De Santillana and von Dechend, *Hamlet's Mill*, 126.
41. *Ibid*, 8, 4.
42. *Ibid*, 177.
43. *Ibid*, 151.
44. *Ibid*, 166, 424.
45. *Ibid*, 176.
46. *Ibid*.
47. *Ancient World-Wide System*, 171 - 180.
48. *Ibid*, 267, 291 - 297; *Star Myths of the World, Volume Two*, 65- 66, 311 - 315.
49. *Star Myths of the World, Volume Four*, 331.
50. *Ibid*, 339.
51. *Ancient World-Wide System*, 305 - 311; see also *Star Myths of the World, Volume Three*, 516 - 517.
52. *Ancient World-Wide System*, 523 - 525.
53. *Star Myths of the World, Volume Three*, 544 - 545.
54. Mahabharata, Book 2, section 67. Ganguli translation.
55. *Ancient World-Wide System*, 277 - 280.
56. Sturluson, *Edda*, 57 - 58.
57. Schwaller, *Esoterism & Symbol*, 1, 3, 75.
58. Icke, *Beyond the Cutting Edge* (2008).
59. *Ibid*.
60. *Ibid*.
61. *Ibid*.
62. *Ibid*.
63. *Ibid*.

Notes

64. *Ibid.*
65. *Astrotheology for Life*, 6.
66. Christopher Knowles interview on *Higherside Chats*, October 20, 2017.
67. Matthew Henry's *Commentary on the Whole Bible*, facsimile reprint of Volume II-I: *First Kings to Esther*, pages 19 - 20.
68. *Star Myths of the World, Volume Four*, 102, 194 - 195.
69. In my 2017 book *Astrotheology for Life*, I wrote on page 4: "Pioneering Swedish folklorist Carl Wilhelm von Sydow (1878 - 1952) coined the term 'oicotype' (sometimes spelled 'oikotype') in 1927 to describe variations upon a story-pattern found in different cultures or different parts of the world. In doing so, he was borrowing a term from botany, describing local or regional variants in a plant species."

In 2019, folklorist Ronald M. James published an article entitled "Nazis, Trolls, and the Grateful Dead: Turmoil Among Sweden's Folklorists," detailing more information about Carl Wilhelm von Sydow and his interaction with a student named Sven S. Liljeblad (1899 - 2000), who appears to have been the one to suggest the new approach that led Liljeblad and von Sydow together to develop what James in his article calls "the Oicotype Method."

Ronald James explains that: "To debut this idea, Liljeblad wrote a treatise on the 'Grateful Dead' motif: a hero sees a corpse on the roadside; people scorn the remains because the man was reviled; taking pity, the hero buries the corpse; the man's spirit dedicates itself to the hero as the Grateful Dead. Folklorist Jan-Öjvind Swahn, a fellow student of von Sydow, describes this as 'the first real bomb under the far too mechanical methodology of the Finnish School.'"

Thus, it appears that Liljeblad must get at least as much credit as von Sydow for the development of the concept of "oicotypes" or <u>patterns in myth and folklore which can be found over and over again in various cultures around the globe</u>.

Obviously, when *Astrotheology for Life* was published in 2017, I did not have access to the information provided in the later article by Ronald James, which was published in 2019 -- the article by James can be found at *Folklore Thursday* (https://folklorethursday.com) and the full URL is listed in the Bibliography.

70. From Fable 77 of the *Fabulae* attributed to Gaius Julius Hyginus (64 BC - AD 17), although the writing style and numerous grammar errors in the text have led scholars to conclude that these *Fabulae* were not written by Hyginus, and thus (not knowing the name of the actual author) they are usually ascribed to "Pseudo-Hyginus." Translation is by Mary Grant, originally published in 1960 and accessed on the *Theoi* website in 2020: https://theoi.com/Text/HyginusFabulae2.html.
71. Pindar, *Nemean Odes*, Trans. Paley: Ode 10, pages 218 - 221.
72. *Ibid*, page 219.
73. Bowden, *Mystery Cults of the Ancient World*, 65 - 66.

74. *Ibid*, 66.
75. From Alcman's fragments, Fragment 2, translated by David A. Campbell. Cited on *Theoi.com* at https://www.theoi.com/Ouranios/Dioskouroi.html and referencing *Greek Lyric, Volume II: Anacreon, Anacreontea, Choral Lyric from Olympus to Alcman*. Trans. David A. Campbell. Loeb Classical Library. 143. Cambridge, Massachusetts: Harvard UP, 1988.
76. Kuhn, *Lost Light*, 156 - 157.
77. *Ibid*, 158.
78. "Shield of Heracles," Trans. Evelyn-White, in *Hesiod, Homeric Hymns, Epic Cycle, Homerica*, 221 - 223. *Thebes* sometimes "Thebe" in this translation.
79. Levine, *Healing Trauma*, 1 - 2. Regarding the assertion that the word "trauma" (typically used for physical wounds) would not begin to be used in the sense of "psychological trauma" until the 1970s, Dr. Levine says on the pages cited here: "I began my career as a scientist in the radical environment of Berkeley, California, in the mid-1960s. While studying the effects of accumulated stress on the nervous system, I began to suspect that most organisms have an innate capacity to rebound from threatening and stressful events. At that time, I had no knowledge of psychological trauma -- the term would not be defined in its modern form for another 15 years."
80. *Ibid*, 7 - 8.
81. Maté, "From Jungle to 'Civilization': How Plant Medicines Can Promote Health in a Toxic Culture," available in *MAPS Podcast*, Episode 37.
82. Levine, *Healing Trauma*, 9.
83. *Epic of Gilgamesh*, Trans. Andrew George, xvii, lx.
84. *Ibid*, Tablet I. 105, found on page 5 of the edition cited.
85. *Ibid*, Tablet II. 40, page 13.
86. *Ibid*, Tablet P. 183 - 184, page 15.
87. *Ibid*, Tablet I. 195 - 202, page 8.
88. *Ibid*, Tablet I. 202, page 8.
89. *Ibid*, Tablet P. 90 - 111, page 14.
90. Meyer, *Nag Hammadi Library*, 48 - 52.
91. *Ibid*, 48.
92. The Book of Thomas the Contender, Trans. John D. Turner. *Gnostic Society Library*, gnosis.org.
93. Maté, *When the Body Says No* (book), 163.
94. Maté, "When the Body Says No: Mind / Body Unity and the Stress-Disease Connection." Talk given at the California Institute of Integral Studies.
95. Maté, "From Jungle to 'Civilization': How Plant Medicines Can Promote Health in a Toxic Culture."
96. *Ibid*.
97. *Ibid*.
98. Tolkien, *Two Towers*, 303 - 304.
99. *Ibid*, 411.
100. *Two Towers*, film.

Notes

101. Levine, *Healing Trauma*, 9.
102. *Star Myths of the World, Volume Two*, 383 - 387.
103. Mahabharata, Trans. Ganguli, 6.16.
104. *Ibid.*
105. *Ibid*, 6. 25.
106. *Ibid*, 6. 21.
107. *Ibid*, 6.23.
108. *Tao Te Ching*, Trans. Victor H. Mair, 141 - 142.
109. *Ibid*, xiii - xiv, 133 - 135.
110. Mahabharata, Trans. Ganguli, 6.26.
111. *Tao Te Ching*, Trans. Victor H. Mair, xv.
112. *Upanishads*, Trans. Swami Nikhilananda, 133 - 150.
113. Gabor Maté interview with Dr. Rangan Chatterjee on *Feel Better Live More* podcast, Episode 37.
114. *Upanishads*, Trans. Mascaró, 59.
115. *Ibid*, 83.
116. Maté, "Psychedelics and Unlocking the Unconscious: from Cancer to Addiction," available in *MAPS Podcast*, Episode 4.
117. Gabor Maté interview with Eric Zimmer. *The One You Feed* podcast, Episode 249.
118. *Udāna: Exclamations*. Trans. Thānissaro Bhikkhu (Geoffrey DeGraff). section cited is from Udāna 1.3, page 28.
119. "A Sketch of the Buddha's Life: Readings from the Pali Canon." *Access to Insight*. 2005. https://www.accesstoinsight.org/ptf/buddha.html
120. "Pabbaja Sutta: The Going Forth." Trans. Thānissaro Bhikkhu. 1997. https://www.accesstoinsight.org/tipitaka/kn/snp/snp.3.01.than.html
121. *Star Myths of the World, Volume Three*, 449.
122. *Star Myths of the World, Volume Two*, 634 - 635.
123. Odyssey, Trans. Buckley, 107.
124. Odyssey, Trans. Fagles, 166 and also Odyssey, Trans. Buckley, 110.
125. *Lost Light*, 46.
126. *Ancient World-Wide System*, 221.
127. *Star Myths of the World, Volume Two*, 277, 280 - 281.
128. *Star Myths of the World, Volume Four*, 346 - 348.
129. Ollestad, *Crazy for the Storm*, 263.
130. *Ibid.*
131. *Ibid*, 266.
132. *Ibid.*
133. *Ibid*, 266 - 267.
134. *Ibid*, 267.
135. *Morgan Hill, California, Earthquake of April 24, 1984*, page 7.
136. *Ibid*, and also *USGS Earthquake Glossary*, "Richter Scale."
137. "Greatest dad saves EVER!!!" (incident described begins at about 0:06 seconds into the clip).

520

138. Ollestad, 263.
139. *Ibid*, 264.
140. *Ibid*, 208.
141. *Ibid*, 264.
142. Pavia and Pavia, *An American Town and the Vietnam War*, 28.
143. *Ibid*.
144. Cited in Carter, *Science and Psychic Phenomena*, 53.
145. Dossey, interview: "The Power of Premontions," 5 - 6. Note that the Institute of Noetic Sciences, founded in 1973, has a deeply suspicious history, clearly closely involved with intelligence agencies and Paperclip scientists.
146. *Star Myths of the World, Volume Three*, 51 - 53, 318 - 322.
147. "Facts & Statistics," *Anxiety and Depression Association of America*.
148. Pratt, Brody and Gu, "Antidepressant Use Among Persons Aged 12 and Over: United States, 2011 - 2014," *NCHS Data Brief No. 283*, August 2017.
149. *Ibid*.
150. Ibid.
151. "Major Depression." *National Institute of Mental Health*.
152. *Ibid*.
153. Geiger and Davis, "A growing number of American teenagers -- particularly girls -- are facing depression."
154. "Major Depression."
155. Levine, 9.
156. Gabor Maté, "Dr. Gabor Maté on Childhood Trauma, The Real Cause of Anxiety and our 'Insane' Culture." Interview with Martin Caparrotta, 23 November 2019.
157. *Ibid*.
158. D'Aulaire and D'Aulaire, *Ingrid and Edgar Parin D'Aulaire's Book of Greek Myths*, 36 - 37.
159. See Orphic Hymn 36.
160. Hudson, *J is for Junk Economics*, 255. Note that public tax is not "rent-seeking," although those who want to privatize everything try to redefine the term "rent-seeking" to apply to the public sector (thus ignoring the fact that rents are a <u>private</u> tax -- a key distinction). Hudson writes elsewhere that:

> Neoliberals [. . .] have re-defined "rent-seeking" to refer only to politicians and labor unions lobbying for "special privileges" such as Social Security, a minimum wage and public programs to meet other basic needs. But these programs have nothing to do with classical rent seeking. They are proper functions of government.

That quotation is from *J is for Junk Economics*, 199.
161. Quotation from Barbiero, *Secret Society of Moses*, 260. Note that Barbiero, quoted in this passage, refers to the families behind the dissolution of the empire and the establishment of feudalism as the "priestly families," according to his theory that they were descended from elite families saved by

Notes

Josephus following the conquest of Jerusalem by Vespasian and Titus. Barbiero believes that these families were descended from the literal and historical Moses of the book of Genesis: obviously, I disagree with Barbiero's theory at this point because I do not believe that Moses was a literal or historical figure (on the contrary, I believe that it can be demonstrated beyond reasonable doubt that Moses is a celestial and metaphorical figure). It should go without saying that I reject all forms of anti-Semitism, racism, and the automatic attribution of criminality to *any* group based on *external* or *inherited* characteristics or heritage of any sort: criminality is a *behavior*, and men and women from any and all backgrounds can be found engaging in criminal behavior which harms other men and women. I am convinced that the vast majority of men and women, of every heritage and background, do not participate in organized crime; on the other hand, to deny the very existence of organized crime would be ridiculous.

162. *Undying Stars*, 265.
163. Hudson, *J is for Junk Economics*, 200.
164. Hudson, *Killing the Host*, 30.
165. Pauwels, *The Great Class War, 1914 - 1918*, 17 - 18.
166. *Ibid*, 18 - 19.
167. *J is for Junk Economics*, 181.
168. *Ibid*.
169. *Ibid*, 181.
170. *Ibid*, 60.
171. *Ibid*, 85.
172. *Ibid*, 199.
173. Koutantou, "Workers protest as Greece sells Piraeus Port to China COSCO," 08 April 2016.
174. *Ibid*.
175. See Michael Hudson's 2018 book entitled *. . . and forgive them their debts: Lending, Foreclosure and Redemption from Bronze Age Finance to the Jubilee Year*.
176. In *Killing the Host*, Michael Hudson writes on page 57:

> The financial sector now occupies the dominant position that landlords did in times past. Debt service plays the extractive role that land rent did in Ricardo's day.

On pages 166 and 167 of *J is for Junk Economics*, he writes:

> Medieval feudalism's seizure of land and natural resources by military conquest and the extraction of groundrent is achieved today by financial means: debt leverage, foreclosure and privatization. Just as feudalism monopolized access to land for housing and food to force an enserfed population to work for subsistence, today's economies block access to housing and education without paying debt service that siphons off labor's income above basic subsistence levels (166).

Notes

and

> Much as warlords seized land in the Norman Conquest and levied rent on subject populations (starting with the Domesday Book, the great land census of England and Wales ordered by William the Conqueror), so today's financialized mode of warfare uses debt leverage and foreclosure to pry away land, natural resources and economic infrastructure. The commons are privatized by bondholders and bankers, gaining control of government and shifting taxes onto labor and small-scale industry (167).

177. Odyssey, Trans. Robert Fagles: Book I, lines 261 - 267, pages 84 - 85.
178. The ancient author Pausanias described Perseus as "admiring her beauty, even in death," speaking of Medusa -- although it should be noted that Pausanias was here trying to euhemerize the account of Perseus slaying Medusa (from his *Description of Greece* or *Guide to Greece*, Book 2 and chapter 21, in paragraphs 4 through 6, during the description of the notable sites in the vicinity of Corinth and Argos). It should be quite obvious that I disagree with the entire general precept of "euhemerization," which attempts to find some ordinary historical persons and events at the basis of all the myths (usually by simply imagining a fictitious set of historical figures who "might have" done this or that ordinary human action, which later "became" a myth). This method of "de-mythologizing" the myths is supposed to have originated with Euhemerus (thought to have lived c. fourth and third centuries BC). Because the figures and episodes in the myths around the globe can be shown to be based on the stars, their origin instead via the "mythologization" of imagined "historical" figures from one particular land or time period (as argued by the euhemerists) can be seen to be extremely dubious. The translation itself, in which Pausanias describes "Perseus, admiring her beauty even in death . . . " is from W. H. S. Jones, in *Pausanias: Description of Greece, Books 1 - 2* (1918), page 358.
179. Pindar's Pythian Ode 12, section 8, Trans. Frederick Apthorp Paley.
180. Odyssey, Book 10, line 582.
181. Odyssey, Trans. Fagles. Book 10, lines 581 - 583, page 246.
182. Walsh, *The Cult of Mithras in Late Antiquity: Development, Decline and Demise ca. AD 270 - 430*, page 15.
183. *Ibid*, 25.
184. Clauss, *Roman Cult of Mithras*, 1990, xx - xxi.
185. *Ibid*, xxi, and also Bjørnebye, "*Hic locus est felix, sanctus, piusque benignus*": *The cult of Mithras in fourth century Rome*, 11.
186. Bjørnebye, 13 and also Clauss, 42.
187. Bjørnebye, 13.
188. Walsh, 28.
189. Beck, "If So, How? Representing 'Coming Back to Life' in the Mysteries of Mithras."
190. *Ibid*.

Notes

191. *Ibid.*
192. *Ibid.*
193. *Ibid.* For the entire text of Porphyry's *On the Cave of the Nymphs in the Thirteenth Book of the Odyssey*, see the *Selected Works of Porphyry*, translated by Thomas Taylor and published in 1823, referenced in the Bibliography; this text by Porphyry is found on pages 171 through 200 of that volume.
194. *Ibid.*
195. *Ibid.*
196. *Ibid*, and quoting Origen's *Contra Celsum* 6.22.
197. *Ibid.*
198. *Ibid.*
199. *Ibid.*
200. *Ibid* -- italics are in the original.
201. Ulansey, *The Origins of the Mithraic Mysteries*, 6.
202. *Ibid*, 11.
203. *Ibid*, 10.
204. *Ibid*, 15.
205. *Ibid*, 19.
206. *Ibid*, 26.
207. *Ibid*, 26 - 28.
208. *Ibid*, 32.
209. *Ibid*, 27 - 30.
210. *Ibid*, 110 - 111.
211. *Star Myths of the World, Volume Two*, 246, 644 - 646.
212. Odyssey, Trans. Robert Fagles, Book 16. 276 - 281, page 346.
213. *Star Myths of the World, Volume Two*, 645.
214. Clauss, 42.
215. Walsh, 9.
216. Ulansey, 4.
217. *Ibid*, citing Renan's 1923 work *Marc-Aurèle et la fin du monde antique*, and translating it himself in the line cited (into English from the original French).
218. Ulansey, 4.
219. Clauss, 61.
220. *Ibid.*
221. The word *felicissimus* is the superlative form of the adjective *felix* in Latin, taking the ending *-us* when describing a masculine singular noun (in this case, a mithraeum, which is masculine) or the ending *-a* when describing a feminine singular noun. The adjective *felix* is usually translated as "happy," which is not incorrect, because our word "happy" (which has had its meaning somewhat watered down through over-use to the point that its origin has been forgotten and thereby diminished) carries the same root as "happen" and "happenstance," and thus the connection to "Fate" or "the way things work

out" (as in our phrase, "as it happens"). In other words, our word "happy" actually carries the connotation of "when things work out favorably" or even "when Fate smiles and permits things to go in a beneficial way" -- and hence there is a connection to our adjective "lucky" (which itself has a connotation that relates to the realm of Fate and the gods, as seen by our occasional reference to a deity known as Lady Luck -- thus "lucky" also carries the connotation of "when things work out favorably," as in: "when Lady Luck smiles upon you"). Thus, we sometimes see the Latin word *felix* translated into English as "lucky." We could also suggest the word "blessed" (in the sense of "blessed by Fate") for the meaning of this word. Perhaps the best translation, however, would be the English word that descends from the Latin: the word "felicitous." Thus, the name of the *Mithraeum of Felicissimus* translates into something akin to "the Mithraeum of Supreme Blessedness" or "the Mithraeum of the Most Felicitous Favor from the mysterious realm of Fate" or "the Mithraeum of Things Working Out in the absolute most happy, lucky or felicitous way possible."

222. Clauss, 98 and 130 - 131 (citing the ancient literalist Church Father, Jerome, who records the seven grades of Mithraic initiation in one of his letters; the seven Mithraic grades are also described by Ulansey on page 19).

223. From a more sinister perspective, hierarchical structures also enable those in control to restrict access to the higher ranks and the "inncer circles" to those newer and more idealistic initiates who can first be observed at the lower ranks passing certain "tests" successfully. Those whose performance appears satisfactory can then be asked to take part in some action or some endeavor which will compromise the candidate in some way (for which, the candidate is told, he has been "specially chosen" due to his superlative performance on the previous challenges), and may be that only *after* they have agreed to this new action or endeavor that they realize that in performing it, they have in some way done something that could deeply compromise their public reputation. Using this tactic, the organization can ensure that by the time newer and more idealistic initiates gain more awareness of what is really going on, they cannot reveal what they know due to threat of that compromising action being revealed more widely. Those judged to be too idealistic or constituted in such a way that it would be inappropriate for this technique to work will, of course, never be approached with the "opportunity" to gain access to the successive "inner circles." For more on this tactic, and the incontrovertible evidence that it is in fact employed in certain secret societies (specifically, intelligence agencies and special military "black ops" units) in the modern day, see the interview with author Douglas Valentine, listed in the Bibliography, and referenced later in the "Concluding Thoughts" chapter of this book.

224. Because Flavio Barbiero's theory posits that an elite group of "priestly families" (which he believes to have been descended directly from a literal and historical figure of Moses) were the primary organizers of the astonishing (and astonishingly successful) long-term plot to gain control of the Roman Empire,

Notes

following the fall of Jerusalem under the Roman armies led by Vespasian and Titus (who later became emperors), my arguments in *The Undying Stars* (which apply aspects of Barbiero's theory) have been criticized by at least one reader as being anti-Semitic, and as falling into the category of right-wing conspiracy which argues that "the Jews" are behind everything.

This accusation is false: I flatly reject anti-Semitism without hesitation or qualification.

Anyone who has read this far in the present volume, and anyone who has read *The Undying Stars* (as well as any of my other books or my more than 1,200 blog posts covering a period of nearly ten years) should know that I do not propagate anti-Semitism and that in fact I repudiate and stand against it and all other forms of racism and bigotry.

They should also be able to see that I view the institution of literalist Christianity as a major force in inflicting trauma and alienation upon individuals (including through doctrines such as the threat of eternal torment in a literal hell, as well as other teachings regarding the relationship between the sexes, the relationship between humanity and nature, the relationship between humanity and the animal kingdom, and teachings about the raising of children and the use of "the rod") as well as a major factor in trying to falsely excuse and falsely "justify" colonialism, imperialism, forced conversions, the obliteration of other cultures and other sacred traditions, slavery, oppression, economic exploitation and repression, feudalism, and genocide.

I do believe that Flavio Barbiero's theory may be correct, in identifying elites from the Hasmonean dynasty of ancient Judea (or Judaea) -- including Flavius Josephus -- as having collaborated with the Flavians (particularly Vespasian and Titus, who both later became emperors of Rome) and using their position to launch the ambitious plan described in *The Secret Society of Moses*.

However, as anyone who reads Barbiero's book (as well as anyone who reads *The Undying Stars*) should realize, if Barbiero's hypothesis is correct, then Josephus was undeniably a traitor to his nation and his people, having collaborated with the Romans and having supplied Vespasian and Titus with access to the hidden wealth of Judea, which enabled those generals to continue to pay their armies and thus to successfully install themselves as emperors (for which they repaid Josephus handsomely, with Vespasian even giving Josephus his own private villa where Vespasian himself had lived prior to Vespasian becoming emperor -- an astonishing reward and one we learn about from the pen of Josephus himself).

The story of Josephus is primarily another example of the elites of one nation working together with the elites of another nation, and showing more loyalty to their fellow elites than to the non-elites of their own home land. According to Flavio Barbiero's theory, which he backs up with enormous amounts of evidence, the descendants of these elite "Flavians" became -- after the deliberate dissolution of the Roman Empire -- the oligarchs who ruled their various fiefdoms throughout Europe, supported by the literalist Christian church. To criticize this system, which oppressed and exploited basically everyone in Europe who was not a member of the "noble" families, is not an example of "anti-Semitism."

On pages 355 through 396 of *The Secret Society of Moses*, Flavio Barbiero presents abundant evidence that the symbols and heraldry which have been used for centuries by these European elites, as well as the symbols and coats of arms associated with the literalist Christian clergy (including the coats of arms of the Vatican and the various Popes) derive directly from ancient Hasmonean symbology and from the symbols associated with various episodes and figures described in the Old Testament (such as towers, eagles, lions, pillars, harps, and so forth) -- all of which I would argue to be celestial in origin. This evidence argues quite strongly in favor of Barbiero's theory, but to write against the excesses of the oppressive and exploitative elites of Europe, or against the later institutions of European colonialism and imperialism, cannot possibly be labeled "anti-Semitism," just because one explores the evidence that the oligarchical families of Europe may have descended from a certain very successful group of elites, some of them elites from the Hasmonean dynasty of Judea and some of them elites from the Flavian dynasty of Rome, conspiring together. In my opinion, in this system, we see collaboration among elites from a variety of backgrounds, ethnicities, and religious beliefs, and they primarily conspire against those excluded from their so-called "elite" circles.

When trying to figure out what is going on, we should more often draw the lines "horizontally" (between "classes" or strata of society) rather than "vertically" (between nations, ethnicities, sexes, and groups of people from different heritages or geographies) -- which is precisely why those who would prefer that men and women never figure out what is really going on are constantly encouraging us to draw "vertical" lines between various groups, a phenomenon which has become completely obsessive in recent decades and which shows little sign of slowing down. The distinction between "vertical" and "horizontal" lines is introduced by historian Jacques R. Pauwels in his book *The great class war, 1914 - 1918*, which is listed in the Bibliography.

225. Barbiero, *Secret Society of Moses*, 157.
226. *Ibid.*
227. *Ibid*, 176.
228. *Ibid.*
229. *Ibid*, 177.
230. *Ibid*, 176.
231. *Ibid*, 176 - 177.
232. *Ibid*, 177.
233. *Ibid.*
234. *Ibid.*

Notes

235. *Ibid*, 178 - 179.
236. *Ibid*, 178.
237. *Ibid*, 186 - 187.
238. *Ibid*, 185 - 186.
239. *Ibid*, 159.
240. *Ibid*, 187.
241. *Ibid*, 188 - 190.
242. *Ibid*, 192.
243. Barbiero, "Mithras and Jesus: Two sides of the same coin."
244. Barbiero, *Secret Society of Moses*, 161.
245. *Ibid*, 163.
246. *Ibid*, 163 - 164.
247. *Ibid*, 163.
248. *Ibid*.
249. *Ibid*, 200.
250. *Ibid*, 205 ff.
251. *Ibid*, 201.
252. *Ibid*, 206.
253. *Ibid*, 214.
254. *Ibid*, 152 - 156, for example.
255. In commentary by Cameron and Hall in their translation of Eusebius, *Life of Constantine*, 207.
256. Clauss, 62.
257. Seneca, *Tragedies*, Trans. Frank Justus Miller, page 753.
258. Ovid, *Metamorphoses*, Trans. Brookes Moore, page 516.
259. *Ibid*, 516 - 517.
260. *Ibid*, 518.
261. Kingsley, *In the Dark Places of Wisdom*, 33 - 34.
262. Barbiero, *Secret Society of Moses*, 163.
263. *Ibid*, 320.
264. *Ibid*, 168.
265. *Ibid*, 169.
266. *Ibid*, 171 - 172.
267. *Ibid*, 409.
268. *Ibid*, 410.
269. *Ibid*, 409.
270. The discussion of the possible meaning of the distinction between "speculative" and "operative" Masonry is found in Barbiero's *Secret Society of Moses* on pages 407 - 414.
271. Levenda, *Unholy Alliance*, 183.
272. *Ibid*, 167.
273. *Ibid*, 73 - 74.
274. *Ibid*, 74.
275. *Ibid*, 74 - 75.

276. *Ibid*, 33.
277. *Ibid*, 155.
278. *Ibid*, 35.
279. *Ibid*, 36.
280. *Ibid*, 78.
281. Note that I am not here arguing that the esoteric in general, and esoteric societies in particular, are inherently right-wing or inherently evil: in fact quite the contrary. The argument I make is that the esoteric ancient system was *deliberately subverted* during the first through fourth centuries in the Roman Empire by those wishing to take for themselves the ancient wisdom (and the natural resources given by nature and the gods), and that secret societies which descend from that particular historical line are *designed* to preserve esoteric knowledge (when in "safe" mode) and to uphold the general conservative system (of the "nobility" and the literalist church) when taking political action. Thus, these societies tend towards what is called the "right-wing" because they are part of a system designed to protect the "old order" (the feudal order instituted after the destruction of antiquity by the rise of Christianity) rather than to overthrow it. It should go without saying that I see this proclivity and goal as the *inversion* of the original intent of the esoteric myths given to humanity. The study of the esoteric and even the creation of esoteric societies are neither of them inherently evil nor inherently right-wing. Both pursuits can theoretically be undertaken without the promotion of violence against others and without the promotion of the privatization of what properly belongs to all the people of a land. However, the thesis being presented argues that those esoteric groups historically descended from the Mithraic organization will have an inherent tilt towards the same methods and the same ends pursued by the Sol Invictus cult upon which they are deliberately patterned and with which they are in fact connected. Note that the very terminology "right-wing" originated during the period of the French Revolution of 1789, when those who sat on the right side of the parliament's central seat were those who supported the *ancien régime* (that is to say, the "old order" of social hierarchy, the royals and the "nobility," and the power and authority of the clergy and the literalist Christian church).
282. Barbiero, *Secret Society of Moses*, 335 - 340.
283. Levenda, 161.
284. *Ibid*, 226 - 231.
285. *Ibid*, 191 - 197, 187 - 191.
286. *Ibid*, 154.
287. *Ibid*, 151.
288. Again, this proclivity is by no means a necessary feature of the study of the esoteric or of the formation of esoteric societies: for more discussion, please see note 281, above.
289. Levenda, 107.

Notes

290. *Ibid*, 15, 267 - 268. Levenda also points to the extensive evidence of the active and extraordinary lengths taken by networks within the Catholic Church to smuggle Nazis (including members of the SS) out of Europe, in some cases dressed in clerical robes, documented by Ladislas Faragó in *Aftermath: The Search for Martin Bormann* (1974); see for instance the discussion on page 15 in *Unholy Alliance*.
291. Jacobsen, *Operation Paperclip*, xii.
292. *Ibid*, 319.
293. *Ibid*, 319 - 320.
294. *Ibid*.
295. *Ibid*.
296. Levenda, 118 - 119.
297. *Aleister Crowley and Western Esotericism*, Eds. Bogdan and Starr, 4.
298. Bogdan, "Envisioning the Birth of a New Aeon: Dispensationalism and Millenarianism in the Thelemic Tradition," in *Aleister Crowley and Western Esotericism*, 89 - 106; quotation is from page 100.
299. Owen, "The Sorcerer and His Apprentice: Aleister Crowley and the Magical Exploration of Edwardian Subjectivity," in *Aleister Crowley and Western Esotericism*, 15 - 52; quotation is from pages 33 - 34.
300. *Hamlet's Mill*, 122 -123.
301. See for instance Eliade, 153, 168, 257 - 258, 329, 352, 395.
302. Beck, "If So, How? Representing 'Coming Back to Life' in the Mysteries of Mithras," and citing Origen's *Contra Celsum*, 6. 22.
303. Bogdan, "Envisioning the Birth of a New Aeon," 99.
304. Lachman, *Aleister Crowley*, 18.
305. Ramayana of Valmiki. Trans. Shastri, 38.
306. *Ibid*, 37.
307. *Ibid*.
308. Levenda, 306.
309. Bain, *Most Dangerous Book in the World*, 70.
310. *Ibid*, 70 - 72.
311. *Ibid*, 21.
312. *Ibid*, 26.
313. *Ibid*, 40.
314. *Ibid*, 55.
315. *Ibid*, 32ff.
316. Owen, "The Sorcerer and His Apprentice," in *Aleister Crowley and Western Esotericism*, 21.
317. "Inana's descent to the nether world." *Electronic Text Corpus of Sumerian Literature*. Eds. Black, Cunningham, Flückiger-Hawker, Robson, and Zólyomi. etcsl.orinst.ox.ac.uk/section1/tr141.htm
318. *Ibid*.
319. *Ibid*.
320. *Ibid*.

321. This celestial interpretation of the story of Inanna's descent and her condemnation to hang as a corpse on a hook in the underworld is explored in *The Ancient World-Wide System*, 446.
322. *Ancient World-Wide System*, 342 - 347.
323. *Star Myths of the World, Volume Four*, 334 - 337.
324. *Lost Light*, 158.
325. *Ibid*, 178.
326. See Ovid's *Metamorphoses*, Book 11, lines 187 and following. In the Brookes More translation referenced earlier, these lines are found in Volume 3, page 518.
327. Freke and Gandy, *Jesus Mysteries*, 151.
328. Mazaheri, "(A Soviet) Superman."
329. Book of the Dead, Trans. Budge, 180 - 183, 177; also Book of the Dead, Trans. Faulkner, plate 32.
330. Valentine, interview with Sam Tripoli, *Tinfoil Hat* podcast, Episode 294.
331. Pauwels, 14ff.
332. Valentine, *Phoenix Program*, 63.
333. Gabor Maté interview with Martin Caparrotta on *Human Window*. 334. Ovid, *Metamorphoses*, Trans. Brookes More, 518.

Image Credits
listed by page number

8. Milky Way depiction, showing location of our solar system. Wikimedia commons.
https://commons.wikimedia.org/wiki/File:LombergA1024.jpg

15. Jacob's Dream, 1860. Wikimedia commons.
https://commons.wikimedia.org/wiki/File:Schnorr_von_Carolsfeld_Bibel_in_Bildern_1860_032.png

31. Artwork from Stellarium.org.

35. and 37. Bell Krater showing Artemis and Actaeon scene. Beazley, *Attic Red-figured Vases in American Museums*, page 113.

51. Heracles battling the Amazons. Wikimedia commons.
https://commons.wikimedia.org/wiki/File:Herakles_Amazones_Staatliche_Antikensammlungen_1711.jpg

54. Heracles battling Cycnus. Wikimedia commons.
https://commons.wikimedia.org/wiki/File:Herakles_Kyknos_Louvre_F36.jpg

56. Heracles and Achelous. Wikimedia commons.
https://commons.wikimedia.org/wiki/File:Herakles_Achelous_Louvre_G365.jpg

58. Hydria depicting struggle between Heracles and Triton. Boston Museum of Fine Art. Photograph by the author.

59. Battle between Zeus and Typhon. Wikimedia commons.
https://commons.wikimedia.org/wiki/File:Combat_de_Zeus_contre_Typhon.jpg

62. Left: Gorgon. Wikimedia commons.
https://commons.wikimedia.org/wiki/File:Kleitias_decorazione_del_vaso_françois_570_ac_ca._gorgoneion_01.jpg
Right: Achilles dragging the corpse of Hector. Wikimedia commons.
https://commons.wikimedia.org/wiki/File:Akhilleus_Hektor_Louvre_CA601_glare_reduced_white_bg.png

64. Dresden Codex image. Wikimedia commons.
https://commons.wikimedia.org/wiki/File:Dresden_codex,_page_2.jpg

68. Vajra thunderbolt-weapon (open tip). Wikimedia commons.
https://commons.wikimedia.org/wiki/File:MET_1992_150_1_S1.jpg

71. Vajra thunderbolt-weapon (closed tip). Wikimedia commons.
https://commons.wikimedia.org/wiki/File:MET_1987_142_297.jpg

83. Heracles and the Hydra. Wikimedia commons.
https://commons.wikimedia.org/wiki/File:Herakles_and_the_Hydra_Water_Jar_(Etruscan,_c._525_BC)_-_Getty_Villa_-_Collection.jpg

91. Apollo and Python, 1589. Wikimedia commons.
https://commons.wikimedia.org/wiki/File:Apollo_doodt_Python_Metamorfosen_van_Ovidius_(serietitel)_RP-P-2014-67-17.jpg

95. Krishna and Kaliya. Los Angeles County Museum of Art. Public domain. https://collections.lacma.org/node/237695

97. Michael defeating the dragon. Wikimedia commons.
https://commons.wikimedia.org/wiki/File:São_Miguel_Arcanjo,_oficina_de_Garcia_Fernandes_(atr.).jpg

98. Michael and the dragon. Wikimedia commons.
https://commons.wikimedia.org/wiki/File:Pere_Garcia_-_Archangel_Michael.jpg

99. Michael and the dragon. Wikimedia commons.
left: https://commons.wikimedia.org/wiki/File:San_Michele_Arcangelo_Bartolomeo_Vivarini_GAC.jpg
right:
https://commons.wikimedia.org/wiki/File:Francesco_pagano_(attr.),_s._michele,_storie,_santi_e_crocifissione,_1492_ca.,_da_ss._michele_e_omobono_01.JPG

110. David and Bathsheba, Paris Bordon (1500 - 1570). Wikimedia commons.
https://commons.wikimedia.org/wiki/File:Paris_Bordone_-_david-and-bathsheba_(2)_-_Walters_Museum_-_Baltimora.jpg

124. & 126. Scenes from Codex Borgia. Wikimedia commons.
https://commons.wikimedia.org/wiki/Codex_Borgia

135. Bhima drinks blood. Wikimedia commons.
https://commons.wikimedia.org/wiki/File:Bhima_drinks_blood.jpg

136. Dendera relief showing Khnum and Heqet. Wikimedia commons.
https://commons.wikimedia.org/wiki/File:DendaraMamisiKhnum-10.jpg

162. Mermaid, 16th century. Wikimedia commons.
https: commons.wikimedia.org/File:Von_dem_Meerfröuwlin.jpg

213. Two scenes showing Incredulity of Thomas. Wikimedia commons.
Left: https://commons.wikimedia.org/wiki/File:Incredulidad_de_Santo_Tomás._(Iglesia_de_Santo_Tomé_de_Toledo).jpg
Right: https://commons.wikimedia.org/wiki/File:L%27incredulita_di_San_Tommaso.jpg

216. Triptych crucifixion Maarten van Heemskerck. Wikimedia commons.
https://commons.wikimedia.org/wiki/File:Maarten_van_Heemskerck_-_Crucifixion_(Triptych)_-_WGA11313.jpg

229. Vishnu and Lakshmi on Shesha Naga (c. 1870). Wikimedia commons.
https://commons.wikimedia.org/wiki/File:Vishnu_and_Lakshmi_on_Shesha_Naga,_ca_1870.jpg

230. Krishna, 15th century. Wikimedia commons.
https://commons.wikimedia.org/wiki/File:A_15th_Century_Hindu_Art,_Hindu_deity_Krishna,_Asian_Art_Museum_of_San_Francisco.jpg

231. Arjuna before Krishna in war-car. Wikimedia commons.
https://commons.wikimedia.org/wiki/File:A_scene_from_the_Mahabharata;_Arjuna_requests_instruction_fr_Wellcome_V0045044.jpg

233. Arjuna and Krishna in war-car. Wikimedia commons.
https://commons.wikimedia.org/wiki/File:Bhagavatgeeta.jpg

253. Seated Buddha statue. Wikimedia commons.
https://commons.wikimedia.org/wiki/File:Seated_Buddha_Amitabha_statue.jpg

257. Buddha and Vajrapani. Wikimedia commons.
https://commons.wikimedia.org/wiki/File:Buddha-Vajrapani-Herakles.JPG

263. Armillary Sphere, 1771. Wikimedia commons.
https://commons.wikimedia.org/wiki/File:EB1711_Armillary_Sphere.png

281. Goddess Athena. Wikimedia commons.
https://commons.wikimedia.org/wiki/File:Anfora_con_atena_polias,_attica,_480-470_ac_ca._02.jpg

289. Mountain range with Ontario Peak. Wikimedia commons.
https://commons.wikimedia.org/wiki/File:Telegraph_Cucamonga_and_Ontario_Peaks.jpg

299. YouTube screenshots from "Greatest dad saves EVER!!!"
(See Bibliography for URL).

356. Tauroctony from Aquileia. Wikimedia commons.
https://commons.wikimedia.org/wiki/File:Kunsthistorisches_Museum_Mithras-Relief.jpg

359. Mithraeum of the Seven Spheres. Wikimedia commons.
https://commons.wikimedia.org/wiki/File:Sette_Sfere_Mithraeum,_Ostia.jpg

363. Cautes and Cautopates. Wikimedia commons.
Left: https://commons.wikimedia.org/wiki/File:MANA_-_Mithrasrelief_2_Cautopates.jpg
Right: https://commons.wikimedia.org/wiki/File:DSC00244_-_Cautes,_dadoforo_di_Mithra_-_sec._III_d.C._-_Foto_di_G._Dall%27Orto.jpg

375. Two tauroctony scenes with arches. Wikimedia commons.
Above: https://commons.wikimedia.org/wiki/File:White_marble_relief_with_Tauroctony_scene_and_dedicated_inscription_(CIMRM_546_-_547),_Vatican_Museums,_Rome_(21137720003).jpg
Below: https://commons.wikimedia.org/wiki/File:Tauroctony_Heddernheim.jpg

423. Diagram of M16 Rifle. Wikimedia commons.
https://commons.wikimedia.org/wiki/File:M16_rifle_left_side_TM_9-1005-249-10.png

452. Mosaic at the Mithraeum of Felicissimus. Wikimedia commons.
https://commons.wikimedia.org/wiki/File:Ostia_antica_mitreo-di-felicissimo_002.jpg

458. Tree of Life diagram. Wikimedia commons.
https://commons.wikimedia.org/wiki/File:Tree_of_life_kircher_hebrew.png
Superimposed on image of Dealey Plaza, Dallas: Google maps, modern day.

460. Warren Commission Exhibit 359. AARC Public Digital Library.
https://aarclibrary.org

462. Masonic illustration from 1874. Wikimedia commons.
https://commons.wikimedia.org/wiki/File:Alle_frimurer_symboler.JPG

488. Ancient Akkadian seal with goddess Ishtar. Wikimedia commons.
https://commons.wikimedia.org/wiki/File:Ishtar_on_an_Akkadian_seal.jpg

513. Jacob's Dream. Wikimedia commons.
https://commons.wikimedia.org/wiki/File:The_Phillip_Medhurst_Picture_Torah_145_Jacob%27s_Dream._Genesis_cap_28_v_12._Stothard.jpg

Cover art:
Perseus with the head of Medusa, Benvenuto Cellini (1500 - 1571). Wikimedia commons.
https://commons.wikimedia.org/wiki/File:03_2015_Perseo_con_la_testa_di_Medusa-Benvenuto_Cellini-Piazza_della_Signoria-Loggia_dei_Lanzi-volta_a_crociera-ordine_corinzio_(Firenze)_Photo_Paolo_Villa_FOTO9260.JPG

Background: Heart and Soul Nebulae. Wikimedia commons.
https://commons.wikimedia.org/wiki/File:Heart_and_Soul_nebulae.jpg

Bibliography

"About H. A. and Margret Rey." Houghton Mifflin Books website.
www.houghtonmifflinbooks.com/features/cgsite/authors.shtml

Augustine. *City of God.* Trans. Gerald G. Walsh, Demetrius B. Zema, Grace Monahan, and Daniel J. Honan. New York: Doubleday, 1958.

Bain, S. K. *The Most Dangerous Book in the World: 9/11 as Mass Ritual.* Walterville, Oregon: Trine Day, 2012.

Barbiero, Flavio. "Mithras and Jesus: Two sides of the same coin." 27 May 2010. *Graham Hancock* website.
https://grahamhancock.com/mithras-and-jesus-barbierof2/

Barbiero, Flavio. *The Secret Society of Moses: The Mosaic Bloodline and a Conspiracy Spanning Three Millennia.* Trans. Steve Smith. Rochester, Vermont: Inner Traditions, 2010.

Beazley, John Davidson. *Attic Red-Figured Vases in American Museums.* Cambridge: Harvard UP, 1918.

Beck, Roger. "If So, How? Representing 'Coming Back to Life' in the Mysteries of Mithras." In *Coming Back to Life: The Permeability of Past and Present, Mortality and Immortality, Death and Life in the Ancient Mediterranean* (e-book). Eds. F. S. Tappenden and C. Daniel-Hughes. Montreal: McGill University Library and Archives, pp 161 - 189.
https://comingbacktolife.mcgill.ca/article/view/2/48

Bjørnebye, Jonas. "*Hic locus est felix, sanctus, piusque benignus*": *The cult of Mithras in fourth century Rome.*
Dissertation for the degree of *philosophiae doctor*, University of Bergen: 2007.

Book of the Dead: An English Translation of the Chapters, Hymns, Etc., of the Theban Recension, with Introduction, Notes, Etc. Trans. E. A. Wallis Budge. Volume 1: 3 Vols. Chicago: Open Court, 1901.

Book of Thomas the Contender. Trans. John D. Turner.
Gnostic Society Library. gnosis.org/naghamm/bookt.html

Bowden, Hugh. *Mystery Cults of the Ancient World.*
Princeton: Princeton University Press, 2010.

Carter, Chris. *Science and Psychic Phenomena: The Fall of the House of Skeptics.* 2007. Rochester, Vermont: Inner Traditions, 2014.

Bibliography

Clauss, Manfred. *Roman Cult of Mithras: The Cult and His Mysteries.* Trans. Richard Gordon. New York: Routledge, 2000. First published in German as *Mithras: Kult und Myterien.* Munich: C. H. Beck'sche Verlagsbuchhandlung, 1990.

D'Aulaire, Ingri and Edgar Parin. *Ingri and Edgar Parin D'Aulaire's Book of Greek Myths.* New York: Doubleday, 1962.

D'Aulaire, Ingri and Edgar Parin. *Norse Gods & Giants.* New York: Doubleday, 1967.

De Santillana, Giorgio and Hertha von Dechend. *Hamlet's Mill: An Essay on Myth and the Frame of Time.* 1969. Boston: Godine-Nonpareil, 1977.

Dossey, Larry. Interview: "The Power of Premonitions: How Knowing the Future Can Shape Our Lives." (No date).
https://dosseydossey.com/larry/interview_Questions-Premonitions.pdf

Egyptian Book of the Dead: The Book of Going Forth by Day. Trans. Raymond O. Faulkner. San Francisco: Chronicle Books, 2008.

Electronic Corpus of Sumerian Literature. Eds. Jeremy A. Black, Graham Cunningham, Esther Flückiger-Hawker, Eleanor Robson, and Gábor Zólyomi. Oxford: 1998.
http://www-etcsl.orient.ox.ac.uk/

Eliade, Mircea. *Shamanism: Archaic Techniques of Ecstasy.* Trans. Willard R. Trask. 1964. Princeton: Bollingen, 1972.

Epic of Gilgamesh: The Babylonian Epic Poem and Other Texts in Akkadian and Sumerian. Trans. Andrew George. London: Penguin, 1999.

Eusebius. *Life of Constantine.* Trans. Averil Cameron and Stuart G. Hall. Oxford: Clarendon, 1999.

"Facts & Statistics." *Anxiety and Depression Association of America.*
https://adaa.org/about-adaa/press-room/facts-statistics

Freke, Timothy and Peter Gandy. *The Jesus Mysteries: Was the "Original Jesus" a Pagan God?* New York: Three Rivers Press, 1999.

Ganser, Daniele. *NATO's Secret Armies: Operation Gladio and terrorism in Western Europe.* Abingdon, Oxon: Frank Cass, 2005.

Geiger, A. W. and Leslie Davis. "A growing number of American teenagers -- particularly girls -- are facing depression." July 12, 2019. *Pew Research Center.*
https://www.pewresearch.org/fact-tank/2019/07/12/a-growing-number-of-american-teenagers-particularly-girls-are-facing-depression/

Gladiator. Dir. Ridley Scott. DreamWorks Pictures, 2000.

Bibliography

Gesenius, Wilhelm. *Gesenius's Hebrew and Chaldee Lexicon to the Old Testament Scriptures.* Trans. Samuel Prideaux Tregelles.
London: Samuel Bagster & Sons, [1857].
https://archive.org/details/hebrewchaldeelexoogeseuoft/page/n6/mode/2up

"Greatest dad saves EVER!!!" Online video clip. YouTube. 24 Aug 2015.
https://youtube.com/watch?v=nj85L2r17rw

Greek Lyric, Volume II: Anacreon, Anacreontea, Choral Lyric from Olympus to Alcman. Trans. David A. Campbell. Loeb Classical Library. 143. Cambridge, Massachusetts: Harvard University Press, 1988.

Hancock, Graham. *America Before: The Key to Earth's Lost Civilization.* New York: St. Martin's-Griffin, 2019.

Hesiod. *The Homeric Hymns and Homerica.* Trans. Hugh G. Evelyn-White. London: Heinemann, 1914.

Henry, Matthew. *Commentary on the Whole Bible.* 6 vols. *Volume II-I: First Kings to Esther.* 1706 - 1721. Facsimile reprint, Ed. Anthony Uyl. Woodstock, Ontario: Devoted Publishing, 2017.

Hudson, Michael. *... and forgive them their debts: Lending, Foreclosure and Redemption from Bronze Age Finance to the Jubilee Year.* Dresden: ISLET-Verlag, 2018.

Hudson, Michael. *J is for Junk Economics: A Guide to Reality in an Age of Deception.* Dresden: ISLET-Verlag, 2017.

Hudson, Michael. *Killing the Host: How Financial Parasites and Debt Destroy the Global Economy.* Dresden: ISLET-Verlag, 2015.

Hyginus. *Fabulae.* Trans. Mary Grant. Humanistic Studies. 34. Lawrence: University of Kansas Publications, 1960.

Icke, David. *Beyond the Cutting Edge.* Presentation at Brixton Academy, London: May, 2008.

Jacobsen, Annie. *Operation Paperclip: the secret intelligence program that brought Nazi scientists to America.*
New York: Back Bay-Little, Brown, 2014.

Jacobsen, Annie. *Phenomena: The Secret History of the U.S. Government's Investigations into Extrasensory Perception and Psychokinesis.*
New York: Back Bay-Little, Brown, 2017.

James, Ronald M. "Nazis, Trolls and the Grateful Dead: Turmoil Among Sweden's Folklorists." *Folklore Thursday.* April 11, 2017.
https://folklorethursday.com/folklore-folklorists/nazis-trolls-and-the-grateful-dead-turmoil-among-swedens-folklorists/

Karate Kid. Dir. John G. Avildsen. Columbia Pictures, 1984.

Bibliography

Kingsley, Peter. *In the Dark Places of Wisdom.*
Point Reyes, California: Golden Sufi Center, 1999.

Knowles, Christopher. Interview with Greg Carlwood. *Higherside Chats,* "Song to the Siren, Invoked Entities & Rebuilding Babylon. 20 October 2017.

Koutantou, Angeliki. "Workers protest as Greece sells Piraeus Port to China COSCO." *Thomson Reuters Business News,* 08 April, 2016.
https://uk.reuters.com/article/uk-eurozone-greece-privatisation-china-c-idUKKCN0X50XD

Kuhn, Alvin Boyd. *Lost Light: An Interpretation of Ancient Scriptures.*
Elizabeth, New Jersey: Academy Press, 1940.

Lachman, Gary. *Aleister Crowley: Magick, Rock and Roll, and the Wickedest Man in the World.* New York: Penguin, 2014.

Lao Tzu. *Tao Te Ching: The Classic Book of Integrity and the Way.*
Trans. Victor H. Mair. New York: Bantam, 1990.

Levenda, Peter. *Unholy Alliance: A History of Nazi Involvement with the Occult.* Third Revised and Expanded Ed. Lake Worth, Florida: Ibis, 2019.

Levine, Peter A. *Healing Trauma: A Pioneering Program for Restoring the Wisdom of Your Body.* Boulder, Colorado: Sounds True, 2008.

"Major Depression." *National Information of Mental Health.*
www.nimh.nih.gov/health/statistics/major-depression.shtml

Mahabharata. Trans. Kisari Mohan Ganguli. First published 1883 - 1896.
Web edition *Internet Sacred Text Archive.*
https://www.sacred-texts.com/hin/maha/

Maté, Gabor. "From Jungle to 'Civilization': How Plant Medicines Can Promote Health in a Toxic Culture." Talk given at the 2017 Psychedelic Science Conference, 21 April 2017, in Oakland, California.
Audio file available at the *MAPS Podcast,* Episode 37, 18 February 2019.

Maté, Gabor. "Dr. Gabor Maté on Addiction." Interview with Eric Zimmer. *The One You Feed,* Episode 249. 16 October 2018.

Maté, Gabor. "Dr. Gabor Maté on Childhood Trauma, the Real Cause of Anxiety and our 'Insane' Culture." Interview with Martin Caparrotta. *Human Window.* July 2019; transcript published 23 November 2019.
https://humanwindow.com/dr-gabor-mate-interview-childhood-trauma-anxiety-culture/

Maté, Gabor. "How Our Childhood Shapes Every Aspect of Our Health." Interview with Dr. Rangan Chatterjee. *Feel Better Live More,* Episode 37. 21 November 2018.

Bibliography

Maté, Gabor. "Psychedelics and Unlocking the Unconscious: from Cancer to Addiction." Talk given at the 2013 Psychedelic Science Conference, 10 April 2013, in Oakland, California. Audio file available at the *MAPS Podcast*, Episode 4, published 04 April 2017.

Maté, Gabor. "When the Body Says No: Mind / Body Unity and the Stress-Disease Connection." Talk given at the California Institute of Integral Studies, 31 October 2015, in San Francisco, California. Audio file available at the *CIIS Public Programs* podcast page. 29 December 2015.
https://soundcloud.com/publicprograms

Maté, Gabor. *When the Body Says No: Exploring the Stress-Disease Condition.* Hoboken, New Jersey: Wiley, 2003.

Mathisen, David Warner. *Ancient World-Wide System: Star Myths of the World, Volume One*, Second Ed. Paso Robles, Beowulf: 2019.

Mathisen, David Warner. *Astrotheology for Life: Unlocking the Esoteric Wisdom of Ancient Myth.* Paso Robles, Beowulf: 2017.

Mathisen, David Warner. *Star Myths of the World, and how to interpret them, Volume Two: Myths of Ancient Greece.* Paso Robles, Beowulf: 2016.

Mathisen, David Warner. *Star Myths of the World, and how to interpret them, Volume Three: Star Myths of the Bible.* Paso Robles, Beowulf: 2016.

Mathisen, David Warner. *Star Myths of the World, and how to interpret them, Volume Two: Norse Mythology.* Paso Robles, Beowulf: 2018.

Mathisen, David Warner. *Undying Stars: the truth that unites the world's ancient wisdom, and the conspiracy to keep it from you.* Paso Robles, Beowulf: 2014.

Mazaheri, Ramin. "(A Soviet) Superman: Red Son -- the new socialist film to watch on lockdown."*The Saker Blog*, 02 April 2020.
https://thesaker.is/a-soviet-superman-red-son-the-new-socialist-film-to-watch-on-lockdown/

Meyer, Marvin W. *The Gnostic Discoveries: The Impact of the Nag Hammadi Library.* San Francisco: HarperCollins, 2005.

Morgan Hill, California, Earthquake of April 24, 1984. Ed. Seena N. Hoose. U.S. Geological Survey Bulletin 1639.
Washington, DC: US Government Printing Office, 1987.
https://pubs.usgs.gov/bul/1639/report.pdf

Odyssey. Trans. Robert Fagles. New York: Viking Penguin, 1996.

Odyssey. Trans. Theodore Alois Buckley. Philadelphia: David McKay, 1896.

Ollestad, Norman, Jr. *Crazy for the Storm: A Memoir of Survival.* New York: Ecco, 2009.

Orphic Hymns. Trans. Apostolos N. Athanassakis and Benjain M. Wolkow. Baltimore: Johns Hopkins University Press, 2013.

Bibliography

Orwell, George. *Nineteen Eighty-Four.* 1949. New York: Signet, 1981.

Ovid. *Metamorphoses.* Trans. Brookes More. Volume Three. Francestown, New Hampshire: Marshall Jones, 1957.

"Pabbaja Sutta: The Going Forth." Trans. Thānissaro Bhikkhu. 1997. *Access to Insight.* https://www.accesstoinsight.org/tipitaka/kn/snp/snp.3.01.than.html

Pausanias. *Description of Greece, Volume I: Books 1-2.* Trans. W. H. S. Jones. Loeb Classical Library. 93. Cambridge: Harvard University Press, 1918.

Pauwels, Jacques R. *The Great Class War, 1914 - 1918.* Toronto: Lorimer, 2016.

Pavia, Tony and Matt Pavia. *An American Town and the Vietnam War: Stories of Service from Stamford, Connecticut.* Jefferson, North Carolina: McFarland & Company, 2018.

Pindar. *Odes of Pindar, Translated into English Prose, with Brief Explanatory Notes and a Preface.* Trans. F. A. Paley. Cambridge: Williams and Norgate, 1868.

Porphyry. *Selected Works: Containing his four books on Abstinence from Animal Food, his treatise on the Homeric Cave of the Nymphs, and his Auxiliaries to the Perception of Intelligible Natures.* Trans. Thomas Taylor. London: Thomas Rodd, 1823.
https://babel.hathitrust.org/cgi/pt?id=mdp.39015046819200&view=1up&seq=5

Pratt, Laura A., Debra J. Brody, Qiuping Gu. "Antidepressant Use Among Persons Aged 12 and Over: United States, 2011 - 2014." *NCHS Data Brief No. 283*, August 2017.
https://www.cdc.gov/nchs/products/databriefs/db283.htm

Ramayana of Valmiki. Trans. Hari Prasad Shastri. Volume I. London: Shanti Sadan, 1952.

Renan, Ernest. *Marc-Aurèle et la fin du monde antique.* Paris: Calmann-Lévy, 1923.

Rey, H. A. *The Stars: A New Way to See Them.* 1952. Boston: Hughton Mifflin, 1988.

"Richter Scale." *USGS Earthquake Glossary.*
https://earthquake.usgs.gov/learn/glossary/?term=Richter%20scale

Rothstein, Edward. "Monkey Business in a World of Evil."
New York Times, March 25, 2010.
https://www.nytimes.com/2010/03/26/arts/design/26curious.html.

Schwaller de Lubicz, R. A. *Esoterism & Symbol.* 1960.
Trans. André and Goldian VandenBroeck. Rochester,
Vermont: Inner Traditions, 1985.

Seneca. *Tragedies.* Trans. Frank Justus Miller. Loeb Classical Library
Volumes. Cambridge: Harvard UP, 1917.
https://www.theoi.com/Text/SenecaPhaedra.html

"A Sketch of the Buddha's Life: Readings from the Pali Canon."
Access to Insight. 2005. https://www.accesstoinsight.org/ptf/buddha.html

Stark, Karl Berhard. "Die Mithrassteine von Dormagen," in *Jahrbücher des Vereins von Alterthumsfreunden im Rheinlande, Heft XLIV und XLV.* Bonn: Kosten des Vereins, 1868. Stark's article is found on pages 1-25.

Strong, James. *Exhustive Concordance of the Bible.*
New York: Eaton & Mains, 1890.

Sturluson, Snorri. *Prose Edda by Snorri Sturluson.* Trans. Arthur Gilchrist
Brodeur. Scandinavian Classics. 5.
New York: American-Scandinavian Foundation, 1916.

Tolkien, J. R. R. *Two Towers.* Lord of the Rings. 2.
New York: Ballantine, 1965.

Two Towers. Dir. Peter Jackson. New Line Cinema, 2002.

Udāna: Exclamations. Trans. Thānissaro Bhikkhu (Geoffrey DeGraff). 2012.
Access to Insight. www.accesstoinsight.org/lib/authors/thanissaro/udana.pdf

Ulansey, David. *The Origins of the Mithraic Mysteries: Cosmology and Salvation in the Ancient World.* Oxford: Oxford University Press, 1989.

Upanishads: Translations from the Sanskrit. Trans. Juan Mascaró.
London: Penguin, 1965.

Upanishads: Katha, Iśa, Kena, and Mudaka. Trans. Swami Nikhilananda.
Volume I. New York: Harper & Brothers, 1949.

Valentine, Douglas. *The Phoenix Program.* 1990.
New York: Open Road, 2000.

Valentine, Douglas. "Vietnam Black Ops with Douglas Valentine." Interview with Sam Tripoli. *Tinfoil Hat with Sam Tripoli* podcast. Episode 294.
26 March 2020.

Walsh, David. *The Cult of Mithras in Late Antiquity: Development, Decline and Demise* ca. AD 270 - 430. Leiden: Brill, 2019.

Index

Abraham 2
Abyss 448 - 449, 451
Achelous 56 - 57
Achilles 62 - 63, 87, 232
Acrisius, Akrisios 348
Acropolis 319, 322
Actaeon, Acteon 35, 37 - 41, 43, 90 - 91
Adam 128, 184, 186 - 188
Adamantine 347
Adonis 159
Æsir 127
Aeaea 279
Aegean 175, 349, 413
Aegis 281
Aeolus 266
Aetna 81
Africa 3, 21, 64, 311, 328, 390, 436
Aftermath 530 n. 290
Agency 406 - 407, 411, 418 - 419, 471, 483 - 484
Ahnenerbe 426
Akkad, Akkadian 349, 489
Alaric I (AD 370 - 410) 104 - 105
Alcaeus 180
Alcimus 388
Alcman (7th century BC) 175, 519 n.75
Alcmene, Alcmena 79, 81, 83, 179, 193
Alexandria 384
Aliens 150
Alienation ii - iv, 165, 182, 184 - 187, 189 - 190, 193 - 194, 196 - 197, 200 - 202, 211, 235, 249 - 250, 304, 309, 316 - 318, 332, 345 - 346, 365, 381 - 383, 403, 409 , 430, 453, 455, 486, 496 - 497, 500, 506, 526 n.224
Algeria 447 - 448
All-seeing eye 462
Almaas, A. H. 201
Alsace 390
Altair 11, 13
America Before 44
American Philological Association 369
American Town and the Vietnam War 305

Amphitrite 277, 279
Amphitryon 79, 81, 179 - 180, 193
Amphorae 54
Amun 112, 498, 517 n.36
Amymone 81 - 82, 86
Anatolia 409, 413
Ancient Order of Druids 433
Ancien régime 329, 529 n.281
Ancient World-Wide System 64, 66 - 67, 87, 92, 96, 101, 118 - 119, 126 - 127, 129, 133, 136 - 137, 166, 187, 229 - 230, 253, 257 - 258, 283 - 284, 493, 517 n.36, 531 n.321.
Anderson Lake 296
Andromeda 44, 60, 83, 179, 350 - 352, 371, 373 - 374, 416 - 417, 483, 499
Angels 2, 13 - 17, 20, 23, 96 - 101, 108, 112, 140, 295, 373, 443 - 444, 473
Ani (c. 1250 BC) 502
Anjali mudra 96, 231, 243, 248
Ankara 413
Antares 86
Anthroposophical Society 433
Antidepressant medications 313
Anti-Semitism 427, 434, 522 n.161, 526 - 527 n.224
Anubis 502
Anunna, Anunnaki 144, 491, 495
Anxiety 209, 313 - 316
Anxiety and Depression Association of America 313
Aotearoa 346
Aphareus 170 - 171, 179
Aphrodite 109, 180
Apollo 79 - 80, 90 - 92, 101, 416
Aquarius 27, 213 - 214, 218, 213 - 214, 218, 265 - 267, 269, 272 - 273, 285, 310, 358
Aquila 11 - 17, 19 - 20, 53, 66, 87 - 89, 111, 125, 169
Aquincum 390
Ara 17, 169, 321 - 322, 349
Arachne 323
Aragon High School 295, 297
Arbogast (d. AD 394) 104

543

Archangel (See *Michael the Archangel*)
Ares 109, 171
Argolic Gulf 80 - 81
Argos 80, 348, 523 n.178
Aries 27, 214, 265, 273, 351, 358 - 359, 364, 371, 374, 377 - 378, 422, 499
Aristocracy 327, 330, 392, 394 - 395, 421, 424, 434, 436 - 437, 440, 473 - 474
Aristotle (385 BC - 323 BC) 121
Arjuna 182, 203, 223 - 227, 230 - 233, 242 - 245, 247 - 249, 276, 317, 487
Arks 129, 349
Armillary spheres 262 - 265
Arnold, Bob (c. 1951 - 1979) 288
Artemis 35 - 41, 43, 90 - 91, 156, 323
Ash Wednesday 492
Ashvattha (See *Sacred fig*)
Ashvineya, Ashvins 182
Assassinations 331, 333, 393 - 395, 398, 427, 457, 459, 461 - 463, 465, 467 - 468, 474, 478, 481, 501, 506 - 508
Asses 122, 373, 416
Astrology 26 - 27, 158, 361, 431, 437, 444
Astrotheology 156 - 157
Astrotheology for Life 156 - 157, 518 n.69
Atheism 447
Athena 84, 171, 276, 278, 281 - 282, 319, 321 - 323, 334, 344, 346 - 348, 350, 383, 405, 410
Athens 319, 322, 338 - 339
Atimetus 380
Atman 233 - 235, 237 - 239, 241, 243, 411
Atrahasis 129
Attic peninsula 35, 349
Atum 112, 198, 517 n.36
Aulis 86
Augustine (AD 354 - 430) 103 - 109, 111, 500
Augustorum 380
Australia 3, 21, 311, 346, 427, 436
Authentic self (See *Essential self*)
Avatars 92, 94, 224, 229
Awakening 251, 260, 274
Axes 69 - 70, 138, 284
Ayahuasca 505

Ayodhya 456
Aztec 120, 127, 138

Baal 155
Bacchus 413 - 415, 512 (See *Dionysus*)
Bailey, Susan 296
Bain, S. K. 479 - 481
Balances (See *Scales*)
Baldr 127, 285, 492 - 493, 495, 497
Ba-neb-Tattu 502
Bankers 329, 523 n.176
Baphomet 480
Barach, Bariyach 114, 517 n.37
Barbiero, Flavio 324 - 325, 386 - 403, 410, 419 424, 430 - 431, 521 - 522 n.224, 528 n.270
Basilicas 396 - 397, 403, 438
Bathsheba 109 - 111
Bats 12, 88 - 89
Bauhaus 27
Bausani, Alessandro (1921 - 1988) 369
Bavaria 329, 425, 427 - 428, 474
Bavarian Illuminati 474
Bavarian People's-state (See *Volksstaat Bayern*)
Beards 17, 51, 56, 62, 65, 82
Beck, Roger 357 - 362, 364 - 365, 368 - 369, 380, 383, 402, 410, 451
Beersheba 1, 2, 4, 142
Belgium 329 - 330, 425, 468
Belshazzar 129
Berenice's Hair (See *Coma Berenices*)
Berkeley 519 n.79
Berlin 27, 353
Berlin, University of 353
Bertilak 284
Bhagavad Gita 63, 203, 224, 228, 234, 241 - 243, 247, 276
Bhagavata Purana 94, 96, 516 n.27
Bharata 134, 222
Bhima 71, 101, 118, 134, 138 - 139, 232
Bhishma 222
Bible ii, 3, 14, 16 - 17, 20 - 22, 26, 41 - 42, 101 - 102, 107 - 109, 111 - 112, 114 - 119, 127 - 132, 135, 138, 140, 142, 148, 151, 157, 163, 165 - 166, 186, 189, 191, 214 - 215, 252, 254 - 256, 279, 282, 311, 404, 415, 446 - 447, 453, 498, 500, 508, 517 n.37, 518 n.67

Biblical inerrancy 446 - 447
Bildad 115
Bilgameš (See *Gilgamesh*)
Bimbisara 252
Bishops 104, 163, 397 - 398, 401 - 402
Bjørnebye, Jonas 355
Black ops 525
Black Sea 388, 413
Black Tezcatlipoca (See *Tezcatlipoca*)
Boaz and Jachin 461, 479
Boddhisatva 274
Bodhi tree 251, 274, 322
Bodhidharma 283, 497
Boeotia, Boeotians 175, 180
Bogdan, Henrik 446 - 447, 453
Bondholders 341, 343, 523 n.176
Book of the Dead (Book of Going Forth by Day) 502
Book of the Law 446
Book of Thomas the Contender 192 - 194, 196, 211, 237, 242
Boötes 63, 87 - 88, 137 - 138, 185
Borgia, Stefano (1731 - 1804) 124
Bormann, Martin (1900 - 1945?) 439, 530 n.290
Bosporus 413
Boston 29, 57, 158
Bou Saada 447, 489
Bowden, Hugh 175
Brahma 225, 455 - 456, 498
Brahman 238, 243, 411
Brazil 27, 29, 44
Brazilian Amazon 27
Bremmer, Jan 365
Brigetium 390
Britain 409
Britannia 390
British Isles 329, 384
Brotherhood of Saturn 433
Brussell, Mae (1922 - 1988) 439
Budapest 390
Buddha 251 - 253, 256 - 258, 260, 268, 273 - 275, 280, 322, 497
Buddhism 67 - 68, 251
Budge, Ernest Alfred Thompson Wallis (1857 - 1934) 502
Building Seven (WTC 7) 332, 479, 508
Bulrushes 349

Cadmus 276
Caesars (tetrarchy) 399
Calaveras Fault 296
California 4, 145, 183, 199, 238, 287, 295 - 297, 309, 366, 519 n.79
California Institute of Integral Studies 199, 366
Calvary 218
Calypso 276, 344
Cambridge, University of 446
Cambridge, Massachusetts 29
Camp King 438 - 439
Campus Martius 384
Cancer (constellation) 88, 262, 273, 359 - 364
Cancer (disease) 238
Canopies 230 - 232
Capes 356, 372
Capitalism 326, 428
Capricorn 27, 169, 213 - 214, 265 - 267, 269, 272 - 273, 358 - 362, 364, 483, 499
Caracalla (AD 188 - 217) 393
Carnuntum 390
Carter, Chris 308
Casseiopeia 60
Castor 168, 170 - 172, 175 - 178, 181, 193, 242
Catholic Church 325, 437, 467
Cautes 363 - 364, 366
Cautopates 363 - 364, 366
Cave of the Nymphs (See *On the Cave of the Nymphs in the Odyssey*)
Caves 19, 81 - 82, 355 - 358, 360 - 361, 383, 397
Central America 3, 64, 119, 131
Central Intelligence Agency 439, 463, 506
Centaurs 32 - 33, 39, 322
Cepheus 60
Cerberus 81
Ceres 415 (See also *Demeter*)
Cessna aircraft 287
Chapman, Patricia 290 - 291, 301 - 304, 466
Charioteers 63, 81, 84, 87 - 88, 223, 230 - 231, 234, 242, 244, 247

545

Chariots 63, 81 - 82, 84, 87, 221, 232 - 234, 239 - 244, 247 - 249, 286, 379, 455, 487
Charybdis 259
Chatterjee, Rangan 235, 241
Chi-rho 400, 402
Childbirth 323, 501 - 502
China 3, 61, 154, 226, 283, 311, 327, 338
Choronzon 448 - 449, 453
Christ 108, 190, 192 - 194, 196 - 198, 200, 202, 209 - 218, 226, 237, 241 - 244, 248, 252, 259 - 260, 268, 273, 286, 317, 487, 492 - 493, 495, 497, 509, 512
Christianity 103 - 106, 111, 143 - 144, 149, 154 - 155, 324 - 326, 334, 336 - 337, 339, 345 - 346, 354, 383 - 384, 386 - 387, 389, 392 - 404, 407, 409, 412, 420, 424, 431 - 437, 440 - 442, 446 - 447, 453, 457, 470 - 471, 473, 476, 480, 500, 503, 506, 536 - 527 n.224, 529 n.281
Christian Science 433
Christmas 193
CIA (See *Central Intelligence Agency*)
Circe 268, 279, 351
City of God 105 - 106, 109, 111, 500
Clauss, Manfred 353, 384
Clift (or Cleft) of the Rock 251 - 256, 280
Cloaks 16, 62
Clouds 7, 16, 19, 31, 63, 15, 180, 222
Clubs 50, 56, 62, 69, 73, 82 - 84, 14, 232, 284
Cobras 93 - 94, 101, 125, 229, 503
Cobra-Kai 145 -147, 160, 162, 412
Codices, Codexes 64 - 65, 67 - 68, 73, 124
Codex Borgia 124
Coffins 493
Coincidences 22, 301, 303, 333, 368, 434, 463, 479
Colonialism 331, 345, 402, 409, 436, 440, 468 - 469, 473, 481, 526 - 527 n.224
Columbus, Christopher (1451 - 1506) 64
Coma Berenices 85, 87 - 88, 90, 125, 137
Commerce Street (Dealey Plaza) 458 - 459, 461

Commodus (AD 161 - 192) 391 - 393
Con 283
Conch shells 96, 221 - 222, 230, 232
Congo, Republic of 468 - 469
Constantine (AD 272 - 337)v103, 339, 392, 397 - 398, 400 - 402, 420, 429, 432 - 433, 500
Constantinople 427
Contra Celsum 362, 451
Copper Age 1
Corona Australis 216, 219, 281
Corona Borealis 53 - 55, 57 -58, 125, 137, 281, 285, 499
Corpses 62 - 63, 87, 350, 491 - 493, 495, 497 - 498, 505, 518 n.69, 531 n.321
Corpus Inscriptionum et Monumentorum Religionis Mithraiacae (CIMRM) 374 - 375
COSCO Shipping Corporation 338
Coyotes 290, 301 - 302
Crabs 83 - 84, 88 - 89
Crazy for the Storm 288 - 289
Cressman, Sandra (c. 1948 - 1979) 287 - 288
Crests 54 - 55, 281 - 282
Cronus 171, 180
Crowe, Russell 391
Crowley, Aleister (1875 - 1947) 443, 445 - 459, 453, 480
Crucifixion 215 - 219, 354, 493 - 495
Crypts 355
Cults (modern) 426, 428, 431, 437, 440, 442 - 443, 447, 508
Cult-niches 358, 364
Cumont, Franz-Valéry-Marie (1868 - 1947) 366 - 368
Curious George 28 - 29, 34
Cybele 413
Cyclopean construction 80
Cyclopes 80, 226, 268, 276
Cygnus 11 - 17, 19 - 20, 168 - 169, 284

Da Mo (See *Bodhidharma*)
Dao De Jing (See *Tao Te Ching*)
Dacia 390
Dallas 457, 461, 463
Damasus (AD 305 - 384) 397
Danaë 348 - 349, 405, 415

Daniel (Bible figure and book) 129 - 130
Danube 388, 390, 395
DAP (See *German Workers Party*)
Darby, John Nelson (1800 - 1882) 453
Dardanelles 413
Dark Rift 10 - 11, 16, 256, 285, 320
Daruma (See *Bodhidharma*)
Dasaratha 456
Daughter of Herodias 254
David 108 - 111, 130 - 132, 163, 215
De Benavarre, Pedro Garcia (1445 - 1485) 99
De Civitate Dei (See *City of God*)
De Santillana, Giorgio (1902 - 1974) 119 - 123, 449, 451
Dealey Plaza 458 - 460, 464 - 465, 472, 478
Decius (AD 201 - 251) 395
Declaration of Independence 77
Dee, John (1527 - 1608) 443 - 445
Delphi, Delphic Oracle 79, 104, 339, 345, 404
Deluge (See *Flood*)
Demeter 174, 408, 496
Democracy 329, 392, 432, 481
Demons 106 - 107, 111, 122, 274, 404, 448, 455 - 456, 491 - 492, 500
Dendera 136 - 137
Deneb 12 - 13
Denethor 242
Denmark 27
Depression 202, 225, 313 - 316
Descendants 89, 131, 214 - 215, 282
Description of Greece 523 n.178
Dessau 27
Detachment 203 - 204, 227 - 228, 249, 273, 275 - 276, 280, 283, 286, 497
Devas 456
Devils 98, 448, 480, 500
Dhritarashtra 221 - 222, 224
Dialogue of the Savior 192
Dictys 349
Didymus 190 - 193, 196, 242
Diocletian (AD 245 - 313) 398 - 399
Dionysus, Dionysos 170, 214, 408, 413 - 417, 419, 486, 512
Dioscuri 170, 172 - 175, 177 - 179, 181, 193
Dispensationalism, Dispensations 453

Divine realm (See *Infinite realm*)
Divine twin 163, 177 - 178, 182, 189, 197
Djeheuty (See *Thoth*)
Domesday Book 523 n.176
Domitian (AD 51 - 96) 387 - 389
Doors 19, 190, 284, 286, 415, 490 - 491
Dorje (See *Vajra*)
Dormagen 369
Dossey, Larry 308 - 309
Doubt 172, 189 - 190, 193, 197 - 200, 202 - 206, 209, 212, 219 - 220, 224 - 228, 241 - 245, 247 - 250, 276 - 279, 409, 512
Doubting Thomas (See *Thomas*)
Dragons 33, 79, 86, 90 - 92, 96 - 101, 112, 144
Draupadi 133 - 134
Dreams 2, 10 - 11, 13, 16, 18, 20 - 22, 31, 66, 131, 141, 163 - 165, 168, 308, 311, 348, 379, 454, 498
Dresden 64
Dresden Codex 64 - 68
Drums 221 - 222, 450, 489, 492, 505
Dulichion 382
Dumuzid 492, 497
Durga 125, 224
Duryodhana 221 - 223
Dushashana 134

Ea (See *Enki*)
Eagles 11 - 13, 66 - 67, 73, 88 - 89, 125 - 126, 527 n.224
Earthquakes 11 - 13, 66 - 67, 73, 88 - 89, 125 - 126, 527 n.224
Echidna 80 - 82, 89 - 90
Ecliptic 158, 262 - 267, 271 - 273
Economic rent (See *Rent*)
Edda 127 - 128, 139, 181
Eden 20, 128, 151, 184
Egoic mind 141 - 142, 149, 181, 196 - 200, 202 - 206, 208 - 209, 212, 219, 228, 235, 237, 241 - 245, 247 - 250, 268, 270 - 271, 275, 280, 283, 286, 295, 298, 304, 312, 317 - 318, 331 - 332, 337, 366, 406, 447, 449, 455, 463, 485 - 487, 495 - 496, 505, 511 - 512
Egypt 3, 43, 61, 65, 97, 112, 127, 129, 136 - 137, 154 - 155, 173, 191, 311, 384, 409, 427, 498, 502, 509

547

Eisner, Kurt (1867 - 1919) 427
Elagabulus (c. AD 204 - 222) 393
Elbe 27
Electryon 179 - 180
Elephants 221 - 222
Eleusinian Mysteries 103, 174, 339, 345, 384, 404
Eliade, Mircea (1907 - 1986) 449, 451, 530 n.301
Elijah 128, 279 - 280
El-Jib 163, 166
Elm Street 458, 460 - 461
Emory, Dave 439
Engelmann, Siefried (1931 - 2019) 480
England 163, 367, 425, 431, 444, 523 n.176
Enki 129, 491
Enkidu 181, 187 - 189, 205, 453
Enlil 490 - 491
Enochian language 443
Enuma Elish 85, 101, 117
Ephebianus, Titus Flavius Hyginus (1st century AD) 384
Ephesians 500
Equinox, The 447
Equinoxes 267 - 269, 271, 358, 361, 376 - 378, 381, 383
Equites, Equestrians 392
Erishkegal, Erec-ki-gala 490
Eros and Psyche 203, 317
Esau 20, 181, 187
Esotericism, Esoteric iii - iv, 111, 140, 143, 147 - 148, 156 - 157, 176, 178, 185, 190, 193, 200, 267, 337, 353, 357, 360 - 362, 364, 380 - 381, 383 - 385, 404, 426 - 427, 429 - 430, 432, 434 - 436, 443, 445 - 456, 459, 461, 464 - 465, 470 - 471, 474, 476, 479, 494, 499, 503, 508, 529 n. 281, 529 n.288
Essential self ii - iv, 142, 164, 178, 181 - 183, 189 - 190, 193 - 205, 208 - 212, 219 - 220, 228, 233 - 245, 247 - 250, 260 - 262, 270 - 271, 275, 278 - 280, 283, 286, 292, 295, 300, 304 - 305, 309, 312, 317 - 318, 331, 337, 365 - 366, 381, 403 + 404, 406 - 407, 409, 411, 418, 430, 435, 454 - 455, 476, 482, 485, 495 - 498, 500, 505, 510 - 512

Etruscans, Etruscan 83 - 84, 195
Euhemerism 523 n.178
Euhemerus (late 4th to early 3rd centuries BC) 523 n.178
Europe 21, 28, 45, 64 - 65, 124, 138, 149, 324, 327 - 331, 345 - 346, 353, 398, 402, 407 - 409, 412, 421, 423 - 425, 429 - 434, 436 - 442, 444, 446, 468 - 469, 508, 527 n.224, 530 n.290
Eurotas 169
Euryale 347
Eurystheus 80 - 81, 84
Eve 102, 128, 184, 186, 188
Evelyn-White, Hugh Gerard (1884 - 1924) 181
Exodus 118, 254, 256, 285, 320
Extrasensory perception 300, 307
ExxonMobil 510

Fagles, Robert (1933 - 2008) 278, 344
Faragó, Ladislas (1906 - 1980) 530 n.290
Farmer, Glenn 290, 302 - 304, 466
Fascism, fascists 45, 330, 435, 441
Faulkner, Raymond O. (1894 - 1982) 502
Federal Bureau of Investigation 288
FedEx 342
Feel Better Live More podcast 235
Fernandes, Garcia (c. 1514 - 1565) 98
Feudalism 149, 324, 326 - 329, 331, 334 - 335, 339, 345, 392, 402, 405, 407, 409, 412, 440, 444, 468, 470, 472 - 473, 521 n.161, 522 n.176, 526 n.224, 529 n.281
Ficus religiosa (See *Sacred fig*)
Fig trees (See also *Sacred fig*)
Find the Constellations 39
First International Congress of Mithraic Studies 367 - 369
Flavia Constans 400
Flavians 387, 526 - 527 n.224
Flood 118, 129, 150, 310
Flutes 92, 95 - 96, 230
Ford, Gerald (1913 - 2006) 463
France 28 - 29, 104, 327 - 329, 383, 425, 448, 529 n.281
Frankfurt 438

Freemasonry 421 - 425, 427, 430 - 434, 440, 461 - 462, 464, 470 - 471, 474, 478 - 479, 503, 528 n.270
Freyja, Freya 154
Frigidus 104
Fuller, J. F. C. (1878 - 1966) 447
Fundamentalism 446, 453

Galactic Center 7 - 11, 86, 166, 261, 270
Galatians 500
Galerius (AD 250 -311) 399
Gandalf 181, 193, 205 - 206
Gandharvas 456
Gandiva 223, 231
Ganguli, Kisari Mohan (1848 - 1908) 134
Ganser, Daniele 331
Garden of Eden (See *Eden*)
Garuda 67
Gate of Cancer 360 - 362, 364
Gate of Capricorn 360 - 362, 364
Gauls 104, 409
Gawaine 284
Gawaine and the Green Knight 284
Gehlen, Reinhard (1902 - 1979) 438 - 439
Gehlen Organization 439
Gemini 168, 262, 273, 359, 363
Genesis 2, 4, 10, 13 - 14, 16 - 17, 20, 85, 101 - 102, 108, 118, 128, 141, 150 - 151, 184 - 187, 210, 310 - 311, 360, 362, 364, 372, 454, 483, 522 n.161
German Workers Party 428 - 429, 432
Germanenorden 427, 429
Germania Inferior, Lower Germania 369
Germany 27 - 28, 45, 59, 64, 104, 245, 330, 367 - 369, 387, 390, 409, 425 - 429, 431 - 432, 435 - 439, 441 - 442, 444 - 445, 469
Gesenius, Wilhelm (1786 - 1842) 114 - 115
Gibeon 131, 163 - 168
Gilgamesh 85, 181, 186 - 189, 205, 453
Gilson, Étienne Henri (1884 - 1978) 105
Giraffes 28
Girdles 284
Gladiator 391

Gladio (See *Operation Gladio*)
Glauer, Adam Alfred Rudolf (See *Sebottendorf, Rudolf*)
Gnosis.org 192
Gnostic 191 - 192
Göbekli Tepe 1
God of the Bible (See *Jehovah*)
Golden Dawn 433, 443 - 445, 458, 474
Golden Party Badge 438
Gollum 206 209
Golgotha (See *Calvary*)
Gondor 242
"Good cop, bad cop" 437
Gooseberry Canyon 290
Gordian III (AD 225 - 244) 393
Gordon, Richard L. 367
Gorgons 61 - 62, 127, 347, 349 - 350, 352, 372, 405 - 406, 410, 418, 466, 484
Göring, Hermann (1893 - 1946) 438
Gospel of Thomas 192
Gospels 189 - 193, 197, 211, 214, 218, 226, 241, 243, 247, 259, 495, 509
Goths (See *Visigoths*)
Gothenburg, University of 453
Graeae, Graiai (See *Gray Sisters*)
Grant, Kenneth (1924 - 2011) 158 - 159
Grant, Mary Amelia (1890 - 1987) 518 n.70
Grassy knoll 459
Grateful dead 518 n.69
Gray Sisters 347
Great Britain 330, 334, 445
Great Square of Pegasus 262, 266, 285, 311, 351 - 352, 371, 374, 416 - 417, 483, 499
Great War (See *World War I*)
Greater Germany 428
Greece, Greek 3, 17, 35, 49 - 50, 60 - 61, 65 - 66, 68, 81, 84, 86 - 88, 108 - 109, 111 - 112, 116, 119 - 120, 125, 138, 147, 154, 156, 166, 168, 170, 174, 178, 191, 214, 232, 256, 259, 262, 266, 278, 284, 311, 319, 323, 338 - 341, 343 - 344, 370, 408, 413, 453, 491, 501
Green Knight 284
Greenwich Mean Time 297
Greenwich Village 29
Gross Domestic Product (GDP) 316

549

Gross-Krotzenburg 355, 390
Gucumatz 283

Hades 172, 176
Hadrian's Wall 384, 390
Hamburg 27
Hamlet's Mill 119 - 123, 127, 449, 451, 454
Hammers 69 - 71, 138 - 140, 184
Hancock, Graham 44
Hanuman 71, 118, 138, 231 - 232
Hands (relating to constellations) 20, 52, 54 - 55, 91, 94, 96, 98 - 100, 118, 129 - 130, 132 - 133, 136 - 137, 165, 190, 211 - 212, 214, 219, 231, 254, 256 - 258, 347, 350, 356, 373, 379, 489
Haran 1, 2, 4, 24, 142
Harpe sword 347, 350 - 351, 372, 483
Hasmoneans 526 - 527 n.224
Hathor 502
Hawaii, University of 369
Healing Trauma 182 - 184, 200, 210, 220, 235, 315, 519 n.79
Health and Human Services, US Department of 313
Heart of Sky 64, 498
"Heat shields" 395 - 396
Hebrew 113 - 114, 128, 282, 349, 517 n.37
Hecate 88
Hector 62 - 63, 87, 232, 256
Heddernheim 375, 390
Heels (relating to constellations) 20, 52, 54, 56, 58, 62, 88 - 89, 101 - 102, 185
Heidelberg, University of 369
Heqet 136 - 137
Henry, Matthew (1662 - 1714) 163
Hephaestus, Hephaestos 347, 373
Hera 79
Heracles 17, 49 - 52, 54 - 62, 65, 79 - 85, 87 - 90, 92, 100, 102, 112, 116, 118, 134, 139, 178 - 180, 193, 232, 281
Hercules 14 - 17, 19 - 20, 44, 46 - 64, 69 - 72, 83, 85, 87 - 90, 112 - 113, 116 - 120, 124 - 139, 142, 165, 167 - 170, 214 - 215, 232, 255, 257 - 260, 262, 265 - 266, 285, 270 - 272, 280 - 282, 284 - 285, 322, 352, 422, 497 - 500, 517 n.36
Heresy 41, 75

Hermes 170, 279, 347, 350, 405, 410, 487
Hermetic Gnosticism 192
Hermetic Order of the Golden Dawn (See *Golden Dawn*)
Hermeticism, Hermetic tradition 192, 458
Hermod 284
Hero Twins 181
Herodias 254
Herodotus (c. 484 - 425 BC) 376 - 384
Hesiod (c. 8th century BC) 81, 179
Hidden realm (See *Infinite realm*)
Higher self (see *Essential self*)
Higherside Chats 158 - 159
Himmler, Heinrich (1900 - 1945) 426, 428, 431, 438
Hinnells, John (1941 - 2018) 367
Hiruko 349
Hitler, Adolf (1889 - 1945?) 426 - 427, 432, 438, 465
Hitler Speaks 426
Hlidskjálf 167
Hollywood 61
Holmes, Sherlock 464
Hooks 347, 350, 372, 491 - 493, 495, 497, 505, 531 n. 321
Horeb 280
Horns 56, 97, 213 - 214, 373
Horsemanship 170, 322
Horses 82, 170, 180, 217 - 218, 221, 230 - 231, 233 - 239, 241, 244, 247, 249, 322, 351, 450, 472
Horus 156, 362, 503
Houghton Mifflin 27 - 29
Houston Street (Dealey Plaza) 460 - 461
Hudson, Michael P. 327, 334 - 335, 342, 344, 521 n. 160, 522 n.175, 522 n.176
Humbaba, Huwawa 453
Humiliation 133, 394, 495
Hunahpu 181, 509
"Hunches" (See *Syncronicities*)
Huracan, Hunrakán 64, 120, 123 - 124, 127 - 128, 138, 498
Hurricanes 119 - 120, 123
Hyades 122
Hydra (constellation) 102, 125, 151, 185
Hydra (monster) 80 - 86, 88 - 90, 92 - 93, 101 - 102, 112, 116, 178

Hydrias 57, 59
Hyginus, Gaius Julius (64 BC - AD 17) 518 n. 70
Hyrrokin 127 - 128

Iceland 127, 409, 431
Icke, David 144, 150 - 157, 454, 477
Idas 170 - 171
"If So, How? [. . .] the Mysteries of Mithras" 357 - 365, 451
Iliad 63, 65, 86, 214, 256, 344
Illuminati (See *Bavarian Illuminati*)
Imperialism 331, 345, 440, 468, 526 - 527 n.224
In Hoc Signo Vinces 400
In the Dark Places of Wisdom 418, 509
Inanna, Inana 489 - 493, 495 - 498, 505 - 506, 509, 531 n.321
Incarnation 176 - 177, 181 - 182, 185 - 186, 267, 270, 357, 383, 385, 403, 456, 487, 494 - 495
Independent Order of Owls 433
India 3, 21, 44, 61, 64 - 66, 71, 88, 92, 101, 116, 118, 125, 133, 155, 170, 182, 221 - 222, 232, 251, 311, 321, 349, 411, 413, 450
Indonesia 437, 468 - 469
Indra 64, 67, 116, 124, 127, 138, 498
Infinite realm   iii, 23, 44 - 45, 94, 111, 141 - 143, 164 - 165, 168, 172, 174, 178, 184 - 186, 243, 262, 270, 283, 285 - 286, 304 - 305, 309, 312, 318 - 319, 322 - 324, 326, 328, 337 - 338, 340, 346, 350, 352 - 353, 403, 406 - 411, 415, 419, 430, 432, 444, 454 - 455, 457, 465 - 468, 476 - 477, 482, 484, 486 - 487, 502 - 503, 510 - 512
Ingsoc 41
Ino (See *Leucothea*)
Insler, Stanley (1937 - 2019) 369
Institute of Noetic Sciences 309, 521 n.145
Intelligence agencies 307, 438 - 439, 441 - 445, 474, 504, 506, 521 n.145, 525 n.223
International Astronomy Union 48, 59, 75

Intervisibility lines, i.v. lines 291 - 293
Invisible realm (See *Infinite realm*)
Iolaus 81 - 82, 84, 87 - 88
Iphicles 81, 180 - 181, 193
Iphigenia 88
Iran 367 - 368, 450
Isaac 2
Isaiah 112, 114, 116, 131, 135, 138
Iseum 384
Ishtar 150, 155, 489
Isis 156, 384, 496, 502
Israel 118, 136, 256
Italy 103, 124, 324, 330, 355, 386, 394, 425, 431, 508
Ithaca 266, 344, 381 - 382
Izanagi and Izanami 349

Jachin and Boaz 461, 479
Jacob 4, 10 - 11, 13 - 25, 31, 49, 62, 66, 85, 117, 140 - 143, 181, 187, 454, 483, 498
Jacob's Ladder (See *Jacob*)
Jacobsen, Annie 307, 438 - 439
Jaguars 125 - 126
Jahrbücher des Vereins [. . .] 369
James, Ronald M. 518 n.69
Japan 3, 311, 330, 349, 463
"Jawbone of an ass" 122, 373
Jehovah 108, 128, 138, 215, 498
Jeremiah 135 - 136, 166
Jeremiah, David Paul 115
Jerome (AD 347 - 420) 525 n.222
Jerusalem 129, 163, 387 - 388, 526 n.224
Jesus (See *Christ*)
Job 115 - 116, 130 - 131
John the Baptist 254
John, Gospel according to 189 - 191, 197 - 198, 203, 211, 219, 226, 243, 247, 259, 286
Jones, William Henry Samuel (1876 - 1963) 523 n.178
Jonestown 475, 508
Joseph 193
Joseph, Michael 457 - 458, 461 - 462
Josephus (AD 37 - 100) 325, 387 - 388, 391, 522 n.161, 526 n.224
Jotunheim, Jotuns 139
Journal of Parapsychology 308
Jove 66, 106, 108 - 109, 138 - 139, 498
Judaism 154

Judea, Judaea 387, 389, 526 - 527 n.224
Jupiter 66, 108 - 109, 122 - 123, 139, 360, 498

Kabbalah 458
Kabeiroi 175
Kalinda 93
Kaliya Naga 93 - 96, 101
Karate Kid (1984) 144 148, 159 - 160, 162, 412
Karna 349
Katha Upanishad, Kathopanishad 233 - 234, 237, 239, 241, 243 - 244, 247
Kauravas 134, 221 - 222, 224
Kelley, Edward (1555 - c. 1597) 443, 445
Kelly, Gerald Festus (1879 - 1972) 455
Kennedy, John F. (1917 - 1963) 331, 333, 457, 459, 462 - 463, 468 - 469, 471, 474, 478, 481, 506, 508
Kennedy, Robert F. (1925 - 1968) 331
Kent, University of 353
Kher-aha 502
Khnum 136 - 138, 498
Kibisis bag or wallet 350
King, Martin Luther, Jr. (1929 - 1968) 77 - 78, 331, 334, 469
Kings (Bible books) 128, 131 - 133, 163 - 165, 280, 411, 419, 479
Kings College London 175
Kingsley, Peter 509
Knights Templar (See *Templars*)
Knowles, Christopher 157 - 161, 454 - 455, 476, 509
Kojiki 349
Kon Tiki 283
Kore 175
Kosmokrator 379 - 380
Krishna 92 - 96, 101, 154, 182, 203, 223 - 233, 242 - 244, 247 - 249, 252, 260, 268, 273, 276, 317, 487, 497
Kshatriyas 134
Kubala 492
Kuhn, Alvin Boyd (1880 - 1963) 176 - 177, 179, 295, 494
Kunstakademie Düsseldorf 27
Kunti 349
Kurus (See *Kauravas*)
Kurukshetra 203, 221, 226, 230, 242, 249

Labors of Heracles 80 - 84, 116, 178
Ladders 2, 4, 9 - 17, 23, 31, 62, 117, 140, 295, 362, 396, 451 - 452, 454, 483 - 484, 498 - 500
Laestrygonians 266 - 269
Laetus, Quintus Aemilius (d. AD 193) 393
Lambesis 390
Lapis lazuli 489 - 490
Latins, Latin 108 - 108, 156, 168, 334, 336, 347, 397, 524 - 525 n.221
Latitude 4, 471, 508
LaVey, Anton (1930 - 1997) 479
Leda 168 - 169, 171
Lemnos 175
Lent 492
Leo 125 126, 265, 272 - 273, 359
Lerna 81
Lernaean Hydra (See *Hydra, monster*)
Leucippas 170
Leucothea 276 - 278, 283 - 284
Levant 4, 409
Levenda, Peter 425 - 429, 431, 437, 443, 445, 465, 467, 530 n.290
Leviathan 112 - 113, 115 - 116
Levine, Peter A. 182, 184, 186, 190, 194 - 195, 199 - 200, 210, 220, 235, 304, 215, 519 n.79
Libra 98, 100, 265 - 267, 269, 273, 358 - 359, 364
Licinius (c. 270 - 324) 400
Lidar 44
Light pollution 3, 5, 158
Liljeblad, Sven S. (1899 - 2000) 518 n.69
Lions 30, 51, 56, 80 - 81, 83, 126, 188, 252, 385, 527 n.224
Lion-skin 51 - 52, 56, 126
Literalism i - iii, 22 - 23, 78, 103, 107, 111, 115, 141, 143 - 144, 148 - 152, 156 - 157, 159, 161, 163, 166, 185, 188, 191, 193, 211 - 212, 228, 250 - 251, 311, 324, 326, 334, 336 - 337, 339, 345 - 346, 386, 389, 392, 394 - 395, 399, 402 - 404, 407, 409, 446 - 447, 453, 457, 470 - 471, 473, 476, 478, 480, 500, 503, 506, 525 n.222, 525 - 527 n.224, 529 n.281
Livianus, Tiberius Claudius 388
Locrians 180

Locusts 118, 122
Loki 88, 139, 495
London 150, 390, 461
London, King's College (See *King's College London*)
London, University of 367
"Lone nut" 463
Longitude 4, 480
"Looking away" 352, 372
LORD (See *Jehovah*)
Lord of the Rings 181, 205, 209, 242
Lorsch 390
Los Angeles 288
Lost Light 176 - 177, 279, 494
Lotuses 69, 71, 229 - 230
Louvre 55
Lovecraft, Howard Phillips (1890 - 1937) 158 - 159
Luke, Gospel according to 190
Lumumba, Patrice (1925 - 1961) 468 - 469, 474
Lynceus 171
Lyra 13, 53, 72 - 73

Ma Wang Dui texts 226 - 227
Maces 50, 63, 69, 71, 221 - 222, 232, 257, 284
Magadhans 252
Magic 158, 161, 179, 426 - 427, 435, 437, 443, 447 - 451, 465, 467, 480
Magic self 447
Mahabharata 63, 101, 133 - 135, 138, 170, 182, 221, 224, 229, 231 - 232, 487
Main Street (Dealey Plaza) 458 - 461
Mainz 390
Mair, Victor H. 225 - 226, 228
Malcolm X (1925 - 1965) 331, 469
Manchester, University of 367
Mandukya Upanishad 238, 243, 411
Manning, Paul (d. 1995) 439
Manson Family 475, 508
Manta rays 12, 88 - 89
Mar Vista 288
Mara, Maara 274
Marcellinus (d. 413) 105
Marcia Aurelia Ceionia Demetrias (d. AD 93) 393
Marcus Aurelius (AD 121 - 180) 391, 393, 503

Marduk 101 - 102, 112, 117, 138, 150, 517 n.36
Mark, Gospel according to 190
Mars 109, 122 - 123, 360
Marsyas 416
Mary 193
Mary Magdalene 108
Marxism 329
Mascara 489
Masonic Emblems 461 - 462
Masonry (See *Freemasonry*)
Maté, Gabor i, 183 - 184, 190, 195, 198 - 205, 212, 235 - 238, 241, 244 - 245, 247, 249 - 250, 267, 274 - 275, 304, 315 - 316, 505, 507
Materialism, Materialist paradigm 300 - 301, 303 - 307, 312, 337, 346
Matthew, Gospel according to 190, 214, 254
Maui 101, 349
Maximian (AD 250 - 310) 399
Maximilian I (1459 - 1519) 423
Maximinus Daia (AD 270 - 313) 400
Maya 64 - 68, 73, 119 - 120, 127 - 128, 138, 181, 283, 498
McCloy, John J. (1895 - 1989) 463
Mediterranean 154, 409, 413
Medusa, Medousa 347 - 352, 405, 410, 466, 523 n.178
Megara 79
Mentor 344
Mercury 122, 360
Merkelbach, Reinhold (1918 - 2006) 387
Mermaids (See *Sirens*)
Mert 502
Mesia 389
Mesopotamia 1, 3, 43, 61, 65, 85, 101, 112, 117, 127, 129, 138, 144, 150, 154, 181, 186 - 189, 257, 349, 450
Metamorphoses 414 - 415, 512, 531 n.326
Mexico 124, 138
Meyer, Marvin W. (1948 - 2012) 192
Michael the Archangel 96 - 101, 108
Midas 374, 413 - 419, 454 - 455, 482, 484 - 486, 499, 510 - 512
Midgard Serpent 101 - 102, 112, 505

553

Milky Way 3, 5 - 17, 19 - 21, 31, 63, 85 - 86, 89, 91, 93, 114, 116, 158, 166 - 169, 256, 261 - 272, 276, 284 - 285, 320, 322, 349 - 352, 373, 376, 416 - 417, 483, 498 - 500, 515 n.3
Miller, Alice (1923 - 2010) 245
Milvian Bridge (See *Battle of the Milvian Bridge*)
Mitchell, William B. (1946 - 1965) 305 - 306
Mitchell, Marjorie 306
Mithraea 354 - 365, 369, 378, 380, 383 - 385, 387 - 388, 390- 391, 396 - 397, 403 - 405, 410, 420 - 422, 451, 483, 524 - 525 n.221
Mithraeum of Felicissimus 385, 451 - 452, 524 - 525 n.221
Mithraeum of the Seven Spheres 357 - 362, 369, 380, 385, 422, 451 - 452
Mithraic grades 385,393, 451 - 452, 454, 483, 525 n.222
Mithraism 347, 353 - 380, 353 - 380, 383 - 398, 401 - 405, 410 - 412, 417, 419 - 422, 424, 429, 432, 437 - 438, 445, 451 - 452, 454, 472, 474, 483 - 484, 498, 506, 524 - 525 n.221, 525 n.222, 529 n.281
Mithras 355 - 357, 359 - 360, 364, 366 - 367, 369 - 380, 388, 390, 398, 405, 422
Mithras-Orion: Greek Hero and Roman Army God 370
"Mithrassteine von Dormagen" 369
Mitres 398
Mitreo delle Sette Sfere (See *Mithraeum of the Seven Spheres*)
Mjöllnir 69 - 71, 138 - 140
MK Ultra 159
Mocking (See *Humiliation*)
Monroe, Marilyn (1926 - 1962) 467
Moon iii, 3 - 4, 25, 28, 154 - 157, 172 - 173, 222, 261, 264 - 266, 268, 272 - 273, 360 - 361, 385, 421, 461
More, Brookes (1859 - 1942) 414
Morgan Hill Earthquake 296 - 297
Moses 118, 254 - 256, 285, 320 - 321, 349, 386, 521 n.161, 525 - 527 n.224
Most Dangerous Book in the World 479

Mount Aetna (See *Aetna*)
Mount Horeb (See *Horeb*)
Mount Olympus (See *Olympus*)
Mount Taÿgetus (See *Taÿgetus*)
Mountains 19, 81, 86, 92 - 93, 109, 128, 131, 166, 170, 251 - 253, 256, 280, 287 - 291, 293 - 294, 298, 300 - 302, 407, 431, 466 - 467, 512
Mourning 490 - 492, 494, 496
Mudras 96, 231, 234, 248
Munich 27, 59, 425 - 428, 439
Munich, University of 27
Museum of Fine Art (Boston) 57
Mycenae 179
Mysteria, Mysteries 103, 174 - 175, 339, 353 - 354, 357, 361, 364 - 366, 377 - 378, 380, 383 - 384, 404, 451

Nachiketa 239 - 241
Nag Hammadi 191
Nag Hammadi Corpus 97, 191 - 192
Nagas 93 - 96, 101, 229
Nahuatl 127
Nakula 170, 182
Namaskaram 231
Nameless Gods 175
Naqab 4
Narayana 94, 224
Natalis Invicti 384
Nathanael 259
National Health and Nutrition Examination Survey 313
Nativity scenes 193
Nazis, Nazi Party 27 - 28, 45, 330, 425 - 426, 428 - 433, 435 - 443, 465, 469, 518 n.69, 530 n.290
Nebraska, University of 192
Nebuchadnezzar 129
Nemean Lion 80 - 81
Nemean Odes (Pindar) 170, 175
Neoliberalism 316, 328, 521 n.160
Neoplatonism 357, 360, 365
Negev 4
Nerañjarā River 251
Netherlands 468
Neti 490
New Testament 3, 22, 26, 97, 101, 108, 135, 149, 156, 189, 193, 199, 215, 286
New York Times 27 - 28, 287

New Zealand 346
Newman, John 469
Newspeak 41, 75 - 77
Nietzsche, Friedrich (1844 - 1900) 329
Night iii, 1 - 7, 9, 11, 13 - 14, 16, 25 - 27, 29 - 32, 35 - 36, 41, 48, 51, 54 - 55, 58 - 60, 79, 84, 87, 101, 108 - 109, 115, 118, 125, 131, 138 - 140, 151 158, 164, 167 - 168, 173 - 174, 180, 188, 206, 222, 229, 261, 264 - 267, 296, 271, 277, 290, 297, 305, 310, 337
Nimrud, Nimrod 155
Nineteen Eighty-Four 41, 75 - 77
Ninshubur, Nincubura 489 - 491
Noah 129, 310
Nobility (See *Oligarchy*)
Nock, Arthur Darby (1902 - 1963) 353
Nonaction 225
Norman Conquest 523 n.176
Norse mythology 64, 87 - 88, 101, 116, 127 - 128, 140, 167, 283 - 284, 311, 409, 492 - 493, 495, 497
North America 3, 172, 491
North Celestial Pole 123, 173
North Pole 172
Northern Crown (See *Corona Borealis*)
Northwestern University 447
NSDAP (See *German Workers Party*)
Nu, Nun 502
Numbers (Bible book) 320, 373
Nuremberg 438
Nut 503
Nymphs 193, 347, 357, 524 n.193
Nysos 170

Oakland 183, 201, 238
Oberursel 438 - 439
Objectification 406, 416, 418, 430, 454, 483 - 485, 487, 505
Odd Fellows 433
Odin 167
Odysseus 259, 266 - 270, 276 - 279, 283 - 284, 344 - 345, 351, 372, 381 - 383, 466, 509
Odyssey 65, 109, 259, 262, 266 - 268, 276, 278, 283, 305, 324, 344 - 346, 351 - 352, 357, 372, 381 - 382, 403, 457, 466, 509

Oicotypes 168, 178, 183, 186, 189, 284, 349, 491, 195 - 196, 518 n.69
Old Testament 108, 140, 149 - 150, 166, 181, 282, 386, 386, 527 n.224
Oldspeak 41, 77
Oligarchy 149, 328, 389, 405, 423 - 425, 429, 431, 433, 435 - 437, 441, 470, 477, 500, 527 n.224
Olive trees 267, 319, 322, 516 n.26
Ollestad, Norman, Jr. 287 - 291, 293 - 295, 298, 300 - 305, 307, 353, 407, 466
Ollestad, Norman, Sr. (1935 - 1979) 288
Olympus 79 - 81, 109, 171 - 173, 177, 180
On the Cave of the Nymphs in the Odyssey 357, 360 - 361, 365
One You Feed 245
Ontario Peak 289 - 291, 300 - 303
Operation Paperclip 438
Operation Rusty 438
"Operative" Masonry 424, 528 n.270
Ophiuchus 18 - 20, 25, 58, 63, 66 - 67, 85 - 87, 89 - 93, 95 - 102, 109 - 111, 113 - 114, 116 - 117, 119, 125 - 126, 129 - 138, 152, 165 - 167, 169, 185, 214 - 219, 229 - 230, 232 - 233, 250 - 253, 255 - 262, 265 - 273, 275 - 276, 280 - 286, 320 - 322, 349, 492 - 494, 497 - 499, 508, 515 - 516 n.26
Oppression i, 41, 46, 75, 77, 149, 153, 155, 157, 160 - 162, 249 - 250, 318 - 319, 323 - 324, 336, 338, 346, 392, 419, 430, 435, 437, 440 - 441, 455, 469, 472 - 473, 476 - 477, 484 - 485, 487, 501, 505, 525 - 527 n.224
Oracle at Aulis (See *Aulis*)
Oracle at Delphi (See *Delphi*)
Order of the Trapezoid 479 - 480
Ordo Templi Orientis (See *OTO*)
Origen (c. AD 185 - 253) 302, 362, 451, 524 n.196, 530 n.302
Orion 11, 370, 503
Orion Spur 8
Orphic Hymns 323
Orwell, George (1903 - 1950) 41, 75 - 77
Osiris 156, 159, 384, 493, 496 - 497, 502 - 503, 509
Ostia 357 - 358, 360, 362, 380, 385, 388, 422, 451

555

Oswald, Lee Harvey (1939 - 1963) 463
Other realm (See *Infinite realm*)
OTO (*Ordo Templi Orientis*) 433
Ovid (43 BC - c. AD 17) 319, 414, 512
Owen, Alex 447 - 448, 451, 480
Owls 319, 433

Pacific island cultures 3, 13, 21, 65, 101, 311, 349, 436
Pacific Ocean 3 - 4, 13
Pactolus, River 374, 416, 486
Paganism 105, 107, 339, 395, 397 - 398, 401
Pagano, Francesco (d. 1506) 99
Pala dress 489 - 490
Paley, Frederick Apthorp (1815 - 1888) 170 - 173, 178
Pāli, Pali Canon 251 - 253, 256
Pamphäes 170
Pan 480
Pandava Mountain 252
Pandavas 122 - 134, 182, 221 - 224
Pannonia 389 - 390, 395
Paperclip 438, 521 n.145
Paris (city) 28, 45, 55
Paris (prince of Troy) 454 - 455
Parmenides, Parmeneides (5th century BC) 509
Passion 354
Pater patrum 397 - 398, 420
Patricians 387, 392, 394 - 395, 503
Patrick, St. Patrick 116
Patrick, Simon (1626 - 1707) 163
Patriot Act 481
Patroclus 62
Paul 500
Pausanias (c. AD 110 - 180) 80, 523 n.178
Pauwels, Jacques R. 329 - 330, 504, 527 n.224
Pegasus 262, 285, 311, 351 - 352, 374, 416 - 417, 483, 499
Peloponnese 80
Pendulum readers 431
Penelope 266, 344 - 355, 381
Pennsylvania 480
Pennsylvania, University of 225
People's State of Bavaria (See *Volksstaat Bayern*)

Peoples Temple 475, 508
Persephone 174, 496
Perseus 60 - 61, 83, 179, 262, 347 - 353, 366, 370 - 374, 376, 378, 405 - 407, 410, 413, 416 - 418, 466, 483 - 484, 487, 498 - 499, 523 n.178
Persia 367, 376
"Persians" 353, 357, 362, 365, 376, 385, 405, 483
Persona 141 - 142, 149, 195 - 197, 206 - 209, 212
Pet Goat 480
Petaluma 309
Peter 108, 396 - 398, 403, 438
Petrifaction, petrification 86, 347 - 348, 405 - 407, 416
Phenomena 307
Phicium 180
Philip I, "Philip the Arab" (AD 204 - 249) 103, 394 - 395
Phocians 180
Phoenix, Joaquin 391
Phoenix Program 506
Phrygia 413 - 414, 416 - 417, 482
Phrygian caps 356, 363, 370 - 372, 374, 416, 483
Phrygianum 396 - 398, 403, 420, 438
Picasso, Pablo (1881 - 1973) 467
Pillars 3, 13, 69, 111, 115 - 116, 131, 163, 282, 450, 458 - 459, 461 - 462, 464, 478 - 479, 516 n.26, 527 n.224
Pillar of Severity 459
Pindar (c. 518 BC - 438 BC) 170, 172, 175, 348
Pippal, Pippala (See *Sacred fig*)
Piraeus 338, 340
Pisces 265 - 267, 269, 293, 311, 358 - 359, 364, 422, 499
Planets iii, 4 - 5, 121 - 124, 158, 172 - 173, 178, 261, 264 - 266, 268, 271 - 272, 360 - 362, 385, 450 - 452
Plato (c. 428 BC - c. 348 BC) 319, 360 - 361
Plymouth Brethren 446, 453
Poetovium 390
Pohl, Hermann (1887 - 1966) 427
Polaris 123, 450
Pollux, Polydeuces 168, 170 - 172, 175, 177 - 178, 181, 193, 242

Polydectes 349, 405 - 406, 487
Polyphemus 268, 276
Ponte Milvio (See *Battle of the Milvian Bridge*)
Pope (*Papa*) 398, 527 n.224
Popol Vuh 64, 181, 283, 509
Porphyry of Tyre (c. AD 234 - 305) 357 - 358, 360 - 362, 364 - 365, 368, 383, 393, 402 - 403, 405, 498, 506, 524 n.193
Ports 335, 338 - 340, 357, 388, 509
Portugal 98
Poseidon 276 - 277, 319, 321 - 322, 334, 348, 408
Postal services 342 - 343, 389
Posture 49, 55 - 56, 58 - 59, 62 - 63, 65, 67, 73, 83, 91, 111, 124, 126 - 127, 217, 244
Potter's wheel 135 - 138
Praetorian Guard 388, 391, 393 - 394, 405, 419
Prague 444
Precession 178, 376 - 382, 403, 471
Premonitions 303, 305 - 308, 312
Privatization 324, 326 - 328, 334 - 340, 342 - 343, 389, 404, 433, 435, 469, 473, 481, 501, 509, 511, 521 n.160, 522 - 523 n.176, 26 n.224, 529 n.281
Protestantism 425, 431, 453
Proverbs 178
Psalms 112, 128, 130 - 131
Psyche (See *Eros and Psyche*)
Psychedelics 199, 238, 505
Psychedelic Science Conference 183, 201
Psychological operations, Psy-ops 149 - 150, 153
Psychological trauma (See *Trauma*)
Ptah 112, 498, 503, 517 n.36
Pterelaos 179
Public domain 335, 337, 341, 343
Pullach 439
Punic Wars 104
Pushpaka 455
Pythia 79 - 80
Python 79, 90 - 92, 101

Quetzalcoatl 126, 283, 497
Quiché Maya (See *Maya*)

Ra, Re 112, 503, 517 n.36
Raffy 28
Rajagaha 252
Rajasthan 95
Rakshasas 455
Rama 456
Ramayana 455 - 456, 511
Rauschning, Hermann (1887 - 1982) 426
Ravana 455 - 456, 511
Reagan, Ronald W. (1911 - 2004) 195, 203
Reconciliation (See *Recovery*)
Reconnection (See *Recovery*)
Recovery ii, iv, 102, 164, 182, 189 - 190, 194, 200, 202, 204 - 205, 210 - 212, 218, 220, 233 - 234, 240, 249 - 250, 261 - 262, 266, 275, 283, 286, 312, 317 - 318, 337, 354, 365, 403 - 404, 411, 435, 454 - 455, 482, 496 - 497, 500, 505 - 506, 509 - 512
Red Sea 118, 256, 285, 320 - 321
Red Tezcatlipoca (See *Tezcatlipoca*)
Regensburg 423
Reichstag fire, Reichstag 27 - 28, 45
Renan, Ernest (1823 - 1892) 383 - 384, 524 n.217
Rent (economic rent) 326 - 327, 335 - 336, 340, 521 n.160
Rentiers 327 - 331, 343 - 344, 346, 392, 433, 477
Reptilians (See *Icke, David*)
Revelation 97 - 98, 100 - 101, 108, 122
Rey, H. A. (1898 - 1977) 27 - 36, 38, 40 - 46, 49 - 51, 53, 56 - 57, 65, 71, 73 - 75, 78, 122 - 123, 312, 370, 372
Rey, Margret (1906 - 1996) 28 - 29, 44 - 45
Rhine 369
Rhine, Louisa (1891 - 1983) 308
Richter, Charles (1900 - 1985) 297
Richter scale 297
Riess, Curt (1902 - 1993) 439
Right-wing 427 - 428, 436, 526 n.224, 529 n.281
Rings 262 - 265, 489 - 490
Rio de Janeiro 27 - 28
Rio Tinto 510
River Pactolus (See *Pactolus*)

557

Rivers 27, 56, 81, 86, 89, 91, 93 - 94, 96, 104, 166, 169, 251, 261, 278 - 279, 285, 335, 351, 374, 416, 486, 499, 536
Rods 100, 118, 256, 285, 321, 490
Roman Empire, Romans, Rome 17, 54, 66, 103 - 106, 108 - 109, 111, 138, 154, 324 - 326, 328, 334, 339, 353 - 355, 357, 362, 369, 384, 386 - 392, 394 - 398, 400 - 042, 404 - 405, 407 - 408, 410 - 411, 413 - 414, 419 - 425, 431 - 438, 440, 442, 444, 446 - 448, 474, 500, 503, 525 - 527 n.224, 529 n.281
Romans (Bible book) 135
Rosetta Stone 42, 78
Rosicrucians 474
Röskva 140
Rube Goldberg 467
Russia 328 - 330, 425, 431, 438, 440, 442, 469
Russian Revolution 329 - 330, 425, 431, 438, 440, 442

Sadhus 413
Sagittarius 5, 9 - 13, 15 - 16, 19, 25, 31 - 40, 43, 86, 90 - 92, 95 - 96, 101, 110 - 111, 116, 122, 156, 167, 169 - 170, 217 - 219, 232, 261 - 262, 265 - 267, 272 - 273, 284 - 285, 321 - 322, 349, 358 - 359, 483, 498 - 499
Sahadeva 170, 182
Sais, Lady of Sais 502
Salomon Brothers Building 479, 508
Same 382
Samothrace 175
Samson 108, 122, 373
Samuel 130, 166
San Bernardino County Sheriff's Department 287
San Francisco 199, 366
San Gabriel Mountains 287
San Jose 296
San Mateo 295
Sanjaya 221 - 222
Sankhya 227
Sanliurfa 1
Sanskrit 63, 88, 92, 101, 133, 155, 221, 229, 233, 237, 258, 455
Santa Monica 287

Sarah 108
Sarapeum 384
Sarcophagi 493
Sardis 416, 512
Sargon of Akkad 349
Satan 98, 479
Saturn 106, 122 - 123, 264, 360, 422, 433
Satyrs 413 - 414, 416
Sashes 277, 283 - 284
Scaevola, Quintus Mucius (d. 82 BC) 106
Scales (or Balances) 97 - 100, 431, 482
Schism206 457
Schwaller de Lubicz, René Adolphe (1887 - 1961) 148
Science and Psychic Phenomena 308
Scorpio 5, 9 - 13, 15, 17 - 20, 31 - 38, 63, 85 - 87, 89 - 93, 95 - 97, 99 - 102, 112 - 114, 116, 122, 125, 151, 167, 169, 185, 216 - 219, 229 - 230, 261 - 262, 265 - 267, 269 - 270, 272 - 273, 281, 349, 358, 483, 498 - 499
Scott, Peter Dale 333, 469
Sea-foam 349
Sebottendorf, Rudolf (1875 - 1945) 427, 429
Segontium 390
Sekhmet, Sekhet 502
Selket, Serqet 502
Semiramis 155
Seneca the Younger (4 BC - AD 65) 413
September 11, 2001 331 - 333, 457, 178 - 182, 484 - 485, 506 - 508
Serifos, Seriphos 349
Serpents, Serpent-halves 33, 59, 62, 79 - 80, 82, 84 - 86, 89 - 90, 92 - 96, 98 - 102, 112 - 113, 115 - 116, 125 - 126, 129, 132, 134, 136 - 137, 144, 151 - 152, 185, 215, 217, 229 - 230, 253, 256 - 257, 259, 281 - 283, 320 - 321, 348, 398, 442, 474, 492 - 493, 505, 515 - 516 n.26
Set, Seth 502
Sethian Gnosticism 191
Severus Alexander (c. AD 208 - 235) 393
Shamans, Shamanism 238, 449 - 452, 454
Shamanism: Archaic Techniques of Ecstasy 449

Shamhat 188
Shaming (See *Humiliation*)
Shango (See *Xango*)
Shem, Ham and Japheth 310
Shepherds 158 - 159, 162, 180, 187 - 188, 492
"Shield of Heracles" 179, 519 n.78
Shields 179 - 180, 281, 347, 350, 400
Shrouds 493
Sif 88
Silenus 413 - 414
Sirens 158 - 159, 162
Siricius (AD 334 - 399) 397
Sitchin, Zecharia (1920 - 2010) 144
Sméagol 206 - 209
Smith, Adam (1723 - 1790) 327
Smith, Richard 287
Smiths 347
Smoking Mirror (See *Tezcatlipoca*)
Snorri Sturluson (1179 - 1241) 127 - 128, 139
Social Darwinism 329
Socialism 328 - 330, 425, 427 - 429, 438, 440, 442, 469
Sol Invictus 353, 374 - 375, 378 - 380, 384, 386, 388 - 389, 391 - 399, 401 - 404, 407, 410, 412, 419 - 421, 424, 432, 435 - 436, 440, 445 - 446, 451, 470, 472, 483, 506, 529 n.281
Sola scriptura 446
Solar disc 127
Solomon 131 - 132, 134, 163 - 165, 168, 215, 252, 260, 282, 374, 411, 415, 454 - 455, 479, 482, 497, 508
Solstices 267, 269, 357 - 364, 376, 381, 383
Solstitial diameter 359
Somatic Experiencing 182
Son of Sam 475
"Sorcerer and His Apprentice" 447, 480
South America 3, 44, 437
South Celestial Pole 123, 173, 263
Southern Crown (See *Corona Australis*)
Sovereign Plumed Serpent 126, 283, 497
Soviet Union 430, 439, 442
Spain 64, 104, 390, 409, 425
Spears 99 - 100, 126, 171, 180, 214, 217 - 219, 256, 281 - 282, 516 n.26

"Speculative" Masonry 424, 432, 528 n.270
Speidel, Michael P. 369
Speyer 423
SS (*Schutzstaffel*) 426, 428, 430 - 432, 438 - 440, 465
St. Albans 390
St. Peter's Basilica 396 - 397, 403, 438
Staatliche Antikensammlungen (Munich) 59
Stark, Karl Bernhard (1824 - 1879) 368 - 369
Star Myths, Volume One (See *Ancient World-Wide System*)
Star Myths, Volume Two 61, 86, 109, 119, 156, 166, 168 - 169, 214, 258, 262, 266 - 269
Star Myths, Volume Three 17, 20, 102, 109, 119, 128, 132, 185, 191, 215, 256, 258, 282, 311, 321, 352, 382
Star Myths, Volume Four 64, 87 - 88, 101, 127 - 128, 283, 285, 493
Stars: A New Way to See Them 29, 34, 38, 42 - 43, 46, 50, 56, 74, 122 - 123
Starr, Martin P. 446 - 447
Stellarium 5, 31 - 32, 264 - 265
Stheno 347
Still small voice 279 - 280, 287
Stones 1, 17 - 21, 23, 80, 86, 141, 171, 207, 347 - 348, 350, 369, 405 - 407, 414, 490, 495
Strong, James (1822 - 1894) 114
Strong's *Concordance* 114, 128, 517 n.37
Suitors 324, 344 - 346, 381 - 383, 457
Sukarno (1901 - 1970) 468 - 469
Sumer, Sumerian 154, 186, 311, 489, 492
Summer Triangle 13, 53
Sun iii, 1, 4 - 5, 7 - 9, 154 - 159, 172 - 174, 221 - 222, 261, 264 - 266, 268, 271 - 273, 323, 326 - 327, 335, 349, 353, 358, 360 - 361, 374, 377 - 381, 384 - 385, 402, 421 - 422, 461
Surya 349
Swahn, Jan-Öjvind (1925 - 2016) 518 n.69
Swastikas 127

559

Swords 38, 50, 53, 63, 69, 73, 84, 112 - 113, 138, 221 - 222, 284, 347, 350 - 351, 356, 372, 483
Symbionese Liberation Army 475, 508
Synchronicities 301
Synoptic gospels 190
Syriza 343
Syros 175

Talaria 347
Tammuz 155
Tao Te Ching 225 - 226, 228, 318
Taphian Isles, Taphians 179 - 180
Tappenden, Frederick S. 358
Tarot 461
Tarshish 128
Tate-LaBianca murders 475
Tauroctony 355 - 336, 358 - 360, 363, 366 - 378, 380, 383, 403, 405, 417
Taurus 273, 370 - 371, 373, 377 - 378, 380, 417
Taxes 324 - 327, 388 - 390, 419, 511, 521 n.160, 523 n.176
Taÿgetus 171
Teleboans (See *Taphians*)
Telemachus 266, 344 - 345, 381 - 382
Templars 430, 474
Temples 103, 141, 188, 251, 319, 326, 343, 348, 354 - 355, 357, 383, 404, 421
Temple at Jerusalem 388
Temple of Solomon 129, 131, 282, 479, 508
Tetragrammaton 108
Tetrarchy 399
Teutonic Knights 430, 474
Tezcatlipoca 120, 123 - 127, 131, 138, 142
Thebes 170, 179 - 180, 348, 519 n.78
Thelema 453 - 454
Theodosius (AD 347 - 395) 103 - 104, 339, 400, 404
Theosophical Society 433
Theosophy 427, 433
Therapnae 170, 172
Theravada 251
Thessaloniki 340
Theurgy 447
Third Dynasty (Ur) 187
Third Reich 427, 429, 432, 436
"Thirteenth zodiac sign" 273, 497
Thjálfi 139 - 140
Thoth 129, 503

Thor 64, 69, 71, 88, 101 - 102, 112, 116, 127, 138 - 140, 142, 498, 505
Thule Society (*Thule Gesellschaft*) 426 - 429, 443, 474
Thunderbolts 63 - 64, 67 - 74, 81, 124, 138, 171, 284
Tiamat 101 - 102, 112, 118
Tibet 67, 431, 437
Tiki 65, 283
Timothy (Bible books) 500
Tiryns 80
Titus (AD 39 - 81) 387 - 388, 391, 522 n.161, 526 n.224
Toland, John (1912 - 2004) 429
Tolkien, J. R. R. (1892 - 1973) 181, 205 - 209, 242
Tolle, Eckhart 201
Toltec 127, 138
Torches 82, 84, 88, 363 - 364
Toronto, University of 357
TRAINOSE 340
Trajan (AD 53 - 117) 388
Trapezoids 479 - 480
Trauma i - ii, iv, 160 - 162, 182 - 184, 186, 189 - 190, 194 - 204, 209 - 210, 220, 226, 235, 237, 239, 241, 244 - 245, 248 - 250, 271, 275, 304, 315 - 319, 328, 331 - 334, 337 - 338, 345 - 346, 365, 381, 383, 406 - 407, 409 - 410, 430, 436, 447, 457, 475 - 478, 481 - 482, 484 - 487, 495, 505 - 511, 519 n.79, 526 n.224
Tree of Life 458 - 459, 461 - 462, 464 - 465, 472, 478, 508
Treviri 390
Trident 319 - 321
Trigonometry 296
Triton 58 - 59
Troy 106, 232, 344
Tsourakis, Constantinos 339
Tuna 101
Tunisia 390
Tupaca 283
Turbans 489 - 490
Turcan, Robert (1929 - 2018) 365
Turkey 413, 427
Turner, John D. (1938 - 2019) 192

Twins, twinning 20, 81, 90, 163, 168, 170, 172, 175, 177 - 178, 180 - 183, 186 - 189, 191 - 194, 196 - 197, 205 - 206, 211, 242, 364, 366
Twin Towers 332 - 333, 478 - 480, 508
"Twisted legs" or "twisted feet" 373
Tyndareus 168, 171
Typhaonium 180
Typhon 59, 63, 67 - 68, 71 - 72, 80 - 82, 89 - 90, 92, 100, 102, 152

Uatchet 502
Ulansey, David 366 - 373, 376 - 380, 383 - 384, 405, 410, 525 n.222
Umbrellas (See *Canopies*)
Unconquered Sun, Unconquerable Sun (See *Sol Invictus*)
Underworld 174 - 177, 284 - 285, 351, 372, 408, 450, 489 - 498, 500, 509, 531 n.321
Undying stars 173
Undying Stars 103, 174, 324, 386 - 387, 526 n.224
Unholy Alliance 425 - 427, 431, 467
United Kingdom 425
United States 173, 291, 296 - 297, 305, 307, 313 - 314, 316, 330 - 331, 341 - 342, 438 - 439, 441, 445, 457, 459, 464, 472
United States Army 291, 305, 395, 438 - 439, 479
United States Military Academy (See *West Point*)
Universität Erfurt 367
Unseen God 347
UPS 342
Upanishads 233 - 234, 237 - 241, 243 - 244, 247, 411
Ur 187
Uraei 503
Urfa 1
Uriah 109
Uruvela 251
Utgarda-Loki 139
Útgardr 139

Vajra 67 - 72, 138, 257 - 258
Vajrapani 257 - 258
Valentine, Douglas 504, 506, 508, 525 n.223

Valentinian Gnosticism 191
Van Heemskerck, Maartin (1498 - 1574) 216 - 218
Vases 35 - 38, 40, 50 - 52, 54 - 58, 83, 232, 372
Vatican, Vatican Hill 124, 396 - 398, 403, 420, 438, 438, 441, 527 n.224
Vayu 118, 138
Vedas 138, 455, 498
Vega 13, 53, 73
Venus 106, 109, 122, 159, 360, 422
Vermaseren, Josef (1918 - 1985) 374
Vespasian (AD 9 - 79) 387 - 389, 391, 522 n.161, 526 n.224
Vestal Virgins 104
Vienna 390 - 391
Vietnam 467, 469, 481, 506, 305, 333 - 334
Vindobona 390 - 391
Vineyards 3, 310
Viracocha 283, 497
Virgo 20, 27, 102, 125 - 126, 137, 185, 265 - 267, 272 - 273, 285, 358 - 359, 364, 381
Vishnu 67, 92, 94, 224, 229 - 230, 455 - 456, 497
Visigoths 104
Vivarini, Bartolomeo (1440 - 1499) 99
Volcanoes 347
Volksstaat Bayern 425, 427
Von Dechend, Hertha (1915 - 2001) 119 - 123, 449, 451
Von Sydow, Carl Wilhelm (1878 - 1952) 518 n.69
Vulcan (See *Hephaestos*)

Wadjet 503
Waldstein, Felix (1865 - 1943) 28
Walsh, David 353, 355 - 357
Walsingham, Francis (c. 1532 - 1590) 444
War-carts 63, 139, 221, 223, 230 - 233
Warren Commission 459, 463
"Wax-on, wax-off" 146 - 147
Weaving 323
Wepwawet 502
West Point 344, 508
When the Body Says No 195

561

"Whirling" form of Hercules 117, 119, 127, 258 - 259, 322
Whirlwinds 117, 119
White, Gordon 158
William the Conqueror (c. 1028 - 1087) 523 n.176
Wind (in myth) 103, 117 - 120, 123, 127 - 128, 131, 138, 280
Wings (in myth) 11, 13 - 14, 17, 62 - 63, 87, 89, 98 - 100, 127, 347, 350 - 351
Wisdom figures 260, 280 - 283, 286
"World-pillar" 450
World Trade Center 332 - 333
World War I 328 - 330, 504
World War II 46, 307, 328, 394, 430, 436, 438 - 439, 445, 457, 463, 474
Writing on the Wall 129 - 130
WTC 7 (See *Building 7*)
Wulff, Wilhelm (1892 - 1979) 431

Xango 64, 69, 71, 138
Xbalanque 182, 509

Yaaga ritual 240 - 241
Yahweh (See *Jehovah*)
Yakshas 456
Yama 233 - 234, 237, 239 - 241, 244, 247, 497
Yamuna 93, 96
Yoga 227
Yoruba 64, 138
YouTube 21, 298 - 299, 457
Yudhishthira 133, 224

Zacynthus 382
Zapruder, Abraham (1905 - 1972) 459 - 460
Zeus 49, 59 - 63, 65 - 68, 71 - 73, 79 - 81, 90, 92, 100, 102, 108 - 109, 112, 116, 120, 123 - 125, 127, 138 - 139, 142, 168 - 172, 177 - 181, 193, 242, 281, 348 - 350, 376, 498
Ziggurat, ziqqurat 450, 454
Zimmer, Eric 245
Zodiac 5, 11, 26, 31, 261 - 262, 264 - 273, 275 - 276, 280, 283, 358 - 361, 363, 375, 377 - 378, 380 - 383, 421 - 422, 397 - 398, 516 n.26
Zodiac murders 475
Zoroastrianism 447

www.ingramcontent.com/pod-product-compliance
Lightning Source LLC
Chambersburg PA
CBHW031304150426
43191CB00005B/71